Introduction to the Hebrew Bible

And Deutero-Canonical Books

Second Edition

John J. Collins

Fortress Press
Minneapolis

INTRODUCTION TO THE HEBREW BIBLE, SECOND EDITION

Cover image: Warriors scaling walls with ladders: bas-relief from the palace in Niniveh, Mesopotamia. Neo-Assyrian, 7th c. B.C.E. © Erich Lessing / Art Resource, NY
Cover design: Tory Herman
Book design: PerfecType, Nashville, TN

Library of Congress Cataloging-in-Publication Data
Print ISBN: 978-1-4514-6923-3
eBook ISBN: 978-1-4514-8436-6

Manufactured in the U.S.A.

Contents

PART ONE: THE TORAH/PENTATEUCH

PART TWO: THE DEUTERONOMISTIC HISTORY

PART THREE: PROPHECY

PART FOUR: THE WRITINGS

Maps

Illustrations

Preface

This book is written out of the experience of teaching introductory courses on the Old Testament or Hebrew Bible at several different institutions over thirty years. The students in these courses have included Catholic seminarians (at Mundelein Seminary and the University of Notre Dame), undergraduates (at DePaul, Notre Dame, and the University of Chicago), master of divinity students of all denominations (at Chicago and Yale), and master of arts students who, like the undergraduates, might have a religious commitment, or might not. They have been predominantly Christian, but have also included good numbers of Jews and Unitarians (especially at Chicago). Most of these students came to the courses with some knowledge of the Bible, but some were unencumbered by any previous knowledge of the subject. This introductory textbook is written to meet the needs of any or all such students. It presupposes a certain level of literacy, and some previous acquaintance with the Bible would definitely be helpful. It is intended, however, as a book for those who are beginning serious study rather than for experts. It is meant to be ecumenical, in the sense that it does not seek to impose any particular theological perspective, but to provide information and raise questions that should be relevant to any student, regardless of faith commitment. The information is largely drawn from the history, archaeology, and literature of the ancient Near East. The questions are primarily ethical, and reflect the fact that people of different faith commitments continue to read these texts as Scripture in the modern world.

The introduction is historical-critical in the sense that it emphasizes that the biblical text is the product of a particular time and place and is rooted in the culture of the ancient Near East. Since much of the Old Testament tells an ostensibly historical story, questions of historical accuracy must be addressed. In part, this is a matter of correlating the biblical account with evidence derived from archaeology and other historical sources. But it also leads to a discussion of the genre of the biblical text. The history-like appearance of biblical narrative should not be confused with historiography in the modern sense. Our best guide to the genre of biblical narrative is the corpus of literature from the ancient Near East that has been recovered over the last two hundred years.

This introduction, however, is not only historical in orientation. The primary importance of the Old Testament as Scripture lies in its ethical implications. In some cases, biblical material is ethically inspiring—the story of liberation from slavery in Egypt, the Ten Commandments, the preaching of the prophets on social justice. In other cases, however, it is repellent to modern sensibilities. The command to slaughter the Canaanites is the showcase example, but there are numerous issues relating to slaves, women, homosexuality, and the death penalty that are, at the very least, controversial in a modern context. In any of these cases, whether congenial to modern sensibilities or not, this introduction tries to use the biblical text as a springboard for raising issues of enduring importance. The text is not a source of answers on these issues, but rather a source of questions. Most students initially see the text through a filter of traditional interpretations. It is important to appreciate how these traditional interpretations arose, but also to ask how far they are grounded in the biblical text and whether other interpretations are possible.

Since this book is intended for students, I have tried to avoid entanglement in scholarly controversies. For this reason, there are no footnotes. Instead, each chapter is followed by suggestions for further reading. These suggestions point the student especially to commentaries and reference works that they can use as resources. Inevitably, the bibliographies are highly selective and consist primarily of books that I have found useful. Many other items could be listed with equal validity, but I hope that these suggestions will provide students with a reliable place to start. Since they are intended primarily for American students, they are limited to items that are available in English.

A large part of this book was written in 2000–2001, when I enjoyed a sabbatical year by courtesy of the Luce Foundation and Yale University. I am grateful to the Luce Foundation for its financial support and for the stimulation of two conferences with other Luce fellows. I am especially grateful to Richard Wood, then dean of Yale Divinity School, for making it possible for me to have a sabbatical in my first year at Yale.

I am also indebted to Samuel Adams, my graduate assistant in the production of this book, to Tony Finitsis, Patricia Ahearne-Kroll, John Ahn, and Matt Neujahr, who served as teaching assistants in my introductory course at Yale and gave me valuable feedback, and to the staff at Fortress, especially K. C. Hanson and Jessica Thoreson, who saw the book through the production process.

The book is dedicated to the students of Yale Divinity School.

Preface to the Second Edition

This revised second edition has updated bibliographies and is presented in a different format from the original.

I have made only minor changes to the text. I have moved the discussion of the book of Jonah from chapter 26 (the Hebrew Short Story) to chapter 20 (Postexilic Prophecy). I have separated out introductory comments on the Deuteronomistic History, Prophecy and the Writings. I have revised my analysis of the flood in chapter 2. Numerous smaller changes are scattered throughout the book.

I would like to thank Joel Baden and Ron Hendel for their comments and suggestions.

I am especially grateful to Neil Elliott and the staff at Fortress for shepherding this revision through the publication process.

Abbreviations

AB	Anchor Bible
ABD	*Anchor Bible Dictionary*. Edited by D. N. Freedman. 6 vols. Garden City, NY: Doubleday, 1992
AnBib	Analecta biblica
ANET	*Ancient Near Eastern Texts Relating to the Old Testament*. Edited by J. B. Pritchard. 3rd ed. Princeton: Princeton University Press, 1969
BA	*Biblical Archaeologist*
BAR	*Biblical Archaeology Review*
BETL	Bibliotheca ephemeridum theologicarum lovaniensium
Bib Int	Biblical Interpretation
BZAW	Beihefte zur Zeitschrift für die alttestamentliche Wissenschaft
CBQMS	Catholic Biblical Quarterly Monograph Series
CC	Continental Commentaries
CEJL	Commentaries on Early Jewish Literature
CHANE	Culture and History of the Ancient Near East
ConBOT	Coniectanea biblica (Old Testament series)
FOTL	Forms of the Old Testament Literature
GBS	Guides to Biblical Scholarship
HSM	Harvard Semitic Monographs
HTR	*Harvard Theological Review*
ICC	International Critical Commentary
ITC	International Theological Commentary
JBL	*Journal of Biblical Literature*
JPS	Jewish Publication Society
JSJSup	Journal for the Study of Judaism Supplement Series
JSOT	*Journal for the Study of the Old Testament*
JSOTSup	Journal for the Study of the Old Testament Supplement Series
LXX	Septuagint (Greek version)
MT	Masoretic text
NCB	New Century Bible
NIB	*New Interpreter's Bible*
NICOT	New International Commentary on the Old Testament
NRSV	New Revised Standard Version

OBT	Overtures to Biblical Theology
OEANE	*Oxford Encyclopedia of Archaeology in the Near East.* Edited by E. M. Meyers. 5 vols. New York: Oxford University Press, 1997
OTL	Old Testament Library
SBL	Society of Biblical Literature
SBLDS	SBL Dissertation Series
SBLEJL	SBL Early Jewish Literature Series
SBLMS	SBL Monograph Series
SBLWAW	SBL Writings from the Ancient World
VTE	Vassal Treaties of Esarhaddon
VTSup	Supplements to Vetus Testamentum
WBC	Word Biblical Commentary
WMANT	Wisssenschaftliche Monographien zum Alten und Neuen Testament

Introduction

INTRODUCTION

The following pages will introduce the different canons of the Hebrew Bible and Old Testament, considerations regarding the text of the Bible, questions about the Bible and history, and methods of biblical scholarship.

What Are the Hebrew Bible and Old Testament?

The writings that make up the Hebrew Bible or Christian Old Testament are by any reckoning among the most influential writings in Western history. In part, their influence may be ascribed to their literary quality, which establishes them as enduring classics—think, for example, of the depiction of the human predicament in the book of Job. But not all books of the Bible are literary classics, nor does their importance depend on their literary merit. The place of the Bible in Western culture derives from the fact that these books are regarded as sacred Scripture by Jews and Christians and are consequently viewed as authoritative in a way that other literary classics are not. The idea of sacred Scripture,

however, is by no means a clear one, and it is taken to mean very different things by different people. Some conservative Christians regard the Bible as the inspired word of God, verbally inerrant in all its details. At the liberal end of the spectrum, others regard it only as a witness to the foundational stages of Western religion.

It is often the case that people who hold passionate beliefs about the nature of the Bible are surprisingly unfamiliar with its content. Before we can begin to discuss what it might mean to regard the Bible as Scripture, there is much that we need to know about it of a more mundane nature. This material includes the content of the biblical text, the history of its composition, the literary genres in which it is written, and the problems and ambiguities that attend its interpretation. It is the purpose of this book to provide such introductory knowledge. If the Bible is Scripture, then the idea of Scripture must be formed in the light of what we actually find in the biblical text.

The Different Canons of Scripture

The Hebrew Bible and the Old Testament are not quite the same thing.

The Hebrew Bible is a collection of twenty-four books in three divisions: the Law (*Torah*), the Prophets (*N^ebi'im*), and the Writings (*K^etubim*), sometimes referred to by the acronym *Tanak*.

The Torah consists of five books: Genesis, Exodus, Leviticus, Numbers, and Deuteronomy (traditionally, the books of Moses).

The Prophets are divided into the four books of the Former Prophets (Joshua, Judges, Samuel, and Kings; 1 and 2 Samuel and 1 and 2 Kings are each counted as one book) and the four books of the Latter Prophets (Isaiah, Jeremiah, Ezekiel, and the Twelve; the Twelve Minor Prophets [Hosea, Joel, Amos, Obadiah, Jonah, Micah, Nahum, Habakkuk, Zephaniah, Haggai, Zechariah, Malachi] are counted as one book).

The Writings consist of eleven books: Psalms, Proverbs, Job, Song of Songs (or Canticles), Ruth, Lamentations, Qoheleth (or Ecclesiastes), Esther, Daniel, Ezra-Nehemiah (as one book), and Chronicles (1 and 2 Chronicles as one book).

The *Christian Old Testament* is so called in contrast to the New Testament, with the implication that the Old Testament is in some sense superseded by the New. Christianity has always wrestled with the theological significance of the Old Testament. In the second century C.E., Marcion taught that Christians should reject the Old Testament completely, but he was branded a heretic. The Old Testament has remained an integral part of the Christian canon of Scripture. There are significant differences, however, within the Christian churches as to the books that make up the Old Testament.

The *Protestant Old Testament* has the same content as the Hebrew Bible but arranges the books differently. The first five books are the same but are usually called the Pentateuch rather than the Torah. Samuel, Kings, Ezra-Nehemiah, and Chronicles are each counted as two books, and the Minor Prophets as twelve, yielding a total of thirty-nine books. The Former Prophets are regarded as historical books and grouped with Chronicles and Ezra-Nehemiah. Daniel is counted as a prophetic book. The (Latter) Prophets are moved to the end of the collection, so as to point forward to the New Testament.

The *Roman Catholic canon* contains several books that are not in the Hebrew Bible or the Protestant Old Testament: Tobit, Judith, Wisdom of Solomon, Ecclesiasticus (or the Wisdom of Jesus, son of Sirach = Ben Sira), Baruch, Letter of Jeremiah (= Baruch 6), 1 and 2 Maccabees. Furthermore, the books of Daniel and Esther contain passages that are not found in the Hebrew Bible. In the case of Daniel, these are the Prayer of Azariah and the Song of the Three Young Men, which are inserted in Daniel 3, and the stories of Susanna and Bel and the Dragon.

The Greek Orthodox Church has a still larger canon, including 1 Esdras (which reproduces the substance of the book of Ezra and parts of 2 Chronicles and Nehemiah), Psalm

151, the Prayer of Manasseh, and 3 Maccabees. A fourth book of Maccabees is included in Greek Bibles but is regarded as an appendix to the canon, while another book, 2 Esdras, is included as an appendix in the Latin Vulgate. These books are called Apocrypha (literally, "hidden away") in Protestant terminology. Catholics often refer to them as "deuterocanonical" or "secondarily canonical" books, in recognition of the fact that they are not found in the Hebrew Bible.

Some Eastern Christian churches have still more extensive canons of Scripture. The books of *Jubilees* and *1 Enoch* attained canonical status in the Ethiopian church.

Why Are There Different Canons of Scripture?

By "canon" we mean here simply the list of books included in the various Bibles. Strictly speaking, "canon" means "rule" or "measuring stick." The word was used in the plural by librarians and scholars in ancient Alexandria in the Hellenistic period (third and second centuries B.C.E.) with reference to literary classics, such as the Greek tragedies, and in Christian theology it came to be used in the singular for the Scriptures as "the rule of faith," from the fourth century C.E. on. In its theological use, canon is a Christian concept, and it is anachronistic in the context of ancient Judaism or even of earliest Christianity. In common parlance, however, "canon" has come to mean simply the corpus of Scriptures, which, as we have seen, varies among the Christian churches.

The differences between the various canons can be traced back to the differences between the Scriptures that became the Hebrew Bible and the larger collection that circulated in Greek. The Hebrew Bible took shape over several hundred years and attained its final form only in the first century C.E. The Torah was the earliest part to crystallize. It is often associated with the work of Ezra in the fifth century B.C.E. It may have been substantially complete a century before that, at the end of the Babylonian exile (586–539 B.C.E.), but there may have also been some additions or modifications after the time of Ezra. The Hebrew collection of the Prophets seems to have been formed before the second century B.C.E. We find references to the Torah and the Prophets as authoritative Scriptures in the second century B.C.E., in the book of Ben Sira (Ecclesiasticus) and again in the Dead Sea

Fig. Int.1 Ezra (?) is depicted in a fresco from the third-century C.E. synagogue at Dura-Europos on the Parthian border. Commons .wikimedia.org

CANONS OF THE HEBREW BIBLE/OLD TESTAMENT

THE HEBREW BIBLE

Torah:

Genesis
Exodus
Leviticus
Numbers
Deuteronomy

Prophets (Former):

Joshua
Judges
Samuel (1 and 2)
Kings (1 and 2)

Prophets (Latter):

Isaiah
Jeremiah
Ezekiel
Minor Prophets ("The Twelve"):
  Hosea, Joel, Amos, Obadiah,
  Jonah, Micah, Nahum, Habakkuk,
  Zephaniah, Haggai, Zechariah,
  Malachi

Writings:

Psalms
Proverbs
Job
Song of Songs
Ruth
Lamentations
Qoheleth (Ecclesiastes)
Esther
Daniel
Ezra-Nehemiah
Chronicles (1 and 2)

PROTESTANT OLD TESTAMENT

Pentateuch:

Genesis
Exodus
Leviticus
Numbers
Deuteronomy

Historical Books

Joshua
Judges
Ruth
1 Samuel
2 Samuel
1 Kings
2 Kings
1 Chronicles
2 Chronicles
Ezra
Nehemiah
Esther

Poetry/Wisdom

Job
Psalms
Proverbs
Ecclesiastes (Qoheleth)
Song of Solomon (Songs)

Prophets

Isaiah
Jeremiah
Lamentations
Ezekiel
Daniel

Hosea	Nahum
Joel	Habakkuk
Amos	Zephaniah
Obadiah	Haggai
Jonah	Zechariah
Micah	Malachi

Apocrypha

1 Esdras
2 Esdras
Tobit
Judith
Additions to Esther
Wisdom of Solomon
Ecclesiasticus (Wisdom
  of Sirach)
Baruch
Letter of Jeremiah
Prayer of Azariah and
  Song of the Three
  Young Men
Susanna
Bel and the Dragon
Prayer of Manasseh
1 Maccabees
2 Maccabees

ROMAN CATHOLIC OLD TESTAMENT

Pentateuch

Genesis
Exodus
Leviticus
Numbers
Deuteronomy

Historical Books

Joshua
Judges
Ruth
1 Samuel
2 Samuel
1 Kings
2 Kings
1 Chronicles
2 Chronicles
Ezra (Greek and Russian
    Orthodox Bibles also
    include 1 Esdras, and
    Russian Orthodox
    includes 2 Esdras)
Nehemiah
Tobit
Judith
Esther (with additions)
1 Maccabees
2 Maccabees
(Greek and Russian
    Orthodox Bibles include
    3 Maccabees)

Poetry/Wisdom

Job
Psalms (Greek and Russian
    Orthodox Bibles include
    Psalm 151 and Prayer of
    Manasseh)
Proverbs
Ecclesiastes (Qoheleth)
Song of Solomon (Songs)
Wisdom of Solomon
Ecclesiasticus (Wisdom of
    Sirach)

Prophets

Isaiah
Jeremiah
Lamentations
Baruch (includes Letter of
    Jeremiah)
Ezekiel
Daniel (with additions)
Hosea
Joel
Amos
Obadiah
Jonah
Micah
Nahum
Habakkuk
Zephaniah
Haggai
Zechariah
Malachi

Scrolls (in a document known as 4QMMT). The book of Daniel, which was composed about 164 B.C.E., did not find a place among the Prophets in the Hebrew Bible, and this has often been taken as an indication that the collection of the Prophets was already fixed at the time of its composition. The preface to the book of Ben Sira also mentions other writings that were regarded as authoritative. There does not, however, seem to have been any definitive list of these writings before the first century C.E. Most references to the Jewish Scriptures in the writings of this period (including references in the New Testament) speak only of "the Law and the Prophets." The Psalms are sometimes added as a third category. The Dead Sea Scrolls include a Psalms Scroll that has additional psalms, and this would seem to indicate that the canonical collection of psalms had not yet been fixed. The first references to a fixed number of authoritative Hebrew writings are found toward the end of the first century C.E. The Jewish historian Josephus gives the number as twenty-two, while the Jewish apocalypse of *4 Ezra* (contained in 2 Esdras 3–14) speaks of twenty-four. It is possible, however, that both had the same books in mind but that Josephus combined some books (perhaps Judges-Ruth and Jeremiah-Lamentations) that were counted separately in *4 Ezra*.

The fixing of the Hebrew canon is often associated with the so-called Council of Jamnia, the discussions of an authoritative group of rabbis in the period after the fall of Jerusalem in 70 C.E. It is misleading, however, to speak of a "Council of Jamnia," since it suggests a meeting like the great ecumenical councils of the Christian church in later centuries. Before the fall of Jerusalem, Rabbi Johanan ben Zakkai established an academy in the coastal city of Jamnia, and this academy assumed a leadership role after the fall. Its discussions, however, had the character of a school or court rather than of a church council. We know that the rabbis debated whether some books (Qoheleth and Song of Songs) "make the hands unclean" (that is, whether they are holy books and should be included among the Scriptures). There seems, however, to have been further discussions of this kind at a later time, and there is no evidence that the rabbis proclaimed a formal list of Scriptures. Nonetheless, it is at this time (70–100 C.E.) that we first find references to a fixed number of authoritative books. It may be that the list adopted consisted of the books that were accepted by the Pharisees already before the fall of Jerusalem.

It is important to recognize that the books that were included in the Hebrew Bible were only a small selection from the religious writings that were current in Judaism around the turn of the era. A larger selection was preserved in the Greek Scriptures that were taken over by the early Christians, but had been already developed in Jewish communities outside the land of Israel, especially in Alexandria in Egypt. According to legend, the Torah had been translated into Greek at the request of Ptolemy II Philadelphus, king of Egypt, in the first half of the third century B.C.E., by seventy-two elders. (The story is told in the *Letter of Aristeas,* a Greek composition from the second century B.C.E.) The translation became known as the Septuagint or LXX (Septuagint means "seventy"). The name was eventually extended to cover the whole collection of Greek Scriptures. These included translations of some books that were written in Hebrew but were not included in the Hebrew Bible (e.g., the book of Ben Sira, 1 Maccabees) and also some books that never existed in Hebrew but were composed in Greek (2 Maccabees, Wisdom of Solomon). There has been some debate as to whether the Jews of Alexandria had a larger collection of Scriptures than the Jews in the land of Israel. But there is no evidence that there ever existed a distinct Alexandrian canon. Rather, the Jews of Alexandria did not set a limit to the number of the sacred writings, as the rabbis did after the fall of Jerusalem. The Jewish community in Alexandria was virtually wiped out in the early second century C.E. Christians who took over the Greek Scriptures of the Jews, then, inherited a larger and more fluid collection than the Hebrew Bible. Centuries, later, there is still considerable variation among the lists of Old Testament books cited by the church fathers.

When Jerome translated the Bible into Latin about 400 C.E., he was troubled by the discrepancies between the Hebrew and Greek Bibles. He advocated the superiority of the Hebrew (*Hebraica veritas*, "the Hebrew truth") and based his translation on it. He also translated the books that were not found in the Hebrew but accorded them lesser status. His translation (the Vulgate) was very influential, but nonetheless the Christian church continued to accept the larger Greek canon down through the Middle Ages. At the time of the Reformation, Martin Luther advocated a return to the Hebrew canon, although he also translated the Apocrypha. In reaction to Luther, the Catholic Church defined its larger canon at the Council of Trent in the mid-sixteenth century.

It should be apparent from this discussion that the list of books that make up the Hebrew Bible and the Christian Old Testament emerged gradually over time. The list was (and to some degree still is) a subject of dispute. The various canons were eventually determined by the decisions of religious communities. Christian theology has often drawn a sharp line between Scripture and tradition, but in fact Scripture itself is a product of tradition. Its content and shape have been matters of debate and are subject to the decisions of religious authorities in the various religious traditions.

The Text of the Bible

Not only did the list of books that make up the Bible take shape gradually over time, but so did the words that make up the biblical text. Modern English translations of the Bible are based on the printed editions of the Hebrew Bible and the principal ancient translations (especially Greek and Latin). These printed editions are themselves based on ancient manuscripts. In the case of the Hebrew Bible, the most important manuscripts date from the tenth and eleventh centuries C.E., almost a thousand years after the canon, or list of contents, of the Hebrew Bible was fixed. The text found in these manuscripts is known as the Masoretic text, or MT. The name comes from an Aramaic word meaning to transmit or hand down. The Masoretes were the transmitters of the text. What is called the Masoretic text, however, is the form of the text that was established by the Ben Asher family of Masoretes in Tiberias in Galilee. This text is found in the Aleppo Codex, which dates from the early tenth century C.E. This codex was kept for centuries by the Jewish community in

Aleppo in Syria. About a quarter of it, including the Torah, was lost in a fire in 1948. It is now in Jerusalem. The Pentateuch is preserved in a tenth-century codex from Cairo. Codex Leningrad B19^A from the eleventh century is the single most complete source of all the biblical books in the Ben Asher tradition. It is known to have been corrected according to a Ben Asher manuscript. The Cairo Codex of the Prophets dates from 896 C.E., and a few other manuscripts are from the tenth century. These manuscripts are our oldest witnesses to the vowels of most of the Hebrew text. In antiquity, Hebrew was written without vowels. The Masoretes introduced the vowels as pointing or marks above and below the letters, as part of their effort to fix the text exactly. There are fragments of vocalized texts from the sixth or perhaps the fifth century C.E. Besides the Tiberian tradition of vocalization, represented by the Ben Asher family, there was also Babylonian tradition, associated with the family of Ben Naphtali. The first printed Hebrew Bibles appeared in the late fifteenth century C.E.

The discovery of the Dead Sea Scrolls in caves near Qumran south of Jericho, beginning in 1947, brought to light manuscripts of biblical books more than a thousand years older than the Aleppo Codex. Every biblical book except Esther is attested in the Scrolls, but many of the manuscripts are very fragmentary. (A small fragment of Nehemiah only came to light in the 1990s). These manuscripts, of course, do not have the Masoretic pointing to indicate the vowels; that system was only developed centuries later. But they throw very important light on the history of the consonantal text.

Fig. Int.2   A page from Deuteronomy in the Aleppo Codex. Commons.wikimedia.org

Fragments of about two hundred biblical scrolls were found in the caves near Qumran. Most of the fragments are small, but the great Isaiah Scroll, 1QIsa^a, contains the whole book. This scroll dates from about 100 B.C.E.; the oldest biblical scrolls from Qumran are as old as the third century B.C.E. Most of the scrolls contained only one biblical book, but three Torah scrolls contained two consecutive books. The Twelve Minor Prophets were contained in one scroll. Many of these texts are in substantial agreement with the text copied by the Masoretes a thousand years later. But the Scrolls also contain other forms of biblical texts. Several biblical texts, including an important copy of the book of Exodus (4QpaleoExod^m), are closer to the form of the text preserved in the Samaritan tradition. (The Samaritan text is often longer than the MT, because it adds sentences or phrases based on other parallel biblical passages, or adds a statement to indicate the fulfillment of a command that has been described.) Moreover, the text of some other biblical books is very similar to that presupposed in the ancient Greek translation (LXX).

Before the discovery of the Dead Sea Scrolls, our oldest copies of Old Testament texts were found in Greek translations. There are fragments of Greek biblical manuscripts from the second century B.C.E. on. The oldest complete manuscripts date from the fourth century C.E. These are Codex Vaticanus and Codex Sinaiticus. Another important manuscript, Codex Alexandrinus, dates from the fifth century. These manuscripts are known as uncials and are written in Greek capital letters.

The Greek translations of biblical books were generally very literal and reflected the Hebrew text closely. Nonetheless, in many cases the LXX differed significantly from the MT. For example, the books of Jeremiah and Job are much shorter in the Greek than in the Hebrew. The order of chapters in Jeremiah also differs from that of the MT. In 1 Samuel 16–18, the story of David and Goliath is much shorter in the LXX. In Daniel 4–6 the LXX has a very different text from that found in the MT. New light was shed on some of these cases by the Dead Sea Scrolls. The Scrolls contain Hebrew texts of Jeremiah that are very close to what is presupposed in the LXX. (Other copies of Jeremiah at Qumran agree with the MT; both forms of the text were in circulation.) It now seems likely that the differences between the Greek and the Hebrew texts were not due to the translators but reflect the fact that the Greek was based on a shorter Hebrew text. This is also true in 1 Samuel 16–18 and in a number of other cases.

Not all differences between the LXX and the MT are illuminated by the Dead Sea Scrolls. The Scrolls do not contain a short text of Job or a deviant text of Daniel 4–6 such as that found in the LXX. Nonetheless, the assumption must now be that the Greek translators faithfully reflect the Hebrew they had before them. This means that there were different forms of the Hebrew text in circulation in the third, second, and first centuries B.C.E. Indeed, different forms of the text of some books are preserved in the Dead Sea Scrolls. In some cases, the LXX may preserve an older form of the text than the MT. For example, the shorter form of Jeremiah is likely to be older than the form preserved in the Hebrew Bible.

What this discussion shows is that it makes little sense to speak of verbal inerrancy or the like in connection with the biblical text. In many cases we cannot be sure what the

Fig. Int.3   A fragment of an Isaiah scroll from Qumran (1QIsaᵇ). Commons.wikimedia.org exact words of the Bible should be. Indeed, it is open to question whether we should speak of *the* biblical text at all; in some cases, we may have to accept the fact that we have more than one form of the text and that we cannot choose between them. This is not to say that the wording of the Bible is unreliable. The Dead Sea Scrolls have shown that there is, on the whole, an amazing degree of continuity in the way the text has been copied over thousands of years. But even a casual comparison of a few current English Bibles (say the New Revised Standard Version, the New English Bible, and the Living Bible) should make clear that there are many areas of uncertainty in the biblical text. Of course, translations also involve interpretation, and interpretation adds to the uncertainty. For the present, however, I only want to make the point that we do not have one perfect copy of the original text, if such a thing ever existed. We only have copies made centuries after the books were originally composed, and these copies often differ among themselves.

The Bible and History

The Bible is a product of history. It took shape over time, and its content and even its wording changed in the process. In this it is no different from any other book, except that the Bible is really a collection of books, and its composition and transmission is spread over an exceptionally long period of time.

The Bible, however, is also immersed in history in another way that has implications for how we should study it. Much of it tells the story of a people, proceeding in chronological order, and so it has at least the appearance of a historical narrative. (One of the most influential biblical scholars of the twentieth century, Gerhard von Rad, once said that the Old Testament is "a history book.") Not all books of the Bible have this history-like appearance. Books like Proverbs and Job have virtually no reference to dates or places that would enable us to locate them in history. But these books are exceptional in the corpus. If we read through the Pentateuch, we follow a story about humanity from the dawn of history, and then the emergence of a particular people, Israel. The story of this people continues in the "Former Prophets" and in Chronicles and Ezra-Nehemiah (and also in the books of Maccabees if we include the Apocrypha). The books of the prophets repeatedly refer to events in that history and are virtually unintelligible without reference to it. Only in the Writings, in some of the Psalms and in the wisdom books (Job, Proverbs, Qoheleth), does the history of Israel recede from view, and even then it reappears in the later wisdom books in the Apocrypha (Ben Sira and Wisdom of Solomon).

For most of Jewish and Christian history, there has been an uncritical assumption that the biblical story is historically true. In fact, for much of this time the Bible was virtually the only source of information about the events in question. In the last two hundred years, however, copious information about the ancient world has come to light through archaeological exploration and through the recovery of ancient literature. This information is often at variance with the account given in the Bible. Consequently, there is now something of a crisis in the interpretation of the Bible. This is a crisis of credibility: in brief, if the Bible is not the infallible, inerrant book it was once thought to be (and is still thought to be by some), in what way is it reliable, or even serviceable at all? This crisis reaches far beyond questions of historicity and reaches most fundamentally to questions of divine revelation and ethical teaching. But historical questions have played an especially important part in bringing it on. In the modern world, there is often a tendency to equate truth with historical fact. This tendency may be naïve and unsophisticated, but it is widespread and we cannot ignore it. If we are to arrive at a more sophisticated conception of biblical truth, we must first clarify the complex ways in which these books relate to history.

Biblical Chronology

It may be useful to begin with an outline of history as it emerges from the biblical text. The story begins, audaciously, with the creation of the world. In Genesis 5 we are given a chronological summary of the ten generations from Adam to the flood. This period is said to last 1,656 years. The patriarchs of this period are said to live prodigiously long lives. Methuselah's 969 years are proverbial, but seven of the ten figures have life spans over 900 years. After the flood, ten more generations are listed rapidly, concluding with Terah, father of Abraham (Genesis 11). This period is allotted 290 years, and life spans drop from an initial 600 in the case of Shem to a modest 148 in the case of Nahor, father of Terah. There follows the period of the patriarchs, Abraham, Isaac, Jacob, and the sons of Jacob, which is narrated in Genesis 12–50. A total of 290 years elapse from the birth of Abraham to the descent of Jacob and his family into Egypt. The sojourn in Egypt is said to last 430 years

in Exod 12:40. After the exodus, the Israelites wander for 40 years in the wilderness. Then they invade the land that would be known as Israel. After a campaign of 5 years, they occupy the land under the rule of the judges for some 470 years. The period of the judges is brought to an end by the transition to kingship under Saul and David, as recorded in 1 and 2 Samuel. According to 1 Kgs 6:1, David's son Solomon began to build the temple in Jerusalem in the fourth year of his reign, 480 years after the Israelites came out of Egypt. This figure is obviously incompatible with the total number of years assigned to the judges.

In the generation after Solomon, the kingdom was divided in two. The northern kingdom of Israel survived for two hundred years until it was conquered by the Assyrians and its capital, Samaria, was destroyed. The southern kingdom of Judah survived more than a century longer until it was conquered by the Babylonians, and Jerusalem and the temple were destroyed. A large number of the most prominent inhabitants of Jerusalem were deported to Babylon. This episode in history is called the Babylonian exile. It came to an end when Babylon was conquered by the Persians. Jewish exiles were then allowed to return to Jerusalem and to rebuild the temple. The period between the Babylonian exile and the end of the biblical era is known as the postexilic period, or as the period of the Second Temple. For most of that time, Judah was a province, subject to foreign rulers, first the Persians, then the Greeks. Judah was ruled in turn by the Greek kingdoms of Egypt (the Ptolemies) and of Syria (the Seleucids). The Maccabean revolt led to a period of Jewish independence that lasted roughly a century, before Judah came under the power of Rome.

The Second Temple was finally destroyed in the course of a revolt against Rome.

The destructions of Samaria and Jerusalem allow us to correlate the history of Israel with the general history of the Near East, since these events are also recorded in Assyrian and Babylonian records. The fall of Samaria is dated to 722 B.C.E. The Babylonians first captured Jerusalem in 597, and the destruction of the temple took place in a second conquest in 586. (A number of other events from the period of the monarchy can also be correlated with Assyrian and Babylonian records.) The chronology of the Second Temple period is relatively secure. The restoration of the Jewish community after the exile is dated to 539. The Maccabean revolt took place between 168 and 164 B.C.E. The Roman general Pompey entered Jerusalem in 63 B.C.E. The first Jewish revolt against Rome broke out in 66 C.E., and

Fig. Int.4 Bishop James Ussher, who dated creation at 4004 B.C.E. Commons .wikimedia.org

the Jerusalem temple was destroyed by the Romans in 70 C.E.

The chronology of the preexilic period is more problematic. If we work back from the dates of the destructions, by adding up

CHRONOLOGY	
Approximate dates implied in Bible for early history:	Modern chronology:
4000 B.C.E. Creation	(Scientists estimate the age of the earth is 4.5 billion years.)
2400 Flood	
2401	
2100 Abraham	The historical value of the stories of the patriarchs is uncertain. Modern scholars have often proposed a date of 1800 B.C.E. for Abraham.
1875 Descent into Egypt	
1445 Exodus	1250 B.C.E. (approx.) Exodus from Egypt (disputed).
	1250–1000 Emergence of Israel in the highlands of Canaan.

CHRONOLOGY		
Approximate dates implied in Bible for early history:	**Modern chronology:**	
1000 David	1000–960 (approx.)	King David. Beginning of monarchy in Jerusalem (disputed).
	960–922 (approx.)	King Solomon. Building of Jerusalem temple (disputed).
(From 922 on, the implied biblical dates are generally compatible with those of modern scholarship.)	922	Division of kingdom: Israel in the north, Judah in the south.
	722/721	Destruction of Samaria, capital of Israel, by the Assyrians. End of kingdom of Israel.
	621	Reform of Jerusalem cult by King Josiah. Promulgation of "the book of the law" (some form of Deuteronomy).
	597	Capture of Jerusalem by Babylonians. Deportation of king and nobles to Babylon.
	586	Destruction of Jerusalem by Babylonians. More extensive deportations. Beginning of Babylonian exile.
	539	Conquest of Babylon by Cyrus of Persia. Jewish exiles allowed to return to Jerusalem. End of exile. Judah becomes a province of Persia
	520–515	Rebuilding of Jerusalem temple.
	458	Ezra is sent from Babylon to Jerusalem with a copy of the Law.
	336–323	Alexander the Great conquers the Persian Empire.
	312–198	Judea controlled by the Ptolemies of Egypt (a Greek dynasty, founded by one of Alexander's generals).
	198	Jerusalem conquered by the Seleucids of Syria (also a Greek dynasty).

CHRONOLOGY		
	168/167	Persecution of Jews in Jerusalem by Antiochus IV Epiphanes, king of Syria. Maccabean revolt.
	66–70 C.E.	First Jewish revolt against Rome. Destruction of Jerusalem temple.
	132–135 C.E.	Second Jewish revolt under Bar Kochba. Jerusalem rebuilt as Aelia Capitolina, with a temple to Jupiter Capitolinus.

the years of the kings of Israel and Judah, we arrive at a date in the mid-tenth century B.C.E. for Solomon. Because of inconsistencies and ambiguities in the biblical record, scholars arrive at slightly different dates, but most place the beginning of his reign in the 960s and its conclusion in the 920s. If the exodus took place 480 years before the building of the temple, this would point to a date around 1445. This in turn would give a date of approximately 1876 for the descent of Jacob's family into Egypt and place Abraham around 2100. The seventeenth-century Irish Anglican bishop James Ussher famously calculated the date of creation as 4004 B.C.E.

Modern scholarship has generally accepted the biblical chronology of the period of the monarchy since it can be correlated with nonbiblical sources at several points. The dates for the exodus and the patriarchs, however, are viewed with great skepticism. The life spans of the patriarchs are unrealistic, ranging from 110 to 175 years. The 430 years in Egypt is supposed to cover only three generations. Most scholars place the exodus in the thirteenth century, on the assumption that the cities of Pithom and Rameses, where the Israelites labored according to Exodus 1, were built by Pharaoh Ramesses II, who ruled

Egypt for almost two-thirds of that century. Many scholars now question whether we can claim any historical knowledge about a patriarchal period or even an exodus. For the present, however, it will suffice to note that both the biblical record itself and the majority view of modern scholarship place the emergence of Israel as a people in the second half of the second millennium B.C.E., and that modern reconstructions favor the last quarter of that millennium, roughly 1250–1000 B.C.E.

One implication of this chronological survey is that Israel was a late arrival on the stage of Near Eastern history. The great civilizations of Egypt and Mesopotamia had already flourished for a millennium and a half before the tribes of Israel appeared on the scene. The history of Israel was shaped to a great extent by its location between these great powers. We shall turn to this broader historical context in the following chapter.

A second implication of the chronological survey is that on any reckoning there is a gap of several centuries between the date when the biblical books were written and the events that they purport to describe. Traditionally, the books of the Torah were supposed to be works of Moses, but it has long been clear that Moses could not have been

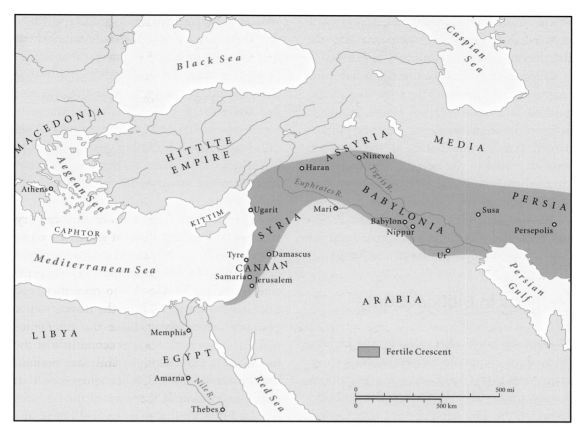

Map. Int.1   The Ancient Near East.

their author. For much of the twentieth century, scholars believed that the stories contained in the Torah were first written down in the tenth century, in the time of David or Solomon, although the final form of the books was clearly much later. Confidence in the supposed tenth-century sources has been eroded, however, as we shall see in chapter 2. While the Torah incorporates material from various centuries, it is increasingly viewed as a product of the sixth century B.C.E. or later. There is then a gap of several hundred years between the literature and the events it describes.

It now seems clear that all the Hebrew Bible received its final shape in the postexilic, or Second Temple, period. The books of Joshua through Kings, which make up the Former Prophets in the Hebrew Bible, are called in modern scholarship "the Deuteronomistic History." These books were edited in light of the book of Deuteronomy, no earlier than the sixth century B.C.E., although the events they describe range, supposedly, from about 1200 B.C.E. to the destruction of Jerusalem. The earliest of the great prophets, Amos, Hosea, and Isaiah, lived in the eighth century. The book of Isaiah, however, includes not only oracles from the original prophet, but much material that was clearly composed after the Babylonian exile. (Accordingly, Isaiah 40–66 is called Second, or Deutero-, Isaiah, and chapters 56–66 are sometimes further distinguished as Third, or Trito-, Isaiah, although, as far as we know, there was only one prophet named Isaiah.) The books of the prophets were all edited in the Second Temple period, although we cannot be sure just when. Most of the books in the Writings were composed in the postexilic period, although the Psalms and Proverbs may contain material from the time of the kingdoms of Israel and Judah.

Methods in Biblical Study

Most of the books that make up the Hebrew Bible were composed in several stages over many centuries (there are some exceptions, mainly among the Writings and the shorter books of the prophets). Books like Genesis and Judges incorporate tales that may have originated as folklore or popular short stories. But these stories were shaped and edited, probably by several different hands, over hundreds of years. Moreover, ancient editors were not always as concerned with consistency as their modern counterparts. Consequently, there are many gaps and inconsistencies in the biblical text, and it seems to reflect several different historical settings.

In light of this situation, it is not reasonable to expect that we can read a book like Genesis as we would read a modern novel. The literary critic Robert Alter, who is a leading advocate of a literary approach to the Bible, speaks of "composite artistry" in the case of Genesis. One can, and should, appreciate the artistry of the finished product. But the reason that this artistry is recognized as composite is that there are problems in the text that cannot be explained on the assumption of a unified composition. If we are to take the composite character of biblical narrative seriously, we cannot avoid some measure of what Alter calls "excavative scholarship"—the attempt to understand the sources, so that we can better appreciate the artistry with which they were put together.

The history of biblical scholarship is in large part a sequence of attempts to come to grips with the composite character of the biblical text. In the nineteenth century, "literary criticism" of the Bible was understood primarily as the separation of sources (source criticism), especially in the case of the Pentateuch. (Source criticism was similarly in vogue in Homeric scholarship in the same period.) This phase of biblical scholarship found its classic expression in the work of the German scholar Julius Wellhausen (1844–1918) in the 1870s and 1880s. We shall consider the legacy of Wellhausen, which is still enormously

Fig. Int.5 Julius Wellhausen. Commons.

wikimedia.org

influential, in chapter 2. The strength of this kind of scholarship was that it was based on very close reading of the biblical text and yielded numerous acute observations about its inner tensions. Many of these observations are still important and require explanation. The weakness, however, was that it tended to expect the text to conform to modern expectations about consistency. It relied on rational analysis of the text but made little use of comparative material from the ancient Near East. Wellhausen can scarcely be blamed for this omission. The great works of ancient Near Eastern literature, such as the creation story *Enuma Elish* and the flood story contained in the Epic of Gilgamesh (see chapter 1) were only first edited and published around the time that Wellhausen was doing his work on the Old Testament.

A reaction against this kind of source-criticism appeared in the work of another German scholar, Hermann Gunkel (1862–1932), in the last decade of the nineteenth century and the first two decades of the twentieth. Gunkel is regarded as the founder of *form criticism*. This method tries to focus on the smaller units that make up the biblical text, such as the individual stories of Genesis. Gunkel drew attention to the importance of literary form or genre. He recognized that the kind of truth that we may expect from a text varies with its genre. For example, we should not read poetry as if it were factual reporting. He also drew attention to the importance of social location (the *Sitz im Leben*) for the meaning of a text. It is important to know the purpose for which a text is composed, whether, for example, it was meant to serve as a cult legend in a sacred celebration or was meant for entertainment around a campfire.

Fig. Int.6   Hermann Gunkel.
Commons.wikimedia.org

Gunkel also made extensive use of the newly available Babylonian literature for purposes of comparison with the biblical material. He did not deny the validity of source criticism as practiced by Wellhausen, but it was not the focus of his attention. Some of the later practitioners of form criticism tended to use the study of literary forms as a source-critical tool and to reconstruct earlier forms of biblical passages that fitted the ideal form. This kind of procedure has rightly been criticized. But Gunkel's basic insights into the importance of literary form and social location, and of comparison with other Near Eastern literature, remain valid and important.

One disadvantage of form criticism was that it tended to break up the biblical text into small fragments. In the mid-twentieth century, a reaction against this fragmentation arose in the form of redaction criticism. Here the focus was on the way in which the smaller units were combined by an editor who imposed his own theological agenda on the material. The classic works of redaction criticism were again by German scholars, Gerhard von Rad (1901–1971) and Martin Noth (1902–1968). Von Rad is best known for his work on the Pentateuch, although he also made important contributions in other areas. His focus, however, was not so much on the final form of the Pentateuch as on the main narrative source, the Yahwist or J source (see chapter 2). His work then still relied heavily on source criticism. Noth demonstrated the editorial unity of the Deuteronomistic History (Joshua through Kings). Redaction criticism was closely bound up with source criticism and form criticism, but it showed the beginnings of a shift of interest that has continued in more recent scholarship, placing the main emphasis on the later rather than on the earlier forms of the text.

The scholarship mentioned thus far all developed in Germany, where the most influential biblical criticism developed in the nineteenth and early twentieth centuries. A different tradition of scholarship developed in North America, which attached great importance to archaeology as a source of independent confirmation of the biblical text. Archaeological discoveries could also help to fill out the context of the biblical material. The dominant figure in North American scholarship through the first half of the twentieth century was W. F. Albright (1891–1971). Albright also made extensive use of the literature of the ancient Near East as the context within which the Bible should be understood. He made especially fruitful use of the Canaanite literature discovered at Ugarit in Syria in 1929 (see chapter 1). Albright's view of the history of Israel found classic expression in the work of his student John Bright (1908–1995). It also found an enthusiastic response among Israeli scholars,

Fig. Int.7   W. F. Albright

who have generally been wary of the analytical approach of German scholarship.

In Albright's lifetime, archaeology was believed to support the essential historicity of the biblical account (not necessarily in all its details), although there were some troubling discrepancies (for example, archaeologists found no evidence of the destruction of a walled city at Jericho in the time of Joshua). In the last quarter of the century, however, the tide has turned on this subject. Discrepancies between the archaeological record and the biblical narrative are now seen to outweigh the points of convergence. We shall discuss various examples of this problem in the course of this book. For the present, it may suffice to say that these discrepancies undermine any simple assumption that biblical texts are historical reports, and direct attention again to the literary character of the biblical corpus. (A lucid account of the discrepancies between the biblical account and the results of archaeology can be found in I. Finkelstein and N. A. Silberman, *The Bible Unearthed.*)

CHRONOLOGY OF MODERN BIBLICAL SCHOLARSHIP

1735	Jean Astruc observes multiple names for the divinity in the Pentateuch.
1805	W. M. L. de Wette dates Deuteronomy later than the rest of the Pentateuch.
1822	Jean-Francois Champollion deciphers Egyptian hieroglyphics for the first time.
1860s	K. H. Graf and A. Kuenen establish a chronological order for the various "sources" in the Pentateuch: (J, E, P, D).
1870s	Discovery of great works of Akkadian literature, such as the creation story Enuma Elish and the Gilgamesh epic.
1878	Julius Wellhausen, in *Prolegmonena to the History of Israel*, presents his classic study of the Documentary Hypothesis and a new source chronology: J, E, D, P.
1890–1920	Hermann Gunkel pioneers Form Criticism, which examines the literary genre of shorter biblical passages and their *Sitz im Leben* (social location).
1920s–30s	Discovery of Ugarit (1929) and the efforts of W. F. Albright to confirm the historical accuracy of the Bible through archaeology.
Mid-20th century	Gerhard von Rad and Martin Noth examine the editorial history of biblical texts through redaction criticism. • American scholarship dominated by Albright and his students: • John Bright's *History of Israel* (1959) provides synthesis of biblical data and ancient Near Eastern history. • Biblical theology movement, emphasizing the "acts of God in history," typified by archaeologist G. E. Wright.
1947–54	Discovery of Dead Sea Scrolls at Qumran
1960s–present	Biblical scholarship characterized by a multiplicity of approaches, including: • the study of religion and literature of Israel in light of Near Eastern, especially Ugaritic traditions, typified by F. M. Cross, *Canaanite Myth and Hebrew Ethic* (1973) • sociological approaches, typified by N. Gottwald, *The Tribes of Yahweh* (1979) • literary approaches, typified by R. Alter, *The Art of Biblical Narrative* (1981) and *The Art of Biblical Poetry* (1985) • feminist/literary approaches, typified by P. Trible, *God and the Rhetoric of Sexuality* (1978) and *Texts of Terror* (1984) • canonical approach to biblical theology, typified by B. Childs, *Introduction to the Old Testament as Scripture* (1979) • revisionist Pentateuchal studies, questioning traditional sources: see overview by E. Nicholson, *The Pentateuch in the Twentieth Century* (1998) • revisionist approaches to Israelite history: see I. Finkelstein and N. A. Silberman, *The Bible Unearthed* (2001)

At the dawn of the twenty-first century, biblical scholarship is characterized by a diversity of methods. Here I will comment only on two broad trends: the rise of literary criticism and the influence of sociological methods.

The Bible is literature, whatever else it may be, and any serious biblical study must have a literary component. Literary scholarship, however, is of many kinds. Beginning in the 1960s, literary criticism of the Bible was heavily influenced by a movement called "New Criticism" in the study of English literature. New Criticism was a formalistic movement that held that the meaning of a text can be found through close examination of the text itself, without extensive research into questions of social, historical, and literary context. The attraction of this method was that it redirected attention to the text itself rather than to archaeological artifacts or hypothetical source documents. Nonetheless, it has obvious limitations insofar as it leaves out of account factors that may help to clarify and explain the text. In general literary studies, a reaction against the formalism of New Criticism has arisen in a movement called "New Historicism," which appreciates the importance of contextual information while still maintaining its focus on the literary text.

Another consequence of the rise of literary criticism has been increased attention to the final form of biblical books. (This has also been encouraged by the theological "canonical approach" advocated in the work of B. S. Childs [1923–2007].) On the whole, this has been a positive development. Some older scholarship was so preoccupied with identifying sources that it lost sight of the actual text as we have it. We should bear in mind, however, that the books of the Bible are not governed by the same literary conventions as a modern novel or treatise. In many cases they are loose compilations, and the conventional book divisions are not always reliable guides to literary coherence. There is more than one way to read such literature. If we are to appreciate the "composite artistry" of biblical literature, then the final form of the text cannot be the exclusive focus of our attention.

Beginning in the last decades of the twentieth century, literary criticism has been influenced by the intellectual trends of postmodernism, which are skeptical of any attempt to reduce a text to a single meaning. All interpretation is perspectival and colored by the social location of the interpreter. Deconstruction, a style of interpretation associated with the French philosopher Jacques Derrida, delights in pulling on the loose threads in the text to recover suppressed meanings. Postmodernism has been invoked in biblical studies in various ways. The most prominent advocate of postmodern perspectives is Walter Brueggemann, who has attempted an ambitious *Theology of the Old Testament* from a postmodern perspective. Brueggemann emphasizes the presence of "counter-traditions" in the text that call into question some of the more prominent themes. Some conservative scholars appeal to postmodernism as a way to evade the implications of historical criticism, but they are seldom willing to embrace the full implications of postmodern indeterminacy.

This introduction is written in the belief that the best guide to the literary character of the biblical text is the comparative literature of the ancient Near East. Gunkel was on the right track when he brought this comparative material into the discussion. Later form

Fig. Int.8 Walter Brueggemann

critics erred when they tried to dissect the text to conform to modern ideas of consistency. Questions of genre and literary conventions are fundamental, but we are dealing with ancient genres and conventions, not those of modern literature (although comparison with modern literature may sometimes have heuristic value).

The second major trend in recent biblical studies is the increased use of sociological methods. These methods, again, vary. They may be viewed as an extension of traditional historical criticism, insofar as they view the text as a reflection of historical situations. Perhaps the most fundamental contribution of sociological theory to biblical studies, however, is the realization that interpretation is not objective and neutral but serves human interests and is shaped by them. On the one hand, the biblical texts themselves reflect the ideological interests of their authors. This insight follows naturally enough from the form-critical insistence on the importance of the *Sitz im Leben*.

On the other hand, the modern interpreter also has a social location. Feminist scholarship has repeatedly pointed out male patriarchal assumptions in biblical scholarship and has made little secret of its own agenda and commitments. Jewish scholars have pointed out that Christian interpretations are often colored by theological assumptions. But no one is exempt from presuppositions and special interests. Postmodernism has contributed some distinctive perspectives to sociological criticism. Notable in this regard are the "ideological criticism" associated with the French philosopher Michel Foucault and the more recent development of "postcolonial criticism" associated with the work of Homi K. Bhabha, which focuses on the perspectives of people who have been conquered and colonized. One of the clearest gains of recent postmodern scholarship has been the increased attention to figures and interests that are either marginal in the biblical text or have been marginalized in previous scholarship. Feminist scholarship has led the way in this regard. The text is all the richer when it is considered from different points of view.

In light of this situation, the interpreter has two choices. One may either adopt an explicitly ideological or confessional approach, or one may try to take account of different viewpoints, and so modify one's own biases even if they can never be fully eliminated. This introduction takes the latter approach. We view the Hebrew Bible/Old Testament as the common heritage of Jews and Christians, not the exclusive property of either. We try to get some distance on the text by viewing it in its historical context, relating it where possible to the history of the time and respecting the ancient literary conventions. In this way we hope to further understanding as to how different interpretations arise. It is of the nature of historical scholarship that it is always subject to revision. One generation learns by criticizing the work of its predecessors but must do so in full consciousness that it will be subject to similar criticism in turn.

Placing the Bible in its historical context is not, however, an end in itself. For most readers of the Bible, this is not only a document of ancient history but also in some way a guide for modern living. The responsible use of the Bible must begin by acknowledging that these books were not written with our modern situations in mind and are informed by the assumptions of an ancient culture remote from our own. To understand the Bible in its historical context is first of all to appreciate what an alien book it is. But no great literature is completely alien. There are always analogies between the ancient world and our own. Within the biblical text itself, we shall see how some paradigmatic episodes are recalled repeatedly as analogies to guide the understanding of new situations. The use of the exodus as a motif in the Prophets is an obvious case in point. Biblical laws and the prophetic preaching repeatedly raise issues that still confront us in modern society. The Bible does not provide ready answers to these problems, but it provides occasions and examples to enable us to think about them and grapple with them.

Before we can begin to grapple with the issues raised by the biblical texts, however, we must know something about the ancient world from which they arose. We turn to this subject in chapter 1.

FOR FURTHER READING

Formation of the Canon

T. H. Lim, *The Formation of the Jewish Canon* (Yale Anchor Reference Library; New Haven: Yale University Press, 2013). An up-to-date critical assessment of the formation of the canon, drawing especially on the evidence of the Dead Sea Scrolls.

L. M. McDonald and J. A. Sanders, eds., *The Canon Debate* (Peabody, MA: Hendrickson, 2002). A comprehensive collection of essays on the formation of the canons of both Testaments.

The Text of the Hebrew Bible

E. Tov, *Textual Criticism of the Hebrew Bible* (3rd ed.; Minneapolis: Fortress Press, 2012). The most comprehensive and up-to-date treatment.

Biblical Chronology

M. Coogan, "Chronology: Hebrew Bible," *ABD* 1:1002–11.

I. Finkelstein and N. A. Silberman, *The Bible Unearthed: Archaeology's New Vision of Ancient Israel and the Origin of Its Sacred Texts* (New York: Free Press, 2001). Readable account of the results of archaeological research and their implications for biblical studies.

Methods in Biblical Scholarship

G. Aichele et al. (= The Bible and Culture Collective), *The Postmodern Bible* (New Haven: Yale Unversity Press, 1995). Comprehensive introduction to postmodern biblical interpretation.

R. Alter, *The Art of Biblical Narrative* (New York: Basic Books, 1981). Pioneering literary approach.

J. Barton, ed., *The Cambridge Companion to Biblical Interpretation* (Cambridge: Cambridge University Press, 1998). Contains essays on various approaches to biblical studies (poststructuralist, political, feminist, etc.).

J. Barton, *The Nature of Biblical Criticism* (Louisville: Westminster, 2007). Basic introduction to historical criticism.

J. Barton, *Reading the Old Testament* (rev. ed.; Louisville: Westminster, 1996). Good critical treatment of literary methodologies.

W. Brueggemann, *Theology of the Old Testament* (Minneapolis: Fortress Press, 1997). Attempt to do biblical theology from a postmodern perspective.

J. J. Collins, *The Bible after Babel: Historical Criticism in a Postmodern Age* (Grand Rapids: Eerdmans, 2005). Critical assessment of recent developments in biblical scholarship.

D. A. Knight, *Methods of Biblical Interpretation* (Nashville: Abingdon, 2004), Essays on major methods and intepreters.

S. L. McKenzie and S. R. Haynes, *To Each Its Own Meaning: An Introduction to Biblical Criticisms and Their Application* (Louisville: Westminster, 1999). Comprehensive survey of modern approaches, including literary and feminist readings.

P. Trible, *God and the Rhetoric of Sexuality* (OBT; Philadelphia: Fortress Press, 1978). Pioneering feminist study.

See also the series of Guides to Biblical Scholarship, published by Fortress Press.

History of Scholarship

W. F. Albright, *From the Stone Age to Christianity* (Baltimore: Johns Hopkins University Press, 1957).

J. Bright, *A History of Israel* (4th ed.; Louisville: Westminster John Knox, 2000).

B. S. Childs, *Introduction to the Old Testament as Scripture* (Philadelphia: Fortress Press, 1979).

I. Finkelstein and N. A. Silberman, *The Bible Unearthed: Archaeology's New Vision of Ancient Israel and the Origin of Its Sacred Texts* (New York: Free Press, 2001).

H. Gunkel, *The Stories of Genesis* (Vallejo, CA: Bibal, 1994).

E. Nicholson, *The Pentateuch in the Twentieth Century: The Legacy of Julius Wellhausen* (Oxford: Clarendon, 1998).

M. Noth, *The Deuteronomistic History* (JSOTSup 15; Sheffield: JSOT Press, 1991).

M. Noth, *A History of Pentateuchal Traditions* (Chico, CA: Scholars Press, 1981).

G. von Rad, *Old Testament Theology* (2 vols.; New York: Harper, 1961).

J. Wellhausen, *Prolegomena to the History of Israel* (Atlanta: Scholars Press, 1994).

PART ONE

The Torah/Pentateuch

P1.1. One of two silver fragments containing scripture verses engraved in archaic Hebrew, including the so-called Priestly Blessing of Numbers 6:24-26; discovered at Ketef Hinnom, Israel.

CHAPTER 1

The Near Eastern Context

INTRODUCTION

This chapter provides an overview of the history of the ancient Near East, the context in which any historical understanding of the Hebrew Bible must be based. We will review aspects of the modern rediscovery of the ancient Near East and aspects of Mesopotamian, Canaanite, and Egyptian mythology especially.

Early History of the Near East

Life in the ancient Near East can be traced back thousands of years before Bishop Ussher's date for the creation of the world in 4004 B.C.E. There was a settlement at Jericho as early as the eighth millennium B.C.E., and village life developed throughout the Near East in the Neolithic period (8000–4000). With the coming of the Early Bronze Age (3200–2200), the first great civilizations emerged in proximity to the great rivers of the region, the Nile in Egypt, and the Tigris and Euphrates that define Mesopotamia (literally, the land "between the rivers") in modern Iraq.

In southern Mesopotamia, around the junction and mouth of the two rivers, the Sumerians are credited with developing the earliest known writing system around 3200 B.C.E. The documents were written with reeds on clay tablets, which were then baked. The Sumerians developed the system of wedge-shaped signs called cuneiform, which was later

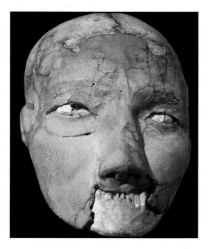

Fig. 1.1 A human skull, recovered in plaster and painted, from Jericho, ca. 6000–4000 B.C.E. Gianni Dagli Orti; ArtResource, NY

Fig. 1.2 Akkadian cuneiform (wedge-shaped) writing: A Neo-Assyrian amulet, ca. 900–600 B.C.E. Museum zu Allerheiligen, Schaffhausen. Commons. wikimedia.org

used in Akkadian writing; but unlike Akkadian, Sumerian was not a Semitic language. The origin of the Sumerians is unknown. They developed city-states (Uruk, Lagash, Umma) that were diverse among themselves. Shortly before 2300 B.C.E. the Sumerians were conquered by Sargon of Akkad, which was slightly further north in Mesopotamia but still south of Babylon. Akkad gave its name to the Semitic language that remained the main medium of Mesopotamian literature for two thousand years (Akkadian). Sargon and his successors ruled the first Mesopotamian territorial state for almost two centuries. Then Akkad fell and neverB.C.E. rose again. Even the location of the city has been lost. After this, the Third Dynasty of Ur united most of Sumer for about a century around the end of the third millennium. Thereafter the Sumerians faded from history, but they bequeathed to the ancient Near East a rich legacy of art and literature.

The second millennium saw the rise of Babylon under **Hammurabi** (eighteenth century B.C.E.), a king most famous for the code of laws that bears his name. Thereafter Babylon's power declined, and it only became dominant again a thousand years later, under Nebuchadnezzar, the conqueror of Jerusalem in the early sixth century B.C.E. Assyria, in northern Mesopotamia, first became powerful in the early second millennium. The Assyrians attained their greatest power, however, first in the Middle Assyrian period in the thirteenth and twelfth centuries and then especially in the Neo-Assyrian period in the ninth and eighth centuries B.C.E.

Egyptian civilization is almost as old as that of Sumer. A form of writing known as hieroglyphics first appeared around the end of the predynastic period (3100 B.C.E.). Stone buildings appeared shortly thereafter. Many of the great pyramids were constructed during the Old Kingdom (2700–2160). The Middle Kingdom extended from 2033 to 1648. For about a century in the middle of the second millennium (1648–1540), Egypt was ruled by foreigners from Asia known as the Hyksos, who were eventually driven out. In the period of the New Kingdom that followed, Egyptian power was extended all the way to the Euphrates. Egypt ruled over Canaan, the region where Israel would emerge, for much of this period. In the mid-fourteenth century, Pharaoh Amenhotep IV abandoned the traditional worship of the god Amun and devoted himself to the worship of the sun and the solar disk (Aten). He changed his name to **Akhenaten** and moved his capital to Amarna. This period is known as the Amarna period. It is important because of the monotheistic character of Akhenaten's devotion, but also because of a hoard of tablets from this period that give information about the state of affairs in Canaan. These are the **Amarna letters**, which were letters sent to the pharaoh by vassals in Canaan. These letters figure prominently in discussions of the origin of Israel. After Akhenaten's death, his successor, Tutankhamun, departed from Amarna and reverted to the cult of Amun.

In this period, the main challenge to Egyptian power in Asia came from the Hittites, a people who lived in Anatolia, or modern Turkey. During the Amarna period, the Hittites established a province in Syria. In the thirteenth century, Ramesses II (1279–1213), who is often thought to be the pharaoh of the exodus, fought an indecisive battle against the Hittites at Qadesh on the Orontes in Syria, but Egypt subsequently lost control of most of Syria and Canaan, although Ramesses later regained it in part.

In between Egypt and Mesopotamia lay the land of **Canaan**, where Israel would carve out its territory along the southern half of the eastern shore of the Mediterranean. Canaan also extended further north, including modern Lebanon and part of Syria. It was not a political unit, except insofar as it was unified as an Egyptian province. Rather, it was a loose configuration of city-states. Later, in the first millennium, the Canaanites in the coastal cities of Tyre, Sidon, and Byblos were known as Phoenicians, from the Greek name for the area.

The biblical texts sometimes use the designation **"Amorite"** as an interchangeable variant for "Canaanite." The name comes from *Amurru*, the Akkadian expression for the land in the west (relative to Mesopotamia). The Amorites appear to have originated in northern Syria. Whether they were nomadic or settled is disputed. They appear in Akkadian texts around the end of the third millennium, when they exerted pressure on the urban centers of Mesopotamia. Before the end of the Third Dynasty of Ur, the king had built a wall to keep out the Amorites. Amorites were involved in the destruction of Ur at the beginning of the second millennium, and rulers with Amorite names are found in several Mesopotamian cities early in the second millennium. Amorite rulers also appear in the west, in Ugarit and Byblos. Amorite expansion to the west had presumably also taken place. In the mid-second millennium there was a kingdom of Amurru in the upper Orontes valley in Syria. Biblical texts sometimes refer to the inhabitants of the land that became Israel as

Fig. 1.3 Bust of Akhenaten, from the temple at Karnak, now in the Cairo Museum. Photo: Jon Bodsworth; Commons.wikimedia.org.

CHRONOLOGY OF ANCIENT NEAR EASTERN HISTORY		
Period	**Mesopotamia**	**Egypt**

Early Bronze Age (3200–2200 B.C.E.)	3200 B.C.E.
	    Sumerians develop first
	        known writing system
	2300 B.C.E.
	    Sumerian city-states (Uruk,
	        Lagash, Umma)
	    Sargon of Akkad conquers
	        the Sumerians
		From 3100 B.C.E.
		    Hieroglyphic writing
		2700–2160 B.C.E.
		    Old Kingdom
		    Age of the Pyramids

Middle Bronze Age (2200–1550 B.C.E.)	18th century B.C.E.
	    Rise of Babylon under
	        Hammurabi
	    Assyrian kingdom becomes
	        an established power
		2160–2106 B.C.E.
		    First Intermediate Period
		2033–1648 B.C.E.
		    Middle Kingdom
		1648–1540 B.C.E.
		    Second Intermediate Period
		    Hyksos rule in Egypt

Late Bronze Age (1550–1200 B.C.E.)	14th century B.C.E.
	    (Canaan: Kingdom at Ugarit)
	1124 B.C.E.
	    Elevation of Marduk under
	        Nebuchad nezzar
		1540–1069 B.C.E.
		    New Kingdom
		Ca. 1350 B.C.E.
		    Amarna Period
		    Akhenaten
		1279–1213 B.C.E.
		    Reign of Ramesses II

Amorites, but this may be a loose use of the term.

From the twelfth century on, the people of northern Syria were called **Arameans**. These were not a unified people, but included several small kingdoms. They became a significant factor in the history of Israel in the first millennium.

One final people should be noted to complete this rapid overview of Israel's neighbors and predecessors. The **Philistines** were sea people who came to Canaan from the Aegean. Their origin remains obscure. They were defeated by Ramesses III about 1190 B.C.E., but they then settled in the coastal towns of Palestine, Ashkelon, Gaza, and Ashdod. Thus the territory they controlled was south of the Canaanite (Phoenician) cities of Tyre and Sidon and immediately adjacent to emerging Israel. The history of the Philistines parallels that of Israel to a great degree, as they were repeatedly subject to the various imperial powers.

Fig. 1.4 The Rosetta Stone, written in hieroglyphic, Demotic, and Greek. Commons.wikimedia.org

The Modern Rediscovery of the Ancient Near East

For much of Western history, these ancient civilizations were known primarily from the accounts of Greek historians such as Herodotus (fifth century B.C.E.) and from references in the Bible. The modern recovery of the native Near Eastern sources began with Napoleon's expedition to Egypt in 1798–1802. Napoleon took with him a group of scholars whom he charged with the task of preparing a record of the country. In the course of their work, they found an inscription on stone in Greek, classical Egyptian (hieroglyphics), and Egyptian demotic script (a popular form of Egyptian from the later half of the first millennium B.C.E.). This inscription became known as the Rosetta Stone. Since the same text was written in both Greek and Egyptian, it became possible to decipher hieroglyphics for the first time. (Names that were identified in all parts of the inscription provided the key.) The decipherment was accomplished by a French scholar, Jean-François Champollion.

The rediscovery of ancient Mesopotamia also began in the early nineteenth century. An employee of the East India Tea Company named Claudius Rich carried out a study of the ruins of Babylon, beginning in 1807. His collection of artifacts, including many cuneiform tablets, was purchased by the British Museum. The first explorations of Assyrian sites (Nineveh, Khorsabad) were carried out in the 1840s by a Frenchman, Paul-Émile Botta, and then, beginning in 1845, by an Englishman, Austen Henry Layard, who excavated palaces at Nimrud and Nineveh. Large quantities of Assyrian sculpture found their way to the British Museum, and some to private collectors in England. The key to the decipherment of Akkadian was provided by an inscription by a Persian king Darius on the rock of Behistun in Persia. The Behistun inscription was written with cuneiform signs in Old Persian, Elamite, and Akkadian. The decipherment was accomplished mainly by H. C. Rawlinson, an Englishman, and Edward Hincks, an Irishman, in the 1850s. In the 1870s, the great works of Akkadian literature such as the creation story ***Enuma Elish*** and the **Gilgamesh Epic** were discovered and first translated. The Babylonian flood story, which was contained in the Epic of Gilgamesh, caused a sensation because of its similarity to the story of Noah and the ark.

Other major discoveries followed in the late nineteenth and early twentieth centuries. These included the Amarna letters, noted above, in 1887. A discovery of major importance for biblical studies was made at **Ugarit** (Ras Shamra), B.C.E. on the Mediterranean coast in northern Syria in 1929. A French archaeologist, Claude Schaeffer, discovered over two thousand texts, written in cuneiform script, in a language that proved to be closely related to Hebrew. These texts date from the fourteenth century B.C.E. and include some myths, or sacred stories, as well as ritual texts, legal records, diplomatic correspondence, and other documents. A few years later, beginning in 1933, another major discovery was made at **Mari**, on the Euphrates, by another French expedition led by André Parrot. More than twenty thousand tablets were discovered. The most important of these date to the eighteenth century B.C.E. More recently, a major discovery of cuneiform tablets was made at **Ebla** Tell Mardikh, near Aleppo in northwestern Syria) by an Italian expedition led by Paolo Matthiae, beginning in 1964. The Ebla tablets date to the third millennium B.C.E. and constitute the largest single find of cuneiform texts from this early period (approximately 1,750 tablets). Another major find of some eight hundred tablets was made at another site in Syria, Emar (modern Meskene), in the mid-1970s.

Aspects of Near Eastern Religion

The worship of gods and goddesses was a significant part of life in the ancient Near East. It is important to bear in mind, however, that religion was not standardized and systematized in the ways that are familiar to us from Christianity and Judaism. Each city-state had its own cult and its own assembly of gods, headed by the chief god or goddess of that city. The city-states were not isolated from each other, however, and there were periods when various cities in a region were unified—as happened, for example, under Sargon of Akkad and under Hammurabi of Babylon. The status of gods rose and fell with the fortunes of their city-states. Throughout Mesopotamian history, beginning in the Sumerian period, scribes tried to impose order on the multiplicity of gods by composing god lists.

There was, moreover, a corpus of literature that circulated widely in the ancient Near East. As part of their training in Akkadian, scribes had to copy out a prescribed body of standard texts. Consequently, the same works could be found at widely different locations at diverse dates. Copies of the Epic of Gilgamesh were found at Emar on the Euphrates, in the Hittite capital in modern Turkey, and at Megiddo in what later became the land of Israel, all in the late second millennium. Other copies come from Assyrian collections centuries later. Modern scholars often refer to such texts as "canonical," but it is important to bear in mind that the "canon" or standard they established was literary, and that it did not involve an orthodoxy in religious belief. Nonetheless, these standard texts were not idiosyncratic and can be taken as representative of Near Eastern beliefs, even if they were not normative in the sense later associated with the Bible.

We may get an impression of the Mesopotamian view of the world by considering some of the myths or stories about the origin of the world and of humanity. The word "myth" is derived from the Greek *mythos,* or story, but is used especially for sacred or traditional stories deemed to have religious import. In modern English usage, "myth" is often opposed to factual truth, but this is unfortunate, as it makes it difficult to take myths seriously. The ancient myths are serious but imaginative attempts to explain life in this world. There are several minor creation stories preserved in Akkadian, many of them in the introductions to ritual texts. Two myths stand out, however, because of their length and wide distribution. These are the myth of **Atrahasis** and the ***Enuma Elish.***

Atrahasis

The story of Atrahasis is most fully preserved in an Old Babylonian version from about 1700 B.C.E. Over seven hundred lines of this version have been published. Other copies come from the library of the Assyrian king Ashurbanipal in the seventh century B.C.E. The text, then, was copied for at least a thousand years.

The story begins at a point before the creation of humankind, "when the gods instead of man did the work, bore the loads." But there was already a hierarchy among the gods. As in other early Mesopotamian myths, the chief gods were Anu (or An in Sumerian texts), Enlil, and Enki. When the gods cast lots and divided the world, Anu took the sky, Enlil the earth, and Enki the waters below the earth. (Each had other gods associated with him.) The labor of agriculture was imposed on a class of gods called the Igigu. The first section of the myth deals with the rebellion of these worker gods, which led the high gods to concede that their workload was too heavy.

Consequently, Enki and the mother-goddess (called Mami/Mama, Nintu and *Belet-ili*) created humanity "to bear the load of the gods." They slaughtered "a god who had intelligence" (probably the god who had the idea for the rebellion), and Nintu mixed clay with his flesh and blood. From this mixture, she fashioned seven males and seven females.

The second section of the myth goes on to give the early history of humankind, culminating in the story of a great deluge. After six hundred years the people became too numerous, and "the country was as noisy as a bellowing bull." Enlil made a complaint in the council of the gods, and a plague was sent to reduce humanity. At this point, the hero who gives his name to the story emerges: "Now there was one Atrahasis whose ear was open to his god Enki" (the name Atrahasis means "very wise"). Enki advised him to have humanity withhold offerings from all the gods except the one who controlled the plague, and eventually that god relented and put an end to the affliction. Enlil made a number of similar attempts to reduce humanity at six-hundred-year intervals, but each time Enki instructed Atrahasis and the danger was averted. (When the other gods forbade Enki to speak to the man, he conveyed his revelation in dreams.) Finally, the gods sent a flood to wipe humanity off the face of the earth. Enki instructed Atrahasis to build a boat that was big enough to ride out the deluge. Atrahasis took his family and livestock on board. The flood lasted seven days and seven nights and wiped out the rest of humanity. The gods, other than Enlil, were horrified at the destruction, but they were mainly affected by the fact that they were deprived of their offerings. When the flood subsided, Atrahasis made an offering in thanksgiving. When the gods smelled the odor, "they gathered like flies over the offering." There were bitter recriminations against Enlil, but he in turn attacked Enki for frustrating the will of the gods. Enki defended himself by saying that he acted so that life would be preserved. In the end, the gods devised a new scheme for population control. Some women would be barren, some children would die at birth, and some categories of priestesses would not bear children at all.

This story is obviously important for understanding the biblical book of Genesis. For the present, however, we are concerned only with the light it throws on Mesopotamian religion. Two of the most prominent features of the story stand in contrast with modern conceptions of God. First, the gods are anthropomorphic: they are conceived and portrayed in the likeness of human beings. They feel hunger, are troubled by noise, are wearied by labor, argue among themselves, and, in the case of Enki, can be deceitful. Second, there is a whole society of gods, analogous to a human society. Especially important is the role of the council of the gods, where the gods deliberate and arrive at decisions. These gods are not fully in control of events. Rather, they react to crises as they develop. Moreover, they are not, as a group, the guardians of a moral order. The crises develop for various reasons: overwork in the case of the Igigu, overpopulation in the case of humanity. The actions that lead to the crises are not necessarily wrong or sinful. The gods react differently to these crises, and the eventual solutions are reached by compromise. While Enki frustrates the designs of Enlil, in the end they arrive at a balance of forces rather than the dominance of any one god. While the main emphasis is on the social character of the divine council, the story also notes that a human being (Atrahasis) can have a personal relationship with a particular god (in this case, Enki).

The Atrahasis story also throws some light on the way in which ancient literature was composed. The first part of the myth draws on the Sumerian myth of Enki and Ninmah, where Ninmah creates seven defective humans and Enki finds useful occupations for them. The story of the flood was also already known in Sumerian sources. It also appears in the story of Gilgamesh. Atrahasis, then, was not entirely an original composition, but was rather fashioned as a new work out of traditional materials.

Enuma Elish

The *Enuma Elish* was composed some centuries later than Atrahasis, probably in the reign of Nebuchadnezzar I of Babylon (1125–1104 B.C.E.). It celebrates the rise of Marduk, god of Babylon, to a position of leadership among the gods. It was only in the time of Nebuchadnezzar that Marduk was granted that status. This myth was widely copied. It was recited on the fourth day of the New Year's festival, the Akitu. It was still copied in the Hellenistic period in the third century B.C.E.

The *Enuma Elish* begins at an earlier point in primordial time than does the Atrahasis story:

> *When skies above were not yet named*
> *Nor earth below pronounced by name,*
> *Apsu, the first one, their begetter*
> *And maker Tiamat, who bore them all,*
> *Had mixed their waters together*
> *But had not formed pastures, nor discovered reed-beds;*

When yet no gods were manifest,
Nor names pronounced nor destinies decreed,
Then gods were born within them.

(trans. S. Dalley, *Myths from Mesopotamia*, 233)

At the beginning, then, only the primordial pair, Apsu and Tiamat, were on the scene. (Both Apsu and Tiamat represent primordial waters. Some scholars think that Apsu represented the fresh waters beneath the earth while Tiamat represented the salt waters, or sea.) The story proceeds with the theogony, or begetting of the gods, which must come before the creation of humanity. Here it is the young gods who create a tumult. Finally, Apsu, with his counselor Mummu, goes to Tiamat and complains:

Their ways have become very grievous to me,
By day I cannot rest, by night I cannot sleep.
I shall abolish their ways and disperse them.
Let peace prevail so that we can sleep.

(Dalley, *Myths*, 234)

Tiamat resists the proposal ("How could we allow what we ourselves created to perish?"), but Mummu supports it. The young gods, however, learn of the plot because of the wisdom of Ea. Ea then devised a spell, put Apsu to sleep, and slew him. He set up his dwelling on top of Apsu. There he begat new gods, Bel and Marduk. Anu, father of Ea, created four winds and gave them to Marduk to play with. But the winds stirred up Tiamat and made some gods restless, and they incited Tiamat to action. Tiamat then prepared for battle and made Qingu leader of her army. Again, Ea discovered what was happening. Ea and Anu in turn tried to confront Tiamat but were intimidated and turned back. At last, Ea urged

Marduk to come forward. Marduk agreed to fight Tiamat on one condition:

"If indeed I am to be your champion,
If I am to defeat Tiamat and save your lives,
Convene the council, name a special fate . . .
And let me, my own utterance shall fix fate instead of you!
Whatever I create shall never be altered!
Let a decree from my lips shall never be revoked, never changed!"
The gods granted his demand:
"You are honoured among the great gods.
Your destiny is unequalled, your word (has the power of) Anu! . . .
May your utterance be law, your word never falsified."

(Dalley, *Myths*, 248-9)

They proclaimed Marduk king and gave him a throne and scepter.

Marduk and Tiamat engaged in battle. He released a wind in her face. When she opened her mouth to swallow it, she could not close her lips. Then Marduk shot in an arrow that slit her heart and killed her. He rounded up the gods who supported Tiamat and smashed their weapons. He cut the corpse of Tiamat in two, put up half of it to make the sky and arranged her waters so that they could not escape. He then proceeded to establish the constellations of the stars as stations for the great gods. He devised a plan to create humankind, to do the work of the gods so that they might be at leisure. Ea then made humankind from the blood of Qingu, the ally of Tiamat. Finally, he gave the command to create Babylon. The gods labored for a year to construct Babylon and the temple Esagila. On its completion, Marduk invited them to a banquet in the temple. The myth ends with a lengthy litany of the names and praises of Marduk.

The *Enuma Elish* celebrates the exaltation of Marduk, god of Babylon, to kingship among the gods. This development evidently corresponds to the emergence of Babylon as a world power, but it is not a simple political allegory. Rather, the story encapsulates a view of the world. Tiamat is a complex and fascinating figure. She is Mother Nature, at one point concerned for the survival of her offspring, at another ready to devour them. She is not evil; indeed, she is only slowly provoked to rage. But since she is a threat to the lives of the young gods, she must be destroyed. If life is to flourish on earth, nature must be subdued.

The story has a clear formula for establishing a successful society. Faced with the threat of Tiamat, the gods realize that they need to unite behind the strong leadership of a king. The kingship of Marduk among the gods carries a strong implication that kingship is also necessary in human society. There is a clear symmetry between the king and his palace and the god and his temple. The myth can easily be read as a story composed to legitimate the rise of monarchy. But a story like this has many meanings, and we should not try to reduce it to a simple political message.

The monarchical kingship of Marduk, even though it is still accompanied by the council of the gods, must be seen as a step in the direction of monotheism. Theoretical monotheism, the belief that only one god exists, was rare in the ancient world, and became possible only with the rise of Greek philosophy. In the Babylonian myth, the reality of other gods is freely granted, but Marduk is preeminent among the gods. In the Bible too, the psalmist will ask, "Who is like you among the gods, O Lord?" (Exod 15:11). There are differences, to be sure, between the biblical and the Mesopotamian views of divinity, but there is also continuity.

Like the Atrahasis myth, *Enuma Elish* drew on earlier sources and was part of a stream of tradition. One of its sources is the Myth of Anzu. There, too, a young hero-god does battle with a monster. In this case, the monster is Anzu, who steals the tablets of destiny. The hero-god Ninurta defeats him by lopping off his wings and proceeds to provide water to the land that had previously been lacking.

The Epic of Gilgamesh

The *Enuma Elish* is almost entirely concerned with the realm of the gods. But Mesopotamian literature also contains one of the most remarkable dramatizations of the human condition that have come down to us from antiquity. This is the Epic of Gilgamesh. This work is called an epic rather than a myth, because the main characters are human, although gods and goddesses also intervene in the action. (Some people refer to the *Enuma Elish* as "the epic of creation," but this usage is loose, and is better avoided). Gilgamesh was regarded in antiquity as a historical character. He may have lived in the third millennium, in Uruk (Warka) in southern Mesopotamia. The epic, however, developed over many centuries. Its relation to history may be similar to that of Homer's epics, which also have a starting point in history but are essentially works of fiction and imagination.

Several stories about Gilgamesh were current in Sumerian before 2000 B.C.E. These were short stories, which eventually served as the bases for episodes in the epic. They included separate stories about Gilgamesh and other main characters in the epic: Enkidu, Humbaba, and the Bull of Heaven. There is a story of the death of Gilgamesh. The flood story seems to have been an independent tale in Sumerian. A composite epic is found in Old Babylonian tablets from the early second millennium. It is not clear, however, whether the whole epic was already unified at this point. Fragments of various parts of the story are found at a wide range of locations in the mid- to late second millennium. The most complete version comes from Nineveh (in Assyria) in the early seventh century B.C.E. It is possible to trace the development of the epic over more than a thousand years.

According to the epic, Gilgamesh, king of Uruk, was two-thirds divine and one-third mortal. He had no rival, but his excessive energy was a problem and made him over-bearing. He would not leave young women alone, and the gods often heard their complaints. Eventually the gods created someone to be a match for him, a primitive man named Enkidu, who lived with the beasts on the steppe. He was discovered by a hunter, who told Gilgamesh about him. Gilgamesh dispatched a harlot with the hunter. They waited for Enkidu at the watering place. The harlot opened her garments and "did for him, the primitive man, as women do." Enkidu lay with her for six days and seven nights. When he tried to return to the animals, however, they shied away from him and he could not keep pace with them. The harlot consoled him:

"You have become [profound], Enkidu, you have become like a god.

Why should you roam open country with wild beasts?
Come, let me take you into Uruk the Sheep-fold . . .
Where Gilgamesh is perfect in strength."
(Dalley, *Myths*, 56)

Enkidu goes to Uruk, where he becomes a well-matched companion for Gilgamesh. He puts on clothes and learns to eat and drink in the human fashion.

Together, Gilgamesh and Enkidu undertake great adventures. First they kill Humbaba, the giant of the forest. When they return to Uruk, Gilgamesh is so resplendent that the goddess Ishtar becomes enamored of him and proposes marriage. Gilgamesh, however, insults her by recalling the misfortunes that have befallen her former lovers. Ishtar persuades Anu, the god of heaven, to give her the Bull of Heaven to punish Gilgamesh and Uruk. But Enkidu subdues the bull and Gilgamesh kills it.

By killing Humbaba and the Bull of Heaven, Gilgamesh and Enkidu win fame and acclamation in Uruk, but they incur the displeasure of the gods. It is decreed that one of them must die, and the sentence falls on Enkidu, who learns of his fate in a dream. Enkidu complains to Shamash, the sun-god, and curses the hunter and the harlot who first brought him to Uruk. Shamash, however, points out all the good things that came to Enkidu because of the harlot. Enkidu agrees and changes the fate of the harlot to a blessing: "Governors and princes shall love you. . . . Because of you, the mother of seven, the honoured wife, shall be deserted."

When Enkidu dies, Gilgamesh mourns bitterly: "Shall I die too? Am I not like

Fig. 1.5 A horned figure (Enkidu?) fights a lion. Cylinder seal impression from ancient Babylon.

Commons.wikimedia.org

Enkidu? . . . I am afraid of Death, and so I roam the country." He decides to visit Utnapishtim, the flood hero (the counterpart of Atrahasis in the Atrahasis story), who was granted eternal life and now lives far away at the ends of the earth. The journey takes Gilgamesh into the mountain in the west where the sun sets, through a dark tunnel to the sunrise at the other side. He comes to the shore of the sea that circles the earth, where he finds an inn kept by an alewife, Siduri. He tells her his story and asks for directions. She sees that his quest is hopeless:

> *"Gilgamesh, where do you roam?*
> *You will not find the eternal life you seek.*
> *When the gods created mankind*
> *They appointed death for mankind,*
> *Kept eternal life in their own hands.*
> *So, Gilgamesh, let your stomach be full,*
> *Day and night enjoy yourself in every way,*
> *Every day arrange for pleasures.*

> *Day and night, dance and play,*
> *Wear fresh clothes.*
> *Keep your head washed, bathe in water,*
> *Appreciate the child who holds your hand,*
> *Let your wife enjoy herself in your lap.*
> *This is the work [of the living]."*
> (Old Babylonian version; Dalley,
> *Myths*, 150)

She does, however, direct him to Urshanabi, boatman of Utnapishtim. Gilgamesh prevails on the boatman to ferry him over to Utnapishtim, who again lectures him on the inevitability of death. When Gilgamesh presses him as to how he obtained eternal life, Utnapishtim tells him the story of the flood. Before Gilgamesh sets out on his return journey, however, Utnapishtim tells him about a plant that grows in the Apsu, the fresh waters beneath the earth, that has the power to rejuvenate or make the old young again. Gilgamesh dives and brings up the plant. On the way back, however, he stops to bathe in a pool, and while he is doing so, a snake carries off the plant. At this point Gilgamesh becomes resigned. When they return to Uruk, he displays the walls of Uruk to Urshanabi, with the implication that the city walls have a permanence that is denied to human beings, even to heroes.

The story of Gilgamesh needs little commentary. It is a poignant reflection on human mortality that belongs to the classics of world literature. In contrast to what we find in the Bible, morality is not a consideration in this story. The exploits of Gilgamesh and Enkidu are neither good nor bad. They win fame for the heroes, but they also bring about their fall. There is a nice appreciation of both the curses and the blessings that attend the harlot.

The gods are sometimes capricious (especially Ishtar), sometimes reasonable (Shamash). In the end, however, death is the great leveler of humanity. As Utnapishtim remarks, death is inevitable for Gilgamesh as for the fool.

The Role of Goddesses

The role of Ishtar in the Gilgamesh Epic draws attention to an aspect of Near Eastern religion that stands in contrast to what we find in the Hebrew Bible. Deities are both male and female; goddesses figure in the stories beside the gods. We have seen the roles of the mother-goddesses Mami/Belit-ili and Tiamat in the creation stories. In general, the roles assigned to the goddesses decline in the second millennium. In Atrahasis, Enki and Mami collaborate to make human beings. In *Enuma Elish*, Ea (the Babylonian counterpart of Enki) makes them alone. There is still a mother-goddess, Tiamat, but she has no role in the creation of humanity, and she is part of the old order that Marduk must defeat. In Sumerian texts, the mother-goddess Ninhursag appears as the third of the triad of most powerful deities, after Anu and Enlil. In the second millennium, however, she is replaced by the wise god Enki, as we see in the Atrahasis myth.

One goddess who did not decline in importance in the second millennium was Ishtar. The name Ishtar derives from the Semitic word *'attar*. A masculine god with this name appears in Ugaritic texts, and the feminine Astarte is known in the Bible. Ishtar was identified with the Sumerian goddess Inanna and is associated with fertility in all its aspects. She is the goddess of thunderstorms and rain, and perhaps because of this association, she is also the goddess of battle. (Gods of thunderstorms were often envisaged as warriors riding the chariots into battle.) Above all, she was the goddess of sexual attraction. She was also associated with the morning star. She is most probably the goddess venerated as the "queen of heaven" (Jer 44:17, 19).

Inanna/Ishtar is associated with the shepherd king Dumuzi (Babylonian Tammuz) in several stories, most notably a story of her Descent to the Netherworld. After a passionate courtship with Dumuzi, they celebrate a sacred marriage. Another phase of the myth deals with the death of Dumuzi. This is described variously in the texts. In some, Inanna mourns him bitterly. According to the story of the Descent of Inanna, however, she is responsible for his demise. Inanna visits the netherworld, where her sister Ereshkigal turns her into a corpse. She is eventually revived and allowed to ascend, but on condition that she find a substitute. She finds that Dumuzi has not been grief-stricken in her absence, and designates him as the substitute to go down to the netherworld. In the end an arrangement is made whereby Dumuzi and his sister spend alternate halves of the year in the netherworld. This arrangement is related to the seasonal cycle of death and rebirth.

The relationship between Inanna and Dumuzi was ritualized in the cultic celebration of the sacred marriage between the king and a priestess representing Inanna. The sacred marriage was a ritual to ensure fertility, of the fields as well as of people. The texts often use agricultural metaphors in connection with Inanna and the sacred marriage (e.g., "Inanna, your breast is your field"). The rejection of Ishtar by Gilgamesh is remarkable in view of the Sumerian tradition of the sacred marriage, but this tradition faded in the second millennium, and the king no longer played the part of the god in the marriage ritual. Ishtar, however, was associated not only with marriage but also with extramarital sex and prostitution. She is not a maternal figure, and despite her marriage to Dumuzi, she remains an unencumbered woman. As such she is a marginal figure, at once a subject of fascination and attraction and of fear. She represents both sex and violence, and even, because of her descent to the netherworld, death. The ambivalence of Ishtar is prominently expressed in the Epic of Gilgamesh. Yet the conclusion of the epic refers to Ishtar's temple as a prominent feature of the city of Uruk, in which Gilgamesh apparently takes pride.

Fig. 1.6 Babylonian relief, nineteenth or eighteenth century B.C.E., of a winged and eagle-footed goddess (Ishtar?); known as the "Queen of the Night"; now in the British Museum. Commons. wikimedia.org

Canaanite Mythology

Our sources for Canaanite mythology are much less extensive than those for Mesopotamia. Until the discovery of the tablets at Ugarit in 1929, we were dependent on the polemical accounts of Canaanite religion in the Bible and some information in Greek sources (especially Philo of Byblos), which are late and problematic. Whether Ugarit is properly described as Canaanite is a matter of dispute, but the gods that appear in the Ugaritic tablets (El, Baal, Anat, etc.) are the same deities that figure in the Hebrew Bible. The Ugaritic texts are the best representatives we have of Canaanite religion in the second half of the first millennium. Here again we should remember that there was no orthodoxy in ancient Near Eastern religion and that different myths, or different forms of these myths, may have circulated in other locations.

In the Ugaritic pantheon, El was king and father of the gods. His decree is wise and his wisdom eternal. The word *El* is familiar from Hebrew, where it is both the common noun for "god" and a designation for the God of Israel (YHWH). El is said to live in a tent on a mountain that is the source of two rivers. He presides over assemblies of "the sons of El," the council of the gods.

By the time the Ugaritic myths were composed, however, El's position among the gods was largely ceremonial. At least in the Baal cycle of myths, Baal emerges as the dominant figure, although his claim to rule is still challenged by Yamm (Sea) and Mot (Death). Three goddesses figure prominently in the stories: Asherah, wife of El; Anat, sister and wife of Baal; and Astarte, who is the least prominent of the three.

The Baal Cycle from Ugarit resembles *Enuma Elish* insofar as it describes a conflict among the gods that culminates in the establishment of a king (in this case, Baal). The two myths may be related. Tiamat in the Babylonian myth is related to the Deep or the Sea (the Hebrew cognate *tᵉhom* is the word used for the Deep in the opening verses of Genesis), and the Sea does battle with Baal in the Canaanite myth. The Ugaritic text does not discuss the creation of the world, but it is often described as cosmogonic (that is, a story of the origin of the world), as it can be read as an account of how things came to be the way they are. The first episode of the myth begins when Yamm (Sea) demands that the assembly of the gods surrender Baal into his power. The gods are intimidated by the violent approach of the messengers, and El agrees to hand Baal over. Baal, however, refuses to submit. Instead, he gets two clubs, fashioned by the divine craftsman, Kothar-wa-Hasis. With these he

> struck Prince Sea on the skull
> Judge River between the eyes.
> Sea stumbled; he fell to the ground;
> his joints shook, his frame collapsed.
> Baal captured and pierced Sea;
> He finished off Judge River.
> (trans. M. D. Coogan and M. S. Smith,
> *Stories from Ancient Canaan*,
> 2ⁿᵈ ed. 113)

Thereupon Astarte proclaims:

> Hail, Baal the Conqueror!
> Hail, Rider of the clouds!
> For Prince Sea is our captive,
> Judge River is our captive.

Another passage in the myth says that Baal finished off Lotan, the fleeing serpent, the seven-headed monster. This is probably another way of referring to the same victory. Lotan appears in the Bible as Leviathan (Job 3:8; 41:1; Pss 74:13-14; 104:26; Isa 27:1).

A second episode of the myth begins with the construction of Baal's house and a celebratory banquet. At first Baal resists the advice of Kothar-wa-Hasis that he should have a window in his house, but after the banquet he changes his mind. (A window was thought to provide an entry for Death: Compare Jer 9:21.)

The third episode of the myth presents a more serious challenge to Baal on the part of

Fig. 1.7   Figurine of a warrior god (Ba'al?) from Syria, ca. 1550–1150 B.C.E. From the Mr. and Mrs. Allen C. Balch Collection, Los Angeles County Museum of Art. Commons. wikimedia.org

Mot, or Death. Baal is terrified and declares that he is Mot's servant forever. The story vividly describes how Death swallows Baal.:

> *One lip to the earth, one lip to the heavens;*
> *. . . his tongue to the stars.*
> *Baal must enter inside him;*
> *He must go down into his mouth like a dried*
>   *olive,*
> *the earth's produce, the fruit of the trees.*
>   (Coogan and Smith, *Stories*, 141)

Baal's death is greeted with widespread mourning. El gets down from his throne and rolls in the dust. Anat gashes her skin with a knife. Both express concern as to what will happen to the people if Baal is dead. El offers to make one of Asherah's sons king in place of Baal. One of them, Athtar, tries out Baal's throne, but his feet do not reach the footstool. Finally, Anat confronts Mot:

> *She seized El's son Death;*
> *with a sword she split him;*
> *with a sieve she winnowed him;*
> *with fire she burned him;*
> *with millstones she ground him;*
> *in the fields she sowed him.*
>   (Coogan and Smith, *Stories*, 148)

Baal then returns to life, and the heavens rain down oil and the wadis (or gullies) run with honey. Finally, there is a tussle between Baal and Mot. Both are strong and fall. The Sun warns Mot that El will be displeased and will undermine his throne, and at that Mot becomes fearful.

While the Baal cycle has much in common with *Enuma Elish*, it does not seem to have the same political implications as the Babylonian myth. Rather, like the myth of Inanna and Dumuzi, it seems to reflect the seasonal changes, at least in the struggle of Baal and Mot. When Baal dies, there is no rain. The wadis dry up and the fields are dry. When he comes back to life, the rain comes again. This story is not concerned with morality any more than the Babylonian myth. Mot is not evil, he is just a power that must be given his due. In the end there is some equilibrium between Baal and Mot. A striking feature of the Canaanite mythology is the violence of the goddess Anat, who not only dismembers Death but also berates the high god El on occasion and threatens to smash his skull if he does not comply with her wishes.

Baal's victory over the Sea is more decisive. We may imagine that the image of a monster with seven heads was suggested by the waves of the sea, beating against the Mediterranean coast. In the Hebrew Bible, we shall find the idea that the work of creation involved setting limits to the sea (Ps 104:9). The sea must be restrained so that dry land can emerge. Both Sea and Death may be considered chaos monsters: they are forces that threaten the survival of life. In this they resemble Tiamat in the Babylonian myth. Baal, like Marduk, is a god who protects life, but Baal has much stronger overtones of fertility.

All the characters in the Baal myth are gods or goddesses. But the Canaanites also had stories with human heroes. One such story tells of a man named Danel, who had no son and besought one from the gods. This Danel is mentioned as a legendary wise man in Ezek 14:14, where he is associated with Noah and Job, and again in Ezek 28:3, where the prophet asks rhetorically, "Are you wiser than Danel." (The name is often translated as "Daniel," by analogy with the hero of the biblical book of Daniel.) In the Ugaritic story,

Danel is depicted as a king or local ruler, who sits at the entrance to the city gate, presiding over legal disputes involving widows and orphans. His prayers are answered, and he is given a son named Aqhat.

The son is given a present of a bow by the divine craftsman Kothar-wa-Hasis, but this wonderful present is a cause of misfortune for Aqhat. It attracts the attention of the goddess Anat. She offers Aqhat gold and silver for the bow, and when he refuses, she offers him immortality: "You'll be able to match years with Baal, months with the sons of El." But Aqhat replies:

> *"Don't lie to me, maiden,*
> *for to a hero your lies are filth.*
> *A mortal—what does he get in the end? . . .*
> *glaze poured on his head,*
> *lime on top of his skull.*
> *As every man dies, I will die;*
> *yes, I too will surely die."*
>
> (Coogan and Smith, *Stories*, 42)

He goes on to insult her by saying that she has no business with a bow, as women do not hunt.

This episode resembles the encounter of Gilgamesh and Ishtar, but Anat is more successful than Ishtar in getting her revenge. She makes her servant Yatpan take the form of a vulture and strike Aqhat on the skull and kill him. In his mourning, the father Danel places a curse on nature:

> *For seven years let Baal fail,*
> *eight, the Rider on the Clouds:*
> *no dew, no showers,*
> *no surging of the two seas,*
> *no benefit of Baal's voice.*
>
> (Coogan and Smith, *Stories*, 47-8)

(Baal's voice was the thunder.) The death of Aqhat, then, results in a crisis in fertility, even if not on the same scale as that which followed the death of Baal. After the seven years of mourning, Aqhat's sister, Pagat, sets out to avenge her brother. She goes to Yatpan's tent and plies him with wine. Unfortunately the ending of the story is lost, but presumably she gets her revenge by killing Yatpan. The motif of the woman who visits a man with the intention of killing him appears again in the book of Judith, in the Apocrypha, at the end of the Old Testament.

The story of Aqhat is fragmentary, and so it is difficult to discern its central purpose. It certainly shows the inevitability of death, even for a hero, just as the story of Gilgamesh did. But it also throws light on some aspects of everyday life in the ancient Near East. For example, when Baal relays Danel's wish for a son to the council of the gods, he petitions:

> *Let him have a son in his house,*
> *an heir inside his palace,*
> *to set up a stela for his divine ancestor,*
> *a votive marker for his clan in the*
> *   sanctuary . . .*
> *to hold his hand when he is drunk,*
> *support him when he is full of wine . . .*
> *to patch his roof when it gets muddy,*
> *wash his clothes when they are dirty.*
>
> (Coogan and Smith, *Stories*, 35-6)

We are told that Pagat "gets up early to draw water," knows the course of the stars, saddles a donkey, and lifts her father onto it. The story then is a portrayal of life in ancient times, whether it had some more specific purpose or not.

episode recalls the revolt of David's son Absalom in 2 Samuel.

Egyptian Religion

As in Mesopotamia and Canaan, religion in ancient Egypt was subject to local variations and had no overarching orthodoxy. The status of deities rose and fell with the fortunes of their cities. The Old Kingdom, in the second half of the third millennium B.C.E., had its capital at Memphis. In the Memphite theology, the preeminent god was the creator-god Ptah. The priesthood of Heliopolis, however, exalted the god Atum as creator. The New Kingdom, in the second half of the second millennium, had its capital at Thebes in Middle Egypt, and here the god Amun came to prominence and was linked with the sun-god Re. Several different gods appear as creators in Egyptian myths: Ptah, Re, Atum, Amun, Khnum, but there is only one creator in any given myth. The multiplicity of creation emerges out of an original unity. Other gods, however, also figure in these myths. The sun-god Re was universally worshiped and appears in almost every creation myth, although his role varies. The process of creation also varied. In the theology of Heliopolis, the sun-god emerged from the abyss on a primal mound and created the first pair of deities by masturbation or spittle. The god Ptah was said to conceive in his heart the things he wanted to create and bring them into existence by uttering a word. The god Khnum, in contrast, was a potter-god who fashioned human beings as a potter fashions clay. The models of creation by a word and of fashioning like a potter appear in the Bible, but on the whole the Bible is much closer to

Fig. 1.8 **Bronze female figurine (Anat). From Syria, second millennium B.C.E.** Walters Art Gallery, Baltimore.
Commons.wikimedia.org

Another cycle of stories from Ugarit tells the tale of a king named Keret or Kirta, who, like Job, saw his numerous family destroyed. The gods grant him a new family, but he is afflicted by illness and has to contend with a challenge to his rule by his son. The latter

the idiom of the Canaanite and Mesopotamian texts than to that of the Egyptian myths.

The Egyptian creation stories place less emphasis on conflict than was the case in *Enuma Elish* or the Baal myth. The main mythical conflict in Egyptian tradition was the conflict of Horus and Seth. Seth is the symbol of chaos and evil (the Greeks identified him with Typhon). He murders his brother and rival, Osiris. Isis, widow and sister of Osiris, recovers his body and conceives his son Horus. Horus engages in many struggles with Seth and eventually defeats him. Horus was the defender of the pharaoh, and the pharaoh was regarded as the living Horus. After death, the pharaoh was identified with Osiris. Osiris became the king of the dead and symbolized the hope for eternal life.

One of the most striking features of ancient Egyptian culture was the pervasive belief in life after death. It is to this belief that we owe the pyramids. Many of the artifacts that stock the Egyptian section of modern Western museums were discovered in tombs, where they had been buried as provisions for the deceased in the afterlife. There is a considerable corpus of Egyptian literature that deals in some way with death and the afterlife. The most ancient corpus of Egyptian religious texts are the Pyramid texts: spells for the protection of the deceased inscribed on the inside walls of the pyramids. In the Middle Kingdom, such spells were inscribed on the panels of wooden coffins and are called the Coffin texts. In the New Kingdom many of these spells appear on papyrus scrolls in Books of the Dead.

One episode in the history of Egyptian religion has often been thought to have influenced the development of monotheism in Israel. This was the religious reform of the pharaoh Amenophis IV, also known as Akhenaten (about 1350 B.C.E.). This pharaoh broke with the traditional cult of Amun at Thebes. He moved his capital to Amarna or Akhetaten, further north on the Nile, and concentrated worship on one god alone, Aten, the solar disk. (This period is known as the Amarna period. It is also famous for the Amarna letters, sent to the pharaoh by his vassals in Canaan, describing conditions there.) Akhenaten declared that all the other gods had failed and ceased to be effective. Aten, identified with Re, the sun-god, had given birth to himself and was beyond compare. He was supreme and all-powerful, the creator and sustainer of the universe. Akhenaten defaced the statue of Amun, sent the high priest of Amun to work in the quarries, and diverted income from the temples of Amun to those of Aten. Scholars dispute whether this cult is properly described as monotheistic. It is not clear that Akhenaten denied the existence of other gods. But it certainly came closer to monotheism than any other cult in the Near

Fig. 1.9   The Egyptian god Khnum (seated, left) models the goddess Ihy on a potter's wheel; relief from the Dendera Temple, Egypt. Commons.
wikimedia.org

East before the rise of Israel. The reforms were short-lived, however. Akhenaten died in the seventeenth year of his rule. After his death, his successor, Tutankhaten, changed his name to Tutankhamun and moved the royal residence from Amarna to the ancient site of Memphis, south of modern Cairo. Akhenaten's monuments were destroyed or concealed and the royal cult returned to the old ways.

Many scholars have wondered whether the religion of Moses was not in some way influenced by that of Akhenaten. YHWH, the God of Israel, is sometimes described with solar imagery, and Psalm 104 has many parallels to Akhenaten's Hymn to the Sun Disk. But on the whole, there is little similarity between the Egyptian solar god and the God of Israel. The Egyptian deity is a timeless, unchanging divinity. Although Christian theologians may also conceive of God as timeless and unchanging, the biblical God of Israel, YHWH (usually pronounced Yahweh), is bound up with his people's history from the beginning, and is revealed through that people's history, as well as through nature. The ways in which YHWH was conceived owe much more to the idiom of Mesopotamian and especially Canaanite myths than to Egypt. These myths were written in Semitic languages that were much closer to Hebrew than was Egyptian.

Conclusion

The material reviewed in this chapter is meant to give an impression of the world of the second millennium B.C.E. and the ways in which people imagined gods and goddesses. The Bible claims that Moses received a new revelation, but even a new revelation was of necessity expressed in language and imagery that was already current. The Hebrew language was a Canaanite dialect, and Canaanite was a Semitic language, like Akkadian.

Fig. 1.10 At left, Anubis (with a jackal's head) brings a deceased person to the underworld, where his soul is weighed against a feather, Thoth (with the head of an ibis) recording the results. He is then led by Horus (with a falcon's head) into the presence of the lord of the underworld, Osiris. From a papyrus *Book of the Dead* by the scribe Hunefer; 19th Dynasty; now in the British Museum. Photo by Jon Bodsworth. Commons.wikimedia.org

Israelite religion, too, did not emerge in a vacuum. Its novel aspects came into being as modifications of beliefs and practices that had been current for centuries. The Hebrew language uses the word *El* for God, and the term inevitably carried with it associations of the Canaanite high god. The biblical creation stories draw motifs from the myths of Atrahasis and *Enuma Elish*, and from the epic of Gilgamesh. In short, much of the language and imagery of the Bible was culture specific, and was deeply imbedded in the traditions of the Near East. Consequently it is necessary to keep the myths and stories of Near Eastern religion in mind when we turn to the biblical text.

FOR FURTHER READING

Citations of Mesopotamian myths in this chapter follow S. Dalley, *Myths from Mesopotamia* (Oxford: Oxford University Press, 1989). Citations of Ugaritic texts follow M. D. Coogan and M. S. Smith, *Stories from Ancient Canaan* (Louisville: Westminster John Knox, 2012).

Other Translations

M. D. Coogan, *A Reader of Ancient Near Eastern Texts: Sources for the Study of the Old Testament* (New York: Oxford University Press, 2012).

B. R. Foster, *From Distant Days: Myths, Tales and Poetry of Ancient Mesopotamia* (Bethesda, MD: CDL, 1995). Literate translation of a wide sample of Mesopotamian literature.

W. W. Hallo and K. L. Younger, eds., *The Context of Scripture,* vol. 1: *Canonical Compositions from the Biblical World* (Leiden: Brill, 1997). Extensive selection of texts from Egyptian, Hittite, Ugaritic, Akkadian, and Sumerian sources, not including laws.

M. Lichtheim, *Ancient Egyptian Literature* (3 vols.; Berkeley: University of California Press, 1975–80). Authoritative translation of Egyptian literature.

S. B. Parker, ed., *Ugaritic Narrative Poetry* (SBL Writings from the Ancient World 9; Atlanta: Scholars Press, 1997). Contains the Ugaritic myths, translated by Mark Smith and others.

J. B. Pritchard, ed., *Ancient Near Eastern Texts* (3rd ed.; Princeton: Princeton University Press, 1969; henceforth *ANET*). This is still the most complete single collection of ancient Near Eastern texts, but individual translations have been superseded in many cases.

M. S. Smith, *The Ugaritic Baal Cycle.* Vol. 1 (VTSup 55; Leiden: Brill, 1994); Vol. 2 (with W. T. Pitard, 2009). Most complete discussion of the Baal myth.

General Sources

Substantial entries on many aspects of the ancient Near East can be found in the following encyclopedias:

D. N. Freedman, ed., *Anchor Bible Dictionary* (6 vols.; Garden City, NY: Doubleday, 1992)

E. M. Meyers, ed., *The Oxford Encyclopedia of Archaeology in the Near East* (5 vols.; Oxford: Oxford University Press, 1997)

J. M. Sasson, ed., *Civilizations of the Ancient Near East* (4 vols.; New York: Scribner, 1995).

Specific Topics

J. Assmann, *The Search for God in Ancient Egypt* (Ithaca, NY: Cornell University Press, 2001). Recent account of Egyptian religion by an influential scholar.

J. Bottéro, *Mesopotamia. Writing, Reasoning and the Gods* (Chicago: University of Chicago Press, 1992). Good introduction to the ancient Near East.

R. J. Clifford, *Creation Accounts in the Ancient Near East and in the Bible* (CBQMS 26; Washington, DC: Catholic Biblical Association, 1994). Good overview of Near Eastern creation myths.

T. Frymer-Kensky, *In the Wake of the Goddesses* (New York: Free Press, 1992), 9–80. Good account of the major goddesses.

T. Jacobsen, *The Treasures of Darkness: A History of Mesopotamian Religion* (New Haven: Yale University Press, 1976). Classic account of Mesopotamian religion.

M. van de Mieroop, *A History of the Ancient Near East* (Oxford: Blackwell, 2004). Clear, up-to-date survey.

A. L. Oppenheim, *Ancient Mesopotamia. Portrait of a Dead Civilization* (Chicago: University of Chicago, 1964). Classic account of Mesopotamian civilization.

Pitard, W. T., "Before Israel: Syria-Palestine in the Bronze Age," in M. D. Coogan, ed., *The Oxford History of the Biblical World* (New York: Oxford University Press, 1998), 33-78. Useful sketch of Canaan in the second millennium, with an eye to relevance for the Bible.

D. B. Redford, *Ancient Gods Speak: A Guide to Egyptian Religion* (New York: Oxford University Press, 2002). Good introduction to Egyptian religion.

D. B. Redford, *Egypt, Canaan, and Israel in Ancient Times* (Princeton: Princeton University Press, 1992). Historical survey of Egypt in the late second millennium.

D. B. Redford, "The Monotheism of Akhenaten," in H. Shanks and J. Meinhardt, eds., *Aspects of Monotheism: How God Is One* (Washington, DC: Biblical Archaeology Society, 1997) 11–26. Lively account of the "monotheistic revolution" of Akhenaten.

CHAPTER 2

The Nature of the Pentateuchal Narrative

INTRODUCTION

The Pentateuch appears in our Bible as a single continuous narrative but clearly includes very diverse materials. In this chapter, we discuss problems with the traditional attribution of the Pentateuch to Moses and indications of multiple authorship. We will also consider what has been the dominant explanation of the Pentateuch's composition among modern scholars, the Documentary Hypothesis, and criticisms that have been raised against it.

The first five books of the Bible (Genesis, Exodus, Leviticus, Numbers, and Deuteronomy; collectively known as the Pentateuch) tell the story of the prehistory of Israel, from creation to the death of Moses on the threshold of the promised land. Genesis 1–11 deals with primeval history, from creation to the flood, and the tower of Babel. Genesis 12–50 is the patriarchal history, the stories of Abraham, Isaac, Jacob, and the sons of Jacob. The Joseph story, in Genesis 37–50, is a distinct block of material within this corpus. It is a transitional story that explains how Israel came to be in Egypt, and thereby sets the stage for the exodus. Exodus 1–18 tells the story of the liberation from Egypt. Then Exodus 19–40 and the book of Leviticus present the revelation at Mount Sinai. The book of Numbers describes the sojourn in the wilderness. Finally, Deuteronomy is the farewell address of Moses.

Mosaic Authorship

These books are traditionally known as the Torah and as the book of Moses. Both of these designations are problematic. The Torah is commonly, but not quite accurately, translated as "Law." Much of the Pentateuch is a presentation of laws, but Genesis and the first half of Exodus consist of narratives. The Hebrew word *torah* has a broader sense than "law" and includes a sense of traditional teaching. The attribution to Moses, however, arises from the prominence of laws in these books. The book of Deuteronomy is introduced as "the words that Moses spoke to all Israel beyond the Jordan" (Deut 1:1), and Moses is again said to be the source of various other parts of Deuteronomy (4:44; 31:24; 32:45). In the books of Joshua and Kings, "the *torah* of Moses" refers to the laws of Deuteronomy (Josh 8:31-32; 23:6; 1 Kgs 2:3; 14:6; 23:5). Later books of the Hebrew Bible, such as Ezra, Nehemiah, and Chronicles, refer to the Torah of Moses, with reference to the laws in Deuteronomy and Leviticus (e.g., Neh 8:1, 13-18). The Torah is commonly regarded as the book of Moses in the Hellenistic period. Ben Sira, who wrote in the early second century B.C.E., refers to "the book of the covenant of the Most High God, the law that Moses commanded us" (Sir 24:23). The Torah is regarded as the book of Moses in the Dead Sea Scrolls, in the New Testament, and in the first-century C.E. Jewish authors Philo and Josephus. The Babylonian Talmud (*Baba Bathra* 14b) says explicitly that Moses wrote the five books named after him. It seems that this tradition had its origin in the book of Deuteronomy and was gradually extended until Moses was regarded not only as the mediator of the laws but as the author of the whole Pentateuch, although there is no basis for this claim in Genesis or in the narrative portions of Exodus.

The problematic nature of the supposed Mosaic authorship was noticed at least as early as the Middle Ages. The medieval Jewish scholar Ibn Ezra (twelfth century) noted that Gen 12:6, which says that "the Canaanites were then in the land," must have been written at a later time, when this was no longer the case. Similarly, Gen 36:31, which refers to

Fig. 2.1 Title page of the commentary on Exodus by the twelfth-century scholar Abraham ibn Ezra; from a fifteenth-century printed edition. Commons.wikimedia.org

"the kings who reigned in the land of Edom, before any king reigned over the Israelites," must have been written after the establishment of the monarchy. Other scholars noted that Moses cannot have written the account of his own death at the end of Deuteronomy. Attention was gradually drawn to various repetitions and contradictions that suggested that the Torah was not the work of any one author, but was rather a compilation of tradition long after the time of Moses. Such observations proliferated in the wake of the Reformation, when the Bible was subjected to a new level of scrutiny. One of the earliest notable critics of the Pentateuch was a Catholic priest, Richard

Simon, in the seventeenth century. Simon argued that the Pentateuch could not have been composed by Moses, but was written centuries later by scribes who drew on archival records. His work was suppressed in France, and he was expelled from his order. Important contributions were made by two great philosophers. Thomas Hobbes, in his master work *Leviathan* (1651), demanded that people be guided by the statements of the biblical books themselves (as opposed to traditional beliefs about them) and held that these books gave considerable evidence about the time in which they were written. In 1670 the Jewish philosopher Benedict Spinoza argued in his *Tractatus Theologico-Politicus* that the Pentateuch and the following books, down to Kings, were compiled by Ezra after the Babylonian exile. Spinoza allowed, however, that Ezra made use of older sources.

A major advance in the study of the Pentateuch is credited to Jean Astruc, a convert to Catholicism who became private physician to King Louis XV. In 1735 Astruc published his "Conjectures about the notes that Moses appears to have used in composing the book of Genesis." Astruc observed that in some passages God is called by the general Hebrew word for god, *Elohim*, while in others he is called by the proper name Yahweh. (Often written without vowels, YHWH, so as not to profane the name by pronouncing it. Jewish tradition substitutes the word *Adonai*, "the Lord." The mongrel form "Jehovah" is a combination of the consonants of YHWH, or JHVH, with the vowels of *Adonai*.) Astruc supposed that different source documents had been woven together in the composition of Genesis.

Astruc's observation was gradually developed by later scholars into a full-fledged documentary hypothesis, which addressed the composition of the entire Pentateuch. The book of Deuteronomy was recognized as substantially a distinct source. A distinction was made between passages that refer to God as Elohim in Genesis. Some of these passages (e.g., Gen 1:1—2:4a, and various passages dealing with genealogies) were recognized as part of a Priestly source (P) that is represented extensively in Leviticus. The remaining narrative material was seen as a combination of Yahwistic source (J, following the German spelling Jahweh) and an Elohistic one (E). For much of the nineteenth century, scholars assumed that the Priestly document was the oldest stratum of the Pentateuch. (In German literature from that time it is called G, for *Grundschrift*, or basic document.) In the 1860s, however, this theory was revised, so that P was viewed as the latest (or next to latest) document, and the order of the sources was established as J, E, D, P (or J, E, P, D). The new order was argued by a number of scholars, notably the German Karl Heinrich Graf and the Dutch scholar Abraham Kuenen. It received its classic formulation, however, from the German Julius Wellhausen in the 1870s and 1880s.

The Documentary Hypothesis, or the view that the Pentateuch is a combination of (at least) four different documents, enjoyed the status of scholarly orthodoxy for about a century. There were always variations of the theory. Some scholars identified additional sources, or subscribed to a Fragment Hypothesis that allowed for greater diversity of authorship. For a long time Scandinavian scholars defended the view that the tradition was transmitted orally down to the late seventh century B.C.E. Some scholars extended the division of sources into the book of Joshua and spoke of a Hexateuch (six books) rather than a Pentateuch. But the four-source theory was by far the dominant view. Only in the last quarter of the twentieth century has it come to be widely questioned. Before we can evaluate these objections, however, we need to appreciate the kind of observations on which the hypothesis was based.

Indications of Multiple Authorship

The different divine names cannot be explained as stylistic variation. In Exod 6:2-3 we read: "God also spoke to Moses and said to him: 'I am YHWH. I appeared to Abraham, Isaac, and Jacob as El Shadday, but by my name YHWH I did not make myself known to them.'" Yet in Gen 4:26 we are told that people began to call upon the name of YHWH in the time of Enosh, grandson of Adam. God is often called YHWH in his dealings with the patriarchs, especially with Abraham. It is apparent, then, that Exod 6:2 comes from a different source than these passages in Genesis.

The variation in divine names is by no means the only indication of multiple authorship. In numerous cases we have doublets, or variant forms of the same story. The account of creation in Gen 1:1—2:3 is quite different from that which follows in the remainder of chapters 2 and 3. Two versions of the flood story are intertwined in Genesis 6–9. Several stories in Genesis appear in more than one form. Abraham identifies his wife, Sarah, as his sister to a foreign king in two separate stories (in chaps. 12 and 20). In a third story, Isaac identifies his wife, Rebekah, as his sister (chap. 26). There are two accounts of God's covenant with Abraham (chaps. 15 and 17), two accounts of Abraham's dealings with Hagar and Ishmael (chaps. 16 and 21), two accounts of the naming of Beersheba (chaps. 21 and 26). The doublets are not confined to Genesis or to the narrative material. There are variant accounts of the crossing of the Red Sea in Exodus 14–15 and different accounts of the revelation of the commandments in Exodus 19–20 and in Deuteronomy. The mountain of the revelation is variously named Sinai or Horeb. The Decalogue (Ten Commandments) is given three times, with some variations (Exod 20:1-17; 34:10-28; Deut 5:6-18). The list of forbidden animals is given twice (Leviticus 11 and Deuteronomy 14). Many further examples could be given.

The argument that these duplications result from the combination of different documents can be illustrated well from the story of the flood. The two versions of the story can be separated as follows:

J: GENESIS 6:5 The Lord saw how great was man's wickedness on earth, and how every plan devised by his mind was nothing but evil all the time. [6] And the Lord regretted that He had made man on earth, and His heart was saddened. [7] The Lord said, "I will blot out from the earth the men whom I created—men together with beasts, creeping things, and birds of the sky; for I regret that I made them." [8] But Noah found favor with the Lord.

J: Noah was a righteous man; he was blameless in his age;

P: [9] This is the line of Noah.—

P: Noah walked with God. [10] Noah begot three sons: Shem, Ham, and Japheth. [11] The earth became corrupt before God; the earth was filled with lawlessness. [12] When God saw how corrupt the earth was, for all flesh had corrupted its ways on earth, [13] God said to Noah, "I have decided to put an end to all flesh, for the earth is filled with lawlessness because of them: I am about to destroy them with the earth. [14] Make yourself an ark of gopher wood; make it an ark with compartments, and cover it inside and out with pitch. [15] This is how you shall make it: the length of the ark shall be three hundred cubits, its width fifty cubits, and its height thirty cubits. [16] Make an opening for daylight in the ark, and terminate it within a cubit of the top. Put the entrance to the ark in its side; make it with bottom, second, and third decks. [17] "For My part, I am about to bring the Flood—waters upon the earth—to destroy all flesh under the sky in which there is breath of life; everything on earth shall perish. [18] But I will establish My covenant with you, and you shall enter the ark, with your sons, your wife, and your sons' wives. [19] And of all that lives, of all flesh, you shall take two of each into the ark to keep alive with you; they shall be male and female. [20] From birds of every kind, cattle of every kind, every kind of creeping thing on earth, two of each shall come to you to stay alive. [21] For your part, take of everything that is eaten and store it away, to serve as food for you and for them." [22] Noah did so; just as God commanded him, so he did.

J: 7 [1] The Lord said to Noah, "Go into the ark, with all your household, for you alone have I found righteous before Me in this generation. [2] Of every clean animal you shall take seven pairs, males and their mates, and of every animal that is not clean, two, a male and its mate; [3] of the birds of the sky also, seven pairs, male and female, to keep seed alive upon all the earth. [4] For in seven days' time I will make it rain upon the earth, forty days and forty nights, and I will blot out from the earth all existence that I created." [5] And Noah did just as the Lord commanded him.

P: [6] Noah was six hundred years old when the Flood came, waters upon the earth. [7] Noah, with his sons, his wife, and his sons' wives, went into the ark because of the waters of the Flood.

J: [8] The clean animals, and the animals that are not clean, and the birds, [came to Noah]

P: and of everything that creeps on the ground, [9] two of each, male and female, came to Noah into the ark [came to Noah], as God had commanded Noah.

J: [10] And on the seventh day the waters of the Flood came upon the earth.

P: [11] In the six hundredth year of Noah's life, in the second month, on the seventeenth day of the month, on that day all the fountains of the great deep burst apart, and the floodgates of the sky broke open.

J: [12] The rain fell on the earth forty days and forty nights.

P: [13] That same day Noah and Noah's sons, Shem, Ham, and Japheth, went into the ark, with Noah's wife and the three wives of his sons—[14] they and all beasts of every kind, all cattle of every kind, all creatures of every kind that creep on the earth, and all birds of every kind, every bird, every winged thing. [15] They came to Noah into the ark, two each of all flesh in which there was breath of life. [16] Thus they that entered comprised male and female of all flesh, as God had commanded him.

J: And the LORD shut him in. [17] The Flood continued forty days on the earth,

P: and the waters increased and raised the ark so that it rose above the earth. [18] The waters swelled and increased greatly upon the earth, and the ark drifted upon the waters. [19] When the waters had swelled much more upon the earth, all the highest mountains everywhere under the sky were covered. [20] Fifteen cubits higher did the waters swell, as the mountains were covered. [21] And all flesh that stirred on earth perished—birds, cattle, beasts, and all the things that swarmed upon the earth, and all mankind. [22] All in whose nostrils was the merest breath of life, all that was on dry land, died.

J: [23] All existence on earth was blotted out—man, cattle, creeping things, and birds of the sky; they were blotted out from the earth. Only Noah was left, and those with him in the ark.

P: [24] And when the waters had swelled on the earth one hundred and fifty days, **8** [1] God remembered Noah and all the beasts and all the cattle that were with him in the ark, and God caused a wind to blow across the earth, and the waters subsided. [2] The fountains of

J: and the rain from the sky was held back; ³ the waters then receded steadily from the earth.

J: ⁶ At the end of forty days, Noah opened the window of the ark that he had made.

J: ⁸ He sent out the dove to see whether the waters had decreased from the surface of the ground. ⁹ But the dove could not find a resting place for its foot, and returned to him to the ark, for there was water over all the earth. So putting out his hand, he took it into the ark with him. ¹⁰ He waited another seven days, and again sent out the dove from the ark. ¹¹ The dove came back to him toward evening, and there in its bill was a plucked-off olive leaf! Then Noah knew that the waters had decreased on the earth. ¹² He waited still another seven days and sent the dove forth; and it did not return to him any more.

J: and when Noah removed the covering of the ark, he saw that the surface of the ground was drying.

the deep and the floodgates of the sky were stopped up.

P: At the end of one hundred and fifty days the waters diminished, ⁴ so that in the seventh month, on the seventeenth day of the month, the ark came to rest on the mountains of Ararat. ⁵ The waters went on diminishing until the tenth month; in the tenth month, on the first of the month, the tops of the mountains became visible.

P: ⁷ He sent out the raven; it went to and fro until the waters had dried up from the earth.

P: ¹³ In the six hundred and first year, in the first month, on the first of the month, the waters began to dry from the earth;

P: ¹⁴ And in the second month, on the twenty-seventh day of the month, the earth was dry. ¹⁵ God spoke to Noah, saying, ¹⁶ "Come out of the ark, together with your wife, your sons, and your sons' wives. [17] Bring out with you every living thing of all flesh that is with you: birds, animals, and everything that creeps on earth; and let them swarm on the earth and be fertile and increase on earth." [18] So Noah came out, together with his sons, his wife, and his sons' wives. [19] Every animal, every creeping thing, and every bird, everything that stirs on earth came out of the ark by families.

J: [20] Noah built an altar to the LORD and, taking of every clean animal and of every clean bird, he offered burnt offerings on the altar. [21] The LORD smelled the pleasing odor, and the Lord said to Himself: "Never again will I doom the earth because of man, since the devisings of man's mind are evil from his youth; nor will I ever again destroy every living being, as I have done. [22] So long as the earth endures, seedtime and harvest, cold and heat, summer and winter, day and night shall not cease."

P: **9** [1] God blessed Noah and his sons, and said to them, "Be fertile and increase, and fill the earth. [2] The fear and the dread of you shall be upon all the beasts of the earth and upon all the birds of the sky—everything with which the earth is astir—and upon all the fish of the sea; they are given into your hand. [3] Every creature that lives shall be yours to eat; as with the green grasses, I give you all these. [4] You must not, however, eat flesh with its life-blood in it. [5] But for your own life-blood I will require a reckoning: I will require it of every beast; of man, too, will I require a reckoning for human life, of every man for that of his fellow man! [6] Whoever sheds the blood of man, by man shall his blood be shed; for in his image did God make man. [7] Be fertile, then, and increase; abound on the earth and increase on it." [8] And God said to Noah and to his sons with him, [9] "I now establish My covenant with you and your offspring to come, [10] and with every living thing that is with you—birds, cattle, and every wild beast as well—all that have come out of the ark, every living thing on earth. [11] I will maintain My covenant with you: never again shall all flesh be cut off by the waters of a flood, and never again shall there be a flood to destroy the earth." [12] God further said, "This is the sign that I set for the covenant between Me and you, and every living creature with you, for all ages to come. [13] I have set My bow in the clouds, and it shall serve as a sign of the covenant between Me and the earth. [14] When I bring clouds over the earth, and the bow appears in the clouds, [15] I will remember My covenant between Me and you and every living creature among all flesh, so that the waters shall never again become a flood to destroy all flesh. [16] When the bow is in the clouds, I will see it and remember the everlasting covenant between God and all living creatures, all flesh that is on earth. [17] That," God said to Noah, "shall be the sign of the covenant that I have established between Me and all flesh that is on earth."

It is clear that the two versions have not been preserved in full. Noah is never instructed to build the ark in J. But the outline of the two stories is clear enough. In one account Noah takes only one pair of animals into the ark. In the other he takes seven pairs. In one account the flood lasts 150 days; in the other, 40 days and 40 nights. Moreover, these two accounts can be aligned with strands or sources elsewhere in Genesis. There are clear links between the Priestly version and the Priestly account of creation in Gen 1:1—2:3,

typified by the command to be fruitful and multiply. The anthropomorphic character of God in the J account (he regrets that he made humankind and is pleased by the odor of sacrifice) is typical of the J source.

The example of the flood should suffice to show that sources are combined in the Pentateuch at least in some cases. It also shows that it is possible to line up consistent features of these sources in different passages. Proponents of the Documentary Hypothesis insist that consistent profiles can be established for

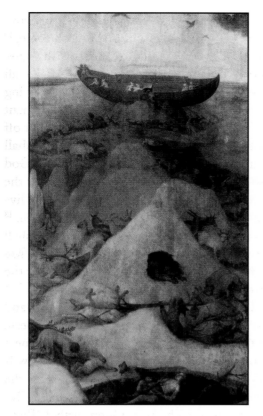

Fig. 2.2 *Noah's Ark on Mount Ararat*
by Hieronymus Bosch (ca. 1514–1516).
Commons.wikimedia.org

each of the four sources, so that we are not dealing just with diverse elements in individual passages, but with strands that run through several biblical books. The continuity of these strands is a major argument for the Documentary Hypothesis.

Profiles of the Sources

The Priestly document is the easiest source to recognize. The rather dry, formulaic style is familiar from the account of creation in Genesis 1. God said "let there be light" and there was light. It is marked by a strong interest in genealogies, in dates (note the precise dating in the Priestly account of the flood), and in ritual observance (the Creator observes the Sabbath by resting on the seventh day). The book of Leviticus is quintessential Priestly material, as is the description of the tabernacle in Exodus 25–31 and 35–40. In P, history is punctuated by a series of covenants, with Noah, Abraham, and finally Moses. P has no angels, dreams, or talking animals, such as we find in other pentateuchal narratives. There is little dispute about the identification of P, although its date remains very controversial. We shall examine this strand of the Pentateuch in more detail in chapter 7.

The D source is also relatively unproblematic. It is found primarily in the book of Deuteronomy, although some scholars now identify Deuteronomic passages also in Genesis and Exodus. There are a few independent passages at the end of Deuteronomy (the Song of Moses in Deuteronomy 32; the Blessing of Moses in chap. 33; the death of Moses in chap. 34), but the main body of the book constitutes the basic D corpus. This material is written in a distinctive style. YHWH is said to love Israel, and Israel is commanded to love YHWH "with all your heart and soul," to listen to his voice, and to do what is right in his sight. YHWH brought Israel out of Egypt "with a strong hand and an outstretched arm." The central theme in Deuteronomy is the covenant, and its most distinctive commandment is that it forbids sacrifice outside of the central sanctuary. Since the work of W. M. L. de Wette at the beginning of the nineteenth century, Deuteronomy has been associated with the reform of King Josiah in 621 B.C.E. Deuteronomy is the subject of chapter 8 below.

The most problematic part of the Documentary Hypothesis is the distinction between the narrative sources, J and E. The distinction emerges clearly in three doublets in Genesis: Gen 12:10-21 (J), with its parallel in 20:1-18 (E; the wife-sister motif); 16:4-14 (J) and parallel in 21:8-21 (E; Hagar and Ishmael); and 26:26-33 (J) and parallel in 21:22-34 (E; controversy at Beersheba). The E accounts use the name Elohim for God and associate revelation with dreams. They reflect on problems of guilt and innocence, and emphasize the "fear of God." E has no primeval history; it begins with Abraham in Genesis 15. Its narrative is built around four figures who all have prophetic traits. Abraham is called a prophet in 20:7 and is said to receive revelations in visions and dreams. Jacob and Joseph also receive revelations in dreams. The call of Moses closely resembles the call of prophets in the later books.

The J source is more colorful. It is familiar from the story of Adam and Eve, with its anthropomorphic God and talking snake. God is described in very human terms. He walks in the garden, regrets that he made humanity, is pleased by the odor of sacrifice, gets angry. Abraham argues directly with YHWH over the fate of Sodom, and the Deity is also represented by "the angel of the LORD" who appears on earth. The call of Abraham in Genesis 12 and the covenant with Abraham in Genesis 15 are ascribed to J. The theme of promise and fulfillment is prominent in this strand. This theme has been especially attractive to Christian theologians, since Christianity has traditionally claimed to be the fulfillment of promises made to Israel. Already in the New Testament, in the Epistle to the Galatians, the apostle Paul appeals to Abraham as a prototype for Christian faith. It is significant that J begins with the story of Adam and Eve and has a substantial treatment of primeval history. Its horizon appears to be wider than that of E, and it is often said to be universalistic in outlook. Abraham is told that in him all the families of the earth will be blessed (Gen 12:3). These features help explain the great interest in J as an author by Christian biblical theologians such as Gerhard von Rad, but J is by no means a Christian construct. In recent years, the integrity of the J source has been defended vigorously by Jewish scholars.

While J and E are clearly distinguished in some passages, they are more difficult to disentangle in others. The story of the sacrifice of Isaac in Genesis 22 is basically an E narrative. Nonetheless, we are told in v. 14 that Abraham called the place "YHWH will provide," and that it is said "to this day" that "on the mount of the Lord it will be provided." The conclusion of the story in vv. 15ff. refers to God as YHWH. Many scholars assume that these verses come from a secondary Yahwistic editor, not the original J. Alternatively, one might suppose that both J and E variants of the story existed, and that an editor took part of the story from E, and the conclusion from J. But the mixture of sources is troubling for the traditional source theory. Again, the story of Jacob's dream at Bethel in Genesis 28 seems to be a combination of E and J narratives. After his dream, Jacob exclaims that "surely YHWH is in this place and I did not know it," but adds, "This is none other than the house of God (Elohim)." In this case, it seems likely that variant forms of the story were spliced together. As a final example of the difficulty of disentangling J and E, we may cite the story of the burning bush in Exodus

Fig. 2.3   Adam, Eve, and a serpent with a human face in the garden of Eden; from the workshop of Cranach the Elder (sixteenth century). Commons.wikimedia.org

3. Moses was guarding the flock of his father-in-law Jethro when he came "to Horeb, the mountain of God (Elohim). There the angel of YHWH appeared to him in a flame of fire out of a bush. . . . Then Moses said, 'I must turn aside and look at this great sight. . . .' When YHWH saw that he had turned aside, God (Elohim) called to him out of the bush." It is possible to explain this passage as the close intersplicing of J and E narratives, but we must assume that the editor took half a verse from one source and the other half from the other. In light of this situation, it is understandable that some scholars prefer to speak of JE, without attempting to separate the sources cleanly. The distinction between J and E becomes even more elusive in the book of Exodus, after the revelation of the name YHWH to Moses. Some scholars now dispute whether E ever existed as a distinct, coherent source.

Dating the Sources

Once it became clear that the Pentateuch was not written by Moses, the dates of its various parts became matters of speculation. One fairly firm point of reference is provided by the date of Deuteronomy. In a groundbreaking dissertation published in 1805, a German scholar, W. M. L. de Wette (1780–1849), demonstrated that "the Book of Deuteronomy differs from the preceding books of the Pentateuch and is the product of a different and somewhat later author." De Wette observed that Deuteronomy 12 restricts sacrificial worship to the one "place that YHWH your God will choose" and calls for the destruction of all the places of worship at the "high places" throughout the country. This law stands in contrast to the practice of Israelite religion throughout much of its history. The book of Genesis describes a time before Moses, when this commandment was presumably unknown, but there were still multiple sacrificial sites after Moses, according to the books of Joshua, Judges, and Samuel. In each of these books, leaders of Israel build altars and offer sacrifices at various locations. Samuel offered sacrifice at Mizpah (1 Samuel 7). Elijah rebuilt the ruined altar on Mount Carmel (1 Kgs 18:30). At least by the time of Elijah, the Jerusalem temple was in existence, and was presumably "the place that the Lord chose." Yet there is no indication that the existence of other places of sacrifice was known to be contrary to Mosaic law. Even prophets such as Amos, who condemn the cult practiced at Bethel and other sanctuaries, never appeal to a law forbidding worship at more than one place. In fact, we only know of two attempts to centralize the Israelite cult and shut down other cult places. The first was by King Hezekiah of Judah, at the end of the eighth century B.C.E. (2 Kings 18), and the second was by his great-grandson, Josiah, in 622 B.C.E., roughly a century later (2 Kings 22). Only Josiah's reform was based on a written law—the "book of the Torah" that had just been found in the temple. De Wette concluded that the law of centralization was an innovation in the time of Josiah, and that the "book of the Torah" in question was Deuteronomy, or at least major parts of it. While the extent of Josiah's law book remains a matter of dispute, the thesis that the law of centralization dates from the time of Josiah seems beyond reasonable doubt. This datum provides an Archimedian point for the dating of biblical narratives and laws. Texts that allow or endorse worship at multiple sanctuaries are most probably older than the time of Josiah. Those that reflect knowledge of this law are presumably later. There is, of course, a possibility that some texts written after the time of Josiah might reject the law of centralization, but in that case we should at least expect them to polemicize against it.

Until recent years, most scholars after de Wette have assumed that the narratives ascribed to J and E are pre-Josianic. Julius Wellhausen, the grandmaster of pentateuchal criticism, put J in the ninth century, E in the eighth, D in the seventh, and P in the sixth or fifth. Wellhausen paid little attention to the dates of J and E. His main argument was that P was later than D. This argument was controversial and remains so more than a century later. We will consider it in detail in chapter 8 when we discuss the relation between the Priestly source and Deuteronomy. In the case of J and E, it seemed obvious that both were pre-Deuteronomic and it was assumed that J was earlier than E.

Gerhard von Rad popularized the view that the J source was older than Wellhausen had supposed. He argued that J should be associated with the reign of Solomon, which he held to be a time of enlightenment, when the tribes of Israel came of age as a state on the international scene. It is widely agreed that J originated in Judah, in the southern part of Israel. Abraham is associated with Hebron, a village near Jerusalem. There are analogies between J's account of Abraham and the story of David. Both are associated with Hebron (David was crowned king there) and both are given covenants that require only that they be faithful to their God. Both Abraham and Isaac are associated with the cult at Beersheba, in southern Judah. Judah is especially prominent among the sons of Jacob. Only J includes the long story from the life of Judah found in Genesis 38, which ends in the birth of Perez, the supposed ancestor of David and the kings of Judah. Judah is said to save Joseph from the older brothers who plan to kill him. In the J account of the covenant with Abraham in Genesis 15, God promises that Abraham's descendants will rule over the land "from the river of Egypt to the river Euphrates." It has been claimed that these were the bounds of the kingdom of David and Solomon. Recent historians have been very skeptical about this claim and doubt that these kings ruled over such an extensive area.

In von Rad's view, however, the Solomonic era was a plateau that could plausibly be understood as a climax of history. The Yahwist was a court historian, who wrote to explain how a people that had been slaves in Egypt attained the status of a kingdom. His explanation was that the Solomonic empire was the fulfillment of a promise made to Abraham centuries earlier. Just as Virgil would later compose an embellished account of Roman origins from the perspective of the Augustan empire, so the Yahwist wrote from the newly attained pinnacle of Solomon's rule.

Von Rad's attractive hypothesis, however, has not stood the test of time. On the one hand, scholars have been increasingly troubled by the lack of any evidence outside the Bible for the glory of Solomon. On the other hand, Genesis 15 is now seen as a very thin thread on which to hang a hypothesis about dating. Even if we were to accept that Solomon's empire extended from the river of Egypt to the river Euphrates, at most this would mean that Genesis 15 was written no earlier than the time of Solomon. It would not guarantee a Solomonic date. Moreover, the lack of overt reference to the Judean monarchy in J is surprising, especially if we are to suppose that J was a court historian. Nonetheless, the southern origin of the J source seems well founded.

The Elohistic source has usually been dated a little later than J, on the assumption that it was created as a northern alternative account of the prehistory of Israel, after the separation of the northern kingdom (Israel) from Judah after the death of Solomon. There are good reasons to associate the E source with the northern kingdom. In Genesis 28 Jacob names the place where he has a dream Bethel, the house of God. Bethel was one of the state temples of the northern kingdom, set up by Jeroboam I, the secessionist king. Jeroboam also built the city of Peniel, which is the site of a struggle between Jacob and God or an angel in Genesis 32. In the E story of Joseph, it is Reuben, rather than Judah, who saves Joseph from his brothers. There is a close analogy between the forced labor imposed on the Israelites in Egypt in Exodus 1 and the corvée, or labor draft, imposed by Solomon and his son Rehoboam, which led to the revolt of the northern tribes. Some stories in the E source are critical of Aaron, the supposed ancestor of the Jerusalem priests. It is plausible, then, that E was composed in the northern kingdom. The prominence of the Arameans in the Jacob story may suggest a date in the ninth century or early eighth century, when the Arameans were the most significant foreign power in relation to Israel. J is generally thought to be slightly older, but the evidence is not conclusive. The editor who put the sources together gave precedence to the J narrative, but some sections, such as Genesis 22 and Genesis 28, could be very well explained on the assumption that E was prior.

Neither J nor E shows any awareness of the Deuteronomic prohibition of worship outside of the central sanctuary in Jerusalem. It is most probable, then, that these sources were compiled before the reform of King Josiah in the late seventh century B.C.E., although some additions could still have been made later.

Criticism of the Documentary Hypothesis

In the last quarter of the twentieth century, many of the established certainties of the Documentary Hypothesis have been called into question. John Van Seters questioned the date of the Yahwist source. One of the central motifs in that source is the migration of Abraham from Mesopotamia to the promised land. Van Seters argued that such a story would make best sense in the period after the Babylonian exile, when Jewish exiles in fact returned from Babylon to Israel. Abraham is not described as a returning exile, and so the analogy is by no means perfect. Nonetheless, the early chapters of Genesis (both J and P sources) show extensive points of contact with Mesopotamia, and while these points of contact are not incompatible with an early date, they can be explained more easily in the exilic period or later than in the early monarchy. It should also be noted that the story of Adam and Eve is never cited in the preexilic prophets, and becomes a prominent point of reference only in the Hellenistic period. This does not prove that the J source was written late, but it does create some misgivings about the supposedly early date of the J strand of Genesis 1–11. It may be that the Primeval History in Genesis 1–11, where most of the Babylonian analogies are found, was a late addition to the J source.

A different line of critique was developed by the German scholar Rolf Rendtorff, a student of von Rad. Rendtorff noted that some influential scholars who continued to affirm the Documentary Hypothesis nonetheless proceeded on quite different assumptions. Hermann Gunkel, the founder of form criticism, treated the stories of Genesis as discrete units, akin to folklore, and paid little attention to the major sources, although he did not deny their existence. Martin Noth, a contemporary of von Rad, analyzed the Pentateuch in terms of five major themes: the promises to the ancestors, the guidance out of Egypt, the wandering in the wilderness, the revelation at Sinai, and the guidance into the arable land. These were traditional themes, which both J and E formulated in their different ways. Implicit in Noth's analysis, however, was the insight that the patriarchal stories are different in kind from the story of the exodus, even if one recognizes J and E strands in both. For most readers, the differences between these blocks or themes are more obvious and more significant than the difference between J and E.

Rendtorff went further than Noth and questioned the entire validity of the J and E sources. Building on Rendtorff's work, his student Erhard Blum has proposed an elaborate alternative to the Documentary Hypothesis. Abandoning the traditional sources, J and E, Blum finds two main stages in the composition of the Pentateuch. The first he calls the "D-Komposition" (K^D), which was the work of editors from the Deuteronomistic tradition. He dates this composition to the generation after the Babylonian exile. The second stage is the "P-Komposition" (K^P), the work of Priestly writers who edited K^D, and so, of necessity, worked even later. This is not to suggest that all of the pentateuchal narratives are as late as the exile. The authors of K^D inherited two main documents. One was an edition of Genesis 12–50 from the exilic period, which was itself a reworking of a composition from the late preexilic period. (Parts of the Jacob cycle, however, are thought to date from the formation of the northern kingdom of Israel, after the death of Solomon.) The second was a "Life of Moses," which had been composed some time after the fall of the northern kingdom, but which, again, incorporated elements that dated from the early monarchy. K^D introduced the theme of the promise to the patriarchs as a means of connecting these two blocks of narrative. K^D began with Gen 12:1-3 and concluded with a narrative of the wandering in the wilderness. The Primeval History (Genesis 1–11) was added by K but also incorporated some older sources. The traditional P material, such as we find in Leviticus, would also have been added at this stage. There have been several other proposals along the lines of Blum's work, but differing in details.

It is clear enough that the patriarchal stories and the Exodus tradition present different accounts of the origin of Israel. The question is whether they were combined already in J and E, or only later by the Priestly writers and Deuteronomists. Perhaps the main issue raised by the work of Rendtorff and Blum is whether the composition of the pentateuchal narratives can be ascribed to Deuteronomistic editors, no earlier than the Babylonian exile. There is an obvious problem with this thesis. The signature element of the Deuteronomic movement was the insistence that sacrifice should be offered only at the central sanctuary in Jerusalem, and centralization of the cult also seems to be presupposed in P. Yet much of Genesis consists of stories of the founding of other cult sites, including the northern sanctuary of Bethel, by the patriarchs. Such stories could only lend legitimacy to the sanctuaries that were condemned to destruction in Deuteronomy. Blum allows that the narratives of Genesis 12–50 had already been put together before the exile, but it is still difficult to see why Deuteronomistic editors would let so much of this material stand while making major modifications in other respects. It is surely more plausible that the pentateuchal narrative was already established and authoritative before Deuteronomy was added. Also, Blum's argument does not do justice to the clear distinction between J and E passages in the patriarchal stories noted above. It remains likely that J and E were composed (not necessarily combined) before the Deuteronomic reform, although some material in the Primeval History may have been added later.

Nonetheless, the recent debates about the Pentateuch show that the reconstruction of earlier forms of the biblical text is a highly speculative enterprise. Perhaps the main lesson to be retained is that these texts are indeed composite and incorporate layers from different eras. We should allow for differences and contradictions between different passages. These differences are not eliminated by the "canonical shape" of the texts. The final editors, Deuteronomists, priests, or whoever they may have been, did not revise the older traditions systematically. Rather, they let stand material with diverse points of view, and were content to add their own distinctive emphases to the mix. The biblical text that resulted from this process is not a consistent systematic treatise. Rather, it is a collection of traditional materials that places different viewpoints in dialogue with one another and offers the reader a range of points of view. It is not a text that lends itself to imposing orthodoxy, or even orthopraxy, despite (perhaps because of) the proliferation of laws. Rather, it should stimulate reflection and debate by the unreconciled diversity of its content.

On any reckoning, the Pentateuch cannot have reached its present form earlier than the postexilic period. While the Priestly strand may have been an independent document, it serves to tie the narrative sources together. It provides the opening chapter of Genesis and connects the narrative with its genealogies and dating formulae. We shall see that some elements in the Priestly strand were added quite late, long after the Babylonian exile. Nonetheless, it is not clear whether Priestly or Deuteronomic editors should be credited

with establishing the shape of the Pentateuch as we have it. The evidence for Priestly editing of Genesis and Exodus is much clearer than that for Deuteronomic editing. This might suggest that the first four books of the Pentateuch were edited by Priestly writers before Deuteronomy was added. The fact that Deuteronomy stands as the last book of the Pentateuch gives the impression that it was added last and not thoroughly integrated with the other books. But much depends here on whether one finds persuasive the arguments of scholars like Blum for Deuteronomic editing of the first four books of the Pentateuch. There were certainly some Deuteronomic additions in the earlier books, but the extent of the Deuteronomic editing remains in dispute. Ultimately there is much to be said for the view that the Pentateuch as it stands is a compromise document, in which Priestly and Deuteronomic theologies were presented side by side, without any clear indication that one should take precedence over the other. In that case, the compiler(s) should not be identified as either Priestly or Deuteronomic, but as mediating the different theological traditions.

In the following chapters I do not attempt to extrapolate theologies of J or E to any significant degree. There are evidently different strands in Genesis, and light can be thrown on some passages by noting their affinities with J or E. The distinction is also useful sometimes in Exodus, but much less often. My goal, however, is not to reconstruct J or E, but to appreciate the pentateuchal narratives as they have come down to us. P and D, in contrast, correspond to well-defined blocks of text and present clear and well-developed theologies. These sources will accordingly be treated in separate chapters.

FOR FURTHER READING

J. S. Baden, *The Composition of the Pentateuch: Renewing the Documentary Hypothesis* (Yale Anchor Reference Library; New Haven: Yale University Press, 2012). Vigorous defense of the Documentary Hypothesis.

J. Blenkinsopp, *The Pentateuch* (New York: Doubleday, 1992). Good history of scholarship. Analysis along the lines of Rendtorff and Blum.

A. R. Campbell and M. A. O'Brien, *Sources of the Pentateuch: Texts, Introductions, and Annotations* (Minneapolis: Fortress Press, 1993). Convenient presentation of the sources throughout the Pentateuch, following the analysis of Martin Noth.

T. Dozeman and K. Schmid, eds., *Farewell to the Yahwist? The Composition of the Pentateuch in Recent European Interpretation* (SBL Symposium Series 34; Atlanta: SBL, 2006). Essays by the leading critics of the Documentary Hypothesis, including Blum.

T. Dozeman, K. Schmid, and B. Schwartz, eds., *The Pentateuch: International Perspectives on Current Research* (Tübingen: Mohr Siebeck, 2011). Essays representing the full spectrum of current approaches.

R. E. Friedman, "Torah (Pentateuch)," *ABD* 6:605–21.

R. E. Friedman, *The Bible with Sources Revealed: A New View into the Five Books of Moses* (San Francisco: Harper, 2003). Staunch defense of traditional source criticism.

E. Nicholson, *The Pentateuch in the Twentieth Century: The Legacy of Julius Wellhausen* (Oxford: Clarendon, 1998). Good review of the history of scholarship, including recent developments.

M. Noth, *A History of Pentateuchal Traditions* (trans. B. W. Anderson; Chico, CA: Scholars Press, 1981). Classic analysis of major themes in the Pentateuch.

R. Rendtorff, *The Problem of the Process of Transmission in the Pentateuch* (trans. J. J. Scullion; JSOTSup 89; Sheffield: JSOT Press, 1990). Influential argument against the Documentary Hypothesis.

A. Rofé, *Introduction to the Composition of the Pentateuch* (The Biblical Seminar 58; Sheffield: Sheffield Academic Press, 1999). Concise, helpful illustration of the issues.

K. Schmid, *Genesis and the Moses Story* (Winona Lake, IN: Eisenbrauns, 2010). Emphasizes the discontinuity between Genesis and Exodus.

J.-L. Ska, *Introduction to Reading the Pentateuch* (Winona Lake, IN: Eisenbrauns, 2006). Clear, helpful exposition of the criticisms of the Documentary Hypothesis.

J. Van Seters, *Abraham in History and Tradition* (New Haven: Yale University Press, 1975)

J. Van Seters, *The Life of Moses* (Louisville: Westminster, 1994). Regards the J source as later than Deuteronomy.

G. von Rad, "The Form-Critical Problem of the Hexateuch," in *The Problem of the Hexateuch and Other Essays* (trans. E. W. Trueman; New York: McGraw-Hill, 1966; German original, 1938). Classic exposition of the J source.

J. Wellhausen, *Prolegomena to the History of Ancient Israel* (1885; reprint Atlanta: Scholars Press, 1994). Classic exposition of the Documentary Hypothesis. Enormously influential.

CHAPTER 3
The Primeval History

INTRODUCTION

In this chapter, we will explore how the first book of the Bible begins, examining the story of Adam and Eve, distinctive themes and emphases in the Priestly story of creation, and the stories of decisive events in the early history of the human race—including the great flood and the Tower of Babel—in Genesis 4–11.

The Primeval History, in Genesis 1–11, is woven from the J and P strands. The contrast between the two is clearly evident in the two accounts of creation with which they begin—the ritualistic Priestly account in Gen 1:1—2:4a, and the colorful, folksy, Yahwistic account in the remainder of chapters 2 and 3. P is responsible for the genealogy in chapter 5, for one strand of the flood story as we have already seen, and for the genealogies of Noah's sons in Genesis 10 and 11. We shall begin by considering the J account of the Primeval History and then consider how it has been shaped by the Priestly editors.

Adam and Eve

The J account begins with one of the most familiar of all biblical narratives—the story of Adam and Eve. There is surprisingly little reference to this story in the remainder of the Hebrew Bible, although there are several allusions to the garden of Eden as a place of remarkable fertility (Isa 51:3; Ezek 36:35; Joel 2:3; et al.). Ezekiel 28:13-16 alludes to a figure who is driven out of "Eden, the garden of God," by a cherub, in the context of a taunt against the king of Tyre, but it is not clear that he had the same story in mind that we now find in Genesis. For clear allusions to Adam and Eve, we have to wait until Ben Sira, in the early second century B.C.E., and the Dead Sea Scrolls.

The Creation of Humanity

The story focuses on the creation of humanity. Little is said about the creation of heaven and earth, except that they are the work of YHWH, and that the earth was not watered initially. The man (*adam* is the generic Hebrew word for human being) is made from the dust of the ground and animated by the breath of life. In the Babylonian myth of Atrahasis, humanity is also made from clay, mixed in that case with the flesh and blood of a slain god. In the biblical story, the breath of God is the element of divine origin in the human makeup. In this rather simple understanding, life comes with the breath and ceases when the breath departs. Then human beings return to the state of clay.

In the Atrahasis story, humanity was created to do agricultural work for the gods. In Genesis the first human being is also charged with keeping the garden of God, but the task does not appear very onerous. The Creator provides for the growth of "every tree that is

Fig. 3.1   The Myth of Atrahasis; cuneiform tablets from ancient Babylon, now in the British Museum. Commons.wikimedia.org

pleasant to the sight and good for food." Luxuriant divine gardens often appear in ancient Near Eastern literature. The most celebrated example is the land of Dilmun, which is described in the Sumerian myth called "Enki and Ninhursag" (see sidebar on p. 71).

We encounter similar imagery in the book of Isaiah in the context of the restoration of an Edenic state in the messianic age. These gardens are often the source of life-giving waters that refresh the earth. This is also the case in Genesis, where a river that flows out of Eden is said to be the source of four rivers, including the Tigris and Euphrates, the great rivers of Mesopotamia.

Two trees are singled out in this garden: the tree of life in the middle of the garden and the tree of the knowledge of good and evil. (The precise meaning of "the knowledge of good and evil" is disputed. It may mean "universal knowledge," or it may mean the power of discernment between good and evil—cf. Isa 7:15-16, which refers to the age by which a child knows how to choose the good and reject the evil.) Symmetry would lead us to expect that if one tree is the tree of life, the corresponding one should be the tree of death, and sure enough, Adam is told that if he eats of it he shall die. The tree is not introduced to Adam under the negative name of death, however, but in its attractive aspect as the tree of knowledge. The plot of the story hinges on the idea that God does not want humanity to eat from the tree of knowledge. The idea that gods jealously guard their superiority over humanity is widespread in the ancient world. It is also found in the Greek myth of Prometheus, the hero who was condemned to torture because he stole fire from the gods to benefit humankind. It should be noted, however, that Adam is not initially forbidden to eat from the tree of life.

The plot is complicated when the Creator decrees that "it is not good that the man should be alone." (In the Atrahasis myth human beings were created in pairs, and in the Priestly account of creation in Genesis 1 they were created male and female.) In the J account, the man is allowed responsible participation in the choice of his mate. In the process, he is allowed to name all the beasts, but none of these is found to be a fit partner for him. The gradual process of creation here is sometimes cited as biblical support for the idea of evolution, but the two concepts are very different. It should be emphasized, however, that the Genesis story by no means conceives of God as an unmoved mover who produces creation fully formed. Rather, the Creator proceeds by a process of trial and error, and engages in unsuccessful experiments. This is also the way creation is imagined in the Babylonian Atrahasis myth.

Finally, Adam finds a partner in the woman who is taken from his rib. Whether the manner in which the woman is created implies the subordination of woman to man is a matter of heated dispute. For two thousand years, the implication of subordination was thought to be obvious. In the words of St. Paul, in the course of his attempt to argue that women should cover their heads when they pray or prophesy: "man was not made from woman, but woman from man. Neither was man created for the sake of woman, but woman for the sake of man" (1 Cor 11:8-9; cf. 1 Tim 2:13, which forbids women to teach or have authority over men, because "Adam was formed first"). Even Paul recognized the anomaly of this claim. He added that though woman came from man, "so man comes through woman, and all things come from God" (1 Cor 11:12) and that "in the Lord, woman is not independent of man, or man independent of woman" (v. 11). In the Genesis text, the emphasis is on the closeness of the bond between man and woman: "This at last is bone of my bones and flesh of my flesh. . . . Therefore a man leaves his father and his mother and clings to his wife, and they become one flesh" (Gen 2:23-24). (Usually in ancient Israel, the woman left her parents' house to live with her husband; either the Genesis text reflects a time when this was not the custom or it simply means that for a man the bond with his wife takes precedence over that with his parents.) Despite all this, however, the reversal of the natural order of birth, by having the woman taken from the man's body, cannot be denied. The order of creation surely implies an order of precedence. In the ancient (and modern) Near East, it was assumed that females should defer to males. But to speak of subordination here is too strong. In the account of the original creation, the emphasis is on the closeness of the bond between male and female.

The man and wife were naked and not ashamed. This notice alerts us to the sexual overtones of the story. Some interpreters even hold that the "knowledge of good and evil" refers to sexual initiation. Immediately after their expulsion from Eden, we are told that Adam "knew his wife, Eve, and she conceived and bore Cain" (Gen 4:1). The verb "to know" often refers to sexual relations in biblical idiom. Genesis does not say explicitly that Adam "knew" his wife in the garden. Later Jewish tradition insisted that he did not, since the garden was holy, like the temple, because of the presence of God. Nonetheless, the motif of the forbidden fruit in Genesis 3 has always lent itself to a sexual interpretation. More fundamentally, however, the nudity of Adam and Eve symbolizes their initial innocence and lack of self-awareness—a state in which human beings are not sharply different from animals. By the end of the story, they will have put on clothes and become human, for better or worse.

The Serpent

Genesis 3, however, introduces another character into the story: "the serpent was more crafty than any other wild animal that the LORD God had made" (3:1). In later tradition, the serpent would be identified as Satan, or the devil. According to the Wisdom of Solomon (a Jewish text, written in Greek around the turn of the era and included in the Catholic canon and Protestant Apocrypha), death entered the world "by the envy of the devil" (Wis 2:24). The New Testament book of Revelation refers to "the ancient serpent, who is called the Devil and Satan, the deceiver of the whole world" (Rev 12:9). (The role of Satan in the tempting of the primeval couple is further developed in an extensive postbiblical literature on the life of Adam and Eve.) The figure of the devil, however, is a latecomer on the biblical scene. When Satan appears in the Hebrew Bible (in the book of Job and again in Chronicles), he is not yet quite "the devil"—in Job he appears among "the sons of God" in the heavenly court. Neither should the serpent in Genesis be interpreted as the devil. Talking animals are a standard device in the literary genre of the fable, which was developed most famously by the Greek writer Aesop. The appearance of a talking snake should alert even the most unsophisticated reader to the fictional nature of the story. The snake articulates the voice of temptation, but it is not yet a mythological figure such as Satan later became.

The Knowledge of Good and Evil

The snake leads the human couple to question the divine prohibition against eating from the tree of the knowledge of good and evil: "You will not die; for God knows that when you eat of it your eyes will be opened, and you will be like God, knowing good and evil." So the woman takes the forbidden fruit and eats, and then offers it to Adam, and he eats. Then "the eyes of both were opened and they knew that they were naked; and they sewed fig leaves together and made loincloths for themselves." The "knowledge of good and evil" that they attain does not quite make them like gods, but it does give them self-awareness, and it sets them apart from the animals.

At this point, light can be shed on the story of Adam and Eve by recalling an episode from the Babylonian Epic of Gilgamesh. When Enkidu, the companion of Gilgamesh, is first introduced, he roams with the wild beasts and eats grass. He is tamed by a harlot, who waits for him at the watering place. Enkidu couples with her for six days and seven nights. When he returns to the beasts, however, they run off, and he finds that he cannot keep pace with them as before. He returns to the harlot, who tells him: "You have become [profound], Enkidu. You have become like a god! Why should you roam open country with the wild beasts?" (trans. Dalley, *Myths from Mesopotamia*, 56). The harlot teaches him to eat human food and drink strong drink. Then he anoints himself with oil, puts on clothes, and becomes human. He sets out for Uruk to meet Gilgamesh and undertake great adventures. On the one hand, his encounter with the harlot leads to loss of his natural strength, but on the other hand, he becomes wise like a god, or at least like a human being.

The story of Enkidu takes a tragic turn. Because he and Gilgamesh kill the Bull of Heaven, it is decreed by the gods that Enkidu must die. He is forewarned of his death in dreams. Bitter, he curses the harlot who changed the course of his life. When Shamash the sun-god hears his curse, however, he reminds Enkidu of the good things that resulted from that change—the food, wine, and garments, and above all the friendship of Gilgamesh. Enkidu relents and pronounces a blessing on the harlot instead.

Adam is told that his death is the direct result of eating from the tree of knowledge. Enkidu's fate is not the direct result of his encounter with the harlot. There is an analogy

Fig. 3.2 A powerful figure vanquishes a lion, a theme common in ancient depictions of Gilgamesh; stone relief now in the Louvre. Commons.wikimedia.org

between the two, nonetheless. Both characters make the transition to the kind of self-consciousness that requires them to wear clothes. Both become conscious of death. Enkidu would presumably have died anyway. This is less clear in the case of Adam, who had the opportunity to eat from the tree of life but failed to do so. Both aspire to being wise like the gods, but when their eyes are opened all they discover is that they are naked and that they will die.

In the Babylonian story, Enkidu's action and its results are mixed. Ultimately, he has to confront death, but he also gains a richness of life unknown to the animals on the steppe. The evaluation of Adam's action in Genesis is severer. First God curses the snake, and condemns it to crawl on its belly and eat dust. Then he tells the woman that he will greatly increase her pain in childbearing (a subject that had not previously been mentioned). Yet she is told "your desire shall be for your husband, and he shall rule over you" (3:16). Finally, the man is told that "because you have listened to the voice of your wife" and eaten from the forbidden tree, the ground is cursed because of him. Consequently, "By the sweat of your face you shall eat bread until you return to the ground, for out of it you were taken. For you are dust, and to dust you shall return" (3:19). God then expels Adam and Eve from the garden, lest they put forth their hands and eat from the tree of life and live forever.

Disobedience and Fall

The story of Adam and Eve is known in Christian theology as "the fall," and it is assumed that the human condition, subject to suffering and death, are consequences of the sin of Adam. Against this, it has been objected that no Hebrew equivalent of the term "fall" is used in the Hebrew Bible in this context. The concept of a fall derives from Greek Orphic traditions and Platonic philosophy. Plato thought of the soul as a pure, spiritual substance, which

falls into the imperfect material world and loses its original perfection. But even if the concept of a fall, as such, is not articulated in the Hebrew Bible, it cannot be denied that Adam and Eve are expelled from Eden as a punishment for eating the forbidden fruit. Moreover, God pronounces curses on the serpent and on the ground because of what Adam and Eve have done. The narrative can still be read, like that of Enkidu, as a coming of age story of the transition from a prehuman to a human state. But unlike the Babylonian story, Genesis judges this transition negatively. Even though no words meaning "sin" or "punishment" are used in the story, it is quite clear that the conditions in which men and women must henceforth live are explained as punishment for disobedience.

These conditions are described in God's words to the serpent, the woman, and the man in Gen 3:14-19. It should be clear that these passages give us only the author's assumptions about the nature of life. They are not descriptions that are universally valid. Still less can they be read as normative accounts of how life must, or should, be. The nature of these passages can be seen clearly in the words addressed to the snake: "Upon your belly you shall go, and dust you shall eat all the days of your life." Snakes do not in fact eat dust; this was simply a misconception on the part of the author. What we have here is an etiology—a story that is told to explain the cause of something. There are numerous examples of such stories in the Bible and in ancient Near Eastern literature. An example that is relevant to Genesis 2–3 is found near the end of the Epic of Gilgamesh. Gilgamesh secures a plant that has the power of rejuvenation—if an old man ate of it, he would become young again. On his return journey, however, he stops to bathe in a pool. A snake smells the fragrance of the plant and carries it off. Thereafter the snake sheds its scaly skin. This episode dooms Gilgamesh's attempt to escape from death, but it also provides an etiology of why the snake sheds its skin. Again, there is a misconception involved, insofar as the story implies that the snake becomes young again.

The curse pronounced on the snake provides an etiology of the way the snake was thought to live. God's words to the woman likewise reflect the author's view of the female condition. There is pain in childbearing, and subordination to a husband who "will rule over you." It is often pointed out that this condition is not the original design of creation. It is a punishment, imposed after Adam and Eve ate from the forbidden tree. It is a mistake to read this passage as if it were the normative expression of God's will for women (as seems to be implied in the New Testament in 1 Tim 2:13-14, which says that woman will be saved through childbearing). In that case, one would also have to conclude that it is God's will that snakes eat dust and that men earn their bread by the sweat of their brow. God's words to the woman simply reflect the common experience of women in ancient Israel and throughout the ancient Near East. The passage is explanatory in nature. It is not prescriptive or normative.

If God's words to the woman paint a grim picture of life, his words to the man are no less severe. The final verdict recalls the words of the alewife Siduri in the Epic of Gilgamesh, when she tells Gilgamesh, "You will not find the eternal life you seek. When the gods created mankind they appointed death for mankind, kept eternal life in their own hands" (trans. Dalley, *Myths from Mesopotamia*, 150). Genesis suggests that this may not have been the original design of the Creator, but nonetheless it is now the inescapable human condition. There is no hint here of any possibility of meaningful life after death. (The common assumption in the Hebrew Bible, as we shall see later, was that after death all people, good and bad, went to the shadowy underworld, Sheol, the counterpart of the Greek Hades.) Where the Babylonian epic, however, simply presents this situation as a matter of fact, the biblical text seeks to explain it by laying the blame on human beings. In part, the problem is disobedience to the divine command. More broadly, however, one could say that the problem is human overreaching. Like the heroes of Greek tragedy, Adam and Eve are guilty of hubris in their desire to be like God, knowing good and evil. One message of this story, which is a common message in ancient Near Eastern literature, is that human beings should know their place and stay in it.

Theological Misconceptions

More than most stories, these chapters of Genesis have been overlain with theological interpretations that have little basis in the Hebrew text. Since the time of St. Augustine,

---

Siduri the Alewife's Advice to Gilgamesh

"You will not find the eternal life you seek. When the gods created mankind they appointed death for mankind, kept eternal life in their own hands."

—(trans. Dalley, *Myths from Mesopotamia*, 150)

Christian theology has maintained the doctrine of original sin—the belief that human beings after Adam are born in a state of sin. There is a partial basis for this idea in the New Testament, where St. Paul asserts that "one man's trespass led to condemnation for all" and "by the one man's disobedience the many were made sinners" (Rom 5:18-19), but there is no suggestion of this in the text of Genesis. In the first century c.e., when Paul wrote, there was some debate in Judaism about the significance of Adam's disobedience. This debate is reflected in apocalyptic writings from the end of that century. In *4 Ezra* 7:48 [118] Ezra asks, "O Adam, what have you done? For though it was you who sinned, the fall was not yours alone, but ours also who are your descendants" (RSV). In the nearly contemporary apocalypse known as *2 (Syriac) Baruch,* Baruch rejects this sentiment and takes a position that is more typical of Jewish tradition: "For though Adam first sinned and brought untimely death upon all men, yet each one of those who were born from him has either prepared for his own soul its future torment or chosen for himself the glories that are to be. . . . Thus Adam was responsible for himself only; each one of us is his own Adam" (*2 Bar.* 54:15, 19; trans. L. H. Brockington, in H. F. D. Sparks, ed., *The Apocryphal Old Testament* [Oxford: Clarendon, 1984]). The story of Adam is paradigmatic, insofar as the temptation to eat forbidden fruit is typical of human experience. One might also suppose that an *inclination* to sin is inherited from one generation to another. But there is no suggestion in the biblical text that guilt is transmitted genetically.

Equally unfounded is the view that the responsibility for sin lay with Eve rather than with Adam. The earliest occurrence of this idea is found in the book of Ben Sira in the early second century b.c.e.: "From a woman sin had its beginning, and because of her we all die" (Sir 25:24). It is repeated in the New Testament in 1 Tim 2:14: "Adam was not deceived, but the woman was deceived and became a transgressor." One may reasonably infer from the text of Genesis that the serpent approached Eve first because she was weaker, but Adam still bears the primary responsibility in the story. The command was given to him before Eve was created. Only after they have both eaten are their eyes opened. Adam and Eve suffer equally from the consequences of their action.

Finally, the words of God to the snake have been invested with theological meaning in Christianity: "I will put enmity between you and the woman and between your offspring and hers; he will strike your head and you will strike his heel." Catholic Christianity has traditionally identified the woman as Mary, her seed as Jesus, and the snake as Satan. The passage is then read as a prophecy of the crushing of Satan and has inspired countless statues of Mary with a snake under her feet. Such allegorical interpretation has its place in a religious tradition, but we should be aware that it is not implied by the Hebrew text. Like the preceding verse, about the snake crawling on its belly and eating dust, this one is an etiology meant to explain a fact of experience—snakes bite people, and people kill snakes.

The Contrast with Modern Values

The story of Adam and Eve is a compelling story, largely because the lure of forbidden fruit rings true to human experience, as does

Fig. 3.3   At left, Adam and Eve are tempted by the serpent; at right, they are expelled from the garden. Fresco in the Sistine Chapel, the Vatican, by Michelangelo Buonarroti (1509). Commons.wikimedia. org

the sense that our enjoyment of paradisiac bliss is likely to be short-lived and doomed to frustration. It should be emphasized, however, that the worldview of this story is antithetical to modern Western culture. While Adam has free range over nearly all the garden, the limit imposed by the divine command is crucial. Obedience to a higher authority is an essential element of the biblical ethic. For modern culture, in contrast, the sky is the limit and people are constantly encouraged to "go for it." One may debate the relative merits of the two approaches to life, but the fundamental difference between them must be acknowledged. Moreover, not everyone in antiquity subscribed to the kind of "philosophy of limit" that is implied in Genesis. The Greek sophists, in the fifth century B.C.E., taught that "man is the measure of all things." In the Gnostic writings of the fourth and fifth centuries C.E., the serpent is viewed positively, as an instructor who wanted humanity to attain wisdom and illumination.

The recognition of human limitation is a common feature of ancient wisdom outside the Bible as well. We have already referred to the theme of hubris in Greek tragedy. Those who aspire to rise too high, to be like gods, are doomed to catastrophe. This theme was also found in Near Eastern myth, and is reflected in the Bible in taunts of Gentile kings. In the book of Isaiah, the king of Babylon is taunted: "How you are fallen from heaven, O Day Star, son of dawn! How you are cut down to the ground, you who laid the nations low! You said in your heart, 'I will ascend to heaven; I will raise my throne above the stars of God . . . I will make myself like the Most High.' But you are brought down to Sheol, to the depths of the pit" (Isa 14:12-14). Ezekiel taunts the king of Tyre by telling him that he was (or thought he was) in "Eden, the garden of God," but was driven out by a cherub (Ezekiel 28). In these cases, as in Greek tragedy, the sin that leads to the fall is simply pride. In Genesis it is disobedience, and the desire for "the knowledge of good and evil." Also in Genesis this is not just the experience of a king or an extraordinary person, but of Adam, the archetypical and paradigmatic human being.

The Date of the Yahwistic Creation Story

Genesis 2:4b—3:24 is generally, and persuasively, regarded as the beginning of the J narrative because of the lively style and anthropomorphic presentation of God. There are some problems with the attribution, however. First, God is not just called YHWH as we might expect, but YHWH Elohim ("the LORD God"). This combination occurs only once in the Pentateuch outside this story, in Exod 9:30 (where the text is not certain). As we have seen in the previous chapter, there are good reasons for regarding the J narrative as generally pre-Deuteronomic. The creation story, however, and indeed all of the Primeval History, echoes Babylonian literature at several points. Such allusions would not be impossible before the exile, but they can be more easily explained in an exilic context or later. Finally, while some prophets, especially Ezekiel, are aware of traditions about Eden, there is no really clear reference to this story until the Hellenistic period, in the book of Ben Sira. There is no foreshadowing in the garden of the later stories of Abraham and Israel, and there are no allusions to the story in the later narratives. The stylistic argument for ascribing the story to J is still a strong one, but the considerations we have noted suggest a relatively late date for the composition of the section of the J narrative that deals with the Primeval History.

The Priestly Creation Story

Whatever the origin of the Adam and Eve story, it stands in sharp contrast to the Priestly account of creation that now forms the opening chapter of the Bible. The opening verse (Gen 1:1) is majestic in its simplicity: "In the beginning, God created the heavens and the earth." Originally, the Hebrew was written without vowels. The vowels were added later as points above and below the consonants. The consonantal text can also be translated as: "In the beginning, when God created the heavens and the earth. . . ." The Babylonian creation myth, *Enuma Elish,* similarly begins with a temporal clause. (There is another possible reflection of the Babylonian myth in Gen 1:2. The Hebrew word for "the deep" [*tᵉhom*] is a cognate of the name of the Babylonian monster Tiamat in *Enuma Elish.*) If the opening words are translated as a temporal clause, it is clear that we are not speaking of creation out of nothing. Already when God set about creating the heavens and the earth, there was a formless void *(tohu wabohu),* and the wind or spirit of God was hovering over the waters. God proceeds to bring order out of chaos simply by uttering commands. There were precedents for creation by divine word in Egyptian mythology, but there is an evident contrast here with Genesis 2 and with the creation mythologies of Mesopotamia. The God of the Priestly writers is more exalted, or more remote, than the God of J.

The creation is arranged in seven days:

1. Light; separation of light and darkness
2. Firmament; separation of lower and upper water

3a. Dry land; separation of water and dry land

3b. Vegetation

4. Sun, moon, and stars; separation of day and night

5. Water and air creatures

6a. Land creatures; human beings

6b. Vegetation given to birds, animals, and human beings as food

7. God rests

The narrative is formulaic. There are frequent pronouncements that "God saw that it was good," and after the sixth day, everything is pronounced "very good." At the same time, the narrative is not fully consistent. The pronouncement that "it was good" is lacking for the second and fourth days, and there are double acts of creation on the third and sixth days. The duplications are necessary to fit the work of creation into six days, thereby allowing the Creator to rest on the seventh, in effect inaugurating the Sabbath day. The fact that the whole process ends in a liturgical observance is typical of the Priestly source. Also typical is the emphasis on separation—of light and darkness, upper waters and lower waters, and so on. In the Priestly creation, everything must be in its proper place.

Human beings are created on the sixth day. While humankind is designated by the masculine word *adam,* both male and female are explicitly included. (The rabbis later speculated that the first human being was a hermaphrodite, both male and female, an idea that is known most famously from Plato's dialogue, the *Symposium.*) Both males and females, then, are created in the image of God. In the ancient Near East, images were very important for cult and worship, as the presence of the divinity was made manifest to the worshipers in the statues. As we shall see when we discuss the Decalogue, or Ten Commandments, in Exodus, no such images were used in the cult of YHWH. Instead, according to the Priestly writer, the presence of God was made manifest in human beings. Moreover, gods in the ancient Near East were often depicted in the form of animals. Such depictions are rejected here. Near Eastern deities were also often depicted in human form. If human beings are made in the divine image, it follows that the Deity has human-like form. In the modern world, we tend to say that God is conceived or imagined in human form—our knowledge of human form comes first and what we say about the Deity is an inference. In the ancient world, however, the divine typically comes first, and human beings are thought to be an imitation of the divine form. This account of creation, then, attributes great dignity to human beings, both male and female. Moreover, humanity is given dominion over the rest of creation. The Priestly account of creation, then, is remarkably humanistic. From a modern perspective, however, it must be noted that human sovereignty over creation has not always been a blessing but has often been abused. It should also be noted that Genesis 1 only allows for vegetarian food. Only after the flood will provision be made for eating meat.

One other commandment is given to humanity in Genesis 1, besides the charge to subdue the earth. They are also commanded to increase and multiply. The Priestly account of creation, then, affirms human sexuality and seems to rule out at the outset an ethic of abstinence and asceticism. This point is important, as the Priestly rules of purity that we shall find in Leviticus have often been taken to suggest a rather negative view of sexuality.

Perhaps the most striking thing about the Priestly creation account, however, is its positive tone. Everything is very good. The origin of sin and evil is not addressed. It is likely, however, that the editor who placed this account at the beginning of Genesis presupposed the Yahwist creation account of Genesis 2–3. The Priestly account is not the whole story. Rather, it supplements the Yahwist account and is meant to forestall a negative interpretation of the human situation, which might be derived from Genesis 3.

If this is correct, then the Priestly account must have been composed after the Yahwist account. There is nothing in this passage to indicate a more precise date. There is a possible allusion to Gen 1:2 in the prophet Jeremiah at 4:23: "I looked on the earth, and lo, it was waste and void." Jeremiah prophesied during the Babylonian crisis, around 600 B.C.E. His vision indicated that the earth was about to be undone and returned to the condition in which it was before creation. But Jeremiah is not necessarily referring to the text of Genesis as we know it. The idea that the earth was "waste and void" before YHWH created it may have been current before it was incorporated in the Priestly account of creation.

Genesis 4–11

Cain and Abel

The Yahwist provides another paradigm of sin in the story of Cain and Abel. Rivalry between brothers is a common theme in folklore, as is conflict between farmer and shepherd. In this case, however, the conflict is initiated by the apparently capricious preference of YHWH for the offering of Abel. The rejection of Cain's sacrifice is not due to any sin on his part; rather, it becomes the occasion of his sin. He is told that "sin is lurking at your door, but you must master it." As in the story of Adam and Eve, there is a vigorous assumption of free will and a realistic appreciation of the force of temptation. Cain murders his brother, but interestingly enough he is not condemned to death. Instead, he is sentenced to wander the earth, and his story becomes an etiology of the Kenite people, itinerants who lived in the desert lands south of Judah.

The Sons of God

The brief notice about "the sons of God" (that is, gods, or heavenly beings) in Gen 6:1-4 is difficult to assign to a source. (The statement in v. 3, where YHWH limits the span of human life, is not necessarily part of the story about the sons of God [Elohim], and may be intrusive.) The episode of the sons of God seems to be a fragment of a polytheistic myth. Like many of the stories in Genesis, it has an etiological aspect: it explains the origin of the Nephilim (literally, "fallen ones"), the "heroes of old." In the Greek and Latin versions, the Nephilim are rendered as "giants"—a translation suggested by the fact that the Giants in Greek mythology (as narrated in Hesiod's *Theogony*) were born of the union of Heaven and Earth. Evidently, such a story was current in ancient Israel, and it was incorporated by the Yahwist as part of the account of the Primeval History.

In itself, the report in Gen 6:1-4 passes no judgment on either the "sons of God" or the

Nephilim, except to note that the latter were famous. This episode is followed, however, by the statement that YHWH saw that the wickedness of humankind was great on the earth; this statement introduces the story of the flood. It may be that the Yahwist, or whoever put these stories side by side, intended to imply a connection, so that the wickedness of humankind resulted from the descent of the sons of God and the rise of the Nephilim. Nothing further is said in Genesis to develop this connection. In later tradition, however, it grew into a full-fledged myth. In the Book of the Watchers (*1 Enoch* 1–36), an apocalyptic work written in Aramaic in the third or early second century B.C.E., the sons of God become "the Watchers," angelic beings who descend to earth in an act of rebellion. The Watchers then impart to humanity all kinds of forbidden knowledge. The giants whom they beget cause great havoc on earth because of their lawless behavior. Eventually, the flood is sent to cleanse the earth. The book of *Jubilees* (written in Hebrew, second century B.C.E.) also makes the connection between the descent of the fallen angels and the spread of wickedness on earth. Unlike *1 Enoch*, however, *Jubilees* claims that the Watchers originally came down to teach men to do what is just and right on earth (*Jub.* 4:15), although they subsequently sinned by entering into unions with the daughters of men. The myth of the fallen angels had a long life in Western tradition and received a classic form in John Milton's epic, *Paradise Lost*. The biblical text, however, contains only the germ of this myth. The Yahwist located responsibility for sin in the actions of human beings rather than in those of fallen angels, and this was also true of the Priestly editor of the Primeval History.

The Flood

According to Gen 6:5, the wickedness of humankind is due to the fact that "every inclination of the thoughts of their hearts was only evil continually." The "inclination" (Hebrew *yetser*) of human beings became a matter of increased speculation in later Jewish tradition. According to the Midrash (or rabbinic commentary) on Genesis, people have two inclinations, one good, one bad, and are still responsible for the one they choose to follow. These inclinations were implanted by God at creation. For the later rabbis, this was a purposeful plan on the part of God. In Genesis, however, we rather get the impression of an experiment gone awry: "the LORD was sorry that he made humankind on the earth, and it grieved him to his heart." In this respect, the Genesis account resembles the Babylonian myth of Atrahasis. There, too, the gods come to regret that they made humanity, and in fact this happens several times. The problem is that human beings multiply too quickly and become too noisy, and so the gods send plague and disease to destroy them. Each time the god Ea comes to the rescue of human beings and reveals a plan to the wise human Atrahasis. Finally, the gods send a flood. Genesis dispenses with the attempts to destroy humanity by disease and goes directly to the flood. It is also characteristic of Genesis that the problem is wickedness rather than population or noise control.

There are two versions of the flood story in Babylonian literature. In one, the flood hero is Atrahasis. In the other, which is part of the Epic of Gilgamesh, he is Utnapishtim. The biblical story is clearly indebted to this story in some form. All the flood heroes, reasonably, cover their vessels with pitch or bitumen. Utnapishtim's ark, like Noah's, comes to rest on a mountaintop, and he sends out birds (a dove, swallow, and raven), to test whether the waters have subsided. When they emerge from the ark, each of the heroes offers a sacrifice. In the Atrahasis myth, when the gods smell the fragrance, they gather like flies over the offering. Nonetheless, the god Enlil is angry that life has survived. The gods reach a compromise so that human population will be controlled by less drastic afflictions (wild beasts, famine, unsuccessful births). In the J account, too, YHWH is pleased by the odor of the sacrifice, but he reacts more generously than his Babylonian counterparts. Humanity is not entirely to blame, "for the inclination of the human heart is evil from youth," and so YHWH resolves that he will never again destroy every living creature as he almost did with the flood.

The Priestly account of the flood is characterized by the typical Priestly interest in precise detail. Noah is given specific measurements for the ark. Only one pair of each kind of animal is taken, reflecting the Priestly preference for binary opposites. Events are dated precisely. The flood occurs in the six hundredth year of Noah's life. He emerges from the ark in his six hundred and first year, in the second month, on the twenty-seventh day of the month. Like the first human beings in the creation story, he is given dominion over the earth and commanded to increase and multiply. Henceforth, humanity is allowed to eat meat: "every moving thing that lives shall be food for you" (9:3). There is a restriction, however: "Only you shall not eat flesh with its life, that is, its blood" (Gen 9:4). Moreover, the fact that humanity is made in the image of God is cited as reason to refrain from murder: "Whoever sheds the blood of a human, by a human shall that person's blood be shed; for in his own image God made humankind" (9:6).

Perhaps the most important detail in the Priestly account of the flood is the covenant that God concludes with Noah at its end. God undertakes not to destroy the earth by flood again and sets the rainbow in the sky as a sign of this promise. The covenant, however, is usually understood to include the commandment to Noah not to eat flesh with the blood in it. In Jewish tradition, these commandments were expanded and were understood to apply also to Gentiles. Typically, they included prohibitions of idolatry, cursing God, cursing judges, murder, incest and adultery, robbery, and the eating of meat with the blood. Gentiles who observed these laws could be regarded as righteous. The Priestly theology was primarily concerned with God's commandments to Israel, but it also recognized the common human framework provided by creation.

The Tower of Babel

The final episode in the J Primeval History is the story of the Tower of Babel (Gen 11:1-9). The people who live in the land of Shinar (Babylon) resolve: "Let us build ourselves a city, and a tower with its top in the heavens, and let us make a name for ourselves." (The tower is an allusion to the ziggurats, or stepped pyramids, associated with Babylonian temples.) Just as YHWH in the story of Adam and Eve seemed distrustful of human knowledge and discouraged its pursuit, here he seems distrustful of technological progress (and even urban development) and hastens to put a stop to it. Again, the story has an etiological aspect.

Fig. 3.4 *Construction of the Tower of Babel* **by Abel Grimmer (1604).** Commons.wikimedia.org

It answers the question why people speak different languages. It is also a derisive explanation of the name of Babylon (Babel = babble). Israelites certainly knew about Babylon from an early time, but the obvious setting in which such a parody would make most sense is the Babylonian exile, or later, when the people of Judah had good reason to resent Babylonian pretensions.

Here again we have some reason to think that the section of J that deals with the Primeval History is a late composition. Thematically, the story of the tower provides an apt conclusion to this phase of history as it reiterates the theme of human limitation and the dangers involved in trying to be like God or to rise to the heavens.

The Priestly Genealogies

The Priestly editors of these narratives tried to integrate them into an unfolding history by inserting genealogies. One genealogy, in Genesis 5, traces the development of humanity from Adam to Noah. In chapter 10 we find a list of the descendants of Noah. Finally, in Genesis 11, the editor fills in the generations from Shem to Abram (Abraham). These genealogies are largely a connecting device in the narrative, but they also provide a way for the editors to posit relationships between the various peoples known to them. Both biblical accounts of creation assume a diffusionist model of the spread of humanity—since there was only one act of creation of humanity, all human beings must be ultimately related. Inevitably, these genealogies are fictional, but they served to bring a sense of order to the diversity of human society and also helped to keep the biblical focus on the story of Israel in perspective. Even the Gentiles, in all their ethnic variations, were made in the image of God.

FOR FURTHER READING

Commentaries

J. Blenkinsopp, *Creation, Un-Creation, Re-Creation: A Discursive Commentary on Genesis 1-11* (New York: Continuum, 2011). Literary-theological discussion of the canonical text with attention to premodern interpretation rather than to sources.

T. E. Fretheim, "Genesis," *NIB* 1:319–426. Good homiletically oriented commentary.

G. von Rad, *Genesis* (trans. J. H. Marks; OTL; Philadelphia: Westminster, 1972). Brief but classic commentary.

C. Westermann, *Genesis 1–11: A Commentary* (trans. J. J. Scullion; CC; Minneapolis: Augsburg, 1984). Best full historical-philological commentary.

Other Studies

G. A. Anderson, *The Genesis of Perfection* (Louisville: Westminster John Knox, 2001). Interesting discussion of the ways in which the story of Adam and Eve was elaborated in later Jewish and Christian tradition.

J. Barr, *The Garden of Eden and the Hope of Immortality* (London: SCM, 1992). Incisive clarification of what the text does and does not say.

B. Batto, *Slaying the Dragon: Mythmaking in the Biblical Tradition* (Louisville: Westminster, 1992), 41–101. Discussion of Genesis 1–3 in light of Babylonian parallels.

P. A. Bird, *Missing Persons and Mistaken Identities: Women and Gender in Ancient Israel* (Minneapolis: Fortress Press, 1997) 123-93. Penetrating analysis of Genesis 1-3 from a feminist perspective.

R. J. Clifford, *Creation Accounts in the Ancient Near East and in the Bible* (CBQMS 26; Washington, DC: Catholic Biblical Association, 1994). Survey of accounts of creation in the Ancient Near East and throughout the Bible.

P. Enns, *The Evolution of Adam* (Grand Rapids: Brazos, 2012). What the Bible does and does not say about evolution.

W. R. Garr, *In His Own Image and Likeness: Humanity, Divinity, and Monotheism* (CHANE 15; Leiden: Brill, 2003). Detailed and penetrating analysis of Genesis 1.

H. Gunkel, *Creation and Chaos in the Primeval Era and the Eschaton: A Religio-Historical Study of Genesis 1 and Revelation 12* (trans. W. K. Whitney; Grand Rapids: Eerdmans, 2006). Translation of 1895 classic that pioneered the use of Near Eastern mythology in the interpretation of the Bible.

R. Hendel, *The Book of Genesis: A Biography* (Princeton: Princeton University Press, 2013). Lively account of the reception-history of Genesis. Includes a chapter on science and fundamentalism.

P. T. Lanfer, *Remembering Eden: The Reception History of Genesis 3:22-24* (New York : Oxford University Press, 2012). Includes a detailed analysis of the Eden story as well as its reception in early Judaism.

C. E. L'Heureux, *In and Out of Paradise: The Book of Genesis from Adam and Eve to the Tower of Babel* (New York: Paulist, 1983). Excellent use of Babylonian parallels.

C. L. Meyers, *Discovering Eve: Ancient Israelite Women in Context* (New York: Oxford University Press, 1988), 72–138. Feminist-historical reading. Questions traditional understanding of the fall. Revised edition: *Rediscovering Eve*, (2012), 59-80.

Mark S. Smith, *The Priestly Vision of Genesis 1* (Minneapolis: Fortress Press, 2010). Literate historical and theological study. Places Genesis 1 in the context of different models of creation and different approaches to biblical study.

P. Trible, *God and the Rhetoric of Sexuality* (OBT; Philadelphia: Fortress Press, 1978). Groundbreaking feminist-literary work.

CHAPTER 4
The Patriarchs

INTRODUCTION

We next examine the stories of Israel's ancestors in Genesis 11–50. We will ask whether aspects of the patriarchal stories help us to place the patriarchs in their culture and time, then look at the stories of Abraham, Jacob, and Joseph, and turn at last to consider aspects of the final Priestly edition of these stories.

A new phase in biblical history is ushered in by the appearance of Abraham, or Abram, as he is initially called. (His name is changed to Abraham in Gen 17:5; his wife is initially Sarai, but her name is changed to Sarah in 17:15.) Abram is first introduced in a genealogical list in chapter 11, which is part of the Priestly source. In 11:31 we are told that he departed from "Ur of the Chaldeans" with his father, Terah, and his wife, Sarai, "to go into the land of Canaan," but settled in Haran on the way. This notice is also part of the Priestly source, but another reference to Ur of the Chaldeans in 15:7 is usually ascribed to J (see Map 4.1). The tradition that the ancestors of Israel came from Haran is also attested elsewhere in Genesis. Haran was a major city in northwestern Mesopotamia, on the river Balikh, an eastern tributary of the Euphrates. The area is also called

Aram-Naharaim (Aram or Syria of the two rivers). It was situated on a major trade route, but this would have been a very roundabout way to get from Ur to the land of Canaan. Ur was a famous and ancient city in southern Mesopotamia that flourished in the third millennium B.C.E. It could be called "Ur of the Chaldeans," however, only after the rise of the Neo-Babylonian Empire in the late seventh century B.C.E. The Chaldeans are only known to history from the ninth century B.C.E., when they appear to the south of Babylonia. The reference to Ur of the Chaldeans may be no older than the Babylonian exile, at a time when the departure of Abraham from there had great significance for Jews who would return from Babylon to Judah. (The reference to Ur of the Chaldeans in 15:7, then, must be a secondary addition, unless we ascribe a very late date to J.)

Fig. 4.1 A lyre player and singer; detail from the decorated chest known as the Standard of Ur, ca. 2600 B.C.E. Now in the British Museum.

Commons.wikimedia.org

Aspects of the Patriarchal Stories

The Patriarchs and History

As we saw in the introduction, the internal chronology of the Bible suggests a date around 2100 B.C.E. for Abraham and a time around 1876 for the descent of his grandson Jacob into Egypt with his family. Only extremely conservative scholars would now take these dates at face value, in view of the prodigious life spans attributed to the patriarchs, but many have tried to set the stories of Genesis against the background of a historical era. It is not unreasonable to expect that even a work of fiction should provide clues as to the time of its composition. Unlike many biblical books, however, the patriarchal stories are practically void of reference to public events that might be known from other sources. There is a rare account of war between kings in Genesis 14.

(The five cities of the plain, Sodom, Gomorrah, Admah, Zeboiim, and Bela or Zoar, rebel against Chedorlaomer, king of Elam, which was east of Mesopotamia.) But none of the kings mentioned in this account is known from any other source. At one time, scholars held that Amraphel, king of Shinar, who is mentioned as an ally of Chedorlaomer, might be the famous Hammurabi, king of Babylon, who reigned around 1850–1800 B.C.E. and is associated with a famous law code (Shinar is often used as a name for Babylon in the Bible). If this were so, we could conclude that Abraham lived, or was supposed to have lived, at the same time. Unfortunately, however, the identification has no real basis and has been generally abandoned. On a more general level, scholars sought to associate the migration of Abraham with a major shift in Near Eastern culture in the early second millennium B.C.E. (This approach is associated especially with the American archaeologist William Foxwell Albright.) At this time, the great urban centers of Mesopotamia, such as Ur, went into decline. Akkadian texts from the time refer to "Amorites" or westerners, who supposedly moved in from the wilderness. These Amorites were also thought to expand to the west into Canaan. It was suggested that Abraham was part of this migration of Amorites. It is not clear, however, that the decline of the urban centers was really due to an invasion of Amorites, and the biblical account does not suggest that Abraham was part of a larger population shift. So the "Amorite hypothesis" has been generally abandoned for lack of evidence.

Since there are no references to known historical events in Genesis, scholars have tried to infer the historical era from the customs and lifestyle described. This attempt

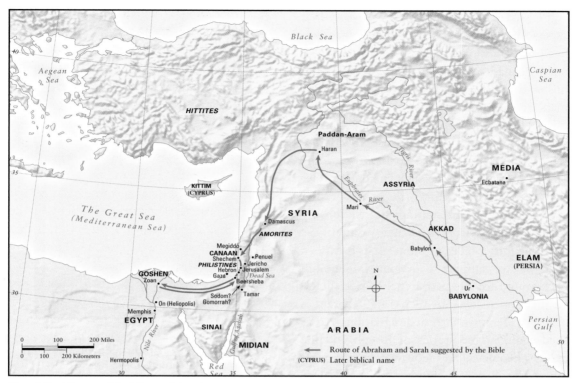

Map 4.1 The world of the patriarchs

was encouraged by the discovery of comparative material from various sites in the ancient Near East, especially Mari on the Euphrates and Nuzi east of the Tigris. Mari flourished around the time of Hammurabi. The kind of society attested there is called "dimorphic" (or "twofold in form") because it involved both a nomadic element and a population settled in towns. This is also the kind of society described in Genesis, where the patriarchs move around from place to place and interact with people settled in towns. But this kind of society was not peculiar to the age of Mari. In fact, it has continued down to modern times, as can be seen from the survival of bedouin to this day. Accordingly, it is not of much help in determining a historical background for

the patriarchal stories. Nuzi, in northern Iraq, also flourished in the mid-second millennium, when it was the capital of a Hurrian kingdom. (The Hurrians were a distinct ethnic group with their own language.) The significance of Nuzi for biblical studies lies chiefly in the realm of law and social customs. For example, a marriage contract found at Nuzi requires a barren wife to provide a slave woman to her husband to bear his children. In Genesis 16 Sarai gives her maid Hagar to Abram to bear him children, since she is barren. Again, it was claimed that in Hurrian society a wife enjoyed special standing and protection when the law recognized her as both wife and sister of her husband. This custom was thought to clarify the stories in Genesis where Abraham and Isaac tell people that their wives are their sisters. But again, the value of these parallels has been questioned. The custom that a barren wife had to provide a surrogate for her husband is also found in Assyrian, Babylonian, and Egyptian texts, over several centuries. The evidence for the alleged Hurrian custom, whereby a wife was also called "sister," is dubious and debatable. In any case, the biblical stories imply no such custom—rather they describe attempts to trick unsuspecting strangers by misrepresenting the relationship between the patriarchs and their women.

One other alleged item that has been thought to support a second-millennium background for the patriarchal stories should be mentioned here. In Gen 14:13 Abram is called a Hebrew, *'ibri,* a designation that is used again in the stories of Joseph and the exodus. People called Habiru or Apiru appear repeatedly in a wide range of Near Eastern texts throughout the second millennium. This term does not refer to an ethnic group but designates people who were on the fringes of society. The Habiru sometimes appear as mercenaries, sometimes as fugitives, sometimes as slaves, sometimes as outlaws. (The corresponding Sumerian term, SA.GAZ, is related to a word for murderer and is sometimes translated as "brigand"; Albright suggested that Apiru originally meant "dusty-footed.") There has been extensive, but inconclusive, debate as to whether "Hebrew" can derive from Habiru. The Hebrews often appear as marginal people in the early books of the Bible. We shall consider the possible Habiru connection again in the next chapter, in connection with the origin of Israel. For the present, it is sufficient to note that even if Abraham were regarded

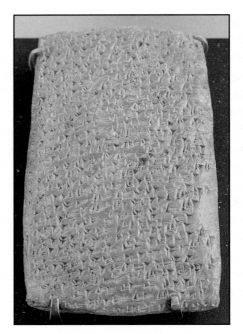

Fig. 4.2   Letter from the king of Byblos to the Pharaoh in Egypt complaining about *Apiru.* EA 362, fourteenth century; now in the Louvre.
Commons.wikimedia.org

as Habiru, this would not point to any specific chronological background, as Habiru are attested throughout the second millennium.

There is then no positive evidence that requires us to set the background of the patriarchs in the early or middle part of the second millennium. Moreover, several considerations tell against such an early background. The Philistines, who are mentioned in Gen 21:32-34; 26:1, 8, 14-15, were one of the Sea Peoples who invaded the coastal plain in the twelfth century, and gave their name to "Palestine." The Arameans, who figure especially in the Jacob stories, are attested only from the end of the second millennium (eleventh century). The earliest mention of the camel as a domesticated animal dates only from the eleventh century, and its use became common only some centuries later. Archaeological evidence suggests that Beersheba was not settled before the twelfth century. Even if we allow that some references may have been added secondarily, this evidence makes it unlikely that these stories originated earlier than the end of the second millennium B.C.E. or the beginning of the first. The stories may still preserve reminiscences of an earlier time. The preference for names that end in *-el* (rather than *-yah*) in the patriarchal stories points to a time before the rise of YHWH as the god of Israel. But the stories cannot be taken as witnesses to pre-Israelite reality in any simple sense.

The Patriarchal Stories as Legends

In fact, the stories of Genesis do not lend themselves easily to historical analysis. As Hermann Gunkel saw clearly, at the end of the nineteenth century, they belong not to the genre of historiography but to that of legend. Gunkel allowed that historical memories may be preserved in legends, "clothed in poetic garb," but he offered several criteria by which the two genres may be distinguished. Legend, according to Gunkel, is originally oral tradition, while history is usually found in written form. Written material is more easily given a fixed form, whereas oral variants of the same tales tend to proliferate. History and legend have different spheres of interest. History treats great public occurrences, while legend deals with more personal and private matters. Even when legends concern matters of great historical import, they still tend to focus on the personal. History would be expected to tell how and for what reasons David succeeded in delivering Israel from the Philistines; legend prefers to tell how the boy David once slew a Philistine giant. The clearest criterion of legend, wrote Gunkel, is that it frequently reports things that are incredible. It is poetry rather than prose, and a different sort of plausibility applies. As poetry, legend aims to please, to elevate, to inspire, and to move. It does not necessarily aspire to tell "what actually happened" in a way that would satisfy a modern historian.

Gunkel went on to distinguish several kinds of legends in Genesis. Etiological legends claim to explain the cause or origin of a phenomenon (e.g., the story of Lot's wife explains the origin of a pillar of salt). Ethnological legends explain the origin of a people or of their customs (the story of Cain explains why Kenites are itinerant). Etymological legends explain the origin of names (there are two accounts of the origin of the name of Beersheba: Gen 21:31; 26:33). Ceremonial legends explain the origin of a ritual (the story of the Passover is an obvious example; the covenant with Abraham in Genesis 17 explains why his descendants practice circumcision). Gunkel did not rule out the possibility that historical reminiscences might be preserved in such legends, but he changed the focus of inquiry, from the events behind the text to the function of the story and its setting in life, or *Sitz im Leben*. His question was, why, and in what kind of setting, was this story told? Many stories were presumably told in a cultic setting—for example, to explain why Bethel was a holy place (Genesis 28)—but some may also have been told simply for entertainment.

The History of Traditions

Building on the work of Gunkel, a movement in German scholarship attempted to trace the history of the oral traditions behind the biblical text. The most influential exponent of this movement was Martin Noth (1902–1968). Noth found a clue to the origin of a tradition in the place with which it was associated. For example, Abraham is repeatedly associated with the "oaks of Mamre" near Hebron, south of Jerusalem. Isaac is associated with Beersheba, further south. Jacob is linked with Bethel, Shechem, and the central hill country. Noth supposed that the traditions about the individual patriarchs originated separately in the different regions.

It is clear, however, that at some point these traditions were linked together to form a genealogy of the ancestors of Israel. Jacob is identified as the father of the people of Israel; his name is changed to Israel in Genesis 32. His twelve sons give their names to the tribes that constitute Israel. Moreover, he is associated with the central hill country, which was the heartland of Israel before the rise of the monarchy. Yet in Genesis priority is given to Abraham, who is associated with the area later known as Judah. There are two periods in biblical history when such a construction would have made sense. One was in the time of David and Solomon, when (at least according to the biblical account) all Israel was united under a Judean monarchy. Scholars of von Rad's generation, in the mid-twentieth century, dated the Yahwist to the reign of Solomon partly for this reason. The other was after the fall of the northern kingdom of Israel in 722 B.C.E., when Judah had reason and opportunity to assert its leadership of all Israel, north and south, and

this remained true into the postexilic period. Both J and E, however, already assume the succession of Abraham, Isaac, and Jacob, and so it is likely that the linkage of the patriarchs was already established at an early time, before these sources were compiled.

There is good reason to think that the linking of the patriarchs in a genealogical succession was an early attempt to define the people of Israel by showing how the tribes were related to each other. It is important that the genealogical links bind Judah and Benjamin (the eventual southern kingdom) to the northern tribes and so create a basis for regarding all Israel as a unity. It is also noteworthy that these stories insist that Abraham and his descendants were not Canaanites. They allegedly came from Mesopotamia via Syria and continued to go back to Syria to seek wives for some generations. The more recent archaeological work in Israel rather suggests that the Israelites emerged out of Canaan. There is no evidence of the intrusion of a different material culture, such as we might expect if they had actually come from another country. The persistent attempt to deny Canaanite origins can be explained as a way of marking a boundary between Israel and Canaan. Since the Canaanites were the Israelites' nearest neighbors, this was the most necessary boundary if Israel were to have its own identity. The patriarchal stories viewed as a whole, then, can be understood as an attempt to define Israel over against its neighbors by positing some relationships and denying others.

Many of the stories in Genesis are folkloric in character, and they surely evolved over centuries. A few features of these stories, however, are significant for their historical background, even if they do not suggest a specific date.

There is no reference in Genesis to an Israelite or Judean king, except for a reference to the "scepter" of Judah in Genesis 49:10. There is no doubt that the final edition of these stories was either under or after the monarchy, but the narrative setting in premonarchic times is consistently maintained. This fact lends some credibility to the view that the stories first took shape before the rise of the monarchy. Also, the religion of the patriarchs is significantly different from that of Deuteronomy or the Priestly source.

Patriarchal Religion

Abraham has a strong personal relationship with a God who makes promises to him and protects him. Isaac is guided by "the God of your father Abraham" (26:24). Jacob has a revelation from "the God of Abraham, your father, and the God of Isaac" (28:13). God tells Abraham, "I am your shield" (15:1). Jacob swears by "the Fear of Isaac" (31:53; cf. 31:42). We read of the Mighty One (or Bull) of Jacob (49:24). The experience of the God of the fathers is not limited to any specific place; the protection of this God follows the patriarchs wherever they go. This form of worship appears to be especially well suited for nomadic or migratory tribes, although some scholars now regard it as a late theological construct.

But the patriarchs also worship God in specific places as manifestations of the God El. *El* was the common Hebrew and Northwest Semitic word for "god," but it was also the name of the high god in the Canaanite myths from Ugarit. In Genesis 14 Abraham gives a tithe to Melchizedek, king of Salem (presumably Jerusalem), priest of El Elyon (God Most High). By so doing, he recognizes, and

lends legitimacy to, an established Canaanite cult. In fact, El and YHWH are recognized as one and the same god in biblical religion. According to the Elohist and Priestly strands of the Pentateuch, the name YHWH was not revealed until Exodus, and so the patriarchs worshiped El in his various manifestations. In contrast, the Canaanite god Baal is not mentioned at all in Genesis, and the patriarchs are never said to worship a goddess. So the patriarchs appear to participate in Canaanite religion in a modified form, or to appropriate it in a selective way. It is possible, of course, that the selectivity is due to later editors, who edited out of the tradition religious observances that might be deemed offensive.

The patriarchs encounter El under different names and in different manifestations. He can be called El-Roi (16:13), or El Shaddai (17:1; 28:3; et al.). In Genesis 28 Jacob has a dream, in which he sees a ladder going up to heaven and the angels of God going up and down on it. When he awakes, he declares, "Surely the LORD is in this place and I did not know it" (28:16), and so he names it Bethel, the house of God. He has another encounter with divinity in Genesis 32, at the ford of the Jabbok. Spirits were often thought to guard points of transition, such as fords, in antiquity, and there is probably an old legend underlying this story. Jacob names the place "Peniel," or "Penuel," "for I have seen God face to face and lived." All these manifestations might be regarded as local spirits, but in Genesis, and probably also in ancient religion, they are regarded as different manifestations of the same god.

There is a striking discrepancy between the manner of worship practiced by the patriarchs and that which is commanded later in the

Bible. Wherever the patriarchs go, they build altars to the Lord. Abram builds an altar by the oak of Mamre and again between Bethel and Ai. Later he plants a tamarisk tree at Beersheba and calls there on the name of the Lord. Isaac builds an altar in Beersheba, and Jacob at Bethel and Shechem. At Bethel, Jacob takes the stone he had used as a pillow and sets it up as a pillar and pours oil on it. Later, in Deuteronomy 12, Israel is commanded to restrict sacrificial worship to the one "place which the LORD your God shall choose." Then: "You must demolish completely all the places where the nations whom you are about to dispossess served their gods on the mountain heights, on the hills, and under every leafy tree. Break down their altars, smash their pillars, burn their sacred poles with fire, and hew down the idols of their gods" (Deut 12:2-3).

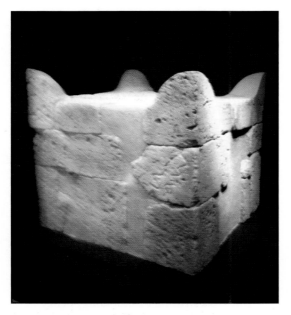

Fig. 4.3 Horned altar from Beer Sheba. Photo by the author

Deuteronomic law did not apply to the patriarchs, who were supposed to have lived before Moses. Nonetheless, the association of the patriarchs with a given shrine marked it as a holy place and gave it legitimacy in the eyes of later tradition. In fact, several stories in Genesis seem to have been preserved in order to legitimate, or establish the holiness of, specific sites. In Genesis 14, Abraham accepts a blessing from Melchizedek, king of Salem, and gives him a tithe of everything he has taken in battle. Salem, or Jerusalem, was an old Canaanite city, with its own religious traditions. Since Abraham acted respectfully toward Melchizedek, however, it was all right for later Israelites or Judeans to worship there. In Psalm 110 the king of Judah is told, "You are a priest forever according to the order of Melchizedek." While it is not clear precisely what this means, it certainly shows that the Judean kings did not entirely repudiate their Canaanite heritage. Melchizedek, king and priest of El Elyon, was an ancestor of whom one could be proud.

Jerusalem, of course, was later regarded as the place that the Lord had chosen. In the books of Kings, and sometimes in the Prophets, great scorn is poured on the rival sanctuary of Bethel, which was one of two state temples erected by King Jeroboam I, when the northern kingdom of Israel seceded from Jerusalem (1 Kgs 12:25-33; the other one was at Dan, on the northern border of Israel). Yet in Genesis 28 we read how Jacob discovered that Bethel was "none other than the house of God and gate of heaven" (28:17). This would seem to establish that Bethel was a holy place, and so lend credibility to Jeroboam's sanctuary. Most of Genesis 28 comes from E, the northern strand of the patriarchal narrative, but vv.

11-16 are clearly Yahwistic (Jacob concludes, "Surely YHWH is in this place, and I did not know it"). It is not clear, however, that the place was identified as Bethel in the J source. The identification of the site of Jacob's dream as Bethel may have been the contribution of the northern, Elohistic, writer. Interestingly, Jeroboam is also said to build Penuel (1 Kgs 12:25), the scene of Jacob's encounter with God (or an angel) in Genesis 32. Here again the Elohist may have been giving support to Jeroboam's actions by associating his sites with the patriarch Jacob.

It is at least clear that the stories of Genesis were not the work of the Deuteronomistic school, which made the centralization of religion into a criterion for true religion. In part, at least, the religion of the patriarchs was the kind of observance that the Deuteronomists sought to suppress. The stories about the patriarchs must have been established as part of Israel's heritage too strongly for the Deuteronomists to repudiate them. It is reasonable, then, to conclude that Genesis reflects a form of popular, family religion that flourished before the Deuteronomic reform. One cannot, however, take these stories as a reliable or full account of Israelite religion in any period. They are stories about a past, which was always idealized to some extent, and may have been edited to some degree besides. They are of some value to the historian of religion, but that value is limited by the lack of explicit historical data.

Genesis as Religious Narrative

Regardless of their historical value, the tales of the patriarchs remain powerful as stories. In large part this is because, like all good folklore, they touch on perennial issues, such as jealousy between a woman and her rival (Sarah and Hagar) or rivalry between brothers (Jacob and Esau). Many of the stories are entertaining—Abraham's ability to outwit the pharaoh or the gentle story of Isaac and Rebekah in Genesis 24. Others are tales of terror, in the phrase of Phyllis Trible—the command to Abraham to sacrifice his only son, or Lot's willingness to sacrifice his daughters to the men of Sodom (Genesis 19). When the stories are read as Scripture, they become more problematic because of a common but ill-founded assumption that all Scripture should be edifying. The stories of Genesis are often challenging and stimulating, but they seldom if ever propose simple models to be imitated.

The Abraham Cycle

The Theme of the Promise

The J account of Abraham begins in Genesis 12. YHWH commands the patriarch to "go forth from your country and your kindred and your father's house to the land that I will show you. I will make you a great nation, and I will bless you, and make your name great, so that you will be a blessing. I will bless those who bless you, and the one who curses you I will curse; and in you all the families of the earth shall be blessed."

This passage introduces the theme of the promise to the fathers, which runs through Genesis and is arguably the unifying theme of the Pentateuch. Some scholars regard it as a late editorial addition, introduced to bring disparate material together. It certainly has an editorial function, but it does not necessarily belong to the latest strata of the Pentateuch. It is sufficient that it belong to the work of the author/editor that we call J. There are no strings attached to the promise. All Abraham has to do is trust in YHWH and obey the command to move.

Both J and P provide a more formal account of the promise to Abraham, casting it in the form of a covenant. The J account is found in Genesis 15 (with some additions that are usually ascribed to E). The point of departure is provided by Abraham's desire for an heir and his distress over being childless. This is a familiar motif in ancient Near Eastern literature. It appears in the Ugaritic stories of Aqhat and Kirta. Abraham, however, is promised more than a child. He is told to "look toward heaven and count the stars, if you are able to count them . . . so shall your descendants be." This promise is formalized in a covenant. Abraham is told to take a heifer, she-goat, ram, turtledove, and young pigeon, and cut each in two. Then a deep sleep and terrifying darkness fall on Abraham, and when the sun has gone down, fire passes between the pieces. Then the Lord formally promises that he will give this land to Abraham's descendants, from the river of Egypt to the great river, the river Euphrates.

The ritual described in this passage relates to the Hebrew idiom for making a covenant, which is to "cut" a covenant. An explanation of the ritual is suggested by a passage in Jer 34:18: "And those who transgressed my covenant . . . I will make like the calf that they cut in two and passed between its parts." In short, the ritual implies a threat—the one who does not abide by the covenant will be cut in two like the sacrificial victim. In the case of Genesis 15, however, no threat is implied. The ritual

merely indicates that it is a formal covenant. The kind of covenant involved here is quite different from that which God makes with Moses and Israel at Mount Sinai. In the latter case, there is a law attached, and the benefits of the covenant are contingent on keeping the law. The covenant with Abraham is really a grant—an unconditional promise. A similar covenant is made with David in 2 Samuel 7, and this is one of a number of correspondences that link Abraham and David. In each case, the promise pertains to the descendants of the recipient. All that is required of Abraham, or of David, is that they trust in the promise. The Priestly account of God's covenant with Abraham, which is found in Genesis 17, introduces another requirement—every male among the descendants of Abraham must be circumcised.

The statement in Gen 15:6, "And he [Abraham] believed in the Lord, and the Lord reckoned it to him as righteousness," has played an important and controversial role in Christian theology. It is cited by the apostle Paul in Gal 3:6. Paul argues that since Abraham is also told that all the peoples of the earth will be blessed in him (Gen 12:3), this shows that Gentiles can be justified by faith, not by the law. This argument later played a fundamental role in the theology of Martin Luther. Needless to say, there is no contrast between faith and law implied in Genesis (although it is true that there is no requirement of legal observance). Faith here is trust in the promise. In Jewish interpretation, the key element is that the promise relates to possession of the land. The promise to Abraham is seen as the original charter for possession of the land of Israel.

The extent of the land, from the Nile to the Euphrates, far exceeds the territory over which the kingdoms of Israel and Judah would later rule. It has sometimes been claimed that the passage reflects, and justifies, the extent of the empire of David and Solomon, but even the biblical text does not claim that they ruled so much (see **Map 12.1**). Second Samuel 8 claims that David placed garrisons in Damascus and received presents from the king of Hamath, but his dominion nonetheless stops well short of the Euphrates. Recent historians are increasingly skeptical about the extent of the supposed empire, for lack of archaeological evidence. In any case, it is clear that the territory promised to Abraham is exaggerated and does not correspond to anything in actual Israelite history. It does, however, establish a key element of later Israelite and Jewish identity. It claims that the land later called Israel was promised to this people by God in a formal covenant. This land includes the territories later ruled by the kingdoms of Israel and Judah. The claim to this territory is presumably no earlier than the time of David, when the tribes of Israel were forged into a unified kingdom (according to the biblical record). It could, however, be much later and reflect the dreams of a greater Israel on the part of the southern kingdom of Judah, after the northern kingdom had been destroyed.

Tales of Deception

Despite the election of Abraham and the promise made to him in Genesis 12, his actions are not always exemplary. On two occasions (Gen 12:10-20; 20:1-7), he passes off his wife as his sister. A very similar story is told about Isaac in Gen 26:6-11. Gen 12:10-20 and 26:6-11 are usually assigned to the J source, while Gen 20:1-7 is from E. The similarity between

the stories suggests a background in oral tradition, where essentially the same story is easily transferred from one character to another. The stories are not simple retellings, however, but present some changes that highlight the central problem.

In Genesis 12 the protagonists are Abram and a nameless pharaoh. Abram goes down to Egypt because of famine, a common experience of Asiatics in the second millennium. Fearing that the Egyptians would kill him to take Sarai, his wife, he says that she is his sister. Pharaoh takes her and deals well with Abram. We are not told that Pharaoh sleeps with Sarai, but neither are we told that he does not. In any case, he is smitten with plagues. Again we are not told how Pharaoh knows that the plagues are because of Sarai. The narrator tells us that the plagues are the work of YHWH. The pharaoh sends Abraham away (rather than kill him), presumably because he fears the power that caused the plague. The most striking feature of this story is Abram's apparent willingness to prostitute his wife and the fact that he is nonetheless rewarded. Morality is obviously not the point of the story. Rather, it is a story of ethnic, or tribal, pride—how our ancestor Abram outwitted the pharaoh. YHWH here appears to be a tribal god who champions his servant Abram no matter what.

In Genesis 20 the protagonists are Abraham and Abimelech, king of Gerar. The reason for passing off Sarah is assumed, on the basis of the earlier story. She is presumed to be irresistibly attractive (although in Genesis 18 she was already old and advanced in years). In this case, God intervenes in a dream to Abimelech to protect Sarah's virtue (dreams are a favorite motif of the Elohist writer). Moreover, Abimelech is greatly concerned to assert his innocence. There is no expression of concern on Abraham's part, but then God tells Abimelech that Abraham is a prophet, so he may be presumed to have known how things would turn out. The simple delight in outwitting a foreign ruler, however, is tempered here by the concern for Sarah's virtue.

The third instance of this motif, in Genesis 26, pairs Isaac with Abimelech, who is now identified as a Philistine. In this case, Isaac announces that Rebekah is his sister, but the Philistines make no move to take her. Eventually, Abimelech sees Isaac fondling Rebekah and concludes that she is his wife. Again, Abimelech seems more concerned than the Hebrew patriarch, apparently out of fear of what might have befallen himself or his people if they incurred guilt. So he warns his people not to touch either Isaac or Rebekah. The concern here is for the guilt incurred in taking another man's wife. Abimelech challenges Isaac about the deception, but a few verses later (26:12) we read that YHWH blessed the patriarch. Deception is apparently permitted for a patriarch if his welfare seems to require it. At this point in the biblical narrative, the motif of election overrides some moral considerations, although there is increased sensitivity about sexual issues.

Later Jewish tradition was troubled by the patriarchal deception and sought to retell the stories so as to avoid offense. The Genesis Apocryphon (cols. 19–20), an Aramaic paraphrase of Genesis found among the Dead Sea Scrolls, has a colorful retelling of the story of Abram and Sarai in Egypt. First, Abram is warned in a dream that the Egyptians will try to kill him, and that Sarai must protect him by saying that he is her brother. The Egyptians are amazed at the beauty of Sarai and describe it to Pharaoh in detail. Sure enough, the pharaoh takes Sarai and tries to kill Abram, but Sarai says he is her brother. Then God afflicts Pharaoh with "a chastising spirit" so that he is unable to approach Sarai, much less have intercourse with her. Finally, Abram is asked to pray for the king, and only then do the Egyptians learn the cause of the affliction—that Sarai is Abram's wife. Pharaoh's outrage is tempered by the fact that he needs Abram to pray for him and expel the evil spirit, and so he sends Abram away with lavish gifts. In this form of the story, the primary concern again is that Sarai not be defiled, but the actual deception is placed in her mouth rather than in Abram's, and it has an honorable and urgent motive.

Fathers and Sons

Another set of issues is raised in the Abraham cycle by the question of an heir who should inherit the promise. At first, Abraham worries that "the heir to my house is Eliezer of Damascus" (Gen 15:2). Then he has a child, Ishmael, by Hagar, Sarah's slave girl. Here again there is an ethnographic aspect to the story: Ishmael becomes the ancestor of a desert tribe. Like the story of Jacob and Esau, the account of Ishmael explains how Israel was defined over against its neighbors by divine choices that seem quite arbitrary. But this story, too, raises moral questions, not only for modern sensibilities.

The story is told twice, with variations, in Genesis 16 (J) and 21 (E). In the J account, the conflict between Hagar and Sarai arises when Hagar becomes pregnant and looks on Sarai with contempt. Abram makes no attempt to defend her but allows Sarai to do

Fig. 4.4 *Hagar and Ishmael in the Desert* by François-Joseph Navez (1820). **Royal Museum of Fine Arts of Belgium.** Commons.wikimedia.org

as she pleases, so that Hagar has to flee. The angel of the Lord intervenes and persuades Hagar to return, by promising that her son will have plentiful offspring, even though he will be "a wild ass of a man" and will live "at odds with his kin." But Hagar is also told to submit to her mistress. We are left in no doubt about Sarai's greater importance in the eyes of the Lord. Abram does not come off well in this story, as he makes no attempt to defend his offspring; but, typically, he is not censured in the text.

The E account locates the conflict later, after Isaac is born and weaned. In this case, Sarah's harshness to Hagar has less justification: she cannot abide the thought that the son of a slave woman would be on a par with her son. This time Abraham is distressed, but God tells him that Sarah is right, and that through Isaac the promise will be transmitted. He then sends Hagar and her child off into the wilderness. The plight of mother and child in the desert anticipates the later wandering of Israel and that of the prophet Elijah. In each case, God comes to the rescue. This time there is no reason for Hagar or Ishmael to return to Abraham, but God causes the boy to prosper in the wilderness. Here again the idea of divine election seems to take priority over human compassion. The story seems to champion ethnocentrism by suggesting that those who do not belong to the chosen people can be sent away. We shall meet a chilling application of the same principle much later in the Bible in the book of Ezra, where Ezra makes the Judean men who have married foreign women send them away with their children. The Elohist softens the story by assuring us that God looked after Hagar and Ishmael. There is no such assurance in the book of Ezra. Once again, the story raises a profound issue, one that will come up many times in the Bible, but it hardly points to a satisfactory solution.

The crowning episode in the narratives about Abraham's heirs is the sacrifice of Isaac in Genesis 22. The basic story, 22:1-14, 19, is generally ascribed to the E source, like the story of Hagar and Ishmael in Genesis 21. Verses 15-18 ("The angel of the Lord called to Abraham a second time . . .") are generally recognized as a secondary addition, which integrates the story into the Yahwistic theme of the promise. There are some problems with the source-critical division, since "the angel of the Lord" is mentioned in v. 11 and v. 14 explains the name Moriah by the phrase "YHWH will see." Evidently, the story has been reworked by different hands, and this helps explain why several different emphases can be detected in it. Nonetheless, the spare artistry of the story has been widely and rightly praised.

The opening verse is exceptional among the stories of Genesis in offering an explicit key to interpretation: "God tested Abraham." The test is eventually aborted, but there is no doubt that Abraham passes. Abraham is commended in v. 12 and again in the redactional addition in vv. 16-18. This is not just any test, however. Abraham is told to take his only son, Isaac, whom he loves, and offer him up as a burnt offering. While the reader is told in advance that this is a test, Abraham is not. To appreciate the force of the story, the awfulness of the command must be taken fully seriously.

Another key to the story is provided by the theme of providence. Abraham tells Isaac that "God himself will provide a lamb for the burnt offering" (v. 8). At this point in the story, this is an understandable attempt to dodge the awful truth, but it is more prophetic than Abraham knows. When the angel of the Lord intervenes, Abraham names the place "the LORD will provide."

Yet another key to the story lies in the repetition of the promise to Abraham in vv. 15-18. While this passage is an editorial addition, it integrates the story into the main theme that now binds the patriarchal stories together.

The fascination of the story, however, lies in the specific content of the command to Abraham to sacrifice his only legitimate son. We do not know how widely human (child) sacrifice was practiced in ancient Israel, but there can be no doubt that it was practiced, down close to the time of the Babylonian exile. Kings of Judah (Ahaz in the eighth century, 2 Kgs 16:3; Manasseh in the seventh century, 2 Kgs 21:6) made their sons "pass through fire," that is, offered them as burnt offerings. There was an installation called the Topheth in Ge (valley) Hinnom outside Jerusalem, where children were burned as victims (hence the name Gehenna for hell in New Testament times). King Josiah destroyed the Topheth in the reform of 621 B.C.E., allegedly so that "no one would make a son or a daughter pass through fire as an offering to Molech" (2 Kgs 23:10). Molech is usually taken to be a Canaanite god, and some interpreters are quick to conclude that child sacrifice was a Canaanite custom. But there is evidence that it was also practiced in the name of YHWH, God of Israel. The eighth-century prophet Micah addresses a Yahwistic worshiper who wonders, "With what shall I come before the LORD, and bow myself before God on high? Shall I come before him with burnt offerings, with calves a year old? . . . Shall I give my firstborn for my transgression, the fruit of my body for the sin of my soul?" (Mic 6:6-8). Micah replies that God requires only justice and kindness, but the question shows that a worshiper of YHWH could contemplate child sacrifice in the eighth century B.C.E. Moreover, child sacrifice appears to be commanded in Exod 22:28-29: "The firstborn of your sons you shall give to me. You shall do the same with your oxen and with your sheep: seven days it shall remain with its mother; on the eighth you shall give it to me" (Hebrew v. 28, English v. 29). This commandment is modified in Exod 34:19-20, which likewise says that "All that first opens the womb is mine," but adds, "all the firstborn of your sons you shall redeem." (Similarly, the firstborn of a donkey could be redeemed by substituting a lamb, but if it was not redeemed, it had to be killed.) Underlying this commandment is the conviction that all life is from God, and that God's right to the firstborn must be acknowledged, in order to ensure future fertility. We should expect that human firstborn sons were normally redeemed, as commanded in Exodus 34, but it is remarkable that the stark commandment in Exodus 22 is left on the books.

YHWH is also said to have commanded human sacrifice in Ezek 20:25-26: "Moreover, I gave them statutes that were not good and ordinances by which they could not live. I defiled them through all their very gifts, in their offering up all their firstborn, in order that I might horrify them, so that they might know that I am the LORD." Ezekiel does not attribute child sacrifice to Canaanite influence. He may have had Exodus 22 in mind. In any case, he provides further testimony that child sacrifice was practiced in Judah down to the time of the exile. The polemic against child sacrifice in Deuteronomy and Jeremiah would not have been necessary if this had not been the case.

Unlike Deuteronomy and Jeremiah, Genesis 22 does not condemn child sacrifice or polemicize against it. On the contrary, Abraham is praised for his willingness to carry it out. He does not have to go through with it, but that may be an exceptional case because of Abraham's exceptional standing. We shall meet a counterpoint to this story in Judges 11, in the story of Jephthah. Jephthah makes a vow to the Lord that if he is victorious in battle, he will sacrifice "whoever comes out of the doors of my house to meet me." The language clearly implies human sacrifice. Unfortunately for Jephthah, he is greeted by his only daughter. He expresses more grief than Abraham and is no less steadfast in fulfilling his vow. Modern commentators often fault Jephthah, since, unlike Abraham, he brought his misfortune on himself by a rash vow. But the Bible does not pronounce his vow rash or pass judgment on him at all. (The New Testament proclaims him, like Abraham, a hero of faith, in Heb 11:32-34). Moreover, he seems to make his vow under the influence of the spirit of the Lord (Judg 11:20-21). In this case, there is no ram in the bushes. The Lord does not always provide a substitute.

While child sacrifice is not repudiated in Genesis 22, it was emphatically rejected by the later tradition. The tradition continued to praise the obedience of Abraham, but there is evident discomfort both with the idea that God gave such a command and with Abraham's willingness to carry it out. On the one hand, it was suggested that the idea of the sacrifice came from Satan, just as Satan incited God to test Job. So the book of *Jubilees*, in the second century B.C.E., has the idea originate with Mastema, leader of the host of demons (*Jub.* 17:16). On the other hand, Targum Neofiti (an Aramaic paraphrase of the Bible from the early Christian period) has Abraham tell Isaac openly that he is to be sacrificed. Isaac responds by asking Abraham to bind him properly so that he may not kick and make the sacrifice unfit. (In Jewish tradition, the sacrifice of Isaac is known as the Akedah, or Binding.) Other Jewish sources from the early Christian era also emphasize that Isaac was a willing victim and that his willingness was meritorious. This interpretation of the story may already be found in a fragmentary text from the Dead Sea Scrolls from the pre-Christian era (4Q225).

Fig. 4.5 *The Sacrifice of Isaac* **by Adi Holzer (1997).** Commons.wikimedia.org

M. J. Gregor; New York: Abaris, 1979], 115.) He went on to cite the story of Abraham as a case in point. This is of course a modern critique, which arises in a world where God is not thought to speak to people on a daily basis and claims of divine revelation are regarded as problematic. We shall find, however, that such a critique is not as foreign to the Bible as we might suppose. Increasingly, as the biblical history unfolds, the authenticity of revelation becomes a problem. We shall find this especially in the debates over true and false prophecy. In the matter of revelation, as in the matter of child sacrifice, we must acknowledge development in the biblical corpus, although that development does not necessarily proceed in a straight line.

The Jacob Cycle

Jacob the Trickster

The story continues to fascinate philosophers and theologians down to modern times. The Danish philosopher Søren Kierkegaard reasoned that Abraham could only be justified by "the teleological suspension of the ethical"—the idea that ethical standards do not apply to a divine command. Immanuel Kant, the great German philosopher of the Enlightenment, offered a more penetrating critique. For Kant, the problem was how one can know whether such a command comes from God in the first place: "There are certain cases in which man can be convinced that it cannot be God whose voice he thinks he hears; when the voice commands him to do what is opposed to the moral law, though the phenomenon seem to him ever so majestic and surpassing the whole of nature, he must count it a deception." (See Kant, *The Conflict of the Faculties* [trans.

Deception is a minor theme in the Abraham cycle, but it figures more prominently in the stories of Jacob. A prime example is presented by the story of Jacob and Esau in Genesis 27. The context is the rivalry between the two brothers that began already in the womb. The success of the younger brother is a well-known folkloric motif. There are other instances in the Bible, such as the story of David. In the case of Jacob and Esau, the rivalry is exacerbated by the fact that Esau is a hunter, while Jacob lives a settled life (compare the story of Cain and Abel). Jacob, however, succeeds by deceiving his aging, blind father and stealing the blessing meant for his brother. He does so with the connivance of his mother. His father, Isaac, cannot revoke the blessing. The story is told in exquisite detail, and no moral judgments are made. One is left to marvel at the strange way in which the blessing is transmitted.

In part, the tale is ethnological. Esau becomes the ancestor of Edom, Judah's neighbor to the south. In part, it is a folkloric tale, with Jacob cast in the role of the trickster, who breaks the rules but is nonetheless attractive and winsome. Such stories provide relief from the earnestness of rule-bound life—the point is not that one should do likewise, but one can get vicarious pleasure from watching Jacob "get away with it." In this respect, the Jacob stories are exceptional in the Bible, where moral earnestness is usually the rule. But while we may appreciate the trickery of Jacob, it is still somewhat troubling that the ancestor of Israel gets his blessing by deceit. Jacob is no saint. The prophet Hosea later says of him, "In the womb he tried to supplant his brother, and in his manhood he strove with God" (Hos 12:3). To some degree, he suffers consequences for his deception. He is himself the victim of deception in his dealings with Laban (Genesis 29–30) and again when he is told that his son Joseph is dead (37:29-35). Nonetheless, he does not lose the blessing. He is not censured for his deception in Genesis, but his moral ambiguity should be kept in mind. This is not the only time that God "writes straight with crooked lines" in the Bible. The manner in which Israel, the tribes descended from Jacob, is said to take possession of the promised land raises more severe moral problems. Increasingly in the Bible, however, and as we shall see even in Genesis, the moral ambiguity of Israel is recognized. The status of "holy people" is an ideal in much of the Bible. It is seldom if ever an actual state.

Jacob's character changes somewhat as he ages. In Genesis 34 we read of the rape of Jacob's daughter Dinah and the sack of Shechem. The protagonist of the story, Shechem, is the figure who gives his name to the town in the central highlands that would figure prominently in the story of early Israel (see Joshua 24). Shechem, we are told, genuinely loved Dinah, despite the fact that he had raped her. His offer to marry her may sound monstrous by modern standards, but not by those of the ancient world. Deuteronomy 22:28 requires a man who seizes a virgin and lies with her to pay a bride-price and marry her. Since he has defiled her, he is not allowed to divorce her. The feelings of the young woman do not seem to be taken into account. The primary consideration is her economic well-being. It would be difficult for a woman who had been raped to find a husband. Shechem's offer of marriage, then, may be construed as sincere and well intended. Moreover, Shechem's father, Hamor, issues an invitation that reverberates through the history of Israel and Judaism down to modern times: "Make marriages with us; give your daughters to us, and take our daughters for yourselves. You shall live with us, and the land shall be open to you" (Gen 34: 9-10).

Jacob's reaction to the incident is low-key, as befits an aging patriarch. His sons, however, are hot-blooded and see only the insult to their family honor. Their reply to Shechem is explicitly acknowledged to be deceitful. They agree to give Dinah in marriage only if every male in Shechem is circumcised. Circumcision becomes one of the distinctive ethnic marks of Judaism in the postexilic period, but the custom was certainly older. Here it is used as a trick, so that Jacob's sons Simeon and Levi can attack the Shechemites when they are still in pain. They kill Hamor and Shechem and plunder the city. They rescue Dinah (but again we are not told whether she wished to be rescued). They even take the wives of the men of Shechem as booty.

Thus far, Genesis 34 might seem to be another case where the Hebrews outwit the Gentiles. The most remarkable aspect of the story, however, is its conclusion. Jacob reproaches Simeon and Levi: "You have brought trouble on me by making me odious to the inhabitants of the land, the Canaanites and the Perizzites; my numbers are few, and if they gather themselves against me and attack me, I shall be destroyed" (Gen 34:30). This statement is remarkably pragmatic. The Canaanites are not demonized here, as they are so often in the Hebrew Bible. There is rather recognition that the Hebrews need to live with them. But the words of Jacob are not the author's final verdict. The sons reply, "Why should our sister be treated like a whore?" (34:31). Honor, too, has its claim. The text leaves the question open. What is remarkable here, however, is the critical spirit that recognizes that there is more than one side to the question.

The story of the sack of Shechem was popular in Second Temple Judaism, when Shechem was the city of the Samaritans, whom the Jews regarded as descendants of Assyrian settlers, even though they worshiped the God of Israel. The story is retold in *Jubilees* 30 without any qualms. The judgment against the Shechemites was given from heaven. Moreover, if any man in Israel wanted to give his daughter or his sister in marriage to a Gentile, he should be stoned to death. The lines between Jew and Gentile are more sharply drawn in the later text. The themes of Genesis 34, circumcision and intermarriage, are central issues in Second Temple Judaism and much less prominent before the exile. The story in Genesis 34 must be taken to reflect some diversity of opinion on relations with Gentiles. Even in the Second Temple period, not all Jews were as hard-line as the author of *Jubilees*.

Judah and Tamar

A more striking example of the emerging critical spirit is found in the story of Judah and Tamar in Genesis 38. Once again, the story has several facets. In one respect, it is a genealogical tale; it explains the strange ancestry by which King David was descended from Judah. It could be taken to have political overtones, since it shows Judah, ancestor of the tribe that dominated the southern kingdom and gave its name to Judaism, in a rather bad light. Mainly, however, it is a morality tale on the dangers of double standards and moral absolutes.

The story begins with Judah's marriage to a Canaanite woman. This is not condemned in the text, but it goes against the practice of the patriarchs hitherto. When their son Er dies, his brother Onan is expected to "go in" to his widow, Tamar, to raise up offspring for him. (This is known as the levirate law. It is spelled out in Deut 25:5-10.) When Onan shirks his duty in this regard, he too dies. Judah then tells Tamar to wait until his youngest son, Shelah, has grown up, but he does not give her to him in marriage. Tamar then decides to take the initiative. She dresses like a prostitute, covering her face, and waits for Judah by the roadside when he is at a sheepshearing. The conquest is easy. There is no implication that Judah does anything extraordinary when he hires a prostitute. He promises a kid from the flock as payment, but she prudently secures pledges from him. When he sends the kid, there is no prostitute there. Only at this point does Judah show embarrassment, that he may be a laughingstock. When Tamar is found to be pregnant, however, Judah suddenly becomes a pillar of rectitude: "Bring her out; let her be burned." (In Deut 22:24 the penalty for fornication is death by stoning. Burning is demanded only in the story of Tamar.) When he sees the pledges, however, he quickly acknowledges that "she is more in the right than I, since I did not give her to my son Shelah." There is no suggestion that Judah should be punished for his action, but the passage is unique in Genesis for its explicit admission that a patriarch was in the wrong. There is also a recognition here of the relativity of law—Tamar's actions are justified because she is pursuing a greater good, the continuation of her husband's line. In fact, one of her twin sons, Perez, becomes the ancestor of King David. An act of deception and prostitution becomes a pivotal link in the transmission of the divine promise. Such is the irony of history.

The Joseph Story

The story of Judah and Tamar is integrated into the longer and more complex story of Joseph, which provides the richest illustration in Genesis of the irony of history and mystery of providence. This story is obviously different in kind from the short, folkloric tales that make up most of the patriarchal history. The Joseph story is a novella, a superb example of early prose fiction. Traditionally, the story has been attributed to the Yahwist (J) with some passages assigned to the Elohist (E). The argument for this division rests on the observation of several duplications. The brothers of Joseph appear as sons of Israel (J) or sons of Jacob (E). First Reuben intervenes to save Joseph's life (E), then Judah intervenes (J). Judah proposes to sell him to the Ishmaelites, but then he is found and taken by Midianite traders, who sell him to the Ishmaelites. He is variously said to be sold in Egypt by the Midianites (37:36) or by the Ishmaelites (39:1). Other minor discrepancies could be added. It has been argued that much of this variation may be deliberate on the part of a sophisticated author. This argument would not apply to the contradiction as to whether he was sold by the Midianites or the Ishmaelites. It may be that the Midianites are introduced secondarily by an editor who wanted to excuse the brothers of the charge of selling Joseph into slavery, which was a crime liable to the death penalty according to Deut 24:7. It should be noted that Joseph says that his brothers sold him into Egypt (Gen 45:4).

The story unfolds through a veritable roller coaster of plot twists. Joseph incurs the hatred of his brothers because he is his father's favorite, and he exacerbates the situation by telling of a dream in which his parents and brothers bow down to him. So when they are away from their parents, pasturing sheep near Shechem, the brothers propose to kill him. First, Reuben intervenes and has him thrown into a pit instead. Then Judah proposes to sell him to the Ishmaelites. This, too, is a crime, but obviously a lesser one. The brothers are relieved of guilt in this regard by the arrival of the Midianites. The brothers then dip Joseph's robe in blood and present it to Jacob as evidence of Joseph's death. This cruel deception echoes Jacob's own deception of his blind father, Isaac. The episode of Judah and Tamar is inserted here and bound to its context by various motifs (e.g., Judah is asked to recognize the pledges he had given to Tamar; Jacob is asked to recognize his son's robe). Mainly, this episode provides space between Joseph's captivity and his rise to prominence in Egypt.

Joseph experiences the transition from captivity to power not once but twice. First, he is overseer of his master's house. This happy situation is disrupted when his master's wife tries to seduce him and then makes a false accusation against him. (This motif has an Egyptian parallel in the Tale of the Two Brothers, where the wife of the elder brother similarly tries to seduce the righteous younger man and then accuses him falsely.) Consequently, Joseph is thrown in prison. He rises again because of his God-given ability to interpret dreams, and now he is placed in authority over all Egypt. He distinguishes himself by storing grain in anticipation of a time of famine. When there is famine in the land of Canaan, his brothers come and fulfill his prophecy by bowing down before him in ignorance of his identity. Joseph tests his brothers, especially with respect to their feelings for their youngest brother, Benjamin, adding to Jacob's distress in the process. In the end, however, he can no longer control himself and discloses his identity (45:1-3). He does not reproach his brothers for selling him into Egypt, because "God sent me before you to preserve for you a remnant on earth, and to keep alive for you many survivors" (45:7). But Joseph is also responsible for causing Jacob and his whole family to go down into Egypt and settle there as shepherds. Moreover, Joseph is

credited with centralizing wealth in the hands of the pharaoh and bringing the people into a state of slavery: "So Joseph bought all the land of Egypt for Pharaoh. All the Egyptians sold their fields, because the famine was severe upon them, and the land became Pharaoh's. As for the people, he made slaves of them, from one end of Egypt to the other" (47:20-21). Only the land of the priests was exempt. One-fifth of all crops was to go to Pharaoh. It would seem, then, that even as Joseph saved his family from famine, he set the stage for their future oppression. But that oppression, in turn, would be the occasion of their greatest deliverance.

Many scholars have tried to find a kernel of history in the Joseph story. There was a time (c. 1750–1550 B.C.E.) when people from Syria, known as the Hyksos, ruled Egypt. The main account of these people is found in the Hellenistic Egyptian historian Manetho, who also calls them "shepherds." Manetho claims that some of the Hyksos settled in Jerusalem when they were expelled from Egypt. We shall consider the story further in connection with the exodus. The career of Joseph, however, bears little resemblance to anything we know of Hyksos rule in Egypt. The Hyksos were a hostile invading force; Joseph is throughout the faithful servant of Pharaoh, and his people settle peacefully in Goshen, away from the settlements of the native Egyptians, "because all shepherds are abhorrent to the Egyptians" (46:34). Any historical reminiscences in this story are incidental.

The purpose of the Joseph story has several facets. First, it is an entertaining story in its own right. We have many such stories from ancient Egypt, such as the Tale of the Shipwrecked Sailor or the Tale of the Two

Brothers. Within the Bible, similar complex novellas can be found in the books of Samuel and in later books such as Ruth and Esther. The Joseph story has a clear theological theme, illustrating the role of divine providence in the history of Israel, despite the unworthy conduct of Jacob's sons. The character of Joseph has an exemplary quality that was often emphasized in later Jewish tradition. It has been suggested that his character is above all that of the ideal courtier, and that he could serve as a model for officials at the royal court in Jerusalem. In the Pentateuch, the story forms a bridge from the patriarchal narratives to the exodus by explaining how the Israelites came to be in Egypt.

As noted already, the Joseph story is different in kind from the other stories in Genesis and for that reason cannot be easily absorbed into one or more of the traditional sources. It has a certain amount of authentic local color. The reforms attributed to Joseph, however, whereby the priests were exempt from the heavy taxation imposed on the people and given an allowance by Pharaoh, fits later Egyptian history rather than earlier. The best parallels are provided by Herodotus and later Greek writers. The Joseph story is unlikely to have been composed as early as the reign of Solomon, as earlier scholars had supposed. The theme of the wise courtier, of which Joseph is the prototype, is especially popular in late Hebrew literature (in the books of Esther and Daniel). It is noteworthy that the heroes of all these stories are Israelites or Jews in the service of foreign kings. Many Jews in fact rose to prominence in the service of foreign kings in the period after the Babylonian exile.

The book of Genesis concludes with the deaths of Jacob and Joseph. Before his death, Jacob blesses his sons. The Blessing of Jacob is an old poem and is an important early catalog of the twelve tribes. We shall consider the tribes further in connection with the history of early Israel, in the books of Joshua and Judges. For the present, two aspects of the Blessing of Jacob should be noted. First, the comment on Simeon and Levi is no blessing: they are condemned as men of violence, presumably because of the sack of Shechem, and doomed to be scattered in Israel. The harshness is especially striking in view of the priestly character of the tribe of Levi. Second, Judah is promised a scepter that will never depart from him. The blessing presumably reflects a Judean perspective, even though it affirms an inclusive view of Israel as embracing all twelve tribes.

The Priestly Edition of the Patriarchal Stories

The Priestly source can be detected only in a few places in the patriarchal narratives. Abram is first introduced in a genealogy (P) in Genesis 11, and we are informed that he was seventy-five years old when he departed from Haran in 12:4. The most significant Priestly addition to the Abraham stories is the account of the covenant with Abraham in Genesis 17. Unlike the J account in Genesis 15, P requires more than faith of Abraham: "This is my covenant which you shall keep, between me and you and your offspring after you: Every male among you shall be circumcised" (17:10). Any male who remained uncircumcised must be cut off from the people. The practice of circumcision is attested in the Near East long before the rise of Israel. There is no reason to doubt that Israelites practiced it from very early times, but it cannot have been a distinctive marker in early Israel. From the time of the Babylonian exile on, however, it acquires central importance as a marker of Jewish identity. The Priestly account of the covenant with Abraham is unlikely to be older than the Babylonian exile. It is characteristic of the Priestly source that the covenant is identified so closely with a ritual requirement. The association has survived down to modern times. The colloquial Yiddish word for circumcision is *bris*, a modification of the Hebrew word for covenant, *bᵉrit*.

Elsewhere in Genesis 12–50 the Priestly source is found primarily in genealogical lists, such as the list of the twelve sons of Jacob in 31:22-26, the descendants of Esau in 36:1-14, and the list of the descendants of Jacob who came to Egypt in 46:6-27. These lists bring order to the narrative by positing relationships, but they also convey a sense or historical reliability by their (fictitious) detail.

FOR FURTHER READING

Commentaries

G. W. Coats, *Genesis, with an Introduction to Narrative Literature* (FOTL 1; Grand Rapids: Eerdmans, 1983). Useful form-critical analysis.

T. E. Fretheim, "The Book of Genesis," *NIB* 1:321–673. Thoughtful homiletical commentary.

G. von Rad, *Genesis* (trans. J. H. Marks; OTL; Philadelphia: Westminster, 1972). Brief but classic commentary.

C. Westermann, *Genesis 12–36: A Commentary* (trans. J. J. Scullion; CC; Minneapolis: Augsburg, 1985); *Genesis 37–50* (trans. J. J. Scullion; CC; Minneapolis: Augsburg, 1986). Best full historical-philological commentary.

Other Studies

R. Alter, *The Art of Biblical Narrative* (New York: Basic Books, 1981). Classic literary reading.

J. S. Baden, *The Promise to the Patriarchs* (New York: Oxford University Press, 2013). Vigorous defense of attribution of the promise texts to the documentary sources rather than to a late redactor.

J.J. Collins, "Faith without Works: Biblical Ethics and the Sacrifice of Isaac," in idem, *Encounters with Biblical Theology* (Minneapolis: Fortress Press, 2005), 47–58.

G. W. Coats, *From Canaan to Egypt: Structural and Theological Context for the Joseph Story* (CBQMS 4; Washington, DC: Catholic Biblical Association, 1975). Discussion of the Joseph story in its literary context.

F. M. Cross, *Canaanite Myth and Hebrew Epic* (Cambridge: Harvard University Press, 1973). Discussion of patriarchal religion in the light of the Ugaritic texts.

I. Finkelstein and N. A. Silberman, *The Bible Unearthed: Archaeology's New Vision of Ancient Israel and the Origin of Its Sacred Texts* (New York: Free Press, 2001), 27–47; up-to-date account of the archaeological record, which frustrates the attempt to salvage history from the patriarchal narratives.

H. Gunkel, *The Legends of Genesis* (trans. W. H. Carruth; New York: Schocken, 1964). Classic exposition of the form-critical approach.

R. Hendel, *Remembering Abraham: Culture, Memory, and History in the Hebrew Bible* (New York: Oxford University Press, 2005), 45–55. Identifies early elements in the patriarchal narratives.

R. Hendel, ed., *Reading Genesis: Ten Methods* (Cambridge: Cambridge University Press, 2010). Ten essays illustrating different approaches to Genesis.

B. Mazar, *The Early Biblical Period: Historical Studies* (S. Ahituv and B. Levine, eds.; Jerusalem: Israel Exploration Society, 1986), 49–62. Classic discussion. Notes that the sites associated with Abraham lie within the bounds of early Israelite settlement (1200–1000 B.C.E.).

P. K. McCarter, revised by R. S. Hendel, "The Patriarchal Age: Abraham, Isaac and Jacob," in H. Shanks, ed., *Ancient Israel: From Abraham to the Roman Destruction of the Temple* (Washington, DC: Biblical Archaeology Society, 1999), 1–31. Sober, balanced discussion of the historical background of the stories, noting early elements.

S. Niditch, *Underdogs and Tricksters* (San Francisco: Harper & Row, 1987). Stimulating treatment of Genesis as folklore.

D. B. Redford, *A Study of the Biblical Story of Joseph (Genesis 37–50)* (VTSup 20; Leiden: Brill, 1970). Important for its mastery of the Egyptian background.

P. Trible, *Texts of Terror: Literary-Feminist Readings of Biblical Narratives* (OBT; Philadelphia: Fortress Press, 1984). Powerful literary reading from a feminist perspective.

CHAPTER 5

The Exodus from Egypt

INTRODUCTION

The exodus is the most celebrated event in the entire Hebrew Bible, though it is not attested in any ancient nonbiblical source. In this chapter, we will examine what we can know about the exodus as history, the revelation of YHWH in the exodus story, and the centrality of the liberation from Egypt for Israelite tradition.

The stories in Genesis are essentially family legends. In the book of Exodus, we encounter a more extended, continuous story that deals with the birth of a people. This story is linked to Genesis by the story of Joseph, but it draws on traditions of a different kind.

The subject matter of this story is the exodus of the Israelites from Egypt. This is the most celebrated event in the entire Hebrew Bible, and the event that is most important for the later identity of Israel and of Judaism. The story is told primarily in the first half of the book, proceeding from the slavery in Egypt to the revelation at Mount Sinai in chapter 19. This is followed by a series of laws in chapters 20–24, beginning with the Ten Commandments and continuing with the collection known as the Book of the Covenant. Then follows the lengthy prescription for the making of the tabernacle or desert shrine and its furnishings. There is a narrative interlude in chapters 32–34, including the story of the golden calf. Then the concluding chapters describe the construction and erection of the tabernacle.

It is much more difficult to distinguish the J and E sources in Exodus than it was in Genesis. Most analyses ascribe only scattered verses to E. After Exodus 6, all sources use the proper divine name YHWH for God in any case. The Priestly strand is very prominent in Exodus. It includes the revelation of the divine name in chapter 6, the account of the Passover in chapter 12, the crossing of the sea in chapter 14, the instructions for the tabernacle (chaps. 25–31), and the account of its construction (chaps. 35–40).

Exodus as History

As we have seen in the introductory chapter, the internal chronology of the Bible suggests a date about 1445 B.C.E. for the exodus. There is little evidence, however, that would enable us to corroborate the biblical account by relating it to other sources. The exodus, as reported in the Bible, is not attested in any ancient non-biblical source. While it might be argued that the escape of the Israelites was inconsequential for the Egyptians, and therefore not recorded, in fact the Egyptians kept tight control over their eastern border and kept careful records. If a large group of Israelites had departed, we should expect some mention of it. For an Egyptian account of the origin of Israel, however, we have to wait until the Hellenistic era, when a priest named Manetho wrote a history of Egypt in Greek. Manetho claimed that Jerusalem was built "in the land now called Judea" by the Hyksos after they were expelled from Egypt. (On the Hyksos see chapter 1 above. They were people of Syrian origin who ruled Egypt for a time and were driven out of Egypt c. 1530 B.C.E.) He goes on to tell a more elaborate tale about an attempt to expel lepers from Egypt. Some eighty thousand of these, we are told, including some learned priests, were assembled and sent to work in stone quarries. They rebelled, however, under the leadership of one Osarseph, who summoned the Hyksos from Jerusalem to his aid. They returned and proceeded to commit various outrages and blasphemies in Egypt but were eventually driven out. Osarseph, we are told, was also called Moses. The account is preserved by the Jewish historian Josephus in *Against Apion* 1.228–52. Manetho probably did not invent this story. Another, slightly earlier, Hellenistic writer, Hecataeus of Abdera, also says that Jerusalem was built by people led by Moses who had been driven out of Egypt. There was a strong folk memory in Egypt of the Hyksos as the hated foreigners from Asia who had once ruled the country. But the idea that Jerusalem had been built by these people is probably a late guess: it provided Egyptians with an explanation of the origin of the strange people just beyond their borders. It is unlikely that Manetho had any reliable tradition about the origin of Israel.

The Egyptians watched their eastern border carefully. About 1200 B.C.E., an Egyptian officer wrote to other officers about an incident involving runaway slaves.

> I was sent forth . . . following after these two slaves . . . When my letter reaches you, write to me about all that has happened to [them]. Who found their tracks? Which watch found their tracks? What people are after them? Write to me about all that has happened to them and how many people you send out after them.

(*ANET*[3], 259)

The biblical account itself offers few specific details that might be corroborated by external evidence. The pharaoh is never named: he remains simply "the king" or "Pharaoh" like a character in a folktale. The most specific references in the biblical text are found in Exodus 1, where we are told that a pharaoh "who knew not Joseph" was concerned at the size and power of the Israelites and set them to work building the cities Pithom and Rameses. Rameses is presumably the city of Pi-Ramesse, which was built on the site of the old Hyksos capital of Avaris. It was reoccupied in the time of Ramesses II (1304–1237 B.C.E.). The location of Pithom (Per-Atum) is uncertain. One of the possible sites was also rebuilt in Ramesside times. Because of this, most scholars have favored a date around 1250 B.C.E. for the exodus. All we can really say, however, is that the biblical account was written at some time after the building of Pi-Ramesse and Per-Atum, and possibly that the author was aware of some tradition associating Semitic laborers with these sites. If the story of the exodus has any historical basis, then the thirteenth century B.C.E. provides the most plausible backdrop.

The existence of Semitic slaves in Egypt in the late second millennium is well attested. More specifically, there is evidence that Habiru or Apiru worked on the construction of the capital city of Ramesses II. (Papyrus Leiden 348 contains an order: "Distribute grain rations to the soldiers and to the Apiru who transport stones to the great pylon of Ramesses.") The Anastasi Papyri show that access to Egypt was tightly controlled in the thirteenth century B.C.E. One passage records the passage into Egypt of an entire tribe during a drought. Another reports the pursuit of runaway slaves who had escaped to the desert. These documents give circumstantial support to the plausibility of an exodus of slaves from Egypt in that period, but they do not, of course, corroborate the specific story found in the Bible. Again, it has been suggested that the story of the plagues contains a reminiscence

of an epidemic in the mid-fourteenth century that is referred to as "the Asiatic illness" (compare the story of the lepers in Manetho). No doubt, plagues were familiar in Egypt, and it is gratuitous to identify the biblical plagues with a specific incident. While parallels such as these suggest that there is a certain amount of Egyptian "local color" in the story, they fall far short of establishing the historicity of the exodus.

Other considerations must be weighed against these elements of local color. The consensus of archaeologists is that the material culture of early Israel, in the central highlands of Palestine, was essentially Canaanite. If there was an exodus from Egypt, then, it must have been on a small scale. Indeed, the claim in Exod 12:37 that about six hundred thousand men, in addition to children, came out of Egypt is hyperbolic in any case. Some scholars now suppose that the biblical account may have "telescoped" several small exoduses, which took place over centuries, into one dramatic narrative. In any case, the claim that early Israel consisted of people who had escaped from Egypt, and their descendants, is problematic in light of the archaeological evidence.

Further, the genre of the stories in Exodus is legendary and folkloristic. The story is replete with miraculous incidents, from the rescue of Moses from the Nile, to the burning bush, to the contest with the magicians of Egypt, to the crossing of the sea. The story of the baby Moses found in the bulrushes is a common folkloric motif. A similar story was told of King Sargon of Akkad (c. 2300 B.C.E.), whose mother also placed him in a vessel of reeds in a river. The final edition of the book of

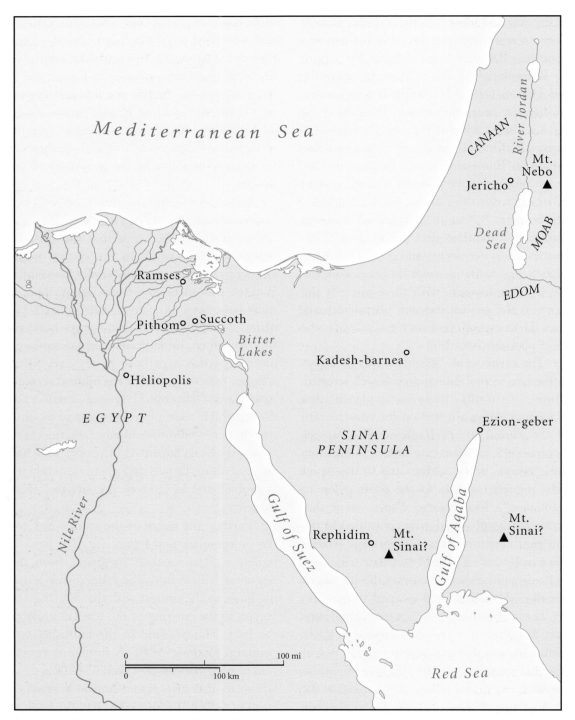

Map 5.1. The landscape of the Book of Exodus.

INTRODUCTION TO THE HEBREW BIBLE

Exodus is no earlier than the Babylonian exile, some seven hundred years after the events it describes. The story was told for cultic reasons, to remind the people of their obligation to worship their God. It is not an exercise in historiography, even by ancient standards, as can be seen readily from the differences in style between the book of Exodus and the books of Kings.

Nonetheless, it seems likely that some historical memories underlie the tradition of the exodus. The name Moses is of Egyptian origin. The word means "child," and it normally occurs as an element in a longer name that begins with the name of a god, such as Ptah-mose, Ra-mose, or Thut-mose. It is difficult to imagine why Israelite tradition should give such a prominent role to someone with an Egyptian name if there were no memory of such a person. It is also unlikely that a people would claim that it had experienced the shameful condition of slavery if there were no historical basis for it.

The memory of the exodus seems to have been especially important in the hill country of Ephraim. When Jeroboam I led the revolt of the northern tribes against Rehoboam, son of Solomon, he allegedly set up golden calves in Bethel and Dan, and told the people, "These are your gods who brought you up out of the land of Egypt" (1 Kgs 12:28). The account in 1 Kings comes from a southern writer and is hostile to Jeroboam, but the reference to the exodus is all the more remarkable for this reason. There is also a parallel between the career of Jeroboam and the beginning of the book of Exodus. Jeroboam was in charge of the forced labor of the house of Joseph under Solomon (1 Kgs 11:28). He rebelled and had to flee to Egypt, but he came up from Egypt after Solomon's death. Moses also encounters a situation of forced labor and has to flee when he kills an Egyptian. The motif of forced labor, then, had special resonance in the time of Jeroboam. As we shall later see, it is clear from the prophets Amos and Hosea that the exodus was celebrated at Bethel during the period of the monarchy. The exodus has been described, with good reason, as the "charter myth" of the northern kingdom of Israel. In contrast, the exodus does not figure prominently in the southern prophets, such as Isaiah of Jerusalem. Also, there are surprisingly few references to the exodus in the books of Judges and Samuel, although these books were edited by Deuteronomists who certainly had a strong interest in the exodus. Jeroboam would not have taken the exodus as his "charter myth" if there were not already a tradition about it, but the story may not have been as prominent in the life of Israel in the period before the monarchy as it later became.

The Revelation of YHWH

There are two major themes in the story of the exodus: the revelation of YHWH and the liberation from slavery. These themes appear to have been originally independent of each other. Several old poetic passages speak of YHWH as the divine warrior who marches out from Mount Sinai, or from some other location in the region south of Israel:

> The LORD came from Sinai and dawned
>   from Seir on us;
> he shone forth from Mount Paran.
> With him were myriads of holy ones;
> at his right a host of his own.
>
> (Deut 33:2)

Or:

LORD, when you went out from Seir,
when you marched from the region of
    Edom
the earth trembled, and the heavens
    poured,
the clouds indeed poured water.
The mountains quaked before the LORD,
    the One of Sinai,
before the LORD, the God of Israel.
         (Judg 5:4-5; see also Ps 68:7-8)

These passages do not speak of an exodus from Egypt. Conversely, the events at Sinai are usually passed over in summaries of the early history of Israel, even in the Deuteronomistic corpus (Deut 26:5-9; Josh 24:2-13). In the poetic passages, Sinai appears to be located south of Israel, in the region of Edom or Midian. It appears that YHWH was associated with a mountain in Midian even before the exodus, and this tradition is also reflected in the story of the burning bush in Exodus 3–4. The oldest poetic passages do not mention the giving of the law in connection with Sinai. In the Elohistic and Deuteronomistic traditions, the mountain where the law is revealed is called Horeb, which means "wilderness"—and may be understood as an unspecified mountain in the wilderness. It appears then that the book of Exodus draws on various old traditions, but it is difficult to say with any confidence when these traditions were combined.

The Burning Bush

There are in fact two revelations on a mountain in Exodus, first in Exodus 3–4 and then in Exodus 19–34. In the first episode, the mountain is called "Horeb, the mountain of God," but the Hebrew word for "bush" *(sᵉneh)* is a wordplay on Sinai. The mountain is located in Midian, which was east of the Gulf of Aqaba. The traditional site identified with Mount Sinai, in contrast, is Jebel Musa, in the Sinai peninsula, west of the Gulf of Aqaba. This identification can be traced back to the early Christian era. The actual location of the site

Fig. 5.1 The traditional site of Mount Sinai (Jebel Musa, in the Sinai Peninsula).

intended in Exodus is disputed. The context of the stories in Exodus would seem to require a location close to Egypt, so in the Sinai Peninsula rather than further east, but the association of Sinai with Midian and Edom requires the location east of Aqaba. It may be that the confusion arises from the combination of traditions that were originally independent, and that the theophanies at Sinai were not originally part of the exodus story.

The opening verses of Exodus 3 at once provide evidence that two sources, J and E, have been combined, and illustrate the difficulty of separating them: "Moses was keeping the flock of his father-in-law Jethro, the priest of Midian; he led his flock beyond the wilderness, and came to *Horeb the mountain of God* (E). There *the angel of the Lord* (J) appeared to him in a flame of fire out of a bush, ... When *the Lord* (J) saw that Moses had turned aside to see, *God* (E) called to him out of the bush ... and Moses hid his face for he was afraid to look at *God* (E)." It seems that J and E had two similar accounts of this incident, and that an editor spliced them together, but there is little to be gained by trying to pry them apart.

The most celebrated part of this passage is the exchange between Moses and God in 3:13-14. When Moses asks for God's name, he is told, "I am who I am" (Hebrew *ehyeh asher ehyeh*). The Greek translators of the Bible rendered this passage as *eimi ho ōn,* "I am the one who is." Beginning with Philo of Alexandria, around the time of Christ, countless generations of theologians argued that the God revealed to Moses was identical with absolute Being, in the sense in which that term was understood in Greek philosophy. The Greek translation became the foundation for a theological edifice that assumed that Greek philosophy and biblical revelation could be correlated and were two ways of getting at the same thing. Historically, however, it is impossible to find this meaning in the Hebrew text. Hebrew simply did not have a concept of Being, in the manner of Greek philosophy. This fact does not invalidate the theological correlation of the Bible with Greek philosophy, but neither does it give it any real support. No such correlation is envisioned in the Hebrew text.

The actual meaning of the Hebrew phrase is enigmatic. The proper Hebrew name for the God of Israel, Yahweh, can be understood as a form of the verb "to be"—specifically the causative (Hiphil) third person singular imperfect. It can be translated "he causes to be." It has been suggested that this name is a way of referring to a creator God. The Deity is often called "the Lord of hosts" (YHWH Sabaoth), and it has been suggested that this means "he causes the hosts (of heaven) to be" or "creator of the hosts." Whether the name was originally understood as a verbal form, however, is uncertain. It often appears in Hebrew names in the form *yahu* or *yaho,* which would not be so easily parsed. In Exodus 3, in any case, the association with the verb "to be" is assumed. The phrase "I am who I am" in effect changes the verbal form to the first person. The phrase may be taken as a refusal to divulge the divine name, in effect brushing off Moses' question. In favor of this suggestion is the fact that Jewish tradition is reluctant to pronounce the divine name. Rather, it substitutes *Adonai,* "the Lord." But elsewhere in Exodus the name YHWH is used freely, and it is explicitly revealed in the Priestly passage in Exodus 6. It may be that the passage is only an attempt to put the divine name YHWH, understood as a form of the verb "to be," in the first person.

In any case, Exodus 3 goes on to give a fuller explanation of the identity of the Deity. He is the God of the ancestors, the God of Abraham, Isaac, and Jacob. The key element, however, is what he promises to do in the future: "I will bring you up out of the misery of Egypt to the land of the Canaanites, the Hittites, the Amorites, the Perizzites, the Hivites, and the Jebusites," in effect fulfilling the promise to Abraham in Genesis 15. The Deity is motivated by the suffering of Israel: "I have observed the misery of my people who are in Egypt, I have heard their cry on account of their taskmasters. Indeed, I know their suffering and I have come down to deliver them" (Exod 3:7-8). YHWH may already have been worshiped in Midian as a god who appeared in fire on the mountain, but henceforth he would be worshiped as the God who delivered the Israelites from Egypt.

Exodus 6 contains a parallel account of the revelation of the divine name, from the Priestly source. Here Moses is told explicitly: "I am YHWH. I appeared to Abraham, Isaac, and Jacob as God Almighty, but by my name YHWH I did not make myself known to them" (6:2). For the Priestly tradition, as for the Elohist, this God was not known to the patriarchs by his proper name. The passage goes on to link the revelation of the name with the promise of liberation from slavery in Egypt. Again, there is an obvious sociopolitical dimension to this liberation. But it also involves a religious commitment: "I will take you as my people, and I will be your God" (6:7). The Israelites will no longer serve the Egyptians, but will serve YHWH instead.

The Liberation from Egypt

The Plagues

The process of liberation begins with the confrontation between Moses and Pharaoh in Exodus 7. Chapters 7–11 narrate a struggle between YHWH and Moses on the one side and the pharaoh on the other. YHWH hardens Pharaoh's heart so that he refuses to let Israel go. Then YHWH smites the Egyptians with a series of plagues. The basic narrative is from the J source, with supplementary additions from P.

The episode of the plagues shows that Exodus is not only the story of the liberation of Israel, but also the story of the defeat and humiliation of the Egyptians. The latter aspect of the story involves nationalistic, ethnic vengeance, which is less than edifying. The plagues affect not only Pharaoh and the taskmasters, but also, even especially, the common Egyptians, who also labored under Pharaoh. The most chilling plague is the slaughter of the firstborn: "Every firstborn son in the land of Egypt shall die, from the firstborn of Pharaoh who sits on the throne to the firstborn of the female slave who is behind the handmill to the firsborn of the livestock" (Exod 11:5). The demand for the death of the firstborn bespeaks the hungry God, whom we have already encountered in Genesis 22. The idea of a destructive force that can be averted by a sign on the doorpost (Exod 12:23) is folkloristic. Muslims have a similar rite, called *fidya*

Fig. 5.2   Ramesses II (1303–1213 B.C.E.); top portion of a granite statue from the Ramesseum in Egypt, now in the British Museum. Photo by the author.

or *fedu* (redemption). At least Exodus appreciates the depth of grief to which this gives rise, but in the end there is little sympathy for the Egyptians. Underlying this episode is the claim made in Exod 4:22-23 (J): "Thus says the LORD: Israel is my firstborn son. I said to you, 'Let my son go that he may worship me.' But you refused to let him go; now I will kill your firstborn son." The notion that Israel is the son of God is an important one, and we will meet it again. In the present context, however, it implies a stark claim of divine election that makes the Egyptians expendable.

The story of the plagues contains an interesting theological notion in the motif of the hardening of Pharaoh's heart. This motif is reflected in both J (Exod 4:21) and P (7:3) sources. God could presumably have softened Pharaoh's heart and had him release the Israelites. The hardening serves to justify the punishments that follow. Pharaoh is held responsible for his hard heart even though it was the Lord who hardened it. In much of the Hebrew Bible the one Lord is responsible for everything, good and bad. Later we will find that the Lord sends an evil spirit on Saul (1 Sam 16:14). Yet the fact that the Lord is in control in no way lessens human responsibility.

Another motif with interesting theological implications is found in Exod 7:1 (P), where God tells Moses: "I have made you a god to Pharaoh." (The NRSV softens the shock of this statement by translating "like a god.") In the context, the point is that Moses is the mouthpiece of God in his dealings with pharaoh. Later tradition, however, speculated that Moses enjoyed a status greater than human. For example, the Jewish philosopher Philo, at the turn of the era, wrote that Moses enjoyed a greater partnership with God than other people, "for he was named God and king of the entire nation" (Philo, *Life of Moses* 1.158). Usually the Hebrew Bible implies a wide gulf between humanity and divinity, but this is not always the case. Hebrew tradition allowed for the possibility that an exceptional person like Moses might be in some sense an *elohim*, "god," or "divine being."

The Passover

Before the Israelites depart from Egypt, they celebrate the Passover. This celebration is found only in the Priestly source. Just as P grounded the Sabbath in the story of creation, so it grounds the Passover in the story of the exodus. YHWH, we are told, "passed over" the houses where the Passover was being celebrated, and that were marked by blood on the doorposts and lintels, when he was smiting the firstborn of the Egyptians (Exod 12:23; the Hebrew verb *pasach*, translated as "passed over," has the same consonants as the name of the festival). The Passover was probably originally a rite of spring practiced by shepherds, but it was associated with the exodus before the Priestly account was composed. P provides the most detailed and explicit account in the Bible of the supposed origin of the Passover in the context of the exodus.

In early Israel, the Passover was a family festival. It is not included in the pilgrimage feasts in the oldest cultic calendars, in Exodus 23 and 34. It was also distinct from the Festival of Unleavened Bread (*Massot*). As we shall see when we discuss Deuteronomy, the celebration was changed by the reform of King Josiah in 621 B.C.E. Then it became a pilgrimage festival to be celebrated at the central sanctuary (Jerusalem) and was combined with the Festival of Unleavened Bread. It is also combined with Unleavened Bread in Exodus 12. Whether the Exodus account assumes that it is celebrated at a central shrine is more difficult to determine. The story is set in Egypt long before there was a temple of YHWH in Jerusalem. It would therefore be anachronistic to speak of a pilgrimage to a central shrine. What Exodus says is that the paschal lamb must be sacrificed by "the whole congregation of the assembly of Israel" (Exod 12:6). This formulation seems to imply that it is not just a family festival, although each family takes its own lamb, but is a collective celebration of the assembled people. It is probable, then, that the

Fig. 5.3 *Israelites Eating the Paschal Lamb on Passover* **by Marc Chagall (1931).** Art Resource, N.Y.
wikipaintings.org

Priestly writers have in mind a celebration at a central point. We shall return to this issue when we discuss the relationship between the Priestly and Deuteronomic sources.

The Crossing of the Sea

The story of the exodus reaches its narrative climax in the episode of the crossing of the sea. According to Exod 13:17-18 (usually ascribed to E), when Pharaoh let the people go, God did not lead them by way of the land of the Philistines, although it was shorter, but by a roundabout way in the desert, toward a body of water that is known in Hebrew as *yam sup*. The conventional translation, "Red Sea," derives from the Greek translation of the Bible, the Septuagint, which was then adopted by the

Latin Vulgate. In modern terms, the Red Sea is the body of water between Africa and the Arabian peninsula, ranging in width from 100 to 175 miles, which splits at its northern end into two gulfs, the Gulf of Suez (20–30 miles wide) between Egypt and the Sinai Peninsula, and the Gulf of Aqaba (east of the Sinai peninsula, 10–20 miles wide). The Hebrew expression *yam sup* is used several times in the Bible to refer to the Gulf of Aqaba (for example, in 1 Kgs 9:26 it is said to be in the land of Edom) and may refer to the Gulf of Suez on a few occasions (for example, in Exod 10:19, where God drives the locusts from Egypt into the *yam sup*). The Hebrew word *sup*, however, does not literally mean "red" but "reed," and some scholars have suggested that in the story of the exodus the *yam sup* was not a great sea but a reedy marsh or lake. The main route from Egypt to Canaan is called "the way of the land of the Philistines" anachronistically in Exodus 13, since the Philistines moved into the area only around the same time as the emergence of Israel. It is easy enough to see why fugitives would avoid this route, because of the presence of Egyptian patrols and border guards. It is difficult, however, to see why they would go toward the Gulf of Suez, still less the Gulf of Aqaba. For this reason, many people have found the suggestion of "the Sea of Reeds" attractive. The situation is further complicated by the fact that the sea of the exodus seems to be distinguished from the *yam sup* in Num 33:8-10 (which is part of the Priestly source but seems to use an old list).

The prose account of the crossing of the sea in Exodus 14 does not identify the sea in question. In 15:4, however, we are told that Pharaoh's officers were sunk in the *yam sup*. Exodus 15:1-18 is a hymn, which is generally believed to contain some of the oldest poetry in the Bible and to be older than the J and E sources. (The argument is based on the use of archaic expressions and similarity to Ugaritic poetry.) A summary form of the hymn is attributed to Moses' sister Miriam in 15:21. The hymn was evidently known in more than one form.

The basic hymn is found in 15:1-12, 18. Verses 13-17 are a later expansion, probably by a Deuteronomic editor, and change the focus of the hymn from the victory over Pharaoh to the triumphal march of Israel into the promised land. The hymn does not actually speak of people crossing through the sea and makes no mention of dry land. The central theme is how YHWH, the Lord, cast Pharaoh and his army into the depths of the sea. It is important to remember, however, that this is a hymn, not a ballad, and that its purpose is to praise God, not to describe a historical event. The imagery of sinking in water is used elsewhere in Hebrew poetry as a metaphor for a situation of distress. In Psalm 69 the psalmist prays:

> Save me, O God, for the waters have
>   come up to my neck.
> I sink in deep mire, where there is no
>   foothold
> I have come into deep waters and the
>   flood sweeps over me.

As the psalm goes on, however, it becomes clear that drowning is not the problem at all. Rather:

> More in number than the hairs of my
>   head are those who hate me without
>   cause;
> many are those who would destroy me,
>   my enemies who accuse me falsely.

Similarly, a psalm found in Jonah 3 says: "The waters closed in over me; weeds [Hebrew *sup*] were wrapped around my head at the roots of the mountains." (Jonah is supposedly in the belly of the great fish, but the psalm was not composed for that context.) In these cases, sinking in the depths is not a description of a physical condition, but simply a metaphor for distress. By analogy, we might suppose that the hymn in Exodus 15 is simply celebrating the defeat of Pharaoh. To say that he and his army sank in the depths like a stone is a metaphorical way of saying that they were completely defeated and destroyed. We do not actually know what defeat of Pharaoh was originally in question, or whether the hymn was composed to celebrate the exodus. It may have been a celebration of the withdrawal of Egypt from Canaan, or it may have had a specific battle in mind. It is poetic language, and it does not lend itself to the reconstruction of historical events.

The biblical prose writers, however, wanted to describe the overthrow of Pharaoh in more concrete, specific terms. The account in Exodus 14 is largely from the Priestly source, but a J account can be reconstructed (only a few verses are attributed to E). The J account reads as follows.

14:5b. The minds of Pharaoh and his officials were changed toward the people, and they said, "What have we done, letting Israel leave our service?" 6. So he had his chariot made ready, and took his army with him. 9. The Egyptians pursued them. 10. The Israelites looked back, and there were the Egyptians advancing on them, and they were in great fear. 13. But Moses said to the people, "Do not be afraid, stand firm, and see the deliverance that the Lord will accomplish for you today; for the Egyptians whom you see today you shall never see again. 14. The Lord will fight for you, and you have only to keep still."

19b. And the pillar of cloud moved from in front of them and took its place behind them. 20. It came between the army of Egypt and the army of Israel. And so the cloud was there with the darkness, and it lit up the night; one did not come near the other all night. 21. The Lord drove the sea back by a strong east wind all night, and turned the sea into dry land. 24 At the morning watch the Lord in the pillar of fire and cloud looked down upon the Egyptian army, and threw the Egyptian army into panic. 25b. The Egyptians said, "Let us flee from the Israelites, for the Lord is fighting for them against Egypt." 27. And at dawn the sea returned to its normal depth. As the Egyptians fled before it, the Lord tossed the Egyptians into the sea. 30. Thus the Lord saved Israel that day from the Egyptians and Israel saw the Egyptians dead on the seashore. 31. Israel saw the great work that the Lord did against the Egyptians. So the people feared the Lord and believed in the Lord and in his servant Moses.

Here again we are not told that the Israelites crossed the sea. We are left with the impression of a tidal wave, which returned and engulfed the Egyptians. One can imagine how this account might have been inferred from the poetry of Exodus 15. The Yahwist adds a few distinctive touches, such as the role of the pillar of cloud.

The Priestly account adds further embellishment to the story. Moses is told to stretch out his hand over the sea so that the waters are divided (cf. Gen 1:6-10, where God separates the waters and gathers the waters under the sky in one place so that dry land appears). The Israelites pass through, but then Moses again stretches out his hand and causes the waters to return on the pursuing Egyptians. This vivid account is the culmination of a long process. It should not be viewed as a historical memory but as one of a series of imaginative attempts to give concrete expression to the belief that YHWH had rescued his people and overthrown the Egyptians.

The sea imagery continues to exercise a powerful effect on the religious imagination of ancient Israel. As we saw in chapter 1, other ancient Near Eastern peoples had stories of combat between a god and the sea or a sea monster. The Ugaritic myth of Baal and Yamm is the one closest to the context of Israel. The battle between Marduk and Tiamat in the Babylonian *Enuma Elish* is also relevant. In the biblical psalms, too, we often find that YHWH is said to do battle with the sea. In Psalm 114 we are told that the sea looked and fled before the Lord. Psalm 77 also says that the waters were afraid, in view of the thunder and lightning of the Lord, as he led his people. One of the most vivid passages is found in Isa 51:9-11, where the prophet asks, "Was it not you who cut Rahab in pieces, who pierced the dragon? Was it not you who dried up the sea, the waters of the great deep, who made the depths of the sea a way for the redeemed to pass over?" Rahab and the dragon were sea monsters, supposedly defeated and slain by YHWH in the process of creation (although this story is never

narrated in the Bible). The exodus, in the view of the prophet, was an event of the same type. It would not be too much to say that the exodus was the creation myth of Israel, and that the sea imagery provided a powerful way to give expression to its mythic character. Just as the ancient Near Eastern myths provided

Fig. 5.4 **A Canaanite statuette of Baal, arm raised to strike; bronze, fourteenth century B.C.E.; in the Louvre.** Commons.wikimedia.org

paradigms, through which various events could be viewed and endowed with meaning, so the exodus became the paradigm for understanding later events in the history of Israel. We shall find that the prophets imagined a new exodus as a way in which Israel might start over and renew its relationship with its God. This motif becomes especially important after the Babylonian exile, either in the form of return from exile or of a final, eschatological deliverance.

One other theme in the accounts of the episode at the sea requires comment. The hymn in Exodus 15 declares, "YHWH is a warrior, YHWH is his name!" The idea that gods are warriors was a common one in the ancient Near East. A major reason why the early Israelites worshiped YHWH was that they believed he was a powerful warrior who could help them defeat their enemies (or simply defeat them on their behalf). Implicit in this image of God is an agonistic view of life, as an arena of constant conflict between competing forces. The book of Exodus makes no pretense that we should love our enemies. This view of God and of life was qualified in the later tradition to a considerable extent, but it has never been fully disavowed. It persists in the last book of the Christian Bible, the book of Revelation, where Jesus comes as a warrior from heaven to kill the wicked with the sword of his mouth (Revelation 19). Some people in the modern world may find the violence of such imagery repellent, but its power cannot be denied. In the context of the exodus, it is the power of God as warrior that gives hope to people in slavery and has continued to give hope to people suffering oppression down

through the centuries. Warrior-gods were also thought to act on behalf of the powerful, and in that case, the imagery can support an oppressive view of the world. In Exodus, however, the warrior God is on the side of the weak, and this imagery has continued to inspire and support liberation movements down to modern times.

Conclusion

In the end, very little can be said about the exodus as history. It is likely that some historical memory underlies the story, but the narrative as we have it is full of legendary details and lacks supporting evidence from archaeology or from nonbiblical sources. The story of the crossing of the sea seems to have arisen from attempts to fill out the allusions in the hymn preserved in Exodus 15. That hymn celebrates some defeat of a Pharaoh, but the references to drowning are poetic and cannot be pressed for historical information.

Regardless of its historical origin, however, the exodus story became the founding myth of Israel (especially in the northern kingdom) and of later Judaism. It is more important than any other biblical story for establishing Israelite and Jewish identity. It is repeatedly invoked as a point of reference in the Prophets, later in the Writings, and in the New Testament. It has served as a paradigm of liberation for numerous movements throughout Western history, from the Puritans to Latin America. It can fairly be regarded as one of the most influential, and greatest, stories in world literature.

FOR FURTHER READING

Commentaries

B. S. Childs, *The Book of Exodus* (OTL; Philadelphia: Westminster, 1974). Excellent discussion of form and redaction criticism. Also contains extensive discussion of history of interpretation and theological significance.

G. W. Coats, *Exodus 1–18* (FOTL 2A; Grand Rapids: Eerdmans, 1999). Technical form-critical commentary. Good for elucidating the structure of passages.

T. Dozeman, *Exodus* (Eerdmans Critical Commentary; Grand Rapids: Eerdmans, 2009). Detailed extensive commentary with attention to literary genres. Finds Deuteronomistic themes throughout Exodus.

M. Greenberg, *Understanding Exodus* (New York: Behrman, 1969). Sensitive commentary from a Jewish perspective.

C. Houtman, *Exodus* (4 vols.; Leuven: Peeters, 1993–2002). Comprehensive commentary. Assumes composite authorship but refrains from source-critical analysis.

C. Meyers, *Exodus* (New Cambridge Bible Commentary; Cambridge: Cambridge University Press, 2005). Affirms a core of reality in the story of Moses and the exodus, while acknowledging complex transmission.

M. Noth, *Exodus* (OTL; Philadelphia: Westminster, 1962). Classic commentary on the history of the traditions.

W. H. Propp, *Exodus 1–18* (AB 2; New York: Doubleday, 1998). Philological commentary. Exceptional for assigning much of Exodus to the E source.

Homiletically Oriented Commentaries

W. Brueggemann, "The Book of Exodus," *NIB* 1:677–981.

T. Fretheim, *Exodus* (Interpretation; Louisville: Westminster, 1991).

Historical Issues

J. Assmann, *Moses the Egyptian* (Cambridge: Harvard University Press, 1997). Discussion of the Akhenaten tradition as the background for Moses.

G. Davies, "Was There an Exodus?" in J. Day, ed., *In Search of Pre-Exilic Israel* (London: T&T Clark, 2004), 23–40. Qualified defense of the historicity of "some kind of Exodus."

W. Dever, *Who Were the Early Israelites and Where Did They Come From?* (Grand Rapids: Eerdmans, 2003), 7–21; forceful argument that the exodus is unverifiable.

I. Finkelstein and N. A. Silberman, *The Bible Unearthed: Archaeology's New Vision of Ancient Israel and the Origin of Its Sacred Texts* (New York: Free Press, 2001), 48–71. Skeptical view of the evidence for the historicity of the exodus.

E. S. Frerichs and L. H. Lesko, eds., *Exodus: The Egyptian Evidence* (Winona Lake, IN: Eisenbrauns, 1991). Useful discussion of the Egyptian background.

R. Hendel, *Remembering Abraham. Culture, Memory and History in the Hebrew Bible* (New York: Oxford University Press, 2005), 57–73. Exodus as cultural memory, preserving some historical elements.

J. K. Hoffmeier, *Israel in Egypt: The Evidence for the Authenticity of the Exodus Tradition* (New York: Oxford University Press, 1997). A conservative view of the historical evidence.

H. Shanks, W. G. Dever, B. Halpern, and P. K. McCarter, *The Rise of Ancient Israel* (Washington, DC: Biblical Archaeology Society, 1992). Useful presentation of the historical issues.

Religious and Literary Themes

B. Batto, *Slaying the Dragon* (Louisville: Westminster, 1992), 102–52. Exodus as myth.

F. M. Cross, *Canaanite Myth and Hebrew Epic* (Cambridge: Harvard University Press, 1973) 112–44. Classic discussion of the Song of the Sea in light of Canaanite myth.

T. B. Dozeman, *God at War: Power in the Exodus Tradition* (New York: Oxford University Press, 1996). Good analysis of Exodus 15.

Enduring Influence of the Exodus Story

J. J. Collins, *The Bible after Babel: Historical Criticism in a Postmodern Age* (Grand Rapids: Eerdmans, 2005), 53–74. Overview of debate over liberationist and postcolonial readings of Exodus.

E. Said, "Michael Walzer's 'Exodus and Revolution,' A Canaanite Reading," *Grand Street* 5 (Winter 1986): 86–106. Sharp critique of Walzer's evaluation of the Exodus.

M. Walzer, *Exodus and Revolution* (New York: Basic Books, 1984). Exodus as antimessianic paradigm for politics.

CHAPTER 6
The Revelation at Sinai

INTRODUCTION

The book of Exodus places the giving of God's laws to Israel at Mount Sinai. As we shall see in this chapter, these laws bear comparison with other ancient Near Eastern treaty forms. We will also observe the importance given to the theophany, or appearance of God, at Sinai; the nature of the laws of the covenant; and the dramatic account of the Israelites spurning God by crafting and offering worship to a golden calf.

As the story of the exodus is told in the book of Exodus, the episode at the sea is followed shortly by another manifestation of God's power at Mount Sinai. It is likely, as we have seen, that the traditions of Sinai and exodus were originally distinct, but in the Bible as we have it they are integrally related. Liberation, or salvation, has its fulfillment in the giving of the law, and the motivation for keeping the law is supplied by the memory of the exodus. This combination of history and law is essential to what we call the Sinai, or Mosaic, covenant. Unlike the covenant of God with Abraham, which was a free grant that required only faith on Abraham's part, the covenant with Israel at Mount Sinai is conditional. The blessings of the covenant are contingent on the observance of the law.

Treaty and Covenant

Much light has been thrown on the structure of the Sinai covenant by analogies with ancient Near Eastern treaties. A large corpus of such treaties, dating over a span of more than a thousand years, has come to light during the last century. Two clusters of these treaties are especially important: a group of Hittite treaties from the period 1500 to 1200 B.C.E. and a group of Assyrian treaties from the eighth century. These treaties are called *vassal* or *suzerainty* treaties. They are not made between equal partners, but involve the submission of one party (the vassal) to the other (the suzerain). While the individual treaties differ from each other in various ways, certain elements remain typical across the centuries.

The essential logic of the treaty is found in the second, third, and sixth elements. The heart of the treaty lies in the stipulations. These are supported by the recollection of the sequence of events that led up to the making of the treaty and by the prospect of blessings or curses to follow. The historical prologue is a distinctive feature of the Hittite treaties. The Assyrian treaties are distinguished by the prominence of the curses.

All the elements of this treaty form are paralleled in the Hebrew Bible, but they are scattered in various books. The most complete parallels are found in Deuteronomy, which also parallels the Assyrian treaties in matters of detail, as we shall see later in chapter 8. In the case of Exodus, the beginning of chapter 20 ("I am the LORD your God, who brought you out of the land of Egypt") combines the introductory preamble with a very brief historical prologue (in a sense, the whole story of the exodus is the historical prologue). The stipulations are amply represented by the Ten Commandments and other laws. Exodus, however, does not address the deposition of the document, the witnesses, or the curses and blessings. (All these elements are found in Deuteronomy.) It does not appear then that the Sinai revelation in Exodus follows the full form of the vassal treaties, although it resembles them in some respects.

The parallels with the Hittite treaties have been especially controversial, since they have potential implications for the date at which the covenant was conceived. The Hittites lived in Asia Minor, in what is now eastern Turkey. They were active in the area of Syria only in the Late Bronze Age (c. 1500–1200 B.C.E.), precisely the time in which Israel is thought to have emerged. At that time they challenged

---

The Hittite Treaty Form

The typical pattern in the Hittite treaties is as follows:

1. The *preamble,* in which the suzerain identifies himself ("I am Mursilis, the Sun, King of Hatti").

2. The *historical prologue,* or history that led up to the making of the treaty. In one such treaty the Hittite king Mursilis tells how he put his vassal, Duppi-Tessub, on his throne, despite his illness, and forced his brothers and subjects to take an oath of loyalty. Another recalls how the Hittites had conquered the land of Wilusa, and how it had never rebelled after that (*ANET* 203–5).

3. The *stipulations,* requirements, or terms of the treaty. These are often couched in highly personal terms. Hittite treaties demand that the subjects "protect the Sun [the Hittite king] as a friend" and report any "unfriendly" words that they hear about him. An Assyrian king, Esarhaddon, demands loyalty to his son Ashurbanipal by telling his subjects, "You will love as yourselves Ashurbanipal." It is essential to these treaties that the vassal "recognize no other lord" or not turn his eyes to anyone else.

4. There is provision for the *deposition or display of the text* of the treaty, and sometimes for its periodic recitation.

5. There is a list of *witnesses* consisting of the gods before whom the treaty oath is sworn.

6. Finally, there is a list of *curses and blessings* that indicate the consequences of observing or breaking the treaty.

Egypt for control of this region. If it could be shown that the Israelite conception of the covenant was modeled specifically on the Hittite treaties, then it would follow that the covenant was indeed a very early element in the religion of Israel. This argument was especially attractive to American scholars of the Albright school. Against this, the tradition of German scholarship viewed the covenant as a late development, fully articulated only in Deuteronomy and later writings.

The argument for Hittite influence rests primarily on the role of history in both Hittite and Israelite texts. Nothing is more characteristic of the Hebrew Bible than the repeated summaries of "salvation history." The primary examples of these summaries, however, are found in Deuteronomy and Deuteronomic texts (see, for example, Deut 6:21-25; 26:5-9; Josh 24:2-13) that are no earlier than the late seventh century B.C.E. Moreover, Deuteronomy has several clear parallels with Assyrian treaties of the eighth century B.C.E. It is possible that Israel developed its interest in the recitation of history independently of the Hittite treaties, and that the similarity in this respect is coincidental. At stake here is the choice between two very different views of the development of Israelite religion. On the account found in the Bible itself, the law was revealed to Moses at the beginning of Israel's history, in the course of the exodus from Egypt. Later generations of Israelites fell away from this Mosaic revelation, but it was recovered at the time of the Deuteronomic reform and became the basis for Second Temple Judaism. On the other view, which is held by many scholars, especially in the German tradition, the exodus was originally celebrated in itself as proof of God's election of Israel. Later the prophets

argued that election should entail responsibility, and this eventually led to the linking of the exodus and law, and the idea that God had made a conditional covenant with Israel. The choice between these two views of Israelite religion will make a difference in our reading of the prophetic books, where the issue is whether the prophets were appealing to an old tradition or were innovators in trying to focus the religion on ethical issues.

The treaty analogies throw some light on the Sinai covenant in any case. The demand for exclusive allegiance in Exod 20:3, "You shall have no other gods before me," is directly comparable to the demands that Hittite and Assyrian sovereigns made on their subjects. Also, the link between the exodus and Sinai in the existing text of Exodus is clear. The Israelites are obligated to obey the law because of what God has done for them in bringing them out of Egypt. The goal of liberation is not individual autonomy but a society regulated by the law revealed to Moses. The treaty analogies serve to underline the political and social character of biblical religion. The parallels between Exodus and the Hittite treaties are not so close, however, as to guarantee that this understanding of the relation between history and law was present already in the time of Moses or in the beginnings of Israelite history.

The Sinai Theophany

In fact, the immediate prologue to the giving of the law in Exodus is not a recitation of history but a description of a theophany (or manifestation of God) on Mount Sinai. We have seen already that Sinai was associated with

Fig. 6.1 Moses receives the tablets of the law and presents them to the people; from the illuminated Grandval-Bibel (ca. 840), now in the British Museum. Commons.wikimedia.org.

theophany before it became the mountain of the law. The account in Exodus 19 exploits the old tradition of YHWH appearing in fire on the mountain and uses it as the backdrop for the giving of the law.

Exodus 19 is clearly composite. Even a cursory reading of the text shows that Moses spends an undue amount of time going up and down the mountain. The separation of sources, however, has proven difficult. Verses 3-8 are generally agreed to be a Deuteronomic insertion. Only here is the word "covenant" used to characterize what happens at Sinai in Exodus 19. Verse 6, which speaks of a priestly kingdom and a holy nation, may derive from the P source. It is also agreed

that v. 2, which gives the stages of the journey to Sinai, is from P. Otherwise there is little agreement about the disposition of the sources. It should be noted, however, that much of the narrative has a cultic character. Much of it has to do with setting limits for the people. They are not to touch the mountain or go near a woman. Moses assumes the role of mediator, but at the end he is invited to bring up his brother Aaron, the priest. The emphasis on the holiness of the mountain and the need for the people to observe limits is a typical concern of the P tradition (we shall find similar priestly regulations later in Ezekiel 44). It seems likely that Priestly redactors have made a greater imprint on this material than was recognized by the traditional source critics. Of course, an interest in holiness and cultic restrictions was not unique to the P source, and the attribution of sources remains uncertain. It is more important for our purpose to recognize the cultic character of this material. This is no eyewitness account of events at Sinai, but a narrative about how people should behave in the presence of the divine that is constructed on the basis of cultic experience.

The revelation on Sinai is framed by another cultic passage in Exodus 24. Here again there are manifold signs of different hands; witness how often Moses is said to ascend the mountain. Some of the ritual is priestly, and the description of the glory (Hebrew *kabod*) of YHWH in vv. 15-18 is usually assigned to the P source. The reference to the "book of the covenant" in v. 7 is Deuteronomic. Verses 9-11, however, which say that seventy elders, as well as Moses, Aaron, Nadab, and Abihu, went up on the mountain and saw the God of Israel, is an old tradition.

It is remarkable for its blunt statement that "they saw the God of Israel" and yet lived. The usual biblical position is that humans cannot see God and live, but there are several notable exceptions in the prophetic literature (Isaiah 6; Ezekiel 1; the story of Micaiah ben Imlah in 1 Kings 22). All these texts, including Exodus 24, are important for the later development of Jewish mysticism. It is not clear here whether the elders are thought to have a meal in the presence of the Lord, in effect cementing the covenant by a communion ritual. The phrase "and they ate and drank" may be a way of saying that they continued to live. The composite text as it stands, in any case, tells how the covenant was sealed with a sacrifice. The blood of the covenant, splashed on the people and on the altar, signifies that the people are joined to God in a solemn agreement. The idea of the blood of the covenant becomes important in the New Testament in connection with the interpretation of the death of Jesus as a sacrifice.

The Laws of the Covenant

In between the theophany on the mountain in chapter 19 and the sacrifices in chapter 24 are two bodies of laws, which constitute, in effect, the stipulations of the covenant. First, there is the Decalogue, or Ten Commandments, in Exodus 20, and this is followed by the so-called Book of the Covenant in chapters 21–23. These two groups of laws are different in kind. The Decalogue is apodictic law: it consists of absolute commandments or (more often) prohibitions, with no conditional qualifications: "you shall not murder, steal," and so on. The Book of the Covenant, in contrast, is casuistic law, of the type "if x, then y." There was a long-standing legal tradition in the ancient Near East, reaching back to the end of the third millennium B.C.E. Famous law codes were associated with the names of the Mesopotamian kings Ur-Nammu (twenty-first century B.C.E.), Lipit-Ishtar (twentieth century), and Hammurabi (eighteenth century). These great law codes are made up primarily of casuistic laws. At one time it was thought that apodictic law was distinctively Israelite, but this position cannot be maintained. The apodictic form seems to be well suited to proclamation in a cultic setting. The casuistic law is more indicative of the actual practice of law.

The Decalogue

The Ten Commandments as found in Exodus 20 are usually attributed to the E source of the Pentateuch. Another series of laws in Exod 34:11-26 is called "the Yahwist Decalogue," although it is clearly not a decalogue. (It is now judged to be a late redactional text.) The closest parallel to Exodus 20 is found in Deut 5:6-21. Other lists of commandments that partially overlap the Decalogue are found in Lev 19:1-18 and Deut 27:15-26. The requirements of the covenant are said to be "ten words" in Exod 34:28; Deut 4:13; 10:4. There is some variation in the way that the Ten Commandments are counted. Jewish tradition distinguishes five positive commandments (down to honoring parents) and five negative. Christian tradition generally distinguishes between obligations to God and obligations to one's neighbor. In some Christian traditions (Catholic, Anglican, Lutheran) the obligations to God are counted as three. (The prohibition of idolatry is subsumed under the first commandment). A distinction is made between coveting one's neighbor's wife and coveting other property. The Reformed tradition groups the commandments as four and six, distinguishing the prohibition of idolatry and regarding the prohibition of coveting as a single commandment. This division of the commandments seems to be most in line with the text of Exodus.

Different lists of the Ten Commandments

Jewish and different Christian traditions number the Ten Commandments differently. The lists contain the same commands.

Jewish Tradition	Catholic, Anglican, and Lutheran Traditions	Reformed Tradition
1. I am the LORD your God who brought you out of Egypt:	1. I am the LORD your God who brought you out of the land of Egypt. You shall have no other gods before me and shall not worship other gods.	1. You shall have no other gods before me.
2. You shall have no other gods before me.	2. You shall not take the name of the LORD in vain.	2. You shall not make any idols (graven images).
3. You shall not take the name of the LORD your GOD in vain.	3. Remember the Sabbath day, to keep it holy.	3. You shall not take the name of the LORD in vain.
4. Remember the Sabbath day, to keep it holy.	4. Honor your father and mother.	4. Remember the Sabbath day, to keep it holy.
5. Honor your father and mother.	5. You shall not kill.	5. Honor your father and mother.
6. You shall not murder.	6. You shall not commit adultery.	6. You shall not kill.
7. You shall not commit adultery.	7. You shall not steal.	7. You shall not commit adultery.
8. You shall not steal.	8. You shall not bear false witness.	8. You shall not steal.
9. You shall not bear false witness.	9. You shall not covet your neighbor's wife.	9. You shall not bear false witness.
10. You shall not covet.	10. You shall not covet your neighbor's house or goods.	10. You shall not covet.

The first four commandments, then, deal with Israel's obligations to YHWH. The first forbids the worship of any other gods. This is not yet monotheism: the existence of other gods is not denied. (The biblical demand that only one god be worshiped is sometimes called henotheism.) Around the time of the Babylonian exile we shall find stronger assertions that YHWH is the only true God, in the prophet we call Second Isaiah, but strict monotheism is developed only in the Hellenistic period, under the influence of Greek philosophy. The prohibition is directly analogous to the requirement in the treaty texts that the vassals serve no other overlord. The restriction of worship to one god was exceptional in the ancient world. The only analogy is found in the so-called Aten heresy in Egypt, when Pharaoh Ahkenaten suppressed the worship of all gods except Aten, the Sun Disk (see chapter 1 above). Many people have supposed that Moses was influenced by the tradition of Akhenaten, but the influence is difficult to demonstrate. Solar imagery is sometimes used for YHWH, but he is not identified with the sun in the way that Aten was. The imagery of YHWH's manifestation on Mount Sinai is much closer to the tradition of the Canaanite god Baal than to that of the Egyptian deity. Egyptian influence on the idea of monotheism cannot be ruled out, but it does not explain very much of the Israelite conception of God.

The rejection of all gods except YHWH was a revolutionary move, whether in the context of ancient Egypt or that of ancient Canaan, all the more so because it forbade the worship of any goddess in Israel. Historically, it served to distinguish Israel most immediately from its Canaanite neighbors. It is clear from the Bible that this distinction was not easy to

Fig. 6.2   King Akhenaten and Queen Nefertiti offer worship to the sun god Aten. Painted relief from Amarna. Commons.wikimedia.org

maintain. Other deities besides YHWH were in fact worshiped in ancient Israel. The prophets and the Deuteronomistic History repeatedly condemn the Israelites for worshiping the Canaanite Baal, the god of fertility. The biblical texts usually imply that there was a clear choice between Baal and YHWH, but in fact many people may have seen no problem in worshiping both. Moreover, we now know that the well-known Canaanite goddess Asherah was worshiped in Judah in connection with YHWH. An inscription found in a tomb at Khirbet el-Qom, near Hebron, south of Jerusalem, in 1968 reads as follows:

Uriyahu the Prince; this is his inscription.
May Uriyahu be blessed by YHWH,
From his enemies he has saved him by
    his Asherah.

The inscription dates from the eighth century B.C.E. A similar inscription was found at Kuntillet Ajrud, a stopover for caravans in the Sinai desert, in 1978. This one is on a storage jar and also dates from the eighth century B.C.E. It is a blessing formula, ending with the words "by YHWH of Samaria and his Asherah." Many scholars deny that Asherah in these inscriptions is the name of a goddess, since the possessive pronoun is not normally used with a proper name. They suggest that the reference is to a wooden image of some kind, a pole or tree, that is mentioned some forty times in the Hebrew Bible. But the wooden image was a symbol of the goddess Asherah, and so the inscriptions testify to the veneration of the goddess in any case. Moreover, more than two thousand figurines of a nude female figure, presumably a fertility goddess, have been found throughout the land of Israel by archaeologists. We also know that a goddess called Anat-Yahu (YHWH's Anat) was venerated by a Jewish community in Elephantine in southern Egypt in the fifth century B.C.E. There can be little doubt that these Jews preserved a cult that they had already practiced in the land of Israel before they immigrated to Egypt.

In light of this evidence, there is some doubt as to whether the demand that Israel worship only YHWH really goes back to the beginning of Israel in the time of Moses. The prophets in the ninth and eighth centuries who demanded the worship of YHWH alone seem to have been a minority. It is possible that the restriction of worship to one god was the result of the preaching of these prophets, and so a relatively late development. But there is no hard evidence for the date of this commandment.

Fig. 6.3 Images painted on a jar found at Kuntillet Ajrud which bears the inscription "YHWH of Samaria and his Asherah."

Neither is there any hard evidence for the date of the second commandment, which forbids the making of idols or images. This commandment complements the previous one, since images played an essential part in the worship of pagan deities. Worshipers in the ancient world did not think that the image was actually a god or goddess, although biblical writers often caricature them in this way (see especially Isa 44:9-20). The Deuteronomistic History in 1 Kings 12 accuses Jeroboam I, the king who seceded from Jerusalem and founded the kingdom of northern Israel, of idolatry by setting up golden calves at the temples at Bethel and Dan, and telling the people: "Here is your god who brought you up out of the land of Egypt" (1 Kgs 12:28). It is unlikely, however, that Jeroboam wanted his people to worship the statues. Rather, as was usual in the ancient Near East, the statue was where the god manifested his presence. In the cult in Jerusalem in the period of the kingdoms there were statues of cherubim, the mythical creatures of Near Eastern art, part human, part animal, part bird. YHWH was thought to be enthroned above the cherubim. The golden calves set up by Jeroboam may also have been supposed to be the thrones of YHWH, rather than the Deity himself. The existence of the golden calves, and of the cherubim, shows that neither Israelite nor Judahite religion completely renounced the making of images. Human figures are portrayed on the jar from Kuntillet Ajrud that carries the inscription referring to YHWH and his Asherah. At some point, the making of images of other deities was forbidden, and we have no

Fig. 6.4 Standing stones and the figure of a devotee from a cult shrine in Hazor, as reconstructed in the Hazor Museum, Israel. Commons.wikimedia.org

evidence that YHWH was ever represented by images or statues. The prohibition in Exod 20:4 refers in the first instance to an image carved from wood or stone. Exodus 20:23 forbids the making of gods of silver and gold. It has been suggested that the origin of this opposition to images lay in an old tradition whereby the deity was represented by standing stones, which were not carved or sculpted. Later the commandment is even extended metaphorically to exclude overly specific interpretations of the divine being.

Verses 5-6 reinforce the prohibition of images: "For I the LORD am a jealous God, punishing children for the iniquity of parents, to the third and fourth generation of those who reject me, but showing steadfast love to the thousandth generation of those who love me and keep my commandments." The jealousy of YHWH is a recurring motif in the Hebrew Bible. The idea that God might punish children for the sins of their parents would later be called into question by the prophet Ezekiel (Ezekiel 18).

The third commandment, prohibiting wrongful use of YHWH's name, refers especially to false or frivolous oaths, considered as an affront to the Deity.

The fourth commandment requires observance of the Sabbath day. The name is derived from a Hebrew verb meaning "to rest." The weekly day of rest would become a distinctive characteristic of Judaism and a subject of mockery among some pagans in antiquity who thought it a sign of laziness. The origin of the custom is unknown. In ancient Babylon, the Akkadian word *shappatu* designated the middle day of the month, the festival of the full moon. The Sabbath is associated with the festival of the new moon in Amos 8:5

and Isa 1:13. It may be that the Sabbath was originally linked to the waxing and waning of the moon, but in the Bible it is independent of the lunar calendar. The rationale given for the observance of the Sabbath in Exodus 20 derives from the Priestly source and links it to the account of creation in Genesis 1.

The remaining commandments concern relations in human society. All societies have laws governing such matters as these. The Bible is distinctive only in the solemnity with which they are proclaimed.

The command to honor father and mother is a staple element of Near Eastern wisdom literature, as we shall see in Proverbs and Ben Sira.

The sixth commandment is usually translated "You shall not kill," but it is clear from the following chapters that a blanket prohibition on all forms of killing is not intended. The Hebrew verb *ratsach* is often used for murder, but also sometimes for unintentional killing. The effect of this law is not to prevent all killing, but to regulate the taking of life and to make it subject to community control.

The prohibition of adultery is concerned with violations of marriage; it does not encompass other kinds of fornication and is distinguished from them elsewhere in biblical law. One should keep in mind that polygamy was permitted in ancient Israel (Solomon was the most famous practitioner). Either men or women could be guilty of adultery, but the man offended against the husband of his partner in sin, while the woman offended against her own husband. Adultery is the subject of several biblical stories. Recall the shock of Abimelech that he might have inadvertently committed adultery against Isaac, and Joseph's virtuous rejection of Potiphar's wife. Warnings

against adultery figure prominently in the wisdom literature, especially in Proverbs 1–9.

The commandment against stealing does not offer any specification of what is stolen. Some scholars have argued that it was originally concerned with stealing persons (kidnapping), but the commandment as it stands is more general.

The importance of truth in witnessing is illustrated by those cases where someone is put to death on the basis of false witness (e.g., the story of Naboth's vineyard in 1 Kings 21). Later laws warn that no one should be put to death on the word of just one witness (Num 35:30; Deut 19:15).

Finally, the tenth commandment supplements the injunctions against adultery and stealing by forbidding even the coveting of another's goods. The most notable aspect of this commandment is surely the inclusion of the neighbor's wife along with his slaves and his ox and donkey. We need not conclude from this that adultery was considered only a property offense. It was also regarded as shameful and an offense against God. But there is no doubt that it was also regarded as a property offense.

The Book of the Covenant

The sweeping, general prohibitions of the Decalogue are followed by a collection of casuistic laws, known as "the book of the covenant" (cf. Exod 24:7). (There are also some apodictic laws in this section.) These laws are more indicative than the Decalogue of the ways in which law was actually practiced in ancient Israel. They qualify the apparent absolute character of the apodictic laws. For example, we are given several cases where killing is permissible, or even commanded, despite the apparent finality of the sixth commandment. It is apparent that these laws were formulated in a settled, agrarian, community; they are not the laws of nomads wandering in the wilderness. We do not know exactly when they were formulated. They are clearly presupposed in Deuteronomy but could have originated either in the premonarchic tribes or in the early monarchy. Various scholars have argued that these laws should be associated with the setting up of the northern kingdom by Jeroboam I in the late tenth century B.C.E. or with the reform of King Hezekiah of Judah in the late eighth, but such suggestions, however plausible they may seem, are only conjectures.

It is not my purpose to comment on all these laws, but to discuss a few illustrative cases. The first issue raised may surprise the reader in the context of the exodus: "When you buy a Hebrew slave. . . ." If Israel had its origin in liberation from slavery, how could buying a Hebrew slave be condoned? But in fact, slavery is taken for granted and remains a problem in varying degrees right through the biblical corpus, including the New Testament (see the Epistle to Philemon). The most common cause of enslavement in the ancient world was debt: people who could not pay their debts were forced to sell their children, or themselves, into slavery. Prisoners taken in battle were also often sold into slavery. From early times, people in the ancient Near East saw the need to set some limits to debt slavery. Babylonian kings traditionally proclaimed an act of "justice" or "equity" (*misarum*) at the beginning of their reigns and at intervals of seven or more years thereafter, remitting debts and causing landholdings to revert to their original owners.

We have an example of such a proclamation in the Edict of Ammisaduqa, a king of Babylon in the seventeenth century B.C.E. (*ANET*, 526–28). It includes a provision for the release of slaves who had sold themselves or their families into slavery. It goes on to state that this does not apply to people who were born in servitude. The law in Exodus is more systematic, insofar as it is not a one-time liberation at the pleasure of the king, but provides that the service of Hebrew slaves be always limited to six years. No such limit is imposed in the case of foreign slaves. Moreover, if the master gives the slave a wife, she and her children remain the master's property, and the slave may decline his liberty because of his family ties. The biblical law, then, is only a modest advance over the Near Eastern precedent. Moreover, women who have been sold into slavery are not granted the same right of liberation after six years. They are granted rights, however, and are entitled to their freedom if these rights are denied. These laws on slavery are revised and liberalized somewhat in Deuteronomy 15 (the distinction between men and women is erased), but the institution of slavery is not questioned.

The rights of slaves are again at issue in Exod 21:20. An owner who beats a slave to death is liable to punishment, but only if the slave dies immediately. Here, as in the laws just discussed, there seems to be an attempt to balance the rights of the slave with the interests of the slave owners. The casuistic form of the laws suggests that they resulted from a process of negotiation. There is an evident concern for the rights of slaves and other people who are vulnerable in society, but there are also compromises with the conventions of society. We do not know how far these laws were ever enforced, but they are designed to be realistic and practical in the society of their time; they are not purely idealistic.

In general, the laws of Exodus stand in the legal tradition of the ancient Near East. The classic example is the case of the ox that gores (Exod 21:28). Laws on this subject are found in the codes of Eshnunna (§§53–54) and Hammurabi (§§250–51) in the early second millennium B.C.E. The Mesopotamian codes differ from the biblical one in placing greater emphasis on monetary compensation. The biblical law requires that an ox that kills a person be stoned and its flesh not eaten, as if the action of the animal had made it taboo. If an ox kills another ox, the price of the live ox and the meat of the dead ox must be divided (Exod 21:35). This prescription corresponds exactly to the Code of Eshnunna §53.

Fig. 6.5 Hammurabi, king of Babylon, receives the law (the Code of Hammurabi) from the god Marduk; detail from a basalt stele; now in the Louvre. Commons.wikimedia.org.

Several laws in this collection deal with the consequences of violence. The most famous is undoubtedly that found in Exod 21:22-25. The first part of this law relates to the case where people who are fighting injure a pregnant woman so that she suffers a miscarriage. This law was later interpreted as prohibiting abortion, a subject that is not otherwise addressed in the biblical laws. The discussion in Exodus goes on to enunciate a general principle: "If any harm follows, then you shall give life for life, eye for eye, tooth for tooth, hand for hand, foot for foot, burn for burn, wound for wound, stripe for stripe." This law has often been derided for inculcating a spirit of vengefulness. In the Sermon on the Mount in the Gospel of Matthew, Jesus cites this law as an example of the old order that he is superseding: "But I say to you, Do not resist any evildoer, but if anyone strikes you on the right cheek, turn the other also" (Matt 5:38-39). But Jesus was enunciating a moral ideal; he was not legislating for a community. Taken in context, "an eye for an eye" is not vengefulness, but moderation. The point is that you may not kill someone who knocks out your eye. In the words of Gilbert and Sullivan's *Mikado*, the object all sublime is to make the punishment fit the crime.

The modern reader cannot fail to be struck by the frequency with which the death penalty is prescribed in these laws. Examples include striking father or mother, or cursing them. It is unlikely that the death penalty was enforced in all these cases, but the laws project a sense of severity. The Jewish historian Josephus, writing at the end of the first century C.E., was proud of this severity and claimed that it showed the superiority of Jewish law to that of the Greeks. Modern reformers who reject the death penalty find no support here, but this is only one of many examples that could be given of the gulf that divides ancient and modern sensibilities on ethical issues.

Several other laws require a brief comment. Exodus 22:16 stipulates that if a man seduces a virgin, he must pay the bride-price for her and make her his wife. The woman is not consulted as to her feelings. The issue is primarily an economic one. A woman who has been defiled would not be able to find another husband (compare the story of the rape of Dinah in Genesis 34).

Exodus 22:21 forbids Israelites to oppress a resident alien, "for you were aliens in the land of Egypt" (so also 23:9). The appeal to the experience in Egypt is exceptional in the Book of the Covenant but is typical of Deuteronomy. The law protecting the poor from their creditors (22:21) is also similar in spirit to Deuteronomy, but there is no reason why such sentiments could not also be found in the older law code. Compare the commands to help the animal of one's enemy in Exod 23:4-5.

Exodus 22:28, "You shall not revile god," uses the Hebrew word 'elohim, which is a plural form, for "God." The Greek translators rendered it by the plural "gods." The philosopher Philo of Alexandria, writing in the first half of the first century c.e., inferred from this that Israelites were forbidden to revile the gods of other peoples lest the Gentiles be incited to revile the God of Israel in return.

We have already commented on 22:29, "The firstborn of your sons you shall give to me," in connection with the sacrifice of Isaac in Genesis 22. The context is the need to give thanks to God by offering the firstfruits, whether of the harvest or of the womb. In Exod 34:20 this commandment is qualified;

the firstborn son must be redeemed by offering something else in his place. This qualification is not found in Exodus 22. It is difficult to believe that any society would systematically require the sacrifice of the firstborn sons, but it may have been proposed as an ideal in early Israel.

The need to give thanks by giving back to God underlies the cultic regulations in Exodus 23. The Sabbath law is spelled out in 23:12. The motivation that is given is practical: so that people and livestock may be refreshed. Similarly the land is to be allowed to rest every seventh year. It is possible that the law in Exodus could be interpreted in terms of rotation of fields—not all the land need lie fallow at the same time. Later, however, this law is clearly taken to refer to a general practice in fixed years.

The cultic calendar in 23:14-17 specifies three major feasts. These were occasions when the males were to "appear before the Lord" by going to a sanctuary. The Hebrew word for such a pilgrimage feast is chag, which is related to the Arabic name for the Muslim pilgrimage to Mecca, the haj. The first is the Festival of Unleavened Bread (massot), which marked the beginning of the barley harvest. The new bread was eaten without leaven, that is, without anything from the harvest of the previous year. It should be noted that this festival was not yet linked with the Passover in the Book of the Covenant. Passover was not a pilgrimage festival but was celebrated in the home. The second festival is here called the harvest festival, and is related to the wheat harvest. It is later known as the Feast of Weeks. Finally, the third festival was that of Tabernacles, or Sukkoth, at the end of the year (in ancient Israel, the year began and ended in the fall).

This was the most important and joyful of the three festivals. In Leviticus it is called simply "the feast of YHWH." In Exodus 23 it is called the festival of ingathering. This was the celebration when all the produce of the fields had been gathered in, including the grapes that were used to make wine.

This cultic calendar will be developed and modified in later biblical law codes. Here we need note only the preponderantly agricultural character of the festivals. Each of them is an occasion for giving thanks to God after a harvest. This is not the calendar of tribes wandering in the desert, but of an agricultural people settled in their land.

One final law must be noted because of its far-reaching effect on later Jewish life: "You shall not boil a kid in its mother's milk" (23:19). It is because of this law that Jews do not combine meat and dairy products in the same meal. No reason is given for the prohibition. Some scholars have speculated that it was intended to reject a Canaanite ritual, and a text from Ugarit was thought to lend support to this view, but it is now clear that the text does not refer to cooking a kid at all. The most plausible explanation of the commandment is the intuitive one: to cook a kid in its mother's milk is unnatural and violates the life-giving character of mother's milk. In this case, as in the laws protecting aliens and the poor, the Covenant Code shows a humane spirit that we will find amplified later in Deuteronomy.

The Golden Calf and the Second Giving of the Law

Another formulation of the laws given at Sinai is found in Exodus 34, especially in vv. 17-26.

This passage is sometimes called the J Decalogue, although it is plainly not a decalogue (despite the reference to "ten words" in 34:28). It is also sometimes called the ritual decalogue because of the prominence of laws concerning cult and sacrifice. It clearly duplicates the laws of Exodus 20–23 at some points. It is now judged to be a late adaptation of earlier texts.

The occasion for the second giving of the law is provided by the story of the golden calf in Exodus 32. The division of sources in this chapter is problematic. It is agreed that 32:7-14 is a Deuteronomic addition, but this passage does not concern the main story line. The remainder of the narrative is variously attributed to J or E, and the confusion springs from conflicting indications in the text. On the one hand, it is extraordinary that Aaron, brother of Moses and high priest, is said to take the lead in making an idol for the people. Aaron was regarded in later tradition as the ancestor of the priestly line that officiated in the Jerusalem temple. The story implicating him in idolatry can only have been composed as a polemic against the Jerusalem temple and its priesthood. This points to a northern origin for this part of the story and would make good sense as part of the E narrative. On the other hand, the golden calf recalls the foundation of the northern kingdom by Jeroboam, after the death of Solomon. In 1 Kgs 12:28-29 we are told that the king "made two calves of gold" and said to the people: "You have gone up to Jerusalem long enough. Here are your gods, O Israel, who brought you up out of the land of Egypt." This is exactly how the people acclaim the golden calf in Exod 32:4. (Neither story actually involves the worship of any god other than YHWH. The plural "gods" reflects the Hebrew word 'elohim, which has a plural

Fig. 6.6 The worship of the golden calf, depicted in a fresco from the walls of the third-century C.E. synagogue at Dura-Europos. Commons.wikimedia.org

form but is also used for God in the singular.) The calves set up by Jeroboam were probably thought of as pedestals, on which the invisible Deity stood, but they are derided as idols in the Deuteronomistic History. Since the golden calf is regarded as an idol in Exodus 32 as well, this story also throws a negative light on the cult established by Jeroboam. Polemic against the northern cult points to an origin in the southern kingdom of Judah. Most probably, the story has been edited more than once. Perhaps a story that was originally intended to condemn the golden calf was revised by a northern editor so as to place the original blame on Aaron, who was revered in the south. As the story now stands, it implies criticism both of the cult that developed in the northern kingdom and of the Aaronic priesthood that flourished in Jerusalem.

The story is also remarkably severe in its tone. The statement that "the people sat down to eat and drink and rose up to play" is cited in the New Testament (1 Cor 10:7) as a paradigm of dissolute behavior that leads to judgment. Even though the celebration is said to be "a festival to the LORD" (Exod 32:5), Moses is enraged by the reveling as well as by the golden calf. The Levites rally to his support and put out the celebration by killing "brother, friend, and neighbor" (32:27). The Levites were the country clergy who served the rural shrines, especially in northern Israel. As we shall see when we discuss Deuteronomy, they were later displaced when the country shrines were suppressed and worship was centralized in Jerusalem, and they were made subordinate to the Aaronide priesthood. Exodus 32 can be read in part as the revenge of the Levites on the line of Aaron. Here the Levites are the true followers of YHWH, and Aaron is the apostate. Indeed, there is little doubt that the Levites were traditionally zealous supporters of the cult of YHWH. The kind of zeal that they exhibit here will be illustrated in Numbers 25, where a priest named Phinehas takes the lead in killing Israelites who have participated in the cult of Baal. YHWH, as we are told in Exod 20:5, is a jealous God. Intolerance of deviant behavior is deeply ingrained in the religion of ancient Israel and in the

Hebrew Scriptures that were accepted as the Old Testament by Christianity.

But there is also a different side of this God, and it is emphasized in Exod 34:6-7, where Moses addresses him in this way: "The LORD, the LORD, a God merciful and gracious, slow to anger, and abounding in steadfast love and faithfulness, keeping steadfast love for the thousandth generation, forgiving iniquity and transgression and sin." This formula is often repeated in the Hebrew Bible (e.g., Num 14:18; Ps 86:15; Neh 9:17) and is one of the central affirmations about God in the biblical tradition. It does not negate the "jealous" character of God, but it qualifies it. It should be noted that the biblical portrayal of God is not unique in the ancient world. A Babylonian prayer to Marduk addresses him as "warrior Marduk, whose anger is the deluge, whose relenting is that of a merciful father" (B. R. Foster, *From Distant Days* [Bethesda, MD: CDL, 1995], 247).

Yet another aspect of the deity is addressed in Exodus 33. This is the elusiveness of the divine presence. In 33:7 we are told that Moses pitched the tent of meeting outside the camp, and that everyone who sought the Lord would go out to it. This is surprising, since much of the second half of the book of Exodus is concerned with the setting up of it "the tabernacle of the tent of meeting," but this is not finally set up until chapter 40. The passage in chapter 33 evidently reflects an older tradition, which involved a less elaborate tent. That it is removed from the camp is significant, as the narrative puts some distance between God and the Israelites. They are told that God will not go with them on their journey to the promised land (33:1-3), but in v. 15 this is qualified, so that his "presence" will go with them. Again, Moses is permitted to see God from behind, but not his face, for no one can see God and live. (We shall find, nonetheless, that some prophets, such as Isaiah, claim boldly to have seen the Lord.) In traditional theological language, the narrative is trying to balance the transcendence and immanence of God—to affirm that God is present while keeping in mind the mysterious nature of that presence. In the narratives about Sinai, God's presence is usually indicated by a cloud. We shall find further refinements of this problem in the Priestly and Deuteronomic writings.

The laws in Exodus 34 duplicate some items from Exodus 20–23 but also modify them at some points. The commandments are interspersed with the cultic calendar. The most significant variation from the earlier laws is that 34:20 says explicitly that "the firstborn of your sons you shall redeem." Unlike 22:29, it does not leave open the question of child sacrifice.

Much of the second half of Exodus is taken up with the account of the tabernacle. Since this material is an integral part of the Priestly cultic system described in Leviticus, we shall defer its discussion to the following chapter.

FOR FURTHER READING

Commentaries

See Chapter 5.

W. H. Propp, *Exodus 19–40* (AB 2A; New York: Doubleday, 2006). Detailed philological commentary.

Other Studies

Sinai pericope

F. M. Cross, *Canaanite Myth and Hebrew Epic* (Cambridge: Harvard University Press, 1973), 145–94. Rich use of Canaanite parallels.

F. Crüsemann, *The Torah: Theology and Social History of Old Testament Law* (Trans. A. W. Mahnke; Minneapolis: Fortress Press, 1996), 27–57. Analysis of literary strata in Exodus 19–24. Posits ultimate shaping by Deuteronomists.

T. B. Dozeman, *God on the Mountain* (SBLMS 37; Atlanta: Scholars Press, 1989). Careful discussion of the various traditions in Exodus 19–24.

Covenant

G. Beckman, *Hittite Diplomatic Texts* (SBLWAW 7; Atlanta: Scholars Press, 1996), 11–118. Extensive collection of Hittite treaties.

J. D. Levenson, *Sinai and Zion: An Entry into the Jewish Bible* (Minneapolis: Winston, 1985), 15–86. Lucid exposition of the analogy between treaty and covenant.

D. J. McCarthy, *Treaty and Covenant* (2nd ed.; AnBib 21A; Rome: Biblical Institute Press, 1981). Balanced discussion of Hittite and Assyrian treaties.

G. E. Mendenhall, *Law and Covenant in Israel and the Ancient Near East* (Pittsburgh: Presbyterian Board of Colportage of Western Pennsylvania, 1955). Influential pioneering demonstration of the parallels between the Mosaic covenant and the Hittite treaties.

Near Eastern law codes

ANET, 159–201.

M. T. Roth, *Law Collections from Mesopotamia and Asia Minor* (SBLWAW 6; Atlanta: SBL, 1997).

Biblical law

A. Alt, "The Origins of Israelite Law," in idem, *Essays on Old Testament History and Religion* (Trans. R. A. Wilson; Garden City, NY; Doubleday, 1968), 101–71. Influential distinction of apodictic and casuistic law.

R. E. Friedman and S. Dolansky, *The Bible Now* (New York: Oxford University Press, 2011). Excellent discussion of what the Bible says, and does not say, about ethical issues that are now controversial.

S. Gesundheit. *Three Times a Year* (FAT 82; Tübingen: Mohr Siebeck, 2012). Study of the festal legislation of the Pentateuch. Demonstrates late redactional origin of Exodus 34.

W. Harrelson, *The Ten Commandments and Human Rights* (Macon, GA: Macon University Press, 1997). Discussion of the lasting significance of the Ten Commandments.

D. A. Knight, *Law, Power, and Justice in Ancient Israel* (Louisville: Westminster John Knox, 2011). Good discussion of social settings of law, informed by legal theory. Argues that there were no law codes in Israel or Judah before the Persian period.

B. M. Levinson, "Is the Covenant Code an Exilic Composition? A Response to John Van Seters," in J. Day, ed., *In Search of Pre-Exilic Israel: Proceedings of the Oxford Old Testament Seminar* (JSOT Sup 406; London: T & T Clark, 2004), 272–325. Lucid defense of the pre-Deuteronomic origin of the Covenant Code.

———, *Theory and Method in Biblical and Cuneiform Law* (JSOTSup 181; Sheffield: JSOT Press, 1994). Collection of essays on various aspects of biblical law.

D. Patrick, *Old Testament Law* (Atlanta: John Knox, 1985). Good introductory survey. Pages 35–61 deal with the Ten Commandments; pages 63–96 with the Book of the Covenant.

J. Van Seters, *A Law Book for the Diaspora: Revision in the study of the Covenant Code* (New York: Oxford University Press, 2003). Strained attempt to read the Covenant Code as a post-exilic composition.

R. Westbrook and B. Wells, *Everyday Law in Biblical Israel. An Introduction* (Louisville: Westminster John Knox, 2009). Brief introductory survey, informed by ancient Near Eastern law.

D. P. Wright, *Inventing God's Law. How the Covenant Code of the Bible Used and Revised the Laws of Hammurabi* (Oxford: Oxford University Press, 2009). Thorough discussion of the Covenant Code.

Goddess worship

J. J. Collins, *The Bible after Babel: Historical Criticism in a Postmodern Age* (Grand Rapids: Eerdmans, 2005), 99–129. Overview of the debate about goddess worship in ancient Israel.

W. G. Dever, *Did God Have a Wife? Archaeology and Folk Religion in Ancient Israel* (Grand Rapids: Eerdmans, 2005). Lively account of the archaeological evidence.

CHAPTER 7

The Priestly Theology
Exodus 25–40, Leviticus, and Numbers

INTRODUCTION

We have encountered the Priestly source in earlier chapters. In this chapter, we examine the core of the Priestly source, including the commandments concerning the tabernacle in Exodus (25–31 and 35–40), the book of Leviticus (and especially the Holiness Code in chapters 17–26), and the book of Numbers, asking about the distinctive theological perspective of this source.

In Genesis and in Exodus 1–24, the Priestly strand consists mainly of editorial additions that link the narrative episodes together by providing dates and genealogies. Longer additions are often related to the inauguration of a ritual (the Sabbath in Genesis 1; the prohibition of eating meat with the blood in it in Genesis 9; circumcision in Genesis 17). There are Priestly narratives of some key episodes (the flood, the crossing of the sea), but there does not appear to have been a separate Priestly narrative of the whole story of Israel's origins. Rather, the Priestly writers accepted the narrative found in the J and E strands and supplemented it at several points to address their own concerns.

The core of the Priestly source is found in the corpus of laws and cultic regulations that begins in Exodus 25 and runs through the book of Leviticus up to Numbers 10, where the Israelites are finally said to set out from the wilderness of Sinai. In this block of material, Moses is given instructions about the sanctuary, the sacrificial system, the consecration of priests, the distinction between pure and impure, and the Day of Atonement. Leviticus 17–26 stands out as a distinct section within the Priestly tradition and is known as the Holiness Code. The early chapters of Numbers provide instructions for the arrangement of the camp in the wilderness, and regulations for various matters, such as suspicion of adultery, the nazirite vow, the Levites or minor clergy, and the celebration of Passover. Taken together, these laws constitute a symbolic system, which embodies a distinct theology within the biblical corpus. The antiquity of this system and the extent of its influence in ancient Israel are highly controversial. In this chapter, we focus on the description of the system. We shall return to the controversial questions of antiquity and importance after we have discussed the book of Deuteronomy in the following chapter.

The Tabernacle (Exodus 25–31; 35–40)

The corpus of Priestly laws begins with the account of the tabernacle in the second half of the book of Exodus. Tent-shrines for deities are attested in the Semitic world. The god El, in the Ugaritic myths, had a tent. The ancient Phoenicians had tent-shrines that they carried into battle. Pre-Islamic Arabs had a tent-shrine called the *qubbah*, a leather tent carried around by nomadic tribes. Such tent-shrines

have survived down to modern times. Most scholars, however, have felt that the tabernacle described in Exodus 26–40 is too elaborate to have been transported in the wilderness, and so the account of its construction in the time of Moses is anachronistic. It may reflect a later, settled shrine, possibly at Shiloh, where the tabernacle is allegedly set up in Josh 18:1 (Shiloh is the site of "the house of the Lord" in the time of Samuel, before the rise of the monarchy and the building of Solomon's temple). Alternatively, it may be an ideal construction, imagined by later Priestly writers. It does not correspond to what we know of the Jerusalem temple, although it incorporates some of its features, notably the statues of winged cherubim guarding the mercy seat (Exod 25:21).

The significance of the tabernacle in the Priestly source is that it provides a way of imagining a central sanctuary even while Israel was wandering in the wilderness. The

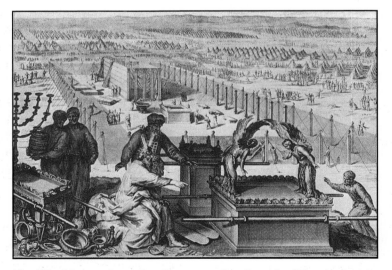

Fig. 7.1 Moses gives direction regarding the ark of the covenant while the tabernacle is constructed in the distance; engraving by Gerard Hoet in *Figures de la Bible* (The Hague, 1728).

presence of God is associated with the ark of the covenant, which is housed within the tabernacle. God is manifested over the mercy seat, between the cherubim that are on the ark (Exod 25:22). The centralization of worship was a major innovation in the reform of King Josiah in 621 B.C.E. and is associated with the promulgation of the laws of Deuteronomy. The Priestly source, as reflected in Exodus 26–40, seems to presuppose this centralization. While there may well have been a tent-shrine in ancient Israel, it is unlikely that it ever served as the focus for the cult of all Israel in the way that the tabernacle does in the Priestly source.

Leviticus

The Sacrificial System (Leviticus 1–7)

Sacrifice is one of the oldest and most basic ways in which people have tried to communicate with the gods. A sacrifice is something that is made sacred by being offered to a god. In the case of animals, and sometimes of human beings, the offering requires that they be killed and so made to pass over into the world of spirit. There is also provision for offerings of inanimate objects, such as cereal.

Various kinds of sacrifices are distinguished in Leviticus 1–7. The burnt offering (*'olah*) literally means "that which ascends." The equivalent Greek term is "holocaust," which means "wholly burned." In such a sacrifice, the victim is given completely to God, as "a pleasing odor." In contrast, the sacrifice of well-being *(shelamim)* was a communion sacrifice in which the victim was eaten by the

worshipers. Since the slaughter of animals was permitted only in the context of sacrifice in early Israel (except for blemished animals and game), these sacrifices were the occasions on which people could eat meat. For most people these occasions were rare and had the character of a celebration. The fat, like the blood, could not be eaten but was deemed to belong to the Deity. (The blood was given to God by being sprinkled on the altar.) The fact that meat was eaten after it had been "made sacred" suggests some form of communion with the Deity, but the biblical texts do not attribute any mystical character to the sacrificial meal.

The cereal or grain offerings (Leviticus 2) were less expensive than the meat sacrifices and so could be offered more frequently. In early Israel these sacrifices were burned. According to Leviticus 2, however, only part of the offering was burned, and the rest belonged to the priests. The livelihood of the priests derived from the offerings of the worshipers. This sometimes led to abuses. A colorful story in 1 Samuel 2 tells how the sons of Eli, the priest at Shiloh, would send their servants to seize portions of the meat that was being offered. The laws in Leviticus regulate the role of the priest in all these sacrifices carefully. Undoubtedly, in ancient times people thought of sacrifices as a way of feeding the gods. This idea is reflected in the Atrahasis myth from Mesopotamia, where the gods are distressed when they are deprived of their offerings. It is also parodied in the story of Bel and the Dragon, which is one of the additions to the book of Daniel in the Greek Bible. In Leviticus, however, there is no suggestion that God needs the offerings in any way. Rather, the sacrificial system provides a symbolic means for people to express their gratitude and indebtedness to God, or to make amends for their sins.

Leviticus prescribes special sacrifices for sin and purification (chaps. 4–7). Leviticus 4 prescribes rituals to be followed in cases where people have committed inadvertent sin. Sin is regarded as an objective fact—it must be atoned for even if it was not committed intentionally. Leviticus also legislates for cases of intentional sin. In some cases, such as robbery or fraud, the sin entails damage done to other human beings, and restitution must be made (6:5). The main emphasis of Leviticus, however, is on atoning for the offense against the Lord by means of a ritual offering.

The Day of Atonement

Perhaps the most vivid example of ritual atonement in Leviticus is found in the ritual for the Day of Atonement in chapter 16. This ritual requires the sacrifice of a young bull and the offering of two goats. The high priest (Aaron) casts lots over the goats and designates one for the Lord and offers it in sacrifice. The other goat is designated "for Azazel" and is driven away into the wilderness. Azazel is not attested elsewhere but is evidently a demon of some sort. In the ancient Near East, all sorts of problems were explained as being due to angry demons that had to be appeased by offerings or other means. In contrast, there are scarcely any references to demons in the biblical writings. (They do appear, however, in Jewish writings of the Hellenistic period, such as the books of Tobit and *1 Enoch*.) Azazel, then, is probably a relic of a stage of Israelite religion when demons were given a more prominent role. It may be that demons were

more important in popular Israelite religion than in the writings that are preserved in the Bible. Little is said about Azazel here, and it is difficult to know just what role he ever played in Israelite religion. He was apparently important enough at some point that he had to be appeased by the offering of a goat. The goat is not killed but is simply sent out into the wilderness, where Azazel presumably lived.

Our purpose in considering Leviticus 16 here is not to speculate on the origin of Azazel, but to reflect on the way in which the ritual works. The priest "shall lay both his hands

Fig. 7.2 A priest hurls a goat into an abyss where Azazel, depicted as a horned demon, awaits; illustration from a fourteenth-century Jewish prayerbook. Commons.wikimedia.org

on the head of the live goat, and confess over it all the iniquities of the people of Israel, and all their transgressions, all their sins, putting them on the head of the goat.... The goat shall bear on itself all their iniquities" (16:21-22). Iniquities (sins) are not material objects that can be packaged and put on an animal's head. They are deeds that people have done (murder, for example), and in many cases they cannot be undone. The action of the priest, then, is symbolic, and the effectiveness of his action depends on the belief of everyone involved. When the ritual is performed correctly, the sins of the people are deemed to be carried away into the wilderness. Just as a judge in a court has the power to declare someone guilty or innocent, the priest has the power to declare sin forgiven. The legitimacy of a court depends on the consensus of a society. Similarly, the effectiveness of a ritual depends on its acceptance within a society. It is assumed in Leviticus that these rituals are prescribed by God and that sin is forgiven because God so declares it. God, however, speaks through the priest.

While we cannot verify the divine acceptance of the ritual, we can assess its effect on the people who practiced it. We can imagine that people who approached the Day of Atonement burdened by a sense of sin would feel a great sense of relief as they watched the goat bearing their sins disappear into the wilderness. Such people might well resolve to avoid sinful conduct in the future, although this is not necessarily the case. We can also understand that an individual who made an offering for sin would be pardoned not only by God but by the society that acknowledged the validity of the ritual. The efficacy of the ritual, however, depends on its acceptance. A person

who did not believe that the goat carried the sin of the people into the wilderness could hardly feel any relief when it went out of sight.

The Priestly laws in Leviticus may give the impression that the sacrifices work automatically, but elsewhere in the Bible we often find an awareness that rituals are only effective when they give expression to genuine human intentions. We shall find that the prophets were often very critical of the sacrificial cult when it was not accompanied by the practice of justice (see especially Amos 5). The psalmists also were aware of the limits of ritual. "For you have no delight in sacrifice," says Ps 51:16-17. "If I were to give a burnt offering you would not be pleased. The sacrifice acceptable to God is a broken spirit; a broken and contrite heart, O God, you will not despise." Leviticus, however, assumes that God is pleased by burnt offerings and that the ritual is effective when it is performed properly.

The Consecration of Priests

The instructions for the building of the tabernacle included directions for the consecration of the sons of Aaron as priests in Exodus 29. The actual consecration is described in Leviticus 8–10. Aaron is given a special tunic and a breastplate equipped with Urim and Thummim, which were used to consult the Lord. We do not know exactly what the Urim and Thummim were. Scholars have speculated that they were some form of dice that could be rolled so as to get either a positive or a negative answer to a question. In any case, it is of interest that the high priest was equipped to engage in divination, which is a function that we associate more usually with prophets. It is also noteworthy that the priests were anointed with oil. Anointing was widely used in the ancient Near East to indicate a raise in status. In Israel the king was anointed. The Hebrew verb "to anoint" is *mashach*. An anointed one is a *mashiach*, the word commonly rendered in English as *messiah*. After the Babylonian exile, when there no longer was a king in Israel, the term "messiah" *(mashiach)* came to designate a future king. But a priest could also be called *mashiach*, and messianic hope for the future sometimes involved the expectation of an ideal priest as well as an ideal king (e.g., in the Dead Sea Scrolls).

Leviticus is at pains to emphasize that the consecration of the priests is stamped with divine approval. At the end of Leviticus 8 we are told that when Moses and Aaron came out from the tent of meeting, the glory of the Lord appeared to all the people. (The glory, or *kabod*, is the standard way in which God manifests himself in the Priestly writings. It may be imagined as a luminous cloud.) Conversely, any improper use of the priesthood is presented as highly dangerous. When Aaron's sons Nadab and Abihu "offered unholy fire" before the Lord (10:1-2), they were consumed by fire. We are not told what made their fire unholy. The point is that any neglect of proper ritual may prove fatal.

Leviticus 8–10 is concerned with the consecration of the sons of Aaron as priests. There was, however, another class of priests in ancient Israel, the Levites. The Priestly account of the consecration of the Levites is found in Numbers 8. According to that account, the Levites (that is, the descendants of the patriarch Levi, son of Jacob) are set aside from other Israelites and consecrated to the Lord, but their position is subordinate to that of the Aaronide priests.

They serve in the tent of meeting in attendance on Aaron and his sons. (The relationship between the Aaronide priests and the Levites is spelled out further in Numbers 18.) The account in Numbers 8 suggests that this was a harmonious arrangement, but there are indications that it was not always so. In Numbers 16 we are told that a descendant of Levi named Korah, supported by descendants of Reuben named Dathan and Abiram, rebelled against Moses and Aaron, saying: "You have gone too far! All the congregation are holy, every one of them, and the Lord is among them. So why then do you exalt yourselves against the assembly of the Lord?" Moses responds: "Hear now, you Levites! Is it too little for you that the God of Israel has separated you from the congregation of Israel, to allow you to approach him in order to perform the duties of the Lord's tabernacle, and to stand before the congregation and serve them? He has allowed you to approach him, and all your brother Levites with you; yet you seek the priesthood as well!" The dispute is resolved when the earth opens and swallows Korah and his followers. Here again the Priestly writers claim absolute, divine authority for the cultic order, and specifically they claim that the Aaronide priesthood is divinely ordained to a higher rank than the Levites. In effect, God has created, and insists upon, a hierarchical order in the regulation of the cult, so that some people are designated as holier than others. We can hardly doubt that the authors of the Priestly source were themselves members of the Aaronide priesthood, the holiest of the holy.

In fact, the relationship between the Aaronide priests and the Levites was considerably more complicated than these passages in the

Fig. 7.3 *The Judgment of Korah, Dathan, and Abiram* by Maria Hadfield Cosway (ca. 1801). Commons.wikimedia.org

book of Numbers suggest. As we shall see in the book of Deuteronomy, another tradition claimed that the Levites were priests. When King Josiah forbade sacrificial worship outside Jerusalem in the Deuteronomic reform of 621 B.C.E., however, the priests who served shrines outside Jerusalem lost their livelihood. They were permitted to go up to Jerusalem, but there the Aaronide priesthood was firmly established. It was at this point that a controversy developed as to whether the Levites were legitimate priests. We shall consider the history of the Levites further in connection with Deuteronomy and in connection with the relationship between Deuteronomy and the Priestly source. For the present, it is sufficient to note that the Priestly writings assume that the Aaronide priesthood takes precedence over the Levites.

The stories of Nadab and Abihu, and of Korah and his followers, bring to mind one other story of instantaneous divine judgment in the book of Numbers. This is found in Numbers 12 and concerns a challenge to the authority of Moses by Aaron and Miriam "because of the Cushite woman whom he had married." In the postexilic period, marriage to foreign women was a controversial issue in Judah. The book of Ezra reports that Ezra forced the Jewish men who had married foreign wives to divorce them and send them away. It is not surprising then that some people would have found the marriage of Moses to a foreign woman to be an embarrassment. The story in Numbers makes the point that no one should question the authority of Moses, regardless of what he may have done. The point is made all the more forcefully by the fact that the people who are rebuked are Aaron and Miriam, sister of Moses (only Miriam is actually punished for her grumbling). There is no suggestion, however, that Moses' marriage to a foreign woman sets a precedent for anyone else.

Each of these stories, where God rebukes Nadab and Abihu, Miriam and Aaron, and Korah and his followers, serves to assert not only the authority of God but also that of God's human surrogates, Moses and Aaron. Religious leaders throughout history have often claimed such divine endorsement, as indeed have political leaders (as we shall see when we discuss the monarchy in Israel and Judah). We shall find in the prophetic literature that there were also good reasons to question such claims, as they served all too neatly the interests of the people who made them.

The Impurity Laws

Leviticus 11–15 deals with various matters that can cause impurity. Impurity, or uncleanness, is not in itself a sinful state, but it renders a person unfit to approach the altar. Accordingly, purity is of great concern for priests. Moreover, the people as a whole are expected to aspire to purity. Some defilement is unavoidable, but it can be removed by ritual action. There is a tendency in Second Temple Judaism for some groups to insist on stricter standards of purity in everyday life, not just in the context of worship. This is the case with the Pharisees and with the sect known from the Dead Sea Scrolls. The prominence given to matters of purity in the book of Leviticus, and the inclusion of Leviticus in the Torah, contributed powerfully to this tendency.

No aspect of these laws has left a more indelible mark on Jewish life through the centuries than the dietary laws that declare some foods kosher or pure and some unclean. We have already encountered the prohibition against cooking a kid in its mother's milk in the Book of the Covenant (Exod 23:19). In the same context, the Israelites are forbidden to eat any meat that is mangled in the field, because "you shall be a people consecrated to me" (23:31). Such concerns are found in the oldest stratum of Israelite laws. More elaborate laws are found in Leviticus 11. Among land animals, those that have divided hooves and chew the cud are permitted. Those that lack either of these characteristics are not. Fish that lack fins and scales are prohibited, as are a list of twenty wild birds (without any stated criteria). All winged insects are "detestable."

These laws have baffled interpreters and embarrassed apologists from ancient to modern times. The traditional, orthodox view is that they reflect the inscrutable will of God, so that no explanation should be sought. Already in the Middle Ages Jewish interpreters such as Maimonides argued that the forbidden animals were carriers of disease—the pig, for example, carries trichinosis. This kind of explanation is still defended in some quarters, but it is not very convincing. It cannot be shown to apply to all the forbidden creatures, and other peoples ate pork without serious consequences. Others have tried to find symbolic explanations for the prohibitions. The *Letter of Aristeas,* written in Alexandria in the second century B.C.E., suggested that chewing the cud was symbolic of recollection, while birds of prey were symbols of injustice. This kind of allegorization is too arbitrary to be convincing. Others have sought an ethical explanation, arguing that the restriction of what humans may eat arises from reverence for life. Some have suggested that the law was meant to limit Israel's access to animals. Only cattle, sheep, and goats, which are bred for the purpose, may be eaten. The pig is excluded because it is disgusting. This kind of explanation makes some sense in the case of the kid in its mother's milk, or in the prohibition of eating meat with the blood. It is difficult to see, however, how reverence for life could lead to classifying animals as abominations or warrant a distinction between fish that have fins and scales and those that do not. In fact, ethical considerations (concern for the effect of actions on other human beings or on animals) are singularly absent from the Priestly code. (It is not unrelated to ethical concerns, since it provides ways to atone for sin, but it is concerned with the rituals, not with the nature of sinful conduct.) We shall see that the purpose of the Holiness Code in Leviticus 17–26 was largely to remedy this lack in the older laws.

The only rationale given in Leviticus is that the Israelites should not defile themselves, but be holy because the Lord is holy (Lev 11:44-45). Holiness is primarily the attribute of God. Human beings are holy insofar as they come close to God. The opposite state is "profane." While the positive character of holiness is difficult to grasp, negatively it implies a contrast with the normal human condition. Holy people and places are set apart and consecrated. Observance of a distinct set of laws makes the Israelites holy insofar as it sets them apart from the rest of humanity. But the concept of holiness in itself does not explain why sheep may be eaten but not pigs.

While any explanation of these laws is hypothetical, many people have found useful the interpretation offered by the anthropologist Mary Douglas. For Douglas, these laws are an attempt to bring order to experience. The problem with animals that have divided hooves but do not chew the cud is that they are anomalous: they deviate from the state that is perceived as normal. The decision as to what is normal is based on observation but draws a line that is arbitrary to a degree. It is characteristic of the Priestly authors that they like clear and distinct dividing lines. By categorizing things in this manner they impose a sense of order on experience, and this in turn gives people a sense of security, which is especially attractive in times of crisis and uncertainty. Such a system can have unfortunate consequences, however, for people who are themselves deemed to deviate from what is considered normal in their society. One of the ways in which a person was seen to be abnormal was by bodily defects. A priest who was blind or lame or had a mutilated face or other deformity was disqualified from service at the altar (Lev 21:16). Animals that were blemished were not acceptable for sacrifice (chap. 22). Anyone who was leprous or had a discharge or was impure from contact with a corpse was to be excluded from the camp (Num 5:1-5) and so, presumably, from the cultic assembly.

Some scholars have also sought to give an ethical character to other impurity laws by arguing that the sources of impurity symbolize the forces of death. Three sources of impurity are discussed in Leviticus 11–15: dead bodies, bodily emissions, and scale diseases. In the case of dead bodies, the association with death is obvious. It is also arguable in the case of scale diseases. We should note, however, that not all diseases are so categorized. Rather, the concern is with leprosy and skin diseases, which involve obvious abnormalities. Moreover, the law also applies to the leprosy of a house—mildew or mold, causing green or reddish spots (14:34-57). Such a house must be scraped and the unclean stones replaced, but this is done under the supervision of a priest. The concern is not only for hygiene but for purity, and the focus is on abnormal growth or coloring, whether in a human being or in a building. Even the defilement of corpses can be understood as distaste for the abnormal, since unburied corpses are in an in-between state and are anomalous in the land of the living.

The attempt to relate impurity to death breaks down most obviously in Leviticus 12, which discusses the impurity caused by childbirth. A woman who bears a male child is ceremonially unclean for seven days, and her time of blood purification is thirty-three days. She is impure for double that length of time if she gives birth to a female. The uncleanness here is caused by bodily emissions, which are messy and do not fit in neatly distinct categories. Compare the discussion of bodily discharges, male and female, in Leviticus 15. Neither the birth of a child nor a discharge of semen can be said to symbolize death. The concern is for an abnormal state or occurrence, but loss of control over the human body may also be a factor. At least, the inclusion of childbirth and of bodily discharges shows that the concern is not with death in a narrow sense, but rather with the edges of life. We are reminded of the limits of human control.

There is no obvious reason why a woman should be impure longer after the birth of a girl than that of a boy. The monetary value placed on a man in Lev 27:1-8 is roughly double that of a woman. It is not unreasonable, then, to suspect that the difference implies that females are inferior in some sense. But greater impurity does not necessarily imply lesser value. A human corpse defiles more than the carcass of an animal. Fear of defilement is very widespread in the ancient world and may indeed be universal. It does not always admit of rational explanation. Impurity laws preserve vestiges of old taboos based on the fear of the unknown. They have more to do with primal fears about life and death and loss of human control over the body than with ethical principles in the modern sense.

The Holiness Code

Leviticus 17–26 is recognized as a distinct block of material within the Priestly corpus. These chapters, called the Holiness Code (H), have a distinctive style and vocabulary. Although the various units are still introduced by the formula "The LORD spoke to Moses saying," they have the character of a direct address by God to Israel, with frequent interjections of the formula "I am the LORD your God." Most importantly, these chapters attempt to integrate ethical commandments of the type found in the Decalogue and emphasized in Deuteronomy and the Prophets, with the more specific cultic and ritual laws of the Priestly tradition.

Slaughter and Sacrifice

Leviticus 17 opens with a remarkable command: "If any Israelite slaughters an animal and does not bring it to the entrance of the tent of meeting as an offering to the LORD, he is guilty of bloodshed" (v. 4). The precise significance of this commandment is controversial. One of the great turning points in the history of the religion of Israel was the Deuteronomic reform of King Josiah in 621 B.C.E., which forbade sacrifice outside the one place that the Lord had chosen (Jerusalem). Since many Israelites lived at some distance from Jerusalem, Deuteronomy allowed that animals could be slaughtered for meat without being sacrificed; that is, it permitted profane slaughter. Leviticus 17 is presented as a law for Israel in the wilderness. It is generally assumed that the law really addresses a much later situation. Since there is only one tent of meeting, most scholars have assumed that H is insisting on the centralization of sacrificial worship, but unlike Deuteronomy it refuses to allow profane slaughter. Such a law would have been difficult to implement. It has been suggested, however, that the tent of meeting here stands for any sanctuary, and that H presupposed the existence of multiple shrines. This would remove the practical difficulty of implementing the law, but the only evidence for multiple sanctuaries in H is the curse in Lev 26:31, where God threatens to lay "your sanctuaries" waste. One can hardly infer from this that H approved of multiple sanctuaries. We shall return to the relevance of Leviticus 17 for the centralization of the cult when we discuss the relationship between the Priestly tradition and Deuteronomy. For the present it is sufficient to note that H takes a purist position on the sacrality of the slaughter of animals. The reason given is to prevent Israelites from offering sacrifices to demons (such as Azazel). H also reiterates emphatically the prohibition against eating meat with the blood in it.

Improper Relations

The next issue raised in the Holiness Code is the distinction of Israel from the nations: "You shall not do as they do in the land of Egypt, where you lived, and you shall not do as they do in the land of Canaan to which I am bringing you" (Lev 18:3). Most of the points at issue involve improper sexual relations. We should not assume that the Canaanites and the Egyptians indulged in all the behavior forbidden to the Israelites. The passage is probably referring to the story in Genesis 9, where Ham, father of both Canaan and Egypt, saw the nakedness of his father, Noah, who cursed Canaan when he awoke. Many of the laws in Leviticus 18 forbid sexual relations between close relatives. Typically Priestly is the prohibition of relations during a woman's menstrual period (18:19). In modern times, the only one of these laws that has been controversial is the statement in 18:22: "You shall not lie with a male as with a woman" (literally, "the lyings of a woman"). The penalties for various offenses listed in chapter 18 are given in chapter 20. Leviticus 18:13 specifies that if a man lies with a male as with a woman, both men have committed an abomination and must be put to death. All of these "abominations" are said to defile the land.

The biblical prohibition of male homosexual intercourse is unique in the ancient world. The Greek philosopher Plato declared that homosexuality was contrary to nature in his dialogue *The Laws*, but here he was going against the consensus of Greek society, and even Plato himself expressed a more positive view of the subject in his earlier dialogue *The Symposium*. The contrast between Jewish and Greek mores in this matter was frequently noted by Jewish writers in the Hellenistic period. Leviticus does not give an argument for the prohibition. It simply declares such intercourse to be an abomination. These are the only passages in the Hebrew Bible where homosexual intercourse is explicitly prohibited, but it also figures in two narratives. In Genesis 19 Lot offers the men of Sodom his two daughters, if only they will refrain from abusing his male guests, but he seems to be concerned over the violation of hospitality and his honor as host. A similar situation recurs in Judges 19, where the master of the

Fig. 7.4 *Lot and His Daughters* by an anonymous artist, ca. 1525–1530. The cities of Sodom and Gomorrah are punished for their wickedness, exemplified in the attempted attack on Lot's guests; in the foreground, Lot's daughters inebriate their father in order to become pregnant from him (see Gen. 19:30-38).

Commons.wikimedia.org

contrast with the ways of other peoples, but this in itself does not explain the specific issues that are chosen. All the issues in Leviticus 18 are sexual, except one. Verse 21 explicitly prohibits child sacrifice, and 20:2-5 prescribes death by stoning as the punishment for this offense. (Chap. 20 also mentions some other offenses, such as consulting mediums and wizards.) Because of this, it has been suggested that procreation is the common theme of chapter 18. Waste of reproductive seed is an issue here, although not every form of nonreproductive intercourse is addressed (for example, intercourse with a wife after menopause is not forbidden). Concern for the waste of reproductive seed was not peculiar to P or H—compare the story of Onan in Genesis 38. The book of Proverbs cautions men to "drink water from your own cistern . . . why should your springs be scattered abroad, streams of water in the streets?" (Prov 5:15-16). There is no prohibition of sex between women (lesbianism) in Leviticus. This omission cannot be explained by the male-centered focus of these laws. The following verse carefully indicates that the prohibition of sex with animals applies to women as well as to men (Lev 18:23; cf. 20:16). Presumably, sex between women did not concern the Priestly legislators because there was no loss of semen involved. In contrast, Rom 1:26-27 condemns "unnatural intercourse" on the part of both males and females.

Procreation, however, is not the only issue here. There is also an intolerable degree of defilement. Not only is the passive male partner condemned to death in Lev 20:13, but also animals with which humans have sexual relations must be killed, although there can be no question of responsibility on the part of the animals. The juxtaposition of the prohibition

house gives over his concubine to a mob to protect his male guest. In the New Testament, the apostle Paul draws a contrast between the "shameless acts" of men with each other and natural intercourse with women (Rom 1:27). Homosexuality is also denounced in several lists of vices in the New Testament (1 Cor 6:9; Gal 5:19; 1 Tim 1:10).

In the context of Leviticus, a number of factors should be noted. There is a deliberate of male homosexuality with that of bestiality and the fact that the death penalty is prescribed for all parties in both cases shows that the issue is not exploitation of the weak by the strong. Neither can the prohibition of male homosexuality be limited to relations with close relatives (the kind of situation addressed in the laws on heterosexual relations). It would be absurd to suggest that the law on bestiality only applied when the animals were part of the extended family!

One other passage in the Holiness Code may throw some light on the prohibition of male homosexuality: "You shall not let our animals breed with a different kind; you shall not sow your field with two kinds of seed; nor shall you put on a garment made of two different materials" (Lev 19:19; cf. Deut 22:9-11). Certain combinations are deemed improper. In Lev 19:19 the concern is with combinations of pairs of different materials; in the prohibition of homosexuality, the issue is combining two of the same kind. In all these cases, however, there is a preoccupation with order, with clear definitions of what is permitted and what is not. The prohibition of male homosexuality must be understood in this context.

Finally, some comment must be made on the relevance of these laws for the modern world. The laws are addressed only to Israelites and are intended to distinguish Israel from other peoples. They seem to be quite unequivocal, however, in their condemnation of male homosexuality. Attempts to restrict their application (e.g., to intercourse with close relatives) seem misguided. Whether one considers any of these laws still binding is another matter. Few people in the modern world worry as to whether their garments are made of different materials. Many other factors besides the teaching of Leviticus would have to be considered in a discussion of the morality of homosexuality in the modern world.

Ethics and Holiness

The strategy of the Holiness Code in revising the Priestly tradition is most clearly evident in Leviticus 19. The chapter begins with the programmatic assertion: "You must be holy, for I the LORD your God am holy." In the Priestly source, holiness was defined primarily by ritual requirements, although reverence for life was certainly implied. In Leviticus 19, however, we find ritual regulations interspersed with ethical commandments of the type familiar from the Decalogue (note the echoes of the Decalogue in 19:2-3, 11-13). Leviticus 19:10 echoes Deuteronomy when it says that the edges and gleanings of the harvest must be left for the poor. Also characteristically Deuteronomic is the reason why one should not oppress the alien: "for you were aliens in the land of Egypt" (19:36). The code does not lessen the importance of ritual and purity regulations, but it puts them in perspective by alternating them with ethical commandments. Holiness is not only a matter of being separated from the nations. It also requires ethical behavior toward one's fellow human beings.

The Cultic Calendar (Leviticus 23)

The cultic calendar in Leviticus 23 differs from those found in Exodus in several significant respects. The older calendars had only three celebrations—Unleavened Bread, Weeks, and Tabernacles. Leviticus lists these three but includes the Passover as a "holy convocation." As we shall see, the Passover was originally a family celebration and became a pilgrimage festival only in the context of the Deuteronomic reform of King Josiah. Two new festivals are mentioned in the seventh month: the celebration that would become known as Rosh Hashanah (the fall New Year's festival) on the first day of the month, and Yom Kippur (the Day of Atonement) on the tenth day. The Priestly calendar gives precise dates for each of the festivals, using the Babylonian calendar that began in the spring. It also stipulates sacrifices and rituals for the celebrations. The fixed dates for the festivals indicate that they are less closely connected to the rhythm of the agricultural year than was the case in the older calendars.

This is a more developed calendar than we find even in Deuteronomy. It cannot have reached its present form until a relatively late date, long after the exile. The book of Nehemiah, which cannot have been written before the late fifth century B.C.E., has an account of the festivals in the seventh month in chapter 8. There is one on the first of the month, but this is followed by the Festival of Tabernacles or Sukkoth. There is no mention of a Day of Atonement on the tenth day. In Nehemiah 9, however, we find that on the twenty-fourth day of the seventh month the people were assembled with fasting and in sackcloth. It may be that the Day of Atonement was celebrated after Sukkoth, but in any case, this account of the festivals in the Second Temple period does not conform to what we find in Leviticus.

Another distinctive observance is added in Leviticus 25. This is the institution of the Jubilee Year. The idea of a sabbatical year was old in Israel. We have already met it in the Book of the Covenant, which stipulated that Hebrew slaves must be emancipated after six

The cultic calendar in Exodus	The cultic calendar in Leviticus 23
Unleavened Bread	Passover
Weeks	Unleavened Bread
Tabernacles (Sukkoth)	Weeks
	Tabernacles (Sukkoth)
	Rosh Hashanah
	Yom Kippur

years, and that fields and vineyards were to lie fallow every seventh year. The law in Exodus is unclear as to whether all fields were to lie fallow in the same year or whether they could be rotated. We shall find that the year was fixed according to Deuteronomy 15. It is also fixed in Leviticus 25. Leviticus adds a further observance in the fiftieth year (after seven weeks of years). There would be general emancipation and the land would lie fallow. This would require that the land lie fallow for two consecutive years, as the forty-ninth year was a sabbatical year. This would seem to involve considerable practical problems. There is no evidence that the Jubilee Year was ever actually observed. The original practice of the sabbatical year was probably a way to avoid overuse of the land and allow it to recover. The laws in Leviticus, however, have a strictly religious rationale: they are a reminder that the land belongs not to the people, but to YHWH.

Blessings and Curses

The Holiness Code concludes with the promise of blessings if the Israelites abide by the laws and the threat of curses if they do not.

Here again there is notable similarity to Deuteronomy. Curses and blessings were an integral part of treaties in the ancient Near East. Curses were especially prominent in Assyrian treaties. We shall discuss the influence of these treaties on the biblical notion of covenant in more detail in connection with Deuteronomy. The blessings in Leviticus 26 are given briefly. They promise a utopian condition of prosperity and peace. Distinctively Priestly is the promise that God will place his dwelling in the midst of the people. The curses are given in more detail and entail war, famine, and pestilence. People will be reduced to eating the flesh of sons and daughters. Again, there is a distinctively Priestly nuance in the prediction that "the land shall enjoy its sabbath years as long as it lies desolate" (26:34). The passage concludes, however, with the assurance that if the people confess their sin and make amends, then God will remember his covenant. "Yet for all that, when they are in the land of their enemies, I will not spurn them, or abhor them so as to destroy them utterly and break my covenant with them; for I am the LORD their God; but I will remember in their favor the covenant with their ancestors whom I brought out of the land of Egypt" (26:44-45). The reference here to the time "when they are in the land of their enemies" clearly presupposes the Babylonian exile.

The Book of Numbers

After the insertion of the Holiness Code, the P source continues in Leviticus 27 (a discussion of vows) and in Num 1:1—10:28. The book of Numbers begins with "a census of the whole congregation of Israelites, in their clans, by ancestral houses" (1:2). In the context, this census is part of the preparation for the journey from Sinai to the promised land. Among other things, it determines the number of males who are twenty years or more and able to go to war. Later we will find that King David takes a census of Israel, and this appears to be an innovation in his time. According to the account in 2 Samuel 4, it resulted in a plague. First Chronicles 21:1 says that it was Satan who incited David to take the census. The Priestly writers, however, have no hesitation on the subject. List making and genealogies are among the favorite activities of P. These lists impose order on reality, and the genealogies establish relationships and places in society. The genealogies became especially important after the Babylonian exile, when Israelite society had been disrupted. According to Ezra 2:59-63, several families were excluded from the priesthood because they could not prove their descent from the genealogical records. The Priestly account retrojects this concern for genealogies and census taking into the wilderness period as part of its construction of an ideal Israel. The journey from Sinai to Canaan is described as an orderly procession, in which the ark of the covenant was the focus of attention. According to P, the Israelites were given precise instructions on the cult and ritual to be observed in the wilderness, and in fact observed them. (In contrast, God, through the prophet Amos, asks: "Did you bring me sacrifices and offerings the forty years in the wilderness, O house of Israel?" [Amos 5:25], with the obvious implication that they did not.) The Priestly account of the wilderness period was evidently not generally known or accepted when Amos prophesied in the eighth century B.C.E.

Fig. 7.5 **The ark of the covenant is depicted in a stone relief from the Roman era, from the synagogue in Capernaum.** Commons.wikimedia.org

Non-Priestly Elements in Numbers

There were, however, older traditions about the wilderness period that can still be found in the book of Numbers, beginning in 10:29. The formula in Num 10:35, "Arise, O LORD, let your enemies be scattered," may reflect the ancient custom of taking one's god into battle (a custom illustrated in 1 Samuel 4–6).

Rebellion in the Wilderness

Numbers 11–12 picks up the theme of rebellion in the wilderness, which was found already in Exodus 16–17 (J). The stories of miraculous food in the wilderness (quails and manna) and the water from the rock (Exodus 17) illustrate Israel's ingratitude for deliverance from Egypt and its complete dependence on divine providence. In the Prophets (e.g.,

Hosea 2), the wilderness period is recalled as an idyllic period when Israel was alone with their God in the desert. It does not appear so idyllic in the account in Exodus and Numbers. It does, however, dramatize vividly human dependence on the Creator and the persistent human failure to appreciate this. The stories in Numbers also use this theme to reinforce the authority of Moses, especially in the story in Numbers 12, to which we have already referred.

Balaam

The colorful character of the Yahwist narrative, in contrast to the rather dry Priestly regulations, is nicely illustrated in the story of Balaam in Numbers 22–24. Balaam is one of the few examples in the Bible of a non-Israelite prophet or seer (24:16 suggests that he falls into ecstasy: "who falls down, but with his eye uncovered"). Balaam is now also known from a pagan source—a plaster inscription discovered in 1967 at Tell Deir Alla in the East Jordan valley that dates from the eighth century B.C.E. The inscription describes Balaam as "a seer of the gods" and attributes to him a prediction that the heavens would be darkened and the ways of birds and animals would be disturbed. The content of this prophecy has no relation to the Balaam texts in Numbers but bears a general similarity to the prophecies of "the Day of the LORD" that we will find in the biblical prophets (e.g., Amos 5:18).

The stories in Numbers 22–24 tell how Balaam was summoned by the king of Moab to curse Israel. (The setting here may throw some light on the oracles against foreign nations that often appear in the biblical prophets, and which may also have originated as curses. We shall return to this phenomenon when we discuss the story of Micaiah son of Imlah in 1 Kings 22, and again in connection with Amos.) Balaam, however, is prevented from performing the task. First, God speaks to him in the night and forbids him to do so (this part of the story is usually attributed to E). Then the angel of the Lord blocks his path. Balaam's donkey sees the angel before Balaam does. This episode is vintage J storytelling (cf. the talking snake in the garden of Eden). The outcome of the story is that the prophet cannot curse Israel because YHWH has not cursed them. The blessing of Israel seems all the more sure because it is put on the lips of a pagan prophet. Balaam is acknowledged as a man of God—indeed he acknowledges YHWH as his God, although he is not an Israelite. The Hebrew Bible seldom appeals to the testimony of Gentiles in this way. (Another example is

found in 2 Kings 5, in the story of Naaman the Syrian.) In the Hellenistic period, however, Jewish writers often attributed praises of Israel and its God to Gentile writers. There is a whole corpus of Jewish oracles attributed to the pagan prophetess, the Sibyl. The oracles of Balaam in the book of Numbers provide a precedent for these later Jewish pseudepigrapha (that is, writings attributed to someone who was not their real author).

One of the oracles attributed to Balaam was especially important in later times: "A star shall come out of Jacob, and a scepter shall rise out of Israel. It shall crush the borderlands of Moab, and the territory of all the Shethites" (Num 24:17). In the Hellenistic and Roman periods, this oracle was taken as a messianic prediction. In the Dead Sea Scrolls, the star was taken to be a priest who would restore the legitimate priesthood, and the scepter as the king who would defeat the enemies of the Jews. Other texts take the star and the scepter as the same figure. The leader of the last Jewish revolt against Rome, in 132–135 C.E., Simon Bar Kosiba, was hailed by Rabbi Akiba as the messiah foretold in this oracle. Because of this, he is known in Jewish tradition as Bar Kokhba (literally, "son of the star").

Phinehas and the Ideal of Zealotry

The older J and E narratives may also have included a brief notice about an incident at Shittim in Moab where the Israelites engaged in the worship of the god Baal (Numbers 25). As this story now stands in Numbers, it bears the distinct stamp of the Priestly writers. The source of the problem is that the Israelites engage in sexual relations with foreign (Moabite) women. In the Priestly edition of the story, the figure who takes the lead in stamping out the apostasy is a priest, Phinehas, son of Eleazar, son of Aaron. When he sees an Israelite man take a Midianite woman into his tent, Phinehas follows them and pierces the two of them with his spear. He did this "because he was zealous for the Lord," and his action is reported as making atonement and stopping a plague among the Israelites. For this God gives him a covenant of peace and an eternal priesthood.

Several points should be noted in this story. The woman is Midianite, although in the context we should expect a Moabite. The significance of a Midianite woman is clear: Moses had married one. The Priestly author wants to make clear that the precedent of Moses does not apply to anyone else. The zeal of Phinehas represents a particular kind of religious ideal that had a long and fateful history in Israel. While it is endorsed by the Priestly source, it was certainly not peculiar to the priests. We shall meet it again in the book of Joshua, in the story of the slaughter of the Canaanites. Much later, in the second century B.C.E., the Maccabees would invoke the model of Phinehas as inspiration for their militant resistance to persecution by the Syrian king Antiochus Epiphanes. The rebels against Rome in the first century C.E. take their name, Zealots, from the same source. Finally, P adds an interesting notice in Num 31:8, 16. The Moabite women, we are told, acted on the advice of none other than Balaam, and the Israelites accordingly killed Balaam with the sword. The Priestly writers were evidently uncomfortable with the idea of a "good" pagan prophet and undermine the older account of Balaam by this notice. It is also axiomatic for the Priestly writer that the women who tempted the Israelites must not be allowed to live.

The Phinehas story underlines some of the fundamental tensions in the Priestly tradition. On the one hand, that tradition was characterized by respect for life, human and animal, as is shown by the prohibition against eating meat with the blood. On the other hand, the violence of Phinehas, like the summary executions of dissidents like Korah, shows an attitude of intolerance, where the demands of purity and holiness take precedence over human life. No doubt the Priestly writers would protest that the laws of purity and holiness are themselves in the service of human life and are intended to make it better. The intolerance shown in this story has its root in the certitude of Phinehas and those he represents that their way is God's way. Where people are convinced that they speak for God, there is no need to compromise or to consider other points of view. Many modern people, religious as well as secular, react to the story of Phinehas with revulsion. At the very least, we must acknowledge that the theology of the Priestly writers (and of other biblical writers besides) is fundamentally at odds with modern democratic and pluralistic sensibilities on this issue. The same is true, to a lesser extent, of the Priestly preoccupation with purity. There are also many people, however, who continue to find the orderly world of the Priestly writers attractive, and who find comfort in its sharp dichotomies between sacred and profane, pure and impure, Israelite and Gentile.

FOR FURTHER READING

Commentaries

P. J. Budd, *Numbers* (WBC 5; Waco, TX: Word, 1984). Good review of history of interpretation.

T. B. Dozeman, "The Book of Numbers," *NIB* 2:3–268. Well informed theological commentary.

E. Gerstenberger, *Leviticus* (trans. D. W. Scott; OTL; Louisville: WestminsterJohn Knox, 1996). Major commentary on Leviticus by a Christian scholar.

B. A. Levine, *Leviticus* (The JPS Torah Commentary; Philadelphia: Jewish Publication Society, 1989). Less technical commentary, from a Jewish perspective.

———, *Numbers 1–20* (AB 4; New York: Doubleday, 1993); *Numbers 21–36* (AB 4A; New York: Doubleday, 2000). Thorough philological commentary.

J. Milgrom, *Leviticus: A Book of Ritual and Ethics. A Continental Commentary* (Minneapolis: Fortress Press, 2004). Condensation of the massive Anchor Bible commentary.

———, *Leviticus 1–16* (AB 3; New York: Doubleday, 1991); *Leviticus 17–22* (AB 3A: New York: Doubleday, 2000); *Leviticus 23–27* (AB 3B; New York: Doubleday, 2001). Exhaustive commentary, informed both by Near Eastern parallels and rabbinic tradition.

M. Noth, *Leviticus: A Commentary* (trans. J. E. Anderson; OTL; Philadelphia: Westminster, 1965). For long the standard historical-critical commentary.

M. Noth, *Numbers* (trans. J. D. Martin; OTL; Philadelphia: Westminster, 1968). Classic historical-critical commentary.

D. T. Olson, *Numbers* (Interpretation; Louisville: WestminsterJohn Knox, 1996). Popular homiletical commentary.

K. D. Sakenfeld, *Journeying with God: A Commentary on the Book of Numbers* (ITC; Grand Rapids: Eerdmans, 1995). Theological commentary with focus on issues of purity and impurity.

Studies

G. A. Anderson, *Sacrifices and Offerings in Ancient Israel: Studies in Their Social and Political Importance* (HSM 41; Atlanta: Scholars Press, 1987). An analysis of the sacrificial system and its social function.

M. Douglas, *Leviticus as Literature* (Oxford: Oxford University Press, 1999). Application of Douglas's anthropological approach to all of Leviticus.

———, *Purity and Danger* (London: Routledge and Kegan Paul, 1966), 41–57. Groundbreaking analysis of the dietary laws.

R. E. Friedman and S. Dolansky, *The Bible Now* (New York: Oxford University Press, 2011), 1–40. Lucid, well-informed presentation of what the Bible has to say on homosexuality.

M. Haran, *Temples and Temple Service in Ancient Israel* (Oxford: Oxford University Press, 1978). Major study of priestly traditions by an Israeli scholar.

J. Joosten, *People and Land in the Holiness Code* (Leiden: Brill, 1996). Exegetical and thematic study of the Holiness Code.

I. Knohl, *The Sanctuary of Silence* (Minneapolis: Fortress Press, 1995). Illuminating study of the Holiness Code.

N. Lohfink, *Theology of the Pentateuch: Themes of the Priestly Narrative and Deuteronomy* (trans. L. M. Maloney; Minneapolis: Augsburg Fortress, 1994). Seminal essays on the Priestly tradition can be found in chapters 1, 4, and 6.

S. Olyan, *Rites and Rank. Hierarchy in Biblical Representations of Cult* (Princeton: Princeton University Press, 2000). Analysis of basic polarities in the Priestly tradition: holy/common, clean/unclean, self/other.

————, *Social Inequality in the World of the Text: The Significance of Ritual and Social Distinctions in the Hebrew Bible* (Göttingen: Vandenhoeck & Ruprecht, 2011), 57—84. Thorough discussion of Lev 18:22 and 20:13.

R. Rendtorff and R. A. Kugler, eds., *The Book of Leviticus: Composition and Reception* (VTSup 93; Leiden: Brill, 2003). Wide-ranging essays on all aspects of Leviticus.

S. Shechtman and J. S. Baden, eds., *The Strata of the Priestly Writings: Contemporary Debate and Future Directions* (Zürich: Theologischer Verlag Zürich, 2009). Collection of essays illustrating current debates.

J. Stackert, *Rewriting the Torah: Literary Revision in Deuteronomy and the Holiness Legislation* (FAT 52; Tübingen: Mohr Siebeck, 2007). Reworks laws from Deuteronomy.

J. W. Watts, *Ritual and Rhetoric in Leviticus: From Sacrifice to Scripture* (Cambridge: Cambridge University Press, 2007). Emphasizes the texts as rhetoric rather than the ritual practice.

CHAPTER 8

Deuteronomy

INTRODUCTION

This chapter examines the final book in the Pentateuch, Deuteronomy. More than any other part of the Bible, Deuteronomy resembles the treaty model known from other ancient Near Eastern cultures. We will look at the distinctive laws in Deteronomy, inquire about the authors who crafted the book, and consider the effects of the Deuteronomic reform that gave rise to it. Finally, we will consider the relationship between Deuteronomy and the Priestly Code.

The book of Deuteronomy takes its name from the Greek translation of a phrase in Deut 17:18, which prescribes that the king should have "a copy of the law" written for him by the Levitical priests. The Greek expression, *deuteros nomos*, means rather "a second law," but this designation of the book is not inappropriate. Deuteronomy is in fact a second formulation of the law, after the one that was given in Exodus. The more usual Hebrew name for the book is taken, as is customary, from the opening phrase: "These are the words. . . ."

Deuteronomy is presented as the farewell address of Moses before the Israelites crossed the Jordan to enter the promised land. Moses recalls the giving of the law on the mountain of revelation, which in Deuteronomy is consistently called Horeb. There are two introductions, which probably reflect two stages

in the composition of the book. The first, in 1:1, says, "These are the words that Moses spoke to all Israel." The second, in 4:44-49, says, "This is the law that Moses set before the Israelites." The word for "law," *torah*, can also mean "instruction," but the translation "law" is justified in the case of Deuteronomy. The two introductions nicely capture the composite character of the book. It is a collection of laws (primarily in chaps. 12–26), but it also has a strongly homiletical character, especially in the long introductory section in chapters 1–11. Accordingly, it has often been characterized as "preached law." It lends itself readily to use in a context of worship.

The book also contains other kinds of material. Chapters 27–28 describe a ceremony in which half the tribes of Israel stand on Mount Gerizim and recite blessings, while the other half stand on Mount Ebal and recite curses. (The two mountains overlook the town of Shechem. Joshua 24 describes a covenant renewal ceremony at Shechem after the Israelites had occupied the land.) Deuteronomy 29:1 marks the beginning of a new speech of Moses: "These are the words of the covenant that the LORD commanded Moses to make with the Israelites in the land of Moab, in addition to the covenant that he had made with them at Horeb." After he has completed this speech, he informs the Israelites that he will not cross the Jordan with them, and appoints Joshua, son of Nun, as his successor. Deuteronomy 32 contains a lengthy song of Moses, which summarizes the Deuteronomic view of Israel's early history. Deuteronomy 33, which is formally introduced as "the blessing with which Moses, the man of God, blessed the Israelites before his death," is an old poem about the tribes, comparable to the blessing of Jacob in Genesis 49. Deuteronomy closes with a brief account of the death of Moses in chapter 34, which is sometimes attributed to the Elohist source.

Apart from the closing chapters, the book has a far more consistent and distinctive style than the other books of the Pentateuch. Even if it was composed in stages, the scribes who contributed to its growth must have come from the same school or tradition. The style is distinctive in the use of direct address and a highly personal tone. There is vacillation between the use of the second person singular and the second person plural (a good example can be found in chap. 12). This has sometimes been taken as a sign of composite authorship, but this is not necessarily so. The variation may be for stylistic reasons, to heighten the sense of personal address in some sections.

> The structure of Deuteronomy as a whole may be summarized as follows:
>
> 1. Motivational speeches, including some recollection of Israel's history (1–11)
> 2. The laws (12–26)
> 3. Curses and blessings (27–28)
> 4. Concluding materials, some of which have the character of appendices (29–34).

The Treaty Model

More clearly than any other biblical book, Deuteronomy is influenced by ancient Near Eastern treaties. We have already noted the debate about the relevance of Hittite treaties from the second millennium to the biblical idea of covenant, in connection with the revelation at Sinai in the book of Exodus. In the case of Deuteronomy, however, much closer parallels are found in the Vassal Treaties of Esarhaddon (VTE), an Assyrian king who ruled in the seventh century B.C.E. (681–669), that were discovered in 1956. (Vassal treaties are those between a superior power and its subjects.) Assyria was the dominant power in the Near East in this era. Esarhaddon's father, Sennacherib, had ravaged Judah and taken tribute, and there is some evidence that Judah was still a vassal of Assyria in Esarhaddon's time.

The influence of the treaty model can be seen on various levels in Deuteronomy. The basic structure of Deuteronomy, which draws on history as a motivational tool and reinforces the commandments with curses and blessings, corresponds to that of the ancient vassal treaties. The recollection of history is

Fig. 8.1 Esarhaddon of Assyria. Stone stele in the Pergamonmuseum, Berlin.

Commons.wikimedia.org

not as prominent in the Assyrian treaties as in the older Hittite examples, but it is not entirely absent. Perhaps the most distinctive element of these treaties is that great emphasis is placed on curses. The Assyrian treaties were essentially loyalty oaths imposed by the king of Assyria to ensure submission to his successor. (In Esarhaddon's case, this was his son Ashurbanipal.) Deuteronomy is similar, in that Moses is handing on authority to Joshua, but the biblical text differs in that the loyalty of the people is pledged to their God, YHWH. Other elements in Deuteronomy that recall the treaty form include the invocation of heaven and earth as witnesses (4:26; 30:19; 31:28; cf. VTE paragraph 3 [line 25]: "You are adjured by the gods of heaven and earth," *ANET*, 534); the deposition of the document (Deut 10:1-5; 31:24-26) and provision for periodic reading (31:9-13) and the making of copies (17:18-19).

The most striking correspondences between Deuteronomy and the treaties concern vocabulary and idiom. In both documents, the word "love" means loyalty, and subjects are commanded to love their lord with all their heart and soul (cf. VTE paragraph 24 [line 266]: "If you do not love the crown prince designate Ashurbanipal . . . as you do your own lives . . ."). Other standard terms for loyalty, both in Deuteronomy and in the treaties, are "to go after," "to fear," and "to listen to the voice of. . . ."

There are further correspondences in detail. VTE 10 (108) warns of seditious talk by "a prophet, an ecstatic, a dream interpreter," among other people. Deuteronomy 13 warns against "prophets or those who divine by dreams" who try to induce people "to go after" other gods. The series of curses in Deut 28:23-35 is paralleled in VTE 39–42 [419–30]. Even the order of the curses of leprosy and blindness is the same in both. In the Assyrian texts this order is determined by the hierarchy of the responsible deities, Sin and Shamash, respectively. Since this hierarchy is irrelevant in the Israelite context, it is clear that Deuteronomy is directly influenced by the treaty texts.

It would not be correct to say that Deuteronomy is formally structured as a treaty text. Rather, it is an address, or homily, that is informed by the treaty analogy and contains many elements of the treaty form. It appeals to history as a motivating factor more often than is the case in the Assyrian treaties. The appeal to history is typified by a passage in chapter 26 that is supposed to be recited in connection with the offering of firstfruits of the land: "My father was a wandering Aramean. He went down to Egypt and lived there as an alien. . . .

The LORD brought us out of Egypt with a mighty arm and an outstretched hand . . . and he brought us into this place, and gave us this land, a land flowing with milk and honey." An earlier generation of scholars, typified by Gerhard von Rad, regarded this passage as the *credo,* or confession of faith, of early Israel, and thought it was a cultic recitation from an early period. More recent scholarship, however, recognizes this passage as typically Deuteronomic and assumes that it was composed for its present context in Deuteronomy.

It has been suggested, quite plausibly, that Deuteronomy is meant to provide an alternative to the Assyrian loyalty oaths: the people of Judah are being told to pledge their loyalty and "love," not to the king of Assyria but to YHWH. Hence the key formulation in Deut 6:4-5: "Hear, O Israel: The LORD is our God, the LORD alone. You shall love the LORD your God with all your heart and with all your soul and with all your might." This is not a theoretical assertion of monotheism. It is an assertion of allegiance. Other gods may exist, but the loyalty of the Israelite is pledged to YHWH alone.

The Date of Deuteronomy

The parallels with the Assyrian vassal treaties constitute a powerful argument that the book of Deuteronomy was not formulated in the time of Moses but in the seventh century B.C.E. In fact, the date of Deuteronomy had become apparent long before the Vassal Treaties were discovered. In 1805 a young German scholar, W. M. L. de Wette, revolutionized scholarship by pointing out the correspondence between Deuteronomy and the "book of the law" that was allegedly found in the temple in 621 B.C.E., in the reign of King

Josiah of Judah. The incident is described as follows in 2 Kings 22–23. In the course of repairs that were being carried out on the temple, the high priest Hilkiah reported: "I have found the book of the law in the house of the LORD." When this book was read to the king, he tore his clothes as a sign of distress and made inquiry of a prophetess named Huldah, "for great is the wrath of the LORD that is kindled against us, because our ancestors did not obey the words of this book, to do according to all that is written concerning us." Huldah confirmed the authenticity of the book and prophesied moreover: "I will indeed bring disaster on this place and on its inhabitants—all the words that the king of Judah has read." From this much we may infer that the book contained curses, or threats of destruction.

Further indication of the contents of "the book of the law of the LORD" can be found in the actions taken by Josiah in 2 Kings 23. We are told that he assembled the people and "read in their hearing all the words of the book of the covenant that had been found in the house of the LORD." All the people subscribed to this covenant. Then he proceeded to purge the temple of the vessels made for Baal and Asherah, and to tear down the "high places" or rural shrines all over the country, where priests had traditionally offered sacrifice. Then the king celebrated the Passover "as prescribed in this book of the covenant. No such passover had been kept since the days of the judges who judged Israel, even during all the days of the kings of Israel and of the kings of Judah." The novelty of this Passover is that it was not a family observance in the home, but a pilgrimage festival celebrated in Jerusalem.

The drift of Josiah's reforms is clear enough. Not only did he prohibit the worship

Fig. 8.2 The Tel Dan altar and high place. Photo by the author

of deities other than YHWH, but he banned sacrificial worship, even sacrifices offered to YHWH, outside Jerusalem, by tearing down the "high places." In effect, he centralized worship in Jerusalem. According to 2 Kgs 18:4, a similar reform had been tried unsuccessfully by King Hezekiah about a hundred years before the time of Josiah. Hezekiah apparently did not have a book to lend divine authority to his reform (2 Chronicles 29–31 attributes a much more elaborate reform to Hezekiah, but its historicity is doubtful).

It was the contribution of de Wette to recognize that the book that was allegedly found in Josiah's time was Deuteronomy, or at least a part thereof. According to Deuteronomy 12: "You must demolish completely all the places where the nations whom you are about to dispossess served their gods on the mountain heights, on the hills and under every leafy tree. Break down their altars, smash their pillars, burn their sacred poles with fire, and hew down the idols of their gods." This was the program of Josiah's reform. Moreover, the Israelites are told: "You shall not act as we are acting here today, all of us according to our own desires, for you have not yet come into the rest and possession that the LORD your God is giving you. When you cross the Jordan . . . then you shall bring everything that I command you to the place that the LORD your God will choose as a dwelling for his name; your burnt offerings and your sacrifices, your tithes and your donations, and all your choice votive gifts that you vow to the LORD." Eventually, the place that the Lord would choose was identified as Jerusalem, a site not occupied by the Israelites until the time of David, some two centuries after Moses, according to the biblical account. But it is apparent that the restriction of sacrificial worship to a single location was an innovation in the time of Josiah (except for the alleged but unsuccessful attempt of Hezekiah).

The account of Josiah's reform in 2 Kings is part of what we call the Deuteronomistic History, which runs through the books of Joshua, Judges, Samuel, and Kings. According to the books of Kings, the first king of the northern kingdom of Israel, Jeroboam, sinned by setting up royal temples in opposition to Jerusalem, one at Bethel and one at Dan. This action is called "the sin of Jeroboam," and it is treated as the original sin of the northern kingdom of Israel. In this Deuteronomistic History, Josiah and Hezekiah (to a lesser extent) are heroes. Accordingly, the account of Josiah's reform must be suspected of being tendentious: it is told to glorify Josiah, with no consideration for other points of view. But the insistence of this history that the law of centralization had not been observed before Josiah's reform is highly significant. It strongly suggests that Deuteronomic law was not an old law that was now rediscovered, but was an innovation in the late seventh century B.C.E. This suspicion is supported by the observation of the close parallels between Deuteronomy and the Vassal Treaties of Esarhaddon. It is possible, of course, that Deuteronomy also includes some older laws, but if so they were reformulated in Deuteronomic idiom. It should also be noted that Deut 29:28 ("The LORD uprooted them from their land in anger, fury, and great wrath") presupposes the exile of the northern tribes to Assyria in 722 B.C.E.

The law of centralization makes good sense in the political context of the late seventh century B.C.E. The northern kingdom of Israel had fallen to the Assyrians a hundred years before. At that time, Hezekiah had tried, with only partial success, to unify the people who worshiped YHWH around the temple in Jerusalem. By the time Josiah came of age, the Assyrian Empire was in decline and the young king felt free to try to expand his control. The centralization of worship in Jerusalem was part of a wider effort to centralize control, and this is reflected in the laws of Deuteronomy. In one respect, the promulgation of the law of Deuteronomy was an exercise in the politics of control.

The Laws of Deuteronomy

The Recollection of Horeb

As in Exodus, the laws in Deuteronomy are presented as divine revelation, originally received by Moses on the mountain. In this case, the mountain is called Horeb, which means simply "the wilderness." This name is sometimes used in Exodus (3:1; 17:6; 33:6). Traditional source criticism ascribed these passages to the E source, with the implication that the mountain of the law was not identified with Sinai in northern tradition. Some recent scholars, however, argue that all references to Horeb are Deuteronomic. It would seem, in any case, that the identification of the mountain of the law with Sinai was not yet universally accepted when Deuteronomy was written.

In Deuteronomy, Moses reminds the Israelites of the original revelation: "how you once stood before the LORD God at Horeb" (4:10). The direct address in Deuteronomy is an attempt to re-create the experience of the original revelation. Moses recalls that the mountain was blazing up to the very heavens, but the primary emphasis of this account is on the verbal character of the revelation: "You heard the sound of words, but saw no form; there was only a voice" (4:12). The content is summarized as "his covenant," "the ten words," and "statutes and ordinances" that Moses should give them to observe when they enter the land. The Ten Commandments in Deuteronomy correspond closely to the formulation in Exodus 20. One significant variation concerns the motivation for keeping the Sabbath day. Where Exod 20:11 grounded this commandment by recalling how God rested on the seventh day of creation, Deuteronomy puts the emphasis on compassion. Not only should the Israelites rest, but so also their slaves and their livestock, for "remember that you were a slave in the land of Egypt." The recollection of the experience of slavery as a reason to be compassionate is typical of the rhetoric of Deuteronomy.

The Statutes and Ordinances

The reform of Josiah seems to have been predominantly concerned with the suppression of non-Yahwistic cults and of all sacrificial worship outside Jerusalem. The book of Deuteronomy as we have it, however, has much broader concerns. We might infer from this that Josiah, too, was engaged in wider social reform, or we might suppose that the book was expanded subsequently by scribes who had broader concerns. One significant aspect of Deuteronomy is the revision of the older code of laws known as the Book of the Covenant (Exodus 21–23). Some of the distinctive emphases of Deuteronomy can be appreciated by comparison with the older code.

Deuteronomy 15:1-11 picks up the laws of sabbatical release. It does not mention the commandment that the land should lie fallow every seventh year. The humanitarian concern for the poor that is cited as a reason for this law in Exod 23:10-11 is addressed elsewhere in Deuteronomy: 24:19-22 commands that something be left for "the alien, the orphan, and the widow" at harvest and grape gleaning. Deuteronomy 15 makes every seventh year an occasion of remission of debts. There were ancient precedents for such amnesties in the ancient Near East. Mesopotamian kings proclaimed acts of "justice" or "equity" (Akkadian *misarum*) involving the remission of debt and other obligations, especially at the beginning of their reigns (see the Edict of Ammisaduqa from Babylon, seventeenth century B.C.E.; *ANET*, 526–28). Deuteronomy makes this a law, to take effect at seven-year intervals, and so makes it independent of royal policy. The remission of debts did not apply to foreigners, who might otherwise take advantage of it. It is primarily a way of reinforcing the cohesion of the people of Israel, but Deuteronomy urges an open and generous attitude.

A more direct comparison with the Book of the Covenant is provided by the law for the release of slaves in Deut 15:12-18. Exodus 21 prescribed that male Hebrew slaves must be set free after six years. Deuteronomy applies this law to all slaves, whether male or female. It retains the provision that a slave may elect to stay with his master "because he loves you and your household, since he is well off with you," but the slave is no longer faced with the choice between his own freedom and remaining with his wife and children, as was the case in Exodus. Deuteronomy also goes beyond the older code in its homiletical exhortation to "provide liberally" for the liberated slave, and it adds the typical Deuteronomic motivation: "Remember that you were a slave in the land of Egypt."

The laws about the remission of debt and the release of slaves underline one of the prominent features of Deuteronomy—humanitarian concern for the poor and the marginal. This kind of concern appears in several other laws. Chapter 19 requires the Israelites to designate cities of refuge where people might flee to avoid revenge for unintentional homicide. Verse 15 requires the word of two or three witnesses for conviction of a crime, in order to protect people who might be wrongfully accused. The humane tendency is further in evidence in the provision that the corpse of an executed criminal must not be left all night on a gibbet (21:22-23), and in laws concerning a neighbor's livestock and the prohibition against taking a mother bird with its young (22:6). Deuteronomy 23:6 says that slaves who have escaped from their owners should not be given back to them. Deuteronomy 24 contains provisions protecting the rights of poor wage earners, aliens, and orphans. Some of these concerns are already found in the Book of the Covenant in Exodus, but they are more developed in Deuteronomy.

Chapter 20 sets humanitarian restraints on war. People may be exempted from service if they are engaged but not married (or if they are newly wed, 24:5), or if they have built a new house, or even if they are afraid. There may be some practical rationale for these exemptions. Halfhearted soldiers might undermine the morale of an army. The laws also require restraint in the conduct of war.

People besieging a town should not cut down its trees. And yet the laws for treating conquered people sound barbarically harsh to modern ears. In "the towns of these peoples that the LORD you God is giving you as an inheritance," the Israelites must not let anything that breathes remain alive. In cities outside the promised land, people who submit peacefully are to be enslaved. If they resist, the males must be put to the sword and the women and children and livestock taken as plunder. Yet again, in 21:10-14 we find a more humane discussion of the treatment of captive women. If a man takes such a woman for himself, he may not sell her thereafter, but must let her go free if he no longer wants her. Ancient warfare was savage, and little mercy was shown to captives. Nonetheless, the Deuteronomic insistence that the Canaanites be annihilated is in jarring conflict with the generally humane attitudes of the book. We shall discuss the Deuteronomic ideal of warfare and the alleged annihilation of the Canaanites further in the following chapter.

The Effects of Centralization

Some of the legal innovations of Deuteronomy result directly from the law of centralization of the cult. Most immediately, the prohibition of sacrificial worship outside Jerusalem radically changed the nature of Israelite religion. On the one hand, the account of Josiah's reform in 2 Kings 23 makes clear that up to this time there was widespread worship of Baal and Asherah, and that there were various cultic practices that Deuteronomy now deemed improper. This picture is now confirmed by archaeology, which has brought to light inscriptions mentioning YHWH's

Fig. 8.3 Terra-cotta figurines of women (or the goddess Astarte?), from Iron-Age Lachish and Ein Shemesh. Israel Museum. Erich Lessing/Art Resource, NY.

Asherah (which is variously interpreted as a goddess or as a cultic object associated with the goddess) and over two thousand terracotta figurines depicting a nude female figure (presumably a fertility-goddess). Some of the practices suppressed by Josiah had venerable histories. The patriarchs in Genesis had consecrated places of worship that were now torn down (e.g., Bethel) and had set up pillars and planted trees by them. Objects consecrated to the sun had allegedly been set up by "the kings of Judah" (2 Kgs 23:11). Even human sacrifice could be justified by appeal to Exod 22:29 ("the firstborn of your sons you shall give to me") and had also been practiced by Judean kings.

The Deuteronomic reform, then, entailed a purge of Judean religion that brought it much closer to monotheism than it had previously been. On the other hand, the worship of YHWH was also transformed. People who lived at a distance from Jerusalem could now offer sacrifice only on the rare occasions when they made a pilgrimage to the temple. Prior to this time, meat was eaten only when it had been sacrificed (except in the case of some wild animals). In light of the difficulties created by the centralization of the cult, Deuteronomy allowed that "whenever you desire you may slaughter and eat meat within any of your towns" (12:15). This change is often described as a "secularization" of Israelite religion. The term is not quite appropriate; society as envisioned by Deuteronomic law would still be permeated by religion. But it is true that some activities that had hitherto been sacral were now treated as profane, and that cultic rituals would henceforth play a much smaller role in the lives of most of the people.

The centralization of the cult also led to the transformation of the Festival of Passover. In the Book of the Covenant, Passover was not listed among the pilgrimage feasts, as it was a family festival, to be celebrated at home. Deuteronomy 16:2, however, requires that the Passover lamb be sacrificed "at the place that the LORD will choose as a dwelling for his name," and it is clearly combined with the Festival of Unleavened Bread. In 2 Kgs 23:21-23 we are told that King Josiah commanded the people to observe the Passover in accordance with the book of the covenant (that is, Deuteronomic law, not the Book of the Covenant in Exodus) and that they did so in Jerusalem, although no such Passover had been kept since the days of the judges.

The place of the Levites in Israelite society was also affected by centralization. The Levites at the country shrines were practically put out of business by the centralization of the cult. Their situation is addressed in Deut 18:6-8, which says that any Levite who chose to go up to Jerusalem could minister at the temple there and share in the priestly offerings. This provision inevitably made for tensions between the Jerusalem priesthood and the newly arrived Levites. According to 2 Kgs 23:9, "the priests of the high places did not come up to the altar of the Lord in Jerusalem, but ate unleavened bread among their kindred." Nonetheless, we shall find in Ezekiel 44 that relations between priests and Levites in Jerusalem remained controversial after the Babylonian exile.

Centralization and Control

The centralization of the cult is the most obvious way in which Deuteronomy brings about a concentration of power in Jerusalem, but it also tends toward a more centrally controlled society in other respects. Chapter 13 contains a warning against prophets and other diviners who might offer rival claims about the will of God. Deuteronomy 18:15-22 allows that there are legitimate prophets, who are prophets like Moses. (The singular form, "a prophet like me," is clearly meant to indicate a type, although it was later understood to refer to an individual who would come at the end of days.) A prophet who speaks in the name of gods other than YHWH is false, but Deuteronomy also recognizes that a prophet may speak falsely in the name of the Lord. The distinction between true and false prophecy would eventually become a major problem, as we shall later see. Deuteronomy 18 offers one simple criterion: a prophecy that is not fulfilled is thereby shown to be false. But prophets did much more than make predictions. The more far-reaching implication of Deuteronomy 18 is that a true prophet is "a prophet like Moses." The book of Deuteronomy was an attempt to express revelation

in written, definitive form, so that it would be the standard against which all other forms of revelation would be measured.

A number of laws in Deuteronomy curtail the power of the father over the affairs of his family. If a man had two wives and came to dislike one of them, he was not free to disinherit her children (21:15-17). If he had a rebellious son who was not amenable to discipline, he must bring him before the elders at the city gate. They may put him to death, but the father does not have the right to do so. Similarly, disputes about the virginity of a bride must be settled in public, by the elders. In all of this, Deuteronomy seeks to limit arbitrary action by the heads of families and impose standard judicial procedures on the society.

Perhaps the most remarkable assertion of control in Deuteronomy, however, concerns the king, in 17:14-20. Deuteronomy makes clear that kingship is something that develops from the people's desire to be like the neighboring peoples. Nonetheless, it is legitimate, within certain limitations. The king may not be a foreigner. He must not "acquire many horses," which would be necessary for building up an army, nor acquire many wives (as Solomon would do), nor acquire much gold and silver. Instead, he should have a copy of this book of the law and read it all the days of his life. Even the king must be subject to the law. Even though Josiah was very young when he began to reign, and was presumably subject to his advisers for a time, it is difficult to believe that he would have promulgated such a restrictive law of the kingship. Most probably, this passage was added later to the book, after the kingship had definitively failed in the Babylonian crisis. It is, however, in accordance with the general tendency of Deuteronomy to bring everything under the influence of the book of the law.

Purity Concerns in Deuteronomy

In contrast to Leviticus and the Priestly Code, purity concerns are not prominent in Deuteronomy. But they are not entirely absent either. Deuteronomy 14 gives a list of forbidden foods that is very similar to what we find in Leviticus 11. In chapter 22 there are prohibitions against cross-dressing (22:5), against plowing with an ox and an ass, and against combining wool and linen in a garment (22:10-11).

Purity is also a consideration in laws concerning marriage and sexual relations. Adultery (sex with the wife of another man) is punishable by death for both partners. Whether this law was actually implemented, we do not know. The prophet Hosea, a century before Deuteronomy, describes a quite different way of dealing with an adulterous wife, by shaming and divorcing her. The law recognizes that a woman is not at fault in case of rape, but if she is unmarried, the penalty for the man is that he has to marry her and cannot divorce her. In this case, the motivation is the woman's well-being, since she would find it difficult to find a husband if she had been defiled. The discussion of divorce in Deuteronomy 24, however, seems to be concerned more with purity. If a man divorces his wife and she becomes the wife of another but is divorced a second time, then the first husband may not marry her again. It should be noted that there is no legislation concerning divorce in the Hebrew Bible. The practice is simply assumed. Verses 1-4 became the focal text for discussions of divorce in later tradition. Verse 1 envisions the case of a man who divorces a woman "because he finds something objectionable about her." Later tradition inferred that divorce was permitted if a man found "something objectionable" about his wife. (Normally, wives were not permitted to initiate divorce in ancient Judaism. An exception to this rule is found among Jews in the south of Egypt in the Persian period and possibly again in the region of the Dead Sea early in the common era, but the latter case is disputed.) In Deuteronomy "something objectionable" most probably implied impurity or sexual misconduct. There was a famous debate about the meaning of the phrase between the rabbinic schools of Shammai and Hillel in the first century B.C.E. The Shammaites attempted to restrict the man's power of divorce to cases of adultery, but the school of Hillel ruled that divorce was permitted "even if she spoiled a dish for him" (Mishnah *Gittin* 9–10). Rabbi Akiba went further: "Even if he found another fairer than she."

The Authors of Deuteronomy

According to the account in 2 Kings 22, the law book promulgated by Josiah had been found in the Jerusalem temple and was presumably ancient. In light of the preceding discussion, there is good reason to regard the finding of the book as fiction, designed to ensure its ready acceptance by the people. The language of the book, which is influenced by the Assyrian treaties, does not permit a date much earlier than the time of Josiah. Moreover, the policy of centralization, which is central to the book, was Josiah's policy, and the book seems to have been either composed or edited to support it.

The elements that deal with centralization, either of the cult or of authority, were surely the work of Josiah's scribes. Other elements in the book, however, such as the discussion of divorce, are not obviously related to centralization. These elements, too, have been edited, since the book has a uniform style, but they suggest that the scribes drew on a legal tradition, which included, but was not limited to, the Book of the Covenant that is now found in Exodus 21–23. The description of a covenant ceremony at Shechem in Deuteronomy 27–28 is also independent of Josiah's policies and can hardly have been composed by people who wanted to centralize worship in Jerusalem. The provenance of these pre-Josianic traditions has been the subject of much scholarly discussion.

That the covenantal ceremony is located at Shechem strongly suggests that some of these traditions had their origin in northern Israel, more precisely in the central highlands of Ephraim. Despite the fact that the place that the Lord has chosen to centralize the cult is certainly Jerusalem, there are no allusions in Deuteronomy to Mount Zion or to traditions that can be associated with Jerusalem. In many respects, Deuteronomy recalls the northern eighth-century prophet Hosea. Hosea also took the exodus as his primary point of reference and referred to Moses as a prophet. He vehemently rejected the worship of deities other than YHWH, especially Baal. He also used the language of love for the relationship between God and Israel, although he spoke of God's love for Israel more than of Israel's obligation to love God. In contrast, there are few points of contact between Deuteronomy and the Jerusalem prophet Isaiah. There was a huge influx of northerners into Jerusalem after the fall of the northern kingdom. (We know from archaeological evidence that the size of the city more than doubled at that time.) It is not unreasonable then to suppose that some of the traditions found in Deuteronomy had originated in the north. Besides prophetic circles, of which Hosea might be representative, Levitical priests have been suggested as the carriers of these traditions. The Levites figure prominently in the covenant ceremony in chapters 27–28 and are mentioned frequently throughout the book. It is unlikely that northern Levites would have promoted the idea that the sacrificial cult should be restricted to Jerusalem, but they may have preserved traditions about a covenant at Shechem and laws that had circulated in northern Israel. These traditions may have been brought south by refugees after the fall of Samaria. It is conceivable that a book containing such material was hidden in the Jerusalem temple and found in the time of Josiah, but this is not a necessary hypothesis.

There can be little doubt, however, that the primary authors of Deuteronomy were Jerusalem scribes, initially in the service of Josiah. The editing of the book presumably went on for some time after Josiah's reign. The historical books of Joshua through Kings were also edited from a Deuteronomic perspective, and so we should imagine a Deuteronomistic school, whose activity continued even after the Babylonian exile. Josiah's scribes would presumably have been familiar with the Assyrian treaties that provide a model for the book in some respects.

Deuteronomy and Wisdom

One other aspect of Deuteronomy suggests a scribal origin. This is the extensive affinity with wisdom literature. We shall discuss wisdom literature in some detail later in this book. The classic biblical example is provided by the book of Proverbs. Wisdom is essentially instructional material, which incorporates traditional proverbs and sayings and has some lengthier didactic compositions. It was an international genre. Biblical wisdom literature is very similar to Egyptian instructions, and there are examples of similar literature from Mesopotamia. These instructions are often addressed to the student in the second person. Typically, they are not presented as divine revelation but as the distillation of human experience. The typical wisdom formula is "Listen, my son, to your father's teaching." We know that in Egypt these instructions were used in the training of courtiers and bureaucrats for the royal court. They were probably used in a similar context in Israel. King Solomon was traditionally regarded as the great patron and exponent of wisdom (see especially 1 Kgs 4:29-34 = 5:9-14 in MT). One section of the book of Proverbs is said to have been copied by "the men of Hezekiah." Hezekiah was king of Judah about a hundred years before Josiah (Prov 25:1).

The parallels between Deuteronomy and wisdom teachings are of various kinds. The "statutes and ordinances" are presented as a kind of wisdom: "You must observe them diligently, for this will show your wisdom and discernment to the peoples, who, when they hear all these statutes, will say, 'Surely this great nation is a wise and discerning people'" (Deut 4:6). The Torah is to be Israel's counterpart to the wisdom teachings of other peoples. Similarly, the judges appointed by Moses in Deut 1:13 are described as "wise, discerning, and reputable."

Several ordinances found in Deuteronomy are paralleled in wisdom writings. Injunctions against removing boundaries (Deut 19:14; 27:17) and falsifying weights and measures (25:13-16) are found not only in Proverbs (20:10, 23; 22:28; 23:10) but also in the Egyptian Wisdom of Amenemope. Both biblical books declare such actions "an abomination to the LORD"; Amenemope declares them an abomination to the Egyptian god Re. Deuteronomy 23:21-23 warns that a person who makes a vow should not postpone fulfilling it, and adds, "but if you refrain from vowing you will not incur guilt." This attitude contrasts sharply with the positive legislation about vows in Leviticus 27. The wisdom book of Qoheleth similarly warns against postponing the fulfillment of a vow and says that "it is better that you should not vow than that you should vow and not fulfill it" (Qoh 5:5). Deuteronomy 23:15, which prohibits sending a runaway slave back to his master, corresponds to Prov 30:10 ("do not slander a slave to his master"). In contrast the Laws of Hammurabi declared that sheltering a runaway slave was punishable by death (Code of Hammurabi 15; *ANET*, 166-67).

Despite these wisdom influences, Deuteronomy is unmistakably a law code, that frequently invokes the death penalty as sanction for its ordinances. It is also presented as revealed law rather than as the fruit of human experience, and it appeals to the distinctively Israelite experience of the exodus rather than to common human nature, as is customary in the older wisdom literature. Nonetheless, it is quite emphatic that the wisdom it presents has a human, earthly character: "Surely, this commandment that I am commanding you today is not too hard for you, nor is it too far away. It is not in heaven, that you should say, 'Who will go up to heaven for us, and get it for us so that we may hear it and observe it?' Neither is it beyond the sea, that you should say, 'Who will cross to the other side of the sea for us, and get it for us, so that we may hear it and observe it?' No, the word is very near to you; it is in your mouth and in your heart for you to observe" (Deut 30:11-14). While the law itself is revealed, no further revelation is necessary in order to understand it. Deuteronomy leaves little space for prophecy or for other forms of revelation such as we will find later in the apocalyptic literature.

The Effects of the Deuteronomic Reform

We have already noted that the centralization of the cult brought about a profound change in the practice of Israelite religion outside Jerusalem. The long-term effects of the reform, however, were more profound than anyone could have anticipated in 621 B.C.E. Less than a generation later, Jerusalem and its temple were destroyed and the leading citizens were taken into exile in Babylon. The Babylonians changed Judean society in ways that Josiah never could. The exiles in Babylon had to live without their temple, but they had "the book of the law," which acquired new importance in this setting. Henceforth, Judaism would be to a great degree a religion of the book. Study of the law would take the place of sacrifice. The synagogue would gradually emerge as the place of worship, first for Jews outside the land of Israel, later even within Israel itself. These changes took place gradually, over centuries, but they had their origin in the Deuteronomic

reform, which put a book at the center of religious observance for the first time.

The increasing emphasis on the written law brought the class of scribes to the fore as important religious personnel. They were the people who could copy the book of the law and edit it and make insertions on occasion. They were also the people who could read and interpret it. The role of the scribes would increase gradually over the centuries, but, again, it had its root in the importance accorded to the book of the law in Josiah's reform.

We do not know when Deuteronomy was combined with the material found in Genesis through Leviticus. According to the most influential scholarly theory, Deuteronomy was originally joined to the historical books, Joshua through Kings. Some time after the Babylonian exile, the book of the law was detached from the historical books and linked with the other accounts of revelation at Mount Sinai and the presentations of the laws. Some Deuteronomic phrases found their way into the earlier books, but the evidence for Deuteronomic redaction of these books is not clear and is much less obvious than the evidence for Priestly editorial work. It would seem, in short, that the books of Genesis through Leviticus were edited by Priestly writers. Deuteronomy was added to this corpus, but there was relatively little Deuteronomic editing in the first four books.

Together with the Priestly edition of the Torah, Deuteronomy was a major influence on Jewish theology in the Second Temple period. The main emphasis of that theology was on the observance of the law. Those who kept the law would prosper and live long in the land. Those who did not keep the law would come to grief. This theology did not go unquestioned in Second Temple Judaism. We find a major critique of it in the book of Job. But Deuteronomic theology should not be construed too narrowly as a legalistic religion. At the heart of it stood the command to love the Lord God with all one's heart and soul. The ordinances and commandments were concerned with human relations, with a strong emphasis on compassion for the disadvantaged in society. Jewish teachers in the Hellenistic period sometimes taught that the whole law could be summed up under two headings, love of God and love of one's neighbor. The saying attributed to Jesus in the Gospels (Matt 22:34-40; Mark 12:28-31; Luke 10:25-28), on the twofold greatest commandment, sums up at least one strand of Deuteronomic theology as it developed in the Second Temple period.

Appendix: The Relationship between Deuteronomy (D) and the Priestly Code (P)

D and P obviously represent two contrasting kinds of theology. The relationship between them, and specifically the chronological relationship, has often been controversial. Up to the mid-nineteenth century, scholars usually assumed that P was the *Grundschrift*, or basic document, the oldest stratum of the Pentateuch. The classic work of Graf and Wellhausen in the second half of the nineteenth century reversed the order and argued that P presupposes Deuteronomy and is the latest stage in the development of the Torah. This order was accepted as standard through most of the twentieth century. In Wellhausen's view,

the Priestly theology reflected the decline of Israelite religion, from the spiritual heights of the Prophets to the legalism of "Late Judaism." The late dating thus became associated with a negative value judgment. Jewish scholars understandably took exception to this view. The classic Jewish response to Wellhausen's approach was that of Yehezkel Kaufmann, who not only defended the spiritual value of the Priestly source but also its early date. The dating remains controversial, more than a century after Wellhausen wrote.

Insofar as the dispute about dating entails value judgments about the spiritual value of the Priestly source or any other material, it is misplaced. The earlier is not superior and the later is not inferior. One could as well argue that the later material represents a higher stage of development, but this again is not logically necessary. The question of chronological order is unrelated to the assessment of value.

Regardless of his prejudice against ritualistic forms of religion (Catholic as well as Jewish), Wellhausen offered serious arguments for the late date of P:

1. The centralization of the cult was an innovation in the time of Josiah. Deuteronomy reflects this innovation and addresses the question of centralization directly. In contrast, centralization is taken for granted in P.
2. Related to this is the question of profane slaughter. Deuteronomy allows the slaughter of animals for food apart from sacrifice, and this permission is clearly related to the restriction of sacrifice to Jerusalem. Profane slaughter is taken for granted in P but is explicitly forbidden in H (Leviticus 17).

Wellhausen reasoned that the acceptance of profane slaughter in P presupposed the Deuteronomic reform.

3. Deuteronomy does not distinguish clearly between priests and Levites, and often refers to "Levitical priests." In the Priestly source, however, the Levites are clearly subordinated to the priests.

4. Finally, the cultic calendar in Leviticus is more developed than that of Deuteronomy.

On the other side of the debate, various arguments have been offered for the antiquity of P. There has been a vast increase in knowledge about the ancient Near East since Wellhausen's time, and it is now clear that laws dealing with ritual and purity, sin and sanction, were an integral part of Near Eastern religion in the second millennium B.C.E. Consequently, interest in such matters can no longer be relegated to a late, supposedly decadent, period of Israelite or Jewish religion. It is now readily admitted that P is a repository of ancient traditions. But this does not require that the document itself be ancient.

The primary argument that has been offered for the antiquity of P is based on the development of the Hebrew language. Several key terms in P either fall out of use in the postexilic period or acquire a different meaning. For example, the Priestly word for the assembly is ʿedah. In postexilic books (Ezra, Nehemiah, Chronicles) the Deuteronomic term qahal is used instead. The word ʿabodah means "physical labor" in P; in Chronicles it means "worship." Some have argued that the book of Ezekiel, from the time of the exile, marks a watershed in this regard. Although it

shares many of the concerns of P, it often uses different terminology. (For a concise exposition of the linguistic evidence, see Milgrom, *Leviticus 1–16*, 3–13.) All of this shows that the language of P was not invented in the exilic or postexilic period. But Priestly, liturgical language is often archaic, and terminology is often preserved in ritual contexts long after it has fallen out of use in popular speech. (Compare the use of Latin in the Roman Catholic Mass up until the Second Vatican Council in the 1960s.) So the retention of archaic language in P does not necessarily prove that the composition is ancient. Indeed, some scholars have argued that P deliberately used archaic or archaizing language. For example, there is no good evidence that Israelites still worshiped at a tabernacle or tent-shrine *(mishkan)* during the monarchy at any time that P could plausibly have been composed. Also the word *nasiʾ*, "prince," was meant to evoke an earlier time, before the monarchy. It should be granted that the language of P is indeed old and not an artificial construct of the postexilic period, but this in itself does not settle the date at which the Priestly laws as now found in the Pentateuch were formulated.

Some scholars have argued that while there is no clear case of Deuteronomic influence on P, there are several cases of Priestly influence on D. For example, Deuteronomy sometimes tells the Israelites to do "as I have commanded them" when the relevant commands are found in Leviticus (e.g., Deut 24:8, with reference to scale disease, which is the subject of Leviticus 13–14). Also the dietary laws in Deuteronomy 14 are said to be adapted from Leviticus 11 (such laws are typical of Leviticus but exceptional in Deuteronomy). But this issue, too, is not as straightforward as it might appear. The presence of some elements of Priestly tradition, such as dietary laws, in Deuteronomy can be explained in various ways. On the one hand, it is possible that these laws were known in Israel apart from the book of Leviticus, even before the Priestly laws were written down. On the other hand, it has often been suggested that these elements were introduced into Deuteronomy by editors who were influenced by P but that they were not part of the original Deuteronomic code.

This latter point highlights an ambiguity in the entire discussion. It is generally granted that Deuteronomy was not complete in its present form at the time of Josiah's reform, but was edited and expanded by scribes for many decades thereafter. It is also likely that the Priestly code evolved over a period of time. Even if we can show that one book, or tradition, depends on the other at a specific point, this does not necessarily mean that the entire book or tradition is later. Wellhausen, in fact, was not so much concerned with the book of Deuteronomy as with the underlying historical event of Josiah's reform and the changes it brought about in Israelite religion.

Even if one grants that P is a repository of ancient tradition and uses archaic language, and that the book of Deuteronomy is influenced by Priestly tradition at some points, Wellhausen's primary arguments remain to be addressed. The central issue has always been whether P presupposes the centralization of the cult. Neither P nor H ever explicitly demands that sacrificial worship be confined to one place, in the manner of Deuteronomy 12. Since the Priestly legislation is presented in the context of Israel's sojourn in the wilderness, it speaks of the tabernacle and the tent of meeting as one central place of worship.

The question is, did the Priestly authors imply that Israel should also have one central place of worship when they came into the land? In the discussion of Leviticus 17 in the previous chapter, we saw that H required that anyone offering sacrifice bring it to the entrance of the tent of meeting. It has been suggested that this only means that sacrifice must be offered at *a* sanctuary, not necessarily at one central shrine. There is little other indication in P or H, however, that they condoned sacrifice at multiple shrines. Another interesting test case is provided by the prescriptions for the celebration of the Passover in Exodus 12. There we are told that the lamb should be sacrificed by "the whole assembly of the congregation of Israel" (Exod 12:6; the words for "assembly," *qahal,* and "congregation," *'edah,* are roughly equivalent; it may be that two variant formulations were combined into one). The language here is most easily taken to mean that the lamb is sacrificed in a cultic assembly. But we have seen that Passover was a family celebration down to the time of Josiah's reform. It would seem then that P presupposes the Deuteronomic transformation of Passover into a pilgrimage festival. Nonetheless, the text is not so explicit as to settle the issue beyond doubt. If indeed P was compiled after Josiah's reform, then the attempt of H to forbid profane slaughter must be seen as a reactionary move in rejection of one of the major changes brought about by Deuteronomy. The stricter Holiness Code was idealistic, but it is unlikely that it was ever enforced.

The changing relations between priests and Levites are also more easily explained if the Priestly legislation is later than Josiah's reforms. Deuteronomy refers to the Levites as "Levitical priests." In Deut 18:1 we are told that the tribe of Levi has no allotment within Israel, but that they may eat the sacrifices that are the Lord's. After Josiah's reforms, however, there were (or were supposed to be) no sacrifices to eat outside Jerusalem. Consequently, Deuteronomy decreed that any Levite could go to "the place that the LORD will choose" whenever he wished and minister there, and receive an equal portion to eat with the other priests (Deut 17:6-8). This arrangement could hardly fail to cause tensions between the priests who were already in Jerusalem and those who came in from the countryside.

According to Deuteronomy, the Levitical priests could serve at the central sanctuary on an equal basis with other priests. The Priestly legislation, however, in Num 3:6-9 and again in Num 18:1-7 is quite explicit: the tribe of Levi is set before Aaron the priest to assist him, but the priesthood belongs only to Aaron and his descendants. The subordinate role of the Levites is also emphasized in Ezek 44:10-14. This text, from the exilic or early postexilic period, blames the Levites for "going astray from me after their idols" and, as punishment, makes them hewers of wood and drawers of water. Ezekiel redefines the "Levitical priests" as the Zadokites, the traditional Jerusalem priesthood. Ezekiel's understanding of the relationship between priests and Levites is essentially in agreement with that of P. The relationship was still problematic at the time of the restoration of Jerusalem after the exile. It is apparent that the Zadokite priests did not welcome the Levites from the country shrines as their equals in ministry, but they did make a place for them in Jerusalem, even if it was a subordinate one.

Finally, Wellhausen was indisputably right that the Priestly calendar in Leviticus 23 is the most developed such calendar in the Hebrew Bible. Not only does it include the Passover among the pilgrimage feasts, but it includes two important festivals that are not found even in Deuteronomy. "In the seventh month, on the first day of the month, you shall observe a day of complete rest, a holy convocation commemorated with trumpet blasts" (Lev 23:24). This is the festival that would be known to posterity as Rosh Hashanah, the New Year's celebration, when the year was deemed to begin in the fall. Then, "the tenth day of this seventh month is the Day of Atonement," or Yom Kippur (23:27). It is inconceivable that Deuteronomy would have omitted these festivals if they were celebrated when it was composed. Moreover, the book of Nehemiah, written no earlier than the end of the fifth century B.C.E., describes the observances of the seventh month in the time of Ezra (probably a little after the mid-fifth century). According to Nehemiah, there was a holy day, marked by a solemn assembly, on the first day of the month, but the next observance was the Feast of Booths or Tabernacles, which Leviticus dates to the fifteenth of the month. There is no mention of Yom Kippur on the tenth of the month, although there is a day of fasting on the twenty-fourth. From this it would seem that the cultic calendar of Leviticus 23 had not yet been finalized in the mid-fifth century B.C.E.

It would be too simple, however, to say that the Priestly source is later than Deuteronomy, without qualification. Both of these sources contain ancient traditions, and both went through extensive redaction over a lengthy period of time. Some of the traditions contained in the Priestly source may be quite old. It seems, however, that the Priestly strand of the Pentateuch was edited after Josiah's reform and was influenced by the centralization of the sacrificial cult and the changes it entailed.

Finally, the Priestly material was integrated with the older pentateuchal traditions (traditionally known as J and E) to a much greater extent than was Deuteronomy. There is good reason to think that the books of Genesis through Numbers were edited by Priestly writers. Deuteronomy, in contrast, was originally linked with the historical books that follow it. We do not know when it was detached from the history and integrated into the Torah as the fifth book of Moses. While some Deuteronomic glosses can be identified in the first four books, there does not seem to have been a Deuteronomic redaction of the Torah on the same scale as the Priestly one. Nonetheless, the climactic position eventually accorded to Deuteronomy ensured that for many people it would provide the lens through which the Pentateuch would be interpreted in later tradition.

FOR FURTHER READING

Commentaries

W. Brueggemann, *Deuteronomy* (Nashville: Abingdon, 2001). Theological and ethical analysis.

R. E. Clements, "The Book of Deuteronomy," *NIB* 2:268–538. Theological and homiletical commentary.

A. D. H. Mayes, *Deuteronomy* (NCB; Grand Rapids: Eerdmans, 1981). Careful, reliable commentary.

P. D. Miller, *Deuteronomy* (Interpretation; Louisville: Westminster John Knox, 1990). Well-informed homiletical commentary.

R. D. Nelson, *Deuteronomy* (OTL; Louisville: Westminster John Knox, 2002). Substantial commentary. Relates the core text to the Assyrian period.

J. Tigay, *The JPS Torah Commentary: Deuteronomy* (Philadelphia: Jewish Publication Society, 1996). Historical-critical commentary informed by medieval Jewish tradition.

G. von Rad, *Deuteronomy* (trans. D. Barton; OTL; Philadelphia: Westminster, 1966). Influential but now dated.

M. Weinfeld, *Deuteronomy 1–11* (AB 5; New York: Doubleday, 1991). The best English-language commentary. Unfortunately incomplete.

Studies

Braulik, G., *The Theology of Deuteronomy: Collected Essays of Georg Braulik OSB* (trans. U. Lindblad; Bibal Collected Essays 2; N. Richland Hills, TX: Bibal, 1996). Essays on Deuteronomy by a major European interpreter.

D. L. Christensen, ed., *A Song of Power and the Power of Song: Essays on the Book of Deuteronomy* (Sources for Biblical and Theological Study 3; Winona Lake, IN: Eisenbrauns, 1993). Wide-ranging collection of essays on Deuteronomy by American and European authors.

Y. Kaufmann, *The Religion of Israel: From Its Beginnings to the Babylonian Exile* (trans. and abridged by M. Greenberg; New York: Schocken, 1977). Classic Jewish counterpoint to Wellhausen.

B. Levinson, *Deuteronomy and the Hermeneutics of Legal Innovation* (New York: Oxford University Press, 1997). Study of the adaptation of the Book of the Covenant in Deuteronomy.

N. Lohfink, *Theology of the Pentateuch: Themes of the Priestly Narrative and Deuteronomy* (trans. L. M. Maloney; Minneapolis: Fortress Press, 1994). Chapters 8–11 are theologically sensitive essays on Deuteronomy.

N. MacDonald, *Deuteronomy and the Meaning of "Monotheism"* (Tübingen: Mohr Siebeck, 2003). Analysis of statements that YHWH is One in Deuteronomy, disputing usefulness of the category "monotheism."

E. W. Nicholson, *Deuteronomy and Tradition* (Philadelphia: Fortress Press, 1967). The use of northern tradition in Deuteronomy.

A. Rofé, *Deuteronomy: Issues and Interpretation* (London: T&T Clark, 2002). A collection of previously published essays on Deuteronomy by the author, with several items on law.

T. C. Römer, *The So-Called Deuteronomistic History: A Sociological and Literary Introduction* (London: T&T Clark, 2007), 45–65. Detailed analysis of 2 Kings 22–23 and Deuteronomy 12, distinguishing layers of redaction. Pages 67–78 are on the parallels with Assyrian treaties.

J. Stackert, *Rewriting the Torah: Literary Revision in Deuteronomy and the Holiness Legislation* (Tübingen: Mohr Siebeck, 2007). Deuteronomy reworks the Covenant Code and is in turn reworked by the Holiness Code.

G. von Rad, *Studies in Deuteronomy* (trans. D. Stalker; SBT 9; Chicago: Regnery, 1953). Emphasizes the role of the Levites.

M. Weinfeld, *Deuteronomy and the Deuteronomic School* (reprint, Winona Lake, IN: Eisenbrauns, 1992). Explores links with wisdom and with Assyrian treaties.

J. Wellhausen, *Prolegomena to the History of Israel* (reprint, Atlanta: Scholars Press, 1994). The classic treatment of the relationship between P and D.

PART TWO

The Deuteronomistic History

Introduction

The books of Joshua, Judges, Samuel and Kings (traditionally known as the Former Prophets) provide the main account that we have of the history of ancient Israel. All history writing is subject to ideological bias, and in the case of these books the bias might also be described as theological. History is viewed through the lens provided by the book of Deuteronomy. Accordingly, these books are known in modern scholarship as the Deuteronomistic History.

The view that the book of Deuteronomy once constituted a literary unit with the historical books was argued in detail by the German scholar Martin Noth in 1943, and has been widely accepted since then, although some scholars have questioned it in recent years. The historical books contain diverse kinds of material, and evidently drew on older sources and traditions. Other scholars before Noth had noticed that some elements in these books were influenced by the book of Deuteronomy. The books of Kings, for example, frequently condemn the kings of northern Israel for continuing "the sin of Jeroboam," the first king of northern Israel, who erected places of worship at Bethel and Dan, as counterattractions to the temple in Jerusalem. This criticism clearly presupposes Josiah's reform and Deuteronomic law. Noth, however, pointed out that similar language and ideology runs through all these historical books, and that this shows that they were edited in a consistent manner. The editor is called Deuteronomistic because history is judged in the light of Deuteronomic theology.

According to Noth, the Deuteronomist divided the history of Israel into four major periods: the time of Moses, the conquest of Canaan under Joshua, the period of the judges, and the monarchy. Key points in this history were marked by speeches. For example, a speech by Joshua in Joshua 1 marks the beginning of the conquest, and another in Joshua 23 marks its conclusion. Samuel's speech in 1 Samuel 12 marks the transition to the time of the monarchy. Solomon's prayer in 1 Kings 8 at the consecration of the temple also marks an important point in the history. Other Deuteronomistic passages take the form of narrative summaries: Joshua 12; Judg 2:11-22; 2 Kgs 17:7-18, 20-23. Subsequent scholars have identified other passages that have structural importance, most notably the promise to David in 2 Samuel 7, which is often recalled in 1–2 Kings.

Noth argued that the entire Deuteronomistic History was composed by one editor, during the Babylonian exile. The purpose of the work would then be to explain the disaster that befell Israel and Judah as divine punishment for their failure (and especially the failure of the kings) to keep the covenant. Other scholars, however, have insisted that this is not the only theme in the history. There is also a positive view of the kingship that is reflected in the promise to David in 2 Samuel 7 and in the account of Josiah's reform. Various alternatives to Noth's single editor have been proposed. The most influential of these in the English speaking world is the view of F. M. Cross that there were two editions of the history. The first edition was in the reign of Josiah. This had a positive view of the monarchy, and was in effect propaganda for Josiah's reform. The second edition was in the Babylonian exile, after the release of King Jehoiachin from prison in 562 B.C.E., which is the last event reported in 2 Kings. The second edition was colored by the destruction of Jerusalem, and placed greater emphasis on the failure of the monarchy. Other scholars have proposed more complex theories. A theory of three editions, one with an historical focus, one prophetic, and one nomistic (emphasizing law), has enjoyed wide support in German scholarship.

For our present purposes, three considerations should be borne in mind in reading these books. First, this history was put together and edited no earlier than the late seventh century B.C.E., several hundred years after the supposed time of the conquest and the judges. The final edition of these books must be dated no earlier than the Babylonian exile, possibly later. It is not suggested that the Deuteronomistic writers invented their history out of whole cloth. They certainly had traditions and sources at their disposal. These traditions, however, were not all historiographical in nature. Their purpose was not necessarily to provide historical information. While the historical books may contain much reliable information about the history of Israel, they must be examined with caution before they can be used as historical sources.

Second, the reconstruction of the history of Israel in these books has a clear ideological character. It is heavily influenced by Deuteronomic theology, and sees a pattern of reward and punishment in history. It is written from a Judean perspective, with a strong belief in the divine election of Jerusalem and of the Davidic dynasty. It is decidedly unsympathetic to the kings of northern Israel. We need hardly add that it has no sympathy for the Canaanites, who are viewed only as a threat to Israel and its covenant. Moreover, the sources on which the Deuteronomists drew often had the character of legend. We should not doubt that these writers tried to give an accurate account of the past, as they understood it. But they also clearly wanted to convey a theological understanding of history, the belief that the course of events is shaped by God in response to human actions. This theological aspect of these books is as important for the modern reader as any historical information they contain.

Third, we must also reckon with the fact that these books contains some diversity of editorial perspective. Some passages have a clearly negative view of the monarchy, others are more positive (we find these conflicting views in 1 Samuel). This diversity is most easily explained by supposing that there were different editions of the book. Moreover, each of the books that make up the history has its own character, which is shaped by the underlying traditions on which it draws, and the different subject matter of each phase of the history. It is typical of biblical literature that these tensions in the text were not smoothed out by a final editor, but were allowed to stand, allowing us to see some of the diverse perspectives that shaped these books.

FOR FURTHER READING

A. F. Campbell and M. A. O'Brien, *Unfolding the Deuteronomistic History* (Minneapolis: Fortress Press, 2000). An analysis of the entire text, identifying redactional layers.

F. M. Cross, *Canaanite Myth and Hebrew Epic* (Cambridge: Harvard University Press, 1973) 99–105. Influential theory of two redactions.

G. N. Knoppers and J. G. McConville, eds., *Reconsidering Israel and Judah: Recent Studies on the Deuteronomistic History* (Winona Lake, Ind.: Eisenbrauns, 2000). Collection of essays representing recent scholarship.

S. L. McKenzie, "Deuteronomistic History," *ABD* 2:160–68. Good summary of the state of the question.

R. Nelson, *The Double Redaction of the Deuteronomistic History* (JSOT 18; Sheffield: JSOT, 1981). Elaboration of the two-redaction theory proposed by Cross.

M. Noth, *The Deuteronomistic History* (JSOTSup 15; Sheffield: JSOT Press, 1991). Classic presentation of the Deuteronomistic ideology of Joshua–Kings.

J. Pakkala, *Intolerant Monolatry in the Deuteronomistic History* (Göttingen: Vandenhoeck & Ruprecht, 1999). Argues that "intolerant monolatry" was a late development in the Deuteronomistic History.

R. F. Person, *The Deuteronomistic History and the Book of Chronicles: Scribal Works in an Oral World* (Atlanta: Society of Biblical Literature, 2010) argues that DTR and Chronicles are competing histories from the Persian period, based on common traditions.

A. de Pury, T. Römer, and J.-D. Macchi, eds., *Israel Constructs Its History: Deuteronomistic Historiography in Recent Research* (JSOTSup 306; Sheffield: Sheffield Academic Press, 2000). Collection of essays representing recent scholarship.

T. C. Römer, *The So-Called Deuteronomistic History. A Sociological, Historical and Literary Introduction* (London: T & T Clark, 2007). Comprehensive discussion and history of scholarship. Defends a three-stage theory.

L. S. Schearing and S. L. McKenzie, eds., *Those Elusive Deuteronomists: The Phenomenon of Pan-Deuteronomism* (JSOTSup 268; Sheffield: Sheffield Academic Press, 1999). Collection of essays critical of loose use of the label "Deuteronomic," with reference to prophetic and other literature.

H. Spieckermann, "The Former Prophets: The Deuteronomistic History," trans. L. G. Perdue, in L. G. Perdue, ed., *The Blackwell Companion to the Hebrew Bible* (Oxford: Blackwell, 2001) 337–52. An example of a recent German approach to distinguishing multiple layers in the Deuteronomistic History.

CHAPTER 9

The Book of Joshua

INTRODUCTION

Following the death of Moses at the end of Deuteronomy, the book of Joshua tells the story of the Israelite possession of Canaan. As we will see in this chapter, this account raises both historical and moral questions. We will discuss current thinking about the origins of Israel in Canaan, then consider aspects of the biblical account of the "conquest" of the land, the settlement of the tribes, and the covenant at Shechem.

The book of Joshua purports to describe how the Israelite tribes took possession of the land of Canaan west of the Jordan. The opening verses of the book are programmatic. The Lord tells Joshua, "My servant Moses is dead. Now proceed to cross the Jordan, you and all the people, into the land that I am giving to them, to the Israelites. Every place that the sole of your foot will tread upon I have given to you, as I promised to Moses. From the wilderness and the Lebanon as far as the great river, the river Euphrates, all the land of the Hittites, to the Great Sea in the west shall be your territory. No one shall be able to stand against you all the days of your life." The territory promised here is essentially the same as that promised to Abraham in Genesis 15, "from the river of Egypt to the great river, the river Euphrates." Later summary statements suggest that Joshua did indeed overrun the entire country. Compare, for example, Josh 10:40: "So Joshua defeated the whole land, the hill country and the Negeb and the lowland and the slopes, and all their kings; he left no one remaining, but utterly destroyed all that breathed."

Closer reading of the book of Joshua suggests a more limited conquest. Most of the action in chapters 2–10 takes place in the small area that would finally be assigned to Benjamin. Chapters 3–6 describe the crossing of the Jordan and the conquest of Jericho. Then chapters 7 and 8 are devoted to the events at Ai, near Bethel, a few miles to the northwest. This is followed by very brief accounts of a covenantal ceremony at Shechem (8:30-35), the surrender of Gibeon (a few miles northwest of Jerusalem), and the defeat of five kings from Jerusalem, Hebron, Jarmuth, Lachish, and Eglon (chaps. 9–10). These victories are followed by the summary in 10:40-43, claiming the comprehensive conquest of the southern part of the country. Chapter 11 describes a campaign against Hazor in the far north. The actual narratives of conquest appear quite spotty as compared with the sweeping claims in the summaries. Moreover, Judges 1 gives a long list of places from which the Canaanites were not driven out, including major sites such as Taanach and Megiddo. There are also troubling inconsistencies. Judges 1:8 says that "the people of Judah fought against Jerusalem and took it," but according to 1:21 "the Benjaminites did not drive out the Jebusites who lived in Jerusalem." Later we will find that Jerusalem was captured only in the time of David.

Also Hazor, which was allegedly captured by Joshua in Joshua 11, is still in Canaanite control in Judges 4 and 5. The biblical evidence for a sweeping conquest, then, is not as straightforward as it might initially appear. Consequently, different models have been proposed to explain the origin of Israel in Canaan.

Four such models have been influential in scholarship in the twentieth century: the immigration model, favored especially by German scholars in the mid-twentieth century; the conquest model, defended especially in North America; the revolt hypothesis, which tries to explain the origin of Israel as social upheaval; and the model of gradual evolution, which suggests that the Israelites originated

Fig. 9.1 The circular platform of a Canaanite cultic place in Stone Age Megiddo. Photo by Marshall Johnson

INTRODUCTION TO THE HEBREW BIBLE

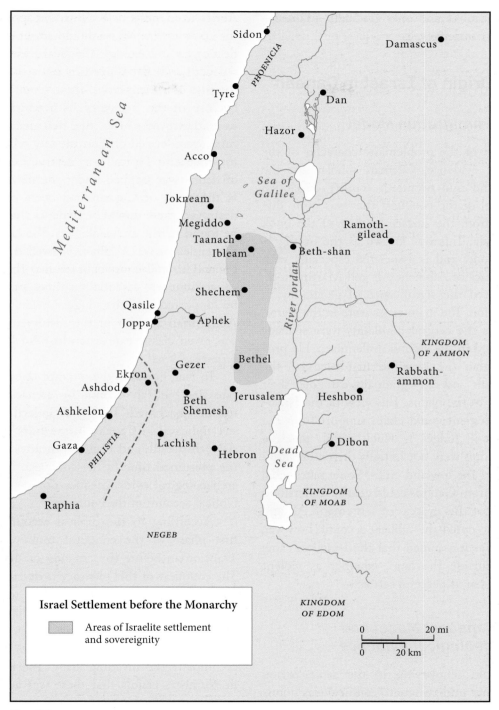

Israel Settlement before the Monarchy

Areas of Israelite settlement and sovereignty

Map 9.1

as Canaanites and only gradually attained a distinctive identity.

The Origin of Israel in Canaan

The Immigration Model

In light of the problematic character of the biblical evidence, German scholars of the early and mid-twentieth century developed a model of the conquest that was quite different from the surface reading of the book of Joshua. This was known as the immigration model and is associated especially with the names of Albrecht Alt and Martin Noth. Alt noted the significance of geography in the region. The main cities were in the plains, whereas the central highlands were sparsely inhabited in the second millennium. He proposed that the Israelites first occupied the highlands and only gradually extended their control to the plains. This view of the Israelite settlement could claim support from the account in Judges 1, which admits that the Canaanites were not initially driven out from many of the lowland cities. Some patriarchal stories from Genesis could also be understood as part of this process of settlement. Alt and Noth accepted the biblical account, however, insofar as it assumed that the Israelites came from outside the land, whether as violent invaders or as peaceful settlers.

The Conquest Model and Archaeological Evidence

American scholarship in the same period (early and mid-twentieth century) was dominated by the rise of archaeology. Unlike the stories of Genesis or Exodus, the account of the conquest in Joshua should admit of verification by archaeology. The Near East is dotted with *tells,* flat-topped mounds that were the sites of ancient cities. These mounds grew because of the frequency with which cities were destroyed. After the destruction, the ruins were leveled off and the city rebuilt on top of them. Typically, a "destruction layer" of debris was trapped under the new floors. If the cities of Canaan had been violently destroyed, there should be evidence that could be found by the archaeologists. The leader in this endeavor was William Foxwell Albright. He and his colleagues believed that the biblical account was essentially correct and could be supported by archaeological evidence. The Albrightian account of the history of Israel was given classic expression in John Bright's *History of Israel.*

In fact, however, the attempt to corroborate the biblical account by archaeological research backfired. There was indeed extensive upheaval in Canaan in the Late Bronze Age (thirteenth and twelfth centuries B.C.E.), the presumed time of the conquest. But the archaeological evidence does not match the biblical account of the conquest.

According to the biblical accounts, the first phase of the conquest took place in Transjordan before the crossing of the river. The conquest of this territory is described in Numbers 21. In Josh 1:12, Joshua tells the tribes of Reuben and Gad and the half-tribe of Manasseh that they may settle beyond the Jordan, although their warriors should accompany the invading army. The account in Numbers claims that there was a settled population in this region and specifically

Fig. 9.2 A Neolithic tower in Jericho, excavated by Kathleen Kenyon, who found evidence the tell was uninhabited in the time of Joshua. Photo by Marshall Johnson

mentions the cities of Heshbon and Dibon. Both of these sites have been excavated and shown to have been unoccupied in the Late Bronze period. It follows that they cannot have been destroyed by the Israelites in the late thirteenth century B.C.E.

Similar results were obtained at Jericho and Ai, the two showpieces of the conquest in Joshua. Neither was a walled city in the Late Bronze period. Of nearly twenty identifiable sites that were captured by Joshua or his immediate successors according to the biblical account, only two, Hazor and Bethel, have yielded archaeological evidence of destruction at the appropriate period. Ironically, the biblical evidence on Hazor is problematic, since it is said to be still in Canaanite hands in Judges 4–5. Archaeology is not an infallible science, and its results are always open to revision in light of new excavations, but a scholar can only make judgments based on the best evidence available at the moment. In light of the available evidence, we must conclude that the account of the conquest in Joshua is largely if not entirely fictitious. The nature and purpose of this fiction is an important question, to which we shall return, but first a little more can be said about the origin of Israel in Canaan.

The results of archaeology have not been entirely negative. Excavations and surveys in the last quarter of the twentieth century have brought to light hundreds of small sites that were established in the thirteenth to eleventh centuries B.C.E., primarily in the central highlands, but some as far north as Galilee and some to the south in the northern Negev. Nearly all these are small, unwalled sites, and most were abandoned by the eleventh century. These settlements are generally assumed to be Israelite, although they do not, of course, provide explicit self-identification. The identification of these settlements as Israelite is suggested first of all by the fact that this region is the stronghold of early Israel according to the biblical account, and it was clearly Israelite in later times. Moreover, we have one piece of nonbiblical evidence that Israel had come into existence in the land of Canaan before the end of the thirteenth century B.C.E. A commemorative stela of the Egyptian pharaoh Merneptah, erected about 1220 B.C.E., boasts of his victories:

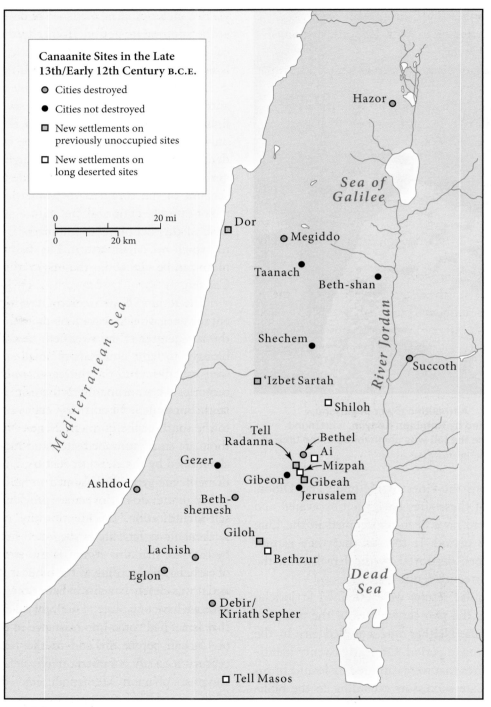

Canaanite Sites in the Late 13th/Early 12th Century B.C.E.

- ◉ Cities destroyed
- ● Cities not destroyed
- ▣ New settlements on previously unoccupied sites
- ▢ New settlements on long deserted sites

0   20 mi

0   20 km

Hazor

Sea of Galilee

Dor

Megiddo

Taanach

Beth-shan

River Jordan

Shechem

Succoth

'Izbet Sartah

Shiloh

Mediterranean Sea

Tell Radanna

Bethel
Ai

Mizpah

Gezer

Gibeon

Gibeah

Jerusalem

Ashdod

Beth-shemesh

Giloh

Lachish

Bethzur

Eglon

Dead Sea

Debir/ Kiriath Sepher

Tell Masos

Map 9.2

Plundered is Canaan with every evil.
Carried off is Ashkelon; seized upon is
Gezer;
Yanaom is made as that which does not
exist;
Israel is laid waste, his seed is not;
Hurru is become a widow for Egypt.
(*ANET,* 378)

It is not clear here whether Israel is a people or a place (like Ashkelon and Gezer), but in either case the inscription shows that an entity called Israel existed in Canaan. There is no record in the Bible of an encounter between Israel and Merneptah. Of course, Egyptian inscriptions are guilty of hyperbole quite as much as the Bible is, and some of the pharaoh's victories may have been imaginary. We can hardly suppose, however, that he would have claimed victory over imaginary places or peoples, especially when they are known to have existed at a later time.

But the evidence for Israelite or proto-Israelite settlements in the central highlands stops far short of confirming the biblical account. The most remarkable thing about these settlements in light of the biblical account is that their material culture is essentially Canaanite. In the words of one prominent archaeologist: "It must be stressed that there is no evidence whatsoever in the material culture that would indicate that these Iron I villagers originated outside Palestine, not even in Transjordan, much less in Egypt or the Sinai. There is nothing in the material remains to suggest that these are 'pastoral nomads settling down'—on the contrary, they appear to be skilled and well-adapted peasant farmers, long familiar with local conditions in Canaan" (W. Dever, *ABD* 3:549–50). Archaeologists of an earlier generation thought they had found some distinctively Israelite features in the central highlands. The typical style of house there is usually referred to as "the four-roomed courtyard house" (consisting of a cluster of rooms around a courtyard). This has often been called "the Israelite-style house," and it was indeed the typical kind of house in ancient Israel. But while this kind of house became common only in the later part of the second millennium, there were some earlier examples, and a growing number of such houses have now been found at sites that were obviously not Israelite. Similarly, the "collar-rimmed jar" is typical of these settlements but not unique to them. The pottery in the new villages is usually of poorer quality than what is found in Canaanite cities such as Gezer, but of the same general type. (One aspect of the material remains of the highland settlements

Fig. 9.3 The Merneptah Stele (or "Israel" stele), ca. 1220 B.C.E.; now in the Egyptian Museum, Cairo.

that may be distinctive, however, is the absence of pig bones, which is of interest in view of the biblical dietary laws.)

Since these villages were not fortified, they lend support to the view that the settlement was a process of peaceful immigration. Unlike the older immigration hypothesis of Alt and Noth, however, the new evidence suggests that the settlers did not come from outside the land, but were of Canaanite origin. If some Israelites had been slaves in Egypt and spent a period wandering in the wilderness, they failed to make an impact on the material culture, at least insofar as we are now aware. These archaeological findings do not prove that no exodus took place, but they suggest that the origin of the people of Israel cannot be explained primarily by the story of escape from Egypt.

The Revolt Model

The hypothesis that Israel had its origins in a social revolution within Canaan was first proposed by an American student of Albright, George Mendenhall, in 1962. Mendenhall was prompted by dissatisfaction with the biblical account rather than by new archaeological evidence. The basic idea for the model, however, was derived from the Amarna letters, which had been found in Egypt in 1888. These were letters written in Akkadian on clay tablets by people in Canaan and addressed to the pharaohs Amenophis III and Amenophis IV, or Akhenaten, in the fourteenth century BCE. The latter pharaoh had launched a religious revolution in Egypt by promoting the cult of the sun-god Aten to the exclusion of other deities (this was the so-called Aten heresy). He evidently did not pay very close attention to the affairs of the Egyptian empire in Canaan. The letters from Canaan frequently complain about groups who were causing turmoil in Canaan and challenging Egyptian authority. These troublemakers are often called Habiru/Hapiru or Apiru/Abiru. This term is also known from a range of other texts over the second millennium. It is not an ethnic term, but refers to people who were, in one way or another, on the margins of society, sometimes as mercenaries, sometimes as slaves, and sometimes just as troublemakers.

Lab'ayu writes to Pharaoh

In this letter from the archives of Amarna, the Canaanite king Lab'ayu defends himself against accusations that he has disloyally allowed his son to associate with 'apiru.

To the king, my lord and my Sun: Thus Lab'ayu, your servant and the dirt on which you tread. I fall at the feet of the king, my lord and my Sun, seven times and seven times. . . . I am a loyal servant of the king! I am not a rebel and I am not delinquent in duty. I have not held back my payments of tribute; I have not held back anything requested by my commissioner. He denounces me unjustly, but the king, my Lord, does not examine my (alleged) act of rebellion. . . . I know the actions of Milkilu [a Canaanite rival] against me! Moreover, the king wrote for my son. I did not know that my son was consorting with the 'apiru. I hereby hand him over to Addaya-(commissioner). Moreover, how, if the king wrote for my wife, how could I hold her back? How, if the king wrote to me, "Put a bronze dagger into your heart and die," how could I not execute the order of the king?

—EA 254

Especially interesting are the references to one Labayu, who allegedly "gave Shechem to the Habiru." Shechem figures prominently in Deuteronomy and Joshua as an early Israelite center, but there is no account of its capture in the book of Joshua.

The Amarna letters date from a time more than a century before the usual date for the exodus, so they cannot be taken as referring to upheavals caused by the emergence of Israel. But conditions in Canaan probably did not change very much over a century or so. The letters show dissatisfaction among the Canaanites with the power structures of the time, and especially with Egyptian rule and the taxation it inevitably implied. Mendenhall suggested that the Israelites who had escaped from Egypt made common cause with these disaffected Canaanites. Israel was not originally an ethnic group but the union of people fleeing oppression, who joined together in the worship of the liberator god YHWH. This revolt hypothesis was developed and given a distinctly Marxist twist by Norman Gottwald.

The revolt hypothesis is in fact compatible with the archaeological evidence, but it has little support in the biblical text. It is true that Canaanite kings are sometimes singled out for destruction (e.g., in Joshua 10), but there is no suggestion in the biblical text that Joshua was engaged in the liberation of Canaan. Gottwald's formulation of the hypothesis is transparently influenced by socialist sympathies, arising out of the disturbances of the 1960s in the United States (he cites a poem in honor of the Viet Cong in the dedication to his book). Consequently, the revolt model is widely viewed as anachronistic, a myth of ancient Israel that conforms to one set of modern ideals. Of course modern ideologies may also influence the preference of scholars for other models, such as the traditional account of violent conquest. Ultimately, any model must be judged on its ability to account for the evidence, regardless of the ideology of the interpreter.

The Gradual Emergence Model

In fairness to the revolt model, however, one must admit that no account of early Israel can reconcile the biblical account and the archaeological evidence. The consensus on the subject at the beginning of the twenty-first century, insofar as there is one, favors the view that the Israelites were basically Canaanites who gradually developed a separate identity. The emergence of Israel as a distinct entity is presumably reflected in the increase in settlement of the central highlands. The people who founded these settlements had apparently migrated from the lowlands. We do not know why. They may have been disaffected with an oppressive society in the Canaanite city-states, as the revolt model suggests. Alternatively, they may have fled because of the instability of life in the lowlands due to the invasion of the Sea Peoples who became the Philistines, and who emerge into history about the same time as the Israelites. Or the migration may have been due to other reasons. The main difference between the model of gradual emergence and the revolt model is that this model does not assume that the Israelites were motivated by egalitarian ideals. It is true that early Israel, according to the Bible, did not have a king, but this may have been due to the relative lack of political organization rather than to ideological reasons. Nonetheless, one must recognize that any view of the emergence of Israel in Canaan that is guided by the archaeological evidence must assume that the highland settlers were people who withdrew from the Canaanite city-states, for whatever reason.

Archaeology as yet has shed no light on the origin of the cult of YHWH. Yet it was this cult, more than anything else, that eventually distinguished Israelites from other Canaanites. (The Hebrew language also evolved, eventually, from a Canaanite dialect to a distinct language.) It is possible that the cult of Yahweh was introduced to the highlands of Canaan by people who had escaped from slavery in Egypt. There were surely some escaped slaves among the early Israelites. Otherwise the biblical story of the exodus is impossible to explain. It is also possible that the cult of YHWH was brought north to Canaan by Midianite traders who worshiped YHWH as a storm-god on the mountains of Midian. If so, we would have to assume that this cult was taken over and transformed in Canaan, so that YHWH was worshiped not primarily as a storm-god but as a god who liberated people from slavery. Much remains uncertain about the origin of Israel in Canaan. What seems clear is that the account of the conquest in the book of Joshua is not historically accurate but is a fiction that was composed for ideological reasons at a much later time. It is the ideology of the book that will concern us in the remainder of our discussion of Joshua.

The Account of the Conquest

Gilgal and Jericho

Some of the early stories in the book of Joshua have a markedly ritualistic character. Before the crossing of the Jordan, Joshua tells the Israelites to sanctify themselves as they had before the revelation at Sinai. The waters part before the Israelites when the priests enter the river, and the people cross on dry ground. This crossing directly recalls the crossing of the Red Sea. It has been suggested, plausibly, that this story reflects a ritual reenactment of the exodus at Gilgal. (The crossing of the Jordan is followed in Joshua 5 by the celebration of the Passover.) We know from the prophets Amos and Hosea that the exodus was celebrated at nearby Bethel in the eighth century B.C.E., and probably from the beginning of the northern kingdom. The detail of crossing on dry land appears only in the latest (Priestly) account in Exodus and presumably derives from that account. The setting up of twelve standing stones *(massebot)* obviously represents the twelve tribes of Israel, as it does explicitly in Exod 24:4, where Moses sets up such pillars at Sinai. The explanation given in Josh 4:21-24, that the stones are a reminder that the Israelites crossed over on dry ground, is surely secondary, and not the original significance of the stones. Standing stones were often a feature of cultic sites in ancient Israel and Canaan, and the connection of the stones at Gilgal with the Exodus may well be secondary. Any reconstruction of the ritual at Gilgal is, of necessity, very hypothetical. For our present purposes, the point to note is that the supposedly historical account of the crossing of the Jordan seems to derive from a ritual celebration of the exodus.

According to Joshua 5, Joshua had all the Israelites circumcised before proceeding to attack Jericho. Such an action is wildly implausible at the beginning of a military campaign (cf. Genesis 34, where the sons of Jacob sack Shechem while the Shechemites are still sore after circumcision). Here again the editor of the story seems to be more concerned with ritual propriety than with historical plausibility. Exodus 12:48 requires that all males be circumcised before celebrating Passover. Here again Joshua seems to presuppose an element in the Priestly tradition.

Before the attack on Jericho, Joshua has a vision of a figure who identifies himself as "commander of the army of the LORD" (5:14). The point is made that Israel does not rely only on its own human resources. Rather, it is engaged in a "holy war," where it is aided by angelic hosts. Consequently, it is crucial that the Israelites keep themselves pure and not create an obstacle to the participation of their heavenly allies. In this view of warfare, ritual preparation is more important than military training. (A similar view of "holy war" is found at a much later date in the Qumran Scroll of the War of the Sons of Light against the Sons of Darkness.) While many people in antiquity attached great importance to ritual in preparation for battle, this is not a practical view of warfare. It is rather a theological theory of warfare, which makes no realistic allowance for the resistance that might be offered by the other side. Joshua is told to remove his shoes in the presence of this figure, as Moses did before the burning bush.

The textbook example of the theological, or ritual, theory of warfare is provided by the account of the siege of Jericho in Joshua 6. The Israelites march around the city for six days, with seven priests bearing seven trumpets of rams' horns before the ark. On the seventh day, the priests make a long blast on the ram's horn, and all the people shout. Then the walls fall down. We shall see in 1 Samuel that it was indeed customary to carry the ark into battle, to symbolize the presence of the Lord. Shouting was also a common tactic in ancient warfare. The Greek idiom for an easy conquest was *autoboei*, "with the very shout." The biblical story, however, has something more in mind. It emphasizes the miraculous character of the

Fig. 9.4 *The Seven Trumpets of Jericho* by James Tissot (ca. 1896–1902). Tissot's painting shows the miraculous Israelite conquest of an obviously inhabited Jericho, something archaeological excavation has shown was highly unlikely. Commons.wikimedia.org

conquest, that victory is given by the Lord, not achieved by human power. If, as the archaeologists have concluded, Jericho was not even occupied in the late thirteenth century, then the biblical writer was free to compose an ideal account of theologically correct conquest, unhindered by any historical traditions.

One striking aspect of both the crossing of the Jordan and of the conquest of Jericho is the prominence of priests, and we have also noted some points of contact with the Priestly traditions in the Pentateuch (the crossing on dry land; the circumcision before Passover). An older generation of critics often tried to trace the sources of the Pentateuch also in Joshua, and spoke of a Hexateuch (six volumes) rather than a Pentateuch. It is now generally agreed that Joshua is part of the Deuteronomistic History (although some scholars regard it as an independent composition. It is quite probable, however, that the sources on which the compilers of Joshua drew had been transmitted by priests. The detailed lists of tribal allocations in the second half of the book are also the kind of material often associated with priests. The relation of Joshua to the actual P strand in the Pentateuch is difficult to assess. The Deuteronomistic History was edited during the exile or later and could well have been influenced by the Priestly source at some points. The ritualistic actions at Gilgal and Jericho, however, have no clear basis in the P source and are more likely to be due to the author's familiarity with ritual practices.

The Moral Problem of the Conquest

The story of Jericho has been something of an embarrassment for conservative biblicists because of the negative findings of archaeological research. A more fundamental problem is posed, however, by the morality exemplified in the story. Joshua instructs the Israelites that "the city and all that is in it shall be devoted to the Lord for destruction" (6:17), with the exception of the prostitute Rahab, who helped the Israelite spies. When the Israelites enter the city, we are told that "they devoted to destruction by the edge of the sword all in the city, both men and women, young and old, oxen, sheep, and donkeys" (6:21). This dedication and destruction is known as *herem*, or the ban. The custom was known outside Israel. King Mesha of Moab, in the ninth century B.C.E., boasted that he took Nebo from Israel, "slaying all, seven thousand men, boys, women, girls and maid-servants, for I had devoted them to destruction for (the god) Ashtar-Chemosh" (*ANET*, 320). The story of the capture of Jericho is almost certainly fictitious, but this does not lessen the savagery of the story. We are not dealing in Joshua with a factual report of the ways of ancient warfare. Rather, the slaughter of the Canaanites, here and elsewhere, is presented as a theologically correct ideal.

The savagery of the destruction here is bound up with its sacral character: the victims are dedicated to the Lord. There may have been some strategic benefit to total destruction; apart from annihilating the enemy, it maintained discipline in the army by preventing the soldiers from engaging in selfish quest for booty (as happens in the case of Achan in Joshua 7–8). We may also suppose that unrestrained killing allowed the soldiers to work themselves into a frenzy of violence and solidified their group solidarity and morale. But such benefits were incidental.

INTRODUCTION TO THE HEBREW BIBLE

The *herem* was essentially a religious act, like sacrifice. It not only condoned indiscriminate slaughter; it sanctified it and gave it legitimation. We may compare the story of the zeal of Phinehas in Numbers 25, where the summary killing of an Israelite with a Moabite woman is rewarded with a covenant of peace and an eternal priesthood.

The brutality of warfare in antiquity is no greater than in modern times, and arguably less. We should not be surprised that the Israelites, like other peoples, gloried in the destruction of their adversaries. What is troubling in the biblical text is the claim that such action is justified by divine command and therefore praiseworthy. (Such claims are not unknown in modern warfare either.) We shall find that claims of this sort are sometimes criticized even within the biblical tradition, especially in the Prophets. They are certainly disavowed by later Jewish and Christian tradition. But the examples of Joshua and Phinehas are still enshrined in Scripture and are therefore likely to lend a cloak of legitimacy to such actions. This is a case where biblical authority is a dangerous and misleading concept. The aura of biblical authority must not be allowed to mask the utter barbarity of the conduct. That barbarity is not lessened by the fact that it was accepted as part of warfare in antiquity, or indeed by the fact that it is often surpassed in modern warfare.

But why is the ideal of *herem*, or dedication to total slaughter, endorsed so enthusiastically by the Deuteronomist? Within the framework of the biblical story, the Canaanites have done the Israelites no wrong. The people of Jericho are not slaughtered because they have oppressed the Israelites (the theory of peasant revolt notwithstanding). They are simply given into the hand of the Israelites by the Lord. Neither were the Canaanites oppressing Judah in the time of Josiah. Moreover, the book of Deuteronomy is notably humane in its legislation for Israelite society. Why then do the Deuteronomists insist on such savage treatment of the Canaanites?

No definite answer can be given to these questions, but a few suggestions may be offered. First, Josiah's reform was, among other things, an assertion of national identity. Judah was emerging from the shadow of Assyria and laying claim to sovereignty over the ancient territory of Israel. The assertion of identity entails differentiation from others, especially from those who are close but different. The ferocity of Deuteronomic rhetoric toward the Canaanites may be due in part to the fact that Israelites were Canaanites to begin with. Moreover, Josiah promoted a purist view of Yahwism that tolerated the worship of no other deities. The Canaanites were perceived as a threat to the purity of Israelite religion. It may be that the violence of Joshua toward the Canaanites was meant to provide a model for the violence of Josiah toward those who deviated from strict Yahwism, although we do not know that he ever engaged in the kind of *herem* that is attributed to Joshua.

Underlying the whole Deuteronomic theology, and indeed most of the Hebrew Bible, is the claim that the Israelites had a right to invade Canaan because it was given to them by God. This claim is found already in the promise to Abraham in Genesis and is repeated constantly. It would not be problematic if the land were empty, but it was not. The God of Israel, it would seem, does not care much for the Canaanites. Jews and Christians traditionally identify with Israel when they read the Bible, and do not give much thought to the Canaanites either. There are of course numerous historical parallels to the conquest of Canaan. The entire history of Western colonialism involved claims of divine authorization for transparently selfish interests. The most glaring example is perhaps the conquest of North America by white settlers of European origin and the near eradication of Native Americans. There is also a troubling analogy in the rise of modern Israel in Palestine and the dispossession of the Palestinians. To be sure, each of those cases has its own complexity, and none is simply identical with the biblical prototype. In each case, including that of ancient Israel, the long-term results have included much that is good. History is always ambiguous. But the ambiguities of history should not blind us to the fact that the unprovoked conquest of one people by another is an act of injustice and that injustice is often cloaked with legitimacy by claims of divine authorization. At the very least, we should be wary of any attempt to invoke the story of the conquest of Canaan as legitimation for anything in the modern world.

The final redaction of the Deuteronomistic History, including the book of Joshua, was done in the Babylonian exile or later. In that situation, the Judeans were not the invincible conquerors, but the hapless victims, a situation in which the Jewish people would unfortunately find themselves more than once in the course of history. Perhaps the fantasy of Joshua's conquests brought some consolation to the Judeans in Babylon, or to those who struggled in the impoverished land of Judah. But it is surely one of the ironies of the biblical story that the people of Israel and Judah suffered the kind of violent conquest that they supposedly had inflicted on the Canaanites, and that the historicity of their own destruction is in no doubt whatsoever.

There is one small note of relief in the story of the capture of Jericho. One household is spared, that of the prostitute Rahab. She is spared because she had assisted the Israelite spies (and thereby betrayed her own people). But it is typical of the Deuteronomistic History that the person who is spared is a person of ill repute. One of the themes of this history is articulated in the Song of Hannah in 1 Samuel 2: the Lord lifts up the poor from the dust and brings low the mighty. This pattern in history applies to Israel as well as to other nations, and it applies when Israel is mighty as well as when it is low. The privilege apparently given to Israel in its early history will be erased when it becomes the domain of kings.

Fig. 9.5 *Joshua Burns the Town of Ai* by **Gustav Doré, 1866.**

The Story of Ai

The story of the attack on Ai is most probably also a fiction designed to give a clear illustration of the Deuteronomist's theology. When the initial attack fails, it is assumed that the reason is not inadequate manpower or strategy, but the displeasure of the Lord. Sure enough, the Lord informs Joshua that Israel has broken the covenant by disobeying a commandment. The specific commandment in question is the ban, which Achan had broken by taking things for himself. The specificity of the commandment is not crucial, however. The point is that a commandment has been broken. After the perpetrator has been executed, the Israelites are able to capture Ai and destroy it. Perhaps the most remarkable aspect of the story is the sense of corporate responsibility. The Israelite army is defeated and some thirty-six people are killed because of the sin of one man. Moreover, not only is Achan executed, but also his sons and daughters and livestock, and even the goods that he had taken are stoned, burned, and buried under a heap of stones. There is a strong sense here that the family is a unit, but there is also a sense of defilement that has spread even to material objects.

The story of Achan is all the more remarkable because Deut 24:16 says explicitly that "parents shall not be put to death for their children, nor shall children be put to death for their parents; only for their own crimes may persons be put to death." The story of Achan is presumably older than the Deuteronomic law. According to Exod 20:5, the Lord punishes children for the iniquity of their parents even to the third and fourth generation, and this was the traditional idea in Israel, roughly down to the time of the Deuteronomic reform or the Babylonian exile. The doctrine of individual responsibility is an innovation in Deuteronomy 24. It is most strongly articulated in Ezekiel 18, in the context of the exile.

The story of Achan provides incidentally a good description of the social structure of ancient Israel. When Joshua is trying to identify the culprit, he first identifies the tribe, then the clan, then the family, or father's house. These were the different levels of kinship groups to which an individual belonged.

The Tribes

The second half of the book of Joshua is dominated by the allotment of territory to the tribes. There are various inconsistencies in this account. According to Josh 14:1-5, Joshua, the priest Eleazar, and the heads of the tribes gathered at Gilgal and divided the land west of the Jordan between eight and a half tribes. (Two and a half tribes had already received an inheritance east of the Jordan. No land was given to the tribe of Levi.) Joshua 18:1-10 says that Joshua alone divided the land among seven tribes that had not yet received an allotment. Some passages suggest that tribes claimed land for themselves (e.g., Judah in 14:6-12; compare the violent migration of the tribe of Dan to the north of Israel in Judges 18), others that it was divided by lot. Some lots included cities that remained in Canaanite control for some time, such as Gezer in the territory of Ephraim. The territories of some tribes (especially Judah and the Joseph tribes, Ephraim and Manasseh) are outlined in more detail than the others. At the end of the book, in Joshua 24, Joshua gathers all the tribes at Shechem to renew the covenant.

Biblical tradition is unanimous that the twelve tribes of Israel were descended from twelve sons of Jacob, who was also called Israel. Such a simple genealogical model, whereby each tribe is descended from one individual, is clearly a fiction, but the tradition that early Israel consisted of associated tribes can hardly be denied. The tribes are listed in several places in the Pentateuch, with some variations. The sons of Jacob are listed in Genesis 29–30 and again in the blessing of Jacob in Genesis 49, in the following order: Reuben, Simeon, Levi, Judah, Zebulun, Issachar, Dan, Gad, Asher, Naphtali, Joseph, and Benjamin. The first six of these have Leah as their mother, the next four have the handmaids Bilhah and Zilpah, and the last two are sons of Rachel. Numbers 26 lists the tribes of Israel in the following order: Reuben, Simeon, Gad, Judah, Issachar, Zebulun, Manasseh, Ephraim, Benjamin, Dan, Asher, and Naphtali (these are the tribes listed in Joshua, in different order). As compared with the lists in Genesis, Levi has fallen out, presumably because it had become a priestly tribe with no territorial allotment of its own, and Joseph had been divided into Ephraim and Manasseh, to maintain the number twelve. Also Gad is transferred to a place among the Leah tribes, so that their number is maintained at six. It has been suggested that the Leah tribes represent an older association, which was gradually enlarged. The youngest children of Jacob, Joseph and Benjamin, acquire their territory in the central highlands, where most of the conquest narratives in Joshua are set. It is evident that some historical changes are reflected in these lists. The list in Genesis 49 is older than that in Numbers 26, on linguistic grounds. But attempts to reconstruct the history of the tribes, for example by supposing that a smaller association of six tribes was gradually expanded, are of necessity hypothetical. It has also been suggested that the tribal lists in Numbers and Joshua reflect administrative districts under the monarchy, but here again clear confirming evidence is lacking. What is clear is that each tribe, with the exception of the priestly tribe of Levi, was identified with specific territory. Presumably the identity of the tribes and their territories evolved over time. The story of the allotment of territory in Joshua 13–19 projects into the early history of Israel the kind of centralized control that came only with the monarchy, and was aggressively pursued by Josiah in his reform in the late seventh century B.C.E.

The Amphictyony Hypothesis

For much of the twentieth century, biblical scholars spoke confidently of a tribal league or amphictyony in the period before the monarchy. The term *amphictyony* is a Greek word that referred to a sacred league that had its center in the shrine of Apollo at Delphi beginning in the sixth century B.C.E. The league consisted of twelve peoples who undertook to maintain and defend the shrine. The members undertook not to destroy any of the towns in the league and had mutual relations, but they did not constitute a political unity. Their primary purpose was the support of the cult at Delphi. Other leagues, with varying numbers of members, were called amphictyonies by analogy with the Delphic league. The analogy was applied to early Israel by Martin Noth in an influential study in 1930 and was widely accepted for a time. It was assumed that the tribes were bound together by covenant and

TRIBAL LISTS IN THE BIBLICAL TEXTS		
Genesis 49	**Numbers 26**	**Joshua**
Leah's offspring:	Reuben	Judah
Reuben	Simeon	Manasseh
Simeon	Gad	Ephraim
Levi	Judah	Reuben
Judah	Isaachar	Gad
Zebulun	Zebulun	Benjamin
Isaachar	Manasseh	Simeon
	Ephraim	Zebulun
Bilhah and Zilpah's offspring:	Benjamin	Isaachar
Dan	Dan	Asher
Gad	Asher	Naphtali
Asher	Naphtali	Dan
Naphtali		
Rachel's offspring:		
Joseph		
Benjamin		

that their delegates came together periodically for a covenant renewal such as we find in Joshua 24.

In the later decades of the twentieth century, however, the amphictyony model was widely rejected. A major problem concerned the existence of a central sanctuary. In Joshua 24 the tribes assemble at Shechem, but later we read of assemblies at other locations, such as Mizpah (Judg 20:1; 1 Sam 7:5) and Gilgal (1 Sam 11:14), while the ark of the Lord was located at Shiloh at the end of the premonarchic period. Never in the book of Judges or in 1 Samuel do we hear of the tribes of Israel rallying to the defense of a central shrine. The model of the amphictyony, then, does not apply to Israelite tribes.

Nonetheless, the Israelite tribes were evidently associated in some way. A vivid illustration of this association is found in the Song of Deborah in Judges 5, which is universally recognized as an old poem, one of the older passages in the Hebrew Bible. This is a ballad commemorating a battle between Israelite tribes and Canaanite kings, "at Taanach, by the waters of Megiddo." The issue concerned the plundering of caravan traders, but our present concern is with the light it sheds on the alliance of Israelite tribes. Ephraim, Benjamin, Machir (= Manasseh), Zebulun, Issachar, and Naphtali all reported for duty. The Transjordanian tribes of Reuben and Gilead (= Gad) and the coastal tribes of Dan and Asher did not. Judah, Simeon, and Levi

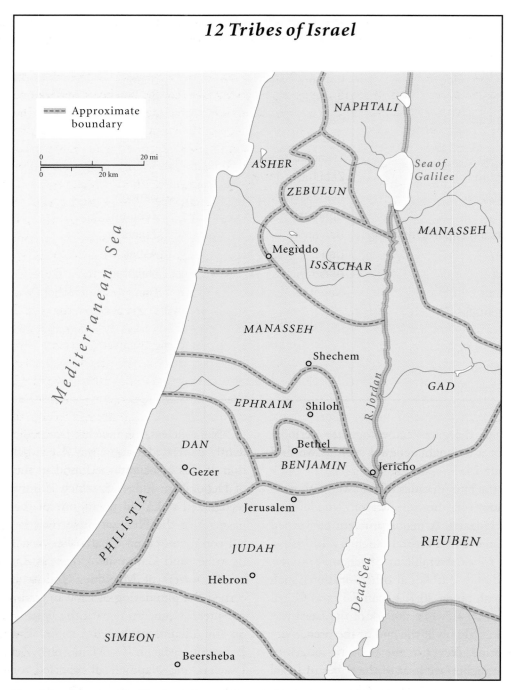

12 Tribes of Israel

Approximate boundary

0   20 mi
0   20 km

NAPHTALI

ASHER

ZEBULUN

Sea of Galilee

MANASSEH

Mediterranean Sea

Megiddo

ISSACHAR

MANASSEH

Shechem

EPHRAIM

Shiloh

R. Jordan

GAD

DAN

Bethel

Gezer

BENJAMIN

Jericho

Jerusalem

JUDAH

REUBEN

Hebron

Dead Sea

SIMEON

Beersheba

PHILISTIA

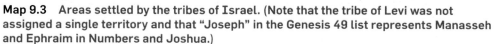

Map 9.3   Areas settled by the tribes of Israel. (Note that the tribe of Levi was not assigned a single territory and that "Joseph" in the Genesis 49 list represents Manasseh and Ephraim in Numbers and Joshua.)

are not mentioned. The song singles out the otherwise unknown entity of Meroz to be cursed because its inhabitants did not come to the aid of the Lord. The song suggests that there was an alliance of tribes who worshiped YHWH (though not necessarily exclusively). There was some obligation of mutual defense, but it is noteworthy that there are no sanctions against the tribes that did not show up, with the exception of Meroz (which may not have been a tribe at all). The alliance did not extend to all twelve tribes. The omission of Judah is significant. Later, under the monarchy, northern dissidents would raise the rallying cry, "What share do we have in David? We have no inheritance in the son of Jesse. To your tents, O Israel" (1 Kgs 12:16; cf. 1 Sam 20:1). The bond between Judah and the northern tribes was weak, and this eventually led to the separation of the two kingdoms after the death of Solomon.

Judah is included in the Blessing of Moses in Deuteronomy 33, but there Simeon is missing. It would seem that the number twelve was not so stable in the premonarchic period as is often supposed. The stories in the book of Judges give little impression of centralized organization and suggest rather that cooperation between the tribes was sporadic.

The Covenant at Shechem

In chapter 24 the book of Joshua concludes with a covenant renewal ceremony at Shechem. The passage is now recognized as Deuteronomic because of its use of characteristic Deuteronomic idiom. It is not an old source incorporated by the historian. It has many of the elements of the treaty form.

The historical prologue is developed at great length. The people are called to witness against themselves (in place of the pagan gods of the Near Eastern treaties). The words of the covenant are recorded in a book, and a stone is set up to commemorate the covenant. The statutes of the covenant are not recited, but they are implied. The main point is that possession of the land is contingent on serving the Lord. The main elements of the covenant that are missing are the blessings and curses. In contrast, blessings and curses are amply represented in the prescriptions for a covenant at Shechem in Deuteronomy 27–28. The prominence of Shechem in these Deuteronomic writings strongly suggests that there was a tradition of covenant renewal at that site. It does not necessarily follow, however, that all twelve tribes were ever involved in such a ceremony. Moreover, we find in Judg 8:33 that Israelites at one point worshiped Baal-berith (Baal of the covenant) and there was a temple of Baal-berith at Shechem. Indeed, Shechem appears to have been a Canaanite city through much of the period of the judges. The tradition of a covenant ceremony at Shechem may have been older than the cult of YHWH.

The need for fidelity to "all that is written in the law of Moses" is also emphasized in Joshua 23, the farewell speech of Moses. Here again we find reiterated the central theme of the book of Joshua, that the land is given to Israel so long as it keeps the covenant. The previous occupants of the land are only a foil for God's gift to Israel. Joshua concedes that the Canaanites have not been wiped out. For that reason, vigilance is necessary: "For if you turn back and join the survivors of these nations left here among you, and intermarry with them, so that you marry their women and they yours, know assuredly that the Lord your God will not continue to drive out these nations before you, but they shall be a snare and a trap for you" (23:12-13). The prohibition of intermarriage is found already in Deuteronomy 7 with reference to the peoples of the land: "Make no covenant with them and show them no mercy. Do not intermarry with them, giving your daughters to their sons or taking their daughters for your sons" (Deut 7:2-3). The prohibition in Deuteronomy mentions specifically seven peoples who lived in the land. It did not necessarily apply to all peoples. Some distinctions between Gentiles were possible. Deuteronomy 23 distinguishes between the Ammonites and Moabites, who may not be admitted to the assembly of the Lord "even to the tenth generation" and the Edomites and Egyptians, who may be admitted after the third. The thrust of Deuteronomy, however, is to maintain a distinct identity, and this could be threatened by intermarriage with any Gentiles. Originally this thrust may have been part of Josiah's attempt to build a national identity in Judah that incorporated the remnant of northern Israel. After the Babylonian exile, however, a significant part of the Jewish people would live outside the land of Israel, and the need for boundaries over against the Gentiles became more urgent. In this context, distinctions between Ammonites and Edomites lost their significance and all intermarriage was discouraged. We shall see that there was a crisis on this issue in the postexilic community that comes to a head in the book of Ezra, but it is an issue that continues to bedevil Judaism down to the present day.

FOR FURTHER READING

Joshua

R. G. Boling, "Joshua, Book of," *ABD* 3:1002–15. Supplements the Boling-Wright commentary. Useful discussions of geography and of the structure of the book.

R. G. Boling and G. Ernest Wright, *Joshua* (AB 6; New York: Doubleday, 1982). Thorough commentary, but now somewhat dated. Assumes more historical value than is usual in more recent scholarship.

R. B. Coote, "Joshua," *NIB* 2:555–716. Strong reading of Joshua as Josianic propaganda.

T. Dozeman, *Joshua 1-12* (Yale Anchor Bible; New Haven: Yale Univ. Press, 2014). Full commentary on Joshua 1–12. Takes Joshua as an independent book, not part of a Deuteronomic history, and locates it in northern Israel in the Persian period.

R. D. Nelson, *Joshua* (OTL; Louisville: Westminster John Knox, 1997). Clear, well-balanced commentary.

J. A. Soggin, *Joshua* (trans R. A. Wilson; OTL; Philadelphia: Westminster, 1972). Older commentary, still useful for its exegetical insights.

Early History of Israel

J. Bright, *A History of Israel* (4th ed.; Louisville: Westminster, 2000). Classic defense of the conquest model.

W. G. Dever, *Who Were the Early Israelites and Where Did They Come From?* (Grand Rapids: Eerdmans, 2003). Straightforward readable account of the archaeological evidence.

I. Finkelstein and N. A. Silberman, *The Bible Unearthed: Archaeology's New Vision of Ancient Israel and the Origin of Its Sacred Texts* (New York: Free Press, 2001), 72–122, 329–39. Up-to-date account of archaeological record.

N. Gottwald, *The Tribes of Yahweh* (Maryknoll, NY: Orbis, 1979). Elaborate formulation of the revolt hypothesis.

G. E. Mendenhall, "The Hebrew Conquest of Palestine," *BA* 25 (1962): 66–87. Original formulation of revolt hypothesis.

M. Noth, *A History of Israel* (trans. S. Godman; New York: Harper & Row, 1960). Classic formulation of the theory of gradual infiltration.

Particular Themes

W. Brueggemann, *Divine Presence amid Violence: Conceptualizing the Book of Joshua* (Eugene, OR: Cascade, 2009). Wrestles with the problem of violence but argues that Joshua is a story of liberation.

J. J. Collins, *The Bible after Babel. Historical Criticism in a Postmodern Age* (Grand Rapids: Eerdmans, 2005), 27–51. Overview of the controversy about early Israel.

———, *Does the Bible Justify Violence?* (Minneapolis: Fortress Press, 2004). Focuses on the moral problem of the conquest story.

J. S. Kaminsky, *Yet I Loved Jacob: Reclaiming the Biblical Concept of Election* (Nashville: Abingdon, 2007). Nuanced account of the biblical doctrine of election.

A. D. H. Mayes, "Amphictyony," *ABD* 1:212–16. Summary of state of the question.

S. Niditch, *War in the Hebrew Bible: A Study in the Ethics of Violence* (New York: Oxford University Press, 1993). Creative study of biblical perspectives on war and its justification.

L. L. Rowlett, *Joshua and the Rhetoric of Violence: A "New Historicist" Analysis* (JSOTSup 226; Sheffield: Sheffield Academic Press, 1996). Interesting study of the rhetoric of Joshua and its social functions.

K. W. Whitelam, *The Invention of Ancient Israel and the Silencing of Palestinian History* (London: Routledge, 1996). Provocative critique of alleged anti-Palestinian bias in biblical scholarship.

Younger, K. L. *Ancient Near Eastern Conquest Accounts: A Study in Ancient Near Eastern and Biblical History Writing* (JSOTSup 98; Sheffield: JSOT Press, 1990). Interesting comparison of Joshua with Mesopotamian conquest accounts.

CHAPTER 10

Judges

INTRODUCTION

In this chapter, we look at the book of Judges and its relationship to history, at the accounts of various "judges" in the period before the monarchy, and at the Deuteronomistic purposes in describing a time "when there was no king" in Israel.

The material we find in the book of Judges is quite different from the content of Joshua. The core of the book consists of stories about local heroes who distinguished themselves in battle with Canaanites, Midianites, or Philistines when "there was no king in Israel." Most of these stories have a folkloristic character. They preserve plausible local color and provide some vivid glimpses of life in early Israel but contain little that can be verified by extrabiblical evidence. The individual stories deal with conflicts in different regions. Ehud fights the Moabites in Transjordan. Deborah and Barak campaign against the kings of Canaan near Mount Tabor in northern Israel. Gideon fights the Midianites in the south. Abimelech is involved in civil war in Shechem. Jephthah battles the Ammonites in Transjordan. Samson is involved with the Philistines. These stories were edited into a sequential (but episodic) narrative by the Deuteronomist. There is a programmatic introduction in 2:11—3:6 that provides an overview of the period from the point of view of the editors. Despite the rather heavy-handed editorializing in chapter 2, many of the stories in the core of the book are quite ambiguous and preserve a range of perspectives. They are not edited consistently to reflect Deuteronomic ideology, but preserve much of their character as independent tales, told for varying purposes.

Judges and History

Since the book of Judges is presented as the history of a period of Israel's early history, some comment on its historical value is required. The summary of the "conquest" in Judges 1, which lists extensive areas in the lowlands

JUDGES IN ISRAEL		
Judge	Opponent(s)	Reference
Othniel	Cushan-rishathaim of Aram	3:7-11
Ehud	King Eglon of Moab	3:12-30
Shamgar	Philistines	3:31
Deborah and Barak	Jabin, king of Canaan, and his general Sisera	Chapters 4–5, which include the "Song of Deborah"
Gideon	Midianites	Chapters 6–8
Abimelech	(Abimelech kills his seventy brothers, becomes king of Shechem)	Chapter 9
Tola		10:1-2
Jair		10:3-5
Jephthah	Ammonites	10:6—12:7
Ibzan		12:8-10
Elon		12:11-12
Abdon		12:13-15
Samson	Philistines	Chapters 13–16

where the Canaanites were not driven out, is widely regarded as more accurate than the picture of sweeping conquest painted in the book of Joshua. (Of course, the fact that Canaanites remained in many of these places does not in any way corroborate the conquest of the areas that the Israelites are said to have taken.) But the account in Judges is not without its problems. It includes contradictory notices about Jerusalem (1:8, 21). Gaza, Ashkelon, and Ekron are all said to be conquered by Judah in 1:18, but they are subsequently known to be Philistine strongholds. At several sites that

are said to remain in Canaanite hands in Judg 1:27-35, the archaeological evidence shows that Canaanite culture in fact persisted (Bethshean, Megiddo, Gezer). In contrast, Taanach, which was not conquered according to Judg 1:27, was apparently destroyed in the thirteenth century and replaced by a village like those in the central highlands. Hazor, which was allegedly destroyed in Joshua 11, and was in fact destroyed at some time during the thirteenth century, still appears in Canaanite hands in Judges 4–5. The prominence of the Philistines in the book of Judges is appropriate to the period. Also the book depicts the land of Canaan in a state of transition from the city-states of the Bronze Age to the emerging national entities of Israel, Philistia, Aram, and so forth. This transition is appropriately located in the period around 1200–1000 B.C.E. Many of the stories in Judges, however, deal with local events, which would be difficult to verify in any case. The historical value of Judges, such as it is, lies more in the general picture of conditions before the rise of the monarchy than in the specific events that are narrated. While some details are of historical value, the greater interest of the book for the modern reader lies in the drama of the stories and the moral issues they raise.

The Deuteronomistic Introduction

After the summary of the situation at the end of the "conquest" in Judges 1, the narrative continues with the death of Joshua in chapter 2. Before Joshua dies, the angel of the Lord makes a cameo appearance, to assure the people that the Lord will not break the covenant, and warn them not to make a covenant with the peoples of the land. Rather, they are to "tear down their altars." This injunction corresponds directly to Deuteronomy 12 and to the policy of Josiah, as described in 2 Kings 23. The peoples who have been allowed to survive provide temptation for Israel. The angel is the mouthpiece of the Deuteronomistic editor. The editor speaks in his own voice in 2:11—3:6. According to this prospective summary of the period of the judges, Israel "did what was evil in the sight of the Lord" by worshiping Baal, Astarte, and other deities. Then the

Fig. 10.1   The goddess Astarte; pottery relief from the Hebron area, ca. 1400 B.C.E. Reuben and Edith Hecht collection, Haifa University, Israel. ArtResource, NY

anger of the Lord was kindled against them, and he gave them into the hand of their enemies. Then the Lord would be moved to pity by their groaning and would raise up a judge to deliver them.

Whenever the judge died, however, the Israelites would relapse into their old ways and the anger of the Lord would be kindled against them again. In the long-term view of the Deuteronomistic History, this pattern would explain the great destructions of Israel and Judah at the hands of the Assyrians and Babylonians. In the shorter perspective of the book of Judges, it would lead to the institution of the monarchy as a way of providing permanent leadership. The monarchy, however, would have its own problems.

The English word *judges* is a somewhat misleading label for the saviors raised up by God. They are primarily military leaders. They are charismatic figures, in the sense that they are not officeholders to begin with, but are chosen for the task of dealing with a crisis because their abilities are recognized. They are not necessarily chosen for their virtue. Jephthah, for example, was the son of a prostitute and had been driven out by his legitimate brothers, so he supported himself by banditry. The skills he learned as an outlaw are precisely what qualified him as a military leader. Samson's major qualification was brute strength. After the crisis had passed, the judge continued to rule Israel for the rest of his life. In normal times, outside of crisis, the judge might well be called upon to act in a judicial capacity by judging cases. We are told that Deborah sat under a palm tree in the country of Ephraim and all Israel came to her for judgment. Samuel, the last of the judges, also acted as a judge in the usual sense of the word. Deborah plays a role in battle, but neither she nor Samuel fight, and so they deviate from the typical pattern.

It is clear that the Deuteronomist imposes a schematic design on Judges that does some violence to the stories that make up most of the book. The judges are typically local heroes, and they lead what is at most a temporary alliance of tribes. Worship of deities other than YHWH does not appear to be an issue for the protagonists in these stories in the way that it is for the Deuteronomistic editor. Neither are they guided by the laws of the covenant nor by the recollection of the exodus. (There are recollections of the exodus in the story of Gideon in Judges 6 and again in the Jephthah story, in Judg 11:12-28, but the relevant passages are clearly Deuteronomistic compositions.) The covenantal context is not an integral part of the stories but is imposed by an editor. The tales themselves give us a glimpse of a pre-Deuteronomic view of Israel, whether it accurately portrays the period before the monarchy or not.

The Early Judges (Chapters 3–5)

The first judge mentioned after the death of Joshua is Othniel, and he is dispatched rapidly in three verses (3:9-11). He is said to go to war against Aram-naharaim (Syria between the Tigris and Euphrates), but this is probably a scribal mistake. Aram does not appear again in the book of Judges. We are not told what tribes supported Othniel, but he was impelled by "the spirit of the Lord." The only apparent effect of the spirit here is that he was successful in battle. After this, the land had rest for the stereotypical forty years.

The second judge, Ehud, is also dealt with briefly, but he is credited with one of the more colorful exploits in the book. His daring assassination of King Eglon of Moab is described in vivid detail. Ehud is a Benjaminite, from the region near Jericho. The Moabites, the people immediately across the Dead Sea, had defeated "Israel" and taken possession of Jericho. It is doubtful that "Israel" here refers to anything more than the tribe of Benjamin, the people of the immediate locality. The assassination of the Moabite king is accomplished by deception, but this kind of deceit is the standard fare of guerrilla warfare and insurgency in all times and places. In this case, Moab is clearly the

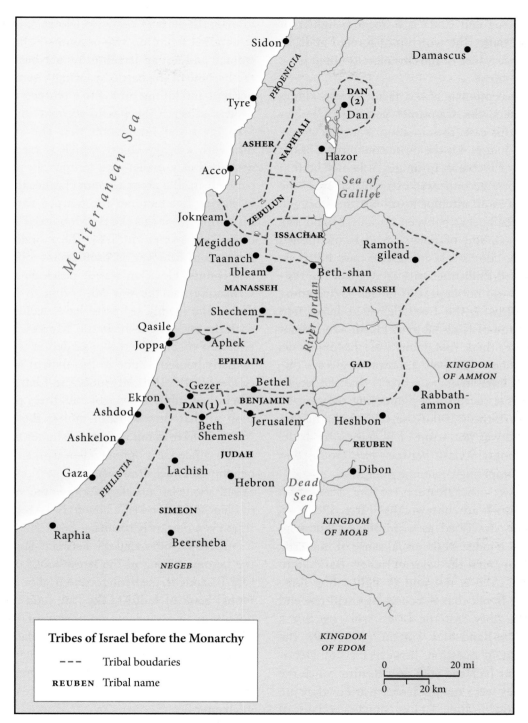

Tribes of Israel before the Monarchy

- - - Tribal boudaries

REUBEN Tribal name

Map 10.1

 JUDGES

oppressor, and Ehud is a freedom fighter or rebel leader. The worship of foreign gods, or the observance of the covenant, is not at issue in the story.

Deception is also a factor in the killing of Sisera, the Canaanite general, in Judges 4. In this case, the situation is more complicated. Judges 4 is the prose counterpart of the Song of Deborah in Judges 5. It may be that the prose account was extrapolated from the poetry in an attempt to fill out the story (cf. the relationship between Exodus 14 and 15). Shamgar, son of Anath, who is mentioned in Judg 5:6, is said in 3:31 to have killed six hundred Philistines with an oxgoad. The Philistines do not appear in Judges 5. According to Judges 4, the Lord delivered Israel into the hand of King Jabin of Hazor. One might assume, then, that Jabin was the oppressor. The song in chapter 5, however, gives a different impression, as it boasts that the Israelites were successfully plundering the caravan routes. If this was the case, then the battle that ensued was not a war of liberation for Israel but simply a clash between two groups that had competing economic interests.

Two other features of the account in chapter 4 are noteworthy. First, Deborah, who is described as a prophetess but who acts as a judge in the usual sense of the term, accompanies the warrior judge Barak into battle. (She is not said to fight.) She forewarns Barak that the campaign will not end in his glory, "for the LORD will give Sisera into the hand of a woman" (Judg 4:9). The woman in question, however, is not Deborah, but Jael, the wife of a Kenite. Since the Kenites were not an Israelite tribe (they are identified in Judg 4:11 as "the descendants of Hobab, the father-in-law of Moses"), Jael is a marginal figure on two accounts—she is a woman and not an Israelite. Yet she becomes the heroine of the battle by luring Sisera into her tent and killing him with a tentpeg while he was asleep. (The poetic account in Judg 5:26 gives the impression that she struck him with a heavy object, which is variously described as a mallet or a tentpeg, in poetic parallelism. The prose account clarifies the act by having her hammer the tentpeg through his temple.) For this she is pronounced "most blessed of women" in 5:24. The morality of her action, however, is problematic on several counts. Her clan was at peace with the Canaanites, so she was not trying to liberate it. She simply seems to have decided to back the winners in the battle. Moreover, the violation of a guest was regarded as a particularly heinous crime in the ancient world. (Compare the story of Sodom in Gen 19:8, where Lot offers his virgin daughters to the mob so that they will not molest the men, "for they have come under the shelter of my roof.") Since Jael's opportunism works to the benefit of Israel, however, no questions are raised about its morality. As in some stories in Genesis, the end (the benefit of Israel) justifies even dastardly means.

There is some analogy between Jael and the heroine of one of the latest books of the Old Testament, the deuterocanonical or apocryphal book of Judith. Like Jael, Judith uses deception to assassinate an enemy of Israel. Unlike Jael, however, Judith could claim to be acting in defense of her own people when they were clearly the victims of aggression. We consider the story of Judith in more detail in chapter 26.

Fig. 10.2 *Jael and Sisera* by Jacopo Amigoni (ca. 1739).
Commons.wikimedia.org

Gideon and Abimelech (Chapters 6–10)

Gideon receives more attention than any other judge in the book except Samson. The occasion is a conflict in the southern part of the country, caused by marauding Midianites. It is clearly a regional conflict that does not involve all Israel; even the neighboring Ephraimites question the wisdom of fighting the Midianites. Gideon is chosen by the angel of the Lord because of his weakness rather than his strength. His visitation by the angel recalls the apparition to Abraham in Genesis 18. Like other judges, he goes to battle under the influence of the spirit of the Lord.

The story of Gideon is marked by tensions between old traditions that do not fit with Deuteronomic ideology and clear interventions by the Deuteronomistic editors. Like the patriarchs, Gideon builds an altar to mark the site of the apparition of the angel of the Lord (6:24; despite the Deuteronomic prohibition of multiple altars). We are told in 7:1 that he was also known as Jerubbaal (meaning "Baal will contend"). This would seem to indicate that he was at one time a Baal worshiper. His sons are still known in chapter 9 as the sons of Jerubbaal, and the people of Shechem are said to revert to the worship of Baal-berit, Baal of the covenant, after Gideon's death. After the defeat of the Midianites, Gideon collects precious metals from his soldiers and constructs an idol, which he erects in his hometown, "so that Israel prostituted themselves to it there, and it became a snare to Gideon and to his family" (8:27). None of this suggests that

Gideon was a devout Yahwist by Deuteronomic standards. He shows himself a ruthless fighter in taking vengeance on the Midianites and also on Israelites who refused to help him. His peculiar method of selecting his elite troups, taking only those who lapped the water like dogs, fits with his image as a ruthless warrior. A small force of men who would act like animals would be more efficient than a larger, more "civilized" army. His ferocity as a fighter, rather than Deuteronomic piety, is what qualifies him as a savior of his people.

In contrast, a few passages cast Gideon in a more orthodox Deuteronomic mold. He recalls the exodus in good Deuteronomic fashion (6:13) and even tears down his father's altar of Baal—an action that seems quite inconsistent with his subsequent idol worship. Another editorial touch can be seen in the report in 6:7 that the Lord sent a prophet to remind the Israelites of the exodus and covenant. Prophets figure prominently in the later historical books, but they seem anachronistic in the context of Judges.

Gideon's success against the Midianites provides the occasion for the first proposal of kingship in Israel. The people invite him to "rule over us, you and your son and your grandson also" (8:22). The people in question are ostensibly all Israel, but only the tribes of Manasseh and Ephraim have been involved in the story. In any case, Gideon declines the offer. There was evidently much ambiguity about kingship in early Israel. Some of the stories in the Deuteronomistic History suggest a process of evolution that naturally led to kingship in Israel as in other peoples in the region. Other passages suggest that there was a tension between the rule of YHWH and the rule of a human king. This is the case in Gideon's reply to the people in Judg 8:23. We shall see this resistance to the kingship articulated more fully in 1 Samuel.

Kingship is also at issue in the story of Abimelech in Judges 9. Abimelech's name ("my father is king") suggests that Gideon may not have been as reticent about kingship as the Deuteronomist would have it. In any case, Abimelech has no reservations about claiming the kingship, and he clears his path by murdering his seventy brothers, except for the youngest, Jotham, who escapes. Like Jephthah in Judges 11, Abimelech is of dishonorable birth; he is the son of a slave woman. Unlike Jephthah, or some other underprivileged figures in the Hebrew Bible, he is not asked to assume leadership but pursues it aggressively, even murderously. The incident evokes Jotham's fable about the trees who tried to choose a king. The olive, the fig, and the vine all decline, because they are engaged in productive activity that brings them honor. Only the bramble wants to be king, and it backs its desire with a threat of violence. The fable is all too easily applicable to power seekers of any age. In the context of Judges, it articulates the deep-seated distrust of monarchy in some strands of Israelite tradition. It should be noted, however, that Abimelech is king of Shechem, not of Israel, and that Shechem appears here to be a Canaanite city with a temple to Baal-berit. One might argue, therefore, that Shechem is simply reverting to being a traditional Canaanite city-state.

The people of Shechem soon tire of Abimelech, and civil war breaks out. According to Judges 9, Abimelech razed the city and burned its tower. The archaeological evidence indicates that Shechem was destroyed in the mid- to late twelfth century. (It had previously been destroyed in the fourteenth century.) Whether this destruction is reflected in the story of Abimelech, we do not know. It is of interest, in any case, that the biblical story provides an instance of the destruction of a Canaanite city that has nothing to do with invaders, whether Israelite, Philistine, Egyptian, or anything else. Internal warfare between Canaanites was also a cause of destruction in Canaan in the Early Iron Age.

Abimelech encounters poetic justice in the end. He is mortally injured when a woman throws an upper millstone on his head—no small feat for a woman! The Deuteronomist, who had little sympathy for Abimelech, renders judgment: "Thus God repaid Abimelech for the crime he committed against his father in killing his seventy brothers," and the curse of Jotham on Shechem is fulfilled.

Jephthah

The story of Jephthah is as gripping as any story in the Hebrew Bible. Jephthah operates in Gilead in Transjordan, and the adversaries are Ammonites. Like Abimelech, he is of dishonorable birth and is expelled by the legitimate children. He rises to prominence as an outlaw, however, and is recalled by the elders because of his prowess as a fighter. He agrees on condition that he will become ruler if he succeeds. (Compare the bargain made by the Babylonian god Marduk in *Enuma Elish*.)

At first, Jephthah takes a diplomatic approach. His speech to the Ammonites is typically Deuteronomic, and makes sense only in the context of Deuteronomic theology. Both parties appeal to the story of the exodus, although they disagree as to which party wronged the other. When negotiations fail, "the spirit of the Lord came upon Jephthah" (11:29). Here as elsewhere the spirit seems to impart superhuman energy and force. (Compare 1 Kings 18:46, where the hand of the Lord was on Elijah and he ran before King Ahab's chariot.) Jephthah makes a vow to the Lord that "whoever comes out of the doors of my house to meet me when I return victorious from the Ammonites shall be the Lord's, to be offered up as a burnt offering" (11:31). There is no doubt in the context that human sacrifice is meant. It would have been absurd to offer the first animal he met, whether fit for sacrifice or not. In the context of ancient Israel, such a vow was an extreme measure, indicating both the extremity of the crisis and the intensity of Jephthah's devotion to YHWH. He evidently did not anticipate that the person in question would be his only daughter. Unlike Abraham, he is given no reprieve. Jephthah is often criticized for making a rash vow, but this criticism is not made in the text, where he appears to act under the influence of the Spirit of the Lord. Neither is he condemned in the tradition; in the New Testament he is celebrated as a hero of faith (Hebrews 11). In the biblical text, his daughter is more heroic than he. She urges him to keep his vow and asks only for time to bewail her virginity. The text is unambiguous that he "did with her according to the vow that he had made" (Judg 11:39). The medieval Jewish commentator David Kimchi held that Jephthah did not kill his daughter but dedicated her to a life of virginity (she asks for time to bewail her virginity, not her early death). A small minority of scholars still holds to this view, but most accept that the daughter's fate is all too clear. While the story in Judges certainly appreciates the tragedy of the outcome, there is no hint that Jephthah did wrong either by making the vow (for which he was rewarded with victory) or in fulfilling it. We shall see a different perspective on the binding force of vows in such circumstances in the story of Samuel and Jonathan in 1 Samuel 14.

The concluding episode of the Jephthah story in Judges 12 tells of a conflict between the men of Gilead and Ephraim. The tribes of Israel fought not only all the neighboring peoples but also one another on occasion. Here again the impression is of local tribal warfare rather than national conflicts between Israel and its neighbors.

Samson

Samson is arguably the most colorful character in the book of Judges, and his story has inspired artistic renderings, from the epic poetry of John Milton to the operatic music of Camille Saint-Saëns. He is marked as a hero from the beginning by his birth to a barren mother, announced by an angel of the Lord. Similar stories are told of Samuel, the last of the judges, and of John the Baptist in the New Testament (Luke 1; the virgin birth of Jesus is related to this pattern but has a heightened miraculous character). He is set aside as a nazirite, who must abstain from wine and strong drink and never cut his hair (cf. Num 6:1-6).

The people with whom Samson interacts are the Philistines. The origin of the Philistines is obscure, but they were part of a wave of "Sea Peoples" that swept through the Aegean and eastern Mediterranean at the end of the Bronze Age, destroying the Mycenaean Greek civilization. They are sometimes said to come from Caphtor (= Crete; see Deut 2:23; Amos 9:7). They also destroyed the Hittite Empire in Anatolia (modern Turkey) and the Canaanite city-state of Ugarit. They were defeated in battle by Ramesses III of Egypt about 1190 B.C.E. Ramesses settled defeated Philistines as mercenaries in the coastal towns of Gaza, Ashkelon, and Ashdod. Subsequently, the Philistines in these cities shook off their Egyptian overlords and formed a powerful local confederation that included the nearby cities of Ekron and Gath. The source of Philistine power came from their early mastery of forging iron (cf. 1 Sam 13:19-21). From an early time, the Philistines accepted the local Canaanite deities, Dagon (father of Baal) and Astarte. The history of the Philistine cities paralleled that of the kingdoms of Israel and Judah. They were conquered by the Assyrians, occupied by the Egyptians, and finally destroyed by the Babylonians, who deported Philistines as well as Judeans. Unlike the Judeans, the Philistines eventually lost their identity, but they did give their name to the country called Palestine. The biblical accounts tend to portray them as barbarians, but in fact they had a rich material culture, which has been amply documented by archaeological excavations in recent years.

The Philistines, then, were emerging as a power at the same time that the tribes of Israel were expanding from the highlands of Canaan. References to them in the books of Genesis and Exodus that imply that they were present at an earlier time are anachronistic. The conflict between Israel and the Philistines comes to a head in 1 Samuel when the Israelites were trying to get control of the lowlands. This conflict was a major reason why the Israelites eventually accepted the rule of a king.

According to Judges 14, the Philistines "had dominion over Israel" in the time of Samson. It is unlikely that they had dominion over all the Israelite tribes, but they controlled the coastal plain and came into conflict with the neighboring tribe of Judah. The story of Samson implies that there was considerable coming and going between Judah and Philistia, and a major feature of Samson's career is his involvement with Philistine women.

The first conflict between Samson and the Philistines in chapter 14 is little more than a family quarrel, arising from the tensions of a marriage across group boundaries. Samson is described as a man of legendary strength, who can tear apart a lion with his bare hands. He is vulnerable, however, to the weaker sex. He tries to take advantage of the Philistines by betting against their ability to answer a trick question, but his wife betrays him. He honors his bet, but at the expense of the Philistines in Ashkelon. The only religious note in all this is that "the spirit of the LORD" comes upon him and enables him to kill thirty men of Ashkelon. As in the case of other judges, such as Jephthah, the spirit of the LORD manifests itself in an outburst of physical force. In these stories, it has nothing to do with wisdom or virtue.

The conflict escalates in chapter 15, because when Samson, after some time, seeks out his wife, he finds she has been given to another. The tribe of Judah becomes involved only because they fear Philistine reprisals if they shelter Samson. They turn him over to his enemies, but again the Spirit of the Lord infuses him with superhuman strength so that he can burst his bonds and slaughter a thousand Philistines with the jawbone of an ass. The Deuteronomist gives him the status of a judge, and he ruled Israel for twenty years. Nothing in the story, however, implies activity outside of Judah and Philistia, and his "judging" seems to consist of outbursts of violent activity.

Samson's downfall inevitably comes from his inability to resist the charms of a Philistine woman, Delilah. He is given ample warning of her treachery, when he repeatedly lets himself be bound and then finds that the Philistines are upon him. Finally, he confides in Delilah that a razor has never come upon his head. Delilah has him shaved while he sleeps, and his strength fails him. He has one last mighty deed, however, when he pulls down the temple of Dagon on himself and his Philistine tormentors. The Deuteronomist portrays this as an answer to prayer. Judges 16:22 hints at a different explanation: his hair had grown back.

The story of Samson is a popular folktale about a legendary strong man, not unlike the Greek tales about the labors of Heracles (Hercules is the Latin form of the name). At no point is Samson motivated by concern for Israel. He shows no awareness of a covenant or of the exodus tradition. He honors his bet, in a way, but he does not seem to be constrained by any moral code except honor and vengeance. His story is preserved in the Bible as part of the lore of Israel, and it is a gripping and entertaining story. The Deuteronomist gives it only a light sprinkling of piety and never suggests that Samson is a moral exemplar. Rather, he is a tragic hero, a person of extraordinary (if brutish) talent who has a fatal weakness in his attraction to Philistine women. The story could easily serve to discourage marriage with foreign women, a favorite Deuteronomic theme, but the readers are left to draw their own inferences in this regard.

Perhaps the final irony of the Samson story is found in the Epistle to the Hebrews (11:32), which includes Samson among those "who through faith conquered kingdoms, administered justice, obtained promises," among other things. Samson could fairly be said to have shut the mouths of lions and put enemies to flight, but his concern for justice is not in evidence in this story. He had faith to the end that God had endowed him

Fig. 10.3 *Samson and Delilah* **by Anton van Dick, seventeenth century. Kunsthistorisches Museum, Berlin.**
Commons.wikimedia.org.

with superhuman physical strength, but this is hardly the kind of faith that is otherwise advocated in the Epistle to the Hebrews. Nonetheless, Samson was often considered to prefigure Christ in later Christian interpretation because of his suffering and the manner in which he meets his death with outstretched arms.

"In Those Days There Was No King"

The last four chapters of the book of Judges are framed by statements that "in those days there was no king in Israel; all the people did what was right in their own eyes" (17:6; 21:25). Reminders that "in those days there was no king in Israel" are also interspersed in the intervening chapters. The stories suggest that when there was no king the society tended to disintegrate. There are two main episodes in these chapters. The first concerns the relocation of the tribe of Dan. The second describes a conflict between Benjamin and the other tribes.

According to Josh 19:40-48, the original territory of the Danites included the city of Ekron, which is known to have become part of the Philistine confederacy, and stretched northward to Joppa. But "when the territory of the Danites was lost to them, the Danites went up and fought against Leshem," which they captured and renamed Dan. Samson was a Danite, and he is located in proximity to the Philistines. According to Judg 1:34, the Amorites repelled the Danites and would not let them come down into the plain. In Judges 18 the Danites are still seeking a terrritory to live in. This time the place they find is called Laish, at the northern extremity of Israel. Laish and Leshem are presumably variant names for the same place.

Later, during the monarchy, Dan was the site of one of the temples set up by King Jeroboam I of the northern kingdom of Israel in opposition to Jerusalem. This was considered an abomination by the Deuteronomistic Historian. The account of the founding of Dan in Judges 17–18 is not flattering. Even though the mission of the Danites is portrayed in terms that recall the initial conquest by Joshua (especially in the matter of spying out the land), we are told twice that the people of Laish were "quiet and unsuspecting." The naked aggression of the Danites is not disguised. Moreover, the cult of YHWH that is established at Dan is of questionable origin. It involves idols that were stolen from the house of Micah in Ephraim, and a Levite who is portrayed as a rather mercenary character. The use of household idols seems to have been a normal part of early Israelite religion, but it was counter to Deuteronomic law. Nonetheless, the story is told without much editorial comment. Readers are free to see for themselves how things were in Israel when there was no king.

The conflict between Benjamin and the other tribes involves one of the "tales of terror" of the Hebrew Bible. Benjamin is not an obvious target for Deuteronomistic polemic as Dan is. Benjamin was the only tribe that remained with Judah after the division of the kingdom. It was also the home tribe of Saul, the first king, who was rejected in favor of David, and this may have given a Judean editor some reason to include such a negative portrayal. In this case, the conflict is entirely within Israel.

The story begins with a Levite from Ephraim who took a concubine from Bethlehem who subsequently left him. When he was bringing her back, they found themselves near Jerusalem at nightfall. Since Jerusalem was then a Jebusite city, however, they pressed on to Gibeah in Benjamin. The assumption that it is safer to lodge among Israelites than among Gentiles proves to be tragically mistaken. The story that unfolds is very similar to the story of Sodom in Genesis 19. The men of Gibeah want to abuse the stranger. The man who has taken him in is horrified and offers them his virgin daughter and the Levite's concubine instead. In Genesis Lot's offer of his virgin daughters is rendered unnecessary by divine intervention. There is no such intervention here. The Levite's concubine is sacrificed to the cause, raped all night, and found dead in the morning. The story is chilling, not only because of the wickedness of the men of Gibeah, but also because of the Levite's willingness to sacrifice his concubine and the host's offer of his virgin daughter. The callousness of the Levite is shown vividly in his words to the concubine the following morning: "Get up, we are going." This part of the story reaches a grisly climax when he dismembers her corpse and sends a piece to each of the tribes. Later, in 1 Sam 11:7, Saul summons the tribes by killing an ox and cutting it up. The outrage of the Israelites against Gibeah is well merited. The conduct of the Levite is scarcely less outrageous but receives no comment in the biblical text.

The fate of Gibeah is not as severe as that of Sodom. The Israelites defeat the Benjaminites, but only after initial setbacks. Eventually all but six hundred Benjaminite men are slaughtered. Even the animals are killed.

Fig. 10.4 *The Levite Finds His Concubine* **by Gustav Doré, 1880.** Commons.wikimedia.org

When the Israelites swear that they will not give their daughters to the men of Benjamin, the future of the tribe seems in doubt. When the people of Jabesh-gilead are slaughtered, however, for failing to come out with the rest of the tribes, their virgin daughters are spared and given to the Benjaminites. Finally, in a scene reminiscent of the Roman tale of the Sabine women, the Benjaminites are allowed to snatch the young women who came out to dance at the festival of the Lord (Tabernacles) at Shiloh, north of Bethel. The book ends on a positive note, insofar as the tribe of Benjamin is restored, but again the price of its restoration is paid at the expense of the women, who are repeatedly treated as disposable commodities in this story. Like many of the stories in Judges, this one is not edifying. It can contribute to moral education by showing the horror of some kinds of behavior. Later tradition would labor to portray the judges in a positive light (as in Hebrews 11). The biblical text, however, seems designed to show the depravity of human, and specifically Israelite, nature and its need for divine mercy and assistance, rather than to exemplify any human virtue.

FOR FURTHER READING

Commentaries

R. Boling, *Judges* (AB 6A; Garden City, NY: Doubleday, 1975). Assumes more underlying historicity than is usual in more recent scholarship.

V. H. Matthews, *Judges and Ruth* (New Cambridge Bible Commentary; Cambridge: Cambridge University Press, 2004). Commentary on canonical text, informed by cultural parallels.

S. Niditch, *Judges: A Commentary* (OTL; Louisville: Westminster John Knox, 2008). Emphasizes folkloristic aspects. Distinguishes an epic-bardic voice, a theological (Deuteronomistic) voice and a humanistic one in chapters 1 and 17–21.

J. M. Sasson, *Judges 1–12* (Yale Anchor Bible; New Haven: Yale University Press, 2013). Distinguished by use of ancient Near Eastern parallels and postbiblical Jewish tradition.

J. A. Soggin, *Judges* (trans. J. Bowden; OTL; Philadelphia: Westminster, 1981). More skeptical than Boling on historical questions.

Historical Issues

B. Halpern, *The First Historians* (San Francisco: Harper & Row, 1988). Innovative study of historiographical method in the Deuteronomistic History, with several examples from Judges.

A. Mazar, *Archaeology of the Land of the Bible, 10,000–586 B.C.E.* (ABRL; New York: Doubleday, 1990) 295–367. Authoritative discussion of the archaeological evidence.

R. D. Miller, *Chieftains of the Highland Clans: A History of Israel in the Twelfth and Eleventh Centuries B. C.* (Grand Rapids: Eerdmans, 2005). Uses an anthropological model to illuminate the society of the Judges.

Literary and Feminist Studies

S. Ackerman, *Warrior, Dancer, Seductress, Queen* (New York: Doubleday, 1998). Study of female characters in the book of Judges, in the ancient Near Eastern context.

Y. Amit, *The Book of Judges: The Art of Editing* (Leiden: Brill, 1999). The main editing of Judges was pre-Deuteronomic.

M. Bal, *Death and Dissymetry: The Politics of Coherence in the Book of Judges* (Chicago: University of Chicago Press, 1988). Provocative feminist literary analysis.

A. Brenner, *A Feminist Companion to Judges* (Feminist Companion to the Bible 4; Sheffield: JSOT Press, 1993). Collection of essays from a feminist perspective.

M. Z. Brettler, *The Book of Judges* (London: Routledge, 2002). Finds various genres in Judges, edited to legitimate the Davidic kingship.

R. D. Miller, *Chieftains of the Highland Clans: A History of Israel in the Twlfth and Eleventh Centuries B.C.* (Grand Rapids: Eerdmans, 2005). Combines archaeological evidence and an anthropological model.

G. Mobley, *The Empty Men: The Heroic Tradition of Ancient Israel* (ABRL; New York: Doubleday, 2005). Lively account of the judges as epic heroes.

P. Trible, *Texts of Terror: Literary-Feminist Readings of Biblical Narratives* (OBT; Philadelphia: Fortress Press, 1984). Groundbreaking feminist study.

G. Yee, ed., *Judges and Method: New Approaches in Biblical Studies* (Minneapolis: Fortress Press, 1995). Uses stories from Judges to illustrate a range of current methodologies (narrative, social-scientific, feminist, deconstructive criticisms among others).

CHAPTER 11
First Samuel

INTRODUCTION

In this chapter, we examine the First Book of Samuel. Different threads of the story—the earlier narrative of the birth and call of the prophet Samuel; the story of the ark of the covenant's capture and recovery; the move to an Israelite monarchy and the trials of the king, Saul; and David's early career in Saul's court and then as an independent mercenary and outlaw—are all part of the story of David's rise to power. As we shall see, different narrative interests are at work in the story.

The two books of Samuel were originally one book in Hebrew and are found on a single scroll in the Dead Sea Scrolls. They were divided in Greek and Latin manuscripts because of the length of the book. In the Greek Septuagint (LXX) they are grouped with the books of Kings as 1–4 Reigns. The Greek text of Samuel is longer than the traditional Hebrew text (MT). Some scholars had thought that the translators had added passages, but the Dead Sea Scrolls preserve fragments of a Hebrew version that corresponds to the Greek. It is now clear that the Greek preserves an old form of the text, and that some passages had fallen out of the Hebrew through scribal mistakes.

First Samuel deals with the transition from the period of the judges to that of the monarchy. The section 1:1—4:1a describes the birth and early career of Samuel. Next, 4:1b—7:1 deals with the Philistine crisis and the capture of the ark. Samuel does not appear at all in this episode. The short section 7:2-17 describes another battle against the Philistines, in which Samuel plays a leadership role. The longer section 8:1—15:35 deals with the beginnings of the kingship under Saul. Then David emerges on the scene, and he dominates the remainder of 1 Samuel and the early chapters of 2 Samuel.

There are various tensions and duplications in 1 Samuel that are obvious even on a casual reading of the text. Samuel disappears from the scene in chapters 4–6, then reemerges in chapter 7. In chapter 8 the choice of a human king is taken to imply a rejection of the kingship of YHWH. Yet the first king is anointed at YHWH's command. There are different accounts of the way in which Saul becomes king (10:17-27; chap. 11) and different accounts of his rejection (chaps. 13 and 15). There are two accounts of how David came into the service of Saul (chaps. 16 and 17). David becomes Saul's son-in-law twice in chapter 18 and defects to the Philistine king of Gath twice in chapters 21 and 27. He twice refuses to take Saul's life when he has the opportunity (chaps. 24 and 27).

It is clear from these duplications that 1 Samuel is not all the work of a single author. Older (nineteenth century) scholarship identified two strands in the book. The first, which included 9:1—10:16; 11; 13–14, had a generally favorable view of the monarchy. The second, including chapters 7–8; 10:17-27; 12; 15, viewed the kingship with grave suspicion. In Martin Noth's theory of the Deuteronomistic History, this second stratum corresponded to the Deuteronomic redaction. Other scholars, however, have argued for a more complex situation. The negative view of the kingship may already have been part of an older, pre-Deuteronomic source that is influenced by the criticism of the prophets. Moreover, there may be more than one Deuteronomistic edition.

Indeed, the Deuteronomistic editor does not seem to have imposed a pattern on the books of Samuel such as we find in Judges or in the books of Kings. There is relatively little distinctive Deuteronomic language. Deuteronomic passages have been recognized in the oracle against the house of Eli in 1 Sam 2:27-36 and 3:11-14, in Samuel's reply to the request for a king in 8:8, and especially in Samuel's farewell speech in chapter 12. (For a fuller list of Deuteronomic passages,

see McCarter, *1 Samuel*, 16–17.) It has been suggested that the Deuteronomists had at their disposal relatively extensive sources that they found congenial and did not need to edit heavily. Nonetheless, the fact remains that two quite different attitudes to the monarchy are interwoven in 1 Samuel. The easiest way to explain this is by supposing that the first Deuteronomistic edition in the time of Josiah was positive toward the monarchy, and that the more negative material was incorporated in a later edition during the exile after the monarchy had collapsed. Both editions may have drawn on older traditions. The net result, however, is a complex narrative that shows the range of attitudes toward the monarchy in ancient Israel and that cannot be easily categorized as ideological propaganda. The books of Samuel present us with sophisticated literature that shows the ambiguous and multifaceted character of human action to a much greater degree than the books we have considered up to this point. The historical accuracy of these stories is moot, since we have no way of checking them. They have the character of a historical novel, which clearly has some relationship to history but is concerned with theme and character rather than with accuracy in reporting.

The Birth and Call of Samuel (1:1—4:1a)

The story of Samuel's birth is similar to that of Samson's but more elaborate. His father had two wives. (Polygamy is never forbidden in the Hebrew Bible. It is usually assumed that the practice faded out in the Second Temple period, but documents found near the Dead

Sea from the Bar Kokhba period in the early second century c.e. provide an example of bigamy even at that time.) The rivalry between the wives adds to the misery of the barren one, Hannah. (Compare the tension between Sarah and Hagar in Genesis.) Eventually, the Lord answers her prayer, and Samuel is conceived. In thanksgiving, Hannah dedicates her son as a nazirite to the Lord. Unlike Samson, who was also a nazirite, Samuel is dedicated to service at the house of the Lord at Shiloh. This was apparently the most important Israelite shrine in the period immediately before the rise of the monarchy. Later the building of the temple in Jerusalem is represented as a break with tradition (2 Sam 7:6-7), on the grounds that YHWH had not lived in a house up to that time but had been going around in a tent-shrine or tabernacle. The structure at Shiloh, however, seems to have been of a more permanent nature. Later the prophet Jeremiah refers to Shiloh as the place where the Lord first made his name to dwell (Jer 7:12). Psalm 78:60 describes the shrine at Shiloh as a *mishkan* or tent-shrine, and Josh 18:1 and 19:51 refer to the tent of meeting there. Some scholars have argued that the tabernacle described in the Priestly source in the Pentateuch was located at Shiloh. The hypothesis is intriguing, but the evidence is not conclusive.

The Song of Hannah in 1 Samuel 2 provides a theological perspective not only on the change in Hannah's fortunes, but also on the ups and downs of the unfolding history. The song is a psalm, such as we find in the Psalter, and was probably not composed specifically for this context. As we shall see, there is in the Psalter a genre of Thanksgiving Psalms (e.g., Psalms 18, 30, 118), that would be appropriate for a context like this. These typically include a description of the distress from which the psalmist was delivered and often contain indications of a ceremonial context (e.g., a call to the other participants to join in the thanksgiving). Hannah's Song does not have these distinctive features of the thanksgiving psalm of the individual. It is a more general hymn of praise, that refers to God's typical ways of dealing with humanity rather than to a specific act of deliverance. It was probably chosen for this context because of v. 5: "The barren has borne seven, but she who has many children is forlorn." The theme of the song is that God exalts the lowly and brings down the mighty. Various incidents in the books of Samuel and Kings can be cited as illustrations of this theme, but it can hardly be said to be the organizing theme of this history. Hannah's Song is the model for the Magnificat, the thanksgiving song of the virgin Mary in the New Testament (Luke 1:46-55).

The manner of Samuel's birth links him with the judges who have gone before, although his career bears little similarity to that of Samson. At this point in the narrative, the priest Eli is judge in Israel according to the Deuteronomistic Historian (1 Sam 4:18 says that he judged Israel for forty years). In fact, however, Eli is described as the chief priest at Shiloh. He never rallies the tribes or acts as a leader of an Israelite confederacy. He is called "judge" here only to fit him into the pattern imposed by the Deuteronomist. He is described as a person of integrity, but his sons are not. The account of the abuses of the sons of Eli in 1 Sam 2:12-17 is a vivid glimpse of life around a temple in ancient Israel. Before Josiah's reform, sacrifice was the occasion for eating meat, and the sacrifices were, in any case, a major source of support for the temple clergy.

If the birth of Samuel links him with the judges, his call in chapter 3 anticipates that of the later prophets. As we shall later see, the call of the prophets takes either of two forms: it can be a vision, as in the calls of Isaiah and Ezekiel, or it can be an auditory experience, where a voice is heard but no form is described. The paradigm example of the auditory call is the story of Moses at the burning bush. Jeremiah is another example. Samuel's call experience is of the auditory type. Unlike Moses or Jeremiah, however, Samuel is not given a mission. Rather, he is given a prophecy of the destruction of the house of Eli. Revelations of coming judgment are very much the stock and trade of the later prophets. Samuel does not function as a medium of such prophecies in the books of Samuel after 1 Sam 4:1, except in the case of Saul. The revelation in chapter 3, however, establishes his credentials as a prophet, and at the end of the chapter we are told that all Israel knew that he was a trustworthy prophet of the Lord, and that he continued to receive and relay the word of the Lord at Shiloh. We shall find that he functions as a prophet in other ways. He is a seer, who can find things that are missing (chap. 9). In a strange interlude in 1 Sam 19:20, he appears as conductor of a band of ecstatic prophets. More importantly, he anoints kings and can also declare that they have been rejected by God. Samuel's interaction with Saul prefigures the interaction between kings and prophets later in the Deuteronomistic History.

The Ark Narrative (4:1b—7:1)

The story of Samuel is interrupted in 4:1b—7:1 by an episode in which he plays no part.

This episode is generally recognized as an independent source document incorporated by the Deuteronomists. The theme of the story is the capture of the ark of the covenant by the Philistines.

The ark is variously called the ark of God, the ark of YHWH, the ark of the covenant, or the ark of testimony. The association of the ark with the covenant is typical of the Deuteronomists; the Priestly writers prefer "the ark of the testimony." In Deut 10:1-5 Moses is told to make an ark of wood as a receptacle for the stone tablets of the covenant. The story in 1 Samuel 4–6, however, makes clear that it is no mere box. It is the symbol of the presence of the Lord. It is carried into battle to offset the superior force of the Philistines, in the belief that YHWH is thereby brought into the battle. (Compare the chant uttered when the ark set out, according to Num 10:35: "Arise, O Lord, let your enemies be scattered.") The ark was also associated with the divine throne as the footstool of the Deity.

The drama of the story in 1 Samuel 4–6 comes from the fact that YHWH's enemies are not scattered before the ark. The Philistines overcome their initial panic and capture the ark. The capture of a people's god or gods was not unusual in the ancient Near East. When one people captured the city of another, they typically carried off the gods, represented by statues, as booty. Even the god of Babylon, Marduk, was carried off in this manner. This was meant to show the superior power of the victor's gods. The defeated people, however, explained things differently. Their gods were supposed to have let themselves be carried off because of anger with their own people. Nonetheless, the capture of the ark in battle was evidently a great shock to the Israelites.

Fig. 11.1 **The ark of the covenant and the broken statue of the Phillistine god Dagon; fresco from the third-century c.e. synagogue at Dura-Europos.** Commons.wikimedia.org

The shock led directly to the death of Eli, and his daughter-in-law named her son Ichabod ("no glory"), for "the glory departed from Israel" when the ark was captured.

The story of the ark, however, has a positive ending for the Israelites. YHWH asserts his power by mysteriously destroying the statue of the Philistine god Dagon and afflicting the people with a plague. As a result, the Philistines send it back. Usually, when victors returned the captured statues of gods, they depicted this as an act of magnanimity on the part of their own superior deities. Here the return is taken to show that YHWH is invincible after all. His apparent capture by the Philistines becomes the occasion for a greater display of his might. Nonetheless, it is significant that shortly after this episode the Israelites begin to ask for a king. The old charismatic religion of the judges, which relied heavily on the Spirit of the Lord, was not adequate for dealing with the Philistines.

The Move to Monarchy (1 Samuel 7–12)

Samuel reappears on the scene in 1 Sam 7:3 and is said to judge Israel after Eli's demise. Like Eli, he also functions as a priest. Unlike the older judges, however, he is not a warrior and does not lead in battle. He secures the success of the Israelites in battle by offering sacrifice, to which the Lord responds with thunder, and this is enough to put the Philistines to flight. This is the Deuteronomistic ideal of how to fight a battle; compare the capture of Jericho, where the Israelites also perform a ritual and the Lord makes the decisive intervention in the battle.

Like Eli, however, Samuel has sons that do not follow in his footsteps, and so the people finally ask for a king. The exchange between Samuel and the people on this subject in 1 Samuel 8 is representative of the negative strand of 1 Samuel and of the Deuteronomistic History. The people are said to have rejected the kingship of YHWH. Moreover, the prediction of "the ways of the king" reflects disillusionment born of centuries of experience. This description of monarchy must have rung all too true after the kingship had been brought to an end by the Babylonians. But the description of the ways of the king is quite in line with the critiques of monarchy by the prophets, beginning with Elijah in 1 Kings 21. We shall find that the ways of the king begin to be exemplified already in the story of David, who takes the wife of a subject, and in a major way in the story of Solomon. The Israelites did not need to wait until the Babylonian exile to discover that monarchy could be oppressive.

There are two accounts of the election of Saul as the first king. The first is a quaint story in which Saul goes to consult the seer Samuel about lost donkeys. This story speaks volumes about early Israelite society. Lost donkeys were a matter of concern for prophets and for future kings. When Samuel meets him, he anoints him as king. This is the first case in which a king is anointed in ancient Israel. Anointing with oil had various connotations. It was thought to give strength, to cleanse or purify, or it could be used for pleasure. In the case of the kingship, it represented strengthening. It is usually assumed that the custom was taken over from the Canaanites, but evidence for the Canaanite usage is lacking. Kings were not anointed in Mesopotamia or in Egypt, but they were among the Hittites. There is also evidence for the anointing of Egyptian vassals in Syria. Other people in Israel were anointed, besides the king, most notably the high priest. The king, however, was "the LORD's anointed"

par excellence. It is from this expression that we get the word *messiah*, from the Hebrew *mashiach*, "anointed."

According to the second account of the election of Saul, he was chosen by lot (1 Sam 10:20). The procedure here is similar to the discovery of Achan in Josh 7:16-18. This appears to be the formal method for discerning the divine will that is favored by the Deuteronomists. It is rendered redundant here by the preceding story of Saul and the donkeys. Another distinctively Deuteronomic note is sounded by the notice that Samuel wrote the rights and duties of the kingship in a book and gave it to Saul. Compare the law of the king in Deut 17:14-20, which specifically requires the king to have a copy of that law and to read it all the days of his life. In this account, the election of Saul is validated by his victory over the Ammonites (1 Samuel 11). Initially, he acts like a judge, summoning the tribes by sending around pieces of the oxen he had cut up. He is then inspired by the spirit of the Lord. (Saul also receives the spirit of prophecy on two occasions, 10:10-13 and 19:23-24, but he does not otherwise act as a prophet.) After the victory over the Ammonites, the people assemble at Gilgal to make him king. There are several steps, then, in the process by which Saul becomes king: divine election, designation by a prophet (Samuel), and finally acclamation by the people.

The accession of Saul is completed by the apparent retirement of Samuel in chapter 12 ("See it is the king who leads you now; I am old and gray"). Samuel's protestation of innocence provides a concise summary of the conduct expected from a good ruler. He should not abuse the people by taking their belongings or defraud them, and he should not take bribes to pervert justice. He seems reluctant, however, to yield the reins of power. He chides the people for asking for a king. In the end, he grants that things will be all right if they do not turn aside from following the Lord but serve him with all their heart. In Deuteronomistic theology, at least as it developed in the Babylonian exile and later, the importance of the kingship is relativized. What is of fundamental importance is keeping the law, regardless of whether there is a king.

The Trials of Saul (1 Samuel 13–15)

Samuel, however, does not stay retired. He clashes with Saul in two incidents, reported in chapters 13 and 15. The first concerns the preparation for a battle against the Philistines. Saul was instructed by Samuel to wait seven days; then Samuel would come and offer sacrifice (cf. 1 Sam 10:8, in what seems to be a different context). Samuel is late, however, and Saul is concerned about the morale of his soldiers, some of whom are deserting. So he presumes to offer the sacrifice himself. No sooner does he do so than Samuel appears and judges him harshly. If he had kept the commandment, his kingdom would have been confirmed, but now it will not continue.

This is clearly a theological reading of the failure of Saul's kingship. According to the Deuteronomists, success comes from keeping commandments, and failure from disobedience. As a prophet, Samuel speaks for God and is not to be questioned. Also implicit in the story is the assumption that success in battle depends on ritual rather than on strategy or force of arms, but the ritual, in turn, is not automatically efficacious but depends on the obedience of the performer. No matter if half the army is deserting, Samuel must be obeyed and the sacrifice must be offered properly. Saul's action, in this episode, is not arrogant or unreasonable. He waits seven days, the time indicated by Samuel, but he is a pragmatist. In the circumstances, his judgment seems unduly harsh.

The clash between Saul and Samuel can also be viewed from other angles. There is a blatant conflict of interest between the two men as to which of them is ultimately in control. Despite his farewell address in the previous chapter, Samuel has not left the scene and seems to be unwilling to yield power to the younger man. All of this is plausible psychologically, although we have no way to verify whether it has any historical basis. There is also, however, a conflict between two theologies. Samuel represents an ethic of unconditional obedience, while Saul represents a moderate pragmatism. From the viewpoint of the Deuteronomists, the trouble with kings was that they took things into their own hands instead of deferring to the word of God as revealed by the prophets. We must bear in mind, however, that the word of God is not manifested directly. It is always mediated by human agents who have their own interests in the proceedings. In this case, the word of God, as pronounced by Samuel, confirms the authority of Samuel over Saul. In the later times when the Deuteronomistic History was written, the theology of obedience favored the authority of the scribes or other religious functionaries over that of secular rulers. The claims of figures like Samuel to speak for God must be viewed with some suspicion in view of their own interests.

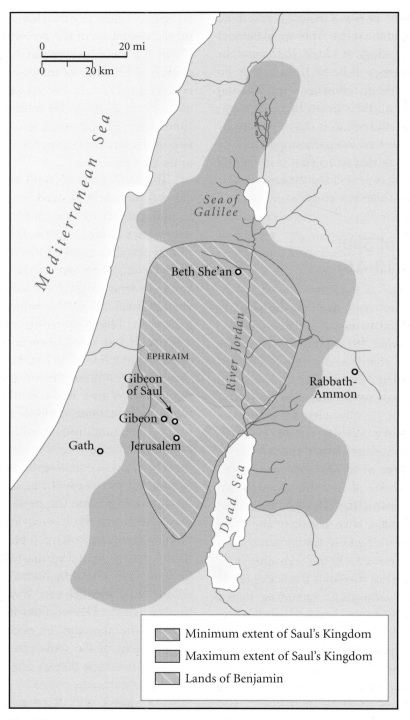

Map 11.1

INTRODUCTION TO THE HEBREW BIBLE

The conflict between Saul and Samuel is resumed in chapter 15. This time Samuel orders Saul to attack Amalek and slaughter every man, woman, and child, and even the animals. Saul partially complies but spares the king and the best of the animals to offer them as sacrifice. Because of this he is again repudiated as king. Saul apparently thought he was in compliance but that he had some discretion as to how he might fulfill the command. The command itself is harsh and inhuman. Even if total slaughter was customary in ancient warfare, it was a base custom, and we should not expect it to be the subject of a divine command. Once again, the issue is authority and control. May Saul, as king, decide such actions for himself, or must he defer to the word of Samuel? The Deuteronomist clearly implies that he must defer. But other perspectives are also possible. The conflict is a power struggle. It is not apparent that Samuel's command, either here or in chapter 13, is for the greater good of the people, unless one assumes, as the Deuteronomist does, that it is always better to obey the prophet who claims to speak for God. Saul might have been forgiven for doubting the authenticity of that claim. But in fact he never questions Samuel's authority in the story. After all, Saul's own authority derived in large part from the word of the prophet.

Samuel's rebuke to Saul has a prophetic ring to it: "Has the Lord as great delight in burnt offerings and in sacrifices as in obedience to the voice of the Lord? Surely, to obey is better than sacrifice, and to heed than the fat of rams" (1 Sam 15:22). There is a close parallel to this in the prophet Hosea: "For I desire steadfast love and not sacrifice, the knowledge of God rather than burnt offerings" (Hos 6:6). Hosea and Samuel agree that sacrifice is no substitute for right conduct, but they have rather different ideas about what constitutes right conduct. For Hosea, it is steadfast love and the knowledge of God. In the context of the prophet's oracles, it is clear that the practice of justice is required, as well as fidelity to YHWH. For Samuel, in contrast, everything comes down to obedience, even if what is commanded is the slaughter of other human beings.

The two stories of conflict between Samuel and Saul in 1 Samuel 13 and 15, frame another engrossing story that illustrates a similar conflict in values. In the battle against the Philistines after the incident at Gilgal, Saul, we are told, laid an oath on the troops, cursing any man who tasted food before the enemy was defeated. (Recall the oath of Jephthah in Judges 11.) His son Jonathan, the hero of the battle up to this point, was unaware of the oath and ate some honey. When he is told of the oath, Jonathan shrugs it off: the men would fight better if they had food. Here again we see a clash between a moderate pragmatism on the one hand and an ethic that attaches great importance to oaths and vows on the other. Jonathan questions the efficacy of oaths as a means to success in battle. It would be better to see that the troops were well fed.

In this case, Saul is cast as the defender of the ethic of obedience. He declares that if Jonathan is guilty he must die. This story, however, ends very differently from either that of Abraham and Isaac or that of Jephthah and his daughter. Jonathan is not executed, and the reprieve does not come from divine intervention. Instead, the troops intervene to rescue Jonathan from his father's oath. In this case, pragmatism wins out.

The stories in 1 Samuel 13–15 capture brilliantly the sense of a society in transition, where deference to custom and to religious authorities collides with a growing sense of pragmatism. The conflict of values, however, is not peculiar to any one period of history. While the Deuteronomist clearly sides with Samuel in his conflict with Saul, the great virtue of the stories is that they are not simplistic but allow us to see more than one side of the issue.

The Rise of David

The second half of 1 Samuel and the opening chapters of 2 Samuel tell the story of David's rise to power. It is widely agreed that the Deuteronomist drew on an older source document here. The "History of David's Rise" is usually identified as 1 Sam 16:14—2 Samuel 5; 1 Sam 16:1-13 is sometimes included. A major turning point in this story is marked by the death of Saul.

What manner of story is this? Like other parts of the books of Samuel, it reads like a historical novel rather than like the kind of chronicle we often find in the books of Kings. It is not historiography in the modern sense of the term. Here again we cannot verify anything about David, because all our sources about him depend on the biblical tradition. Some scholars have gone so far as to question whether David ever existed, but most would regard this as undue skepticism. The ruling family in Judah for some four hundred years was known as the "house of David." This title has now been found in an inscription from Tel Dan. It is possible that a royal house could have a mythical ancestor. It is more likely, however, that David was a historical person, like Omri, who gave his name to a dynasty in

Fig. 11.2 **The Tel Dan inscription, a ninth-century B.C.E. Aramaic inscription in which the king of Aram claims to have defeated "the house of David"—our earliest extra-biblical reference to David; now in the Israel Museum.** Commons.wikimedia.org

northern Israel. That said, we have simply no way of checking whether the historical David bore any resemblance to the figure described in the biblical narratives.

We should expect that the story of King David would have been of interest primarily to the house of David and its supporters. It is surprising, then, that the story does not bear a stronger imprint of the royal ideology of Judah, which hailed the Davidic king as "son of God" or even as an *elohim*, "god" (see the discussion of the royal ideology in chapter 12 below). The books of Samuel claim no divine status for David. On the contrary, he emerges as all too human. The difference over against Judean royal ideology can be explained in either of two ways. Some suppose that this story was composed at a very early time, either in the reign of David or shortly thereafter—before the royal ideology developed. Alternatively, this story may come from a later time. It can scarcely have been composed by the Deuteronomists; it does not contain much that is distinctively Deuteronomistic. Its view of the monarchy, however, is rather similar to that of Deuteronomy, insofar as the kingship is portrayed as a human and fallible institution. It does not, in short, appear to be a court history. The author or authors were clearly sympathetic to David and to the dynasty he founded, but they show more distance from their subject than we might expect if they were court scribes in the pay of the king. We can say little about the origin of this story, except that it was available when the Deuteronomists compiled their history.

Related to this is the question of the genre of the story. One influential hypothesis is that it was composed as an apology for King David—that is, a propaganda document intended to refute charges that might be brought against him. Specifically, it shows that David was not an outlaw, a deserter, or a Philistine mercenary, that he was not implicated in Saul's death or in the deaths of some of Saul's family and followers. A model for such an apology is proposed in the "Apology of Hattusilis." Hattusilis was a thirteenth-century B.C.E. Hittite king who usurped the throne. His apology argued that he had been loyal to his predecessor until the latter had turned against him. His ascent to the throne reflected the will of the gods. Similar themes appear in the history of David's rise.

Nonetheless, for the modern reader, at least, the story conveys the impression that David at various times was an outlaw, a deserter, and a Philistine mercenary, and he was at best conspicuous by his absence when Saul was killed. If this is apologetic literature, it is exceptionally subtle, and, indeed, it is only partially successful. It argues that David was chosen by the Lord and succeeded by divine providence, but it also paints a very credible picture of a young opportunist who could be quite unscrupulous. The appeal of this story lies precisely in the ambiguity of its hero. He is chosen by God, but he is by no means flawless or innocent. The story has more the character of historical novel than of political propaganda. It is a theological historical novel that takes a historical character and develops a story about him that illustrates the ways of human nature but takes the course of events to illustrate the ways of God.

The Election of David

As in the case of Saul, there is more than one account of how David became king. First he is anointed by Samuel (1 Sam 16:1-13). This story follows a familiar biblical pattern in the exaltation of the lowly (cf. the Song of Hannah). Saul was taken from the lowly and recently humiliated tribe of Benjamin; David is the youngest of the sons of Jesse and initially thought to be of no account. The moral is articulated by Samuel: "The Lord does not see as mortals see. They look on the outward appearance, but the Lord looks on the heart" (16:7). Yet the story of Saul would seem to show that the Lord, too, can make a mistake.

First Samuel 16:14-23 gives a different account of the discovery of David. He is picked out because of his skill as a musician. Saul has now lost the Spirit of the Lord, and instead is afflicted by "an evil spirit from the Lord" (16:14). In modern parlance, this would be described as a psychological illness, perhaps manic depression or bipolar disorder. It should be noted that evil spirits are supposed to come from the Lord. In

Fig. 11.3 David is anointed by Samuel in a fresco from the third-century C.E. synagogue at Dura Europos. Commons. wikimedia.org

Deuteronomic theology, there is no other power that might be responsible for them. Saul's behavior becomes increasingly erratic, but this is quite intelligible in view of the way he has been frustrated by Samuel. David is summoned to court to soothe the king by his music. Saul, of course, is unaware that David has been anointed as his replacement.

Yet another account of the discovery of David follows in the story of his combat with Goliath in 1 Samuel 17. There are actually two stories here. The first is found in 17:1-11, 32-40, 42-48a, 49, 51-54. The second is found in 17:12-31, 41, 48b, 50, 55-58; 18:1-5, 10-11, 17-19, 29b-30. The verses that make up the second story are missing from the Old Greek translation, as found in Codex Vaticanus. It is generally agreed that in this case the Greek preserves the older form of the text. The second story is an independent account of the combat. It introduces David as if he were previously unknown. Moreover, he is still a shepherd, rather than a musician at Saul's court. This popular variant of the story must have been interpolated into the Hebrew text at some time in the Second Temple period.

Few stories in the Hebrew Bible have such popular appeal as that of David and Goliath. It has become the proverbial story of the underdog. It has much in common with the classic Near Eastern myth of the combat of Marduk and Tiamat *(Enuma Elish),* with the Philistine in the role of the chaos monster. There is no suggestion, however, that David and Goliath are more than human. David triumphs by wit and agility over the huge but rather immobile Philistine. The Deuteronomist sees another dimension in the conflict. Goliath comes with sword and spear, but David comes in the name of the Lord of hosts (17:45). As in the story of the exodus, YHWH is the God of the underdog and outsider, and no human power can prevail against him.

Despite its legendary character, the story of Goliath fits the most plausible scenario of David's rise. He was successful in battle and outshone his master, King Saul. Hence the popular acclaim: Saul has killed his thousands, but David his tens of thousands. David, at this point, is still supposedly Saul's loyal servant, but rivalry between the two men is inevitable. Their relationship is complicated by the friendship between David and Saul's family. We are told that Jonathan, Saul's son, loved David as himself (18:1). Much has been made of the relationship between David and Jonathan as a possible biblical model of a positive homosexual relationship. Homosexual attraction is certainly a factor in male bonding, especially in all-male institutions like the army (down to current times). (Homoerotic overtones have also been suspected in the story of Gilgamesh and Enkidu in the Epic of Gilgamesh.) But if there is a sexual dimension in this relationship, it is never acknowledged explicitly.

David also has relationships with Saul's daughters. The marriage with the elder daughter, Merab (18:17), is part of the secondary Goliath story. It is not found in the Old Greek. The story of Michal is more easily intelligible if there was no marriage to the elder daughter. Michal, like Saul, is eventually a tragic character. In 1 Samuel 18 the initiative for the marriage comes from Michal, who loves David, with Saul's approval. David, then, cannot be accused of marrying for expediency. When David is estranged from Saul, Michal becomes the wife of another man, but David recalls her after Saul's death, when he is trying to secure the kingship over all Israel. After the kingship has been consolidated, however, she is cursed with childlessness, ostensibly for disapproving of David dancing before the ark. The story may be intended to defend David from allegations that he used Michal and dumped her when he no longer needed her, but it is difficult not to read between the lines and suspect that he was motivated by political expediency.

The stories of interaction between David and Saul in 1 Samuel 19–24 provide the closest analogies to the genre of apology, or justification of the actions of a king who might be accused of usurping the throne. Saul repeatedly tries to kill David for no reason other than jealousy. Saul's own family, Jonathan and Michal, side with David in the conflict. Saul commits an outrage by slaughtering the priests of Nob (a shrine north of Jerusalem, near Gibeah) for befriending and defending David. Nonetheless, when David has Saul at his mercy, he refrains, declaring, "I will not raise my hand against the Lord's anointed" (24:10). Even Saul acknowledges that "you are more righteous than I" (24:17). Finally, Saul acknowledges that David will succeed to the kingship and asks only that David not kill his descendants and "wipe out my name from my father's house." It was not unusual in the ancient world (nor indeed at much later times) for a new king to wipe out anyone who might pose a challenge to his throne. Yet we find that Saul pursues David again in chapter 26, and David again refrains from killing Saul when he has an opportunity.

David as Outlaw and Mercenary

The later chapters of 1 Samuel, however, paint a more complex picture of David as bandit leader and mercenary. He is forced into these roles by the constant threat of violence from Saul. Nonetheless, David emerges as an opportunist who can tailor his loyalties to the circumstances in which he finds himself. He continues to pursue his career as a military leader, and this is in large part why Saul fears him and tries to eliminate him.

When David is not in the service of a king, he must support his troops by whatever means available. In 1 Samuel 25 he does this by demanding a protection payment from a sheep farmer in Carmel: "Now your shepherds have been with us, and we did them no harm, and they missed nothing all the time we were in Carmel" (25:7). The farmer is named Nabal, which means "fool." His folly lies in his failure to recognize the threat posed by the bandit's demand. In contrast, his wife, Abigail, is clever and beautiful, and she intervenes to buy David off. When Nabal hears what happened, he dies suddenly, and David takes Abigail as a wife. The story is told in such a way as to imply that the Lord was with David, that Nabal was not only a fool but a mean and ungracious person, and that Abigail was properly generous and appreciated David. Nonetheless, the story looks all too familiar to anyone familiar with novels or films about godfathers and gangsters in the modern world. Frequent invocation of the name of the Lord cannot hide the fact that David is engaged in extortion.

In 1 Samuel 22 David leaves his parents with the king of Moab for safekeeping. In chapter 27 he enters the service of the Philistine king of Gath, who allows him to settle in the town of Ziklag. From there he staged raids on peoples to the south. The text is careful to insist that he only pretended to stage raids on Judah, and in fact this is quite credible in the context, since Judah was his power base. But the fact that the people whom he slaughtered, in acts of naked aggression, were Amalekites, does little to redeem his moral character in the eyes of the modern reader. Rather, the picture we get is of an unscrupulous opportunist.

Finally, David is called on to join the Philistines in battle against Israel. He declares his willingness, and the king of Gath does not doubt his loyalty. Other Philistine commanders, however, are distrustful, and so David is sent back. Thus he is saved from the dilemma of either fighting against his own people or being disloyal to his current master. Here again the story serves as an apology to defend David of complicity in the death of Saul. The apology justifies his actions only in part. There is no indication that he was unwilling to fight against Saul, in the circumstances. The biblical author evidently shares the judgment of the king of Gath that David is as blameless as an angel of God (29:9), but a more skeptical interpretation of his actions is also possible.

First Samuel ends with the death of Saul and Jonathan. Saul's career has deteriorated long before this point. The pathos of his situation is shown in chapter 28 when he disguises himself to consult the witch of Endor, although he had supposedly banished all such wizards and mediums in good Deuteronomic

Fig. 11.4 *Abigail and David,* illustration in a fifteenth-century manuscript of *Fleur des histoires* by Jean Mansel.

Commons.wikimedia.org

fashion. The episode provides a fascinating glimpse of unofficial religious practice in ancient Israel. The woman calls up the spirit of Samuel, but he provides no consolation to Saul. Instead, he reiterates the judgment of the Deuteronomists that Saul was rejected for his disobedience.

The death of Saul has a certain aura of heroism. He falls on his sword rather than be captured by the Philistines. Suicide has generally been condemned in Jewish and Christian tradition, but some cases have always been admired—most notably the mass suicide of the Zealots at Masada at the end of the Jewish revolt against Rome in the first century C.E. There is no hint of disapproval of the suicide of Saul. For all his faults, he is recognized as a champion of Israel in its struggle with the Philistines and other neighboring peoples.

FOR FURTHER READING

Commentaries

A. G. Auld, *I & II Samuel: A Commentary* (OTL; Louisville: Westminster John Knox, 2011). Posits underlying "Book of Two Houses" on which both Samuel and Chronicles. Late composition.

A. G. Auld and E. Eynikel, *For and against David. Story and History in the Books of Samuel* (Leuven: Peeters, 2010). Collection of essays representing a spectrum of approaches.

B. Birch, "1 and 2 Samuel," *NIB* 2:949–1383. Good homiletical commentary.

Campbell, A. J. *1 Samuel* (FOTL; Grand Rapids: Eerdmans, 2003). Systematic form-critical analysis. The text is more theology than history.

H. W. Hertzberg, *I and II Samuel* (trans. J. S. Bowden; OTL; Philadelphia: Westminster, 1964). Classic exegetical commentary.

D. Jobling, *1 Samuel* (Berit Olam; Collegeville, MN: Liturgical Press, 1998). Postmodern commentary focusing on issues of race, class, and gender.

R. Klein, *1 Samuel* (WBC 10; Waco: Word, 1983). Detailed commentary, with good attention to textual issues.

P. K. McCarter, *1 Samuel* (AB 8; New York, Doubleday, 1980). Excellent scholarly discussion of textual and literary issues.

Literary Analyses

D. M. Gunn, *The Fate of King Saul* (Sheffield: JSOT Press, 1980). Idem, *The Story of King David* (Sheffield: JSOT Press, 1978). Sensitive literary readings.

Literary-Historical Analyses

B. Halpern, *David's Secret Demons: Messiah, Murderer, Traitor, King* (Grand Rapids: Eerdmans, 2001). Ingenious attempt to extract historical information from 1 and 2 Samuel.

M. Leuchter, *Samuel and the Shaping of Tradition* (New York: Oxford University Press, 2013). Diverse interpretations of Samuel in the biblical and postbiblical traditions.

S. L. McKenzie, *King David: A Biography* (New York: Oxford University Press, 2000). A readable narrative of David's life in historical context.

P. D. Miller and J. J. M. Roberts, *The Hand of the Lord: A Reassessment of the "Ark Narrative" of 1 Samuel* (Baltimore: Johns Hopkins University Press, 1977). Influential reading of the ark narrative in light of ancient Near Eastern stories about the capture of deities.

CHAPTER 12

Second Samuel

INTRODUCTION

The Second Book of Samuel picks up the story of David's rise to power, which climaxes in YHWH's solemn promise to ensure David's house in perpetuity. In this chapter, we will explore the contours of royal ideology in Judah, as well as the interests at work in the rise of David, his conquests, and his fall: the disastrous affair with Bathsheba and war with his son Absalom. We wil consider at last the nature of the Psalms attributed to David.

Like 1 Samuel, 2 Samuel incorporates extensive source documents that have been only lightly edited by the Deuteronomist. The key passage in the Deuteronomistic edition of the book is the account of the promise to David in 2 Samuel 7, although here, too, the editor is adapting an older source. The history of David's rise, which dominated the second half of 1 Samuel, is continued in 2 Samuel 1–5. Second Samuel 9–2 Kings 2 is often identified as the Court History of David, or the Succession Narrative, but some scholars think that a number of distinct documents are combined in those chapters. The account of the rebellion of Absalom in 2 Samuel 13–20 is a tightly structured narrative, which may be a distinct unit. First Kings 1–2 is an apology for the accession of Solomon to the kingship.

The Conclusion of David's Rise

The story of David's rise to power is completed in 2 Sam 1:1—5:10. David mourns ostentatiously for Saul, even killing the messenger who brought Saul's crown to him. The lament ("how the mighty are fallen") is a moving poem. David is clearly the implied speaker, even apart from the narrative context. This does not necessarily mean that it was composed by David. We have several compositions in the book of Psalms that are related to episodes in David's life. David was regarded as the composer of psalms par excellence, as Solomon was the composer of proverbs. The lament for Saul and Jonathan could have been composed much later and placed on David's lips.

David moves quickly to consolidate his position as the heir apparent. He goes first to Hebron, where he is anointed king by his own tribe, Judah. (The supposed anointing by Samuel when he was still a boy was evidently insufficient.) Hebron is near David's hometown of Bethlehem. It was associated with Abraham in Genesis. It may be that David was anointed there because of the association with Abraham, but some scholars think that the tradition about Abraham was invented later, and that Abraham was modeled on David rather than the reverse.

David's claim to monarchy was not undisputed, however. At the same time, Ishbaal, son of Saul, became king over the rest of Israel, with the support of the general Abner. (Ishbaal means "man of Baal." The fact that a son of Saul, the king of Israel, had a name honoring Baal indicates that other deities besides YHWH were worshiped in Israel at this time.) There follows "a long war between the house of Saul and the house of David" (3:1). Eventually, Abner quarrels with Ishbaal and offers to bring all Israel over to David. He is murdered, however, by David's general Joab in revenge for the killing of Joab's brother. David makes public lamentation for Abner but takes no punitive action against Job at this time. Once again, David escapes blame for the death of a rival. When Ishbaal is murdered shortly thereafter, David not only disavows responsibility but executes the murderers who had sought and expected his favor. Eventually, the only living heir to the house of Saul is the crippled son of Jonathan, who is no threat to David (see 2 Samuel 9, where David shows kindness to him "for Jonathan's sake"). His name, Mephibosheth, is probably a euphemism, concealing the name

of Baal (*bosheth* means "shame"). The name is given as Meribaal in 1 Chron 8:34 and 9:40. The dismantling of the house of Saul is finally completed in 2 Samuel 21. This entire strand of the narrative fits perfectly with the view that the Rise of David is an apologetic or propaganda document. But again it is not difficult to read the story against the grain and arrive at a rather unfavorable picture of David.

The rise of David reaches its climax in 2 Samuel 5. He is again acclaimed as king at Hebron, this time by all Israel. Then he captures Jerusalem, the Canaanite city that was still in the hands of the Jebusites at this time. Jerusalem was an ideal capital for David because it was easy to defend and it had not hitherto been associated with any Israelite tribe, although it was in the territory of David's own tribe, Judah. The acclamation of David is complete when he is acknowledged by the king of Tyre.

Fig. 12.1 David dances ecstatically before the ark of the covenant; terra-cotta; Rome, seventeenth century. Now in the Victoria and Albert Museum. Commons.wikimedia.org

INTRODUCTION TO THE HEBREW BIBLE

The account of the bringing of the ark to Jerusalem is often regarded as the conclusion of the Ark Narrative in 1 Samuel. It makes excellent sense in its present context, however. The ark was the traditional symbol of the presence of YHWH. By bringing it to Jerusalem, David made the old Jebusite city the center of worship for the tribes of Israel that worshiped YHWH. David is ostentatious in his public celebration of the event, leaving no doubt about his devotion to YHWH. The disapproval of Michal, daughter of Saul, is of little consequence at this point. The house of Saul is no longer a factor in the kingship of Israel.

The Promise to David

Second Samuel 7 is one of the key passages not only in the Deuteronomistic History but in the Hebrew Bible as a whole. The promise to David that is narrated here is the foundation charter of the Davidic dynasty and is a frequent point of reference in later writings. It would eventually become the basis for messianic hope, that is, the hope that the Davidic kingship would be restored and would last forever.

The setting of the promise is when the king is settled in his house and has rest from his enemies. Palace and temple were often associated in the ancient Near East. The same Hebrew word, *hekal*, is used for both. Accordingly, David worries that his "house of cedar" is grander than the tent-shrine of the Lord.

At this point, the prophet Nathan appears on the scene. David is said to have consulted the Lord on previous occasions (e.g., 2 Sam 2:1). There were various ways in which this

might be done. One might, for example, consult a priest, who might then use a ritual method of divination. With the rise of the monarchy, however, we find that kings typically have prophets in their service for this purpose. We shall discuss the social location of prophecy in some detail in connection with the narratives about prophets in the books of Kings. For the present, it suffices to note that Nathan is in David's service, although he can on occasion exercise considerable independence. His initial reaction is precisely what we should expect a retainer to tell his employer: "Go do all that you have in mind, for the LORD is with you."

Nathan, however, has second thoughts, and he receives a second oracle for David. YHWH insists that he has never wanted a house. He likes the mobility of a tent. It is not for David to build him a house. Rather, he will build David a house, in the sense of a dynasty. His son will reign after him. While his descendants will be punished for their iniquities, YHWH promises that he will not take the kingdom away from them as he took it from the house of Saul: "Your house and your kingdom shall be made sure forever before me; your throne shall be established forever" (7:16).

Central to this oracle is the play on the double sense of "house." David may not build a house (= temple) for YHWH, but the Deity will build a house (= dynasty) for David. It was not unusual in the ancient Near East for the founder of a dynasty to build a temple for his patron god. The oddity of this passage is the rejection of the offer to build a temple. Scholars have tried to explain this rejection in various ways. Some suggest that this oracle was meant to explain why it was Solomon rather than David who built the temple. But 7:13a ("he shall build a house for my name") is widely recognized as a secondary addition. Not only does it interrupt a passage about the future kingdom, but it is marked as an insertion by a technique called "repetitive resumption"—the phrase that immediately precedes the insertion is essentially repeated immediately after it: "*I will establish his kingdom.* He shall build a house for my name, *and I will establish the throne of his kingdom forever.*" That the house will be built "for my name" is a trademark of Deuteronomistic theology. Presumably, then, the reference to Solomon was added by a Deuteronomistic editor, and the basic oracle was older. It should also be noted that the Deuteronomists provide a different explanation for David's failure to build the temple in 1 Kgs 5:3-4: "David could not build a house for the name of the LORD his God because of the warfare with which his enemies surrounded him." Yet the premise of 2 Samuel 7 is that the Lord had given him rest from his enemies.

The basic oracle is a virtual charter document for the Davidic dynasty, and was presumably promulgated and transmitted by the royal court. Some scholars have argued for a date in the time of David, before Solomon built the temple, on the grounds that the oracle rejects the proposal to build a temple. Such an early date is not necessary, however. While the oracle explains why David did not build the temple, it does not reject the idea of a temple in perpetuity, even without the insertion in v. 13a. Rather, the point is that the need for a temple was not urgent. Indeed, as we have seen, there is some evidence that there had already been a temple, a "house of God," at Shiloh, but that structure either was or contained a tent-shrine. The temple proposed in 2 Samuel 7 and the one eventually built by Solomon were regarded as of a different order. David was concerned to maintain continuity with the traditional cult of the tribes. He moved the tent-shrine to his new capital but did not alter the shrine itself. A temple could be built a generation later, when the tribes had gotten used to the monarchy and to the new capital in Jerusalem.

The role of the Deuteronomists in the composition of 2 Samuel 7 is controversial. On the one hand, the promise to David is certainly important in the Deuteronomistic view of Israel's history. Despite the tension with 1 Kings 5, the notion of "rest" is typically Deuteronomic—cf. Deut 12:10. So is the statement that God "brought Israel up out of the land of Egypt" (7:6) and the construction of a period of judges between the exodus and the monarchy. The oracle assumes the story of David's origin as a shepherd and says that he was designated a *nagid,* or prince, rather than king (7:8). Accordingly, some scholars argue that 2 Samuel 7 is simply a Deuteronomistic composition, although it may comprise more than one stage. (The affirmations that the kingdom would last forever cannot be exilic or later, but are plausible in the time of Josiah.) On the other hand, it is unlikely that the Deuteronomists would have invented an unconditional promise that the kingdom would last forever. In Deuteronomic theology, covenants are conditional. The fortunes of the king depend on his observance of the law. The idea that God had promised David an everlasting dynasty by the oracle of Nathan was probably an established tradition in Jerusalem. The present formulation of the promise has been edited by the Deuteronomists, probably in more than one stage.

Whatever the origin and authorship of the oracle, it contains one of the major themes in the Hebrew Bible. While this theme is often called the Davidic covenant, the word *covenant* is not used in this passage (though it is used with reference to God's promise to David in Ps 89:3). The oracle is more accurately described as a divine promise. There are analogies with ancient Near Eastern treaties, but on the whole the oracle has the character of an unconditional grant rather than of the vassal treaties that we discussed in connection with the Mosaic covenant. The nearest biblical analogy is provided by the covenant with Abraham in Genesis 15, which also had the form of an unconditional grant. Nathan's oracle does provide for the punishment of a rebellious king: "When he commits iniquity, I will punish him with a rod such as mortals use, with blows inflicted by human beings. But I will not take my steadfast love away from him as I took it from Saul" (7:14-15). Punishment for transgression is certainly in line with Deuteronomic theology. But we also find such provisions in Near Eastern treaties. Even if a king were executed, his son might be allowed to succeed him.

In Nathan's oracle, too, the essential point is that the Davidic dynasty will last forever. In fact, it lasted some four hundred years, which might be regarded as a reasonable approximation of "forever." (Compare *1 En.* 10:10, which states of the offspring of the fallen angels that "they hope that they will live forever and that each of them will live for five hundred years.") Nonetheless, when the Davidic kingdom was finally brought to an end by the Babylonians, the promise was thought to stand. If there was no king in the present, then God's promise must be fulfilled in the future by the restoration of the Davidic line. This is the origin of the hope for a messiah, or anointed king, understood as one who is to come and change the course of history.

The relationship between YHWH and the king is defined as that of father and son: "I will be a father to him, and he shall be a son to me" (2 Sam 7:14). There is no suggestion here that the king does not have a human father; the relationship is presumably one of adoption. Egyptian royal theology made a stronger claim that the king was divine, the incarnation of the god Horus. In the area of Syria and Palestine, the claim that the king was the adopted son of a god was more typical. Kings of Damascus in the ninth century B.C.E. took the name or title of "Son of Hadad" (Hadad was another name for Baal). At least one Syrian king was called "Son of Rakib" (*ANET,* 655; Rakib-El is a god known from Aramaic and Phoenician inscriptions). The claim that the Davidic king was son of YHWH is also found in the Psalms, most explicitly in Ps 2:7, where the king is said to be begotten by God. In 2 Samuel 7 the idea that the king is God's son is linked directly to the idea that he should be chastised. (The idea that sons should be chastised is a favorite theme of the book of Proverbs.)

An eternal dynasty

A thirteenth-century Hittite grant to one Ulmi-Teshshup promises: "After you, your son and grandson will possess it, nobody will take it away from them. If one of your descendants sins . . . the king will prosecute him at his court. . . . But nobody will take away from the descendant of Ulmi-Teshshup either his house or his land."

Excursus: The Royal Ideology of Judah

As we have seen, the formulation of 2 Samuel 7 is shaped by Deuteronomistic editors in the late seventh century B.C.E., but the idea of a promise to David is probably older. This may be an appropriate point to digress on the question of the understanding of kingship in ancient Israel, and more especially in Judah and Jerusalem, before the Deuteronomic reform.

The main window we have on older views of the monarchy is provided by certain psalms. We shall discuss the Psalms in detail in a later chapter. For the present we note that several of them deal with the kingship, and at least some of these are likely to date from the pre-exilic period. These include Psalms 2, 45, 72, and 110. Moreover, two psalms speak of the promise to David in terms reminiscent of 2 Samuel 7. These are Psalms 89 and 132.

Some of these psalms depict the kingship in mythological terms that are unsuspected in 2 Samuel. Psalm 2 implies that the king in Jerusalem is the rightful ruler over all the kings of the earth. If the Gentile nations resist, the Lord derides them. The authority of the king comes directly from God. The psalmist reports the decree of the Lord: "You are my son, this day I have begotten you." This way of viewing the relationship between the king and God is indebted to Egyptian tradition. Egypt had ruled over Jerusalem in the second millennium B.C.E., and the traditions about kingship were passed down through the Jebusites, who inhabited Jerusalem before David conquered it. Some scholars hold that this formula was recited by a prophet when a new king ascended the throne, and the suggestion is attractive, although it cannot be verified. What is striking in Psalm 2 is the kind of authority the king is supposed to enjoy: the nations are his inheritance and the ends of the earth are his possession. No king in Jerusalem ever actually reigned over such an empire, even bearing in mind that the world known to the psalmist was smaller than ours. Of course, the claim is deliberately hyperbolic, but it shows that the Jerusalem monarchy had delusions of grandeur.

The theme of divine sonship reappears in Psalm 110. In this case, the king is addressed as *Adonai*, "my lord"—the phrase that came to be substituted for the divine name in later Judaism. YHWH bids him sit at his right hand. (This is probably a reference to the king's throne in the temple.) The Deity continues: "From the womb of dawn, like dew I have begotten you" (Ps. 110:3; the Hebrew is corrupt and must be reconstructed with the help of the Greek. The NRSV follows the Hebrew, reading, "Your youth will come to you" instead of "I have begotten you"). In this case, the psalmist adds an intriguing detail: "You are a priest forever according to the order of Melchizedek." Melchizedek was the priest-king of Salem (presumably Jerusalem) in Genesis 14 who blessed Abraham and to whom Abraham gave a tithe of all that he had. Melchizedek was a Jebusite, which is to say a Canaanite. He was priest of El Elyon, a Canaanite deity who was identified with YHWH in the Bible. If the Davidic kings claimed to be "according to the order of Melchizedek," this meant that they affirmed continuity with the old Canaanite religion that had been practiced in the city for centuries before David captured it. We may infer that they took over the Canaanite understanding of the kingship, at least to some degree, and that understanding in turn had been influenced by Egyptian traditions. (Melchizedek appears again as a mysterious figure, without father or mother, in Heb 7:3, which emphasizes his priesthood. In the Dead Sea Scrolls, in a scroll known as 11QMelchizedek, he is an angelic figure who executes judgment on God's behalf.)

An even more startling view of the kingship appears in Psalm 45. This seems to be a song for a royal wedding. It begins with unabashed praise (flattery?) of the king: "you are the most handsome of men . . . gird your sword on your thigh, O mighty one!" The praise reaches its climax in v. 6: "Your throne, O God, endures forever and ever. Your royal scepter is a scepter of equity. You love righteousness and hate wickedness, therefore God, your God, has anointed you with the oil of gladness above your fellows." Here the king is addressed as *elohim*, "God." This does not mean that he is put on the same level as the Most High. He is carefully distinguished from "God, your God," who has anointed him and on whom he depends. But the king is clearly regarded as something more than a regular human being. He is a divine being in some sense.

Psalm 45 also emphasizes the obligation of the king to uphold truth and righteousness. This obligation is also clear in Psalm 72. That psalm stops short of addressing the king as a

Fig. 12.2 **Abraham is offered hospitality by King Melchizedek (thirteenth-century mosaic in the Basilica of San Marco, Venice. Did Melchizedek figure in Davidic claims to legitimacy?** Commons.wikimedia.org

god, but it prays that he may live as long as the sun and moon, and have dominion from sea to sea.

Seen against the background of these psalms, Nathan's oracle paints a much more modest picture of the king. True, he is like a son to God, but nothing is said of him being begotten by God, even metaphorically. As "son of God," he is subject to chastisement, a point not noted in these psalms. Second Samuel 7 represents a toned-down, even demythologized, form of the royal ideology, and this is exactly what we would expect in the Deuteronomistic History.

There are, however, two other psalms that are closely related to 2 Samuel 7. Psalm 89 is a complex psalm that falls into three parts: vv. 1-18, 19-37, and 38-51. These parts may have been composed on different occasions. The first part contains a simple statement of the Davidic covenant: "I have sworn to my servant David: I will establish your descendants forever and build your throne for all generations." This is an unconditional promise and quite compatible with 2 Samuel 7, but not necessarily dependent on it. The rest of vv. 1-18 goes on to praise God as creator, in mythical terms ("you crushed Rahab like a carcass"). The second part of the psalm elaborates the promise to David. The king is allowed to share in YHWH's control over nature ("I will set his hand upon the sea," v. 25). He will call God "father," and God will make him the firstborn, the highest of the kings of the earth. This section goes on to make provision for the event that "his children forsake my law." The content of the psalm here corresponds almost exactly to 2 Samuel 7 and is most likely dependent on it. The reference to "my law" probably presupposes the Deuteronomic reform. The final

part of the psalm envisions a situation where God has rejected the king and apparently renounced the covenant. The most plausible setting for this part of the psalm is the Babylonian exile. Taken as a whole, the psalm recalls the covenant with David in terms that are fully in agreement with 2 Samuel 7, to remind God of his promise and ask him to honor it.

Psalm 132 is a celebration of the moving of the ark to Jerusalem, which also narrates YHWH's promise to David. It departs from 2 Samuel 7 at one very significant point. It affirms that "the LORD swore to David a sure oath from which he will not turn back: one of the sons of your body I will set upon your throne" (v. 11). This time, however, their reign is conditional: "If your sons keep my covenant and my decrees that I shall teach them, their sons also forevermore shall sit on your throne" (v. 12). While the psalm does not use characteristic Deuteronomic language (such as reference to the name of God), it seems to presuppose Deuteronomy in two key respects: the insistence that the king must keep "my covenant" and "my decrees" in v. 12, and the statement that the Lord has chosen Zion as his resting place in vv. 13-14. Despite the attempt of some scholars to date this psalm very early, even in the time of David, it surely belongs to the last years of the monarchy. There is no evidence that the kingship of David's line was originally conceived as conditional. It is much easier to suppose that we have here an extension of Deuteronomic theology that not only makes the kings subject to punishment but makes the whole line subject to rejection. Nonetheless, the psalmist expresses confidence that the promises to David and Zion are still valid and does not show the kind of distress that we find in the last part of Psalm 89. This optimistic tone is more easily explained if the psalm was written in the latter years of the monarchy, before the collapse.

We shall consider the royal ideology of Judah again at various points in the prophetic corpus, especially in connection with Isaiah of Jerusalem. For the present, we may conclude that before the Deuteronomic reform, the kings in Jerusalem were quite exalted. The king was "son of God" or even a god. He was the rightful ruler of the whole earth. He was chosen and anointed by God without any conditions attached. The promise of an everlasting dynasty is affirmed in 2 Samuel 7, but the kings are said to be liable to punishment for their offenses. Psalm 132 shows that some people drew out the implications of Deuteronomy and held that the promise of a lasting dynasty was subject to the condition that the kings observe the covenantal law.

The royal ideology is extremely important for the development of messianism in postexilic Judaism and its adaptation in early Christianity. The promise to David provided the main basis for belief that the Davidic kingdom would one day be restored. Moreover, the royal ideology provided the basis for the view that the messiah is Son of God and may even be spoken of as "God." Psalm 110 ("The Lord said to my lord, 'Sit at my right hand'") was taken as proof in early Christianity that the Messiah must ascend to heaven (Acts 2:34-36). It should be noted, however, that messianic hope was not always widespread in Second Temple Judaism. It only became prominent in the last century before the common era. The typical Jewish hope for a Davidic messiah was political in character and involved the restoration of the dynasty and kingdom in Jerusalem. Christianity would claim that the messianic

prophecies of the Old Testament were fulfilled in Jesus, but Jesus did not restore the kingdom of Judah in accordance with Jewish expectations. The Christian belief that Jesus was the messiah required a considerable reinterpretation of Jewish messianism.

The Conquests of David

Chapters 8 and 10 describe the wars of David, in which he allegedly subjugated all the surrounding peoples—Philistia, Moab,

Fig. 12.3 Large stone structure in central Jerusalem, dated to the tenth to ninth centuries B.C.E., identified by archaeologist Eilat Mazar as the palace of David. Photo by the author

Ammon, Edom, but also the Arameans as far as Damascus and the Euphrates. Modern scholarship is skeptical of these claims. Not only are they not supported by extrabiblical evidence, but the Bible itself does not claim that these peoples were under Israelite control in later generations. David may be credited with containing the Philistines and bringing an end to the conflict between Philistines and Israelites. He may also have conducted campaigns against neighboring peoples, but it is unlikely that he established lasting control of these areas. Second Samuel 24 describes a census taken by David that allegedly included Tyre and Sidon and all the cities of the Canaanites, but does not extend to Arameans or other neighboring peoples. Moreover, it is quite clear from the account of the reign of Solomon in 1 Kings that Tyre was never subject to Israel. The claims made for David in 2 Samuel 8 and 10 are at best hyperbolic, and their historical value is suspect. It may be that the author was influenced by the promise made to Abraham in Gen 15:18-21: "To your descendants I give this land, from the river of Egypt to the great river, the river Euphrates." The descendants of Abraham certainly did not control all this territory at any time after the reign of Solomon, and Solomon was not a warrior, so the author may have reasoned that the promise was fulfilled in the time of David.

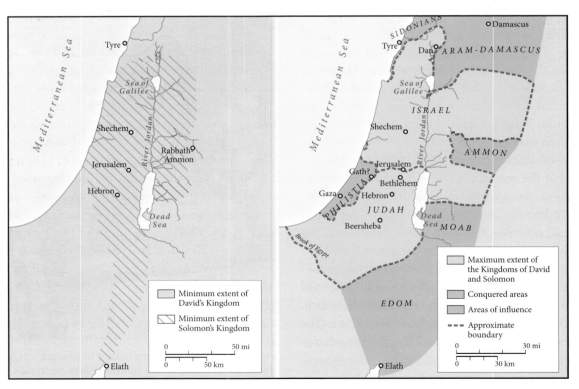

Maps 12.1, 12.2

Fig. 12.4 Stepped structure, shown by archaeologist Eilat Mazar to be connected to the large stone structure in Fig. 12.3 as part of a massive royal palace. Photo by the author.

The Bathsheba Affair

Like many people in positions of power, from ancient times to the present day, David also had other conquests in mind. The story of his encounter with Bathsheba is set in the spring of the year, "when kings go out to battle." King Saul had been killed in battle, but David is wise enough to retire from fighting in person. He seeks other outlets for his energies. The story has several stock motifs. The woman bathes where she can be seen. Her husband, Uriah, carries the instructions for his own murder. David does not initially want to have

the man killed, and tries hard to cover up his adultery by getting him to sleep with his wife. Uriah, however, is undone by his own piety and respect for tradition: he refuses to sleep with his wife while his companions are on a military campaign. David has his general Joab set Uriah up to be killed in battle, and after an appropriate interval for mourning, takes Bathsheba and marries her.

At this point the prophet Nathan enters the scene. He would hardly have needed a special revelation to figure out what had happened. Bathsheba was pregnant, and David's responsibility was clear from the fact that he married her. What is remarkable is the courage of the prophet in confronting his king. He might, after all, have been given the next message to convey to Joab. Equally remarkable is the way that he confronts the king. Later prophets, such as Elijah or Amos, confront kings for wrongdoing but do so by denouncing them harshly. Nathan takes a softer approach. He tells the king a parable. Like many of the parables in the Gospels, this one induces the hearer to pass judgment on himself. It should also be noted that Nathan does not refer to any specific law or remind the king about the exodus or Israelite tradition. The story assumes a common sense of justice, grounded perhaps in natural law, or at least in the common traditions of the ancient Near East. Kings were specifically supposed to uphold justice, and especially to defend the more vulnerable members of society (cf. Pss 45:7; 72:2). But anyone should know that it is wrong for a rich man to take from a poor man, and the story adds pathos by the fact that it involves the killing of a little ewe lamb. The approach of the prophet presupposes that the king is ultimately a person of goodwill, that he has the decency to deplore injustice. Nathan's technique would not work for an Elijah or an Amos who had adversarial relations with the kings of their day. But where the parable can work, it is more likely to lead the listener to repentance than the fiery denunciations characteristic of later prophets.

The child born to Bathsheba dies. If this is punishment for David's sin, we must feel that the punishment is misplaced. It is characteristic of David that he escapes the consequences of his actions by well-timed repentance. Moreover, Bathsheba becomes the mother of David's eventual heir, Solomon. Once again, providence works in unexpected ways, and the Lord seems to write with crooked lines. As we have seen already in the story of Jacob, the blessing of the Lord is not necessarily reserved for virtuous people.

The pattern of sin, repentance, and misplaced punishment is evident again in the last story in 2 Samuel, the story of the census in chapter 24. The purpose of the census is not stated explicitly, but it is transparent—it is a prelude to taxation. Hence the resistance even of David's loyal henchman, Joab. David, characteristically, repents after the deed is done. Yet he is offered his choice of punishment, and it falls primarily on the people (even if we assume that David was grieved by their suffering). Supposedly, seventy thousand people died. Again, the punishment is misplaced. David does not lose the favor of the Lord. The upshot of this incident is that he acquires the threshing floor of Araunah the Jebusite and builds an altar to the Lord. This threshing floor is later identified as the site of Solomon's temple (1 Chron 22:1; 2 Chron 3:1).

David and Absalom

David, however, does not get off scot-free. Second Samuel 13–20 tells a tragic family saga. It begins with the incestuous rape of David's daughter Tamar by her brother Amnon. Another brother, Absalom, bides his time but eventually kills Amnon in revenge. Absalom then has to flee. He is eventually brought back to Jerusalem, through the good offices of Joab, but it takes another two years before he is reconciled with his father. We must assume that this experience is part of what motivates Absalom to seek the kingship by conspiracy. David has to flee from Jerusalem in mourning. Absalom enters Jerusalem and symbolizes his usurpation of David's throne by going

Fig. 12.5 The prophet Nathan confronts Bathsheba and David, their dead son at their feet. The Latin inscription declares, "You shall not commit adultery." Bronze bas relief by Henri de Triqueti (ca. 1837), Church of the Madeleine, Paris.

Fig. 12.6 *The Death of Amnon at Absalom's Banquet* by Gaspare Traversi (ca. 1752). Commons.wikimedia.org

in to his concubines. He meets his downfall, however, by following the advice of David's counselor, Hushai the Archite, and going into battle in person. His demise is comical—he gets caught in a tree by the long hair that was his pride. David, typically, takes no pleasure in his death but laments the loss of his son.

The story shows David in a very favorable light. He does not wish the death of any of his sons, neither Amnon nor Absalom, regardless of what they have done. This portrayal may serve the interest of royal propaganda, but it is also a credible human story. The portrayal of Absalom is not unsympathetic. We can appreciate his outrage at the rape of his sister, and even his impatience with the administration of the aging king. If his intercourse with his father's concubines seems outrageous, this is due to the advice of Ahithophel. Absalom seems naïve in his willingness to go into battle in person and in his vanity about his hair, which leads to his downfall. In the end, however, the story focuses on David rather than on Absalom. David is also portrayed as compassionate and forgiving toward his enemies. He refuses to punish Shimei, who had cursed him, and he accepts Mephibosheth's explanation of his conduct. Yet when a man named Sheba of the tribe of Benjamin (Saul's tribe) attempts to secede from Judah (chap. 20), David acts decisively to put down the revolt. As in several previous incidents, however, Joab and his brother Abishai, the sons of Zeruiah, are the ones who shed the blood. If there is guilt because of the violence, it can be imputed to them rather than to David. The story of the Gibeonites in chapter 21 also has a strongly apologetic character. David disposes of the heirs to the house of Saul, except for the cripple Mephibosheth. But he claims that this was necessary because of bloodguilt on the house of Saul, which was causing a famine. Moreover, David makes a show of goodwill toward the memory of Saul and Jonathan by giving them a proper burial.

The action of the king is ruthless, but the story justifies it and covers it with a gloss of piety. The reputation of the king is defended and enhanced. Nonetheless, the story of Absalom should not be viewed only as political propaganda. It is a moving story of the dilemma of a father whose son has turned against him.

The story of Absalom is a tale of human action, with little divine interference. (In 17:14 we are told that Absalom chose the advice of Hushai over the advice of Ahithophel because the Lord had so ordained.) The humanistic character of the story has led some people to suppose that it is related to the wisdom literature, such as we find in the book of Proverbs. Many scholars have supposed that the Absalom story was composed at the royal court; a similar setting has often been proposed for Proverbs. One of the striking things about this story is the prominent role of counselors and advisers. Amnon is coached by Jonadab; Absalom is advised by Ahithophel and then by Hushai. At one point, we are told that "the counsel that Ahithophel gave was as if one consulted the oracle of God" (16:23). All these counselors are clever; they are not necessarily good. Jonadab, who advises Amnon how to get his sister Tamar at his mercy, is described as "very wise," but his wisdom seems to be quite amoral. The same may be said of Ahithophel, who switches from one master to another and commits suicide when his counsel is not accepted. Hushai is portrayed positively because he acts in David's interest, but he has no scruple in misleading Absalom. The conduct of these counselors is probably a reasonable reflection of the roles such people played at royal courts in the ancient world. We shall see later that there was often tension between counselors and prophets who competed for the ear of the king. The Absalom story does not necessarily view all wisdom negatively, but it does not depict it as a moral good in the way that we shall find in the book of Proverbs.

The Psalms of David

The closing chapters of 2 Samuel contain two poetic compositions ascribed to David. According to 1 Sam 16:18, David was a skillful musician. In later tradition he would become the author of psalms par excellence. A composition found in the Dead Sea Scrolls credits him with 3,600 psalms and 450 songs (11Q5 col. 27)—a total rivaling the productivity of Solomon in 1 Kgs 5:12 (1 Kgs 4:32 in English versions). The psalm attributed to him in 2 Samuel 22 is also found in the Psalter as Psalm 18. It is a thanksgiving psalm, which praises God for delivering the psalmist from the waves of death. It is notable for a description of a theophany of YHWH as a storm-god in 2 Sam 22:8-16.

The shorter poem, called "the last words of David," is notable in several respects. It mentions the "everlasting covenant" that was described at some length in 2 Samuel 7. But it also claims that "the spirit of the Lord speaks through me" (23:2). David, in effect, was a prophet, and he was widely regarded as such in antiquity. The composition from the Dead Sea Scrolls that lists the works of David says that David composed all his psalms and songs in the spirit of prophecy. This text also says that he was wise.

Even if we suspect that much of the portrayal of David in the books of Samuel originated as political propaganda, the character of David as depicted is exceptionally appealing.

No other character in the Hebrew Bible is so well rounded. Here we have a fully human figure who is no saint by later standards. He is a hot-blooded individual who is guilty of murder, adultery, and sundry forms of extortion and exploitation. But he is also an emotional figure, whose grief for his friend Jonathan or for his son Absalom is moving. Even if the biblical authors tried to excuse and justify his actions, they nonetheless portrayed him as a man who was very fallible and even sinful.

Later tradition enhanced the legend of David by crediting him with prophecy and the composition of psalms. In the process, it often depicts him as more pious than he appears in the books of Samuel. (We shall see this tendency in the books of Chronicles.) The charm of the biblical character, however, is precisely his human fallibility. It is this appreciation of the imperfection of human nature that marks the story of David as one of the finest pieces of literature to come down to us from antiquity.

FOR FURTHER READING

Most of the literature cited in the previous chapter deals with both books of Samuel. In addition, note:

Commentaries

Campbell, A. J., *2 Samuel* (FOTL; Grand Rapids: Eerdmans, 2005). Systematic form-critical commentary.

P. K. McCarter, *II Samuel* (AB 9B; New York: Doubleday, 1984). Standard historical-critical commentary.

Davidic Covenant and Royal Ideology

A. Y. Collins and J. J. Collins, *King and Messiah as Son of God* (Grand Rapids: Eerdmans, 2008), 1–47. Discussion of the royal ideology of Judah and its Deuteronomistic modification.

F. M. Cross, *Canaanite Myth and Hebrew Epic* (Cambridge: Harvard University Press, 1973), 229–65. Influential treatment in light of Canaanite traditions.

J. Day, ed., *King and Messiah in Israel and the Ancient Near East* (JSOTSupp 270; Sheffield: Sheffield Academic Press, 1998). Collection of essays on royal ideology and messianic hope.

M. Hamilton, *The Body Royal: The Social Implications of Kingship in Ancient Israel* (Leiden: Brill, 2005). Careful study of the royal ideology of Judah in its Near Eastern context, with emphasis on bodily imagery.

T. N. D. Mettinger, *King and Messiah: The Civil and Sacred Legitimation of the Israelite Kings* (ConBOT 8; Lund: Gleerup, 1976). Discussion of the establishment of the Davidic dynasty, with a particular focus on 2 Samuel 7.

S. Mowinckel, *He That Cometh* (trans. G. W. Anderson; Nashville: Abingdon, 1955). Classic study of royal ideology in the ancient Near East, and the development of messianic expectation.

W. Schniedewind, *Society and the Promise to David* (New York: Oxford Univ. Press, 1999). Traces the history of the interpretation of 2 Samuel 7 down to the Second Temple period.

Literary Study

J. Barton, "Dating the 'Succession Narrative,'" in J. Day, ed., *In Search of Pre-Exilic Israel* (London: T&T Clark, 2004), 95–106. Dates the narrative to the seventh or eighth century B.C.E. on the basis of its style.

C. Conroy, *Absalom Absalom! Narrative and Language in 2 Sam 13–20* (AnBib 81; Rome: Pontifical Biblical Institute Press, 1978). Elegant study of the Absalom story.

Historicity

A. Faust, "Did Eilat Mazar find David's Palace?" *BAR* 38/5 (2012): 47–52. Critical examination of claim to have found David's palace, arguing that the structure was constructed before the time of David.

I. Finkelstein and N. A. Silberman, *The Bible Unearthed: Archaeology's New Vision of Ancient Israel and the Origin of Its Sacred Texts* (New York: Free Press, 2001), 149–68. Skeptical view of David's reign.

CHAPTER 13

1 Kings 1–11
Solomon and the Divided Monarchy

INTRODUCTION

The first part of 1 Kings describes the dramatic and fateful aftermath to David's reign; the succession of Solomon and, upon the succession of his son Rehoboam, the rebellion of Jeroboam and the division of the kingdom.

The Deuteronomistic History continues in the books of Kings. Here again the division between books is artificial and late. First Kings begins with the old age and death of David, which concludes the story of David begun in 1 Samuel. The reign of Ahaziah in northern Israel straddles the division between 1 and 2 Kings. The first eleven chapters of 1 Kings deal with the accession and reign of Solomon. Thereafter 1 and 2 Kings chronicles the parallel histories of the northern kingdom of Israel and the southern kingdom of Judah.

A number of sources are explicitly identified in the books of Kings. First Kings 11:41 refers the reader to "the book of the acts of Solomon." There are several references to "the book of the annals of the kings of Judah" (14:29; 15:7, 23; et al.) and the corresponding annals of the kings of Israel (14:19; 15:31; 16:5, 14; et al.). None of these source

books has survived. It is possible that they are entirely fictional, introduced to give an aura of authenticity to the account, but it seems likely that the author had some records of the kings of Israel and Judah at his disposal. It is widely assumed that chronicles were maintained at the royal courts of Israel and Judah, as there were in Egypt and Mesopotamia (for examples see *ANET*, 265–317). The best-known example of such a royal chronicle is the Babylonian Chronicle, which may be roughly contemporary with the Deuteronomistic History. Lists of kings were compiled in Mesopotamia from ancient times. Historical information was also recorded in royal inscriptions. The Near Eastern accounts are generally presented as lists of events, with little narrative elaboration. The books of Kings have much more developed narrative than the Mesopotamian chronicles, but they are generally less expansive than the stories in the books of Samuel. The books of Kings also draw on some sources of a different character, most notably in the legends about the prophets Elijah and Elisha, which probably circulated independently before they were incorporated into the Deuteronomistic History.

The hand of the Deuteronomistic editors is more obvious in the books of Kings than in those of Samuel. The reigns of the various kings is reported in a formulaic way. A typical introduction to a king of Israel reads: "In the x year of PN [proper name], king of Judah, PN the son of PN began to reign over all Israel in Samaria, and reigned for x years. He did what was evil in the eyes of YHWH." The introductions to the kings of Judah commonly add to this information the king's age at accession and the name of his mother. (The differences between the formulae for the two kingdoms supports the view that the Deuteronomist is adapting source documents.) The end of a king's reign is likewise formulaic: "Now the rest of the deeds of PN, and all that he did, are they not written in the book of the annals of the kings of Israel? And PN slept with his fathers and his son reigned in his stead." The Deuteronomist allows that some kings of Judah (Hezekiah, Josiah) did what was good in the eyes of YHWH, but they are distinctly exceptional. The consistent theological evaluation of the kings is a trademark of the Deuteronomist. So also are the criteria for the evaluation—primarily whether a given king allowed sacrificial worship outside the Jerusalem temple. The first king of northern Israel, Jeroboam, established temples at Bethel and Dan as rivals to Jerusalem, and all the northern kings promoted worship outside Jerusalem. Accordingly, they were said "to walk in the sin of Jeroboam." Other important Deuteronomistic themes in the books of Kings are the theology of the temple expounded by Solomon in his prayer in 1 Kings 8 and the continuity of the Davidic dynasty in the southern kingdom.

The Succession to David (1 Kings 1–2)

The opening chapters of 1 Kings are often regarded as the conclusion of the Court Narrative or Succession Document in 2 Samuel. More specifically, they are an apology for the succession of Solomon to the kingship. Since he is the younger brother, his succession is not by any established right. Rather, it is brought about by palace intrigue. Adonijah, who might be thought to have a better claim to the throne than Solomon, makes a false start by having himself hailed as king without David's approval. Solomon, however, has the support of his mother, Bathsheba, and the prophet Nathan. David's support is decisive. Solomon is accepted by the people as the legitimate king.

The enthronement of a new king was often the occasion of a bloodbath in the ancient world, and indeed also in much later times. Solomon acts ruthlessly to eliminate anyone who might be considered a threat. Adonijah, the general Joab who had supported him, and Shimei, who had cursed David, all meet sudden death. The narrative provides an apology for Solomon's actions by trying to forestall criticism. Solomon, we are told, became king because that was the will of David (although the king was evidently old and infirm). Moreover, David had specifically advised him to eliminate Joab and Shimei. David tells him to "act with the wisdom that is in you." Solomon becomes legendary for wisdom. In this case, however, his wisdom is a kind of street-smartness that leads him to kill his enemies before they kill him. Joab, we are told, deserved to die because of the way he had killed other generals, but he had suffered no consequences for these actions while he was of service to David. Adonijah would have been spared if he had refrained from further agitation, by asking for David's concubine in marriage. Even Shimei would have been spared if he had abided by the terms offered him by Solomon. Nonetheless, the ruthlessness of Solomon's actions comes through loud and clear. He takes both Adonijah and Joab from the altars where they had sought refuge. He promises Bathsheba that he will grant her request for Adonijah but reverses himself when he hears what she asks. In light of this unscrupulous *Realpolitik*, the beginning of David's farewell address in 1 Kings 2 is ironic: "Keep the charge of the LORD your God, walking in his ways and keeping his statutes, his commandments, his ordinances, and his testimonies, as it is written in the law of Moses" (1 Kgs 2:3). This is the Deuteronomic ideal for a king. According to 1 Kgs 2:4, the promise of an eternal dynasty is conditional on the obedience of Solomon's heirs. It is evident, however, that the Deuteronomist had a source, or traditions, about Solomon that showed that he was not greatly concerned about the law of Moses. He had more pressing concerns in the need to eliminate anyone who might present a threat to his kingship.

The Reign of Solomon (1 Kings 3–11)

The reign of Solomon is described in 1 Kings as a golden age. "Judah and Israel were as numerous as the sand by the sea; they ate and drank and were happy. Solomon was sovereign over all the kingdoms from the Euphrates to the land of the Philistines, even to the border of Egypt; they brought tribute and served Solomon all the days of his life" (1 Kgs 4:20-21). Or again: "Thus King Solomon excelled all the kings of the earth in riches and in wisdom. The whole earth sought the presence of Solomon to hear his wisdom, which God had put in his mind. Every one of them brought a present, objects of silver and gold, garments, weaponry, spices, horses, and mules, so much year by year" (10:23-24). He is said to have entered into marriage alliances with all the surrounding peoples, Moabite, Ammonite, Edomite, Sidonian, and Hittite, and even to have received a daughter of the pharaoh in marriage. He engaged in extensive building projects in Jerusalem, including his own palace, a house for Pharaoh's daughter, and, most famously, the temple. He is also credited with building up Hazor, Megiddo, and Gezer. He engaged in international trade and imported gold from Ophir (possibly in southern Arabia) and Tarshish (Spain?). The queen of Sheba (modern Yemen?) came to visit laden with precious goods.

Modern historians are skeptical about this account of Solomon's grandeur. Archaeology has shown that Jerusalem was a very small place until the end of the eighth century B.C.E., when it suddenly expanded, swollen, perhaps

Fig. 13.1 The southern wall of the wall of Herod's temple (first century c.e.), with remains of Seleucid-era construction in the foreground. Behind the three blocked gates on the right is a vaulted area known as Solomon's Stables, now occupied by a Muslim prayer hall below the Al-Aqsa Mosque. Commons.wikimedia.org

by refugees after the fall of the northern kingdom. Prior to that time, it is argued, Jerusalem could have been no more than a local chiefdom, not unlike the traditional Canaanite city-states. The claim that all the territory from the border of Egypt to the Euphrates gave tribute to Solomon corresponds to the promise made to Abraham in Genesis 15. (Note also the references to Amorites, Hittites, Perizzites, Hivites, and Jebusites in 1 Kgs 9:20; and cf. Gen 15:19.) Scholars of an earlier generation accepted the historicity of Solomon's empire and argued that the promise in Genesis 15

was formulated after the fact and could therefore be dated to Solomon's reign. More recent scholars are skeptical (see the maps in chapter 12). The promise may only reflect the aspirations of the Judean kings, and the claims made for Solomon may have been inferred from the promise. The great wealth that Solomon supposedly enjoyed (1 Kgs 10:14) has left no trace in the material remains. Solomon's fabulous empire is now regarded by many scholars as a fiction, a dream of glory from a later time.

The issue, however, is controversial and is likely to remain so. Part of the problem is

262 INTRODUCTION TO THE HEBREW BIBLE

that the most likely place for Solomon's palace and temple is on the site where Herod's temple later stood. This Temple Mount is one of the holiest sites of both Judaism and Islam. It is now impossible to excavate under it, and so it is impossible to verify the claims of Solomon's building projects in Jerusalem. Aside from Jerusalem, Hazor, Megiddo, and Gezer have been excavated extensively. At each of these sites, archaeologists identified a stratum as Solomonic. Characteristic of this stratum were huge gateways with six chambers. Some structures were also identified as stables. Some recent scholars, however, have called the dating of these gates and structures into question, arguing that they could come from the ninth century rather than the tenth. This issue is still contested. In part it depends on whether archaeologists are willing to use the biblical account as a key for interpreting their findings.

Those who defend the historicity of Solomon's splendor argue that the critics are arguing from silence. Such arguments are hazardous, especially when an important site like the Temple Mount is off-limits to the archaeologists. New evidence may yet come to light that would support the historicity of the biblical account. In 1993 and 1994, fragments of an Aramaic inscription were found at Tel Dan in northern Galilee, which mentions "Beth David," the house of David (see Fig. 11.2 above). We know that the kingdom of northern Israel was known as "the house of Omri" and the kingdom of Damascus as "the house of Hazael." This inscription, which dates to the second half of the ninth century B.C.E., confirms that the kingdom of Judah was known as "the house of David." The more

skeptical critics, who have questioned whether David or Solomon ever existed and whether there ever was a united monarchy, have made various attempts to question the authenticity of this inscription or the interpretation of the words. In the eyes of most scholars, however, this inscription stands as a warning about the dangers of arguing too much from silence.

Scholars who defend the historicity of the account of Solomon's reign also point to some features of the narrative that suggest that the author or editor had some good historical sources. There is a list of Solomon's high officials in 1 Kgs 4:2-6 (cf. the list of David's officers in 2 Sam 23:8-39). First Kings 4:9-19 lists Solomon's twelve officers and their districts. The account of the king's building activities in 9:15-18 also has a list-like character. These lists reflect the kind of records produced by scribes as part of the administration of a kingdom. It is, of course, possible that a later scribe invented such lists to give an impression of historical authenticity, but it is not apparent that they serve any ideological purpose for the Deuteronomist. Moreover, there are some tensions in the narrative that suggest that the editors inherited a portrait of Solomon with which they were not entirely comfortable. We notice in 1 Kgs 4:6 that one of Solomon's officers is in charge of forced labor. In 10:20-22 the editor carefully states that Solomon conscripted the Amorites and other non-Israelites who were left in the land, "but of the Israelites Solomon made no slaves." It is apparent, however, from the revolt of the Israelites after Solomon's death that this was not the case. The editor's attempt to gloss over Solomon's use of Israelite forced labor shows that there was a tradition on the matter that

Fig. 13.2   Ruins of distinctive six-chambered gates at Gezer (gates of Solomon?). Photo by the author

had to be addressed. There is also tension between the portrayal of Solomon as a wise king who loved the Lord and the reports that he sacrificed at the high places and worshiped other gods (1 Kgs 3:3). The Deuteronomist did not invent the account of Solomon's reign out of whole cloth. That account lauds Solomon despite the fact that some of his practices were in flagrant violation of Deuteronomic law. Of course, it does not follow that the pre-Deuteronomistic portrait of Solomon must be historically reliable, but at least it must be relatively old, certainly preexilic, a product of the royal court in Jerusalem.

Three aspects of the account of Solomon require further comment. These are his wisdom, the building of the temple, and his worship of foreign deities.

The Wisdom of Solomon

The wisdom of Solomon is proverbial. The book of Proverbs is attributed to him, at least in part, as is the deuterocanonical (or apocryphal) Wisdom of Solomon, which was written in Greek in Alexandria around the turn of the era. Kings were supposed to be wise, but no other king is credited with wisdom to this degree. As we shall see, wisdom literature was associated especially with scribes at the royal court. It may be that Solomon established a scribal school in Jerusalem. If he actually ruled over an empire, as 1 Kings claims, then he would have needed scribes to handle the administration. Other kingdoms, especially pharaonic Egypt, were well equipped with scribes. The hypothesis that he established a scribal school would explain his strong association with wisdom. There is, however, no actual evidence to support it, and nothing is said about such a school in the biblical text. Some scholars think that Jerusalem was too small a place in the tenth century to need a scribal school, and that the need for scribes would only have arisen in the time of Hezekiah, some two centuries later.

Scholars of an earlier generation attributed a lot of literary activity to Solomon's court. The Yahwist was supposed to have composed the J source of the Pentateuch there, depicting Solomon's kingdom as the fulfillment of the promise made to Abraham. The German scholar Gerhard von Rad, in the mid-twentieth century, spoke of a Solomonic enlightenment, stimulated by newfound wealth and by international relations. As we have seen, however, such an early date for the J source is now widely rejected. The debate at the beginning of the twenty-first century is not whether we can speak of an enlightenment in Solomon's reign, but whether we can even assume much literacy in Jerusalem at this early stage.

First Kings addresses the wisdom of Solomon in chapter 3, and again in 5:19-14 (MT 4:29-34). First Kings 3:3-14 reports a dream in which the Lord invites Solomon to "ask what I should give you." Solomon asks for an understanding mind to govern the people. The Lord grants his wish but also grants the things for which he did not ask, riches and honor all his life. These things were supposed to be the gifts of wisdom in any case: "long life is in her right hand; in her left hand are riches and honor" (Prov 3:16). The account of Solomon's dream is clearly a Deuteronomistic composition. It concludes with a conditional promise:

"If you will walk in my ways, keeping my statutes and my commandments, as your father David walked, then I will lengthen your life" (1 Kgs 3:14).

The story of Solomon's dream is followed by an illustration of his wisdom in the judgment of the two women who each claim that a child is theirs. The wisdom of the solution does not necessarily leave the modern reader awestruck. It depends on the assumption that the woman who was not the real mother would let the child be killed. But in any case, the story highlights one aspect of the king's supposed wisdom—his ability to give a discerning judgment.

A different kind of wisdom is highlighted in chapter 5. Here wisdom is encyclopedic. It consists of mastery of proverbs and songs but also of an exhaustive knowledge of nature. The passage shows one kind of material that was valued as wisdom in early Israel. This kind of encyclopedic knowledge is not especially prominent in the biblical wisdom books, but it is implied in some passages in the book of Job (Job 28; 38–39). There is nothing distinctively Israelite about this wisdom. Solomon is compared with other legendary wise men of the ancient world. The queen of Sheba could appreciate such wisdom when she came to visit. We shall find that the biblical book of Proverbs was influenced by Egyptian wisdom at some points. Wisdom was an international phenomenon, fostered especially at the royal courts.

The Temple

Arguably the most important achievement attributed to Solomon was the building of the temple. The materials for the temple were obtained in Lebanon, and at least some of the work was done by Phoenician crafts-men (1 Kgs 7:13-47 describes the work of one Hiram of Tyre, which was also the name of the king of Tyre). The price of Phoenician help was substantial. According to 1 Kgs 9:11 Solomon ceded twenty cities in Galilee to Tyre in a land-for-gold swap. The fact that Solomon needed to do this raises some question about his fabulous wealth.

It is not surprising that the temple con-formed to the typical plan of temples in Syria-Palestine. The basic plan of the temple was a rectangle, 100 cubits long and 50 cubits wide (approximately 165 x 84.5 feet). There were three main sections: the *ulam*, 'or vestibule, the *hekal* or main room (the same word is used for the temple as a whole), and the *debir* or inner sanctuary (the Holy of Holies). There were doors to the second and third chambers. Vari-ous small chambers were located along the sides of the temple. Two bronze pillars, called Jachin and Boaz, stood in front of the tem-ple. There was also a molten sea, which was

a circular object supported by twelve statues of oxen. The symbolism of these objects is not explained, but the sea recalls the prominence of Yamm (Sea) in the Ugaritic myths. In the inner sanctuary there were two enormous cherubim made of olivewood. These hovered over the ark, which represented the presence of God, who was often said to be enthroned above the cherubim. (The cherubim were hybrid, winged creatures, with features of vari-ous animals. Such hybrid creatures were pop-ular in Near Eastern, especially Assyrian, art.)

In the ancient world, a temple was thought to be the house of the god or goddess, and the deity was supposed to live there. While the god or goddess was present in the temple, no harm could befall the city. The Lament for the Destruction of Ur in the early second millen-nium B.C.E. complains that the various deities abandoned their temples (*ANET*, 455–63). Later we shall find that Ezekiel has a vision of the glory of the Lord leaving Jerusalem before it is destroyed by the Babylonians. The

Fig. 13.3 Detail from *The Judgment of Solomon* **by Nicolas Poussin (1649); in the Louvre.** Commons.wikimedia.org

theology associated with Solomon's temple in the preexilic period can be seen in the Psalms. We do not know how far this theology was developed in the time of Solomon or how consistently it was maintained. Insofar as it coincides with common Near Eastern temple theology, we can assume that it was typical also of the Jerusalem temple.

The psalmists sometimes speak unabashedly about the temple as the dwelling place of YHWH. "How lovely is your dwelling place, O Lord of hosts! My soul longs, indeed it faints, for the courts of the Lord" (Ps 84:1-2; this psalm also notes, quaintly, that birds built their nests in the temple). According to Psalm 46, Jerusalem is "the city of God, the holy habitation of the Most High. God is in her midst, she shall not be moved." The presence of the Lord is a great source of security: "Therefore we will not fear, though the earth should change, though the mountains shake in the heart of the sea" (46:2). Again, Mount Zion is said to be God's holy mountain "in the far north" (Mount Zion was not in fact in the north, but traditionally the holy mountain of Baal, Mount Zaphon, was associated with the north). The psalmist supposes that any enemies who attack Jerusalem will flee in panic. It may be that this psalm was inspired by the fact that Jerusalem was not destroyed by the Assyrians, as Samaria was (see 2 Kings 18–19), but it is also possible that this belief in "the inviolability of Zion" was more ancient. The importance of the temple for the people of Judah is amply evident in the Psalms: "for a day in your courts is better than a thousand elsewhere. I would rather be a doorkeeper in the house of my God than live in the tents of wickedness" (84:10).

In light of the temple theology that we find in the Psalms, the theology attributed to Solomon in 1 Kings is modest indeed. The main articulation of this theology is found in his prayer in 1 Kings 8, and it is clearly the work of a Deuteronomistic writer. Solomon recalls the promise to David but understands it as conditional: "There shall never fail a successor before me to sit on the throne of Israel, if only your children look to their way, to walk before me" (8:25). He then goes on to reflect on the basic problem of a temple: "But will God indeed dwell on the earth? Even heaven and the highest heaven cannot contain you, much less this house that I have built" (8:27). This dilemma is resolved by the Deuteronomic compromise: God makes his *name* dwell there. The name still represents the presence of God, but it stops short of saying that God actually dwells in the temple, and so it protects the transcendence of God. Solomon goes on to explain the temple as a place where people can have access to God, to bring their requests and atone for their sins. Presumably, it would also be possible to pray to God elsewhere, but the temple provides a point of focus that is helpful to the people. Nothing is said to suggest that the city is protected by the presence of God in the temple. The temple has become a house of prayer, closer to the understanding of the later synagogue than to the ancient understanding of the house of God's dwelling.

Solomon's prayer at the consecration of the temple may have been written in the Babylonian exile or later, when the myth of the inviolability of Zion had been shattered. The temple, however, remained the central focal point of Jewish worship throughout the biblical period. While Deuteronomy demythologized the temple by saying that God's *name* lived there, rather than the Deity himself, it increased the centrality of the temple by declaring it to be the only valid place for sacrificial worship. We shall have many occasions to consider the place of the temple in Second Temple Judaism, not least in the context of the books of Chronicles, which attach great importance to the temple cult and give a somewhat different account of its origin from what we have seen in 1 Kings.

Solomon as Idolater

The Deuteronomists evidently took pride in the legendary splendor of Solomon, but one part of the Solomonic tradition was offensive to the editors. Not only did Solomon offer sacrifice at high places (1 Kgs 3:3), but he "loved many foreign women" from the nations with whom the Lord had forbidden intermarriage. Moreover, he also succumbed to the worship of their gods and goddesses (11:5-8). Solomon's behavior makes good sense if indeed he was actively engaged in international affairs. One of the ways in which kings in the ancient world cemented alliances was by giving and taking each other's daughters in marriage. The claim that Solomon had seven hundred princesses among his wives, then, is a tribute not to his sexual energy but to his diplomacy. The success of this strategy required that the wives be kept happy and that provision be made for the worship of their gods and goddesses. So we are told that Solomon built temples for Moabite and Ammonite deities. There is a parallel to Solomon's career in this regard in the reign of Herod the Great almost a thousand years later. Herod was also a great builder, and he had little scruple about building shrines to pagan deities, although he was careful not to do so in Jewish territory. We can be confident that the tradition of Solomon's promotion of

pagan deities was not invented by the Deuteronomist. Whether it is an accurate reflection of the reign of Solomon or not, it shows that there was a tradition of tolerance in Jerusalem toward the gods and goddesses of neighboring peoples, prior to Josiah's reform. This should hardly surprise us, given the Canaanite background of Jerusalem and the tradition that its kings were "after the order of Melchizedek."

While the Deuteronomists are unlikely to have invented Solomon's worship of foreign deities, they could use it for their purposes. It was because of this, we are told, that God raised up enemies against Solomon, such as Hadad the Edomite (11:14). More importantly, it is the reason why the united monarchy did not persist. Ten tribes were allowed to secede under the leadership of Jeroboam the son of Nebat because Solomon worshiped Astarte, goddess of the Sidonians, Chemosh the god of Moab, and Milcom the god of the Ammonites (11:33). Nonetheless, the kingdom is not taken away entirely from Solomon and his heirs. The promise to David remains, despite Solomon's failure to keep the laws. It is somewhat ironic that the only tribe left under the kingdom of Judah is Benjamin, the tribe of Saul.

The Division of the Kingdom

The Deuteronomistic explanation of the division of the kingdom is placed on the lips of a prophet, Ahijah the Shilonite, who performs a symbolic action by tearing his robe in twelve pieces and giving ten to Jeroboam (1 Kgs 11:30-31). From this point on, prophets play a more prominent role in the history. One of their functions is to make or depose kings. We shall find several examples of symbolic actions in the books of the prophets, notably in Hosea, Isaiah, Jeremiah, and Ezekiel. The symbolic actions of the prophets have been described as a kind of street theater, a vivid form of communication that was sometimes more effective than words.

It is quite clear from the narrative, however, that the tribes that broke away from Solomon's son Rehoboam were not motivated by concern about the worship of other gods. The issue that sparked the revolt was the oppressive practice of forced labor, or corvée, introduced by Solomon. The old men in his retinue advised Rehoboam to lighten the burden on the people, while the young men told him to intensify it. He chose the latter course, and the schism resulted. Jeroboam had been in charge of all the forced labor of the house of Joseph. When he rebelled, with the encouragement of the prophet, he fled to Egypt. There is a clear parallel here between the forced labor of Solomon and the oppression of the Israelites in Egypt in the exodus story. The same Hebrew word, *mas* or *missim*, is used to refer to the corvée in both stories. After Solomon's death, Jeroboam comes up from Egypt. When he becomes king, he makes the recollection of the exodus central to the cult at the royal sanctuaries in Bethel and Dan (12:28). Jeroboam may have drawn a parallel with an older tradition about the exodus to lend legitimacy to his revolt, but it is also possible that the celebration of the exodus became central to the cult of YHWH only at this time.

It is also apparent that the northern tribes, or at least some of them, regarded Judah as a foreign body. The battle cry of Jeroboam ("What share do we have in David?") echoes that of Sheba, son of Bichri, in 2 Sam 20:1. Henceforth, the northern tribes would constitute the kingdom of Israel proper. It may be significant that the rebellion was launched at the old center of Shechem, rather than at Hebron, where David had been crowned. Kingship in the north would remain much closer to the kind of charismatic leadership we saw in Judges than would the dynasty in the south. There were frequent coups and upheavals. The northern kingdom clearly took the exodus as its national myth and celebrated it in the cult. In Judah, by contrast, little attention appears to be paid to the exodus story until the reform of Josiah.

Jeroboam built up Shechem as the first capital of the northern kingdom. (The seat of government was moved to Tirzah at an early point in the monarchy.) His action that most concerns the Deuteronomist, however, was the construction of two shrines, one at Bethel, just north of the border and not far from Jerusalem, and one at Dan in the far north. These locations were evidently chosen for geographic reasons. Bethel was associated with Jacob, who had allegedly given it its name, "house of God." Whether Jeroboam was drawing on an old tradition about the sacrality of Bethel, or whether the story of Jacob was invented to give legitimacy to the site, we cannot be sure.

The account of Jeroboam's actions bears the clear imprint of the Deuteronomist and is decidedly unsympathetic to the northern leader. He is virtually accused of idolatry in setting up the two golden calves. (The story of the golden calf in Exodus 32 was surely a polemic against the cult established by Jeroboam, although that story is complicated by the fact that the guilty part is Aaron, the ancestor of the Jerusalem priesthood. See the discussion in chapter 6 above.) It is unlikely, however, that Jeroboam was guilty of idolatry.

Fig. 13.4 "My little finger is thicker than my father's loins. Now, whereas my father laid on you a heavy yoke, I will add to your yoke. My father disciplined you with whips, but I will discipline you with scorpions." Hans Holbein the Younger's portrait of Rehoboam, Great Council Chamber of Basel Town Hall (ca. 1526–1528). Commons.wikimedia.org

The deity may have been thought to stand on the calves, just as he was thought to sit above the cherubim in the Jerusalem cult. Jeroboam's crime in the eyes of the Deuteronomists was that he promoted sacrificial worship outside Jerusalem. This is what is called, in the remainder of the history, the sin of Jeroboam. In fact, Jeroboam was more closely attuned to the traditions of the tribes than was Rehoboam, whose capital had been a Jebusite stronghold little more than a generation earlier.

The Deuteronomists provide an explicit judgment on Jeroboam in 1 Kings 13, where a man of God is said to prophesy that a Davidic king named Josiah would one day tear down the altar at Bethel. The explicit mention of Josiah here leaves no doubt but that this king's reform is the climax of the history. This episode is followed by a strange legend about how

the man of God was eaten by a lion because he was tricked into disobeying God's orders. This story probably originated as a popular legend. The Deuteronomist uses it to show the perils of disobedience in a colorful way. An even more explicit judgment is pronounced in chapter 14 by Ahijah the Shilonite. Jeroboam is to have no male descendant, ostensibly because of his promotion of worship outside Jerusalem. Anyone who has read the books of Samuel must appreciate the irony when Jeroboam is told that he has not been like "my servant David, who kept my commandments and followed me with all his heart, doing only that which was right in my sight" (14:8). The moral ambiguity that enriched the portrait of David in the earlier books is lost here. Ahijah proceeds to prophesy the destruction of the northern kingdom and the exile of the people "beyond the Euphrates" because of the sin of Jeroboam (14:15-16). At this point, the Deuteronomistic History tends to reduce everything to one cause and to become simplistic. We shall find a more complex and compelling analysis of the problems of northern Israel in the eighth-century prophets.

The early kings of Judah fare no better than their northern counterparts in the judgment of the Deuteronomists. Rehoboam initially desists from fighting against Jeroboam because of the word of a prophet (12:24). Yet we are informed later that there was war between Rehoboam and Jeroboam continually (14:30), and that it continued throughout the reigns of their immediate successors. The Deuteronomist moves rapidly through several reigns. Here it would seem that the editors adapted a chronicle that gave basic information about each king and inserted judgments based on Deuteronomic criteria. The campaign of Pharaoh Shishak (14:25-26) is also known from Egyptian sources. Its inclusion here serves no theological purpose, and it supports the view that the Deuteronomistic editors had ancient annals at their disposal. The editorial judgments on the kings are heavy-handed. Among the early kings, only Asa of Judah receives a positive notice for suppressing some cultic practices, although he did not interfere with the high places. The succession of the Davidic kings proceeds smoothly, in accordance with the divine promise. In the northern kingdom, however, we have a coup in the second generation, in fulfillment of the judgment on the house of Jeroboam, and another two generations later, because Baasha continued "to walk in the way of Jeroboam." Zimri, the usurper who killed the son of Baasha, reigns only seven days. The first real

dynasty in northern Israel is established by Omri (16:16-17; c. 885 B.C.E.).

Omri is the first king of Israel or Judah to leave an imprint in nonbiblical sources. The Moabite Stone, which was discovered in 1868, tells of the conflict between Mesha, king of Moab, and Omri, who humbled Moab for many years but was eventually defeated (*ANET*, 321). The inscription is remarkable for the similarity it shows between the religion of Moab and that of Israel. Mesha acts at the behest of his god Chemosh, just as the Israelites act at the behest of YHWH. Most remarkable is that Mesha boasts of having slaughtered every man, woman, and child in Nebo, "for I had devoted them to destruction for (the god) Ashtar-Chemosh." Omri's son, Ahab, is mentioned in the Monolith

Fig. 13.5 The Moabite Stone (or Mesha Stele), ca. **840** B.C.E.; in the **Louvre.** Commons.wikimedia.org

Inscription of the Assyrian king Shalmaneser as having contributed two thousand chariots and ten thousand footsoldiers to an Aramean coalition that halted an Assyrian advance (*ANET*, 279). Assyrian records continued to refer to Israel as "the house of Omri" long after Omri's descendants had ceased to rule. Omri and Ahab were kings to be reckoned with. There is much more evidence outside the Bible for their power and influence than was the case with Solomon.

It is Omri who bought and fortified the hill of Samaria, which remained the capital of Israel from that time forward. Archaeology has shown that it was a splendid city. The royal acropolis was a huge rectangular enclosure that covered an area of four acres, the size of a typical town of the time. It was paved with a thick lime floor and surrounded by a wall of fine ashlar masonry. One of the buildings on the acropolis contained a hoard of carved ivories, the most important collection of artwork from ancient Israel. The Omride dynasty also either built or expanded Hazor and Megiddo, and fortified them with massive walls. Huge, ornate pillar capitals, in the style called proto-Aeolic, were found at Samaria, Hazor, and Megiddo.

The southern, Deuteronomistic, editor dismisses Omri summarily: "Omri did what was evil in the sight of the LORD; he did more evil than all who were before him" (16:26). His son Ahab proves to be a much more colorful character: "And as if it had been a light thing for him to walk in the sins of Jeroboam son of Nebat, he took as his wife Jezebel, daughter of King Ethbaal of the Sidonians, and went and served Baal and worshiped him" (16:31). The advent of Ahab and Jezebel sets the stage for a major confrontation between the devotees of YHWH and the cult of Baal, and the first sustained discussion of prophecy in the Hebrew Bible.

FOR FURTHER READING

Introductory Discussion

S. W. Holloway, "Kings, Book of 1–2," *ABD* 4:69–83.

Commentaries

M. Cogan, *1 Kings* (AB 10; New York: Doubleday, 2000). Standard historical and philological commentary.

V. Fritz, *1 & 2 Kings* (Continental Commentary; Minneapolis: Fortress Press, 2003). Assumes more than one exilic redaction of Deuteronomistic History. Good use of archaeology.

G. Hens-Piazza, *1-2 Kings* (Nashville: Abingdon, 2006). Literary-theological commentary.

B. O. Long, *1 Kings, with an Introduction to Historical Literature* (FOTL 9; Grand Rapids: Eerdmans, 1984). Form-critical commentary. Helpful analysis of literary structure.

R. D. Nelson, *First and Second Kings* (Interpretation; Atlanta: John Knox, 1987). Concise homiletically oriented commentary.

C.-L. Seow, "The First and Second Books of Kings," *NIB* 3:1–296. Concise scholarly commentary with some homiletical reflections.

M. A. Sweeney, *First and Second Kings: A Commentary* (OTL; Louisville: Westminster John Knox, 2007). Comprehensive commentary. Posits final exilic edition, but also detectable earlier stages.

S. J. de Vries, *1 Kings* (WBC 12; Waco: Word, 1985). Substantial discussion of textual and compositional issues.

J. T. Walsh, *1 Kings* (Berit Olam; Collegeville, MN: Liturgical Press, 1996). Focus on literary issues.

Historical Background

W. G. Dever, "Histories and Non-Histories of Ancient Israel: The Question of the United Monarchy," in J. Day, ed., *In Search of Pre-Exilic Israel* (London: T&T Clark, 2004), 65–94. Defense of the historicity of the United Monarchy on the basis of the archaeological evidence.

I. Finkelstein and N. A. Silberman, *The Bible Unearthed: Archaeology's New Vision of Ancient Israel and the Origin of Its Sacred Texts* (New York: Free Press, 2001), 169–205; *David and Solomon: In Search of the Bible's Sacred Kings and the Roots of the Western Tradition* (New York: Free Press, 2006). Skeptical view of the reign of Solomon. Argues that the supposedly Solomonic cities were built at a later time.

A. Mazar, *Archaeology of the Land of the Bible, 10,000–586 B.C.E.* (ABRL; New York: Doubleday, 1993), 375–402. Supports the traditional view of the archaeological evidence for Solomon's reign.

J. M. Miller and J. H. Hayes, *A History of Ancient Israel and Judah* (Philadelphia: Westminster, 1986), 189–286. Helpful citation of nonbiblical evidence.

M. B. Moore and B. E. Kelle, *Biblical History and Israel's Past: The Changing Study of the Bible and History* (Grand Rapids: Eerdmans, 2011), 202–65. Overview of the debate about the historicity of David and Solomon.

N. Na'aman, "Cow Town or Royal Capital? Evidence for Iron Age Jerusalem," *BAR* 23/4 (1997): 43–47. Discussion of the status of Jerusalem in the tenth–ninth centuries B.C.E.

H. Shanks, "Where Is the Tenth Century?" *BAR* 24/2 (1998): 56–61. A record of the debate about whether the Solomonic cities should be dated to the tenth or ninth century.

Studies

G. N. Knoppers, *Two Nations Under God: The Deuteronomistic History of Solomon and the Dual Monarchies,* vol. 1: *The Reign of Solomon and the Rise of Jeroboam* (HSM 52; Atlanta: Scholars Press, 1993). Elaboration of the two-redaction view of the Deuteronomistic History.

J. D. Levenson, *Sinai and Zion* (Minneapolis: Winston, 1985), 89–184. Lucid exposition of Zion theology.

S. L. McKenzie, *The Trouble with Kings: The Composition of the Book of Kings in the Deuteronomistic History* (VTSup 42; Leiden: Brill, 1991). Modified version of the two-redaction theory of the Deuteronomistic History, positing later additions rather than earlier sources.

C. L. Meyers, "Temple, Jerusalem," *ABD* 6:348–69. Informative descriptive article on the temple.

R. R. Wilson, "Unity and Diversity in the Book of Kings," in S. M. Olyan and R. C. Culley, eds., *A Wise and Discerning Heart: Essays in Honor of B. O. Long* (Brown Judaic Studies 325; Providence: Brown University Press, 2000), 293–310. Discussion of the literary problems of the books of Kings.

KINGS OF ISRAEL AND JUDAH

Judah	Israel
Rehoboam (922–915) Abijah (Abijam) (915–913) Asa (913–873)	Jeroboam (922–901) Nadab (901–900) Baasha (900–877) Elah (877–876) **Omride Era** Omri (876–869)
Jehoshapat (873–849) Jehoram (849–843) Ahaziah (843/2)	Ahab (869–850) Ahaziah (850–849) Jehoram (849–843) **Jehu Dynasty** Jehu (843–815)
Athaliah (842–837) Joash (837–800) Amaziah (800–783) Uzziah (Azariah) (783–742)	Jehoahaz (815–802) Jehoash (802–786) Jeroboam II (786–746)
Jotham (742–735)	**Assyrian Intervention** Zechariah (746–745) Shallum (745) Menahem (745–737) Pekahiah (737–736)
Ahaz (735–727 or 715) Hezekiah (727 or 715–687)	Pekah (736–732) Hoshea (732–723) **Fall of Samaria (722)**
Manasseh (687–642) Amon (642–640) Josiah (640–609) Jehoahaz (609) Jehoiachim (609–598) Jehoiachin (598–597) **First capture of Jerusalem by Babylonians** (597) Zedekiah (597–587) **Destruction of Jerusalem (586)**	

CHAPTER 14

1 Kings 12—2 Kings 25
Tales of Prophets and the End of the Kingdoms of Israel and Judah

INTRODUCTION

In this chapter, we examine stories of prophets in the last chapters of 1 Kings and in 2 Kings, including the stories of Micaiah ben Imlah, Elijah, and Elisha; what these tell us about the nature of prophecy and its relationship to the monarchies in north and south; the prophecy-inspired coup that brought Jehu to the throne; and the end of the northern kingdom and the fortunes of Judah in the Assyrian crisis.

The narratives in 1 Kings 17–22 and 2 Kings 1–9 stand out from their context in the books of Kings. They depart from the annalistic series of reports on the reigns of kings and provide more developed narratives in which the central characters are prophets. These stories most probably circulated independently before they were incorporated into the Deuteronomistic History. Most of them concern the figures of Elijah and Elisha, and these probably circulated together. They are highly legendary stories. While they refer to known historical figures and events, their miraculous character cautions against treating them as historical sources. They are primarily of interest for the light they shed on the place of prophecy in Israelite society under the divided monarchy.

Micaiah ben Imlah

An impression of what might be called the normal context of prophecy in ancient Israel may be gleaned from the story of Micaiah ben Imlah in 1 Kings 22, one of the prophetic stories that does not involve Elijah or Elisha. This story ostensibly tells of the death of King Ahab. Initially, however, the king of Israel is not identified, although his counterpart,

Jehoshaphat of Judah, is named. Only in v. 22 do we learn that the king is supposed to be Ahab. Thereafter, he is anonymous again, until the editor refers to "the rest of the acts of Ahab" in v. 39. The formulaic statement that "Ahab slept with his ancestors" in v. 40, however, would normally imply that his death was uneventful. It seems likely, then, that the story originally referred to an anonymous "king of Israel," who was only secondarily identified as the great Ahab.

The story is set in a time of good relations between Israel and Judah, but in a time of intermittent war between Israel and Aram (Syria). The kings of Israel and Judah agree to launch a campaign against the disputed city of Ramoth-gilead. Before they do so, however, the king of Judah proposes that they "inquire first the word of the Lord." It should be noted that that there is no mention of Baal here, as we might expect from the other narratives about the reign of Ahab. This might be explained by the involvement of the king of Judah.

In order to consult the Lord, the king of Israel assembles four hundred prophets. We shall see that similarly large numbers of prophets are "on call" at the royal palace in the story of Elijah. Most prophets were not isolated individuals, as we might think from the canonical prophetic books. They were members of a guild and operated en masse. The prophet who went his own way was the exception. One of the functions of prophets in the early period seems to have been to whip up enthusiasm at the beginning of a campaign. Here the prophets hold a virtual pep rally for the king. Not only do they affirm that he should go up, and promise that God will give him victory, but they symbolically act out

the battle. One Zedekiah son of Chenaanah, whose name indicates that he was a prophet of YHWH, made himself horns of iron to illustrate how the king would rout his enemies. All of this took place at the threshing floor of the entrance to the gate of Samaria. The threshing floor was an open space like a town square where public assemblies were held. Later, in the prophetic books, we often find "oracles against the nations" proclaiming woes upon the enemies of Israel. The rally on the threshing floor of Samaria illustrates the *Sitz im Leben*, or setting in life, of such oracles.

Micaiah is identified from the beginning as a dissident. "I hate him," says the king, "for he never prophesies anything favorable about me, but only disaster." Political and personal sympathies have a bearing on the content of prophecy. The messenger who goes to fetch Micaiah is exceptionally candid: "The words of the prophets with one accord are favorable to the king; let your word be like the word of one of them and speak favorably." This is tantamount to an admission that the prophets as a group tell the king what he wants to hear. Micaiah, inevitably, does not. He claims to have had a vision of all Israel scattered like sheep without a shepherd. The implication is that the king will be killed in battle.

The most interesting aspect of this story, however, is how Micaiah explains his disagreement with the other prophets. We might have expected him to accuse them of conspiring, as they surely had in light of the messenger's comment. To do so, however, might undercut belief in prophecy altogether. Instead, Micaiah reports an extraordinary vision of his own. He saw the Lord sitting on his throne. According to one strand of Israelite tradition, a human being could not see God and live (cf.

Exod 33:20). Micaiah, however, represents a tradition that we shall meet again in Isaiah 6 and Ezekiel 1, in which prophets claim to have had visions of God. (This tradition is at the root of the later development of Jewish mysticism.) We cannot fail to notice the similarity between the Lord, on his throne, surrounded by his host, and the kings of Israel and Judah on their thrones on the threshing floor of Samaria. God is imagined in the likeness of a human king, but more exalted. The prophet becomes privy to the deliberations of the heavenly council. The Lord consults his heavenly courtiers, and his question is remarkable: "Who will entice Ahab, so that he may go up and fall at Ramoth-gilead?" The Lord is setting the king up for disaster, just as he had set up the pharaoh in the exodus story by hardening his heart. The solution is provided by a "spirit" that volunteers to be a lying spirit in the mouths of the prophets. We saw in 1 Samuel how the Lord sent an evil spirit upon King Saul. Here he sends a lying spirit into the mouths of the prophets. Micaiah does not deny that his fellow prophets are inspired. The problem is that the spirit of inspiration may be deceitful.

The four hundred prophets who prophesied success for the king relied on their ecstatic behavior as evidence that they were inspired. But if inspiration itself can be deceitful, whom should the king believe? Both he and Micaiah adopt an attitude of "wait and see." The king does not have Micaiah killed on the spot, as he might have had, but has him imprisoned, pending the outcome of the battle. Micaiah agrees that if the king returns from the battle, "the LORD has not spoken through me." In the event, Micaiah is vindicated, but it is too late by then for the king to do anything about it.

The story of Micaiah ben Imlah illustrates both the way prophecy worked in Israelite society and the problems that were inherent in it. The prophets claimed to speak the word of the Lord, and this is what made their utterances powerful. But sometimes they disagreed and contradicted each other. How then could one decide which one was right? We shall revisit this problem when we discuss the book of Jeremiah. Ultimately, the only satisfactory way to know whether a prophecy was right was to wait and see, and that might well be too late, as it was in the case of Ahab. The king would have been better advised to decide whether to go to war on the merits of the case: was this a necessary war, that he should risk his life to pursue it? The fact that prophets told him he would be successful (or that he would be killed) was not sufficiently reliable to be the basis for his decision.

Elijah

The figure of Elijah dominates 1 Kings 17–19, 21, and 2 Kings 1–2. The stories about Elijah are closely related to those about Elisha. Each prophet performs a miracle on behalf of a widow by causing her store of oil to increase (1 Kgs 17:8-16; 2 Kgs 4:1-7). Each raises a child from the dead (1 Kgs 17:17-24; 2 Kgs 4:18-37). The stories about Elijah, however, reflect a greater level of theological interest than those about Elisha. Elijah is engaged in polemic against the worship of Baal, and he emerges as a champion of social justice, whereas Elisha is more simply a wonder-worker. Accordingly, some scholars regard the Elisha stories as older than those about Elijah. There is some doubt about the historicity of

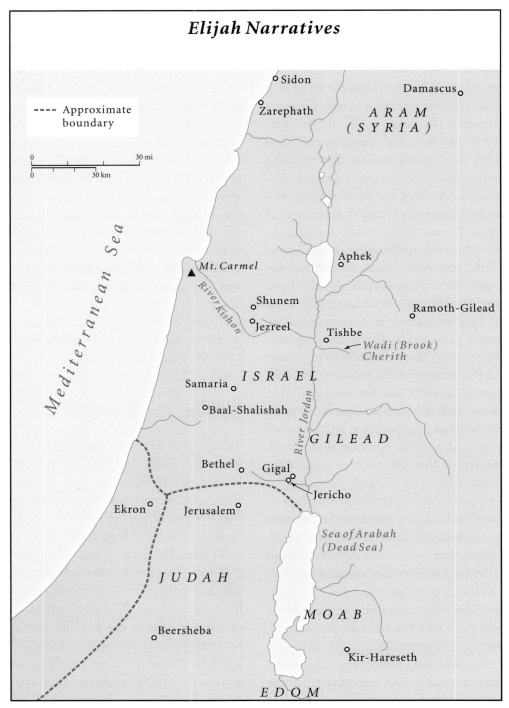

Elijah Narratives

Sidon

Damascus

Zarephath

A R A M
(S Y R I A)

Approximate
boundary

0 ——————— 30 mi
0 ——————— 30 km

Mediterranean Sea

Aphek

▲ *Mt. Carmel*

River Kishon

Shunem

Ramoth-Gilead

Jezreel

Tishbe

Wadi (Brook)
Cherith

I S R A E L

Samaria

River Jordan

Baal-Shalishah

G I L E A D

Bethel

Gigal

Jericho

Ekron

Jerusalem

Sea of Arabah
(Dead Sea)

J U D A H

M O A B

Beersheba

Kir-Hareseth

E D O M

Map 14.1

Elijah. His name means "YHWH is my god," and the stories about him have obvious symbolic significance. The historicity of the stories cannot be checked in any case. They are of interest primarily for the picture they paint of life and religion in the kingdom of northern Israel.

The extent to which these stories were edited by Deuteronomists is disputed. The charge against Ahab in chapters 17–19 is that he "followed the Baals," not that he walked in the sin of Jeroboam. Elijah offers a burnt offering on Mount Carmel, despite the Deuteronomic restriction of sacrifice to Jerusalem. Some have gone so far as to suggest that the Elijah cycle was incorporated in 1 Kings later than the Deuteronomistic edition of the work. But the Deuteronomists also condemned the worship of Baal, and the sacrifice on Mount Carmel was integral to the story. In any case, the stories surely originated in northern Israel before Josiah's reform. Ostraca found at Samaria show that "Baal" was a common element in proper names, and this supports the view that his worship was widespread. It is clear from the prophet Hosea that Baal worship continued to flourish in the eighth century, down to the end of the northern kingdom. The strongest case for a Deuteronomistic insertion can be made in chapter 19, where Elijah goes to "Horeb the mountain of God" and takes on the character of "a prophet like Moses" (cf. Deut 18:15).

The conflict between the cult of YHWH and that of Baal comes to a head in 1 Kings 17 because of a drought, which Elijah interprets as a punishment on Ahab because of the worship of Baal. Baal was a storm-god, the "rider of the clouds," and as such he was supposed to provide rain, which made fertility and life possible. In the Baal cycle of myths from Ugarit, when Baal is swallowed up by death the earth dries up and the gods lament, "Baal is dead, what will happen to the peoples?" When he comes back to life, "the heavens rain down oil, the wadis run with honey." In the words of the prophet Hosea, the dispute in Israel concerned which god provided "the grain, the wine, and the oil," YHWH or Baal (cf. Hos 2:8). This is also the issue in the Elijah stories.

In 1 Kings 17 Elijah performs two miracles that show that it is YHWH rather than Baal who gives life. One concerns the multiplication of oil and meal. The second involves the raising of a dead child. In each case,

Fig. 14.1 Elijah and the widow of Zarephath, sketches by Russian artist Alexander Andreyevich Ilyanov (1806–1858). Commons .wikimedia.org

Elijah emphasizes that he acts by the power of YHWH. The roots of the conflict are further clarified in chapter 18. Here we are told that Jezebel had been killing off the prophets of YHWH. Many people in ancient Israel probably saw no conflict between the worship of YHWH and Baal. Elijah appears as a zealot, who refuses to tolerate the worship of any god except YHWH. The story suggests, however, that Jezebel may also have been intolerant in her promotion of Baal. Such conflicts between rival cults were relatively rare in antiquity. The best-known example before the time of Elijah was the attempt of Pharaoh Akhenaten to promote the worship of the sun-god Aten to the exclusion of all others. The conflict had clear political implications. We are told that four hundred fifty prophets of Baal and four hundred prophets of Asherah ate at Jezebel's table (that is, were supported by Jezebel; 18:19). The picture of a huge retinue of prophets at the royal court conforms to what we have seen in the story of Micaiah ben Imlah. If the worship of Baal and Asherah required such a retinue, there was a practical reason for excluding the equally numerous prophets of YHWH. From the king's perspective, Elijah is a "troubler of Israel" because he is interfering with royal policy. From the prophet's perspective, it is Ahab who troubles Israel by religious policies that lead to drought and disaster.

The contest between Elijah and the prophets of Baal is dramatic. The challenge posed by Elijah is that "the god who answers with fire is indeed God." The prophets of Baal use various techniques to whip themselves into ecstasy. (The practice of gashing oneself was evidently practiced by some prophets in Israel also. One of the latest passages in the prophetic corpus, Zech 13:5-6, envisions a

time when people will be ashamed to admit that they are prophets and will deny it. "And if anyone asks them, 'What are these wounds on your chest?' the answer will be, 'The wounds I received in the house of my friends.'" Such wounds were evidently a trademark of prophecy.) Elijah mocks the prophets of Baal and suggests that their god is asleep. No one's prayers are answered all the time. Devotees of Baal presumably felt that their prayers were answered some of the time, or they would not have persisted in worshiping him. The biblical story, however, is polemical and is not concerned with fair representation of the opponents. The manner in which Elijah produces fire, by pouring water on the offering and in a trench, makes one suspect that some trickery (involving a flammable liquid) is involved. Magicians all the world over have seemed to perform miraculous deeds by sleight of hand. But in truth we do not know whether there is any historical basis for this story. The narrator wished to give the impression that a decisive test was carried out, which proved beyond doubt that YHWH was God. Elijah seizes his advantage by having all the prophets of Baal slaughtered.

Elijah is impelled by the hand of the Lord, which imbues him with strength and enables him to outrun the king's chariots. He manifests a kind of charismatic religion, such as we saw in some instances in the book of Judges. The massacre of the prophets is in the spirit of the *herem*, the total slaughter that was commanded on some occasions in the books of Joshua and 1 Samuel, and of which the Moabite king Mesha boasted in his inscription. (Compare the judgment on King Ahab for sparing Ben-hadad of Damascus in 1 Kgs 20:42.) In later tradition, Elijah was remembered as a figure of zeal and was even identified with Phinehas, the paradigmatic zealot of Numbers 25. This readiness to slaughter one's opponents in the name of God is quite credible in the context of the ninth century B.C.E. (and indeed all too credible even in our own times). It is hardly, however, a religious ideal that we should wish to emulate in the modern world.

One other aspect of Elijah's contest is troubling. He and the prophets of Baal agree that "the god who answers with fire is indeed God." But is this an adequate criterion for identifying God? As we have seen in earlier chapters, YHWH was originally worshiped as a god who manifested himself in fire on a mountain. The early theophanies, or manifestations, of YHWH are very similar to those of the Canaanite storm-god Baal. In the Bible, however, YHWH differs from Baal above all by his ethical character. This difference is not apparent in the story of Elijah on Mount Carmel in 1 Kings 18.

This story, however, is followed immediately by another one, in chapter 19, that serves as a corrective, and that is at least in part the work of a Deuteronomistic editor. Elijah has to flee from the wrath of Jezebel, and he betakes himself southward, to the wilderness. He is fed miraculously in the desert, as Israel was during the exodus. (This motif is anticipated already in 17:6, where he is fed by the ravens.) Then he proceeds for forty days and forty nights to "Horeb the mountain of God"—the name for the mountain of revelation in Deuteronomic tradition. The forty days and nights correspond to the forty years spent by the Israelites in the wilderness. The motif is picked up in the New Testament with reference to the temptation of Jesus.

Fig. 14.2 *The Prophets of Baal Are Slaughtered,* **engraving by Gustav Doré (1866).** Commons.wikimedia.org

At the mountain, Elijah has an experience similar to that of Moses in Exod 33:21-23. Moses was not allowed to see God's face, but he was allowed to see his back. Elijah does not see God in human form, but he does experience a theophany. The Deity, we are told, was not in the wind, the earthquake, or the fire that were the typical trappings of a theophany, even in the account of the revelation on Mount Sinai in Exodus 19. Instead, God was in "a sound of sheer silence" (1 Kgs 19:12). Of course, a sound of silence is a contradiction in terms, but the point is made eloquently that God must not be confused with the forces of nature. The word translated "sound" also means "voice." In Deuteronomic theology, Israel at Horeb "stood at the foot of the mountain while the mountain was blazing up to the very heavens, shrouded in dark clouds. Then the Lord your God spoke to you out of the fire. You heard the sound of words but saw no form; there was only a voice" (Deut 4:11-12). The theophany to Elijah in 1 Kings 19, then, corrects the impression that might have been given by chapter 18, that God is manifested primarily in fire or in the power of nature. Instead, the Deuteronomist insists, God is manifested primarily by the voice and the words of commandment.

But while the Deuteronomist corrects the theology of the traditional story by relativizing the importance of the fire, there is no correction of the ethics of Elijah. The virtue of his (murderous) zeal is affirmed, and he is given a new mission, to anoint a new king in Syria and to anoint Jehu as king of Israel. In fact, it is Elisha who anoints Jehu, but Elisha derives his authority from Elijah. As we learn in 2 Kings, Jehu acts with the same kind of zeal as Elijah in slaughtering the enemies of YHWH. Elijah is also told to anoint Elisha as his successor. He is not actually said to anoint the younger prophet, but he casts his mantle over him, which has the same effect. The act of anointing does not have to be taken literally. The essential point is that he confers authority on Elisha and appoints him to the task of prophecy.

A different kind of story is told about Elijah in 1 Kings 21. Here the issue is not Baal worship but social injustice. Ahab wants the vineyard of Naboth the Jezreelite, which is beside his summer palace. He offers to buy it, but Naboth refuses because it his ancestral heritage. Ahab broods in frustration, but Jezebel takes action. She has false accusations brought against Naboth and has him stoned. Ahab takes possession of the vineyard. The situation is reminiscent of the incident of David and Bathsheba. There also a king wanted something that belonged to another man and eventually resorted to murder to get his way. There also the king was confronted by a prophet. There is a striking contrast, however, between the approach of Nathan and that of Elijah. Nathan induced David to condemn himself by appealing to values that the king shared. Such an appeal may not have been possible in the case of Ahab. In any case, Elijah makes no attempt to win the king over but pronounces a judgment, in effect a curse, on both Ahab and Jezebel. In fact, the coup that terminated Ahab's line came not in his lifetime but in that of his son. The Deuteronomist explains this by saying that Ahab humbled himself and was given a reprieve.

The confrontation between Elijah and Ahab, however, sets a pattern that is often repeated in the books of the prophets. The prophets whose oracles are preserved in these books are in most cases "troublers of Israel" (at least down to the Babylonian exile). Their relations with the kings of Israel and Judah are usually adversarial. The issue of Naboth's vineyard is also representative of the concerns of many of those prophets, especially those of the eighth century B.C.E. Isaiah pronounces woes on those who "add house to house and field to field" (Isa 5:8), and similar issues dominate the book of Amos. At issue was not only the possession of particular plots of land but the character of Israelite and Judean society, where the independent landowners were increasingly forced into servitude and wealth was concentrated in the hands of the upper classes. Like Elijah, these prophets insist on the worship of YHWH alone, but they also insist that the worship of YHWH entails a commitment to social justice.

The end of Elijah's earthly career is described in 2 Kings 2. His affinity with Moses is underlined in the incident where he parts the waters of the Jordan. Then he is taken up to heaven in a fiery chariot. Elijah shares with Enoch the distinction of being taken up alive to heaven. (Moses was sometimes believed to have been taken up. Even though he is explicitly said to have died in Deut 34:5-6, no one knew his burial place.) Because Elijah had not died, it was believed that he would come back to earth "before the great and terrible Day of the LORD" (Mal 4:5). This belief is first attested in the book of Malachi, about 400 B.C.E. It was well established by the Hellenistic period, as can be seen from Sir 48:10 and the Dead Sea Scrolls (4Q558, and by allusion in 4Q521). According to the New Testament (Mark 9:11; Matt 17:10), Elijah is supposed to come before the Messiah. In Revelation 11 one of the two witnesses who appears before the end-time is modeled on Elijah. (He has power to shut up the sky so that no rain may fall.) In Jewish tradition, a place is set for Elijah at the Passover in anticipation of his return.

Elisha

Elisha inherits a double portion of Elijah's spirit, and some of his miraculous deeds are very similar to those of his mentor. Nonetheless, the careers of the two prophets are quite different. Elisha is not engaged in conflict with the cult of Baal, and he never fights for social justice as Elijah did in the case of Naboth's vineyard. Some of his miracles are, at best, amoral. He curses small boys who jeer at him, so that they are mauled by she-bears (2 Kgs 2:23-25). He makes an iron ax head float on the water (6:1-7). He prophesies that the Lord will enable the kings of Israel and Judah to ravage Moab, although there is no evident moral issue at stake. He also discloses the secret plans of the king of Aram and performs various miracles to aid the Israelites in battle against him. These stories are concerned with manifestations of supernatural power with little concern for moral issues.

One notable feature of these stories is the way in which people cross state boundaries. Elijah had been commanded to anoint Hazael as king of Aram in 1 Kings 19. Elisha carries out that command, or at least tells Hazael that the Lord has said he should be king (2 Kgs 8:13). There is no apparent moral reason for the choice of Hazael, who is emboldened by the prophet to murder the ailing king, Benhadad, and who will do much evil to Israel. The encounter with Hazael comes about because the king wants to consult Elisha. The prophet's reputation as a person with access to supernatural knowledge and power transcends ethnic and cultic boundaries. We have several instances in these stories of people seeking help from the gods of other peoples. A king of Israel, Ahaziah, inquires of Baalzebub, the god of Ekron (a Philistine city) in 2 Kings 1, and is condemned by Elijah as a result. The most elaborate story of an appeal to a god of another people is the story of Naaman the Syrian in 2 Kings 5. In this case, the story climaxes in the confession that "there is no God in all the earth except in Israel" (2 Kgs 5:15). At the same time, the story shows that people who are not Israelites can benefit from the power of YHWH. (Compare the story of Jesus and the Canaanite woman in Mark 7:24-30.)

Perhaps the most remarkable episode in these chapters is found in 2 Kgs 3:26-27. When the king of Moab saw that he was losing a battle with Israel, he took his firstborn son, who was to succeed him, and offered him as a burnt offering on the city wall. We have seen that human sacrifice was also offered in Israel, in exceptional circumstances. (An example is found in 1 Kgs 16:34, where Hiel of Bethel is said to have sacrificed two of his sons as foundation offerings when he built Jericho.) The extraordinary point in the case of the king of Moab is that the sacrifice was efficacious, even though it was presumably offered to a pagan god. "Great wrath" came upon Israel, and they withdrew. This is a rare case where the Bible admits, at least implicitly, the power of a pagan god.

In all of the Elisha stories, and in some of the Elijah stories, divine action is recognized especially by the supernatural power involved. They show little of the moral concerns that dominate most of the Hebrew Bible. While the stories are legendary, and their historicity cannot be pressed, they provide a fascinating glimpse of popular religion. People turned to gods and to holy men when they were sick or faced with a crisis because of drought, famine, pestilence, or war. When they did, they were primarily concerned with the reputation of the god or of the holy man to deliver them. If the god, or the prophet, of a neighboring people was thought to be especially powerful, they would turn to him. This kind of popular religion does not get much notice in most of the Hebrew Bible, but it was evidently alive in the time of Jesus, where the same mentality is reflected in the miracle stories in the Gospels.

Jehu's Coup

The career of Elisha reaches its climax in 2 Kings 9, in the story of Jehu's coup. The story is memorable primarily for its bloodthirsty character. King Ahaziah of Judah is killed as well as Joram of Israel. Jezebel faces her fate with some grandeur, dressing for the occasion. Her fate is gruesome nonetheless. She is thrown from an upper window, and the dogs eat her flesh. Throughout this story there is a concern for the fulfillment of prophecy, in this case the prediction of Elijah in 1 Kgs 21:23. The story testifies to the hatred of Jezebel in the circles that preserved the stories of Elijah and Elisha. Even more gruesome is the beheading of Ahab's seventy sons by the leaders of Samaria. In the end, Jehu kills all who were left of the house of Ahab and everyone who was associated with the royal house. He also slaughters the kin of Ahaziah of Judah, whom he meets on the way. Finally, he kills every worshiper of Baal in Samaria. This whole bloodbath is justified by "the word of the LORD that he spoke to Elijah" (10:17). In view of the way that Jehu's actions are justified by appeal to prophecy, it seems quite plausible that the prophetic stories were edited at the court of one of his descendants. (Four of his descendants reigned in Samaria, and the dynasty lasted a hundred years.) The Deuteronomistic editor added only a characteristic note of disapproval: even though Jehu allegedly stamped out the worship of Baal, he still walked in the sin of Jeroboam, by maintaining places of worship outside Jerusalem (2 Kgs 10:29). The "sin of Jeroboam" was not an issue at all in the stories in 1 Kings 17–2 Kings 9.

Some question about the historicity of Jehu's coup is raised by the inscription from Tel Dan that mentions the house of David, which (as reconstructed by Finkelstein and Silberman) seems to indicate that the Syrian king who was responsible for the inscription (most probably Hazael) claimed credit for the deaths of the Israelite and Judean kings. It is possible that he regarded Jehu as his instrument, and so, therefore, the accounts are not incompatible. We should also note that the inscription is largely reconstructed, and that the parts in brackets in the sidebar are conjectural. In any case, the question of historicity does not significantly alter the moral issues raised by the story in 2 Kings.

The Tel Dan inscription has been reconstructed as follows:

"[I killed Jeho]ram son of [Ahab] king of Israel, and [I] killed [Ahaz]iahu son of [Jehoram kin]g of the House of David. And I set [their towns into ruins and turned] their land into [destruction]."

(Finkelstein and Silberman, *The Bible Unearthed*, 201)

Jehu's dynasty rivaled that of Omri in longevity. It did not match its prosperity, however. According to 2 Kings 10, the Lord began to trim off parts of the territory of Israel, through the agency of Hazael of Damascus. Moreover, Jehu had seriously ruptured relations between Israel and Phoenicia by killing Jezebel, and with Judah by killing Ahaziah and his kinsmen. Even in northern Israel, the attempt to justify his bloody coup was not entirely successful. About a hundred years afterward, toward the end of Jehu's dynasty, the prophet Hosea announced that God would punish the house of Jehu for the bloodshed of Jezreel. This judgment did not bespeak any sympathy for the house of Omri but acknowledged that the way in which Jehu carried out his coup was blameworthy. We shall find a similar judgment on the Assyrian Empire by the prophet Isaiah (Isaiah 10). Assyria, according to the prophet, was "the rod of YHWH's anger." Nonetheless, Assyria was guilty because of the arrogant way in which it carried out the divine judgment.

The End of the Kingdom of Israel

After the account of Jehu's coup, the narrative of 2 Kings reverts to the annalistic format of 1 Kings. (Annalistic notices are also interspersed in the prophetic narratives to provide a chronological framework.) The succession of kings in Judah normally went smoothly because of the strength of the Davidic dynasty. The only exception concerned the one supreme ruler who was a queen. Athaliah, mother of the murdered Ahaziah, seized the throne in Judah (2 Kings 11) and tried to wipe out all rivals. But one of the sons of Ahaziah was saved from the slaughter. After seven years, he was crowned king in a palace coup and the queen was executed. Athaliah was a granddaughter of King Omri of Israel (2 Kgs 8:26) and was therefore the only non-Davidic ruler of Judah during the period of the Davidic dynasty. Her successor, Jehoiada, tore down a temple of Baal. We may infer that the cult of Baal had been introduced into Jerusalem by the Omride queen.

The period of the Jehu dynasty in northern Israel (roughly from the mid-ninth century B.C.E. to the mid-eighth) was troubled mainly by wars with Syria (Aram). The high point of Syrian dominance was the latter half of the ninth century, when Hazael was king in Damascus. (This is the period reflected in the Tel Dan inscription.) Israel's fortunes improved during the long reign of Jeroboam II (786–746 B.C.E.). According to 2 Kgs 14:25, Jeroboam restored the borders of Israel, from the border of Lebanon to the Dead Sea (the Sea of Arabah). The claim in 14:28, however, that he also "recovered for Israel Damascus and Hamath" seems highly improbable and is not supported by any other evidence. The prophet Amos is said to have prophesied in the reign of Jeroboam, and his oracles shed a much less favorable light on this reign than we might expect from the brief notice in Kings.

The reign of Jeroboam was paralleled in Judah by that of Uzziah or Azariah, who reigned fifty-two years according to 2 Kgs 15:1. (The actual duration of his reign is disputed, but it lasted more than forty years. Uzziah became a leper and had to cede his throne to his son, Jotham. Both kings seem to have been overshadowed by their northern counterpart. An inscription marking the final resting place of Uzziah's bones has survived (Miller and Hayes, *History*, 310).

After the death of Jeroboam, there was rapid turnover of rulers in northern Israel. Six kings ruled in the space of just over twenty years. Four of these were assassinated. Zechariah, son of Jeroboam, was assassinated after a few months on the throne, and his assassin, Shallum, survived only a month. Menahem

(745–737) had to deal with a new factor in Israelite history, the encroachment of the Assyrian Empire. Menahem paid a heavy tribute to the Assyrian king Tiglath-pileser and in return was confirmed on his throne (2 Kgs 15:19). King Joash, father of Jeroboam, had already paid tribute to Assyria at the beginning of the eighth century, but the Assyrian threat had receded at that time. Assyrian power posed a much more serious threat in the 730s than it had sixty years earlier. Menahem's son, Pekahiah, was assassinated by one Pekah, son of Remaliah, who is mentioned in Isaiah 7. The statement that Pekah reigned for twenty years (15:28) must be a mistake. Modern historians credit him only with a short reign of three or four years. During his reign, Tiglath-pileser of Assyria captured territory in the north of Israel, in Gilead, Galilee, and Naphtali, and took the people captive to Assyria (Damascus

Fig. 14.3 **Assyrian king Tiglath-pileser, stone panel from 728 B.C.E. from the Central Palace in Nimrud; in the British Museum.** Commons.wikimedia.org

Fig. 14.4   A winged figure gestures in blessing; from the Great Palace of Sargon II of Assyria, ca. 716–13 B.C.E.; in the Louvre. Commons.wikimedia.org

was destroyed at this time). Shortly thereafter Pekah was assassinated by Hoshea, the last king of Israel. He ruled for nine years, paying tribute to Assyria, but in the end he made the disastrous mistake of conspiring with Egypt and withholding tribute. In 722 Samaria was destroyed by the Assyrians and the area was placed under direct Assyrian rule.

There are numerous Assyrian inscriptions from this period, and they often mention Israel. Unfortunately, we have no historical texts from the Assyrian king Shalmaneser V, who was ruler when Hoshea rebelled. We do, however, have inscriptions from his successor, Sargon II, which provide information about the disposition of Israel after the destruction. Sargon informs us that Samaria had withheld tribute. He states, "I besieged and conquered Samaria, led away as booty 27,290 inhabitants of it." "The town I rebuilt better than it was before and settled therein people from countries which I myself had conquered. I placed an officer of mine as governor over them and imposed upon them tribute as is customary for Assyrian citizens" (*ANET,* 284–85; Miller and Hayes, *History,* 338).

The account in 2 Kgs 17:5-6, 24 is essentially in agreement with this but is astonishingly brief from a historical point of view. Presumably, there was no Israelite chronicle of these events. The Deuteronomists, writing in the south about a century later, were primarily interested in a theological explanation of the events: "This occurred because the people of Israel had sinned against the LORD their God, who had brought them up out of the land of Egypt, from under the hand of Pharaoh, king of Egypt" (17:7). The people of Israel had sinned by worshiping other gods and by having high places, complete with pillars and poles. Most of all, "Jeroboam drove Israel from following the LORD and made them commit great sin" (17:21) by promoting sacrificial worship outside Jerusalem. The disaster had been foretold by the prophets. Whatever we think of the cultic practices of northern Israel, the Deuteronomistic explanation of the destruction of that kingdom is simplistic. Many other factors were involved, primarily Assyrian expansionism and military power. Internal problems in Israel contributed to the problem, but these too were more complex than the failure to anticipate Josiah's reform and Deuteronomic law. We shall have occasion to consider the problems of Israelite society when we discuss the prophecies of Amos and Hosea.

The biblical account and the Assyrian records agree that people from other places were settled in Samaria. According to 2 Kings 17, the new settlers encountered problems (the Lord sent lions among them) that they attributed to the god of the land, whose worship was neglected. Accordingly, a priest of YHWH was sent back. He lived in Bethel and taught the people how they should worship the Lord. According to 17:33, "they worshiped the LORD but they also served their own gods, after the manner of the nations from among whom they had been carried away." All of this bears directly on the characterization of the people who lived in Samaria when the Deuteronomistic History was compiled. Despite the admission that they worshiped the Lord in addition to their foreign deities, the editors insist, "They do not worship the LORD and they do not follow the statutes or the ordinances or the law or the commandment that the LORD commanded the children of Jacob" (17:34). In short, their way of worshiping the Lord was not satisfactory. In the view of the Deuteronomistic editors, the new inhabitants of Samaria were not legitimate descendants of ancient Israel, and they were not partners in the worship of YHWH. This judgment on

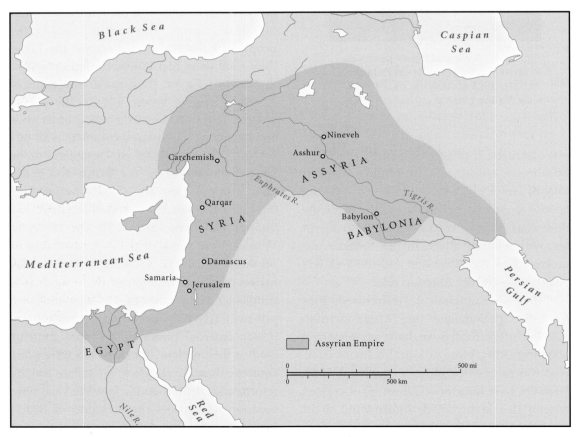

Map 14.2   The Extent of the Assyrian Empire at its zenith.

INTRODUCTION TO THE HEBREW BIBLE

the people of Samaria would be a source of conflict after the Babylonian exile, in the time of Ezra and Nehemiah, and would complicate relations between Jews and Samaritans in the Second Temple period and later.

Judah in the Assyrian Crisis

In Judah, the Assyrian era saw the reign of Hezekiah, the first king to meet the unqualified approval of the Deuteronomists. Hezekiah evidently conducted a reform that was similar to the one later carried out by Josiah. He removed the high places, broke down the pillars, and cut down the sacred poles. He even destroyed the bronze serpent, Nehushtan, that had allegedly been made by Moses in the wilderness (Num 21:6-9). It is difficult to judge the scope of Hezekiah's reform, or even the point at which it took place. According to 2 Kgs 18:1, Hezekiah began to reign in the third year of Hoshea and Samaria fell in the sixth year of his reign. This would require a date around 727 B.C.E. for his ascent to the throne. But Sennacherib's invasion, which is known to have taken place in 701, is said to have been in the fourteenth year of Hezekiah (18:13). This would place his accession in 715. Moreover, he is said to have been twenty-five when he began to reign (18:2), although his father, Ahaz, is said to have died at age thirty-six, and so would only have been eleven when Hezekiah was born! Some of these figures are evidently mistaken.

We know from archaeology that the size of Jerusalem was greatly expanded during Hezekiah's reign. There was presumably an influx of refugees from the north. The suppression of the high places can be understood as part of a strategy of centralization and tightening control in light of the Assyrian threat. There is a much more elaborate account of Hezekiah's reforms in 2 Chronicles 29–32, but the value of Chronicles as a historical source is controversial. We shall return to that issue when we discuss the books of Chronicles in chapter 22.

If indeed Hezekiah attempted to suppress the high places and the worship of foreign gods, he had little success. All these cults were flourishing a century later when Josiah undertook his reform. It may be that there was a relapse in the time of Hezekiah's successor, Manasseh, or it may be that Hezekiah was not thorough in carrying out his reform.

Sennacherib's Invasion

It is uncertain whether Hezekiah was already on the throne at the time of the destruction of Samaria. Jerusalem escaped destruction at that time, presumably by dutifully paying its tribute. Sargon II, who resettled Samaria, claimed in an inscription to be "the subduer of the country of Judah which is far away" (*ANET*, 287). The main narrative in 2 Kings is concerned with events after the death of Sargon in 705 B.C.E. Hezekiah had made preparations for rebellion. These included the construction of the Siloam tunnel, to bring the water from the Gihon spring to a more secure location (the construction of the tunnel is the subject of a famous inscription, *ANET*, 321). He also formed an alliance with other kings in the area. Inevitably, the rebels relied to a considerable degree on Egyptian support. The new Assyrian king, Sennacherib, had to attend to rebellions in various areas, including Babylon, but in 701 he turned his attention to Syria-Palestine. The campaign is described in his inscriptions

(*ANET*, 287–88) and in 2 Kings 18–19. The account in Kings is repeated in Isaiah 36–37. The first paragraph of the Kings account (2 Kgs 18:13-16) is not found in Isaiah.

Sennacherib describes plundering Hezekiah's cities, besieging Jerusalem, and demanding tribute from the king. The tribute included thirty talents of gold, eight hundred talents of silver, and Hezekiah's own daughters, concubines, and male and female musicians. The biblical account says that Hezekiah paid thirty talents of gold and three hundred talents of silver (2 Kgs 18:14). (The Assyrian records are boastful and prone to exaggeration.) But the biblical account says that Hezekiah gave the Assyrians all the silver that was in the house of the Lord and in his own palace, and that he stripped the gold from the doors and doorposts in the temple. There is, then, reasonable correspondence between the Assyrian account and 2 Kgs 18:14-16. The Assyrian records also confirm that Hezekiah was neither killed nor deposed, and that Jerusalem was not destroyed.

The biblical account continues, however, with a colorful and problematic narrative. Assyrian emissaries come up to Jerusalem from Lachish and taunt the king. Their speech is surely a Jewish composition, probably

> Sennacherib describes his dealings with Hezekiah as follows:
>
> As to Hezekiah, the Jew, he did not submit to my yoke, I laid siege to 46 of his strong cities, walled forts and to the countless small villages in their vicinity and conquered (them) by means of well-stamped (earth)ramps, and battering-rams brought (thus) near (to the walls) (combined with) the attack by foot soldiers, (using) mines, breeches as well as sapper work. I drove out (of them) 200,150 people, young and old, male and female, horses, mules, donkeys, camels, big and small cattle beyond counting, and considered (them) booty. Himself I made a prisoner in Jerusalem, his royal residence, like a bird in a cage. I surrounded him with earthwork in order to molest those who were leaving his city's gate. His towns which I had plundered, I took away from his country and gave them (over) to Mittini, king of Ashdod, Padi, king of Ekron, and to Sillibel, king of Gaza. Thus I reduced his country, but I still increased the tribute. (*ANET*, 288)

Fig. 14.5   The Siloam inscription, discovered in 1880, records the construction of Hezekiah's tunnel ca. 701 B.C.E. Commons.wikimedia.org

Deuteronomistic, but it throws vivid light on ancient perceptions of war. The struggle between nations is a struggle between their gods. The might of the god of Assyria is shown by the actual defeat of a long list of peoples, including northern Israel. These peoples might explain the course of events differently. Israelites might say that their God was angry and did not defend them. It was difficult, however, to refute the Assyrian taunt that their God was not able to deliver them.

Moreover, the Assyrians argue that YHWH must be displeased with Hezekiah for tearing down the high places. For the Deuteronomists, the reverse was true. It was true, however, that the Judeans had little hope other than divine intervention. Egypt was a broken reed, which always encouraged the small states in Syria-Palestine to resist the Mesopotamian powers, but never did much to assist them in practice. Hezekiah simply did not have the military power to withstand the Assyrians.

Two other features of the Assyrian's speech should be noted. First, Aramaic was by now the common language of the Near East, and Hezekiah's officials could speak it. Second, the Assyrian appeal to the Judean soldiers shows a fine irony: he promises to take them to "a land like your own land, a land of grain and wine, a land of bread and vineyards, a land of olive oil and honey, that you may live and not die" (2 Kgs 18:32). This is a decidedly optimistic view of Assyrian exile! A similar choice between life and death is presented to the people during the Babylonian crisis a century later, in Jer 21:8-9, another passage where Deuteronomistic editing is probable.

Faced with humiliation and disaster, Hezekiah consults the prophet Isaiah. This is a rare mention of a canonical prophet in the historical books. (Jonah is mentioned briefly in 2 Kgs 14:25.) Since this material is repeated in the book of Isaiah, we shall discuss Isaiah's response in that context, in light of Isaiah's whole career. For the present, it is sufficient to note that Isaiah tells the king not to fear and predicts that God will deliver Jerusalem for the sake of his servant David. It should be noted, however, that the prophet also says that the Judeans would have to eat what grows of itself for a year, and then what grows from

that. Only in the third year would they be able to sow and reap in a normal manner.

The manner of the deliverance is miraculous. The angel of the Lord struck down 185,000 in the camp of the Assyrians. Sennacherib had no choice but to return home. What are we to make of this as a historical report?

It is certainly surprising that Sennacherib did not destroy Jerusalem. Various explanations are possible. An epidemic in the Assyrian army might have given rise to the tradition that the angel of the Lord had intervened. There is a report in Herodotus (2.141) that the Assyrian army was ravaged by a plague of mice at the border of Egypt, but Herodotus's report is also quite fantastic and does not inspire much confidence. According to 2 Kgs 19:9, Sennacherib heard that "King Tirhakah of Ethiopia" had set out to fight against him. (Tirhakah became pharaoh of Egypt only c. 690 B.C.E., but he had been a general in the Egyptian army long before that.) Sennacherib claimed victory in the battle (*ANET*, 287), but the victory may have been less decisive than he claimed. Another possibility is suggested by the words of Isaiah in 2 Kgs 19:7: "I will put a spirit in him so that he shall hear a rumor and return to his own land." No doubt, Sennacherib could have conquered Jerusalem, but it would have taken time. He may have had pressing affairs back home. Timely submission by Hezekiah may have saved the city and his own life.

The account in 2 Kings, however, presents us with two quite different outcomes of the episode. In the first, Hezekiah had to scrape the gold off the temple to pay off the Assyrians. In the second, the Assyrian army was devastated and went home in defeat. Some scholars have argued that Sennacherib invaded Judah twice. The mention of Tirhakah as king, which he became only about 690 B.C.E., lends a little support to this view, but not enough. There is no other archaeological or historical evidence for a second campaign. Thus it is most likely that we have two reports of the same incident from different vantage points.

There is no doubt that Judah was brought to its knees by the Assyrians. For the survivors in Jerusalem, however, the more remarkable thing was that the city was not destroyed. This unexpected deliverance is celebrated in the story of the angel of the Lord. It contributed to the myth of the inviolability of Zion, which we have seen in connection with the temple ideology. According to Ps 46:5, "God is in the midst of the city; it shall not be moved; God will help it when the morning dawns." Psalm 48 tells how kings who came up against Jerusalem were seized with panic and fled. It is possible that these psalms were inspired by the fact that Sennacherib did not destroy Jerusalem. More probably, the belief that the city was protected by YHWH was older, but it was powerfully reinforced by this deliverance. A century later, the confidence inspired by this myth would prove to be false when the city was destroyed by the Babylonians.

The End of the Kingdom of Judah

The "good" King Hezekiah is followed in 2 Kings 21 by Manasseh, who reigns for fifty-five years and does "more wicked things than all the Amorites did, who were before him" (21:11). Manasseh does everything of which the Deuteronomists disapprove, restoring the high places that Hezekiah had torn down, erecting altars for Baal, and even making his son "pass through fire" as a burnt offering. He

is also said to have practiced soothsaying and dealt with mediums. How far these practices were traditional in Judah and how far they were introduced by Manasseh under Assyrian influence, is disputed. At least the high places and the worship of Baal were traditional, although the cult of Baal was not as widespread in Judah as it was in northern Israel. The Deuteronomists paint Manasseh in lurid colors, in part to explain why there were so many abuses when Josiah came to the throne, and in part to explain the fate that ultimately befell Judah, despite the reforms of Hezekiah and Josiah. According to 21:10-15, it is because of the sins of Manasseh that the Lord resolves to destroy Jerusalem.

We have already discussed the reforms of Josiah in connection with the book of Deuteronomy. The account indirectly gives a vivid picture of religion in Judah before the reform, with widespread worship of Baal and Asherah. The reforms represent the climax of the Deuteronomistic History. The first edition of the work was probably promulgated during the reign of Josiah. We might expect that the reform would earn Judah a reprieve in the eyes of the Lord, but this is not what happens. When the pharaoh goes to meet the king of Assyria at the Euphrates, Josiah goes to meet him at Megiddo, and, we are told, the pharaoh killed him. The parallel account in 2 Chron 35:20-24 makes clear that Josiah went to fight the pharaoh, although it is not at all clear why he should have done so. Chronicles explains that Josiah was killed by archers in battle. The account in Kings is ambiguous. The pharaoh may have had Josiah executed for whatever reason. In any case, the premature death of the reforming king confounds the expectations of Deuteronomic theology.

The editors, however, provide an explanation. In 2 Kgs 22:20 the Lord tells Josiah: "I will gather you to your ancestors, and you shall be gathered to your grave in peace; your eyes shall not see all the disaster that I will bring on this place." Josiah is to be spared the destruction of Jerusalem by the Babylonians. The problem with this explanation is that death at the hands of the pharaoh was hardly a peaceful demise.

The actual account of the destruction of Jerusalem is quite terse. (An even terser account is found in the *Babylonian Chronicles*; see Miller and Hayes, *History*, 380–81.) Babylon now replaced Assyria as the invading power, under the leadership of Nebuchadnezzar II. Josiah's son Jehoiakim submitted for a while but then revolted. He died before he could be punished. His son Jehoiachin promptly surrendered and was taken prisoner to Babylon in 597 B.C.E., together with thousands of the upper echelon of Judean society. Jehoiachin's uncle, Zedekiah, was made king in his place. He served Babylon for a time but eventually succumbed to the temptation to rebel. His punishment was brutal. His sons were killed before his eyes,

and his eyes were then put out. Jerusalem was destroyed and the temple burned down. The Babylonians allegedly carried into exile "all the rest of the population" except for some of the poorest people, who were left to be vinedressers and tillers of the soil (25:12).

The Deuteronomistic explanation of these disastrous events is simple, even simplistic: "Surely this came upon Judah at the command of the LORD, to remove them out of his sight, for the sins of Manasseh" (24:3). The assumption is that the course of history is controlled by YHWH, so whatever happens must reflect his will. But it is also assumed that the course of history is determined by the behavior of Israel and Judah. Babylonian policy and Near Eastern politics are of little account. It was a merit of this explanation that it encouraged the Jewish people to look to themselves for the cause of their misfortunes, rather than to pity themselves as the victims of history. As Shakespeare would say, "The fault, dear Brutus, is not in our stars but in ourselves that we are underlings." But ultimately, this explanation of history would not prove satisfactory. It placed too much blame on the victims. Some of the most creative and powerful voices in the Hebrew Bible (the prophet we call Second Isaiah, Job) will challenge and undermine this theology of history.

The Deuteronomistic History, however, ends on a positive note. After thirty-seven years of exile, King Jehoiachin was released from prison and treated with respect by the king of Babylon. Life would go on. Jewish exiles would return to Jerusalem. The destruction of the states of Israel and Judah would set the stage for the emergence of Judaism as a worldwide religion.

The Conquest of Jerusalem

Year 7, month of Kislimu: The king of Akkad moved his army into Haddi land, laid siege to the city of Judah, and the king took the city on the second day of the month Addaru. He appointed in it a [new] king to his liking, took heavy booty from it, and brought it into Babylon.

(*Babyonian Chronicle*, trans. A. Leo Oppenheim; *ANET*, 564.

FOR FURTHER READING

Commentaries

The commentaries of Fritz, Hens-Piazza, Nelson, Seow, and Sweeney listed in chapter 13 also cover 2 Kings.

M. Cogan and H. Tadmor, *II Kings* (AB 11: New York: Doubleday, 1988). Good historical and philological commentary.

T. R. Hobbs, *2 Kings* (WBC 12; Waco: Word, 1985). Thorough literary and historical discussion.

B. O. Long, *2 Kings* (FOTL 10; Grand Rapids: Eerdmans, 1991). Form-critical commentary. Clarifies literary structure.

Historical Issues

J. Bright, *A History of Israel* (4th ed.; Louisville: Westminster John Knox, 2000). Classic treatment. Assumes historical reliability of biblical record but also draws extensively on other Near Eastern sources.

I. Finkelstein and N. A. Silberman, *The Bible Unearthed: Archaeology's New Vision of Ancient Israel and the Origin of Its Sacred Texts* (New York: Free Press, 2001), 206–25, 229–95. Up-to-date archaeological information.

L. L. Grabbe, ed., *Good Kings and Bad Kings* (London: T&T Clark, 2005). Essays on Judah in the seventh century, with special focus on Josiah.

H. Hagelia, *The Dan Debate: The Tel Dan Inscription in Recent Research* (Sheffield: Sheffield Phoenix, 2009). Overview of the debate about the Tel Dan inscription and defense of the editors' interpretation.

J. M. Miller and J. H. Hayes, *A History of Ancient Israel and Judah* (Philadelphia: Westminster, 1986), 314–415. Valuable for citation of primary sources.

R. A. Young, *Hezekiah in History and Tradition* (Leiden: Brill, 2012), 9–150. Important discussion of chronology of Hezekiah.

Literary and Redactional Studies

The books of Knoppers and McKenzie listed in chapter 13 are also relevant here.

A. Rofé, *The Prophetical Stories* (Jerusalem: Magnes, 1988). Innovative study of the prophetic narratives from a form-critical perspective.

M. A. Sweeney, *King Josiah of Judah: The Lost Messiah of Israel* (New York: Oxford University Press, 2001). A speculative attempt to reconstruct the aims of Josiah, drawing on prophetic sources as well as 2 Kings.

S. J. de Vries, *Prophet against Prophet* (Grand Rapids: Eerdmans, 1978). Detailed examination of 1 Kings 22 and the prophetic legends.

R. R. Wilson, "How Was the Bible Written? Reflections on Sources and Authors in the Book of Kings," in S. Dolansky, ed., *Sacred History: Sacred Literature: Essays on Ancient Israel, the Bible and Religion in Honor of R. E. Friedman* (Winona Lake, IN: Eisenbrauns, 2008), 133–43. Discussion of Deuteronomistic editing of the Elijah and Elisha stories.

PART THREE

Prophecy

P3.1   A winged lamassu from the Great Palace in Nimrud; in the Louvre. Commons.wikimedia.org

Introduction

The word *prophecy* comes from the Greek *prophētēs,* "proclaimer," and refers to one who speaks on behalf of a god or goddess. The roles of such spokesmen or spokeswomen vary from one culture to another, and various terms are used to describe them. Prophets typically receive their revelations in a state of ecstasy, either by seeing visions or by direct inspiration. In the Hebrew Bible, the most frequent term for such intermediaries is *nabi'.* The etymology of this word is disputed, but it most probably means "one who is called" (from the verb *bo',* "to come"). Other figures, who are called "seers" *(ro'eh, chozeh)* or "men of God" are also subsumed under the category prophecy. In general, prophecy is distinguished from divination, which attempts to discern the will of the deity by various means, such as the examination of the liver of a sacrificial victim or observing the flight of birds. (In principle, the distinction is between spontaneous inspiration, presumably by a deity, and ritual consultation, which requires human initiative. In practice, the line between prophecy and divination is not always clear.) The book of Deuteronomy condemns anyone "who practices divination, or is a soothsayer, or an augur, or a sorcerer, or one who casts spells, or who consults ghosts or spirits, or who seeks oracles from the dead" (Deut 18:10-11). It is safe to infer that all of these practices were current in ancient Judah before Josiah's reform. Moreover, some forms of divination were deemed acceptable in Israel, most notably the use of Urim and Thummim (probably some kind of pebbles or sticks) by the priests (see Num 27:21; Deut 33:8). Divination of this kind was a priestly, rather than prophetic, function, and the main references to it are in 1 Samuel in stories about Saul and David (e.g., 1 Sam 14:18-19; 23:9-12). Beginning with David and Nathan, the kings of Israel and Judah seek to know the will of the Lord by consulting prophets rather than by divination.

Prophecy in the Ancient Near East

Even though prophecy has often been regarded as a distinctively Israelite phenomenon, it was widespread in the ancient Near East, although the actual form of prophecy varied from one society to another. One major source of information is found in the royal archives of Mari on the Euphrates, in northern Mesopotamia, from the eighteenth century B.C.E. Prophetic activity is mentioned in some fifty letters (of a corpus of eight thousand) and in twelve economic and administrative texts (out of twelve thousand). While the proportion of texts referring to prophetic activity is small, the texts in question come from a wide area, from Syria to Babylon. The prophetic figures, who are both male and female, are most often called *apilu/apiltu* "answerer," or *muhhu/muhhutu* "ecstatic"; but some other terms, including *nabu* (cognate of Hebrew *nabi'*), are also used. The manner in which these figures receive their messages from the deities is not always indicated. Several receive revelation in dreams. A number receive them in temples. The *muhhu* goes into ecstasy. In one instance, a *muhhu* eats a raw lamb in public and then proceeds to deliver his message. Because of the nature of the Mari archive, the oracles of these figures deal predominantly with the affairs of the king. They typically assure the king of success or warn of dangers. They sometimes warn that cultic acts have been neglected. A few letters remind the king of his obligation to see that justice is done. The messages are presented as being in the self-interest of the king. While these prophecies were taken seriously, they seem to have been regarded as inferior to technical divination and were subject to confirmation by court diviners.

Another major source of information about Near Eastern prophecy is found in Assyrian archives from the seventh century B.C.E. Here the most common titles are *muhhu/muhhutu*, "ecstatic" (a variant of the title in the Mari letters), and *raggimu/raggimtu*, "proclaimer." Here again, the texts come from royal archives and deal predominantly with the affairs of the king. Typically they provide assurance of divine support in time of crisis (e.g., in crushing a rebellion), often telling the king to "fear not." Unlike the situation at Mari, the Assyrian prophets do not seem to have been subject to verification. They are presented, and apparently accepted, as the words of a god or

Fig. P3.2 Clay models of livers, for training in divination; from the royal palace in Mari, nineteenth or eighteenth century B.C.E.; in the Louvre. Commons.wikimedia.org

goddess: "Ishtar of Arbela has said . . ." or "the word of Ishtar of Arbela. . . ." We should not think, however, that all Assyrian oracles were favorable to the kings or accepted as authentic. One of the treaty texts of King Esarhaddon requires the vassal to inform the king of any negative utterance by a proclaimer, ecstatic, or inquirer. The Assyrian kings do not seem to allow for the possibility that a negative oracle might be authentic.

One noteworthy feature of the Assyrian oracles is that more than two-thirds of them are preserved in collections on tablets. The oracles were copied for posterity by scribes, who identified the prophetic speakers but evidently believed that the words retained validity beyond their original situations. These oracle collections provide an important analogy for the biblical prophetic books, which likewise preserve for later generations words that were spoken in quite specific situations. In the case of the Assyrian oracles, the preservation may have been motivated by the desire to remind people of the promises of divine support that had been given to the ruling dynasty.

Apart from these Mesopotamian archives, our evidence for ancient Near Eastern prophecy is sparse, although it is sufficient to show that the phenomenon existed. The tale of the Egyptian Wen-Amon, from the eleventh century B.C.E., reports a case of ecstatic prophecy in the Canaanite or Phoenician coastal city of Byblos (*ANET*, 26). We have already encountered prophets of Baal and Asherah in the books of Kings. A plaster inscription from Tell Deir Alla in Jordan, from about 700 B.C.E., refers to Balaam, son of Beor, a "seer of the gods" (cf. Numbers 22–24). An inscription from Syria from about 800 B.C.E. reports how King Zakkur of Hamath prayed to Baal-shamayn during a siege, and Baal answered him by means of visionaries, and told him to "fear not." The scantiness of this evidence reflects the general scarcity of material from Syria and Canaan. Nonetheless, the evidence

that has survived is sufficient to show that prophecy was a widespread phenomenon throughout the ancient Near East.

Prophecy in Israel

The study of prophecy in ancient Israel has usually focused on the great personalities of the prophets whose oracles are preserved in the books that bear their names. The sociologist Max Weber defined the prophet as "a purely individual bearer of charisma, who by virtue of his mission proclaims a religious doctrine or divine commandment" (M. Weber, *Economy and Society* [ed. G. Roth and C. Wittich; 2 vols.; reprint, Berkeley: Univ. of California Press, 1978], 1:439). The "purely individual" label is misleading, however. As we have seen from the tales of the prophets in the books of Kings, prophets in ancient Israel typically belonged to guilds or groups and were often maintained and supported by the royal establishment. (Some prophets may also have been attached to the temples.) The prophets who gave their names to the biblical books were exceptional, insofar as they typically stood apart from these guilds (e.g., Amos) and sometimes were in conflict with them (e.g., Jeremiah). Weber's definition, of course, was based on these biblical prophets, not on the broader historical phenomenon in ancient Israel. Even the biblical prophets, however, cannot be described as "purely individual." Some, like Isaiah, worked in close relationship with the royal court and the temple. All operated within the conventions of Israelite society and presupposed traditions that were shared by their audiences. All were passionately engaged with the events of their time. No prophet could function in isolation from society. The effectiveness of their message required an audience that accepted the legitimacy of prophecy and that shared at least some of their basic convictions.

It is of the essence of prophecy that the prophets addressed specific situations in highly concrete terms. Their message cannot be appreciated without consideration of its historical context. Nonetheless, like many of the Assyrian prophecies, the biblical oracles come to us embedded in collections that were made for later generations. Moreover, the biblical prophetic books are often edited with later situations in mind. There is then an inevitable tension between the words of the prophets in their original context and the "canonical shape" given to their oracles by later editors. Much of the history of scholarship over the last two hundred years has been concerned primarily with the original words of the prophets. In recent years, the pendulum has swung toward a focus on the final form of the prophetic books in their canonical context. (This tendency is especially evident in attempts to treat the twelve minor prophets as a unit. We will return to this at the end of chapter 20.) Both interests are clearly legitimate, and even necessary, but it is important to recognize the tension between them. The historical prophets whose oracles are preserved in these books were often highly critical of the political and religious establishments of their day. The scribes who edited their books, however, were part of the establishment of later generations. Consequently, they often try to place the older oracles in the context of an authoritative tradition. In some cases, this has a moderating effect on oracles that may seem extreme outside (or even in) their historical context. In other cases, the editorial process may seem to take the edge off powerful prophetic oracles and dull their effect. The preference of an interpreter for the original prophets or for the canonical editors often reflects his or her trust or distrust of political and religious institutions in general.

In the following chapters, I try to do justice both to the historical prophets and to their later editors. In order to do this, however, it is necessary to depart from the canonical order of the books and begin by considering the prophets in their historical context. We shall, however, also take note of the ways in which their oracles were edited, and at the end of part 3 we shall reflect on the nature and purpose of the collection of the prophetic books.

FOR FURTHER READING

J. Blenkinsopp, *A History of Prophecy in Israel* (2nd ed.; Louisville: Westminster John Knox, 1996). Reliable historical and literary introduction to the prophets and their books.

T. Collins, *The Mantle of Elijah: The Redaction Criticism of the Prophetical Books* (Sheffield: Sheffield Academic Press, 1992). Overview of the redaction of the prophetic books.

J. Day, ed., *Prophecy and the Prophets in Ancient Israel* (London: T&T Clark, 2010). Wide-ranging collection, addressing both the phenomenon of prophecy and individual prophetic books.

D. V. Edelman and E. Ben Zvi, *The Production of Prophecy: Constructing Prophecy and Prophets in Yehud* (London: Equinox, 2009). A collection of essays with various suggestions about the formation of the prophetic books after the exile.

L. L. Grabbe and Martti Nissinen, eds., *Constructs of Prophecy in the Former and Latter Prophets and Other Texts* (Atlanta: SBL, 2011). Collection of essays on various construals of prophecy in the biblical tradition.

H. B. Huffmon, "Prophecy, Ancient Near Eastern," *ABD* 5:477–82. Overview of evidence for prophecy in the ancient Near East.

K. Koch, *The Prophets* (M. Kohl; 2 vols.; Philadelphia: Fortress Press, 1984). Vivid, distinctive interpretation of the Prophets.

M. Nissinen, ed., *Prophecy in Its Ancient Near Eastern Context: Mesopotamian, Biblical and Arabian Perspectives* (Symposium Series 13; Atlanta: SBL, 2000); *Prophets and Prophecy in the Ancient Near East* (Leiden: Brill, 2003). Excellent collections of essays on prophecy in the ancient Near East.

T. Overholt, *Channels of Prophecy: The Social Dynamics of Prophecy* (Minneapolis: Fortress Press, 1989). Prophecy in cross-cultural and interdisciplinary perspective.

S. Parpola, *Assyrian Prophecies* (Helsinki: Helsinki University Press, 1998). Primary edition of Assyrian prophetic texts.

D. L. Petersen, *The Prophetic Literature: An Introduction* (Louisville: Westminster John Knox, 2002). Focuses on literary aspects of the prophetic books.

———, ed., *Prophecy in Israel* (Issues in Religion and Theology 10; Philadelphia: Fortress Press, 1987). Collection of classic essays on prophecy.

A. Rofé, *Introduction to the Prophetic Literature* (The Biblical Seminar 49; Sheffield: Sheffield Academic Press, 1997). Concise introduction to the critical questions.

C. R. Seitz, *Prophecy and Hermeneutics: Toward a New Introduction to the Prophets* (Grand Rapids: Baker, 2007). Plea for a canonical approach, emphasizing canonical order.

O. H. Steck, *The Prophetic Books and Their Theological Witness* (trans. J. D. Nogalski; St. Louis, MO: Chalice, 2000). Emphasis on literary and theological aspects of the prophetic books.

J. Stökl, *Prophecy in the Ancient Near East: A Philological and Sociological Comparison* (Leiden: Brill, 2012). Notes that Israelite prophets were more critical of rulers than other Near Eastern prophets.

M. A. Sweeney, *The Prophetic Literature* (Nashville: Abingdon, 2005). Synchronic introduction to prophetic books, but with attention to diachronic dimensions.

R. L. Troxel, *Prophetic Literature. From Oracles to Books* (Oxford: Wiley Blackwell, 2012). Introduction to the formation of the prophetic books.

G. von Rad, *Old Testament Theology* (trans. D. M. G. Stalker; 2 vols.; New York: Harper & Row, 1961–65), 2:3–315. Influential introduction to the Prophets from the perspective of the history of the traditions.

R. R. Wilson, *Prophecy and Society in Ancient Israel* (Philadelphia: Fortress Press, 1977). Fundamental study of Israelite prophecy in sociological and anthropological perspective.

CHAPTER 15
Amos and Hosea

INTRODUCTION

We turn in this chapter to consider two eighth-century prophets of the northern kingdom, Amos and Hosea.

Amos

The Prophet

The preface to the book of Amos identifies him as a shepherd from Tekoa, and dates his prophecy to the time of King Jeroboam, son of Joash (785–745 B.C.E.) of Israel and the roughly contemporary King Uzziah of Judah. Tekoa is in Judah, some ten miles south of Jerusalem. Yet Amos seems to have prophesied at Bethel, which was one of the royal sanctuaries of the northern kingdom. Bethel was at the southernmost edge of the northern kingdom, only ten to eleven miles north of Jerusalem, so Amos did not have to travel very far to preach there. Nonetheless, the geography raises questions about Amos's political loyalties. Did he regard the boundary between Israel and Judah as insignificant because all were one people of YHWH? Or was he a Davidic loyalist who was especially critical of

the cult at Bethel because of the separation of the northern kingdom from Jerusalem? There is no doubt that the book was edited in the southern kingdom and presents a Judean perspective in its canonical form. This perspective is clear in the introductory saying in 1:1 ("The LORD roars from Zion . . ."; cf. Joel 3:16) and in the concluding promise that the Lord will raise up "the fallen booth of David" (Amos 9:11-15). It is not at all clear, however, that the eighth-century prophet Amos was promoting Davidic rule, or that he was concerned with the relations between the two kingdoms. He was also critical of "those who are at ease in Zion" (6:1). It might have been more difficult, however, for a man from Tekoa to preach in Jerusalem on the doorstep of the king than in Bethel where he was at some distance from the royal court.

The date assigned to Amos raises another intriguing question. Amos prophesied the destruction of the northern kingdom. His

Fig. 15.1 Tekoa in Israel. Konstantin Hoshana

prophecy was fulfilled by the Assyrian destruction of Samaria in 722 B.C.E. But the Assyrian threat was not in evidence during the reign of Jeroboam and developed only in the reign of Tiglath-pileser III, whose reign began about the time of Jeroboam's death. Amos never mentions Assyria in his oracles, but a few passages refer to the punishment of exile, which was typical Assyrian policy (5:5, 27). Of course victors had always taken captives in war, from the earliest time, and had used or sold them as slaves. The innovation of the Assyrians was mass deportation as a way of subduing an area by resettling it. At least some passages in Amos, such as 5:27, seem to envision mass deportation. These oracles are more easily explained if they are dated somewhat later, when Assyria was a threat to Israel. Amos 6:2, which invites comparison of Israel with Calneh, Hamath, and Gath, must be interpreted in light of the Assyrian conquest of these regions in the 730s. Alternatively, the

allusions to later events and to the specifically Assyrian practice of mass deportation may have been added later, in the course of the transmission of the book.

The prophecy of Amos is also dated "two years before the earthquake." This earthquake is also mentioned in Zech 14:5, but it cannot be dated precisely. That such a precise date is given, however, suggests that the prophetic career of Amos was quite short, perhaps no more than a single season. Alternatively, this date may indicate only the beginning of the prophet's career.

Apart from the introductory preface, there is only one biographical notice in the book of Amos. This is found in 7:10-14 and relates an encounter between Amos and the priest of Bethel. The placement of this notice is probably due to the fact that the story was transmitted in connection with Amos's visions at Bethel. Some scholars have seen a parallel between this incident and the confrontation between an anonymous Judean prophet and Jeroboam I by the altar of Bethel in 1 Kings 13. If the episode in Amos were invented on the model of that passage, however, we should expect that the prophet would address the king directly. The account of the reign of Jeroboam II in 2 Kings makes no mention of Amos and gives a relatively benign account of Jeroboam.

Whatever its origin, the story of the encounter with the priest of Bethel is remarkable in several respects. Amos was preaching that divine punishment was about to befall the kingdom of Israel. The priest Amaziah was understandably nervous about this and worried lest the king think he endorsed the preaching of Amos and was party to a conspiracy. He is all the more irritated by the fact that Amos is a Judean. Therefore he tells him to go back to where he came from, for Bethel is a royal sanctuary and loyal to Jeroboam. The response of Amos has given rise to much commentary: "I am no prophet, nor the son of a prophet." The Hebrew literally reads: "No prophet I" (the term for "prophet" is *nabi'*). Some scholars translate, "I was no prophet," since Amos goes on to say that he was a herdsman and a dresser of sycamores until the Lord called him. But Amos does not say that he became a *nabi'*, and Amaziah calls him not a *nabi'* but a *chozeh* (seer). The point is that Amos is not a member of a prophetic guild, of the "sons of the prophets" who ate at the king's table (such as we saw in the story of Micaiah ben Imlah in 1 Kings 22). He is a freelancer, so to speak, and therefore he is not beholden to the king and does not care whether Bethel is a royal temple. He was also probably a person of independent means. We do not know how extensive his flocks or trees were, but he is

evidently not in the service of anyone else, and he seems to be well informed on the affairs of Israel, and to some extent on international events. The translation "I am not a prophet" is somewhat misleading. Amos certainly claims to be a spokesman for YHWH. The issue is what kind of prophet he is.

The style of Amos's prophecy is in the tradition of Elijah rather than that of Nathan. He is confrontational and abrasive. There is no attempt to win over the people he condemns. The prophecy that Amaziah's wife would become a prostitute could only enrage the priest. It may also have functioned as a curse that was intended not only to predict but to bring about what was predicted. We do not know what happened to Amaziah. It is unlikely that he lived long enough to be taken into exile. Jeroboam certainly did not die by the sword. That this prophecy was not fulfilled argues strongly for its authenticity. Why would a later editor have ascribed to Amos a prophecy that was manifestly incorrect? The editors may have felt, however, that Amos's prophecies were substantially fulfilled by the Assyrian conquest, and may have added the references to the exile of Israel to clarify the point, or interpreted them in this light.

The Oracles of Amos

The book of Amos can be divided into three parts. After the introductory verses, the book begins with a series of oracles against various nations, concluding with Israel (1:3—2:16). The middle part of the book (chaps. 3–6) contains a collection of short oracles. The last part (chaps. 7–9) consists of a series of vision reports, with the account of the confrontation with Amaziah.

The Oracles against the Nations

Oracles against foreign nations were the stock in trade of ancient Israelite prophets. We have seen an illustration of the situation in which such oracles might be uttered in the story of Micaiah ben Imlah in 1 Kings 22, where the prophets conduct a virtual pep rally before the start of a military campaign. There are long sections of such oracles in other prophetic books (e.g., Isaiah 13–19; Jeremiah 46–51). The nations mentioned here are Israel's immediate neighbors. The list has been expanded in the course of transmission. The most obvious addition is the oracle against Judah. The focus on "the law of the LORD" is Deuteronomic and stands in sharp contrast with the highly specific charges in the other oracles (e.g., "They sell the righteous for silver and the needy for a pair of sandals"). The oracles against Tyre and Edom are also suspect (both have shortened endings, and the oracle against Tyre repeats language from the previous oracles). Regardless of the number of nations included, the structure of this section is clear enough. Israelite prophets were expected to denounce foreign nations. The shock comes when Amos denounces Israel just like all the others.

The oracles are formulaic ("For three transgressions and for four" is an idiom meaning "for the numerous transgressions"). The grounds for the denunciations are generally humanistic. Damascus threshed Gilead (in Transjordan) with sledges of iron. Gaza sold entire communities as slaves to Edom. The Ammonites ripped open pregnant women in Gilead. Each of these cases could be read as instances of aggression against Israel, but Amos's concerns are not nationalistic. So he condemns Moab "because he burned to lime the bones of the king of Edom" (2:1). This is a crime of one Gentile against another and can only be viewed as a crime against humanity. Amos operates with a concept of universal justice, such as we often find in the wisdom literature. His horizon is broader than the specific revelation to Israel.

The accusations against Israel are likewise humanistic in nature: they trample the poor into the dust of the earth (2:7). To be sure, they also evoke the laws of the Pentateuch; specifically, the reference to garments taken in pledge (2:8) recalls Exod 22:25 and Deut 24:17. The condemnation of father and son who sleep with the same girl (2:7) is at least in accordance with the spirit of the laws in Leviticus 20. The entire condemnation of Israel has been read as an example of a "covenant lawsuit" or *ribh* (the Hebrew word for disputation). YHWH reminds the Israelites of the favors he has shown them ("I destroyed the Amorites before them"), and threatens them with punishment because of their disobedience. The structure of the argument, which appeals both to the recollection of history and to the consequences of obedience or disobedience, is similar to the "covenant form" derived from ancient Near Eastern treaties, especially in the book of Deuteronomy. Some scholars suspect, however, that the similarity to Deuteronomy is due to Deuteronomistic editors. The concern for prophets and nazirites in vv. 11-12 seems out of context in Amos. The oracle against Israel is similar to those against the other nations except for vv. 9-12, precisely the verses that give the passage a Deuteronomic, covenantal flavor.

The point at issue here is important for understanding the ethics of a prophet such as Amos, and his place in the history of Israelite religion. One view of the subject regards the covenant as foundational, and assumes that such a covenant was known already in the beginnings of Israel, before the rise of the monarchy. On this view, prophets such as Amos were traditionalists, calling Israel back to the observance of its original norms. This view has generally been favored in American scholarship, under the influence of the Albright school. The other view sees the covenant as found in Deuteronomy as a late development, influenced by the preaching of the prophets. On this view, the prophets were highly original figures who changed the nature of Israelite religion and influenced its ultimate formulation in the Bible. This view has been championed by many (but by no means all) German scholars, from the time of Wellhausen. The second view does not deny that the exodus was celebrated in the Israelite cult before the rise of the prophets, or that there was a concept of the election of Israel from early times. The issue is whether that concept of election entailed moral obligation or was tied to a corpus of laws in the earlier period. The originality of the prophets need not be exaggerated in any case. The concepts of justice and righteousness were well established throughout the ancient Near East long before the rise of Israel (cf. the Code of Hammurabi). The preaching of the prophets certainly drew on ancient tradition. The issue is whether these traditions were formulated in a way similar to what we now find in the book of Deuteronomy.

The sources of Amos's thought are likely to remain controversial, but we can at least get a sense from his oracles of the nature of the cult at Bethel, which he criticized strongly, and of the popular understanding of the exodus tradition in the northern kingdom. It is clear that Amos differed sharply from his contemporaries on the role and nature of the cult, and on the implications of the election of Israel. The people of Israel in the mid-eighth century b.c.e. did not share the understanding of exodus and covenant that we find in Deuteronomy. If there was an older covenantal tradition, it had been lost from view. The preaching of Amos can be understood as shaping the development of a covenantal tradition more easily than as harking back to a tradition that had been forgotten.

The Central Oracles

The understanding of the exodus and of the election of Israel is brought to the fore immediately in Amos 3:2: "You alone have I known of all the families of the earth; therefore I will punish you for all your iniquities." This brief oracle could be read as an abbreviated covenant lawsuit: "You alone have I known; therefore you should have kept the commandments, but since you did not, I will punish you." It is more likely, however, that Amos is alluding to and subverting the common Israelite understanding of the exodus. If YHWH has known Israel alone, this should be good news. It should lead to a promise of divine blessing and support, such as was given to Abraham and David. As in the series of oracles against the nations, Amos subverts the expectations of his hearers. There is no doubt that the exodus had been celebrated at Bethel from the time of Jeroboam I. Amos does not dispute that YHWH brought Israel out of Egypt, but he questions the significance attached to it. For him, election only means greater responsibility. Israel has less excuse for its misconduct than other peoples.

The sayings in Amos 3:3-8 are a rare quasi-philosophical reflection on the premises of the prophecies. Amos does not claim that his revelation is a bolt from the blue or that he is telling his audience anything that they could not know by themselves. The reasoning is similar to what we often find in Near Eastern wisdom literature, and that we shall meet again in the book of Proverbs. Things do not happen randomly. Actions have predictable consequences. Consequently, disaster does not befall a city "unless the LORD has done it"(3:6). In the context there is no reference to any specific disaster, but the comment is ominous. Disaster will surely befall Samaria and all of the kingdom of Israel. It is the contention of Amos that this can happen only because of the Lord, presumably as a punishment. Amos may be described as a mono-Yahwist, if not a strict monotheist. He believes that everything that happens can be attributed to the Lord. He acknowledges no other forces that might be responsible. The passage also offers a brief but evocative comment on the compulsion that led him to prophesy: just as one cannot help but be afraid if a lion roars, so one cannot help but prophesy if the Lord speaks (3:8). We shall find a similar sense of compulsion in the case of Jeremiah, where we shall have occasion to reflect further on the nature of the prophetic vocation.

Two themes predominate in the central oracles of Amos. One is social injustice, a topic already broached in the condemnation of Israel in chapter 2. Colorful examples are found in 4:1-3, which caricatures the women of Samaria as "cows of Bashan" (Bashan was a fertile area in Transjordan), and 6:4-7, which derides those who lie on beds of ivory and drink wine from bowls. The latter passage describes an institution called *marzeach*. (A form of the word is found in Amos 6:7, where

Fig. 15.2   Intricate ivory decoration from Samaria depicting a falcon-headed god (Horus, associated with monarchy?) kneeling next to a seated Maat figure; Israel Museum, Jerusalem.
Erich Lessing/ArtResource, NY

it is translated "revelry" in the NRSV.) This was an old Canaanite institution known at Ugarit in the fourteenth century B.C.E. It involved a banquet that lasted several days with copious drinking of wine. At least in some contexts, the occasion was the commemoration of the dead and possibly communion with them. Such celebrations involved great expense. The luxury of Samaria is confirmed by archaeology. One of the most spectacular finds was a collection of ivories, which came from furniture and inlaid walls in the royal palaces (cf. the "beds of ivory" of Amos 6:4). Amos even condemns music as part of the excessive luxury. Those who were at ease, whether in Zion or Samaria, enjoyed their leisure at the expense of the poor, who were forced into slavery when they could not pay their debts. It should be noted that Amos's objection to the *marzeach* was not based on its Canaanite origin, but on the extravagance and indulgence associated with it.

The other recurring theme is condemnation of the cult, especially at Bethel. "Come to Bethel and transgress; to Gilgal and multiply transgressions" (4:4). It is possible to read this pronouncement from a Deuteronomistic perspective: the cult at Bethel was inherently sinful because it was not in Jerusalem. No doubt, this is how the passage was read by many after Josiah's reform. The original concerns of Amos, however, were different. They emerge most clearly in 5:18-27. This famous passage pronounces woe on those "who desire the day of the LORD" (5:18). There has been much debate as to what is meant by "the Day of the LORD." In later times it came to mean the day of judgment. Already in the time of Amos it could refer to a day of divine intervention in battle. In this context, however, it clearly refers to a cultic celebration, perhaps the Festival of Tabernacles or Sukkoth, which was known as "the feast of YHWH" in later times. Tabernacles was celebrated at the end of the grape harvest. It was a joyful festival, marked by drinking wine. The "Day of YHWH" was also a celebration of the greatness of YHWH, and, by implication, the greatness of his people Israel. It was a day of light, in the sense of being a joyful occasion and a celebration of the blessings of Israel.

Amos, however, was not one to join lightly in a celebration. For him the Day of the Lord was darkness and not light, gloom with no brightness. The festival was not a joyful occasion, and insofar as it evoked the presence of the Lord it should carry forebodings of judgment rather than confidence of salvation. Amos is sweeping in his rejection of the sacrificial cult, in all its aspects. He rejects grain offerings as well as animal sacrifice, and dismisses the liturgical music as mere noise. Instead, he asks that "justice roll down like waters."

Criticism of the sacrificial cult is a prominent theme in the eighth-century prophets, and it was directed against the cult in Jerusalem as well as that in Bethel (cf. Isa 1:12-17; Mic 6:6-8; Hos 6:6). Debate has centered on the question whether the prophets wanted to abolish the cult entirely or only to reform it. It is difficult to imagine that anyone in antiquity could have envisioned the worship of a deity without any organized cult, or without offerings of some sort. But the prophets are not addressing the problem in the abstract. They are reacting to the cult as they knew it. In the case of Amos, the rejection is unequivocal. He does not say that sacrifice would be acceptable if the people practiced justice. The rhetorical question, "Did you bring to me sacrifices and offerings the forty years in the wilderness?" clearly implies the answer no. Amos presumably did not know the priestly laws of Leviticus, which envision an elaborate cult in the wilderness. More fundamentally, however, the question implies that people could serve God satisfactorily without sacrifices and offerings. This is not to say that Amos would necessarily have objected to any form of cultic worship, only that he considered the actual cult that was practiced in Israel to be offensive in the sight of the Lord.

The critique of the cult puts in sharp focus the question of what is important in religion. For many people, both in ancient and modern times, to practice a religion means to go to the temple or church and to participate in the rituals. For Amos, however, to serve God is to practice justice. The slaughter of animals, and the feasting and celebration that accompanied sacrifice, did not contribute to that goal. On the contrary, it gave the people a false sense of security, since they felt they were fulfilling their obligations to their god when in fact they were not. For this reason, sacrifices, even if offered at great expense, were not only irrelevant to the service of God, but actually an impediment to it. To call for the reform of the cult might still give the impression that it was important and perpetuate the misplaced values of Israelite society. Consequently, Amos is radical in his rejection. The service of God is about justice. It is not about offerings at all.

The Visions

Chapters 7–9 report a series of five visions, each of which warns of a coming judgment. In the case of the first two visions (locusts and fire), the prophet appeals successfully on behalf of "Jacob" (Israel) because "he is so small." The locusts, we are told, would eat "the latter growth after the king's mowing"—the share of the crop that was left for the people after the king's taxes. The preaching of Amos is directed against the upper classes because of their exploitation of the poor. Yet the poor would suffer even more than the rich from a punishment that might be inflicted on Israel as a whole. But while the Lord relents in two cases, he does not relent forever, and the prophet eventually acquiesces. In 7:8-9, however, he places the emphasis on those elements in Israel that he held responsible for the coming disaster—the sanctuaries that would be made desolate and the house of Jeroboam. Jeroboam himself did not fall by the sword, but his son Zechariah was murdered, and the kingdom remained in turmoil for the short time it survived.

The message of Amos is summed up concisely in 8:1-2. The vision involves a wordplay in Hebrew. He sees "a basket of summer fruit" (Hebrew *qaytz*) and is told that "the end" (Hebrew *qetz*) is coming on Israel (the Hebrew root, *qatzatz*, means "to cut off"). The expectation of "the end" later comes to be associated especially with apocalyptic literature, such as the book of Daniel. (The word *eschatology*, the doctrine of the last things, is derived from the Greek word for "end," *eschaton*.) Eventually it comes to mean the end of the world. In Amos it means simply the end of Israel. In fact, a few decades after Amos spoke, the kingdom of northern Israel was brought to an end by the Assyrians and was never reconstituted.

The reasons for this judgment on Israel are familiar by now. The leaders of Israel trample on the needy and bring the poor to ruin. To a great degree, Israel was defined by its ruling class. These were the people who identified themselves as Israel and celebrated the special status of Israel in the cult. Amos does not charge them with cultic irregularities. They observe new moon and Sabbath even if they do so impatiently. Their crimes are committed in the marketplace, where they cheat and in their dealings with the poor. For Amos the marketplace rather than the temple is the place where the service of God is tested. The idea that the land itself is affected by the sin of its inhabitants is one that we shall meet again in the later prophets.

The final vision concerns the destruction of the temple at Bethel. According to Amos, the Lord would strike his people precisely where they gathered to worship him in their mistaken way. The most striking passage in this chapter, however, is found in 9:7-8: "Are you not like the Ethiopians to me, O people of Israel?" The cult at Bethel clearly involved the celebration of the exodus as the defining experience of Israel. The people who celebrated it either did not think it entailed covenantal obligations or paid no heed to them. The significance of the exodus was that it marked Israel as the special people of YHWH, who would guarantee their well-being. Amos does not question the tradition that God brought Israel out of Egypt, but he radically questions its significance. It was the same God who brought the Philistines from Caphtor (Crete) and the Arameans from Kir (location unknown, but cf. Amos 1:5; 2 Kgs 16:9, each of which refers to Syrians being taken captive to Kir). For Amos, YHWH is the God of all peoples and responsible for everything that happens, good and bad. The movements of the Arameans and Philistines were just as providential as those of the Israelites. In the eyes of God, Israel is no different than the Ethiopians.

The final word of Amos is found in 9:8a-b: "The eyes of the Lord are upon the sinful kingdom, and I will destroy it from the face of the earth." It is unthinkable that the prophet from Tekoa would have added "except that I will not utterly destroy the house of Jacob." To do so would have taken the sting out of the oracle of judgment. For a later editor, however, the addition was necessary. After all, Judah was also part of the house of Jacob. Amos, however, did not dilute his oracles of judgment with any glimmer of hope. In this he was exceptional. Most of the prophets alternate between words of doom and words of consolation. The oracles of Amos, however, were like the Day of the Lord, gloom with no brightness in them.

The Judean Edition of Amos

Amos found little acceptance from the political and priestly leadership of the northern kingdom, naturally enough. His oracles were preserved in Judah. No doubt, people were impressed that the destruction he had predicted was actually brought about by the Assyrians, a mere generation later. The final edition of the book was probably after the Babylonian exile. A few passages stand out as editorial markers. These include the superscription in 1:1, explaining who Amos was, and the verse asserting the priority of Jerusalem as the abode of God in 1:2. The oracle against Judah, "because they have rejected the law of the Lord" (2:4), betrays the influence of the Deuteronomic reform. The book is punctuated by doxologies, short passages giving praise and glory to God (4:13; 5:8-9; 9:5-6). Perhaps the most notable editorial addition, however, is found in 9:11-15, which promises that "on that day" the Lord will raise up the booth of David that is fallen. The phrase "on that day" often indicates an editorial insertion in the prophetic books. Such passages give the whole book an eschatological cast, insofar as they purport to speak about a time in the indefinite future when the conditions of history will be radically altered. That the booth of David is said to be fallen indicates that this passage dates from a time after the Babylonian exile when the Davidic dynasty had been brought to an end. This passage is rightly considered messianic. It looks for a restoration of the kingship in Jerusalem under the Davidic line and expects that this restoration will be accompanied by a transformation of nature (the mountains will drip sweet wine). A similar transformation of nature is predicted in another messianic oracle in Isaiah 11.

The oracle against Judah in Amos 2 gives a good indication of how the book was read in the later tradition. Amos had spoken of specific situations in the northern kingdom, but above all he had established the principle that wrongdoing is punished by the Lord. The fate of Israel stood as an example for Judah, an example that was more fully appreciated after Judah was destroyed by the Babylonians. But unlike the original prophet, the editors ended on a note of hope. Judah, after all, survived its destruction, and the hope remained that YHWH would yet fulfill his promise to David.

One interesting modification of the prophetic message is found in 9:9-10, which says that only "the sinners of my people" will die by the sword. Amos made no such discrimination, and neither, indeed, did the Assyrians. By the time of the Babylonian exile, however, more consideration was given to the merits of the individual, as we shall see especially in Ezekiel 18. In the postexilic period, the fate of Israel became an example not only to the people as a whole but also to individual Judeans.

Hosea

Hosea was a younger contemporary of Amos. (The reason why his book is placed first

Fig. 15.3.   Ruins of ancient Samaria. Photo by Marshall Johnson

among the Minor Prophets lies in the statement in 1:2: "When the LORD first spoke through Hosea," which was taken by the rabbis to mean that Hosea was the first of the prophets through whom the Lord spoke.) According to the superscription of the book (1:1), he prophesied in the reign of Jeroboam of Israel, but in the reigns of Uzziah, Jothan, Ahaz, and Hezekiah of Judah. Since even Uzziah's reign extended after the death of Jeroboam, it is clear that the editor had a Judean perspective, even though Hosea was a northern prophet. It is uncertain whether Hezekiah came to the throne before or after the destruction of Samaria in 722. There is no reflection of that event in the prophecies of Hosea, although there are several allusions to the turbulent history that led up to it. The prophet may have died before the final onslaught, or he may have perished in the course of it.

The book of Hosea falls into two main sections. The first three chapters are framed by two accounts of the prophet's marriage to a promiscuous woman, which serves as a metaphor for the relationship of YHWH and Israel. In between is a long poetic oracle that develops the metaphor in an indictment of Israel. Chapters 4–14 comment on the political and religious affairs of the northern kingdom in the last decades of its existence. The opening chapter, which is in the third person, was presumably recorded by one of the prophet's disciples. The hand of the Judean editors who preserved the oracles is only occasionally visible, in the form of short glosses. Examples of Judean redaction can be seen in 1:7 (the Lord will not have pity on Israel but will on Judah); 1:10-11, which calls for the reunification of Judah and Israel; and in 3:5, which

says that the Israelites will seek the Lord their God and David their king.

The Marriage Metaphor

The opening words of the Lord to Hosea are arresting, to say the least: "Go, take for yourself a wife of whoredom and have children of whoredom, for the land commits great whoredom by forsaking the LORD." This command has bewildered modern commentators as much as it must have astonished Hosea. Some medieval Jewish commentators thought the whole experience was a prophetic vision. Some modern commentators have also tried to deny that the episode has any historical value. We shall find, however, that one of the ways in which prophets communicated with their audience was by symbolic action. (We have already seen an example of this in the story of Micaiah ben Imlah in 1 Kings 22. A memorable example is provided in Isaiah 20, where the prophet catches the attention of the people of Jerusalem by going naked and barefoot for three years.) Hosea's marriage must be seen in that context. It is exceptional in the degree to which it involves his whole family, but it is quite typical insofar as it uses nonverbal communication to convey its message. Some scholars have suggested that Hosea discovered his wife's promiscuous disposition only after he married her, but the symbolism of the action requires that she was known to be promiscuous from the start. Because of this, some have thought that she must have been a prostitute, perhaps even a sacred prostitute who played a ritual part in the cult of the Canaanite god Baal. Recent scholarship, however, has cast severe doubt on whether prostitution played any part in the cult of Baal.

In any case, the book of Hosea does not say that the woman in question, Gomer, played any such role. She may have been a prostitute, or she may have been a woman with a reputation for promiscuous behavior.

The children of Hosea and Gomer are made to bear the prophet's message by symbolic names. The first was named Jezreel, the name of the summer palace of the kings of Israel. It was at Jezreel that Jehu had slaughtered Jezebel and the royal family (2 Kings 9). Jeroboam II and his short-lived son Zechariah were the last kings of the line of Jehu, and this oracle must date from their time. There may have been many acts of bloodshed at Jezreel during the time of the Jehu dynasty. The most conspicuous one, however, was the bloody coup that involved the murder of Jezebel. According to 2 Kings, Jehu acted with the sanction of the prophet Elisha, but his bloodshed nonetheless warranted punishment in the eyes of Hosea.

The second child is named *lo' ruchamah*, which may be translated "not pitied" or "not loved" (the name is related to the Hebrew word for womb, *rechem*). The point is that Israel will no longer be pitied. The third child receives an even harsher name, *lo' 'ammi*, "not my people." The phrase echoes the common formula for divorce ("she is not my wife") and reverses the common formula for marriage. The optimistic conclusion to the chapter is surely supplied by an editor. Hosea, unlike Amos, prophesied salvation on occasion, but in this case the prophecy undermines the symbolism of the children's names, or rather puts it in the wider perspective of ongoing Judean history.

The way in which Hosea uses his wife and children as props for his message is troubling for the modern reader. Neither their welfare nor indeed the prophet's own is treated as of any consequence. We are given the impression of a prophet who is completely obsessed with his message, so that it takes over his whole life. In general, the Hebrew Bible is far more concerned with the welfare of the people as a whole than with that of the individual.

The use of the marriage as metaphor for the relationship between God and Israel raises again the question of the covenant. It is clear that Hosea, like Amos, saw this relationship as conditional. It entailed certain ethical and cultic requirements. If Israel failed to comply, the relationship could be broken off. All of this corresponds to the understanding of the Mosaic covenant that we have seen in the books of Exodus and Deuteronomy. Yet it is also clear that the people addressed by the prophets did not share that understanding, and so the question remains whether the prophets were invoking a traditional understanding of the covenant that had been neglected, or were shaping the idea of covenant in new ways. Hosea notably does not use the analogy of international treaties in the developed way that we find in Deuteronomy, although some of his references to covenant may have had political treaties in mind (we shall return to this point below under "The Critique of Royal Politics"). In chapter 2, Hosea uses marriage as his guiding metaphor. This quite original way of formulating the relationship between God and Israel would become one of the basic models for understanding that relationship in biblical tradition.

The marriage metaphor is developed at length in chapter 2. This long poetic oracle is presented as a legal indictment (Hebrew *ribh*). It is sometimes called a "covenant lawsuit," but the metaphor is one of divorce proceedings rather than of treaty violation. It begins with a formal declaration of divorce: "She is not my wife, and I am not her husband." The grounds for divorce are the wife's adultery, which would definitely qualify as "something objectionable" in the terminology of Deut 24:1. In ancient Israel, only the husband could initiate divorce, and the view of adultery was usually one-sided, a point that is noted later by Hosea (4:14). The punishment for adultery here is startling: "I will strip her naked, and expose her as in the day she was born." This punishment is not attested elsewhere in the Hebrew Bible, except in Ezek 16:37-39, which may be influenced by Hosea (cf. also the story of Susanna 1:32). In biblical law the punishment for adultery is death by stoning (Deut 22: 23-24; both Ezekiel and Susanna also envision an ultimate death penalty). In Genesis 38 Judah condemns his daughter-in-law Tamar to be burned for fornicating while she was the widow of one of his sons and promised to another. Whether any of these punishments was actually carried out in ancient Israel we do not know. The punishment of stripping allows the prophet in Hosea 2 to speak metaphorically of the stripping of the land, to make her like a wilderness and turn her into parched land, by destroying the trees and crops that were her clothing. In fact, Israel was laid bare by the Assyrians already in the 730s and again more drastically in the final assault on Samaria (722).

The adultery of Israel consisted of worshiping Baal, the Canaanite god, who was widely revered in the northern kingdom of Israel. (Compare the Elijah stories in 1 Kings. A high proportion of Israelite names in the ostraca found in Samaria included the name of Baal.) Baal was attractive because he was a fertility deity, the "rider of the clouds" and bringer of rain. People believed that he was the deity who provided "the grain, the wine, and the oil," the main benefits people expected from the worship of a god or goddess. Hosea insists to the contrary that YHWH is the deity who provides these goods. (Compare the story of Elijah and the prophets of Baal, where the conflict initially concerned the power to provide rain.)

Hosea differs from Amos in two crucial respects. First, the primary sin of which Israel is accused is not social injustice but idolatry. Hosea is also concerned about social justice, as we shall see, but it plays a secondary role in his prophecy. In contrast, one would not know from the book of Amos that the worship of Baal was a problem in northern Israel at all. The second way in which Hosea differs from Amos is that he vacillates between judgment and oracles of salvation. The prophecy in Hosea 2 ends with an idyllic vision of restoration. The wilderness was, on the one hand, naked land, a place of death and therefore punishment. But it was also the place where Israel had encountered YHWH in the exodus tradition. Moreover, the Hebrew word for wilderness, *midbar*, could also refer to the steppe land outside a town where young couples might go courting. Hosea recalls the wilderness period of the exodus as the courtship of YHWH and Israel. If Israel is again reduced to wilderness, this is not only a punishment; it is also an opportunity for a new beginning: "therefore I will allure her, and bring her into the wilderness, and speak tenderly to her" (2:14). The Valley of Achor, where Achan was stoned in Joshua 7, would now be a door of hope (*Pethach Tikvah*, the name of a modern suburb of Jerusalem). Israel would no longer address its god as "baal," which meant "lord, husband," but was also the name of the god, but as "*'ishi*," "my man/husband," with a connotation of partnership rather than subordination. In effect, YHWH and Israel would renew their marriage. Hosea's vision, which balances judgment with hope, may have been influenced by the fact that Israel survived the initial Assyrian invasion in the 730s, and for a time could hope for a new beginning.

Hosea 3 is a brief first person account of Hosea's marriage. It is not clear whether it refers to his initial marriage to Gomer. The word "again" in v. 1 may be an editorial gloss, in view of the fact that the marriage has already been reported once. That he pays a bride-price for her suggests that this is the initial wedding. It is remarkable that the prophet is told to "love" this woman. The verb may only mean

to enter into a relationship with her. (In the treaty texts, vassals are often commanded to "love" their overlords.) But it may also require an emotional relationship, such as Hosea imagines in the case of YHWH and Israel. Alternatively, this passage may imply that Gomer was unfaithful to him, even after they had children together. In any case, he punishes her by a period of abstinence. The symbolism of this punishment is that Israel will have to be "without king or prince, without sacrifice or pillar." As we shall see in the later oracles, Israel repeatedly sought salvation by changing kings and by offering sacrifices. In Hosea's judgment, both courses of action were futile and were no substitute for the sincere worship of YHWH.

The marriage metaphor for the relationship between God and Israel is not without

Fig. 15.4 **Bronze relief depicting a mother and her children as refugees from the city of Lachish, besieged by the Assyrian forces of Sennacherib; from the palace of Ashurbanipal in Nineveh; in the British Museum.** John J. Collins.

INTRODUCTION TO THE HEBREW BIBLE

its problems. The prophet takes the common cultural assumptions about the roles of husband and wife as his point of departure. On these assumptions, the adulterous wife could be humiliated and even put to death. It is not the purpose of Hosea 1–3 to say how husbands should treat their wives, faithful or otherwise. The prophet's concern is to explain how YHWH reacts to Israel's behavior. The use of human analogy is one of the most distinctive and appealing aspects of Hosea's prophecy, but it runs the danger of making God conform to the cultural norms of the time. Should God behave like a jealous or outraged husband? Hosea was not unaware of the problem of using human analogies for God, as we shall see in our discussion of chapter 11, but he does not reflect on it in his use of the marriage metaphor. Moreover, there is always the danger that people may take the conduct ascribed to God as exemplary. If God can strip and expose Israel, may not a human husband punish an unfaithful wife in like manner? Hosea does not draw such a conclusion. He does not, as far as we can tell from the text, humiliate Gomer in public, much less have her condemned to death. But there is little doubt that the very negative use of female imagery in the Prophets has contributed to negative stereotypes of women, and even to physical abuse on occasion. Hosea's imagery is not as extreme as what we find in Ezekiel, but nonetheless it calls for sensitivity in interpretation and should not be used to justify abuse of women in any sense.

Chapters 4–14

The main corpus of oracles in Hosea begins with another indictment: There is no faithfulness or loyalty and no knowledge of God in the land. Instead, there is "swearing, lying, murder, stealing, and adultery." All these sins are mentioned in the Decalogue. Accordingly, many scholars see here another "covenant lawsuit." Hosea, at least, holds that Israel's relationship with God requires loyalty and is violated by these sins. He links law and covenant explicitly in 8:1: "they have broken my covenant and transgressed my law." (The word for law here is *torah*, which may also mean instruction, but it is clear that the instruction entails prescriptions for conduct.) There is a close relationship between Hosea and Deuteronomy. Both condemn the worship at the high places, in similar language. Both use the exodus as a major point of reference. Both speak of the danger of "forgetting" God (Hos 2:13; 8:14; 13:6; Deut 6:12; 8:14, 19). Both emphasize the love of God. They differ insofar as "love" in Deuteronomy refers to the loyalty of a vassal, whereas Hosea conceives it on the analogy of the love between husband and wife or father and son (chap. 11). Hosea stands in the same tradition as Deuteronomy and shares much, though not all, of its understanding of the covenantal relationship.

Like Deuteronomy, Hosea makes clear that while the covenant requires the observance of laws, it more fundamentally requires an underlying attitude of faithfulness, loyalty, and "knowledge of God" (cf. the emphasis on the love of God in Deut 6:5). The laws to which Hosea refers in 4:2 are not distinctive. Murder, stealing, and adultery were unacceptable in any society. All the more should they be unacceptable in Israel, which regarded itself as the chosen people of YHWH. The idea that human behavior affects the fertility of the land is an ancient one that was also incorporated in the biblical concept of the covenant.

Hosea may have had predecessors in this tradition. In 6:5 he says that God had "hewn Israel by the prophets," and in 12:13 he claims that it was by a prophet (Moses) that God brought Israel up from the land of Egypt. In 9:7-8 he complains that people dismiss the prophet as a fool, when in fact he is the watchman who gives warning of impending disaster. He may have seen himself in the tradition of Elijah and Elisha, but in fact he seems quite different from them, and he even condemns "the bloodshed of Jezreel" that Elisha had instigated. There may have been many prophets, however, whose words are not preserved in the Bible. In any case, Hosea seems to regard prophets as the true guardians of the heritage of Moses and the exodus, even though the court prophets manifestly did not play this role, and Hosea himself seems to condemn prophet and priest alike in 4:5.

Priesthood and Cult

Hosea is scarcely less vehement than Amos in his criticism of the priests and their cult. His charges against the priests are outlined in 4:4-14. (There seems to be personal animosity between prophet and priest that is expressed most pungently in 4:5: "I will destroy your mother!") The priestly instruction *(torah)* should provide the people with knowledge. For Hosea, "knowledge of God" means understanding what God really requires. The priests mislead the people by encouraging the sacrifices and offerings, which provide their livelihood. Hence the charge that they feed on the sin of the people—the more sin offerings the people bring, the better for the priests. They have forgotten the *torah* of God, not necessarily in the sense

that they do not remember what the laws are but in the sense that they have forgotten what is important. Thus far Hosea's critique is in line with that of Amos: the sacrificial cult distracts the people from the real service of God. Hosea, however, has other charges too. He disapproves of divination by means of rods, and of the cult at the high places. Presumably that cult involved the worship of other deities, such as Baal, hence the metaphor of whoredom. It would seem, however, that some literal prostitution also went on at the high places, not necessarily as part of the ritual but as part of the festivities surrounding the cult. At this point, Hosea comments on the inequality of popular attitudes toward adultery. The women should not be punished, because the men are guilty too. Criticism of male dominance is rare in the Hebrew Bible but not unknown (cf. also the story of Judah and Tamar in Genesis 37).

Hosea returns to the question of sacrifice in chapter 6. In this case, he mocks the occasional proposal of the people to "return to the LORD" in the hope of being restored. (The idiomatic expression in 6:2: "After two days he will revive us; and on the third day he will raise us up," means "he will restore us shortly." In Christian tradition this verse has often been read as a prediction of the resurrection of Christ on the third day.) Hosea dismisses such gestures as fickle and misguided: "for I desire steadfast love and not sacrifice, the knowledge of God rather than burnt offerings." Hosea is not interested in reforming the sacrificial cult any more than Amos was. Sacrifices are not what the Lord wants, and those who offer them are misled into thinking they have fulfilled their obligations when they have not.

The Critique of Royal Politics

Unlike Amos, Hosea does not dwell on the theme of social injustice. He comments repeatedly, however, on the political intrigue that racked the kingdom of Israel in the final decades of its existence. The death of Jeroboam II was followed by rapid turnover in the monarchy. Jeroboam's son, Zechariah, was murdered, and his murderer, Shallum, was murdered in turn a month later by Menahem. At this very time, Assyria was beginning to establish its dominion west of the Euphrates under Tiglath-pileser III (745–727). By 738 it had taken tribute from most of the states of Syria and northern Palestine, including Israel. Menahem of Israel was among those who submitted. The tribute was heavy, but it purchased peace and a measure of stability for a few years. After Menahem's death, his son Pekahiah was murdered, and Pekah ben Remaliah took the throne. Pekah became leader of an anti-Assyrian coalition and attempted to force Judah, under King Ahaz, to join. This policy led to the Syro-Ephraimite war (2 Kings 16; cf. Isaiah 7). Judah appealed to Assyria for help. Tiglath-pileser moved down the coast, destroying the coalition. He overran the Israelite territories in Galilee and Transjordan and destroyed Hazor and Megiddo. He deported some of the population to Assyria (see 2 Kgs 15:29-31). Samaria was spared because Pekah was murdered by Hoshea ben Elah (15:30), who immediately surrendered and paid tribute (15:30). Less than a decade later, after the death of Tiglath-pileser, Hoshea too withheld tribute (724). When the new Assyrian king, Shalmaneser, invaded, Hoshea promptly submitted, but he was imprisoned for treason because he had sent messengers to Egypt and withheld tribute (17:4). Shalmaneser proceeded to besiege Samaria and finally to destroy it.

Hosea finds little to approve in this tragic history. His basic critique is that Israel repeatedly looked for political solutions instead of turning to the service of YHWH. The repeated assassinations and palace coups indicated only fickleness. "They made kings, but not through me; they set up princes, but without my knowledge" (8:4). In a vivid passage in chapter 7, he compares the conspirators to adulterers, who become "sick with the heat of wine" when a new king is crowned (7:5) and ultimately "devour their rulers" (7:7). The repeated violation of treaties also shows their lack of fidelity (6:7; 10:4; 12:1) and is symptomatic of their infidelity toward their God. In an intriguing passage (12:2-3), he suggests that Israel/Jacob was wayward from the beginning: "In the womb he tried to supplant his brother, and in his manhood he strove with God." Hosea knew the traditions about Jacob now found in Genesis 25 and 32, but he did not regard them as a matter of pride for the descendants of Jacob.

Hosea is scathing about attempts to seek help from Egypt and scarcely less so of attempts to appease Assyria. "Ephraim has become like a dove, silly and without sense; they call on Egypt, they go to Assyria" (7:11). The complaint that "Ephraim went to Assyria, and sent to the great king" (5:13) could refer to any of the times that Israel submitted to Assyria. Since the passage is also concerned with Judah, the most likely reference is to the time of the Syro-Ephraimite war. The reliance on Egypt is especially ironic in view of Israel's origin. Hosea remarks caustically: "they shall return to the land of Egypt, and Assyria shall be their king" (11:5). The return to Egypt carries double meaning. They return to Egypt to look for help, but this only brings on the wrath of Assyria, and so they end up in servitude again—their condition in Egypt before the exodus.

It is not clear just how Hosea thought Israel should have responded to the Assyrian threat. Most probably, he believed that if Israel focused on the service of YHWH and avoided international intrigue, the threat would not have arisen in the first place. This judgment may be naïve from a historical point of view. Assyria would have demanded tribute in any case. But the prophet was right that Israel only ensured its own destruction by its attempts to resist Assyria and to form coalitions against it, and that attempts to solve its problems by changing kings were futile.

The Understanding of God

No book of the Hebrew Bible is so rich in metaphorical expressions as Hosea. Often the metaphors are applied to Israel, either to express YHWH's affection for her ("like grapes in the wilderness," 9:10) or her wayward behavior ("a luxuriant vine," 10:1). Even more striking is Hosea's use of metaphor to portray God. We have already explored one such metaphor, the jealous husband. In chapter 11 Hosea develops another: the loving father. Here God remembers Israel as a child whom he taught to walk and lifted to his cheek. So now, despite their disobedience, he cannot bring himself to destroy them. "How can I give you up, Ephraim? How can I hand you over, O Israel? How can I make you like Admah? How can I treat you like Zeboiim? I will not execute my fierce anger; I will not again destroy Ephraim;

for I am God and no mortal, the Holy One in your midst, and I will not come in wrath" (11:8-9). (Admah and Zeboiim were cities destroyed with Sodom and Gomorrah.) On the one hand, God is portrayed in very human terms as someone who can be overcome by emotion. On the other hand, he is "God and no mortal" (*adam*, "man" in the generic sense of human being). What then is the difference between God and a human being? It is not that humans are guided by emotion, and God is not, but that God can overcome the more destructive emotions and be guided by the better, whereas human beings often succumb to the worst. We have no better way to imagine God than in the likeness of human beings, but we should attribute to God what is best in human nature and then some, not human weakness or malevolence.

Unfortunately, the generous promise "I will not again destroy Ephraim," made perhaps when Samaria survived the invasion of Tiglath-pileser, was not fulfilled. It is contradicted outright in 13:9: "I will destroy you, O Israel, who can help you?" God will not ransom them from the power of Sheol: "O Death, where are your plagues? O Sheol, where is your destruction? Compassion is hidden from my eyes" (13:14; this verse is cited in 1 Cor 15:55, in a very different sense). In the end, God's burning anger seems to prevail. The contradictions in Hosea's prophecy arose from the changing fortunes of Israel in its final years. They also illustrate one of the fundamental problems of all human speech about God. On the one hand, there is the conviction, eloquently expressed by Hosea, that God is good and must be imagined in accordance with the highest ideals of humanity. On the other hand, there is belief that God is revealed in history, and specifically in the history of Israel. The first conviction leads to the assertion that God is merciful and compassionate, but this conviction is often hard to reconcile with the death and destruction to which human beings are subject and which were all too often the fate of Israel.

The Judean Edition of Hosea

Like the book of Amos, Hosea was preserved and edited in the south, after the fall of Samaria. His prophecies of destruction had been fulfilled and stood as a warning to Judah. Hosea himself had commented on Judah as well as Israel on occasion, although he was primarily concerned with the northern kingdom, and specifically with the Israelite heartland of Ephraim. So, for example, he comments on the sickness of both Israel and Judah in the context of the Syro-Ephraimite war (5:13). A number of passages, however, contrast Judah with Israel, and these are likely to come from the Judean editors. Hosea 1:7 assures the reader that God will have pity on the house of Judah. Hosea 3:5 inserts a reference to "David, their king," that is inconsistent with Hosea's attitude toward kings of any sort. Hosea 4:15 warns Judah not to become guilty by worshiping at Gilgal or Bethel, probably reflecting the Deuteronomic condemnation of worship outside Jerusalem. Perhaps the most obvious editorial contribution to the book, however, is the positive ending, which promises restoration if only the people will return to the Lord. The final saying ("those who are wise understand these things") is typical of the wisdom literature and shows the hand of the scribes who were finally responsible for the edition of the book. From the viewpoint of these scribes, the oracles provided a moral lesson on the consequences of following "the ways of the Lord." This lesson could be applied to individuals as well as to kingdoms.

FOR FURTHER READING

Amos

J. Barton, *The Theology of the Book of Amos* (Cambridge: Cambridge Univ. Press, 2012). Discussion of major themes in historical context. Also attention to reception history.

M. D. Carroll R., *Amos. The Prophet and His Oracles: Research on the Book of Amos* (Louisville: Westminster John Knox, 2002). Wide ranging history of research.

M. L. Chaney, " 'Bitter Bounty': The Dynamics of Political Economy Critiqued by the Eighth-Century Prophets," in N. K. Gottwald and R. A. Horsley, eds., *The Bible and Liberation* (Maryknoll, NY: Orbis, 1993). Takes the social critique realistically.

D. J. A. Clines, "Metacommentating Amos," in idem, *Interested Parties: The Ideology of Writers and Readers of the Hebrew Bible* (JSOTSup 205; Sheffield: Sheffield Academic Press, 1995), 76–93. Critical questioning of the perspective of Amos.

W. J. Houston, "Exit the Oppressed Peasant? Rethinking the Background of Social Criticism in the Prophets," in J. Day, ed., *Prophets and Prophecy in Ancient Israel* (London: T&T Clark, 2010), 10–116. Nuanced discussion of social background.

J. Jeremias, *The Book of Amos* (trans. D. W. Scott; OTL; Louisville: Westminster John Knox, 1998). Commentary with emphasis on the composition of the book.

P. J. King, *Amos, Hosea, Micah: An Archaeological Commentary* (Philadelphia: Westminster John Knox, 1988). Excellent summary of pertinent archaeological evidence.

J. L. Mays, *Amos: A Commentary* (OTL; Philadelphia: Westminster, 1969). Concise, clear commentary.

S. M. Paul, *Amos* (Hermeneia; Minneapolis: Fortress Press, 1991). Detailed philological commentary.

M. A. Sweeney, *The Twelve Prophets* (Berit Olam; Collegeville, MN, 2000), 1:189–276. Helpful exegetical commentary.

H. W. Wolff, *Amos the Prophet* (trans. F. R. McCurley; Philadelphia: Fortress Press, 1973). Associates Amos with wisdom circles.

———, *Joel and Amos* (trans. W. Janzen, S. D. McBride, and C. A. Muenchow; Hermeneia; Philadelphia: Fortress Press, 1977). Influential redaction-critical commentary.

Hosea

G. I. Davies, *Hosea* (Grand Rapids: Eerdmans, 1992). Good exegetical commentary.

J. Day, "Hosea and the Baal Cult," in Day, ed., *Prophets and Prophecy*, 202–24. Clarification of aspects of Hosea in light of the Baal cult.

J. A. Dearman, *The Book of Hosea* (NICOT; Grand Rapids: Eerdmans, 2010). Conservative historical commentary.

B. E. Kelle, *Hosea 2: Metaphor and Rhetoric in Historical Perspective* (Atlanta: SBL/Leiden: Brill, 2005). Interprets Hosea against the background of the Assyrian period.

J. L. Mays, *Hosea* (OTL; Philadelphia: Westminster, 1969). Clear, concise commentary.

C.-L. Seow, "Hosea," *ABD* 3:291–99. Good summary of the critical issues.

Y. Sherwood, *The Prostitute and the Prophet: Hosea's Marriage in Literary-Theoretical Perspective* (JSOTSup 212; Sheffield: Sheffield Academic Press, 1996). Innovative attempt to apply the literary approach of Jacques Derrida (deconstruction) to a prophetic text.

M. A. Sweeney, *The Twelve Prophets* (Berit Olam; Collegeville, MN, 2000), 1:1–144. Helpful exegetical commentary.

R. N. Weems, "Gomer: Victim of Violence or Victim of Metaphor," *Semeia* 47 (1989): 87–104. Penetrating feminist critique of the prophetic use of female metaphors.

M. Weinfeld, "Hosea and Deuteronomy," *Deuteronomy and the Deuteronomic School* (Winona Lake, IN: Eisenbrauns, 1992), 366–70. Exposition of literary and theological links between Deuteronomy and Hosea.

H. W. Wolff, *Hosea* (trans. G. Stansell; Hermeneia; Philadelphia: Fortress Press, 1974). Influential redaction-critical commentary.

G. A. Yee, "The Book of Hosea," *NIB* 7:197–297. Homiletical commentary with feminist sensitivity.

E. Ben Zvi, *Hosea* (FOTL; Grand Rapids: Eerdmans, 2005). Treats Hosea as a coherent composition from the Persian period.

CHAPTER 16

Isaiah, Micah, Nahum, and Zephaniah

INTRODUCTION

We continue our exploration of the prophetic books in this chapter by turning to the eighth-century prophets Isaiah and Micah and, following the demise of Assyrian power in the seventh century B.C.E., Nahum and Zephaniah.

The oracles of Amos and Hosea focused on the northern kingdom of Israel and had the story of the exodus as a major point of reference. At approximately the same time, other prophets, Isaiah and Micah, were active in the southern kingdom of Judah. For these prophets the primary traditions were those of David and Zion.

Isaiah

The book of Isaiah is arguably the most complex book in the Hebrew Bible. It is introduced as "the vision of Isaiah son of Amoz, which he saw concerning Judah and Jerusalem in the days of Uzziah, Jotham, Ahaz, and Hezekiah, kings of Judah." The death of Uzziah is dated variously from 742 to 734 B.C.E. A major episode in the book concerns the invasion

of Sennacherib in 701 B.C.E. Isaiah, then, according to the superscription, was active for more than thirty years, possibly for as much as forty. The extent of his activity in the days of King Uzziah may be questioned. The vision in chapter 6, which is usually taken to be his call vision, is dated to the year of that king's death. Uzziah may only have been mentioned in the superscription because he is mentioned in chapter 6. Chapters 7–8 have their setting in the time of the Syro-Ephraimite war, in the reign of Ahaz (735–734), when Syria and northern Israel tried to compel Judah to join a coalition against Assyria. There is also reference to a campaign of the Assyrian king Sargon against Philistia in 712, in Isaiah 20.

Only a small part of the book of Isaiah, however, can be associated with the prophet of the eighth century. Chapters 40–66 clearly relate to the Babylonian exile and its aftermath.

Cyrus of Persia, who lived in the sixth century B.C.E., is mentioned by name in Isa 44:28 and 45:1. With the rise of critical scholarship in the late eighteenth century, scholars were unwilling to believe that a prophet who lived in the eighth century would have prophesied so specifically about the sixth. (Some conservatives still fight a rearguard action on this question.) It was more reasonable to assume that these oracles were composed by an anonymous prophet who lived in the sixth century. This prophet was dubbed "Second Isaiah" or "Deutero-Isaiah," although there is no evidence that he spoke in the name of Isaiah. At the end of the nineteenth century, the German scholar Bernhard Duhm argued that chapters 56–66 should be distinguished as the work of a third prophet, dubbed "Third Isaiah" or "Trito-Isaiah." For the last century or so, it has been customary to refer to chapters 1–39 as "First Isaiah."

Not everything in chapters 1–39 can be attributed to the eighth-century prophet, however, and this was clear to Duhm and to others before him. The oracles against Babylon in chapters 13–14 are most naturally dated to a time after Babylon had replaced Assyria as the dominant power. The provenance of some of the other oracles against foreign nations is uncertain. Isaiah 24–27, often called "the Isaiah apocalypse," is usually dated to a time after the exile, by analogy with other late prophetic writings. Chapters 34 and 35 are similar to Second Isaiah in tone and theme. Several shorter passages in chapters 1–39 appear to date from a time after the Deuteronomic reform (2:1-4) or after the end of the monarchy (11:1-9). Passages introduced by the phrase "on that day" (e.g., 7:18-25; 11:10-11) are usually thought to be editorial additions.

In recent years, many scholars have labored to find signs of intelligent editorial intentions in the way the book was put together. The final edition was certainly later than the Babylonian exile, and it was guided by thematic rather than historical interests. Even though the vision in chapter 6 is usually thought to describe the call of the prophet and the beginning of his mission, it does not stand at the beginning of the book. (Contrast the books of Jeremiah and Ezekiel in this regard.) It may be that it originally introduced a separate booklet consisting of Isa 6:1—8:22. The final editors, however, were less concerned with the career of Isaiah than with the theme of judgment. This theme is revisited at the end of the book, in chapter 66. The story of the envoys from Babylon in chapter 39 provides a bridge to the second half of the book, which addresses the Babylonian exile. Some scholars argue that the book should be divided after chapter 33, since chapters 34 and 35 admittedly resemble Second Isaiah. Chapters 36–39 can be read as an introduction to the remainder of the book, which is concerned with the final destiny of Zion. Against this, however, it must be noted that chapters 36–39 refer to events in the Assyrian period at the end of the eighth century and are the last chapters in the book that can be related to the career of the eighth-century prophet. A number of scholars have recently argued that Second Isaiah was responsible for editing the earlier chapters, and that he presented his work as an extension of that of the older prophet. It is quite likely that Second Isaiah was familiar with the oracles of Isaiah and may well have had them in mind as "the former things" that had come to pass (42:9). There is a clear allusion to Isaiah 11 in 65:25 ("The wolf and the lamb will feed together"). But Second Isaiah also echoes the prophecies of Jeremiah, as we shall see, and on the whole his oracles are very different from those of the eighth-century prophet. Chapters 40–66 were probably attached to chapters 1–39 because of their common concern for the fate of Jerusalem. But the book as a whole is not tightly structured by modern standards. Some chapters are grouped together because of either common subject matter (chaps. 7–8) or a common theme (the oracles against the nations in chaps. 13–19). Chronology is sometimes a factor. (Material relating to the Syro-Ephraimite war comes early in the book; the crisis with Sennacherib at the end of "First Isaiah.") In other cases, the reason for the placement of oracles is difficult to discern (e.g., chaps. 2–4, 24–27). While we can identify some principles in the editing of the book, the degree of intentionality should not be exaggerated.

In the present chapter, our concern is with the prophet of the eighth century. We shall reflect on the final shape of the book later in connection with the sections that date to the postexilic period.

Isaiah's Vision

Two main sections in the book of Isaiah provide biographical or quasi-biographical information about the prophet. The first is in chapters 6–8, and the second is in chapters 36–39.

Near the end of chapters 6–8, the prophet gives a command to "bind up the testimony,

Fig. 16.1 Sennacherib, "sitting on the throne of judgment," authorizes the destruction of the Israelite city of Lachish as vanquished enemies bow before him; bronze relief from the Palace of Sennacherib in Nineveh; at the British Museum.
Photo by the author.

seal the teaching among my disciples" (8:16). Similarly, in 30:8 he says, "Go now, write it before them on a tablet, and inscribe it in a book." There is also a reference to a sealed book (by way of analogy) in 28:11, and in 8:1 the prophet is told to write the name of his son on a tablet. These are among the earliest references to writing in the Hebrew Bible. Apparently the prophet had a group of disciples who were entrusted with preserving his "testimony." It is plausible to suppose that the testimony in 8:16 is the narrative of the preceding chapters, or at least that it contained some form of the prophet's oracles to Ahaz. It is equally plausible that additions were later made to this testimony (e.g., in the passages beginning "on that day"). Chapter 7 is written in the third person and does not pretend to be the prophet's own account. But whatever the origin of these chapters, they do much to establish the persona of the prophet as it is presented in the book.

The vision in chapter 6 is not necessarily Isaiah's first prophetic experience. It is similar to the vision of Micaiah ben Imlah in 1 Kings 22, which is certainly not an inaugural vision. Isaiah's vision, however, explains how he was entrusted with a mission, and is the only such account in the book, and so it is usually taken as his call vision. (Besides, the dating to the year of Uzziah's death points to a very early point in his career.) Like Micaiah, Isaiah claims to have seen the Lord seated on his throne. This claim stands in defiance of another biblical tradition, that mortals cannot see God and live (cf. Exod 33:20). We shall find a more elaborate call vision in the book of Ezekiel. In contrast, other prophets experience an auditory call, by hearing only, as Moses did at the burning bush. The call of

Amos does not seem to have involved a vision. Jeremiah's call is also of the auditory type. It is not possible to make any neat distinction between northern and southern prophecy in this regard. Isaiah and Ezekiel were both in Jerusalem, but Micaiah ben Imlah was at the northern court. We may perhaps conclude that the visionary tradition was strong in Jerusalem, but it was not unknown elsewhere. It is impossible to verify whether or how the prophets actually experienced these visions, or whether the accounts were composed by later editors. It is clear in any case that the report of a vision such as this was a powerful claim for the legitimacy of the prophet and helped to establish his credentials.

Unlike the vision of Micaiah, that of Isaiah is set in the Jerusalem temple, where YHWH was believed to be enthroned above the cherubim (cf. Isa 37:16). Micaiah had seen the host of heaven. Isaiah sees "YHWH of hosts," one of his favorite designations for God. The seraphim are "burning ones," representatives of the host in attendance on YHWH. The composition of this host would become a subject of great fascination in later apocalyptic and mystical literature. There are many depictions of winged creatures in Near Eastern art, often with bodies in animal or even human form. Isaiah 14:29 and 30:6 speak of "flying seraphim" in a context that suggests that they are a kind of serpent. In Num 21:6-9 the word is used with reference both to poisonous snakes and to the bronze serpent (Nehushtan) made by Moses. In the time of Isaiah, Nehushtan was still preserved in the temple, and this may have given rise to the idea that seraphim attended the divine throne. Here the seraphim proclaim the holiness of God in a form that influenced the liturgical traditions of both

Fig. 16.2   A winged *lamassu* from the Great Palace in Nimrud; in the Louvre. Commons.wikimedia.org

Judaism (the *q'dushah*) and Christianity (the *trishagion* or *sanctus*). God is often called "the Holy One of Israel" in Isaiah, in all sections of the book.

The implications of the holiness of God become clear in the following verses. Isaiah confesses that he is a man of unclean lips, living among an unclean people, and so he is unworthy to see the Lord. It is not apparent that Isaiah is guilty of any specific violation. Rather, the point is that any human being is impure in relation to God. The gulf between the Holy One and humanity is one of the key themes of Isaiah's prophecy. Isaiah is purified, but at a cost. His lips are touched with a burning coal (suggested by the burning of incense in the temple). The implication is that the human condition can only be purified by the painful and radical remedy of burning. This will have implications for the fate of the people of Judah.

The discussion in the divine council is rather similar to what was reported by Micaiah ben Imlah. The Lord asks for a volunteer to do his bidding. In this case, unlike that of Micaiah, the prophet volunteers. He is given a strange message to convey:

> Keep listening, but do not comprehend;
> keep looking, but do not understand.
> Make the mind of this people dull,
> and stop their ears, and shut their eyes,
> so that they may not look with their eyes,
> and listen with their ears,
> and comprehend with their minds,
> and turn and be healed.
> –Isaiah 6:9-10

In fact, Isaiah's mission to Ahaz failed, in the sense that Ahaz did not accept his advice. But according to chapter 6, the mission was supposed to fail. Failure was part of the commission, before Ahaz came on the scene at all. There is an obvious analogy here with the hardening of Pharaoh's heart in the book of Exodus. Judah is being set up for punishment. The mission of the prophet only increases the guilt, as now there is no excuse. There is certainly a measure of self-justification in this account of the prophet's commission. It was not through any fault of the prophet that his message had no effect. But Isaiah claimed that the lack of response to his preaching was itself part of a divine plan. As Amos might have said, if something bad happens, this too is the work of the Lord.

The prophet asks how long he must carry out this frustrating mission. The answer implies that he must continue until Judah is utterly destroyed and "the LORD sends everyone far away"—a reference to the Assyrian policy of deportation. Even if a remnant survives, it will be burned again. We shall meet the motif of the remnant again in Isaiah. Here it should be noted that the prospect of being reduced to a "stump" was not an inviting one. The final statement, that "the holy seed is its stump," is an obvious gloss. Judah was in fact reduced to a small remnant by the Babylonians, a little more than a century after Isaiah's time. On that occasion, however, the remnant provided the "holy seed" for the restoration of Judah after the exile. From the perspective of the postexilic editor, then, the destruction was not absolute. The image of the stump left room for a new beginning. We shall find a similar image in Isaiah 11.

The Encounter with Ahaz

The account of Isaiah's encounter with Ahaz is set in the context of the Syro-Ephraimite war, when the kings of Israel and Syria tried to coerce Judah into joining a potentially disastrous coalition against Assyria. (The account in Isaiah 7 does not mention the purpose of the attack but depicts it as wanton aggression.)

The prophet meets the king "near the conduit of the upper pool," where he was presumably checking the water supply in anticipation of a siege. Isaiah is accompanied by his son Shear-yashub (meaning "a remnant shall return"). Isaiah's children, like those of Hosea, are walking billboards bearing their father's message. In the following chapter, we shall meet Maher-shalal-hash-baz ("hasten for spoil, hurry for plunder"). The implication of the name Shear-yashub is that *only* a remnant shall return. At a time when no Judeans had been taken into exile, this seems like a disastrous prospect. Later, of course, the survival of a remnant would be the seed of hope. But

the initial force of the child's name was to prophesy deportation and exile. Ironically, this aspect of Isaiah's prophecy was fulfilled more accurately in the later Babylonian crisis than in the prophet's own time.

Isaiah's prophecy to Ahaz begins like the typical Assyrian prophecies of the day, "Do not fear." The campaign of the Arameans and northern Israelites would fail. (The reference to sixty-five years in 7:8b is a gloss, which may refer to further deportations in the seventh century when Ashurbanipal came to the throne.) Ahaz must have faith and trust that the crisis will pass: "If you do not have faith, you will not be made firm" (7:9; the Hebrew is a wordplay on the root "amen"). The underpinning of this advice is to be found in the Zion theology in the Psalms, which we have already considered in connection with Solomon's temple. Psalm 46 declares that "God is our refuge and strength . . . therefore *we will not fear*, though the earth should change, though the mountains shake in the midst of the sea." It goes on to say that "God is in the midst of the city," and that "the LORD of hosts is with us." But in fact, "when the house of David heard that Aram had allied itself with Ephraim, the heart of Ahaz and the heart of his people shook as the trees of the forest shake before the wind" (Isa 7:2). Isaiah challenged Ahaz to believe the proclamation of the psalm, which was easy to recite in times of peace but difficult to accept when there was an enemy at the gates.

In support of this oracle, Isaiah offers Ahaz a sign. The king demurs, saying that he will not put the Lord to the test, but the answer is hypocritical. The sign would make it more difficult for him to reject the prophet's advice. The actual sign is one of the most

Fig. 16.3 A prophet (Isaiah?) points to Mary and Jesus, mother and child, in a second-century fresco from the Christian catacomb of Priscilla in Rome. As medieval interpreters pointed out, the prophet in Isaiah 7 would necessarily have looked to the near horizon to be relevant to King Ahaz. Commons.wikimedia.org

controversial passages in the Old Testament: "The young woman is with child and shall bear a son, and shall name him Immanuel." The Hebrew word for "young woman" is *'almah*, which can, but does not necessarily, refer to a virgin (the unambiguous Hebrew word for virgin is *bᵉtulah*). The cognate Ugaritic word is found in a similar birth announcement in a text called "Nikkal and the Kotharat": "Behold! A maiden shall bear a son." The Greek translation of Isaiah, however, uses the word *parthenos*, which unambiguously means "virgin." This Greek reading was cited in the New Testament as a proof text for the virgin birth of Jesus (Matt 1:23). Consequently, the

text was a battleground for Jewish and Christian interpreters for centuries. The medieval Jewish interpreters (Ibn Ezra, Rashi) rightly argued that in order for the sign to be meaningful for Ahaz it had to be fulfilled in his time, not seven hundred years later.

Various suggestions have been offered for the identity of the young woman. One candidate is the wife of the prophet. In Isa 8:3, Isaiah goes in to "the prophetess" and she conceives Maher-shalal-hash-baz, but then she can hardly have been the mother of Immanuel, at about the same time. The more likely candidate is the wife of the king. The name Immanuel, "God is with us," is an allusion to the royal ideology; compare Psalm 46:7: "the LORD of hosts is with us" (cf. also 2 Sam 7:9; 1 Kgs 1:37; 11:38; Ps 89:21, 24). The birth of a royal child would have greater import for Ahaz. There has been much debate as to whether the child in question was Hezekiah, but the chronology of the period is confused and problematic. It may be significant that 2 Kgs 18:7 says of Hezekiah that "the LORD was with him."

There is no reason to think that Isaiah was predicting a miraculous birth. The sign was simply that the birth of a child in the time of crisis was an assurance of hope for the future of the dynasty. Isaiah predicts that the child "shall eat curds and honey by the time he knows how to refuse the evil and choose the good. For before the child knows how to refuse the evil and choose the good, the land before whose two kings you are in dread will be deserted." The most obvious implication of this message is that the crisis will pass within a few years. Milk and honey were the original trademarks of the promised land (Exod 3:8, 17; 33:3). Fat and milk were generally regarded as signs of abundance in the ancient Near East, and milk and honey were used in cultic activity in Mesopotamia. Isaiah then is assuring Ahaz that the Davidic line will survive and prosper. Such a rosy prediction, however, would be difficult to reconcile with the ominous names of the prophet's children, and in fact there is also another side to it. This is brought out in a series of additions to the passage, each introduced by the formula "on that day." Isaiah 7:21-25 explains that "on that day" everyone will eat curds and honey because the population will be decimated. Moreover, the vineyards will be ravaged and there will be little agriculture, but cattle will be let loose and people will live off the natural produce of the land. They will still have milk and honey, but not the vineyards and wine to which they have become accustomed. Ahaz might not appreciate a diet of milk and honey, but it would nonetheless be good, even wonderful. We sense here the same kind of irony that is implied in the name "A Remnant Shall Return." Isaiah was not prophesying easy deliverance, but he was affirming that the promises to David would be honored.

The negative side of the prediction is developed in chapter 8. The name of the prophet's second child is interpreted as a prediction of the destruction of Samaria and Damascus. But there is also judgment against Judah, exacerbated by the refusal of Ahaz to heed the prophet's advice. The people have rejected the waters of Shiloah by failing to put their faith in the promises to David and Zion (cf. the reference in Ps 46:4 to the streams that gladden the city of God). Ahaz showed his lack of faith by appealing to Assyria for help. Therefore the Lord will bring upon them the floodwaters of Assyria, which will be destructive, though not fatal. Like Hosea, Isaiah rejects the attempts of the king and his counselors to solve their problems by political means: "Take counsel together, but it shall be brought to naught; speak a word, but it will not stand, for God is with us" (8:10). The presence of the Lord requires complete reliance on him. Isaiah's advice would have been difficult for any ruler to follow. It required that he simply put his faith in the Lord, not try to defend himself by making alliances, and certainly not by appealing to Assyria. In Isaiah's estimation, YHWH was more to be feared than either the Syrian-Israelite coalition or Assyria.

The Ideal King

There is, however, a very positive oracle appended to chapters 7–8 in 9:1-7 (MT 8:23—9:6). The context is the invasion of Zebulun and Naphtali—the northeastern part of northern Israel. There is no mention of the destruction of Samaria. The reference, then, in 8:23 is to the Assyrian annexation of this territory in 732 B.C.E., not to any later invasion. The oracle predicts a bright future for this region. Isaiah 8:23, however, has the appearance of an editorial edition, designed to put the negative prediction of the previous passage in a broader historical perspective. This is followed by a poetic oracle, announcing that people who walked in darkness have seen a great light, for "unto us a child is born." The "child" is given hyperbolic names: Wonderful Counselor, Mighty God, Everlasting Father, Prince of Peace.

This passage has generated an enormous amount of controversy. In Christian tradition it is read as a messianic prophecy and used in the Christmas liturgy with reference to the birth of Christ. Some scholars argue that it was originally composed as a messianic prophecy—that it was composed after the Davidic dynasty had been brought to an end by the Babylonians and was a prediction of the restoration of the Davidic line. There is no indication in the passage, however, that, the line had been cut off, or that a restoration of the kingship is involved. Many scholars hold that the oracle was originally part of an enthronement liturgy. Compare Psalm 2, where the king (who is also called *mashiach*, "anointed one"), is told, "You are my son, this day I have begotten you." There are also Egyptian analogies for such an enthronement liturgy, but it should be noted that these, like Psalm 2, address the new king directly. The names given to the child can then be taken as the throne names of the king. We have seen in connection with the discussion of 2 Samuel 7 above that the king is addressed as *elohim*,' "god." The reference to the authority placed on his shoulders supports the view that the reference is to enthronement rather than birth. Justice and righteousness are familiar themes of the royal ideology. The possibility cannot be excluded, however, that the poem celebrates the birth of a child in the royal household. A famous analogy for such a birth poem is found in Virgil's Fourth Eclogue, which is admittedly several centuries later and in a different cultural context.

There is no doubt that the oracle is referring to a Davidic king—it refers explicitly to the throne of David and his kingdom in 9:7. The question then arises how the advent of a new Davidic king in Jerusalem would have heralded salvation for the northeastern part of the kingdom of (northern) Israel in 732 B.C.E. or shortly thereafter. The Israelites in that region would surely have looked to Samaria rather than to Jerusalem for deliverance at that time. But the fact that this oracle is placed editorially after the reference to the subjugation of Zebulun and Naphtali is no guarantee that it was composed in that context. Indeed, such an oracle would make much more sense after the fall of Samaria. We know from archaeological evidence that Jerusalem was greatly expanded at that time, presumably by refugees from the north (cf. 9:3: "You have multiplied the nation"). When there was no longer a king in Samaria, it was possible to rekindle dreams of Davidic rule over all of Israel, as it had been in the beginning. If Hezekiah came to the throne in 715 B.C.E., as is suggested by Isa 36:1 (= 2 Kgs 18:13), his enthronement would provide a plausible setting for this poem. (The reference to the miraculous defeat of the oppressor, "as on the day of Midian," in Judges 7, would have to be proleptic—the anticipation of a victory that had not yet occurred.) The chronology of Hezekiah's reign is problematic, however, and so the matter must remain in doubt.

But can such a positive oracle be credibly attributed to Isaiah? It is certainly possible that a fragment of an enthronement ritual was inserted into the book of Isaiah by an editor, in view of Isaiah's obvious engagement with the Davidic house. The language of the poem, however, is quite compatible with Isaianic authorship. The Immanuel prophecy in chapter 7 indicates that Isaiah believed in the possibility of a just king who would live up to the claims of the royal ideology. The poem preserved in 9:1-7 celebrates the advent of just such a king. This king is not a messiah in the later sense of the term—that is, a future king who would restore the Davidic line. He was rather a successor to the throne who was still at the beginning of his reign, when one might hope for great things. This concept of an ideal king is at the root of later messianic expectation. Whether this oracle was originally uttered by Isaiah or not, the theme of ideal kingship is one of the aspects of the book that has had greatest influence on later tradition.

This theme comes to the fore again in 11:1-9, which is one of the most widely cited messianic texts in the Dead Sea Scrolls and other Jewish literature from around the turn of the era. In this case, however, there is an indication that the Davidic line has been interrupted and must be restored. The metaphor of the shoot sprouting from the stump implies that the tree has been cut down (cf. Job 14:7: "For there is hope for a tree if it is cut down, that it will sprout again, and that its shoots will not cease"). The king in question, then, is more properly called a messiah. It is possible that Isaiah could have uttered such an oracle after the devastation of Judah by Sennacherib, but it is easier to suppose that it comes from a time after the exile, possibly from the period of the restoration, when some people seem to have hoped for a restoration of the Davidic line. The new king would be characterized by wisdom but above all by the fear of the Lord. Even if this oracle is late, however, it taps into the traditional royal ideology, which also informed the preaching of Isaiah. The hope for a righteous king is found in another oracle of uncertain provenance in 32:1.

The motif of the holy mountain (11:9) also appears in 2:1-5. This motif is especially prominent in Third Isaiah (Isaiah 56–66). While the motif of the holy mountain is old, the idea that *torah,* whether "law" or "instruction," radiates from Jerusalem is typical of the Second Temple period and is probably later than the Deuteronomic reform. The explanation of this oracle is complicated by the fact that it is also found, with only minor variations except for the last verse, in Mic 4:1-5. This suggests that it was a traditional oracle of uncertain attribution. Here again we have a relatively late oracle that revives old ideas of a mythical kingdom of universal peace. These oracles are an important element in the final shaping of the book of Isaiah, and they pick up optimistic themes of the royal ideology and Zion theology, which also informed the preaching of the eighth-century prophet.

Themes in the Preaching of Isaiah

The narrative of Isaiah's encounter with Ahaz during the Syro-Ephraimite war is balanced in chapters 36–38 with his encounter with the more receptive Hezekiah during the invasion of Sennacherib toward the end of his career. We shall return to that episode below. In between, the chronological setting of the oracles is only occasionally apparent. The oracle in 1:1-9, which says that Zion is left like a booth in a vineyard, brings to mind the campaign of Sennacherib, when the Assyrian king boasted that he shut up Hezekiah in Jerusalem like a bird in a cage. A setting during the Syro-Ephraimite war has also been suggested, but the question, "Why do you continue to rebel?" is more appropriate to the time of Hezekiah. Here again the prophet held that Judah only brought trouble on herself by attempting to solve her own problems. Isaiah 20, which tells how the prophet went naked for three years as a sign that King Sargon would take Egyptian and Ethiopian captives, is dated to the Assyrian campaign against Philistia in 712 B.C.E. The lesson for Judah is that it was futile to

Fig. 16.4 **A tunnel hewn into rock during the reign of Hezekiah brought water inside the fortified walls of Jerusalem.** Photo by: Tamar Hayardeni. Commons.wikimedia.org

rely on Egypt for help. Apart from these occasional historical allusions, the oracles have been loosed from their historical contexts. It is difficult in many cases to tell whether an oracle came from Isaiah or was added to the collection because it was judged to be thematically appropriate.

Some of the oracles in the early part of the book recall the preaching of Amos. Isaiah 1:1-10 insists on the futility of animal sacrifice: "I have had enough of the blood of bulls." Like Amos, Isaiah appears to reject the cult absolutely: "Trample my courts no more . . . your new moons and your appointed festivals my soul hates" (vv. 12-14). To be sure, he hates them because of the wrongdoing of the people, but he does not entertain the possibility of sacrifices offered by righteous people. The sacrificial cult is a distraction from the real service of the Lord, which is to defend the orphan and plead for the widow. The demand that people "wash yourselves, make yourselves clean" is not intended to substitute one ritual

for another. The washing is metaphorical. (This verse was, however, invoked later as a warrant for ritual washings, which proliferated in Judaism around the turn of the era, and for early Christian baptism.) The critique of the cult is repeated in 29:13, which says that the people honor God with their lips, while their heart is far from him. This passage is quoted in the New Testament in Matt 15:8-9 and Mark 7:6-7.

Isaiah comes close to Amos's concern for social justice in chapter 5. The Song of the Vineyard is an extended allegory. It is introduced as a love song and may have been modeled on a song for a wedding by a friend of the groom, in which the bride was compared with a fertile vineyard (for similar imagery cf. Song 2:15; 4:16; 8:11-12). But the love is short-lived in this song. The vineyard yielded sour wild grapes instead of grapes for wine. Because of this the owner of the vineyard decides to remove its wall and make it waste, and even command the clouds not to rain on it. The allegory is somewhat forced. No vineyard owner would blame his vineyard for its failure to produce good fruit. Isaiah uses the song as an indictment of Israel and Judah.

The choice of the image of the vineyard may be determined by the kind of offenses that Isaiah was condemning: those who joined house to house and field to field. The story of Naboth's vineyard (1 Kings 20) comes to mind. More typically, however, the small landowners were forced to mortgage their property to pay their debts, and so the land came to be concentrated in fewer and fewer hands. The vineyard was a symbol of luxury. It produced the wine that fueled the drunkenness of the wealthy. Consequently, when we are told in Isa 7:23 that "every place where there used to be a thousand vines, worth a thousand shekels of silver, will become thorns and briars," we must realize that from the prophet's perspective this was not altogether bad. The stripping of the land has much the same function in Isaiah that it had in Hosea. It is the painful but necessary condition for a new beginning.

The Song of the Vineyard has some structural similarity to the covenant lawsuit. Israel, or Judah, is indicted for failing to do justice, and condemned to punishment. Unlike Amos and Hosea, however, Isaiah does not use the exodus story as his frame of reference. He operates within the traditions of the Davidic monarchy and Zion, but these also presupposed the practice of justice and righteousness (see, for example, Pss 45:4, 7; 72:1-4).

One of the most characteristic themes of Isaiah's preaching is the condemnation of human pride and the demand for humility before the majesty of God. In Isa 2:12 Isaiah articulates his vision of "the Day of the Lord," which has lost its reference to a festival day and is simply the day of judgment: "For the Lord of hosts has a day against all that is proud and lofty, against all that is lifted up and high, against all the cedars of Lebanon, lofty and lifted up; against all the oaks of Bashan." On this day, the haughtiness of people shall be humbled. People shall enter the holes of the ground in terror. He is especially derisive of the women of Jerusalem who walk daintily and adorn themselves with jewelry (3:16-24; compare the tirade of Amos against the "cows of Bashan"). He is also dismissive of the rulers and counselors who trust in their own competence (3:1-5), and relishes the prospect of the breakdown of the ruling order (3:1-5). The destruction wrought by the Assyrians, then, served to remind people of the abject condition of humanity and the majesty of God. Moreover, the lowliness of humanity is not just a result of sinful behavior. It is intrinsic to the human condition: "Turn away from mortals, who have only breath in their nostrils, for of what account are they?" (2:22).

Isaiah speaks with respect of the awesome military might of Assyria. See 5:26-30, where he compares it to a young lion. Such power must serve a divine purpose. In 10:5-19 he describes Assyria as the rod of YHWH's anger. It executes YHWH's punishment on Israel and Judah. But Isaiah well knew that this was not how the Assyrians saw their role or what they proclaimed in their propaganda. In their eyes there was no difference between Samaria and Damascus or between Jerusalem and anyplace else. Such pride also required punishment. It was as if an instrument should think itself more important than its maker. The extension of this oracle in vv. 20-27 was probably added by a later editor, but the lesson it draws is close enough to the message of Isaiah: one should not fear the Assyrians; their time would also come.

The theme of bringing down the proud is perhaps the most consistent theme that unites the various oracles in Isaiah 1–39. A classic example is found in 14:12-20, a passage of uncertain provenance. It evokes the myth of the Day Star, son of Dawn, who tried to set his throne above the stars of El and was cast down to the Pit. This is probably a reflection of an old Canaanite myth of Athtar, the Day Star, who tried to sit on the throne of Baal in Ugaritic myth (Zaphon, mentioned in 14:13, was the mountain of Baal). The pattern is that the higher they rise, the lower they fall. It is essentially the same pattern that we found in the story of Adam and Eve, who tried to be like gods knowing good and evil, only to find that they were naked.

Distaste for human arrogance also underlies the prophet's critique of Jerusalemite politics in chapters 29–31. Isaiah had an especially strong distaste for the class of "wise men" who functioned as political advisers. So he predicts that "the wisdom of the wise shall perish" (29:14; cf. 1 Cor 1:19). These people allegedly "hide a plan too deep for the Lord" (Isa 29:15). The complaint is that they are overconfident in their wisdom and dismissive of the prophet, and tell him to prophesy "smooth things" (30:10). Isaiah insists that YHWH, too, is wise and has his own plan. The counselors, however, do not consult the Lord, which is to say that they do not pay attention to the prophet.

The recurring element in the plan of the "wise" is to seek help from Egypt (30:1-5; 31:1-3) and trust in horses and chariots. Isaiah formulates the problem concisely: "The Egyptians are human, and not divine; their horses are flesh, and not spirit" (31:3). The contrast between flesh and spirit goes to the heart of Isaiah's theology. That which is merely flesh, which is to say mortal, human, is of no avail. The human role is to trust: "in returning and rest you shall be saved, in quietness and in trust shall be your strength" (30:15). But such trust goes against the grain of a basic human instinct to take control of our own destiny. For the people of Jerusalem, this meant to acquire horses and form alliances. But their efforts typically ended in futility.

The Invasion of Sennacherib

The part of the book of Isaiah conventionally ascribed to First Isaiah is concluded by the narrative about Sennacherib's invasion in chapters 36–38 and the visit of the Babylonian envoys in chapter 39. This narrative is also found in 2 Kings 18–20. The most notable difference between the two accounts is that 2 Kings also includes a short notice in vv. 13-16 that says that Hezekiah submitted to the Assyrian king and paid him tribute. As we have seen in the discussion of 2 Kings, this account is essentially in agreement with the claims of the Assyrian annals. Isaiah 38:9-20 also contains a psalm attributed to Hezekiah that is not found in 2 Kings. It is usually assumed that the account is imported into the book of Isaiah from 2 Kings. That the Assyrian envoy refers to the destruction of the high places by Hezekiah may be taken to support Deuteronomistic authorship. Against this, some have noted that 2 Kings juxtaposes two contradictory accounts, and the shorter account, which corresponds to the Assyrian records, is more likely to be original. The story of the deliverance of Jerusalem may have originated independently and been incorporated secondarily into the Deuteronomistic History. It was also added to the book of Isaiah because of the role the prophet plays in it.

We have already discussed this narrative in the context of 2 Kings. Here our concern is with the portrayal of the prophet Isaiah. There are two interventions by the prophet. First, in Isa 37:2-4 Hezekiah sends delegates to Isaiah to ask him to intercede. There are parallels for consulting a prophet in time of crisis as early as the Mari texts from the mid- second millennium b.c.e. (Compare the delegation to the prophet Jeremiah in Jeremiah 21. In both cases the king expresses a hope that the Lord will intervene.) Isaiah does not elsewhere intercede for the people, but compare the

Fig. 16.5 Officials from the court of Sennacherib, ca. 700 B.C.E.; stone relief from Nimrud, now in the Honolulu Academy of Arts. Commons.wikimedia.org

intercession of Amos in Amos 7. The response of Isaiah on this occasion is in accordance with his oracle to Ahaz in Isaiah 7 and with the typical Assyrian prophecies of the era insofar as it tells the king not to fear. He provides a more explicit assurance to Hezekiah than he did to Ahaz, however, in promising that the Assyrian king will return home because of rumors in his own land.

The second intervention, in 37:21-35, is at Isaiah's own initiative. It has three parts. First there is a poetic taunt song, professing the contempt of Zion and her God for the invader (cf. the dismissal of the nations in Psalm 2). Other taunt songs can be found in the book of Isaiah (e.g., 14:4-21, presented as a taunt against Babylon), but we should expect an oracle addressed to Hezekiah here rather than a lengthy poem. Isaiah 37:26, "Have you not heard that I determined it long ago . . ." anticipates the rhetoric of Second Isaiah (e.g., 40:21). The prediction that YHWH will put a hook in the nose of the Assyrian

king anticipates the oracle against Gog in Ezek 38:4. This taunt song is an unequivocal affirmation of the traditional Zion theology, whereby YHWH defends his city against his enemies. It has a triumphalist tone that is difficult to reconcile with the other prophecies of Isaiah, and is likely to be a later composition.

The following oracle in vv. 30-32 is considerably more nuanced. Here Isaiah gives the king a sign, as he did with Ahaz. In this case, the sign is a prediction of what will happen. For two years people will have to eat what grows of itself, because it will not be possible to grow crops. Compare the reference to eating curds and honey in Isaiah 7. Only in the third year will it be possible again to plant and reap. This prediction is similar to Isaiah's use of the remnant theme in connection with the Syro-Ephraimite crisis. A remnant will survive, but it will not enjoy the kind of easy deliverance suggested by the taunt song.

Finally, in vv. 33-35 Isaiah predicts that Sennacherib would not enter or conquer Jerusalem. It is quite possible that Isaiah made such a prediction. The narrative presents Hezekiah as a righteous king who prays in time of crisis, in contrast to Ahaz who lacked faith. Isaiah affirmed the traditional belief that God would be with the Davidic dynasty and its city, but he did not imply that the people would be unscathed or would not suffer. Another oracle that may relate to the crisis under Sennacherib is in 29:1-7. In that case, the prophet predicts that the city would be besieged, as it once was by David, but that its enemies would suddenly be dispersed. In fact, Jerusalem was not destroyed, and its escape was remembered as a miracle.

While the narrative may have preserved some memory of Isaiah's oracles, however, the portrayal of the prophet here is very different from what we find in the rest of the book. Here he provides only reassurance. Even other oracles that probably relate to this crisis, however, such as 1:2-9 and 29:1-8, speak of punishment (for rebellion, in chap. 1) and of suffering inflicted by God to bring Jerusalem down to the dust (chap. 29). The judgmental side of the prophet's persona has been eliminated in the narrative of chapters 36–39. Further, in chapter 38 we find the prophet making a remedy for Hezekiah when he is sick and acting as a healer. In this he recalls the portrayal of Elijah and Elisha in the books of Kings and conforms to the type of the "holy man." His role as an intercessor, both for the people and for Hezekiah, is in accordance with this type. Whether Isaiah was actually a "holy man" of this type, we do not know. Such a portrayal was not suggested by anything in chapters 1–35.

The account of the envoys from Babylon provides a transition to the second half of the book, which is focused on the Babylonian exile. It seems unlikely that the Babylonians would send envoys such a distance merely to wish the king well. If there was any such visit, it is likely to have happened before Sennacherib's campaign, to seek the support of Judah against Assyria. The prediction that the king's own sons would be taken prisoner was not fulfilled in the case of Hezekiah, but the royal family was taken prisoner to Babylon approximately a century later. It is unlikely that either chapter 39 or chapters 36–38 were composed to provide a bridge between Isaiah 1–35 and 40–66. The bridge they provide is of a very limited nature. The foreshadowing of the Babylonian exile was as relevant to the concerns of the Deuteronomistic History as it was to the editors of the book of Isaiah. Nonetheless, the mention of Babylon provides some connection between the two main parts of the book.

Micah

Roughly contemporary with Isaiah was Micah of Moresheth, a small town about twenty-three miles southwest of Jerusalem. According to the superscription of the book, he prophesied in the days of Jotham, Ahaz, and Hezekiah, and his oracles concerned both Samaria and Jerusalem. In contrast to Isaiah, Micah was a rural prophet and not so closely engaged with the Davidic dynasty. As in the case of all the prophetic books, however, we must reckon with a process of edition and supplementation that may have gone on for centuries. A clear example of this is found in Mic 4:10, where Zion is told to writhe like a woman in labor, "for now you shall go forth from the city and camp in the open country; you shall go to Babylon. There you shall be rescued, there the LORD will redeem you from the hands of your enemies." The initial prophecy that the city would be undone, and that its inhabitants would have to camp in the open country, may well have been uttered by Micah. It is quite compatible with the critique of the ruling powers by the rural prophet. The extension of the prophecy to include the Babylonian exile and the subsequent restoration must have been added by a postexilic scribe, who felt impelled to update the oracle in the light of subsequent history.

The actual extent of the supplementation of the oracles of Micah is a matter of controversy. One scholarly tradition, developed in Germany in the late nineteenth century and still widely influential, attributes only material in chapters 1–3 to the eighth-century prophet, and that with minor exceptions, most notably the prophecy of restoration in 2:12-13. These chapters consist primarily of judgment oracles. The more hopeful oracles in chapters 4–5 are usually dated to the early postexilic period. Chapters 6–7 are also regarded as later additions. At least the conclusion in 7:8-20 was added to adapt the collection to liturgical use. This kind of analysis may go too far in denying the prophet any hope for the future. At least a few passages in chapters 4–7 are likely to come from the eighth century. In contrast to this approach, some recent commentaries have tried to defend the essential unity of the book (Hillers, Andersen and Freedman). There can be little doubt, however, that the oracles underwent a process of transmission and that the book, like those of the other preexilic prophets, was given its present form after the Babylonian exile.

The Social Critique

The opening oracle invokes an old tradition of the theophany of the divine warrior. In Judges 5 the imagery of storm and earthquake were used to express the terror caused by YHWH going to help his people in battle. In Micah they describe the terror of YHWH coming to judge his people. The wrath is directed against both Samaria and Jerusalem. The focus on the capital cities is significant. The offenses are primarily charged to the ruling class. Jerusalem is derisively called a "high place." Micah makes no distinction between the guilt of the two kingdoms. In 1:6 he prophesies that Samaria will be made a heap. In 3:12 he predicts that "Zion shall be plowed as a field;

Jerusalem shall become a heap of ruins." The latter prophecy is cited in Jer 26:18, where its nonfulfillment is explained by the fact that Hezekiah repented. Micah says that he will go naked and barefoot as Isaiah did, but where Isaiah symbolized the captivity of Egyptians and Ethiopians, Micah's action is a gesture of mourning for the destruction of Judah. The statement that "it has reached the gate of my people" recalls the invasion of Sennacherib (cf. Isaiah 1), but it more likely refers to the Syro-Ephraimite war, in view of the date ascribed to Micah and his concern for Samaria as well as Jerusalem.

The initial charge against Samaria and Jerusalem is idolatry. Jerusalem is compared to a high place; Samaria is accused of prostitution (cf. Hosea). More typical of Micah, however, is the accusation of injustice. The statement that "they covet fields, and seize them; houses and take them away," refers to the same phenomenon noted in Isa 5:8, which is addressed to those who add house to house and field to field. The punishment will fit the crime. Their own houses and fields will be seized by the invaders. Micah's condemnation of the exploitation of the poor is more biting even than that of Amos. The rich "tear the skin off my people and the flesh off their bones; eat the flesh of my people . . . chop them up like meat in a kettle" (3:2-3). The punishment to come will be a response of YHWH to the cry of the poor. Like Amos, Micah disassociates himself from the professional prophets (3:5-12). These people, we are told, give oracles for money (3:11; rulers and priests are similarly venal). They cry "peace" when they have enough to eat, and mislead the people by saying "surely, the LORD is with us" (3:11). If Isaiah saw this Davidic slogan as ambiguous, Micah sees it as a misleading illusion. We have no narrative of the call of Micah as we have of Amos. It seems safe to assume that he did not consider himself to be a *nabi'*. Like Amos, his preaching encountered opposition and some people tried to suppress it (2:6). It has been noted that the formula "thus says the LORD" occurs only once in chapters 1–3, and that Micah sometimes speaks in his own name (3:1). Nonetheless, he also speaks in the name of the Lord (e.g., 1:6: "I will make Samaria a heap"), and he claims to be filled with power, with the spirit of the Lord, to denounce the sin of Israel (3:8).

The critique of the cult in chapter 6 is also in line with what we have seen in the other eighth-century prophets and is plausibly attributed to Micah. This passage is cast in the form of a *ribh*, or legal disputation, and can be viewed as a covenant lawsuit. God reminds his people Israel that he brought them up from the land of Egypt and redeemed them from slavery. There is a clear implication that Israel should have responded by serving the Lord with justice and has failed to do so, but the offenses and consequent punishment are not spelled out. While the exodus played no part in the preaching of Isaiah of Jerusalem, it figured prominently in the oracles of Amos and Hosea, even though Amos, like Micah, came from the southern kingdom. Micah, too, addressed Israel as well as Judah. Many scholars assume that the appeal to the exodus here is the work of a Deuteronomistic editor, but this is not necessarily so.

Micah 6:6-8 considers the misguided reasoning of an Israelite, or Judean, worshiper. The assumption is that God will be impressed by the cost of the sacrifice. Even human sacrifice is contemplated. As we have seen in connection with Genesis 22, human sacrifice was practiced in ancient Israel and Judah. King Manasseh of Judah, son of Hezekiah, was said to have made his son "pass through fire," which is to say that he sacrificed him as a burnt offering (2 Kgs 21:6). Human sacrifice, however, is much less likely to have been an option in the postexilic period. Micah's critique of sacrifice is essentially the same as that of the other prophets we have considered. It indicates a misunderstanding of what YHWH wants, which is "to do justice, and to love kindness, and to walk humbly with your God" (6:8).

Most of the positive oracles in chapters 4–5 are likely to have been added by postexilic editors when the time of judgment had passed and the need was for consolation and hope. Micah 4:1-5 repeats an oracle found in Isa 2:1-5, with a variation in the concluding verse. The imagery of *torah* going forth from Jerusalem and the peoples streaming thereto fits better with the aspirations of Second Temple Judaism than with what we know of the eighth century. The oracle probably circulated anonymously. That it is associated with two eighth-century prophets is striking but probably coincidental. A more difficult case is presented by Mic 5:2-5, which predicts the advent of a ruler from Bethlehem of Judah, the ancestral home of David. Many scholars take this as a postexilic prediction of a restoration of the Davidic line, and the obscure statement in v. 3, "the rest of his kindred shall return," can be read as supporting this interpretation. But the focus on Bethlehem, as opposed to Zion, may be significant. Micah of Moresheth may have felt that the Davidic monarchy could be redeemed if it returned to the humble roots symbolized by the ancestral village. The prediction of a ruler from Bethlehem would then be a rejection of the ruling king and the

Jerusalem court, but not of the Davidic line. The oracle would still have been read in a messianic sense in the postexilic period. In the later context, Assyria would be understood as the archetypal enemy. The fantasy of a final defeat of invading nations appears frequently in the later prophetic and apocalyptic books (e.g., the prophecy of Gog in Ezekiel 38–39).

The Final Edition

The books of Amos and Hosea end on optimistic notes with hopeful prophecies for the future. The final edition of Micah also balances judgment with hope but concentrates the optimistic prophecies in chapters 4–5. There is also a prediction of restoration at the end of the book of Micah (7:12). In part, however, this prediction is cast as a prayer, appealing to God to shepherd his people. The final appeal is to the mercy of God, to pardon iniquity. This appeal is backed by recalling the promise to Abraham (7:20), but there is also a confession that the fulfillment of that promise is impeded by the sin of Abraham's descendants and can be implemented only by an act of mercy.

The End of Assyria

In the second half of the seventh century B.C.E., Assyria went into decline. First, Egypt revolted successfully. Then, after the death of the Assyrian king Ashurbanipal in 627 B.C.E., Babylon asserted its independence. In the following years, Assyria was challenged by the Medes from the east and the Babylonians from the south. The decline in Assyrian power permitted a resurgence of Judean nationalism and allowed King Josiah to carry out his reforms. In 614 the city of Ashur fell to the Medes. Nineveh, the Assyrian capital, was destroyed by an alliance of Medes and Babylonians in 612.

Nahum

It was only natural that the fall of Assyria should be celebrated in Jerusalem. The occasion is marked in a short collection of oracles attributed to the prophet Nahum, who is said to come from an otherwise unknown place called Elkosh. Nahum begins with an oracle of assurance for Judah that draws on much of the traditional imagery of the divine warrior (1:2-15). Nonetheless, it comes as something of a shock to read that "a jealous and avenging God is the LORD, the LORD is avenging and wrathful; the LORD takes vengeance on his adversaries and rages against his enemies." No less than Hosea, Nahum projects human emotions onto God. Unlike Hosea, however, he makes no attempt to discriminate which emotions are worthy of God. Nahum certainly had tradition on his side. YHWH is portrayed as a jealous God in Exod 20:5. The violence attributed to YHWH here is often directed against his own people. Nahum may be forgiven a certain glee in seeing it directed against the long-time enemy of Judah. Nahum 1:15 refers to the messenger who brings good tidings, an image that we shall meet again in Second Isaiah in the context of the end of the Babylonian exile. Here the "good tidings" is not the liberation of Jewish exiles, but simply the destruction of the oppressor.

Nahum 2 is addressed to Nineveh itself. Nahum paints a vivid picture of the terror of

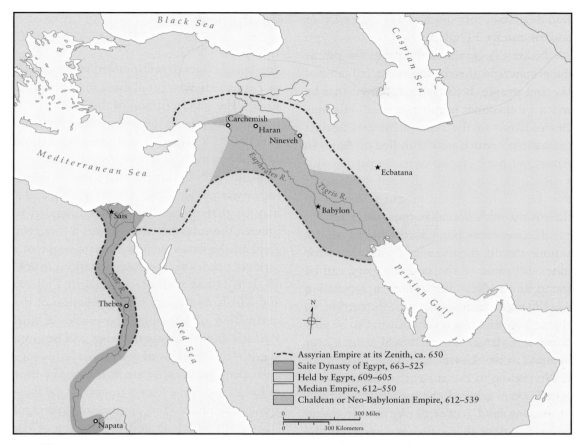

Map 16.1

warfare: "Hearts faint and knees tremble, all loins quake, all faces grow pale" (2:10). The most distinctive aspect of this oracle, however, is the prophet's assumption that YHWH is responsible for the destruction of Nineveh, even though it is carried out by Babylonians and Medes. As Amos might have said, can disaster befall a city if YHWH did not cause it?

The third chapter is a taunt song pronounced over Babylon as a mock lament. Here again we get a vivid poetic description of the sack of a city. Remarkably, he refers to Nineveh as a prostitute. Hosea had used this image with reference to Israel because of the worship of other gods, especially Baal. Later, in the New Testament, the book of Revelation refers to Rome as a harlot, primarily because of her trade (Revelation 17–18). The metaphor is surprising in the case of Assyria, which had relied on force to acquire its wealth. The punishment of Nineveh is like the punishment of Israel in Hosea 2: "I will let the nations look on your nakedness." Nahum goes on to remind the Assyrians of what they had done to the Egyptian capital, Thebes, which they had sacked in 663 B.C.E. Nineveh's fate is well deserved, "for who has ever escaped your endless cruelty"? (Nah 3:19).

Nahum is exceptional among the preexilic prophets in that he utters no criticism of his own people. It has been surmised that he was a professional prophet, a *nabi'*. His oracles conform to the type of "oracles against the nations," which were parodied by Amos in Amos 1–2. Such oracles were compatible with a naïve nationalism, devoid of self-criticism. It may be unfair, however, to judge Nahum on the basis of such a small corpus of oracles.

The most troubling aspect of his oracles is undoubtedly their vengeful tone. The same tone, and some of the same imagery, can be found in the New Testament, in Revelation 17–18, which fantasizes the destruction of Rome. Vengefulness is certainly not to be proposed as a virtue, but we should at least bear in mind what Assyria had done to provoke it. No regime in the ancient world was more brutal, even granted the pervasive brutality of ancient (and modern!) warfare. It would be hard to deny that justice was served in the destruction of Nineveh. But then the execution of justice, especially in a violent way, often begets more oppression. Isaiah saw this when he called Assyria the rod of YHWH's anger, which was itself guilty of excess (Isaiah 10). Earlier, Hosea had denounced the bloodshed of Jezreel (Hosea 1), even though it had been sanctioned by Elisha (2 Kings 9). The Babylonians who ravaged Nineveh would not stop there. They would shortly treat Jerusalem as savagely as the Assyrians had treated Samaria. Nahum, however, shows no awareness of that looming disaster.

A more forgiving attitude toward Assyria is found in the book of Jonah, which we will consider at the end of the prophetic corpus.

Zephaniah

The fall of Nineveh is also noted in the oracles of Zephaniah, who prophesied in the reign of Josiah. The superscription of the book, exceptionally, supplies a genealogy to the third generation. Zephaniah was descended from one Hezekiah, who is not identified, at least explicitly, with the king of that name. Nahum's father was named Cushi ("Ethiopian"), and it may be that the genealogy was intended to prevent the inference that he was a foreigner. Zephaniah's oracle against Assyria is one of a series of oracles against foreign nations in 2:4-15. It is linked with oracles against Philistia and Moab, and a very brief prediction of the destruction of Ethiopia. The oracles against Philistia and Moab say that they will be given over to "the remnant of my people." This suggests that these oracles are later than the time of Josiah and come from a time after the Babylonian conquest. The prophet complains of "the taunts of Moab and the reviling of the Ammonites" (2:8), and this too points to a time after the destruction of Jerusalem. The oracle against Assyria complains that Nineveh had boasted, "I am, and there is no one else" (2:15). We find a similar charge against Babylon in Isa 47:8. It is not clear whether any of these oracles against other nations can be attributed to Zephaniah. Such oracles were frequently inserted into prophetic collections by the editors.

The main concern of Zephaniah, in any case, was not with Nineveh but with Jerusalem, which is the target of the oracles in 1:2—2:3, and again in 3:1-20. The dominant motif is the Day of the Lord. As in Amos, the Day of the Lord is both a festival day and a day of judgment. The festival connotation is shown by Zeph 1:7: "The Lᴏʀᴅ has prepared a sacrifice, he has consecrated his guests." For the people this was a happy occasion, when they would in effect hold parties in connection with their sacrifices. But like Amos, Zephaniah also sees it as a day of punishment. Two charges are brought against the people in chapter 1. The first is idolatry. People, and even priests, worship Baal, bow down to the host of heaven, and swear by Milcom (the god of Ammon) as well as YHWH (the reference to Milcom could also be read as *malkam*, "their king"). The second is more distinctive: "I will punish the officials and the king's sons and all who dress themselves in foreign attire" (1:9). Adoption of foreign dress appears again as a source of conflict much later in the Maccabean crisis in the second century ʙ.ᴄ.ᴇ. but is not otherwise an issue in the Hebrew Bible. Zephaniah probably spoke early in the reign of Josiah, before the Deuteronomic reform. It is unlikely that the reference here is to Josiah's sons, since the king was very young when he came to the throne. The phrase may be a general reference to the royal house. The foreign style that was fashionable was probably Assyrian, since Assyria was still the overlord. This is the most explicit indication in the Hebrew Bible that adoption of Assyrian customs was an issue in seventh-century Judah. Some scholars argue that many of the abuses addressed in the Deuteronomic reform (such as the worship of the host of heaven) were due to foreign influence in this period.

Zephaniah returns to his indictment of Jerusalem in chapter 3. He denounces it as a "soiled, defiled, oppressing city." Officials, prophets, and priests alike are accused of infidelity. The priests are accused of doing violence to *torah*, which in this context probably refers to priestly instruction rather than to the Torah, or Law. The point is that the priests betray the things they are responsible for: that which is sacred, and instruction. All these people will be punished "on that day." Like Isaiah, however, Zephaniah expects the Lord to leave a remnant (3:13). These will be "a people humble and lowly," a designation reminiscent of Micah 6. It is a plausible inference that Zephaniah and this "humble" people would have supported Josiah's reform, which swept away idolatrous worship and foreign influence from Jerusalem. Zephaniah has clear links to the eighth-century prophets Amos, Isaiah, and Micah. His book is a link in the chain of development that led from the preaching of these prophets to the Deuteronomic reform.

Like most prophetic books, Zephaniah has been edited to end on a positive note. From the viewpoint of the postexilic editors, the condemnation of Jerusalem should not be the last word. So they appended an oracle proclaiming that the Lord has taken away the judgments against Jerusalem. Zephaniah himself had said that the Lord was within Jerusalem, in accordance with the royal ideology (3:5) although he saw this presence as dangerous. The editor saw it as assuring. Since the Lord is in its midst, Jerusalem need fear disaster no more. The postexilic origin of this closing oracle is clear in 3:20, which speaks of gathering Judah and bringing it home.

FOR FURTHER READING

Isaiah

J. Barton, *Isaiah 1–39* (Old Testament Guides; Sheffield: Sheffield Academic Press, 1995). Good popular introduction.

J. Blenkinsopp, *Isaiah 1–39* (AB 19; New York: Doubleday, 2000). Excellent historical-critical commentary.

B. S. Childs, *Isaiah* (OTL; Louisville: Westminster John Knox, 2001). Theological commentary on the entire book of Isaiah, with concern for editorial shaping, intertextuality, and the unity of the book.

R. E. Clements, *Isaiah 1–39* (NCB; Grand Rapids: Eerdmans, 1980). Solid redaction-critical commentary.

J. J. Collins, "The Sign of Immanuel," in J. Day, ed., *Prophecy and the Prophets in Ancient Israel* (London: T&T Clark, 2010). Analysis of Isaiah 7.

M. J. de Jong, *Isaiah among the Ancient Near Easter Prophets* (Leiden: Brill, 2007). Comparison of the earliest stages of Isaiah with Neo-Assyrian prophecies.

R. F. Melugin and M. A. Sweeney, eds., *New Visions of Isaiah* (JSOTSup 214; Sheffield: Sheffield Academic Press, 1996; reissue Atlanta: SBL, 2006). Diverse essays on the formation of the book of Isaiah.

D. L. Petersen, *The Prophetic Literature: An Introduction* (Louisville: Westminster John Knox, 2002), 47–96. Discussion of literary issues in light of recent scholarship.

C. R. Seitz, *Zion's Final Destiny: The Development of the Book of Isaiah* (Minneapolis: Fortress, 1991). Redactional study of the place of Isaiah 36–39 in the development of the book.

M. A. Sweeney, *Isaiah 1–39, with an Introduction to Prophetic Literature* (FOTL 16; Grand Rapids: Eerdmans, 1996). Form-critical and redactional analysis.

G. M. Tucker, "The Book of Isaiah 1–39," *NIB* 6:27–305. Homiletical commentary with a form-critical perspective.

H. Wildberger, *Isaiah 1–12* (trans. T. H. Trapp; CC; Minneapolis: Fortress Press, 1991); *Isaiah 13–27* (trans. T. H. Trapp; CC; Minneapolis: Fortress Press, 1997). Classic form and redaction-critical commentary.

H. G. M. Williamson, *The Book Called Isaiah: Deutero-Isaiah's Role in Composition and Redaction* (Oxford: Clarendon, 1994). Analysis of the composition of the book, ascribing an editorial role to Deutero-Isaiah.

———, "The Messianic Texts in Isaiah 1–39," in J. Day, ed., *King and Messiah in Israel and the Ancient Near East* (Sheffield: Sheffield Academic Press, 1998), 244–50. Concise discussion of the potentially messianic texts.

———, *Variations of a Theme: King, Messiah and Servant in the Book of Isaiah* (Carlisle: Paternoster, 1998). Fuller discussion of messianic themes in Isaiah.

R. A. Young, *Hezekiah in History and Tradition* (Leiden: Brill, 2012), 151–91. Historical background of the messianic oracles.

Micah

F. I. Andersen and D. N. Freedman, *Micah* (AB 24E; New York: Doubleday, 2000). Extensive historical-philological commentary. Defends the unity of the book.

D. R. Hillers, *Micah* (Hermeneia; Philadelphia: Fortress Press, 1984). Concise commentary. Regards Micah as a prophet of a revitalization movement. Also defends the unity of the book.

J. L. Mays, *Micah* (OTL; Philadelphia: Westminster, 1976). Solid exegetical commentary, with interest in redactional development.

W. McKane, *Micah: Introduction and Commentary* (Edinburgh: Clark, 1998). Complex philological and redaction-critical commentary.

D. J. Simundson, "The Book of Micah," *NIB* 7:531–89. Helpful homiletical commentary.

M. A. Sweeney, *The Twelve Prophets* (Berit Olam; Collegeville, MN, 2000), 2:337–416. Helpful exegetical commentary.

H. W. Wolff, *Micah the Prophet* (trans. R. D. Gehrke; Philadelphia: Fortress Press, 1981). Concise summary of the views developed in Wolff's commentary.

———, *Micah* (trans. G. Stansell; CC; Minneapolis: Augsburg, 1990). Detailed form- and redaction-critical commentary.

E. Ben Zvi, *Micah* (FOTL 21B; Grand Rapids: Eerdmans, 2000). Form-critical analysis, emphasizing postexilic composition.

Nahum and Zephaniah

A. Berlin, *Zephaniah* (AB 25A; New York: Doubleday, 1994). Careful commentary on philological, textual, and poetic issues.

D. L. Christiansen, *Nahum* (Yale Anchor Bible 24F; New Haven: Yale University Press, 2009). Detailed philological commentary.

M. H. Floyd, *Minor Prophets, Part 2* (FOTL 22; Grand Rapids: Eerdmans, 2000), 1–78 (Nahum), 163–250 (Zephaniah). Form-critical analysis.

J. J. M. Roberts, *Nahum, Habakkuk, and Zephaniah* (OTL; Louisville: Westminster, 1991). Philological and textual analysis.

M. A. Sweeney, *The Twelve Prophets* (Berit Olam; Collegeville, MN, 2000), 2:417–50 (Nahum), 491–526. Concise exegetical commentary.

———. Sweeney, *Zephaniah* (Hermeneia; Minneapolis: Augsburg Fortress, 2003). Detailed exegetical commentary.

E. Ben Zvi, *A Historical-Critical Study of the Book of Zephaniah* (BZAW 198; Berlin/New York: de Gruyter, 1991). Thorough study in historical context.

CHAPTER 17

The Babylonian Era
Habakkuk, Jeremiah, and Lamentations

INTRODUCTION

This chapter examines the prophetic responses to the catastrophe occasioned by the rise of Babylon: Habakkuk, Jeremiah, and the book of Lamentations.

The prophetic books of the Hebrew Bible cluster around the great catastrophes that befell the kingdoms of Israel and Judah. Nahum and Zephaniah are somewhat exceptional in this regard. Nahum prophesied on the occasion of the fall of Assyria. Zephaniah was a little earlier in the reign of Josiah. This was a transition era in the ancient Near East, between the decline of Assyria and the rise of Babylon. Neither Nahum nor Zephaniah addressed the problems presented by the rising power. These prophets, however, were contemporaries of the young Jeremiah, whose later career would be dominated by the shadow of Babylon. Before we turn to Jeremiah, we shall consider briefly another "minor" prophet, Habakkuk, whose short book is also set against the backdrop of the coming of Babylon.

Habakkuk

The book of Habakkuk is exceptional in that there is no superscription giving the dates of the prophet's activity. There is a clear indication of his time, however, in 1:6: "For I am rousing the Chaldeans, that fierce and impetuous nation. . . ."The Chaldeans were a tribe of Aramean origin that appeared in lower Mesopotamia early in the first millennium B.C.E. and became one of the dominant elements in the Neo-Babylonian Empire that was founded by Nabopolassar (626–605 B.C.E.) and expanded by Nebuchadnezzar II, the destroyer of Jerusalem. After the fall of Nineveh in 612, the control of the western part of the Assyrian Empire lay between Egypt and Babylon. In 609, Pharaoh Neco led an army to assist the Assyrians against Babylon at Carchemish on the Euphrates. King Josiah of Judah went to meet him at Megiddo, but the pharaoh killed him (2 Kgs 23:29). According to 2 Chron 35:20-27, Josiah was killed in battle, but there is no mention of a battle in 2 Kings. It may be that Josiah was executed, for whatever reason. In any case, the Babylonians were victorious at Carchemish and could now proceed to consolidate their control over Syria-Palestine. The prophecy of Habakkuk takes place against the backdrop of these events.

Habakkuk is also exceptional in the prophetic books in that it offers a sustained reflection on the problem of injustice. Habakkuk begins on a reflective note that is more typical of the psalmists than of the prophets: "How long, O LORD, shall I cry for help?" (cf. Pss 4:2; 13:1; et al.). The problem is that of theodicy, the justice of God, a frequent topic in the wisdom literature. The wicked surround the righteous and treat them violently, but God does nothing about it. Some scholars think the prophet is referring to the Assyrians, but this is unlikely. Assyrian oppression was not a factor in Judah for a long time before the rise of the Chaldeans. It is far more likely that Habakkuk is referring to internal injustice in Jerusalem. We find similar complaints in this period in the oracles of Jeremiah.

The immediate response of the Lord is to announce that he is rousing the Chaldeans. The oracle in 1:5-11 gives a vivid and striking picture of a ruthlessly efficient army. Five hundred years later, this oracle is interpreted in the Dead Sea Scrolls as referring to Rome (in the pesher, or commentary, on Habakkuk, which is one of the earliest extant biblical commentaries). Rome, too, had a ruthless military machine. The prophet, however, is not

persuaded that the Babylonian invasion will resolve the problem of injustice. The Babylonians, like the Assyrians before them, treated subject peoples as of little consequence—as a fisherman might treat fish. Habakkuk complains that God has made people like the fish of the sea and put them at the mercy of the Babylonians. Once again, God is silent while the wicked swallows those who are more righteous, even if they are not without fault. It is very unusual for a prophet to take God to task. The paradigmatic biblical figure who questions divine justice is Job. Habakkuk is much more restrained in his rhetoric, but he raises the appropriate questions.

In 2:1 Habakkuk takes the position of a watchman. We meet this image again in Ezekiel. The watchman is usually on the lookout for approaching danger. Here he watches for a reply from God. At first he is given only a preparatory reply. The vision that he receives

Fig. 17.1 The beginning of the Habakkuk pesher (or commentary), 1QpHab, from Qumran, first century B.C.E.; at the Israel Museum. Commons.wikimedia.org

is for an appointed time. It will not be fulfilled immediately. The prophet must have patience to wait, but the time will not be long. This verse is often picked up in later tradition in the context of apocalyptic expectations of divine intervention. It is expounded in the commentary on Habakkuk in the Dead Sea Scrolls to explain why the "end" or divine intervention did not come when it was expected. (This phenomenon, of the delay of the end, would often be repeated throughout history.) The final verse of this passage, "the righteous shall live by his [or 'its'] faithfulness," is cited in the New Testament and is used as a summary of Pauline theology (Rom 1:17; Gal 3:11; Heb 10:38). The Hebrew text is ambiguous: it may refer to the reliability of the vision or to the faithfulness of the righteous person. Habakkuk affirms both: the vision is reliable and the righteous person must wait faithfully for its fulfillment.

The remainder of this chapter is an indictment of the proud and the wealthy. Here again there is some ambiguity. Similar charges are brought against King Jehoiakim of Judah in Jeremiah 22. Since the arrogant in Habakkuk "gather all nations for themselves and collect all peoples as their own" (2:5), the reference is more likely to be to the Babylonian king Nebuchadnezzar. Habakkuk is affirming that Babylon will be punished in turn, just as Isaiah had predicted that Assyria would be (Isaiah 10). The description of the greedy, who "open their throats wide as Sheol, like Death they never have enough," recalls the figure of Mot or Death in the old Ugaritic myth who opened his mouth with one lip to earth and one to heaven in order to swallow Baal. The comment on the uselessness of idols in

2:18-19 seems out of context here. This kind of polemic against idolatry is especially associated with Second Isaiah (cf. Isa 44:9-20).

The content of the vision is finally disclosed in chapter 3, but it is not presented in the form of a vision report. Instead, we are given a traditional poem about the theophany of the divine warrior, familiar from such texts as Deut 33:2-3; Judg 5:4-5; Ps 68:7-8. It is typical of these poems that YHWH comes from a mountain in the south, and this recalls a very early stage of the religion of Israel, before the Deity was thought to have made his home in Jerusalem. The appearance of the divine warrior is accompanied by the convulsion of nature (cf. Nah 1:3-5). The prophet (or the traditional poet) asks, "Was your wrath against the rivers . . . or your rage against the sea?" While this motif may recall the exodus (cf. Pss 77:16-18; 114:3-6, this is not a necessary association. The reference is to the cosmic convulsions caused by the appearance of YHWH. The exodus was one example among many, and Habakkuk does not elsewhere refer to the exodus tradition. There is a clear reference, however, to the Davidic kingship: the purpose of the theophany is so that God can save his people and his anointed (3:13).

The recollection of the theophany of the divine warrior apparently reassures the prophet. The book ends on a note of confident hope: "though the fig tree does not blossom, and no fruit is on the vines . . . yet I will rejoice in the Lord, I will exult in the God of my salvation." The concluding verse, which refers to a choir leader and stringed instruments, seems to indicate that the book, or at least the last chapter, was used in a liturgical context, as was also the case with Micah. Unfortunately, we know nothing of the occasions on which it may have been used.

While the prophecy of Habakkuk is grounded in a specific historical situation, the problem of theodicy and the general descriptions of the righteous and the arrogant are easily transferable to other contexts. More than any other prophet, Habakkuk comes close to the reflective attitude of wisdom teachers. In the end, however, he appeals to a vision of the future to resolve the problem of injustice in the present. We shall find that this move is especially typical of apocalyptic literature in the later part of the Second Temple period, especially in its emphasis on patient waiting. It is significant in this regard that Hab 2:3 ("There is still a vision for the appointed time," or, by slight emendation, "The vision is a witness for the appointed time") is cited not only in the Dead Sea Scrolls but also, indirectly, in Dan 11:35, in the context of the expectation of the "end."

Jeremiah

According to the superscription (Jer 1:1), Jeremiah was "son of Hilkiah, of the priests who were in Anathoth," and began to prophesy in the thirteenth year of Josiah (627 B.C.E.). Anathoth was located no more than three miles northeast of Jerusalem. According to 1 Kgs 2:26-27, when he became king, Solomon banished the priest Abiathar to Anathoth for supporting his brother Adonijah. Presumably, Jeremiah came from this priestly line. A man named Hilkiah was high priest in Jerusalem at the time of Josiah's reform (2 Kings 22), but he cannot have been from the priests of Anathoth. Jeremiah continued to prophesy until the fall of Jerusalem to the Babylonians.

The Composition of the Book

The book that bears the name of Jeremiah rivals that of Isaiah in complexity, although the period of its formation does not cover as wide a time span. To begin with, there are obvious differences between the Hebrew text preserved in the Masoretic Bible and the Greek (Septuagint or LXX) translation. The Greek text is about one-eighth shorter than the Hebrew. Most of the differences concern single verses, but some longer passages are also absent from the Greek (33:14-26; 39:4-13; 51:44b-49a; 52:27b-30). Also the block of oracles against foreign nations, which appears at the end of the book in Hebrew (chaps. 46–51), is found in the Greek after 25:13 (25:14 is lacking in the Greek). The historical appendix in chapter 52 is borrowed from 2 Kgs 24:18—25:21. Older scholarship inclined to the view that the Greek translators had abridged the book. One of the fragmentary Hebrew copies of the book found at Qumran (4Q Jerᵇ), however, corresponds to the Greek, and so it now appears that the Greek preserves the older form of the book, while the Hebrew was expanded and rearranged secondarily.

The complexity, however, goes beyond textual issues. It has long been realized that there are three kinds of material in the book: poetic oracles, conventionally designated (A); narratives about Jeremiah, especially in the second half of the book (B); and sermonic prose passages that bear a strong resemblance to Deuteronomic style (C). The oracles against the nations are yet a fourth kind of material. The narratives about Jeremiah are often attributed to his assistant Baruch, although this, of course, cannot be conclusively proved. These narratives also show some signs of

Deuteronomistic editing. The C material is the work of Deuteronomistic editors but may nonetheless contain paraphrases or recollections of actual oracles of the prophet, as well as new material. There is, however, a wide spectrum of opinion on the origin of the material in the book. Some scholars, primarily American, regard the whole book as a reliable witness to the words and life of Jeremiah, with few exceptions. Others regard it as largely a product of anonymous scribes in the postexilic period. The view that distinguishes A, B, and C material as indicated above remains the most helpful starting point, although the actual formation of the book was probably more complicated than this.

Some light may be shed on the formation of the book by an incident reported in chapter 36. In the fourth year of Jehoiakim, or 605 B.C.E., Jeremiah received a divine command to take a scroll and write on it all the words spoken to him "against Israel and Judah and all the nations." So Jeremiah called Baruch, son of Neriah, who was evidently a scribe, and who wrote down the words at Jeremiah's dictation. (A seal impression has been found with the name "Baruch" followed by the words "the scribe.") Baruch was instructed to read the scroll in the temple on a fast day, since Jeremiah was barred from the sanctuary. Baruch did so. The officials who heard it became concerned and felt that it must be reported to the king. They told Baruch and Jeremiah to go and hide themselves while they took the scroll and read it to the king. As the king heard it read, he cut off columns of the scroll and burned them in the fire. Jeremiah, however, dictated the words again to Baruch, who wrote them on another scroll, "and many similar words were added to them" (36:32).

Fig. 17.2 A seal including the words "Baruch ben Neriyahu, the scribe"; now in the Israel Museum.
Commons.wikimedia.org

Many scholars have argued that the substance of this scroll is found in Jer 1:1—25:13a (25:13a refers to "everything written in this book"). These chapters do not, however, contain the unedited oracles of Jeremiah, and they contain some material that is explicitly later than 605, such as 21:1-10, which relates to the reign of Zedekiah, who was made king by the Babylonians in 597. It may be, however, that the oracles of Jeremiah transcribed by Baruch formed the basis of these chapters, which was then edited by Deuteronomistic scribes, to illustrate how the people had failed to listen to "his servants the prophets." In the second half of the book, apart from the oracles against the nations, prose narrative predominates. Whoever may have been the author of these narratives, they constitute a presentation of the prophet that attempts to enlist his authority in support of a particular interpretation of the Babylonian conquest. They cannot be taken as an objective account of the historical events.

There is a rough chronological order in the book, apart from the oracles against the nations, but it is not imposed consistently. The episode in the reign of Zedekiah in chapter 21 appears out of sequence, and there are two prose accounts of Jeremiah's temple sermon (chaps. 7 and 26). It is possible to explain the placement of some chapters, but no one as yet has given a comprehensive explanation of the order of the book. The reason, perhaps, is that Jeremiah, like other prophetic books, is primarily a collection of oracles and of narratives about the prophet. Attempts to impose a thoroughgoing redactional logic on the book are anachronistic and misunderstand the nature of this kind of literature.

The Call of Jeremiah

The call of Jeremiah in chapter 1 follows the pattern of the call of Moses in Exodus rather than that of Isaiah. First, there is no vision involved. It is an auditory experience. Second, Jeremiah protests his unsuitability for the mission, as Moses does in Exod 4:10-17. Finally, the Lord encourages the chosen one and confirms him in his mission. The Lord touches Jeremiah's mouth (1:9). He assures Moses that "I will be with your mouth" (Exod 4:12). Jeremiah is presented as "a prophet like Moses," who is raised up by YHWH and given his words to speak, in accordance with the Deuteronomic model in Deuteronomy 18. At the least, the account of his call shows the marks of Deuteronomistic editing. This does not apply to the opening stanza, however: "before I formed you in the womb I knew you, and before you were born I consecrated you; I appointed you as a prophet to the nations." The designation of Jeremiah as a prophet to the nations is somewhat puzzling. Most of his oracles are addressed to Judah and Jerusalem. The oracles against foreign nations are generic pieces that could have been composed by any prophet. Jeremiah 51:59-64 reports that Jeremiah sent a scroll to Babylon by means of Seraiah, brother of Baruch, with orders to throw it into the Euphrates, bearing prophecies of disasters that would befall the city. If Jeremiah regularly prophesied against other nations, however, this aspect of his prophecy has been obscured by the edition of his oracles, where the oracles against other nations are segregated in a section by themselves.

It is also noteworthy that his mission includes building and planting as well as plucking up and tearing down. The book of Jeremiah includes hopeful oracles about the restoration of Jerusalem, primarily in the so-called book of consolation in chapters 30–33. These oracles have undoubtedly been shaped by editors, but they contain a core of poetic oracles that probably go back to the prophet himself. The editors of the book, in any case, wanted to give the impression that his mission had a hopeful aspect from the start. It may also be significant that the hopeful oracles are placed before the narrative of the fall of Jerusalem. This adds to the impression that restoration was always part of the plan, even before the destruction. In the view of the editors, the legacy of Jeremiah concerned not only the destruction of Jerusalem but also the survival and ultimate restoration of a community in Babylon (cf. Jer 24:6, which promises to plant the exilic community and not pull them up).

Jeremiah and the Deuteronomic Reform

Some of the early oracles of Jeremiah are reminiscent of those of Hosea. He recalls the origin of Israel as YHWH's bride in the wilderness (Jer 2:1) and uses the metaphor of divorce (3:1; cf. Deuteronomy 24, which forbids a man to take back a woman he has divorced after she has been with another man). The complaint here is twofold: worship of the Baals and other gods, and seeking political alliances with Egypt and Assyria. At this point, Jeremiah is reiterating themes from the prophetic tradition. He addresses northern as well as southern Israel (3:12) and holds out the prospect of repentance. The polemic against the worship of other gods would presumably have been congenial to the Deuteronomic reform, as would the prediction that God would reunite northern Israel with Jerusalem if it repented (3:14). The only passages that refer to the reform explicitly, however, are in sermonic prose and are part of the Deuteronomistic edition of the book. Jeremiah 3:6-11 says that Jeremiah preached "in the days of King Josiah" that Judah was repeating the cultic adultery that had led to the destruction of the northern kingdom. Jeremiah 11:1-8 appeals to "the words of this covenant," which can only mean the Deuteronomic law. There are also clear overtones of Deuteronomy in the prose account of Jeremiah's temple sermon in 7:1—8:3, which takes the people to task for trusting in "these deceptive words: 'This is the temple of the LORD, the temple of the LORD, the temple of the LORD.'" Josiah had torn down the places of worship outside Jerusalem, but this only added to the importance of the Jerusalem temple as the one center of legitimate worship, and so indirectly strengthened the Zion theology. Jeremiah's sermon in 7:1—8:3 can be read as an indictment of the people for not truly following the requirements of Deuteronomy by practicing justice and avoiding the worship of other gods. As a result, YHWH would do to Jerusalem what he had done to Shiloh, the long defunct shrine of the premonarchic period. This episode is also recounted in the quasi-biographical narrative in chapter 26, where it is dated to the first year of King Jehoiakim, son of Josiah. In this case, the focus is on the controversy engendered by the prophecy that the Lord would make the Jerusalem temple like Shiloh. This passage, too, has Deuteronomic overtones. The destruction is threatened if the people "will not listen to me, to walk in my law that I have set before you and to heed the words of my servants the prophets" (26:2-5). The first year of Jehoiakim was an appropriate time to express concern over the fate of Josiah's reform. Not only was Josiah prematurely dead, but the choice of "the people of the land," Jehoahaz (Shallum), was deposed by the Egyptians, who put his brother Jehoiakim in his place (2 Kgs 23:30-35). It is very plausible that Jeremiah delivered oracles condemning the facile temple theology and predicting that Jerusalem would be made like Shiloh. The Deuteronomic language of the sermon, however, is probably an interpretation of his oracles by Deuteronomistic editors.

Jeremiah certainly shared basic values of the Deuteronomic reform—opposition to the worship of deities other than YHWH and to social injustice. There is some evidence, however, that he was reluctant to identify the law of the Lord with the contents of a book promulgated by scribes. The clearest evidence of this point is found in a poetic oracle in Jer 8:4-12. The opening verses are reminiscent of Isa 1:2-3: birds and animals know how to behave, but sinful people do not. Jeremiah complains that the people are blinded by false security. They say, "we are wise, and the law of the Lord is with us" (8:8). The law of the Lord here is surely the law promulgated by Josiah. But according to Jeremiah, this law has been vitiated: "the lying pen of the scribes has made it into a lie." There is evident animosity between the prophet and the scribes. Both claimed to speak for God. The claim that the Deuteronomic law was the definitive expression of the will of God implied a restriction of the role of the prophet. If the law was contained in a book, then the rest was interpretation, and for that role the scribe was better equipped than the prophet. The charge that the scribes had falsified the Torah and made it into a lie can be understood in various ways. Jeremiah may have been aware that the scribes added to the original scroll that was allegedly found in the temple. It is more likely, however, that in his view they falsified it by absolutizing it and leading those who had it to trust too easily in their own wisdom.

This is not to say that Jeremiah was opposed to the reform or its principles. He certainly shared basic values of the reformers. The family of Shaphan, Josiah's secretary at the time of the reform, is depicted as befriending and protecting Jeremiah. Ultimately, his oracles were preserved and edited by Deuteronomists. The editors undoubtedly viewed the prophet through the lens of their own theology and made him sound more Deuteronomistic than he had actually been. Nonetheless, it is remarkable that they preserved his biting criticism of the scribes, and this fact inspires some confidence that they did not deliberately distort his message.

A Sense of Impending Doom

One of the most distinctive features of Jeremiah's prophecy is the acute sense of impending disaster that informs much of his poetic oracles. The first prophecies reported in the book take the form of vision reports, similar to those of Amos, in which the Lord asks him what he sees. The first vision (1:11-12) involves a wordplay on the word for an almond tree, which has the same consonants in Hebrew as the verb "to watch" (cf. the wordplay on "summer fruit" in Amos 8:1-3). This is followed by another vision, of a boiling pot tilting over from the north. The foe from the north, in the oracles of Jeremiah, is Babylon, which would approach Judah from the north, through Syria. These visions are not likely to be any earlier than the battle of Carchemish in 605 B.C.E., which opened the way to Syria and Palestine for the Babylonians.

More than any other biblical writer, Jeremiah evokes the sheer terror of military conquest from the victim's point of view: "My anguish, my anguish! I writhe in pain! Oh, the walls of my heart! My heart is beating wildly; I cannot keep silent; for I hear the sound of the trumpet, the alarm of war" (4:19). He sees the coming devastation in cosmic terms: "I looked on the earth, and lo, it was waste and void" (4:23). (This verse is often taken as an allusion to the opening of the Priestly account of creation in Gen 1:2. Both passages could be using the same stock phrase, but in any case, Jeremiah's vision implies the undoing of creation.) The announcement of impending doom is the dominant message in these oracles. The prophet also upbraids the people for various offenses, and he sometimes calls for repentance, but most of his oracles give the impression that doom is inevitable, and that the important thing is for people to come to terms with that fact. Accordingly, he is especially scathing to those who proclaim peace when there is no peace (8:11). The prophet uses some striking metaphors for the condition of Judah. In chapter 13, he is told to bury a soiled loincloth. (The location is probably the village of Parah, near Anathoth, rather than the Euphrates, which was several hundred miles away, but there may be a wordplay on the name Euphrates.) When he retrieves it after many days, it is, naturally, ruined and good for nothing. So, by implication, is Judah. In chapter 19, he smashes a potter's jug as a symbol for the way the Lord will smash Judah. Both of these symbolic actions are reported in the sermonic prose of the Deuteronomistic editors, but they probably recall acts performed by the prophet.

The Critique of the Kingship

While the coming disaster might be inevitable, Jeremiah does not hesitate to lay blame on various leaders and to hold them responsible: "from the least to the greatest, everyone is greedy for unjust gain; from prophet to priest everyone deals falsely. They have treated the wound of my people carelessly, saying, 'Peace, peace,' when there is no peace" (8:10-11). He devotes only passing remarks to the priests and the cult, but he says enough to show that he shared the basic attitudes of earlier prophets. So he asks in 6:20: "Of what use to me is frankincense that comes from Sheba, or sweet cane from a distant land? Your burnt offerings are not acceptable, nor are your sacrifices pleasing to me."

The most biting social criticism in the book is found in 22:18-17, in an oracle addressed to King Jehoiakim, son of Josiah, who was installed as a puppet king by the Egyptians after his brother Jehoahaz (Shallum) had been deposed: "Woe to him who builds his house by unrighteousness and his upper rooms by injustice; who makes his neighbors work of nothing and does not give them their wages."

Jehoiakim is concerned with the trappings of royal rank, such as the splendor of his palace. Jeremiah contrasts this with Josiah's concern for justice. (He does not address the fact of Josiah's violent death.) Accordingly he predicts a shameful end for Jehoiakim: "With the burial of an ass he will be buried." In fact, Jehoiakim died before Jerusalem fell to the Babylonians, and so escaped humiliation. The oracle, however, is reminiscent of the invective of Elijah or Amos. It was not calculated to win over the king but to denounce him and possibly to curse him.

The sharp critique of Jehoiakim raises the question of Jeremiah's attitude to the Davidic line. The oracle on Jehoiakim is followed by another on his son Jehoiachin (Coniah), who was only eighteen when he began to reign and had to surrender to the Babylonians three months later. Jeremiah hurls no accusations against the young king. Even if he were the signet ring on the hand of the Lord, as kings claimed to be, he would be shown no mercy. The oracle in 22:28-30 can be read as sympathetic to the young king, doomed to a life of exile, but the last verse is chilling in its finality: "Record this man as childless, a man who shall not succeed in his days; for none of his offspring shall succeed in sitting on the throne of David and ruling again in Judah." So much, it would seem, for the promise to David. Jeremiah was not opposed to kingship in principle. Josiah ate and drank, but he practiced justice and righteousness (cf. the comments on righteous kingship in 22:1-5). The comment on Jehoiachin is simply a realistic assessment of his prospects. In fact, none of his offspring ever sat on the throne of David. The last king of Judah, appointed by the Babylonians when Jehoiachin was taken into exile, was his uncle, Zedekiah.

Nonetheless, a few passages in Jeremiah entertain a brighter future for the Davidic line. In 23:5-6 the Lord promises: "I will raise up for David a righteous Branch, and he shall reign as king and deal wisely . . . and this is the name by which he will be called: 'The LORD is our righteousness.'" There is a word-play here on the name Zedekiah ("Righteous-ness of YHWH") with the implication that the last king did not live up to his name. The phrase "the days are surely coming" seems to indicate a break in the continuity of the king-ship. Either Jeremiah affirmed that the line would be restored after an interruption, or, more probably, an editor supplied this hope, to balance the pessimistic oracle on Jehoiachin. There is a further elaboration of this oracle in 33:14-18, which affirms that the proph-ecy will be fulfilled "in those days and at that time," which is to say, in God's good time. The later passage adds that there will always be a Davidic king and a Levitical priest. The bal-ancing of the kingship with the priesthood is typical of postexilic Judaism. The passage in chapter 33 is not found in the Greek trans-lation and is certainly a late addition to the text. The designation of the future king as the "Branch" became an important way of refer-ring to the Messiah in later times.

The Critique of the Prophets

Like Micaiah ben Imlah, Amos, and Zepha-niah, Jeremiah is critical of the professional prophets (23:9-40). The problem is not that they prophesy by Baal, like the prophets of Samaria, but that they strengthen the hands of evildoers by prophesying peace. Unlike Mic-aiah ben Imlah, Jeremiah does not attribute false prophecy to a lying spirit from YHWH.

He denies that it is authentic prophecy at all: these prophets have not stood in the council of the Lord. He makes a distinction between the dream of a false prophet and the vision of a true one. This distinction would be difficult to maintain on a purely phenomenological basis. A prophetic vision, especially one received at night, is difficult to distinguish from a dream. The difference between true and false proph-ecy is a matter of evaluation of the contents, not a formal distinction between different media of revelation.

The issues between Jeremiah and his con-temporary prophets are clarified in the prose narratives in chapters 27 and 28. The incident is set in the reign of Zedekiah, when envoys had come to Jerusalem from several neigh-boring states, presumably to foment rebellion. Jeremiah makes himself a yoke to symbolize that Judah must submit to the yoke of Bab-ylon. The sight of the prophet parading as a symbol of submission must have been galling to any Judean who entertained hopes of inde-pendence. According to the narrative, Jeremi-ah's explanation of the symbolism would have added to the offense. The Lord has power over the whole earth, and it is he who has given it to "Nebuchadnezzar of Babylon, my servant" (27:6). To describe the conqueror of Jerusalem as the servant of YHWH would have been little better than calling Hitler the servant of God in modern times.

Jeremiah's message of submission brought him into conflict with other prophets, who were predicting that the Lord would bring back the exiles and the temple vessels from Babylon. One Hananiah broke Jeremiah's yoke, prophesying that the Lord would break the yoke of the king of Babylon. Jeremiah replaced his wooden yoke with a yoke of iron.

Fig. 17.3 Lion frieze from the Ishtar Gate, Babylon, dedicated by Nebuchadnezzar II; now in the Pergamon Museum, Berlin. Commons .wikimedia.org

His response to Hananiah, however, offers another criterion for distinguishing between true and false prophecy: "The prophets who preceded you and me from ancient times prophesied war, famine, and pestilence against many countries and great kingdoms. As for the prophet who prophesies peace, when the word of that prophet comes true, then it will be known that the Lord has truly sent that prophet" (28:8-9). This is an argument from tradition. No doubt there were many prophets before Hananiah who had prophesied peace, but Jeremiah (or the Deuteronomistic editor) did not regard them as true prophets. Besides, the prophecies of disaster had most often been fulfilled. Jeremiah does not deny outright the possibility that a prophecy of peace might be valid, but the presumption seems to be against it. At the least, a prophet who predicted disaster could not be accused of currying favor with anyone or of acting in his own interest. His integrity was beyond reasonable doubt. Ultimately, only time would tell whether a particular prediction was right. By then, of course, it would be too late to be of much help. (This is

the same criterion that is given in Deut 18:22.) In this case, time would prove Jeremiah right. (He gives some supporting evidence by predicting the death of his rival Hananiah.) There can be little doubt, however, that the disagreements between prophets during the Babylonian crisis contributed to the eventual decline in prophecy in the postexilic period.

The Attitude to Babylonian Rule

The confrontation between Jeremiah and Hananiah raises the question of the political stance of the prophet during the Babylonian crisis. The poetic oracles in the first half of the book make clear that he appreciated the magnitude of the coming disaster and saw it as a punishment for the sins of Judah. For his position during the actual crisis, however, we are dependent on prose narratives that are certainly edited to some degree. According to these accounts, Jeremiah consistently advocated submission to Babylon and incurred the wrath of his contemporaries as a result. While these accounts have some basis in the recollection of Jeremiah, they also dovetail with the interests of the Jewish community in Babylon after the deportation.

Already in the time of Jehoiakim, before the initial capture of Jerusalem, Jeremiah is said to have prophesied that Judah would serve Babylon for seventy years (25:11; cf. 29:10). The number is typological, as can be seen from an oracle against Tyre in Isa 23:15-17 and from an inscription of the Assyrian king Esarhaddon, which says that Marduk decreed that Babylon should be desolate for seventy years, but relented and allowed it to be restored after eleven. Jeremiah also prophesied that Zion would be made like Shiloh (chap. 26), and for this some people wanted to put him to death. His friends at court (primarily the son of Shaphan) prevailed by invoking the precedent of Micah of Moresheth, but another prophet, Uriah son of Shemaiah, was not so fortunate. Even though he fled to Egypt, he was brought back and executed. Prophesying bad tidings to the king was a dangerous business.

After the initial deportation in 597 B.C.E., Jeremiah allegedly sent a letter to the exiles (chap. 29) telling them to settle in Babylon and seek its welfare, "for in its welfare you will find your welfare" (29:8), despite the words of some prophets to the contrary. In chapter 24, the Jewish community in Babylon is contrasted with those who remained in the land under Zedekiah. Jeremiah is shown two baskets of figs, one good and one bad. The good figs represent the exiles, while the bad represent Zedekiah and his officials. The exiles are destined for good: "I will plant them and not pluck them up" (cf. 1:10). These passages clearly reflect the viewpoint of the exilic editors of Jeremiah's oracles.

The issues become more acute during the final siege of Jerusalem. In Jeremiah 21 Zedekiah asks the prophet "to inquire of the LORD on our behalf" in the hope that the Lord would do a mighty deed as he was believed to have done a century earlier when Sennacherib was advancing. Jeremiah provides no comfort. On this occasion, the divine warrior is on the side of the Babylonians. This response proceeds on the assumption that YHWH is the Lord of all history, and that whatever happens is his will. To discern the will of the Lord on this occasion, all Jeremiah or Zedekiah had to do was look over the city wall at the Babylonian army and draw their own conclusions.

But Jeremiah does not only predict disaster. He goes on to counsel treason and desertion: "See, I am setting before you the way of life and the way of death. Those who stay in this city shall die by the sword, by famine, and by pestilence; but those who go out and surrender to the Chaldeans . . . shall have their lives as a prize of war" (21:8-10). The reference to the way of life and way of death is a clear allusion to Deut 30:15. In that case, the way of life was to keep the commandment of the Lord. By implication, the will of God was now to surrender to the Babylonians. A similar narrative is found in Jer 37:3-10, on the occasion of hopes raised by the advance of an Egyptian army. The message attributed to Jeremiah in these passages goes against the grain not only of national pride but of the human instinct for self-assertion. Nonetheless, it must be admitted that submission was the only way to self-preservation for Judah in face of the Babylonian army.

Naturally, the officials in Jerusalem took exception to Jeremiah's prophecies of doom on the grounds that he was discouraging the soldiers who were left in the city. According to a narrative in chapter 38, they lowered him into an empty but muddy cistern to await a slow death. He was rescued, however, by a eunuch in the royal court who prevailed on the king to allow his release. Zedekiah appears in these narratives as a pathetic figure. He vacillates over the liberation of slaves in the seventh year as commanded by Deuteronomy (Jer 34:8-22). He is eager to consult Jeremiah but afraid of his own officials and also afraid that if he surrenders he will be handed over to the Judeans who had deserted. Jeremiah assures him that if he surrenders he will be allowed to live (38:17; cf. 34:4-5). In the end, however, Zedekiah suffered a cruel fate. His sons were executed before his eyes, and then he was blinded and taken prisoner to Babylon (52:10-11).

There is little doubt that Jeremiah consistently preached the inevitability of the Babylonian conquest. Jerusalem had no alternative to submission. But there is equally little doubt that these narratives were edited by members of the exilic community who claimed the authority of Jeremiah for their policy of submission. The Babylonians are said to have treated the prophet with respect after the conquest and offered to take him to Babylon. He declined, but he also resisted those who advocated flight to Egypt after the governor Gedaliah was murdered (chaps. 42–43). There are echoes here of the Deuteronomic principle that Israel should not return to Egypt, from which it had once been liberated. Nonetheless, he was finally forced to flee. He continued to be critical of the community in Egypt because of alleged idolatry (chap.

44). The discussion of the worship of the queen of heaven in this context gives an interesting insight into Judean popular religion, even after the fall of Jerusalem.

Whether Jeremiah himself was actually so loyal to Babylon, however, is open to question. There is at least one piece of discordant evidence. Chapters 50 and 51 consist of oracles against Babylon that are attributed to Jeremiah. For an illustrative sample, see 51:34:

> King Nebuchadrezzar of Babylon has
>   devoured me,
> he has crushed me;
> he has made me an empty vessel,
> he has swallowed me like a monster;
> he has filled his belly with my delicacies,
> he has spewed me out.
> "May my torn flesh be avenged on
>   Babylon,"
> the inhabitants of Zion shall say,

Fig. 17.4   The Ishtar Gate, dedicated by Nebuchadnezzar II. Commons.wikimedia.org

"May my blood be avenged on the inhabitants of Chaldea,"
Jerusalem shall say.

Like the other oracles against foreign nations, this one may be anonymous. In part, at least, the oracles against Babylon are set in the context of its conquest by the Medes and Persians, half a century after the time of Jeremiah (see, for example, 51:28). At the end of these oracles, however, a narrative account claims that Jeremiah "wrote in a scroll all the disasters that would come on Babylon" and gave them to Seraiah, brother of Baruch, when he accompanied Zedekiah to Babylon, and told him to submerge it in the Euphrates, saying, "Thus shall Babylon sink, to rise no more." It is possible that all this anti-Babylonian material was added late to the book, after the fall of Babylon to the Persians. If it includes any reminiscences of the words of Jeremiah, however, he cannot have been quite as docile toward the Babylonians as he is portrayed in the prose sections of the book.

Hope for the Future?

In Jer 30:1 the prophet is told to "write in a book all the words that I have spoken to you. For the days are surely coming when I will restore the fortunes of my people, Israel and Judah." The following chapters contain words of consolation, which stand in sharp contrast to the predictions of "war, famine, and pestilence" that dominate the book. The oracles, we are told, concern Israel as well as Judah. Jeremiah 31:2-6 tells the "virgin Israel" that she shall again plant vineyards on the mountains of Samaria, and that there will be a call in the hill country of Ephraim to go up to Zion. This oracle would make good sense in the context of Josiah's reform, which sought, among other things, to rally the remnants of northern Israel around the Jerusalem cult. In 31:15 the prophet speaks of Rachel weeping for her children who were no more, presumably the lost tribes of northern Israel. (The verse is cited with a very different reference in Matt 2:18, in connection with the slaughter of the innocent children.) The following oracle ("I heard Ephraim pleading") alludes to Hosea 11—Ephraim is YHWH's son, and YHWH is moved for him. Again 31:9 speaks of YHWH becoming a father to Israel and having Ephraim as his firstborn. We have seen that Jeremiah drew motifs from the oracles of Hosea in his early oracles, in chapters 2 and 3. It is plausible, then, that some oracles in this section date from early in the prophet's career and envision the restoration of northern Israel.

Several other oracles in this section, however, suggest the period of restoration, at the end of the exile. Second Isaiah addresses the Judean community as "Jacob, my servant" (Isa 44:1; cf. Jer 30:10), despite the northern associations of Jacob. The oracles in Jeremiah, too, switch easily from Jacob to Zion. The idea that the Lord had ransomed Jacob, and that they would come and sing aloud in Zion (31:11-12), is very similar to what we find in Second Isaiah. It is likely that some of these oracles were added after the time of Jeremiah to relate the prophecies to the restoration from Babylon.

This section was also expanded by some prose additions. Jeremiah 31:29 cites the proverb "The parents have eaten sour grapes and the children's teeth are set on edge," which is also cited in Ezekiel 18. One of the best-known prophecies in the book follows in Jer 31:31: "The days are surely coming, says the

LORD, when I will make a new covenant with the house of Israel and the house of Judah." This passage is part of the C stratum of the book, the Deuteronomistic sermonic prose. It has many echoes of Hosea—the metaphor of YHWH as husband and the covenantal/marriage formula, "I will be their God and they shall be my people" (cf. the reverse formula in Hos 1:9). The most striking aspect of the new covenant is that it will be written on the people's hearts. It will, in effect, be an unbreakable covenant. We find here a significant shift in expectations about the future. It was of the essence of the Sinai covenant that it demanded free choice and therefore entailed the possibility of a negative response. But this covenant is judged to have failed. The new internalized covenant will be foolproof, but at a price. A situation where people are programmed, so to speak, to behave in a certain way would no longer correspond to human history as we know it. There is always some tension between utopian thinking, the dream of a perfect society, and free will, which inevitably leads to imperfection. This tension will grow stronger in the apocalyptic writings of the Second Temple period.

At least one passage suggests that Jeremiah entertained hope for the future even in the darkest hours before the fall of Jerusalem. Chapter 32 reports an incident where Jeremiah's cousin approached him and asked him to buy a field in Anathoth, to keep it in the family. He did so, as a sign that "houses and fields and vineyards shall again be bought in this land" (32:15). Later, when the siege of Jerusalem was temporarily lifted, he attempted to go to receive a share of family property, but he was arrested on suspicion of deserting to the Babylonians (37:11-16). He vigorously denied the charge. His initial refusal to go to Egypt, and his attempt to persuade others not to leave (chap. 42), can also be seen as a sign of stubborn hope. It would have been in character for Jeremiah to preach doom when everyone else was clinging to hope but to entertain hope when everyone else was in a state of despair.

Jeremiah 33:10-13 speaks of a time when people would again bring offerings to the Jerusalem temple and recite psalms in praise of the goodness of the Lord (Ps 136:1). The same psalm is recited in Ezra 3:11, when the foundation of the new temple is laid. The prophecy in Jeremiah may have been written after the fact. Regardless of its origin, however, it is one of the most beautiful visions of hope in the Hebrew Bible: "In the towns of Judah and the streets of Jerusalem that are desolate, without inhabitants, human or animal, there shall once more be heard the voice of mirth and the voice of gladness, the voice of the bridegroom and the voice of the bride, the voices of those who sing, as they bring thank offerings to the house of the LORD."

The Confessions of Jeremiah

I have left until last a series of passages in chapters 11–20 that seem to have a more personal character than the other oracles and are often singled out as the "confessions" or "laments" of Jeremiah. These passages are 11:18-23; 12:1-6; 15:10-21; 17:14-18; 18:18-23; and 20:7-18. They resemble the individual laments found in the Psalms (e.g., Psalms 3, 5, 6, 7). Consequently, some commentators regard them as anonymous additions to the book and unreliable witnesses to the prophet Jeremiah. But we should hardly be surprised if the prophet expressed himself in traditional forms, and these laments have their own distinctive features, which at least in some cases relate to the experience of prophecy. We can never be certain that they were composed by Jeremiah, but they certainly contribute to the persona of the prophet as it is presented in the book. They also provide a reflection on the experience of prophecy that is without parallel in the biblical corpus.

The passages in question share a number of features, although they use them in various ways. The prophet calls on God, reports some of the speech of his enemies, declares his own innocence, and prays for vengeance. The complaint in 12:1-6 is of a general nature, reminiscent of Habakkuk: "Why does the way of the wicked prosper?" Jeremiah, characteristically, does not just want an explanation. He asks that God do something about it and set them aside for the slaughter. Other passages are more directly personal. According to 11:18-23, Jeremiah's enemies planned to have him killed—an idea supported by several of the quasi-biographical narratives in the book. The prophet was at first unaware, "like a lamb led to slaughter," but is outraged by the discovery. Jeremiah is not the "turn the other cheek" kind of prophet. He reacts with passion: "Let me see your vengeance on them." He is more explicit in his demand for vengeance in 18:19-23: "Give their children over to famine, and mow them down by the sword's edges. May their wives become childless widows. May their men be slain by Death." There is no concept here of loving your enemies, but there is certainly a passion for justice.

The other poems relate more directly to the experience of prophecy. Jeremiah 15:10-21 begins on a bitter note: "Woe is me, my mother, that you bore me." This sentiment is repeated in 20:15, where it is contrasted with the joy of his father when he was born. The bitterness is due to the fact that nobody likes him, everybody curses him. He should hardly have been surprised, given the tenor of his oracles, but, as he insists, he has not actually wronged anyone. His unpopularity (to put it mildly) comes from the exercise of his vocation as a prophet. This has alienated him from merrymakers: "Under the weight of your hand I sat alone." We are given a picture of the prophet as a brooding figure, incapable of participating in the pleasantries of life. Despite his joy in the word of the Lord, he feels the pain of isolation and resentment, and he asks why he should have to undergo this. A further indication of his isolation is found in chapter 16, where he is forbidden to take a wife or to have children, to symbolize the fact that children born in Jerusalem at that time were likely to perish. Other passages indicate ambivalence even about the prophetic calling, which he had said was his delight. In 17:16 he insists that he did not desire the day of disaster, which he was fated to predict. His predicament is most vividly presented in 20:8-9. The word of the Lord has become a source of reproach and derision. Yet, "If I say, 'I will not mention him, or speak any more in his name,' then within me there is something like a burning fire shut up in my bones; I am weary with holding it in, and I cannot." Jeremiah prophesies because he cannot help himself. We may compare the brief comment in Amos 3:8: "The lion has roared, who will not be afraid? The LORD God has spoken, who can but prophesy?"

These passages raise forcefully the question of the motivation of a prophet like Jeremiah. Not only does he not stand to gain anything, but he opens himself to abuse and possible death. The reassurance he receives from the Lord in 15:19-20 is modest: the prophet will serve as YHWH's mouthpiece, and his enemies will not prevail over him. The Lord promises to deliver him out of the hands of the wicked. But the deliverance is qualified. There is no promise here of any reward after death, or of much by way of public recognition in his lifetime. Jeremiah did not suffer a violent death, but he died in exile against his will. Ultimately, the motivation of the prophet comes from the fire in his bones—the compulsion to speak what he believes to be true. This compulsion is formed by a tradition in which he was brought up, but evidently not everyone who was brought up in that tradition felt the compulsion in the same way. We might speak here of an ethical imperative, an obligation to do the right thing whether it is in our personal interest or not. The understanding of what is the right thing is shaped by tradition, but something more is involved that compels the prophet to go against the culture of his time and against other understandings of the same tradition.

Lamentations

The book of Lamentations has traditionally been ascribed to Jeremiah. Significantly, this attribution is not found in the Hebrew Bible, where Lamentations is separated from Jeremiah and placed among the Writings. It is, however, found in the LXX, which may depend on a lost Hebrew original. The book is ascribed to Jeremiah in the Targums and in the rabbinic literature. The consensus of modern scholarship is that Jeremiah was not the author. If he were, it would be difficult to explain why this is not claimed in the Hebrew

Bible. On the other hand, if the lamentations were originally anonymous, it is easy to understand why they might have been associated with Jeremiah. The prophet was a witness to the fall of Jerusalem, uttered mournful prophecies (e.g., 9:1: "O that my head were a spring of water, and my eyes a fountain of tears, so that I might weep day and night for the slain of my people"), and was said to have written laments (2 Chron 35:25).

Most scholars assume that Lamentations was composed shortly after the fall of Jerusalem when grief was still fresh. They are highly stylized poems that stand in a long tradition of laments for cities that dates back to the end of the third millennium. There are several Sumerian works in the genre, of which the most famous is probably the Lament for Ur (*ANET*, 455). The Hebrew lamentations are carefully constructed. All five poems are shaped in some way by the Hebrew alphabet. Poems one, two, and four are simple acrostics of twenty-two stanzas each; that is, the first word of each stanza begins with a consecutive letter of the Hebrew alphabet (which has twenty-two letters). The third poem is more complex and stands out as the center of the book. There each stanza has three lines, and each line begins with the appropriate letter (so there are three lines with *aleph*, three with *beth*, etc.). The fifth poem is not an acrostic but has twenty-two lines corresponding to the number of letters in the alphabet. The poems then are not spontaneous outpourings, but they are no less authentic for that.

It is likely that Lamentations was used in mourning rituals from an early time. The earliest evidence for mourning rituals related to the fall of Jerusalem is in Jer 41:5, which tells how eighty men from Shechem, Shiloh, and

Samaria shaved off their beards, tore their garments, lacerated their skin, and came to make offerings at the house of the Lord, after the murder of the governor Gedaliah. Zechariah 7:3 indicates that people mourned and fasted in the fifth month (Ab) in the years after the restoration, and a fast in that month is also mentioned in Zech 8:19. Later Jewish custom used Lamentations in the liturgy of the 9th of Ab, which marked the destruction not only of the first temple, but also that of the second temple by the Romans in 70 c.e., and also the defeat of Bar Kokhba, who led the last Jewish rebellion against Rome in 132 c.e. Lamentations was thus taken as a lament for all the disasters of Jewish history. In Christian tradition, selections from Lamentations are chanted in the Matins of Holy Week.

The book consists of five poems. The first personifies Zion as a woman. The first half of the poem describes her affliction from an observer's point of view. In the second half, beginning in v. 12, Jerusalem herself is the speaker. Noteworthy is the explanation offered for the disaster: "because the Lord has made her suffer for the multitude of her transgressions" (1:5). Jerusalem herself attributes her suffering to "that which the Lord inflicted in the day of his fierce anger" (1:12). She confesses that "the Lord is in the right, for I have rebelled against his word" (1:18) and echoes Hosea by saying that she called to her lovers, but they deceived her (1:19). The city also complains of the gloating of her enemies and prays that a like fate may come upon them. The second poem reiterates how the Lord has destroyed Israel and Judah, and has even disowned his own sanctuary. Some of the blame is placed on prophets who saw false visions (2:14). But the confession of guilt is outweighed by

the expression of suffering. The author tells of children crying for food and starving to death. The poet stops short of accusing the Lord of excess, but one might draw that inference from his question: "Look, O Lord, and consider! To whom have you done this? Should women eat their offspring, the children they have borne? Should priest and prophet be killed in the sanctuary of the Lord?" (2:20). The motif of cannibalism is repeated in 4:10. This motif is common in ancient accounts of sieges and times of disaster, but the frequency of the motif does not necessarily mean that such things did not happen.

The third poem is the centerpiece of Lamentations. Here the speaker is an anonymous "man who has seen affliction" (3:1). Again, the suffering is construed as punishment: "Is it not from the mouth of the Lord that good and bad come"? (3:38). In this case, however, the poet also professes confidence that "the steadfast love of the Lord never ceases" (3:22). It is good to be chastised in youth, for the Lord will not be angry forever. Therefore, the people should examine their ways and return to the Lord. This is a time-honored response to adversity in the Hebrew tradition. It scarcely addresses the situation of the thousands who perished in the destruction of Jerusalem. It is precisely this response to suffering that will be put in question in the book of Job. Here again, the poet's submissiveness toward God does not prevent him from praying for vengeance on his earthly enemies.

The fourth poem reverts to a more critical form of complaint. The chastisement of Jerusalem has been greater than that of Sodom, which at least was over quickly (4:6). Again the horrors, including cannibalism, are described in detail. Those killed in battle were better off than those left to starve. Listed among the losses is "the LORD's anointed, the breath of our life" (4:20). Whether the king in question was Jehoiachin or Zedekiah, it is difficult to imagine Jeremiah referring to him in such terms. In this poem the guilt of Jerusalem is qualified: "It was for the sins of her prophets and the iniquities of her priests" (4:13). Moreover, the poem concludes by announcing that the punishment of Zion is accomplished, but that of Edom is about to come.

In the final poem, the confession of guilt recedes further. "Our ancestors have sinned; they are no more, and we bear their iniquities" (5:7). This sentiment comes close to the proverb, "the fathers have eaten sour grapes," which is vehemently rejected in Ezekiel 18, and is said not to apply to the future in Jeremiah 31. In this poem the emphasis is on innocent suffering: women raped, men abused, people starving. The poet concludes by asking God to restore the people, "unless you have rejected us utterly and are angry with us beyond measure" (5:22). Here again there is a hint that this degree of suffering cannot be fully explained as just punishment from God.

The book of Lamentations is cherished mainly for its poetic expression of unspeakable horror. As such, it has lent itself readily to recurring situations in every century, not least the twentieth. There is anger toward taunting neighbors but surprisingly little toward the Babylonians, who were the main agents of Jerusalem's misery. The reason is presumably that the Babylonians were believed to act on behalf of the God of Israel. It is not unusual for victims of violence to blame themselves and view the violence as punishment. The biblical reactions to the fall of Jerusalem take this attitude to an extreme. Only occasionally does Lamentations hint that the punishment is "beyond measure" or indeed unjustifiable in its severity. For a more thorough reflection on the justice of God, we will have to wait for the book of Job. Lamentations fills its role in the canon by testifying to the depth of human suffering and expressing the basic human emotion of grief.

FOR FURTHER READING

Habakkuk

F. I. Andersen, *Habakkuk* (AB 25; New York: Doubleday, 1991). Detailed philological commentary.

M. H. Floyd, *Minor Prophets Part 2* (FOTL 22; Grand Rapids: Eerdmans, 2000), 79–162. Form-critical analysis.

R. D. Haak, *Habakkuk* (VTSup 44; Leiden: Brill, 1992). Detailed study of text and historical context.

T. Hiebert, "The Book of Habakkuk," *NIB* 7:623–55. Brief homiletical commentary.

J. J. M. Roberts, *Nahum, Habakkuk, and Zephaniah* (OTL; Louisville: Westminster, 1991). Textual and philological analysis.

M. A. Sweeney, *The Twelve Prophets* (Berit Olam; Collegeville, MN, 2000), 2:451–90. Concise exegetical commentary.

Jeremiah

L. C. Allen *Jeremiah: A Commentary* (OTL; Louisville: Westminster, 2008). Literary and theological commentary on the canonical form of the book.

J. Bright, *Jeremiah* (AB 21; Garden City, NY: Doubleday, 1965). Helpful but dated commentary. Regards much of the book as historically reliable.

W. Brueggemann, *A Commentary on Jeremiah: Exile and Homecoming* (Grand Rapids: Eerdmans, 1998). Theological and homiletical commentary.

R. P. Carroll, *Jeremiah* (OTL; Philadelphia: Westminster, 1986). Regards most of the text as the product of later editors.

S. Davidson, *Empire and Exile: Postcolonial Readings of the Book of Jeremiah* (London: T&T Clark, 2011). Reading of selected passages in Jeremiah from the perspective of the exiles.

W. L. Holladay, *Jeremiah* (2 vols.; Hermeneia; Philadelphia: Fortress Press, 1986–1989). Detailed commentary. Exceptional confidence in the historical reliability of the book.

P. J. King, *Jeremiah: An Archaeological Companion* (Louisville: Westminster, 1993). Useful collection of pertinent archaeological evidence.

J. R. Lundbom, *Jeremiah* (3 vols. AB 21A–C; New York: Doubleday, 1999–2004). Emphasis on rhetorical criticism.

———, "Jeremiah, Book of," *ABD* 3:707–21. Summary of critical issues.

W. McKane, *Jeremiah* (2 vols.; ICC; Edinburgh: T&T Clark, 1986–1996). Thorough commentary, with extensive attention to the composition of the book.

M. Leuchter, *The Polemics of Exile in Jeremiah 26–45* (Cambridge: Cambridge University Press, 2008). Views Jeremiah 26-45 as a supplement by scribes in the exile, continuous with the thought of Jeremiah.

P. D. Miller, "The Book of Jeremiah," *NIB* 7:555–1072. Judicious commentary with homiletical reflections.

E. Nicholson, *Preaching to the Exiles: A Study of the Prose Tradition in the Book of Jeremiah* (Oxford: Blackwell, 1970). Argument for the Deuteronomistic character of the prose narratives.

K. M. O'Connor, *The Confessions of Jeremiah: Their Interpretation and Role in Chapters 1–25* (SBLDS 94; Atlanta: Scholars Press, 1988). Study of the confessions in their literary context.

——— *Jeremiah. Pain and Promise* (Minneapolis: Fortress, 2011). A study of Jeremiah in the light of trauma and disaster theory.

D. L. Petersen, *The Prophetic Literature: An Introduction* (Louisville: Westminster John Knox, 2002), 97–135. Focuses on literary aspects of the book.

C. J. Sharp, *Prophecy and Ideology in Jeremiah: Struggles for Authority in the Deutero-Jeremianic Prose* London: T&T Clark, 2003. Analysis of the prose narratives in Jeremiah. Argues that two politically distinct groups vied for control of Jeremiah's legacy in the exilic period.

L. Stulman, *Jeremiah* (Nashville: Abingdon, 2005). Theological-literary commentary taking the book as a coherent whole.

———, *Order Amid Chaos: Jeremiah as Symbolic Tapestry* (The Biblical Seminar 57; Sheffield: Sheffield Academic Press, 1998). A study of the literary structure of the book.

Lamentations

A. Berlin, *Lamentations* (OTL; Louisville: Westminster John Knox, 2002). Close analysis of poetic features.

D. R. Hillers, *Lamentations* (rev. ed.; AB 7A; New York: Doubleday, 1992). Brief textual and philological commentary.

——, "Lamentations," *ABD* 4:137–41. Discussion of critical issues in the interpretation of the book.

T. Linafelt, *Surviving Lamentations. Catastrophe, Lament and Protest in the Afterlife of a Biblical Book* (Chicago: University of Chicago Press, 2000). Wide-ranging study of Lamentations and its influence as "literature of survival."

C. R. Mandolfo, *Daughter Zion Talks Back to the Prophets. A Dialogic Theology of the Book of Lamentations* (Atlanta: SBL, 2007). Lamentations 1–2 as a counterstory to the "marriage-metaphor" in the Prophets.

K. M. O'Connor, "Lamentations," *NIB* 6:1013–72. Concise commentary with theological reflections.

R. Salters, *Lamentations: A Critical and Exegetical Commentary* (ICC; London: T&T Clark, 2011). Detailed historical-critical commentary.

C. Westermann, *Lamentations: Issues and Interpretation* (trans. C. Muenchow; Minneapolis: Fortress Press, 1994). Good introduction and commentary, with discussion of lament genre in the ancient Near East.

CHAPTER 18

The Exilic Period
Ezekiel and Obadiah

INTRODUCTION

The prophets of the exilic period, Ezekiel and Obadiah, draw our attention in this chapter.

Ezekiel was a younger contemporary of Jeremiah. He, too, was from a priestly family, most probably a Zadokite from Jerusalem. As such, he had a higher social standing than the prophet from Anathoth. For that reason, he was included among the elite of the land who were deported to Babylon in the company of King Jehoiachin in 597 B.C.E. (2 Kgs 24:15). He was already in Babylon when he had the vision reported in chapter 1, which is usually assumed to be his inaugural vision. That vision is dated to "the thirtieth year," which is correlated in the following verse with the fifth year of the exile of King Jehoiachin. It is reasonable to suppose, then, that the reference is to the thirtieth year of the prophet's life. On this assumption, he was a grown man when he was deported to Babylon. After his call as a prophet, he became a figure of some importance among the exiles. We find him on occasion sitting in his house "with the elders

of Judah sitting before me" (8:1; cf. 14:1; 20:1). Jeremiah was also consulted in Jerusalem, even by the king, but he was generally viewed with hostility by the officials. Ezekiel did not have any such officials to contend with and seems to have been viewed with respect by the exilic community.

The book of Ezekiel is more highly structured than other prophetic books. The most obvious division in the book comes at the end of chapter 24, which marks the destruction of Jerusalem. Up to this point, the great majority of the oracles pronounce judgment on Judah and Jerusalem. Chapters 1–11 are framed by the great visions of the glory of the Lord in chapters 1 and 8–11. The departure of the glory from Jerusalem marks the end of a section of the book. The oracles of judgment in chapters 12–24 are marked by extended and colorful allegories, and end again with the destruction of Jerusalem. There follows a collection of oracles against foreign nations in chapters 25–32. The remainder of the book, chapters 33–48, prophesies consolation and restoration (chap. 33 repeats the commission of Ezekiel as a sentinel from chap. 3, and also the discourse on individual responsibility from chap. 18). The sequence then is judgment on Jerusalem, judgment on foreign nations, consolation for Jerusalem. (Compare the order of the Greek edition of the book of Jeremiah, where the oracles against the nations were also placed in the middle.) The Jewish historian Josephus, who wrote at the end of the first century c.e., said that Ezekiel wrote two books (*Ant.* 10.5.1[79]). It is usually assumed that he was distinguishing the book of judgment (chaps. 1–24) from the book of consolation (chaps. 25–48; the doom of foreign nations was a source of consolation for Israel). There were other writings in circulation in the name of Ezekiel at the turn of the era, however, and it may be that Josephus had one of them in mind. (Fragments survive of an Apocryphon of Ezekiel in Greek and of a Hebrew prophetic work based on the book of Ezekiel, which was found among the Dead Sea Scrolls.)

One of the distinctive features of the book is the frequency with which date formulae are used. There are fifteen such formulae in all, counting the reference to the thirtieth year in 1:1. They range from the fifth year of the exile (1:2) to the twenty-fifth (40:1), mostly in chronological order. Two formulae in the oracles against the nations are out of chronological sequence. Ezekiel 29:1 is dated to the tenth year, although 26:1 was already in the eleventh. More significantly, 29:17 is dated to the twenty-seventh year of the exile (571/570 b.c.e.). This is the latest date in the book. The

passage in question is a revision of the prophecy in 26:7-14, that Nebuchadnezzar would take Tyre, which had not been fulfilled. The predilection for exact dating in the book is one of the many features that relate the book of Ezekiel to the Priestly tradition. We should not necessarily assume that all elements outside of the oracles against the nations are in chronological order. In at least a few cases, early predictions correspond suspiciously well to what eventually happened. For example, chapter 11, which is part of a sequence dated to the sixth year of the exile (592/591), states that Jerusalem officials will not die in Jerusalem but will be judged at the border of the land (cf. 2 Kgs 25:18-21). An undated prophecy in Ezekiel 12 says that the prince would be taken to Babylon but would never see it, a clear reference to the fate of Zedekiah, who was blinded before he was taken into exile (2 Kgs 25:7).

The book also has a kind of architectonic unity. It begins with visions of the destruction of Jerusalem. It ends with an elaborate vision of its restoration. There is no doubt that the book exhibits a deliberate order. Whether that order was imposed by the prophet himself or by a disciple is a matter of controversy. The Greek translation, which is the oldest extant form of the book, is shorter than the Hebrew text (only fragments of the Hebrew have been found at Qumran). The differences are mainly a matter of glosses in individual verses, but they show that the book did go through an editing process. The bulk of the prophecies, however, must be dated to the early exilic period. A number of the predictions regarding foreign nations were not fulfilled. (Besides the prediction of the fall of Tyre, the prophecy that Nebuchadnezzar would conquer Egypt in 29:8-12 was unsuccessful.) Persia is mentioned in passing as an ally of Tyre (27:10) and of Gog (38:5), but there is no reflection in the book of the capture of Babylon by Cyrus. The main doubts about authenticity concern the prophecies of restoration at the end of the book, especially the long vision of the restoration of Jerusalem in chapters 40–48. In part, this vision reflects the struggle for control of the sanctuary after the return of the exiles (chap. 44), but it may be that a prophecy of Ezekiel was updated and expanded. It should be noted, however, that there are scarcely any references of a biographical or quasi-biographical nature in the second half of the book.

Ezekiel differs from other prophets in the prominence of his priestly concerns. Like the Holiness Code in Leviticus, he does not distinguish between moral and ritual laws, and much of his prophecy deals with issues of holiness and purity. Like Jeremiah, he has a distinct persona that emerges in the book, but it is a different persona from that of his contemporary. Ezekiel's reaction to the fall of Jerusalem is to recoil in horror at the impurity

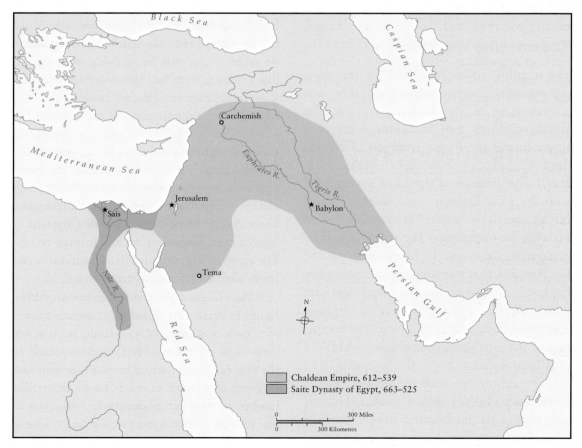

Map 18.1

of the city, which he sees as the primary cause of its downfall. There is little sense that conversion is possible before the destruction. The objective of the prophet's mission is that the people should recognize the hand of the Lord in the fate that befalls them (hence the recurring statement that "you shall know that I am the Lord"). The book is also noteworthy for the prominence of symbolic actions and for the vivid, even bizarre, symbolism of many of the visions.

Chapters 1–11: Glory and Destruction

The Opening Vision

The opening vision of Ezekiel is the most complex of all prophetic visions, and it became a cornerstone of later Jewish mysticism. The vision combines two traditions. First is a storm theophany, in the tradition of Mount Sinai (cf. Judg 5:4-5; Ps 68:7-9; Hab 3:3-15; et al.). The presence of the Lord is associated with fire. (The Hebrew word *hashmal,* which NRSV translates "amber," is used in Modern Hebrew for electricity.) The cloud is said to come from the north. In Jeremiah it was the foe, Babylon, that was supposed to come from the north. The more plausible association here is that the storm-god Baal was traditionally associated with Mount Zaphon (the mountain of the north), and the abode of YHWH in Zion was said to be "in the far north" in Ps 48:1. In accordance with the imagery of the storm-god, YHWH rides a chariot (Hebrew *merkabah*). Later Jewish mysticism is known as Merkavah mysticism, because it is concerned with visions of the divine throne-chariot.

The second tradition that informs Ezekiel's vision is that of the divine throne in the Jerusalem temple, where YHWH was enthroned above the cherubim (cf. the vision of the divine throne in Isaiah 6). These were hybrid creatures, combining features of various animals and endowed with wings, of a type often depicted in ancient Near Eastern art. The beings seen by Ezekiel are inspired by this tradition but are exceptionally bizarre. In their midst was something like burning coals of fire. Burning coals also figured in the vision of Isaiah (Isa 6:6). The Deity is enthroned above the living creatures, separated from them by a dome. Unlike Isaiah or Micaiah ben Imlah, however, Ezekiel does not simply see the Lord. He sees "something like" a throne, on which there was "something that seemed like a human form" but that was fiery and dazzling in appearance. This, we are told, was "the appearance of the likeness of the glory of the Lord." The glory (*kabod*) was the symbol of the presence of God in the Priestly tradition. Ezekiel is at pains to emphasize the transcendent, surpassing nature of this God, who cannot be perceived clearly by human eyes. Throughout the book, Ezekiel is addressed as "son of man," meaning "mortal human being." The emphasis on the prophet's humanity contrasts with the awesome majesty of God.

The vision of the prophet is not an end in itself. As in the case of Isaiah, it is the occasion of a commissioning. Like Isaiah, he is given little hope of success. He is told to preach to the people of Israel, whether they hear or refuse to hear. They shall at least "know that there has been a prophet among them," which is to say, they will have been given a fair warning. The prophet is given a written scroll, which he eats, to symbolize the way he internalizes the message. The same motif was found, but not so vividly portrayed, in Jer 15:16: "Your words were found and I ate them, and your words became to me a joy." Also similar to Jeremiah is the emphasis on the way the prophet must be hardened to endure his mission. Jeremiah becomes "a fortified wall of bronze" (Jer 15:20); Ezekiel's forehead is harder than flint (Ezek 3:9). Jeremiah is never mentioned by name in the book of Ezekiel, but there are many points of contact between the two books.

The nature of the prophet's task is spelled out clearly in Ezek 3:16-21, by analogy with the role of a watchman. The watchman is bound to give warning of an impending danger. Whether anyone heeds that warning is not his responsibility. This view of the prophet's mission is closely bound up with Ezekiel's emphasis on individual responsibility, which we shall find more fully expounded in chapter 18. Both the watchman analogy and the teaching on individual responsibility are repeated in chapter 33, at the beginning of the oracles of consolation.

The vision is formally concluded by the departure of the glory of the Lord. The mobility of the divine chariot-throne is significant. It means that God can appear in Babylon as well as in Jerusalem. We shall later find that this mobility enables YHWH to leave his temple before it is desecrated. Ezekiel is also mobile. Although he was initially said to be among the exiles by the river Chebar, he is now transported there by the Spirit of the Lord. He had presumably been transported away from there in his vision. We shall later find that he sees things happening in Jerusalem, even though he is in Babylon. The prophet Elijah was also said to be transported by the Spirit of the Lord (1 Kgs 18:12).

Symbolic Actions

In 3:22-23 Ezekiel has another encounter with the glory of the Lord. On this occasion he is told to perform a series of symbolic actions. During this period, the prophet is dumb except when he is impelled to prophesy. More than any other prophet, Ezekiel exhibits phenomena that are associated with unusual psychological conditions, and that seem to call for psychological analysis. There have been many attempts to diagnose his condition. One famous philosopher, Karl Jaspers, suggested that Ezekiel was schizophrenic. Any such attempt to diagnose an ancient figure about whom we have very limited evidence is problematic, but there is no doubt that Ezekiel's personal life and his psychological condition were deeply affected by his prophetic calling.

The first symbolic action, in chapter 4, calls for the prophet to build a model of a city under siege. Next he was to lie on his left side and "bear the iniquity of the house of Israel" for 390 days. Then he was to lie on his right side for 40 days, to "bear the iniquity" of the house of Judah. He was to be bound with cords so that he could not turn from one side to the other. We do not know how the prophet carried out these commands. One tradition of interpretation, going back to Maimonides, a great Jewish philosopher in the Middle Ages, argued the action was only within the context of the vision—that the prophet did not carry it out physically. It is of the essence of the symbolic actions of the prophets, however, that they are public signs, performed so as to attract the attention of bystanders. They have aptly been compared to street theater as a way of engaging public interest. We must assume, then, that Ezekiel did the things described.

To lie on one side for 390 days would require (or cause!) a pathological condition, but we do not know whether he was allowed to leave his position periodically or to move.

By lying in these positions, the prophet is said to "bear the iniquity" of Israel and Judah in turn. "Bear the iniquity" is a technical term in the Priestly laws of the Pentateuch. In Lev 16:21-22 the scapegoat is said to "bear the sins" of the house of the people of Israel and carry them away to the desert. In Lev 10:17 the priests are given the sin offering "to bear the iniquity of the congregation." The scapegoat bears iniquity in the sense of removing it. The priests also remove it, in the sense of atoning for it. (In Exod 34:7 God is said to bear iniquity for some people while visiting it on others.) It is doubtful, however, whether Ezekiel is thought to atone for the sin of Israel by his ordeal of lying on his side. Rather, he seems to bear the punishment of the people in the sense that he illustrates and dramatizes it. There is no implication that people are relieved of their guilt simply by looking at Ezekiel. They might be relieved if they were moved by his symbolic action to recognize their condition and repent of their sins. Primarily, the prophet's action is meant to help them recognize their guilt and their impending punishment. The 390 days and 40 days represent the number of years allotted for the punishment of Israel and Judah. Neither figure was historically accurate. The kingdom of Israel was never restored, and the Babylonian exile lasted more than forty years.

Ezekiel is given further instructions about his diet while performing these actions. (That he is allowed to prepare and eat food suggests that he was allowed some freedom of movement.) Two points are significant in this instruction. First, his food is rationed, as it would be in time of siege. Second, he is to prepare it over human dung. The point is to show that the food is unclean. Ezekiel's reaction is visceral: "Ah LORD God! I have never defiled myself; from my youth up to now. . . ." He is allowed to substitute animal dung, which has been used as fuel in the poorer countries of the Middle East down to modern times. It is not clear that human dung would make the food unclean, but it is unlikely to have been a fuel of choice for a priest like Ezekiel. Lands outside Israel were considered unclean in any case, so the uncleanness was a corollary of exile. What is clear from the exchange between the prophet and the Lord is that for a Zadokite priest like Ezekiel, defilement was a fate worse than death.

Ezekiel is given one further symbolic action to perform at this point. He is told to shave his head and his beard with a sword and divide the hair to symbolize the fate of the inhabitants of Jerusalem. One-third would die of pestilence or famine, one-third would fall by the sword, and one-third would be scattered. It has been noted that this fate corresponds to the curses of the covenant, especially as they are formulated in Lev 26:23-33, where the Israelites are threatened with sword, pestilence, famine, and exile if they disobey the laws. (Note especially the motif of eating one's children in both passages; Ezekiel goes further by saying that children will eat their parents.) The reason for such horrors is that "you have defiled my sanctuary" (Ezek 5:11). The logic of both passages is informed by the use of curses in Near Eastern treaties, especially by the Assyrians. The Annals of Ashurbanipal report how Arab rebels were reduced to eating their own children because the Assyrian gods "inflicted quickly upon them all the curses written down in their sworn agreements" (*ANET*, 299–300). The lesson of the symbolic action is elaborated in an oracle in chapter 6.

All of these visions portray the impending destruction of Jerusalem. The main explanation given is the cultic abominations, whether those of the high places or the defilement of the Jerusalem temple. The main emphasis, however, is on the announcement of inevitable doom. Ezekiel was speaking to the exiles in Babylon, who no doubt cherished hopes for the success of rebellion in Judah. Ezekiel disabuses them of any such illusions. Chapter 7 contains a powerful series of oracles in the tradition of Amos. The end has come upon the four corners of the land (cf. Amos 8:2). Ezekiel uses alliteration and repetition to drive the point home. Ezekiel 7:10 evokes Amos's famous oracle on the Day of the Lord: "See the day! See it comes! Your doom has gone out."

The Abominations in the Temple

Ezekiel 8 records a remarkable vision dated to the sixth month of the sixth year of the exile (fall 592 B.C.E.). Ezekiel sees a figure who bears a great resemblance to the figure on the throne in chapter 1 (like fire below the loins, and like gleaming amber above). In this case, the figure is presumably an angel, or a member of the heavenly court other than YHWH. This figure lifts the prophet by a lock of his hair. (In Akkadian visionary literature, this is sometimes an angry gesture, but that does not seem to be the case here.) Ezekiel is then transported to Jerusalem, to the temple courts. (This motif reappears in the story of Bel and the Dragon, an apocryphal addition to the book of Daniel, where Habakkuk is transported from Israel to Babylon to feed Daniel in the lions' den.) The transportation is said to be "in visions of God." It is, then, a visionary experience. We should not suppose that the prophet actually went to Jerusalem.

The vision of abominations in the temple is not necessarily an accurate depiction of what was happening there. Rather, it represents a fantasy of Ezekiel, what he imagined was going on in the temple, so as to explain the catastrophe that befell it. The glory of the God of Israel is there, in the inner court. But there is also "the image of jealousy that provokes to jealousy." This is presumably a statue of another deity, that offends the jealous God, YHWH. According to 2 Kgs 21:7, King Manasseh had set up a sculptured image of Asherah in the temple. Josiah had this burned in the Kidron Valley at the time of the Deuteronomic reform, but it is possible that either another statue had been installed or that Ezekiel imagined that it had been restored. The visionary character of the experience is shown by the statement that Ezekiel dug through a wall, something he could hardly have done with impunity in the actual temple. The account vacillates between portraying seventy elders gathered together in one place and assigning them each a chamber. The "loathsome animals" recall the unclean creatures of the dietary laws of Leviticus 11 and suggest the prophet's priestly preoccupation with impurity. It is noteworthy that the offenders are said to include "Jaazaniah son of Shaphan." Shaphan had played a prominent role in Josiah's reform, and his family protected Jeremiah (Jer 26:24; 39:14). Ezekiel may have wished to indicate that idolatry was rampant even among traditional Yahwists, or the reference may indicate some animosity between the Zadokite priesthood and the Deuteronomic

Fig. 18.1 The goddess Astarte; terra-cotta figurine adorned with gold and inset rubies. From Babylon, third century B.C.E.; now in the Louvre.

Commons.wikimedia.org

reformers. (Note, however, that 11:1 refers to Jaazaniah, son of Azzur. There may have been more than one Jaazaniah, but there is also reason to suspect textual corruption.)

Ezekiel observes a number of idolatrous practices. There is no parallel for veneration of loathsome animals in Israel or Judah. "Women weeping for Tammuz" refers to a Mesopotamian ritual that can be traced back to ancient Sumer in the third millennium, where it marked the death and descent into the netherworld of the shepherd-god, Dumuzi. This ritual was observed in the Near East for thousands of years. Whether it was observed in Jerusalem we do not know. Ezekiel would certainly have been familiar with it from Babylon. Worship of the sun was practiced in Judah in the seventh century. Josiah is said to have suppressed it, destroying horses and chariots

dedicated to the sun and deposing priests who made offerings to it (2 Kings 23). Whether "putting the branch to their nose" (Ezek 8:17) is a reference to a ritual is much disputed. No such ritual is known. It may be that the text should be emended to read, "putting the branch to my nose"—an idiomatic way of saying, "provoking me." There is also a reference to "filling the land with violence" in 8:17. Since all the other offenses are cultic, some scholars have thought that this is an insertion. In any case, it is clear that Ezekiel is primarily disturbed by cultic offenses. Whether in fact any of these "abominations" was practiced in Jerusalem in this period, we do not know. It is not implausible that some Babylonian practices should have been adopted after the Babylonian conquest. What the vision primarily shows, however, is the kind of offenses that Ezekiel thought would trigger the massive destruction of Jerusalem that was to come. The reason why people are said to have indulged in those practices is that they think the Lord has abandoned the land and will not see (8:12). As we shall see, Ezekiel claims that YHWH does abandon the land after the final destruction of Jerusalem, but in no case would it be safe to infer that "the LORD does not see."

The Vision of Destruction

The same figure who had guided Ezekiel in his vision now summons "the executioners of the city." These are six angelic figures accompanied by "a man dressed in linen, with a writing case at his side." The linen dress is typical of priests, but the figure in question is clearly heavenly, what we might call a recording angel. This figure is commanded to go through Jerusalem and mark the foreheads of those who oppose the "abominations" with a *taw,* the last letter of the alphabet, which had the shape of an X in the Old Hebrew alphabet. The marking recalls the smearing of blood on the lintels and doorposts of the Israelites in Egypt, so that the angel of destruction would pass them by (Exod 12:23). In this case, however, the distinction is not between Israelite and Egyptian, but between the people of Jerusalem. The implication is that the people who are killed are sinners. This is a dangerous concept, which is surely not defensible. (The underlying logic, with regard to suffering in general, is criticized in the book of Job.)

As Ezekiel sees it, the slaughter in Jerusalem is the work not of the Babylonians but of YHWH. It is pitiless in its execution of old and young, male and female. The prophet is moved to cry out in protest, but he does not contest the explanation given: "The guilt of the house of Israel and Judah is exceedingly great; the land is full of bloodshed and the city full of perversity; for they say, 'The LORD has forsaken the land, and the LORD does not see'" (10:9). In short, Jerusalem is destroyed because the inhabitants deserve it. This explanation is essentially similar to what we find in the Deuteronomists, but there are some distinct nuances in Ezekiel. He is especially concerned with the defilement of the temple, which leads to its utter violation. He is also exceptional in the degree to which he portrays God as pitiless. Ezekiel's way of dealing with the catastrophe that befell Jerusalem seems to be to persuade himself that it was utterly defiled so that destruction was the only remedy. Some of the most violent denunciations of Jerusalem are found in this book. The violence of the rhetoric seems to make the violence that befell the city more acceptable.

The destruction is completed in chapter 10, when the angel spreads burning coals over the city. In Isaiah's vision burning coals were used to purify the prophet's lips. Here, too, the burning can be understood as purgation. Jerusalem will rise again, in the last section of the book. For the present, however, the destruction is severe and complete. In conjunction with the destruction, the glory of the Lord abandons Jerusalem. This is in accordance with an ancient belief that no temple was destroyed unless its god had abandoned it. The Sumerian Lament for Ur gives a long list of deities who had abandoned the city (*ANET,* 455). Shortly after the time of Ezekiel, the mother of Nabonidus, the last king of Babylon, explained the desolation of Haran and its temple by saying that Sin, the moon-god, became angry with his city and temple and went up to heaven (*ANET,* 560). The departure of YHWH is described in elaborate detail. The glory of the Lord rises up from the temple and comes to rest on the Mount of Olives (Ezek 11:23). The entire destruction and abandonment are described without reference to the Babylonians.

In Ezekiel's view the responsibility for the destruction of Jerusalem was borne primarily by the people who had remained in the city with Zedekiah after the first deportation. These people had grown cynical: "The city is the pot, we are the meat." Ezekiel twists the saying to highlight the violence done within the city by its leaders. They are not doomed to perish in Jerusalem but "at the borders of Israel." This seems to be a reference to the fact that the leaders who were captured after the fall of Jerusalem were taken to the king of Babylon at Riblah in Syria and executed there (2 Kings 25). They were thus denied even the limited consolation of death in the land of Israel.

In contrast to those who stayed in the land, the exiles in Babylon are regarded as the hope for the future. These people were written off by those left behind, on the grounds that they had "gone far from the LORD" and the land was left to those still in Israel (11:15). Ezekiel suggests, however, that divine presence is no longer bound to the land of Israel. YHWH is "a little sanctuary" for the exiles in Babylon (11:16). This phrase is admittedly obscure. The NRSV translates "a sanctuary for a little while," but the sense seems to be that YHWH is present to them to a limited degree. Babylon was no substitute for Zion, and ultimately restoration would be necessary, but it was better to be an observant Yahwist in Babylon than an idolater in Jerusalem. The idea that any kind of "sanctuary" or access to the divine presence was possible in exile would be enormously important for the development of Judaism in the postexilic period.

The latter part of chapter 11 touches on themes that are developed more fully in the second half of the book. The exiles will be restored and will purge Jerusalem of abominations. God will give them a new spirit and a heart of flesh instead of stone (11:19). The basic idea here is similar to the new covenant in Jeremiah 31. In order for a people to keep the covenantal laws, human nature will have to be refashioned in a radical way.

Chapters 12–24: Oracles of Judgment

Chapters 12–24 contain some twenty-five oracles, mostly introduced by the formula "The word of the LORD came to me." There are no visions in this section, although some of the oracles use highly pictorial language. The first oracle relates to a symbolic action, similar to those in chapter 4. The prophet symbolizes exile by digging through a wall and carrying an exile's baggage. The sign relates specifically to the fate of the prince, Zedekiah, whose blindness is also prophesied. The warning of impending fate presents an opportunity for repentance, but there is little expectation that it will be heeded. The role of the prophet is to bear testimony rather than to convert people. The few who survive the disaster "will know that I am the LORD" (12:16).

False Prophecy

The remainder of chapter 12, all of chapter 13, and 14:9-11 deal with problems related to prophecy. Ezekiel's complaint is similar to that of Jeremiah. Prophets mislead the people by saying "peace" when there is no peace (13:10). Ezekiel does not examine the issue of false prophecy in as much detail as Jeremiah, and he is not fully consistent in his comments on it. On the one hand, false prophets prophesy out of their own imagination, when the LORD has not sent them (13:3; cf. Jer 23:21). On the other hand, he allows that if a prophet is deceived, YHWH has deceived him (Ezek 14:9; cf. 1 Kings 22), although that prophet is still condemned. The criticism of other prophets extends to the activities of women who engage in some kind of prophetic activity, although it seems more akin to magic and witchcraft than to the activities of the male prophets (13:17-19: they sow bands on wrists and make veils, and are accused of "pursuing lives," presumably by voodoo-like activities). Moreover, people complain that the words spoken by prophets like Ezekiel (and

Jeremiah?) are not fulfilled, although "the days are prolonged" (12:22). Unfortunately for Jerusalem, the fulfillment of the oracles of judgment came all too soon.

The Useless Vine

One of the most striking features of this section of the book of Ezekiel is the use of metaphor and allegory to describe the situation of Israel. In chapter 15 Jerusalem is compared to a vine. This is a time-honored metaphor. According to Psalm 89, Israel was a vine brought out of Egypt that took deep root and filled the land. According to Hosea, it was a luxuriant vine that yielded fruit. It was a symbol of prosperity and fertility. The blessing of Jacob in Gen 49:11 pictured Judah "binding his foal to the vine, his donkey's colt to the choice vine." In Numbers the spies sent to scout out the land cut a branch with a cluster of grapes as evidence of the desirability of the land (Num 13:23). The Song of Songs (8:12) refers to the beloved as a vineyard. Even the Song of the Vineyard in Isaiah 5, which is an oracle of judgment against Israel and Judah, assumes that a vineyard should be a good thing. The comparison with the vine was normally considered to be an honorable one in the case of Israel.

It comes as something of a shock, then, when Ezekiel asks what the vine is good for. In all the cases cited above, the reference was to the cultivated vine, which yields grapes for wine. The wild vine, however, is useless, and this is the analogy that the prophet has in mind. Not only does Jerusalem have no intrinsic value; it is a vine that has been burned, so that, in the brutal formulation of 15:5, it can never be used for anything. Ezekiel expresses a disdain for Jerusalem that goes far beyond anything that we found in Isaiah or Jeremiah.

The Promiscuous Woman

That disdain finds its most extreme expression in chapter 16. The metaphor of sexual promiscuity has an obvious precedent in Hosea 2, but there are significant differences between the two oracles. Ezekiel is addressing Jerusalem rather than Israel, so there are no exodus and wilderness motifs here. Jerusalem is reminded of its Canaanite origin in the period before the rise of Israel. The specific connections with Amorites and Hittites should not be pressed; the point is that Jerusalem was at one time a pagan (non-Yahwistic) city. Ezekiel views that condition as one of abhorrence. (The way Jerusalem is pictured as "flailing about in your blood" reflects the distaste of the purity-obsessed priest for blood and bodily fluids.) It was YHWH who made it possible for her to grow and become beautiful, and who adorned her with ornaments. Ezekiel 16:9, which says that YHWH pledged himself to Jerusalem and entered into a contract or covenant with her, implies the metaphor of marriage. The beauty of the young woman, however, becomes an occasion for prostitution. Ezekiel is primarily concerned with idolatry, but he also notes the practice of human sacrifice (16:20-21). Diplomatic relations with Egypt, Assyria, and Babylon in turn are also viewed as prostitution, with little regard for the circumstances of Judah's dealings with these powers. Jerusalem was worse than a whore, because she gave rather than received payment for her services.

The punishment of unfaithful Jerusalem in this oracle is severer than the fate of Israel in Hosea. Not only will she be stripped naked in public, but "they shall bring a mob against you, and they shall stone you and cut you to pieces with their swords" (16:40). The violence of this picture is undoubtedly inspired by the actual fate of Jerusalem, but it also carries the implication, or even a presupposition, that this is what a promiscuous woman deserves. Death by stoning was the punishment for adultery in biblical law (Deut 22:23-24). Stripping is the punishment in Hosea 2 (and later in the story of Susanna). There is no precedent for cutting in pieces as a punishment. There may be an allusion here to the Levite's concubine in Judges 19, who was cut in pieces after she had been raped, but this was not a punishment. Feminist scholars have quite rightly expressed concern that such rhetoric may seem to sanction violence against women. Some go so far as to describe it as pornographic. Of course, this is not the point of the oracle. The passage is an allegory and deals with the punishment of Jerusalem, not of actual women. But the allegory accepts as its premise that an adulterous woman deserves to be stoned or hacked to pieces, and the vivid imagery may well have contributed to violence against women, promiscuous or not, over the centuries. It may not be fair to characterize Ezekiel as a misogynist. We know too little of his personal life, but he is grief-stricken at the death of his wife, whom he describes as "the delight of my eyes" (24:15-18). It is unfortunate that his use of female imagery is predominantly negative and associates women primarily with promiscuity and impurity. The allegory of chapter 16 is problematic at best, and it suggests deep-seated problems in the kind of priestly theology that informs the prophet's preaching.

The prophet further expresses his disdain for Jerusalem by associating it with Samaria and Sodom (v. 46). The promise that all three cities will be restored (vv. 53-63) is surprising in the context, and we must wonder whether it was originally part of the allegorical oracle. There is a clear allusion to Hosea 2, however, in the promise that "I will remember my covenant with you in the days of your youth" (Ezek 16:60; cf. Hos 2:15-23). Even the restored Jerusalem, however, will still be tainted by the association with Samaria and Sodom.

Female imagery figures again in the oracle in chapter 23 on the two women, Oholah (Samaria) and Oholibah (Jerusalem; the names can be read as "her [own] tent" and "my tent is in her," respectively, with the implication that YHWH's residence was in Jerusalem). Again, both cities/women are accused of lusting for Assyrians and Babylonians, which is hardly a fair description of the historical relationships. It is true that both cities were defiled by the foreign armies, but rape rather than lust would be the appropriate metaphor. Yet, according to the prophet, YHWH turned in disgust from them. Unfortunately, men have often turned in disgust from women who were raped, and accused them of "wanting it." Ezekiel's accusations against Samaria and Judah are more complex than this. While the guiding metaphor is adultery, in the form of idolatry, there are also charges of human sacrifice and of profaning sanctuary and Sabbaths (23:36-39; note, however, that in 20:25-26 human sacrifice is included among statutes of YHWH that were not good, which he had given Israel "to horrify them"). Yet here again the violence of the punishment (stripping and disfiguring, vv. 25-26) constitutes a dangerous allegory. Whatever Ezekiel's attitude to actual women may have been, the disgust for the personified Jerusalem that he attributes to

YHWH and his sanction of violence against her provides a very unfortunate model for male-female relations.

Political Allegories

Two other allegories in this section of the book are much less controversial for the modern reader, although they may have been quite controversial in their time. Chapter 17 propounds a "riddle" or *mashal* (the Hebrew expression for any kind of figurative speech, allegory, parable, or proverb). An eagle came to Lebanon and took the top of a cedar. The reference is transparent: Nebuchadnezzar of Babylon carried off King Jehoiachin of Judah. The seed planted in his place is Zedekiah. The point of the allegory concerns Zedekiah's switch of allegiance to the second eagle, Egypt. The moral is not only that such conduct is foolish and leads to disaster, but that it violates an oath and breaks a covenant. Even though the covenant was with the king of Babylon, it is an offense against YHWH to break it. Ezekiel held a low opinion of Zedekiah. In 21:25 (MT 30), he describes him as a "vile, wicked, prince of Israel."

Chapter 19 contains two further political allegories in the form of dirges. First Judah is portrayed as a lioness (19:2; cf. Gen 49:9). One of her cubs (Jehoahaz, 2 Kgs 23:30-34) was taken to Egypt. Another (Jehoiachin or Zedekiah?) was taken to Babylon. The second allegory portrays Judah as a vine in a vineyard (19:10). Its strongest stem was plucked off and burned. Again, this could refer either to Jehoiachin or to Zedekiah. This pair of allegories is simply a lament. It may carry the implication that the kings brought their fate upon themselves by their pretensions to power, but even that lesson is not spelled out very explicitly.

Individual Responsibility

The most important contribution of this section of Ezekiel (and arguably of all of Ezekiel) to the theological tradition is the teaching on individual responsibility in chapter 18. This teaching was already touched on in chapter 3, in connection with the commission of the prophet. In 14:12-20 the prophet insists that a land cannot be spared because of righteous individuals (cf. the discussion between God and Abraham about the fate of Sodom in Genesis 18). Even if Noah, Daniel, and Job were in such a land, they would only save their own lives. (Daniel is also mentioned in Ezekiel 28. The reference is probably to a legendary figure who appears as Dan'el in the Ugaritic story of Aqhat. The hero of the biblical book of Daniel was supposed to be a younger contemporary of Ezekiel.) The fullest treatment of the theme of individual responsibility is found in chapter 18.

In this oracle the prophet sets out to refute the popular saying "The parents have eaten sour grapes, and the children's teeth are set on edge." The same proverb is cited, and refuted, in Jer 31:29-30. According to this proverb, the people of Jerusalem were not punished for their own sins but for those of their fathers—notably those of Manasseh in the previous century. Ezekiel argues, to the contrary, that everyone is punished or rewarded for his or her own sins. He proceeds to give examples of righteous fathers and unrighteous sons, and the reverse. Neither the virtue nor the vice of the father is laid to the son's account. Everyone stands or falls on his or her own merits.

In the process, Ezekiel lays out more fully than anywhere else in the book what constitutes righteousness or wickedness. A sinner is one who engages in idolatry or in worship at the high places, defiles his neighbor's wife, and does not observe purity laws, but also one who oppresses the poor, takes interest on loans, or performs unjustly in any way. Ezekiel's concern for purity and related issues is evident on every page of the book. His concern for social justice is not so often spelled out, but receives due prominence here. In this regard, Ezekiel resembles the Holiness Code, where moral and ritual requirements are placed side by side (see Leviticus 19; the taking of interest is prohibited in Lev 25:36). The righteous do more than avoid these offenses. They also feed the hungry and cover the naked. The ideal of righteousness, then, is a well-rounded one, and not as narrowly focused on purity issues as we might have inferred from some passages in Ezekiel.

Ezekiel insists that "the person that sins shall die." We have seen that the vision of the destruction of Jerusalem in chapter 9 seemed to take this principle quite literally: only the righteous were spared. Nonetheless, it is clear that Ezekiel does not think that sinners are struck down automatically. He allows for the possibility that a wicked person may repent or that a righteous person may stray from virtue. Further, there is no suggestion of significant life after death, so even the righteous die eventually. "To live" here most probably means to be right with God, and "to die" means to be in disfavor. But in light of the vision in chapter 9, we must also reckon that those who lived unrighteously were liable to premature destruction.

Ezekiel's teaching on individual responsibility is often viewed as a watershed text in the Hebrew Bible. Prior to Ezekiel's time, corporate responsibility was the norm. When Achan was convicted of violating the ban on booty in Joshua 8, not only was he executed, but also his entire family and even his animals. The case of Achan was admittedly exceptional. In the normal application of law in ancient Israel, only the wrongdoer was punished. But the covenant of God and Israel, and most of the preaching of the prophets, concerned corporate entities. The blessings and curses of the covenant applied to the people as a whole, without exceptions for individual behavior. Jeremiah suggested that individuals could save their lives during the siege of Jerusalem by deserting to the Babylonians, but he did not suggest that the Babylonian soldiers would discriminate on the basis of virtue. The novelty of Ezekiel's teaching was that it called for such discrimination, by God if not by the Babylonians. The lives of Noah, Daniel, and Job would be spared even if the rest of the world were destroyed. (There was in fact an ancient precedent for such exceptions in the case of Noah!) The prophet was still greatly concerned for the welfare of Israel as a whole, but he showed a new concern for individual justice in the eyes of God.

To the modern reader raised in an individualistic culture, this teaching of Ezekiel seems clearly right. It would not have been so obvious to the ancients. According to Exod 20:5, YHWH is a jealous God, punishing children for the iniquity of parents even to the third and fourth generations. Moreover, it is an experiential fact that the behavior of parents has consequences for their children, as the sons and daughters of alcoholics can well attest. Moreover, such a simple correlation of virtue and reward, vice and punishment, lends itself to self-righteousness on the part of the successful and to unfair blame of the less fortunate. We have seen some evidence of that problem in Ezekiel's assumption that the exiles in Babylon were superior to those who perished in the destruction of Jerusalem.

In all, then, the philosophical and theological merit of Ezekiel's doctrine of individual responsibility is suspect. But the teaching had unquestionable pastoral merit. The attitude reflected in the proverb, blaming misfortune on the sins of the fathers, did the exiles no good. It was better for all to take responsibility for their own fate and to use it as an incentive to live better and more righteously. It was with good reason, then, that Ezekiel insisted on this doctrine. He returns to it yet again in chapter 33, which repeats some material from chapter 18.

The Final Blow

The most moving incident in the book of Ezekiel is undoubtedly the passage that concludes the "book of judgment," 24:15-27. The prophet is told that God will take away "the delight of his eyes," but he must not mourn. That evening his wife died. It seems clear from the passage that he loved his wife and wanted to mourn but was prevented by what he perceived as a divine command. The death of his wife is treated as a sign of the destruction of Jerusalem, which he also loved deeply but could not mourn.

The inability to mourn is viewed as a pathological condition in modern psychiatry. It reflects not indifference but a depth of trauma that leaves the person numb. (In the case of Ezekiel, it also leaves him temporarily dumb.) This incident throws a new light on Ezekiel's vehement condemnations of Jerusalem. The destruction of the temple was a great trauma, not only because of his attachment to it but because his tradition taught him that YHWH loved Zion. If YHWH nonetheless destroyed it or allowed it to be destroyed, Jerusalem must have been vile to deserve such a fate. So Ezekiel could rationalize his inability to mourn. The vehemence of his denunciations of Jerusalem bespeaks his deep disillusionment and his desperate desire to vindicate what he perceived as the action of his God.

Chapters 25–32: The Oracles against the Nations

The oracles against foreign nations in Ezekiel are mostly set after the fall of Jerusalem. The first cluster of oracles (chap. 25) refers to Israel's immediate neighbors, Ammon, Moab, Edom, and the Philistines. They are accused of mocking Jerusalem after its fall and, in the case of Edom, of "acting vengefully." Such accusations are common in the exilic and early postexilic literature. There are oracles against Moab in Jeremiah 48 and against Ammon in Jer 49:1-16. The entire book of Obadiah, a total of 21 verses, is taken up with oracles against Edom, including one that invokes the Day of the Lord (v. 15) with a brief conclusion promising salvation on Mount Zion. Edom is also the target of Isaiah 34 and Jer 49:7-22. The condemnation of Edom is taken up again in Ezekiel 35.

The main cluster of oracles in this section of the book is directed against Tyre, the Phoenician coastal city to the north. Tyre is also accused of rejoicing at the fall of Jerusalem, apparently because it anticipated opportunities of plunder. But Tyre had little time to rejoice. It was besieged by Nebuchadnezzar for thirteen years. It eventually submitted to Babylon, but it was not destroyed or pillaged as Ezekiel had prophesied. The failure of the prophecy is acknowledged in 29:17-18. Ezekiel predicted that Nebuchadnezzar would carry off plunder from Egypt as compensation for his effort against Tyre, and that Egypt would be desolate for forty years (29:13). This, too, did not happen. Egypt remained independent until it was conquered by the Persians in 525 B.C.E. In fact, the only prediction that Ezekiel got fully right was the destruction of Jerusalem. Nonetheless, his oracles were preserved and enshrined in Scripture.

The oracles against Tyre are striking for their use of mythic patterns, which reflect a view of the human condition that goes far beyond the historical circumstances of their composition. The basic pattern is one of hubris, or arrogant pride, leading to a fall. It is familiar from Greek tragedy (which developed about a century later), and is often represented in the Bible (e.g., the stories of Adam and Eve and the Tower of Babel, and the allusion to Lucifer, son of Dawn, in Isaiah 14). The finest expression of the pattern is in Ezek 28:2: "Because your heart is proud and you have said 'I am a god; I sit in the seat of the gods, in the heart of the seas,' yet you are but a mortal, and no god, though you compare your mind with the mind of a god." Tyre was an island fortress; hence the confidence that it was as inaccessible as the home of the gods. (In Ugaritic myth the high god El was said to dwell "at the source of the floods, in the midst of the headwaters of the two oceans,"

ANET, 129.) Daniel, as we have seen already, was also a figure of Ugaritic myth. Especially interesting is the allusion in v. 13 to "Eden, the garden of God." Ezekiel evidently knows some form of the story of expulsion from Eden ("so I cast you as a profane thing from the mountain of God"). His form of the story, however, is quite different from what we have in Genesis. The figure in the garden is not naked but adorned with precious stones, and the garden is equated with "the mountain of God." Nine of the stones appear on the high priest's breastplate in Exod 28:17-20, and the mountain of God is usually Zion, the location of the temple. It would seem, then, that Ezekiel knew a form of the story that associated Eden with Zion and the Adam figure with a high priest. The present passage, however, is concerned not with Zion or the priesthood, but with the king of Tyre.

The oracles against Tyre dwell at length on the wealth of Tyre, derived from its trading, especially in chapter 27. (According to 28:13, Tyre accepted slaves as payment in some cases.) There is evident envy in these oracles. They arise out of the mutual grudges between neighboring cities. The desire for revenge and the gloating over the fall of another are not among the most edifying material in the Bible. Nonetheless, these oracles have had a profound impact on later tradition, not least because of their influence on the book of Revelation in the New Testament, especially on the vision of the destruction of Rome in Revelation 17–18.

The oracles against Tyre are followed by a short piece against Sidon (Ezek 28:20-23) and a series of oracles against Egypt, including one that speaks of "the Day of the Lord" in 30:2-3. Part of the resentment against Egypt was due to the false hope it had inspired in

Judah. In the end, we are told in chapter 32, Egypt will be consigned to Sheol, the netherworld, with Assyria and other fallen powers of the past. While this prediction did not come true as soon as Ezekiel expected, it did, of course, come true eventually. One of the abiding insights of these oracles is that all human power eventually collapses. This insight is also fundamental to the apocalyptic literature of the Second Temple period.

Chapters 33–48: Oracles of Restoration

The last section of the book of Ezekiel is dominated by prophecies of restoration. This section is introduced in 33:1-20 by a discourse on the prophet as watchman and on individual retribution that is closely related to material in chapters 3 and 18. This is followed in chapter 34 by an oracle that begins with condemnation of the "shepherds" of Israel. "Shepherd" was a common metaphor for king in the ancient Near East and was also applied to the king of the gods (e.g., Marduk). The shepherds condemned here are the kings who had brought disaster on Judah by their policies, from Jehoiakim to Zedekiah. More than half the oracle, however, looks to the future. The key promise here is in vv. 23-24: "I will set up over them one shepherd, my servant David, and he shall feed them . . . and I, the LORD, will be their God, and my servant David shall be prince among them." This is a messianic oracle, in the sense that it promises a restoration of the Davidic line. The designation "prince" is characteristic of Ezekiel. This was the term used in the Priestly strand of the Pentateuch to refer to the lay leader of the tribes in the wilderness period

(Exod 16:22; Num 4:34; 31:13; 32:2). He also uses the term "king" for the future ruler (Ezek 37:24). We shall see that the role of the prince is quite restricted in Ezekiel 40–48, but this may reflect a later perspective. The hope in 35:23-24 is simply for a just king who would live up to the ideals of the kingship.

A New Spirit

Ezekiel did not envision, or want, a simple return to the status quo before the destruction. In 34:25-31 he speaks of a covenant of peace that would entail a transformation of nature, banishing wild animals and making the earth fertile. There is a similar prophecy in 36:1-12, which also promises an increase in population. The later part of chapter 36 addresses some of the presuppositions of this transformation. YHWH is primarily concerned with the sanctity of his holy name. In order to be restored, Israel must be purified. Therefore "I will sprinkle clean water upon you" (36:25), for a ritual cleansing. Moreover, "a new heart I will give you, and a new spirit I will put within you; and I will remove from your body the heart of stone and give you a heart of flesh. I will put my spirit within you and make you follow my statutes" (vv. 26-27). In Ezekiel's view the old creation had failed. He does not say how Israel, or humanity, had come to have a heart of stone. It is presumably akin to the evil inclination of humanity before the flood (Gen 6:5). Not only would the new creation give people a better disposition, however. It would remove the hazards of free will by making people obey the laws. Here, as in Jeremiah's concept of a new covenant, we find the totalitarian tendency of utopian thinking. Human nature as we know it inclines to evil. Only by

Fig. 18.2 Ezekiel's vision of the valley of dry bones; fresco from the third-century c.e. synagogue at Dura-Europos. Commons.wikimedia.org

radically redesigning human nature can good behavior be guaranteed.

The Valley of Dry Bones

One of the most memorable of Ezekiel's visions is that of a valley full of dry bones in chapter 37. The imagery may have been suggested by the Zoroastrian custom of laying out the dead to be picked clean by vultures. If so, this vision must be later than the time of Ezekiel, although it is faithful to his style. There was no tradition in Israel of the resurrection of the dead. Such a belief was held by the Zoroastrians from an early date. Ezekiel uses the vision of resurrection only metaphorically. He does not suggest that the individual dead will come back to life, only that "the whole house of Israel" will be restored, and that this would be as great a miracle as the resurrection of the dead. In later times, this vision would be reinterpreted as referring to literal resurrection.

The earliest evidence for such reinterpretation is found in a text in the Dead Sea Scrolls that is a reformulation of passages from the book of Ezekiel (4Q386).

This vision is followed by a symbolic action, in which the prophet writes on a stick: "For Judah and the Israelites associated with it." The restoration must include all Israel, north and south, under "my servant David." The restored dynasty would last forever, and YHWH would dwell in the midst of them. The word translated "dwelling" in the NRSV is *mishkan*, the term for the tabernacle or tent-shrine in the Priestly strand of the Pentateuch.

Gog of the Land of Magog

In chapters 38–39 we encounter a new kind of prophecy. The novelty is not formal. It is a judgment oracle like other oracles against foreign nations. The novelty lies in the fact that the enemy addressed is not an actual entity in the contemporary world of the prophet but a legendary figure who takes on mythic proportions. The name Gog is most probably derived from Gyges of Lydia in western Asia Minor, who lived about a century before the time of Ezekiel. He is known from Assyrian texts, where he is called *gugu,* and from the Greek historian Herodotus (book 1). Gyges had absolutely no contact with Israel, and it is unlikely that Ezekiel knew much about him. His country is called Magog (= the place of Gog; the name appears in the list of nations in Gen 10:2, among the descendants of Japheth). He is prince of Meshech and Tubal, vaguely known peoples of Asia Minor. The figure described in these oracles only takes his name from Gyges. He is a figure of myth and fantasy.

In Ezekiel 38 Gog becomes the leader of an army of the nations, including Persia and Ethiopia. Again, these are nations with whom Israel had had very little contact in Ezekiel's time. He is led to do this by YHWH, but, like Assyria in Isaiah 10, he also has his own thoughts on the matter. The entire episode is set "in the latter years"—an indefinite future time.

Gog is identified as the enemy "of whom I spoke in former days by my servants the prophets" (38:17). He is said to come "out of the remotest parts of the north" (38:15), which suggests that he is identified as the "foe from the north" in the prophecy of Jeremiah. If so, this constitutes a reinterpretation of the older prophecy, which clearly referred to Babylon in its own context. This kind of reinterpretation is more likely to have been the work of Ezekiel's disciples than of the prophet himself, although the style of the chapter is consistent with that of the rest of the book.

Gog becomes the principal actor in the mythical conflict between the nations and Zion. This conflict is presupposed in Psalm 2: "Why do the nations conspire and the peoples plot in vain . . . against the LORD and his anointed?" His fate is a variant of the myth of the inviolability of Zion. Gentile armies that come up against Jerusalem are routed (Ps 48:4-5). This myth had received some confirmation from the fact that Jerusalem survived the invasion of Sennacherib, but one would have expected that it would have been demolished by the Babylonian army. The prophecy does not, to be sure, speak specifically of Jerusalem, but the pattern is the same. Gog will be killed "on the mountains of Israel." The expectation of victory over the nations by the power of YHWH had not materialized in the Babylonian invasion. The prophecy insists that it will be fulfilled, in a definitive way, in the future.

It is not enough that Gog be defeated. His entire host must be annihilated. They are buried in the land of Israel, and the land is cleansed. Then there is a gruesome feast. The birds and wild animals are assembled to "eat the flesh of the mighty, and drink the blood of the princes of the earth" (39:18). This is a sacrificial feast, as if Gog were a sacrificial victim. The drinking of blood, however, is extraordinary, especially in a book concerned with ritual purity to the degree that Ezekiel is. It is quite literally a bloodthirsty vision, which sets no limits to the destruction that is wished upon the nations. Here again Ezekiel has left his mark on later tradition. In Rev 20:8 the army of Satan in the final conflict is called Gog and Magog, while "the great supper of God" consists of the flesh of kings and the mighty, but also of all both small and great (Rev 19:17-19).

The banquet brings ritual closure to the drama of the final battle. We shall meet the motif of a final banquet again in one of the additions to the book of Isaiah (Isa 25:6-10). This motif is sometimes called the messianic banquet, but neither Ezekiel 39 nor Isaiah 25 speaks of a messiah in this context. The banquet is, however, part of the pattern of the old combat myth in which the good god defeats his enemies. This myth provides a way of imagining a satisfactory future that is increasingly prominent in Second Temple Judaism, especially in the apocalyptic literature.

The New Jerusalem

The final vision of the book of Ezekiel occupies nine chapters, almost one-fifth of the book. It is written in the style of Ezekiel, and a nucleus of it may come from the prophet himself. On some matters, however, such as the role of the prince, its position seems to be developed beyond that of the earlier chapters, and some passages would seem to fit better in the context of the restoration, some decades after the time of Ezekiel (e.g., chap. 44). It is nonetheless very much in the tradition of Ezekiel and continuous with his interests. It also provides a fitting conclusion to the book, which began with the departure of the divine presence from Jerusalem.

Formally, the vision is similar to the temple vision in chapters 8–11. The prophet is taken on a guided tour by an angel. Jerusalem is not mentioned by name but is referred to as "the city." It is located in a consecrated area that runs from the Jordan to the sea, separating the territories of Judah to the south and Benjamin to the north. Within this area, strips of land are set aside for the priests, the Levites, the city, and the prince. The temple is located in the middle of the territory of the priests. The area of the city proper is declared profane, and

it occupies only half as much territory as that of the priests. The city of Jerusalem is clearly subordinated in importance to the temple area. This sanctified city has an Edenic character. A river flows out from it that makes the waters of the Dead Sea fresh (47:1-12; compare the river that flows out from Eden in Gen 2:10).

In Ezekiel's view, failure to protect the sanctity of the temple was a major cause of the disaster that had befallen Jerusalem. In the future, "no foreigner, uncircumcised in heart and flesh," would enter the sanctuary (Ezek 44:9). Levites and ordinary Israelites were restricted to the outer court. A sharp distinction is made between Levites and Zadokite priests. At the time of Josiah's reform, the Levites from the country shrines were invited to go up to Jerusalem and minister at the temple there. Ezekiel is not so welcoming. The Levites, we are told, must bear their punishment for contributing to the apostasy of Israel in the past, by worshiping outside Jerusalem, and allegedly participating in idolatry. They are allowed to perform menial services in the temple but not to serve as priests. Pride of place in the new order is reserved for the Zadokite priests, who are credited with preserving the sanctuary when the rest of the people sinned, and who alone would be allowed to enter the inner court. They are given special linen garments and are not to wear anything that causes sweat. But they are to remove these garments when they go into the outer court "so that they may not communicate holiness to the people with their vestments" (44:19).

The purpose of these rules is to make a clear separation between the sacred and the profane, and so to preserve the special character of the holy. But inevitably these regulations also create a hierarchical structure, in which some people hold more power than others. The Levites are to a great degree disenfranchised, while power is vested in the hands of the Zadokite priests.

There is still a role in this vision for the "prince," the title given in chapters 34 and 37 to the Davidic king. In the new order, the prince has a place of honor but very little power. His main role is to provide victims and offerings for the altar (46:11-15). In this respect, his role is curtailed in a way that was not apparent in chapters 34 and 37.

Ezekiel's vision was never realized in Jerusalem. Ezekiel was a visionary, and visionaries seldom have the power to implement policy. Nonetheless, some of the tendencies in this vision continue to be prominent in Second Temple Judaism. We shall find in the books of Zechariah and Ezra that the high priest wielded a new level of power in Jerusalem after the exile. To a great degree, he became the primary Jewish ruler. Even texts that speak of a kingly messiah sometimes indicate that he must be subordinate to the high priest. (This is the case in several texts in the Dead Sea Scrolls, which, like Ezekiel, give pride of place to the Zadokite priests.)

Fig. 18.3 The Temple Scroll from Qumran (11Q20). Commons.wikimedia.org

Ezekiel's vision was also the model for several utopian prescriptions for a New Jerusalem in Second Temple times. A long section of the Temple Scroll from Qumran is devoted to regulations for an ideal temple. There is also a fragmentary vision of a New Jerusalem in Aramaic among the Dead Sea Scrolls. The book of Revelation, which is often influenced by Ezekiel, does not offer the kind of detailed instructions found in Ezekiel 40–48, but it does offer a vision of "the holy city, the new Jerusalem, coming down out of heaven from God, prepared as a bride adorned for her husband" (Rev 21:2).

Obadiah

A quite different perspective on the exilic period is provided by the book of Obadiah, which reflects conditions in Judah after the disaster. At 21 verses, Obadiah is the shortest book in the Bible. It follows the Book of Amos in the arrangement of the twelve prophets in the Hebrew Bible. This placement is due to thematic considerations: Obadiah is largely concerned with Edom, which is mentioned in Amos 9:12. The order in the Greek Bible (LXX) is Hosea, Amos, Micah, Joel, Obadiah. Obadiah is linked to Joel by the motif of the Day of the Lord.

Structure and Unity

The short book falls into two parts. Verses 1-14 consist of oracles of vengeance against Edom for wrongs done to Judah. Verses 15-21 contain a more general prediction of judgment on all the nations, followed by the restoration of Judah. It is possible that all of this short book was composed by a single author, but many scholars see the eschatological oracles in vv. 15-21 as additions. In the latter view, there was a tendency to add such oracles throughout the prophetic corpus in the course of the editing of the collection. In any case, there is an analogy between the judgment on Edom and the more general judgment on the nations, and this gives coherence to the book.

Historical Context

The historical context of the first part of the book can be inferred with some confidence from the accusations against Edom in v. 11:

> "On the day that you stood aside,
> on the day that strangers carried off his wealth,
> and foreigners entered his gates
> and cast lots for Jerusalem,
> you too were like one of them."

The occasion is one when Jerusalem was destroyed by a third party. By far the most likely occasion is the destruction of Jerusalem by the Babylonians in 586 B.C.E.. Some scholars object that there is no mention of an Edomite invasion in the historical books of the Hebrew Bible, and neither is there any archaeological evidence for it. Edom figures prominently, and negatively, however, in the prophetic books of the postexilic period. Jewish resentment against Edom in this period must have had some foundation. Later, in the rabbinic period, Edom is often used as the archetypal enemy of Judaism and becomes a code name for Rome. Some scholars suggest that it was a symbolic enemy already in Obadiah. The charges in v. 11 are quite specific, however, and they probably reflect historical experience. If this is correct, the oracles of Obadiah, or at least those in the first part of the book, were probably composed in Judah after the fall of Jerusalem. They are then contemporary with the Lamentations of Jeremiah, and count among the very few witnesses to life in Judah during the Babylonian exile.

The Theology of Obadiah

Obadiah, like Nahum, is one of the few prophetic books that does not criticize Israel or Judah. It is in large part a call for vengeance on Judah's enemy Edom. The book has often been criticized for vindictiveness, but the association of justice with vengeance is found throughout the Old Testament and especially in the prophetic corpus. If Obadiah seems especially vindictive, this is due to the brevity of the book, which allows this theme to dominate to an unusual degree. The desire for vengeance was not unprovoked. The underlying assumption is that one people should not exploit the misfortune of another, and that such exploitation is especially heinous in the case of neighbors and relatives. By Christian standards, vengeance is never good. The Old Testament also contains a strand that reserves vengeance to God (see Deut 32:35: "Vengeance is mine and recompense"). But vengeance remains a very human emotion, and it is better to acknowledge it and address it than to pretend it does not exist.

Obadiah ends with a prophecy of the restoration of Judah and Jerusalem that appeals to the old Zion theology found, for example, in Pss 46 and 48, which view Zion as the holy mountain of the Lord. In accordance with the usual expectation of postexilic prophecy, only a remnant will be saved, but none at all shall be saved from Edom, the house of Esau (v. 18).

FOR FURTHER READING

Ezekiel

D. I. Block, *The Book of Ezekiel* (2 vols.; NICOT; Grand Rapids: Eerdmans, 1997–1998). Thorough commentary informed by ancient Near Eastern parallels.

L. Boadt, "Ezekiel, Book of," *ABD* 2:711–22. Overview of the critical issues.

K. Pfisterer Darr, "The Book of Ezekiel," *NIB* 6:1075–1607. Literary approach with homiletical reflections. Useful overview of scholarship.

E. F. Davis, *Swallowing the Scroll: Textuality and the Dynamics of Discourse in Ezekiel's Prophecy* (JSOTSup 78; Sheffield: Almond, 1989). Ezekiel's oracles as literary compositions.

J. Galambush, *Jerusalem in the Book of Ezekiel: The City as Yahweh's Wife* (SBLDS 130; Atlanta: Scholars Press, 1992). Study of an important motif.

M. Greenberg, *Ezekiel 1–20* (AB 22; New York: Doubleday, 1983).

———, *Ezekiel 21–37* (AB 22A; New York: Doubleday, 1997). Detailed historical and philological commentary. Takes a "holistic" approach, which affirms the unity and integrity of the book.

R. M. Hals, *Ezekiel* (FOTL 19; Grand Rapids: Eerdmans, 1989). Form-critical analysis.

P. M. Joyce, *Ezekiel: A Commentary* (London: T&T Clark, 2007). Attributes most of the book to Ezekiel, but with some additions in chaps. 38–39 and elements of 40-48.

J. S. Kaminsky, *Corporate Responsibility in the Hebrew Bible* (JSOTSup 196; Sheffield: Sheffield Academic Press, 1995). Sets Ezekiel's teaching on individual responsibility in perspective, in light of the full biblical tradition.

J. E. Lapsley, *Can These Bones Live? The Problem of the Moral Self in the Book of Ezekiel* (Berlin: de Gruyter, 2000). Exegetical study of the tensions in Ezekiel's understanding of the moral self.

J. D. Levenson, *The Theology of the Program of Restoration of Ezekiel 40–48* (HSM 10; Missoula, MT: Scholars Press, 1976). Excellent analysis of chapters 40–48.

M. Lyons, *From Law to Prophecy: Ezekiel's Use of the Holiness Code* (London: T&T Clark, 2009). Argument that Ezekiel used the Holiness Code.

J. L. Mays and P. J. Achtemeier, eds., *Interpreting the Prophets* (Philadelphia: Fortress, 1987), 157–236. Essays on aspects of Ezekiel by R. R. Wilson, M. Fishbane, C. A. Newsom, W. Lemke, and M. Greenberg.

A. Mein, *Ezekiel and the Ethics of Exile* (Oxford: Oxford Univ. Press, 2001). Comprehensive study of Ezekiel's ethics.

M. Odell, *Ezekiel* (Macon, GA: Smyth & Helwys, 2005). Literary-theological commentary.

D. L. Petersen, *The Prophetic Literature: An Introduction* (Louisville: Westminster John Knox, 2002), 137–68. Focus on literary aspects of the book.

S. Tuell, *Ezekiel* (NIBC; Peabody, MA: Hendrickson, 2009). Critical evangelical commentary. Attributes chaps. 40–48 to a different hand.

W. Zimmerli, *Ezekiel* (trans. R. E. Clements; 2 vols.; Hermeneia; Philadelphia: Fortress Press, 1979–1983). Classic form and redaction-critical commentary. Distinguishes numerous editorial additions to the text of Ezekiel.

Obadiah

J. Barton, *Joel and Obadiah* (OTL; Louisville: Westminster John Knox, 2001), 113–58. Lucid exegetical commentary.

P. Raabe, *Obadiah* (AB 24D; New York: Doubleday, 1996). Historical and philological commentary.

M. A. Sweeney, *The Twelve Prophets* (Berit Olam; Collegeville: Liturgical Press, 2000), 1:277–300. Helpful exegetical commentary.

H.-W. Wolff, *Obadiah and Jonah* (trans. M. Kohl; CC; Minneapolis: Augsburg, 1986). Form- and redaction-critical commentary.

E. Ben Zvi, *A Historical-Critical Study of the Book of Obadiah* (Berlin: de Gruyter, 1996). Focuses on the original *readers* of the book.

CHAPTER 19

The Additions to the Book of Isaiah

INTRODUCTION

We saw in chapter 16 that the present book of Isaiah included materials from different periods. Here we return to Isaiah to discuss materials from successive periods after the exile, a so-called Second and Third Isaiah, as well as the "Apocalypse" in chapters 24–27 and the final formation of the book in our Bible.

Modern scholarship has been aware, for at least two hundred years, that some parts of the book of Isaiah cannot have originated with the eighth-century prophet. Chapters 40–66 come from a time during or after the Babylonian exile. Cyrus of Persia, the king who overthrew Babylon in 539 B.C.E., is twice mentioned by name (Isa 44:28; 45:1). Since the work of the great German scholar Bernhard Duhm at the end of the nineteenth century, it has been conventional to distinguish between First Isaiah (chaps. 1–39), Second (Deutero-) Isaiah (chaps. 40–55), and Third (Trito-) Isaiah (chaps. 56–66). It is now generally agreed that these distinctions are too simple. Second Isaiah (chaps. 40–55) remains a distinctive and coherent bloc of material. The line between Second and Third Isaiah is

blurred by chapters 60–62, which are closely related to Second Isaiah in style and in spirit. As we have already seen, only a small part of chapters 1–39 can be attributed to Isaiah of Jerusalem. Chapter 35 seems to belong with Second Isaiah. Chapters 24–27, often dubbed "the Apocalypse of Isaiah," are likely to be later than anything in chapters 40–66. Some scholars argue that "First Isaiah" was edited by "Second Isaiah." There are some themes that run through the entire book, such as the interest in Zion/Jerusalem, the designation of God as "the Holy One" and "King" of Israel, and the symbolism of light (2:5; 42:6; 49:6; 60:1). The theme of the new exodus in Isa 11:15-16 is typical of Second Isaiah but atypical of First Isaiah. The mention of the Babylonians at the end of chapter 39 builds a bridge to the second half of the book with its focus on the Babylonian period. Chapter 40 hearkens back to chapter 6, with its report of voices in the divine council. At the end of the book, 65:25 ("the wolf and the lamb shall feed together") alludes back to chapter 11.

Thus numerous links bind the various parts of the book of Isaiah together. These continuities cannot be explained by postulating an "Isaianic school" that was still active a century and a half after the death of the prophet. Rather, we have an anonymous prophet from the period of the exile who was well versed in the oracles of his predecessors and who claimed that ancient prophecies were being fulfilled in his day. The same prophet may have had a hand in editing or transmitting the older oracles of Isaiah. It should be noted, however, that this prophet's interest in older prophecy was not limited to the oracles of Isaiah. He shows an even stronger interest in those of Jeremiah. So, while the placement of the oracles of the exile in the book of Isaiah is not accidental and serves a purpose, it is not inevitable either. This prophet, whom we call Second Isaiah for the sake of convenience, is very much a distinct individual, speaking in a specific time and place. He is not an exegete, concerned with the meaning of the older oracles. He is concerned with the momentous events of his own time and refers to older prophecy in the context of addressing those events.

Second Isaiah

The opening words of Second Isaiah, "Comfort, comfort my people," are among the best-known lines in the Bible because they are used in the text of Handel's *Messiah* (in the King James translation, "Comfort ye, comfort ye my people"). They also mark a major point of transition in the history of Hebrew prophecy. Up to this point, the prophets whose oracles are preserved in the canonical Scriptures prophesied "war, famine, and pestilence" in the phrase of Jeremiah (Jer 28:9) and delivered primarily oracles of judgment. Prophets who attempted to reassure the people were judged to be false prophets in most cases (with some exceptions, to be sure). Now we find a prophet whose main theme is consolation, who is accepted as a genuine prophet of YHWH.

The difference, of course, is the change of historical circumstances. Judah and Jerusalem had been ravaged. Only a remnant had been left. The prophecies of judgment had all been fulfilled. Moreover, Second Isaiah prophesied at one of the most hopeful moments in the history of Israel and Judah. Cyrus of Persia conquered Babylon in the fall of 539 B.C.E. He changed not only the power structure of the Near East but also the policy toward subject peoples in his empire. We know something of his policy from an inscription on a clay barrel known as the "Cyrus Cylinder" (*ANET,* 316). The last king of Babylon, Nabonidus, had been hugely unpopular with the priests of Babylon. He was devoted to the moon-god Sin, but he neglected the worship of other deities such as Marduk. He moved his residence from Babylon to Teima in the Arabian desert and remained there for ten years. Because of his absence, the New Year's (Akitu) festival could not be performed in Babylon, which outraged the Babylonian priests. Cyrus exploited their discontent in his inscription. He claimed that it was Marduk who had called him and led him to Babylon to restore his cult. In fact,

Fig. 19.1   The so-called Cyrus Cylinder; in the British Museum.
Photo by the author

Cyrus did not ravage Babylon, and he restored the Babylonian gods to their shrines. He found it more effective to win over the people of Babylon rather than to subdue them. His Persian successors would not always be so enlightened or so successful in dealing with their subject peoples.

According to the book of Ezra, the policy of Cyrus toward the Judeans was rather similar to his policy toward the Babylonians. An edict cited in Hebrew in Ezra 1:2-4 declares, "Thus says King Cyrus of Persia: YHWH the God of heaven has given me all the kingdoms of the earth, and he has charged me to build him a house at Jerusalem in Judah. Any of those among you who are of his people—may their God be with them!—are now permitted to go up to Jerusalem in Judah, and rebuild the house of the Lord, the God of Israel—he is the God who is in Jerusalem." The authenticity of this edict has been questioned, but

it is certainly the case that Cyrus authorized Judeans to return from Babylon to Jerusalem and to rebuild the temple there. Since he told the Babylonians that he was chosen by Marduk, we should not be surprised that he told the Judeans that he was chosen by YHWH. Whether he did or not, it seemed self-evident to a prophet of YHWH such as Second Isaiah that such a turn of events could only have been brought about by the God of Israel.

The euphoria of (at least some) Judeans at the edict of Cyrus rings loud and clear in Second Isaiah. Some scholars think that the prophet predicted the rise of Cyrus and the release of the Judeans. It is easier to suppose that he prophesied after the fact. The setting is most probably Babylon. There is no awareness in chapters 40–55 of the problems that would confront the exiles when they returned to Judea. We should suppose then that these oracles were delivered within a year or so of the fall of Babylon.

The oracles of Second Isaiah are not as diverse a collection as those we have found in other prophetic books. They consist of a series of short poems. There is no consensus on the actual delimitation and number of these poems; one scholar distinguished as many as seventy in chapters 40–66. A more reasonable approach defines longer units of approximately chapter length in most cases. There is a shift in tone beginning in chapter 49. Chapters 40–48 are filled with the expectation of a new era to be inaugurated by Cyrus, with a certain amount of gloating polemic against the Babylonians. Chapters 49–55 are concerned rather with the Jewish community and its internal problems.

The New Exodus

The opening oracle in Isa 40:1-11 is set in the divine council, like Isaiah's call vision in chapter 6. The speaker is not identified but is apparently a member of the divine council, a heavenly or angelic being. The command to comfort the people is in the plural. The prophet is presumably included, but the commission is a more general one (unlike the situation in Isaiah 6).

The message of comfort in Isa 40:1-2 acknowledges the familiar idea that the exile was a punishment for sin, but it adds a novel twist: not only has Jerusalem served her term, but she has been punished "double for all her sins." This is the first suggestion in the Hebrew Bible that the punishment of YHWH is excessive. The point, as we shall see, is not to question the justice of God, but to open up

the possibility that the suffering may have a purpose other than punishment for sin. This possibility will be explored further in the Servant Songs, to which we shall return below.

Another voice cries out in v. 5: "In the wilderness prepare the way of the LORD." The immediate reference is to the wilderness separating Babylon from Jerusalem, but the motif of the wilderness suggests that the return from Babylon will be a reenactment of the exodus. Israel is given the opportunity to begin anew (cf. Hosea 2). The motif of the highway suggests that the return will be a triumphal procession of YHWH to his city. There is also a suggestion of a new creation because of the way in which the order of nature will be reversed.

The third voice (Isa 40:6) proclaims the transcendent power of God. The statement that the people are grass is probably a gloss added by a scribe, but it only draws out the obvious implication of the oracle. The contrast here between the word of the Lord and ephemeral grass is essentially the same as the contrast in 31:3 between spirit and flesh.

The final movement of this oracle casts Zion and Jerusalem in the role of heralds, passing on the good news to the cities of Judah from their perch on Mount Zion. The emphasis is not on the return of the exiles, but on the return of their God.

The theme of the new exodus is revisited two other times in Second Isaiah. In 43:16 the prophet speaks in the name of the Lord "who makes a way in the sea, a path in the mighty waters"—a clear allusion to the exodus story. Yet a few verses later he says, "Do not remember the former things or consider the things of old. I am about to do a new thing. . . . I will make a way in the wilderness and rivers in the desert . . . for I give water in the wilderness . . . to give drink to my chosen people" (43:18-20). There are clear allusions here to the wandering in the wilderness (cf. Numbers 20 for the motif of water in the wilderness). They are not presented as reminiscences of the past, however, but as projections of the future. The exodus is not to be regarded as "a thing of old" but as a pattern of divine intervention that is being reenacted in the present.

Perhaps the most striking instance of this typological understanding of the exodus (and of history more generally) is found in Isa 51:9-11, which calls on "the arm of YHWH" to awake as in the days of old. The prophet first recalls creation: "Was it not you who cut Rahab in pieces, who pierced the dragon?" This is not the account of creation that we find in Genesis, but one that we know only from passing allusions in Hebrew poetry, such as Job 26:12 or Ps 74:13-14. It is closely related to the stories of Baal and Yamm in the Ugaritic myths and less directly to the Babylonian myth of Marduk and Tiamat. Second Isaiah juxtaposes this myth with the exodus: "Was it not you who dried up the sea, the waters of the great deep; who made the depths of the sea a way for the redeemed to cross over?" (Isa 51:10) The implication is that the exodus and the battle with the dragon at creation are analogous events. But here again the prophet is not interested in ancient history. Both creation and exodus provide a model for what is happening in the present. When "the ransomed of the Lord" return to Zion, the dragon is pierced and the waters of the deep are once again dried up.

The Polemic against Idolatry

For Judeans in Babylon, one of the galling aspects of their situation was the apparent failure of their God and the superiority of the Babylonian deities. One aspect of Babylonian worship that attracts a lot of attention in Second Isaiah is divination—the prediction of the future by ritual means. With the fall of Babylon and the restoration of Jerusalem, however, the situation was reversed. Second Isaiah claims that this is what YHWH had predicted all along. So he challenges the Babylonian gods: "Set forth your case . . . bring your proofs. . . . Tell us the former things, what they are, so that we may consider them, and that we may know their outcome; or declare to us the things to come. Tell us what is to come hereafter, that we may know that you are gods. . . . You indeed are nothing and your work is nothing" (41:21-24; cf. 41:26-27). The Jewish prophet claims that YHWH had predicted these things beforehand: "The former things I declared long ago, they went out from my mouth and I made them known; then suddenly I did them and they came to pass" (48:3). It is not clear what prophecies he has in mind. Some scholars think he is alluding to some of the oracles of First Isaiah. It is also possible that some of Second Isaiah's own prophecies were delivered before the actual fall of Babylon. In that case, the success of the prediction confirms both the legitimacy of the prophet and the superiority of his God. The prophet boasts that it is YHWH "who frustrates the omens of liars, and makes fools of diviners; who turns back the wise, and makes their knowledge foolish; who confirms the word of his servant, and fulfills the prediction of his messengers" (44:25-26).

The claims that Second Isaiah makes for his God are stronger than any we have hitherto encountered in the Hebrew Bible. He categorically denies that any other gods have power, and comes close to denying their existence: "Before me no god was formed, nor shall there be any after me. I, I am the Lord, and besides me there is no savior" (43:10-11); "I am the first and I am the last; besides me there is no god" (44:6; cf. 46:9: "I am God, and there is no other"). Because of statements like these, Second Isaiah is arguably the first real monotheist in the tradition. Earlier Yahwism was henotheistic in the sense that only one God was worshiped, but the existence of others was not denied. Even Second Isaiah seems to grant the pagan gods a limited form of existence on some occasions: "Bel bows down, Nebo stoops, their idols are on beasts and cattle. . . . They cannot save the burden, but themselves go into captivity" (46:1–2). But statements like this are mere mockery. The prophet denies that there is any reality to these gods beyond the idols made by their worshipers.

The critique of idols in Second Isaiah must be seen against the background of the role of statues in Babylonian worship. The cult image was the basic means of representing the presence of the deity. These images were usually made of precious wood and either covered with garments or plated with gold. In the great majority of cases, they had human shape and proportions. They had staring eyes made of precious stones, and elaborate garments that were changed ceremonially. These statues were the focus of the sacrificial cult, and they were carried in processions. When the images were carried off by conquerors, the gods were thought to go with them. The statues were consecrated in ceremonies that supposedly opened their eyes and mouths, and thereafter were treated as if they were alive. Food was placed before them twice a day. The "leftovers" were sent to the king or consumed by the temple clergy. The care and proper clothing of these statues was a major activity of the temple personnel.

Many scholars now think that there were cult images in the Jerusalem temple prior to Josiah's reform. The biblical tradition, however, is staunchly aniconic, and the roots of this tradition are old, even if it was not always normative. In ancient times the Deity was represented simply by standing stones. Later he was thought to be enthroned invisibly above the ark in the Jerusalem temple. To the Jewish exiles, the care lavished on wooden statues was simply ridiculous. Second Isaiah inaugurates a long tradition of satire against idols. He focuses on the process by which they were made. "A man cuts down a tree, makes a fire with part of it to warm himself and heat his food, and makes the rest into a god and calls on it to save him" (44:9-20). Of course the prophet is not being fair to the Babylonians. The statue was not the god or goddess, but only the instrument by which their presence was mediated to the worshiper. In Israelite religion the temple served the same purpose without representing the Deity so directly. It may well be that many Babylonian worshipers ignored the niceties of their theology and simply identified the deity with the image. But in any case, the fact that these images were manmade provided an easy target for the ridicule of the Jewish prophet. There are several such idol parodies in the later books of the Old Testament. A particularly entertaining example is found in the story of Bel and the Dragon in the Greek additions to the book of Daniel. Another caustic example is found in the apocryphal Letter of Jeremiah (= Baruch 6).

While the prophet's mockery is aimed at the Babylonian gods, he does not acknowledge any gods besides YHWH. Despite his enthusiasm for Cyrus of Persia, he never mentions Ahura Mazda, the god of the Zoroastrians. In fact, there is a subtle rejection of the Persian deity in 45:7. In Zoroastrian theology, Ahura Mazda presided over warring forces of light and darkness. According to Second Isaiah, it is YHWH who forms light and creates darkness. There is only one legitimate God for all people.

A Hidden God

If YHWH was the true God after all, and was now vindicated by the turn of events, how was his apparent failure in the period of Babylonian ascendancy to be explained? For the prophet, it must have been part of a deliberate plan. "Truly, you are a God who hides himself, O God of Israel, the Savior" (45:15). By withdrawing from history for a time, YHWH

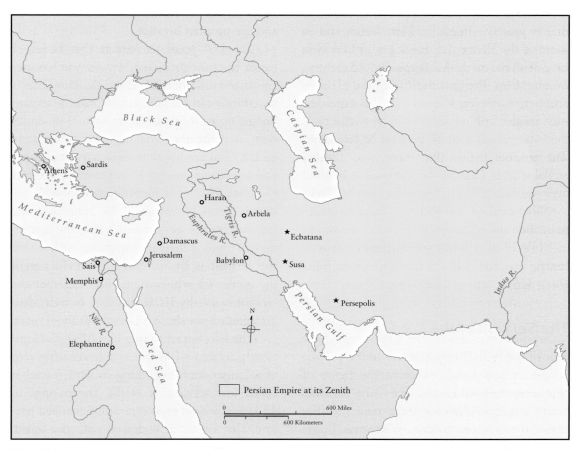

Map 19.1

could make his revelation all the more spectacular. To be sure, his withdrawal was partly due to anger with his people; but Babylon, like Assyria before it, was arrogant and excessive in its conduct (47:6). The reversal of fortunes brought about by the fall of Babylon would catch the attention of the nations. So YHWH calls, "Turn to me and be saved, all the ends of the earth! For I am God and there is no other. . . . To me every knee shall bow, every tongue shall swear. Only in the LORD, it shall be said of me, are righteousness and strength" (45:22-25; cf. 45:5-7).

This call to the ends of the earth reflects the universalistic strand of the Zion theology that is present already in First Isaiah and in some of the Psalms (cf. Isa 2:2-4). YHWH is king of all the earth. All people should come to worship him. The universalism of the Hebrew prophet, however, should not be confused with modern pluralism. What he envisions is the subordination of all peoples to Jerusalem and its God. The prophet gloats over the fall of Babylon in chapter 47, just as Ezekiel had over the fall of Tyre. His vision may still reasonably be called universalistic, since he wants to include the whole universe in the dominion of YHWH. But it has nonetheless an ethnocentric emphasis. It is universalism on Yahwistic terms, centered on Mount Zion.

The Servant of the Lord

One of the best-known features of the prophecy of Second Isaiah concerns the figure of "the servant of the LORD." The word "servant" occurs numerous times in these oracles. At the end of the nineteenth century, however, Bernhard Duhm singled out four passages that he believed were derived from a distinct source:

42:1-4; 49:1-6; 50:4-9; and 52:13—53:12. These passages have generally been known as the Servant Songs. Duhm's idea that they come from a distinct source, however, is now generally rejected. These passages are an integral part of the prophecy of Second Isaiah, and some of them are integral parts of longer passages. Nonetheless, the Servant Songs continue to be a focus of research. The servant in question has been variously identified as a collective figure (Israel) or as an individual. Several individual identifications have been suggested. The most widely supported are Moses, who is often called the servant of the Lord in the Deuteronomic tradition, Cyrus, and the prophet himself.

The first point to note is that Israel, or Jacob, is explicitly called "my servant" in several oracles: 41:8; 44:1-2; 44:21; 45:4. This is also the case in 49:3, in one of Duhm's Servant Songs, unless one resorts to textual emendation, as some do. One can also understand 43:10, "You are my witnesses, says the LORD, and my servant whom I have chosen," to refer to Israel. No other identification of the servant is given. However, 44:26, "who confirms the word of his servant and fulfills the prediction of his messengers," suggests rather that the servant is the prophet. The evidence of the book as a whole, then, indicates that the servant is usually Israel, but that an individual interpretation cannot be ruled out in all cases.

The first Servant Song in 42:1-4 is at least closely related to 42:5-9 and is arguably part of a longer unit, beginning in 41:1 (Israel is called "my servant" in 41:8). The passage in 42:1-4, however, paints an individualized picture. The servant is endowed with the Spirit, as a prophet would be, and entrusted with a mission to the nations, as Jeremiah was. He is depicted as a gentle figure who does no violence but "faithfully brings forth justice." The mission to establish justice on earth suggests a royal figure rather than a prophet, and so it has been suggested that Cyrus is the servant in this passage. Cyrus, however, was not quite this gentle. It is also possible to understand the figure here as Israel, cast partly in the role of a prophet. Israel could also be called on to establish justice in a way that a prophet could not.

The role of the prophet is elaborated in 42:5-9. While the word *servant* is not used in this passage, the person addressed is "called," and given as "a covenant to the people, a light to the nations." (The latter phrase is used again with reference to the servant in 49:6.) The mission includes liberating people from captivity. Again, the oracle could well refer to Cyrus. If it refers to Israel, then we might take it that Israel is supposed to be instrumental in the release of other captives, as she herself was liberated. If we assume that the captives are the Judeans in exile, then the servant seems to have a mission to Israel.

The same tension between the idea of the servant as Israel and as someone with a mission to Israel is in evidence in 49:1-6, where the servant is explicitly addressed as Israel in v. 3. Here again there are reminiscences of Jeremiah. The servant is called before birth, formed from the womb (cf. Jer 1:5). Like Jeremiah, the servant struggles with feeling that he labors in vain. The tension arises in v. 5, which says that YHWH formed the servant "to bring Jacob back to him, and that Israel might be gathered to him." The most natural reading of the text suggests that the servant has a mission to restore Israel. It is possible, but more difficult, to take the text to mean that the role of the servant entails the restoration of Israel, that

Israel is restored by virtue of being the servant. It may be that the servant is an ideal Israel, or an idealized remnant within Israel, that acts as a leader toward the rest of the people.

The mission of the servant is not only to Israel. He is also a light to the nations. The divine plan in the restoration of Israel is not concerned only with the welfare of one people, but with the conversion of the entire world.

In chapter 49, as in chapter 42, it is problematic to isolate the so-called Servant Song from the surrounding passages. Isaiah 49:7 is addressed to "one deeply despised, abhorred by the nations," assuring him that kings and princes would be startled because of what the Lord would do. This points forward to the beginning of the fourth Servant Song in 52:13-15. The "covenant to the people" and the release of prisoners in 49:8-9 hearkens back to 42:6-7. These links suggest that at least three of the servant songs, those in chapters 42, 49, and 52–53, have the same figure in mind.

Duhm's third Servant Song, 50:4-9, stands apart from the others, and in fact does not use the word "servant" at all. The figure, who speaks in the first person, is a teacher, or prophet, who listens faithfully to the word of the Lord and endures much resistance and abuse. Again, Jeremiah would seem to be the model here (cf. Jer 15:15-21). In this case, the reference is most probably to the prophet himself.

The longest and most famous Servant Song begins at 52:13 and runs through chapter 53. The first few verses, 52:13-15, are an introduction in the name of the Lord that summarize the servant's story: he was deformed beyond recognition but will be restored and exalted to the astonishment of kings. The main body of the poem in 53:1-10 is spoken by a collective group. If the servant is thought to be an individual, this group could be the Jewish community. If the servant is Israel, the speakers are the kings, whose astonishment is noted at the end of chapter 52. Again, they comment on the abject state of the servant, but now they add an explanation: "Surely he has borne our infirmities and carried our diseases . . . he was wounded for our transgressions, crushed for our iniquities, upon him was the punishment that made us whole." Moreover, we are told that the servant was "cut off from the land of the living, stricken for the transgression of my people" (53:8). His life is made an offering for sin. The final verses, 11-12, are spoken again by YHWH, confirming that he will indeed atone for others, and that because of this, "I will allot him a portion with the great."

Since the servant is said to be done to death, he can hardly be the prophet himself. He could conceivably be a prophet, and the poem could be composed by his disciples, but this is an entirely hypothetical scenario. It is equally hypothetical to identify the servant with a royal figure (the heir to the throne?) and suppose that he had died "for the sin of my people." The explanation that requires least hypothetical speculation is that the servant is Israel, described metaphorically as an individual. In the exile, Israel was deformed beyond recognition, and might even be said to have died (cf. Ezekiel's vision of a valley full of dry bones). In this case, the people whose iniquities he bore are the other nations. On this explanation Second Isaiah breaks radically with earlier tradition by explaining the exile not as punishment for the sin of Israel, but as vicarious punishment for the sins of other peoples. One of the problems of the poem is the statement that "he shall see his offspring and prolong his days" in 53:10, even though he was earlier said to be cut off from the land of the living. This is less of a problem if the servant is Israel than if he is an individual. There is no hint of individual resurrection anywhere else in Second Isaiah. Admittedly, no interpretation of this song is without problems, and it is easy to understand why many commentators insist that the servant must be an individual. Any individual interpretation, however, requires that we imagine a history for that individual for which we have no other information.

Regardless of whether the servant is individual or collective, the interest of the passage lies primarily in the idea of vicarious suffering: the idea that the sufferings of one person or people can atone for the sin of another. One analogy that comes to mind here is that of the scapegoat in Leviticus 16, which was said to bear the sins of the people and carry them into the wilderness. A closer analogy is provided by Ezekiel, who was said to bear the sin of the people by lying on his side in a symbolic action (Ezekiel 4). As we saw in the case of Ezekiel, the efficacy of such action depends on the reaction of the people for whom it is performed. In the context of Second Isaiah, the dynamic of the action is that the onlookers are astonished by the exaltation of the servant, after he had seemed beyond hope. It is this astonishment that leads to their conversion: compare Isa 45:20-25, where the ends of the earth are expected to turn to YHWH because of the astonishing salvation of Israel. The purpose of the exile, then, was to get the attention of the nations, so that they would become aware of YHWH and be astonished by the sudden revelation of his power. Israel was like a sacrificial victim, a lamb led to the slaughter (53:7; cf. Jer 11:19). By obediently going along with the divine plan, Israel makes righteous the many people who observe what happened. No one is automatically saved by the suffering of the servant, but it creates an opportunity for people to recognize their true situation and convert accordingly.

If the servant in this passage is indeed Israel, then it is problematic that there is no admission of any sin on his part that merited punishment in the exile. Even when Second Isaiah says that Jerusalem was punished double (chap. 40), he does not suggest that it was without guilt. The picture of the servant in chapter 53, then, is idealized, and may not be identical with the entire people. The importance of this passage, in any case, is that it introduces the possibility of a positive understanding of suffering. This idea would prove extremely fruitful in later tradition. The book of Daniel draws on Isa 52:13—53:12 to explain the deaths of the martyrs in Maccabean times (Dan 11:33). The idea that suffering in this life can lead to exaltation hereafter gains currency in the Dead Sea Scrolls and other literature around the turn of the era. This idea would be crucial to the understanding of the death of Jesus in early Christianity. Isaiah 53 is read in the traditional liturgy of Good Friday.

Oracles of Reassurance

The Jewish community in Babylon did not always measure up to the prophet's idea of the righteous suffering servant. In 48:18 he complains, "O that you had paid attention to my commandments! Then your prosperity would have been like a river." In 48:9 he insists that it is only for his name's sake that YHWH defers his anger. It is apparent from 50:4-9 that the prophet encountered considerable resistance to his message, and we know from other sources that not all Judeans in Babylon were eager to return to their burned-out homeland. The repeated urging of the prophet to "depart, depart, go out from there" (52:11), is made necessary by the reluctance of the people. Most of the poems in chapters 49–55, however, are oracles of consolation. It is evident that there was a certain measure of cynicism in the community of exiles: "Zion says: 'the LORD has forsaken me'" (49:14). The prophet counters that YHWH can no more forget Jerusalem than a mother can forget her child. In 54:11-12 he promises that Jerusalem will be rebuilt with precious stones. Moreover, God will make a permanent covenant with Jerusalem like the covenant with Noah after the flood, promising that his covenant of peace with it would never be revoked.

Second Isaiah's vision of restoration has no place for a renewed monarchy. The restoration, after all, was by permission of the Persians, and they were not about to grant Judah its independence. The prophet does refer once to the promise to David in 55:3-5. The everlasting covenant will be renewed, but with the people as a whole rather than with a royal dynasty. The covenant with David, then, is not void, but it finds its fulfillment in the restoration of a Jewish community to Jerusalem. The prophet insists that no word of the Lord goes unfulfilled, although the ways of God are often mysterious to human beings.

Third Isaiah

Some of the oracles in Isaiah 56–66 are close to those of Second Isaiah in spirit and tone. These oracles are found in chapters 60–62.

Chapter 60 is a joyful prediction of the restoration of Jerusalem, familiar from Handel's *Messiah:* "Arise, shine, for thy light has come." The prophet envisions an open city: "Your gates shall always be open; day and night they shall not be shut, so that nations shall bring you their wealth, with their kings led in procession" (Isa 60:11). As we have seen in Second Isaiah, this is a universalistic vision, but a Zion-centered one. There is a place for all the nations in the restored order, but it is a subordinate place. Kings will be led in subjection in a triumphal procession. The descendants of those who had oppressed Jerusalem will be forced to bow down. Nonetheless, the contrast with the vision of the future in the last chapters of Ezekiel is striking. The Ezekiel tradition was concerned to create a holy city where Judeans would be separated from Gentiles. The Isaianic tradition also envisions a holy city, but one where Gentiles enhance the glory of Jerusalem by serving it. The poetry of this oracle is lyrical:

> The sun shall no longer be your light by
> day,
> nor for brightness shall the moon give
> light to you by night;
> but the LORD will be your everlasting
> light,
> and your God will be your glory. (Isa
> 60:19)

This is one of many passages in which the last chapters of Isaiah provide imagery that would be picked up much later in the book of Revelation. According to Rev 21:22, the New Jerusalem "has no need of sun or moon to shine on it, for the glory of God is its light."

The euphoric tone continues in Isaiah 61, where the prophet claims to be anointed and endowed with the Spirit of the Lord. Prophets are not usually said to be anointed in the Hebrew Bible. Elijah is commanded to anoint Elisha as prophet in his place (1 Kgs 19:16). The anointing is metaphorical; he performs it by throwing his mantle over Elisha. In the Dead Sea Scrolls, however, prophets are often referred to as anointed ones, and specifically "anointed of the Spirit" in reference to Isaiah 61. The mission of the prophet here is closely related to that of the servant in Second Isaiah—to bring good news to the oppressed and liberty to captives (cf. 42:7; 49:9). The "year of the LORD's favor" is an allusion to the Jubilee Year of Leviticus 25, but here it seems to have the character of a final, definitive jubilee. It is also the day of God's vengeance. In the Dead Sea Scrolls, this motif has a central place in the Melchizedek Scroll (11QMelchizedek), where it refers to a final, eschatological day of judgment. Isaiah 61:1-2 figures prominently in the New Testament as the text for Jesus' inaugural sermon in Nazareth (Luke 4:18-19).

The remainder of Isaiah 61 provides comfort for "the mourners of Zion" by promising them a glorious future, gilded by the wealth of the nations. In chapter 62, however, we get a sense that the promised glory did not materialize as fast as expected. The prophet urges those "who remind the LORD . . . to give him no rest until he establishes Jerusalem" (62:6-7). The tone of this chapter is still confident: the Lord has sworn, and so the restoration is assured. Nonetheless, the very need for insistent assurance hints at the problems that would be encountered by the people who returned to Jerusalem and the gap that would be apparent between the glorious promises and the modest fulfillment.

A Divided Community

Many of the other oracles in this section of the book of Isaiah have a very different tone, one of bitter recrimination that reflects disputes within the community. These oracles also presuppose a situation after the return to Judah, and are thereby distinguished from Second Isaiah. Chapter 57 complains that "the righteous perish and no one takes it to heart." The reasons for this situation are not as clear as we might wish. The prophet accuses some unidentified people of fornicating "under every green tree," practicing human sacrifice, and making illicit offerings to Molech (57:5-10). All of this sounds like the traditional polemic of the prophets against syncretistic cultic practices before the exile. It is not clear whether these accusations should be taken literally or who the people in question may be.

The question of the prophet's opponents arises again in chapters 65 and 66. In chapter 65 the opponents are accused of provoking the Lord continually, by sacrificing in gardens, spending the night in tombs, and eating swine's flesh. Moreover, they tell others, "Do not come near me, for I am too holy for you" (65:5). This latter statement brings to mind the regulations for the Zadokite priests in Ezek 44:19, who are told to remove their vestments after they serve at the altar, "so that they may not communicate holiness to the people with their vestments." This has led some scholars to suppose that the polemic in Isaiah 65 is actually directed against the Jerusalem priesthood after the exile by people who felt excluded by the demands of holiness. We need not suppose that the Zadokite priests were actually guilty of eating swine's flesh or of human sacrifice; these charges may have

been hyperbolical rhetorical abuse. Other scholars think it more likely that the oracles are directed against people who were actually reviving some of the old rituals that had been practiced before the exile, and which in fact may never have died out. These people would have been at the other end of the spectrum from the Zadokite priesthood.

There is some evidence of tension between Third Isaiah and the Jerusalem priesthood. In 66:1-2, the prophet asks, in the name of the Lord: "'Heaven is my throne and the earth is my footstool; what is the house that you would build for me, and what is my resting place? All these things my hand has made, and so all these things are mine,' says the LORD. But this is the one to whom I will look, to the humble and contrite in spirit, who trembles at my word." This passage clearly dates from the period after the exile, when the temple was being rebuilt. (We shall discuss this historical episode in connection with the book of Haggai.) The opening question echoes Solomon's prayer at the consecration of the temple in 1 Kgs 8:27: "But will God indeed dwell on the earth? Even heaven and the highest heaven cannot contain you, much less this house that I have built!" Solomon goes on to explain the value of the temple as a place where people could make their offerings. There is no such explanation in Isaiah 66. The implication of the question would seem to be that the temple is unnecessary, or at least not very important. The Isaianic prophet here stands in the tradition of the prophets who had questioned the value of sacrifices (cf. especially Mic 6:6, where the requirements of the Lord emphasize justice and humility). He was not necessarily opposed to the rebuilding of the temple; he was just not as impressed with it as some of his contemporaries. It is unlikely that he opposed the temple cult; he makes a favorable reference to it in 66:20, when he speaks of Israelites bringing a grain offering in a clean vessel. But like Micah, Amos, and the other prophets, he held that cultic offerings were no substitute for humility and justice.

The passage continues, however, with some of the most startling verses in the Hebrew Bible. The Hebrew text juxtaposes a series of participles, literally "slaughtering an ox, killing a man; sacrificing a lamb, breaking a dog's neck; presenting a grain offering, offering swine's blood." The NRSV translates: "Whoever slaughters an ox is like one who kills a human being; whoever sacrifices a lamb, like one who breaks a dog's neck; whoever presents a grain offering, like one who offers swine's blood." On this interpretation, some of the hallowed practices of the Jewish cult were morally equivalent to murder or profanity. But the Hebrew can also be construed in another way: "The one who slaughters an ox also kills a man; the one who sacrifices a lamb also breaks a dog's neck; the one who presents a grain offering also offers swine's blood." On this interpretation, the problem is not that the cult itself is perverse, but that there is a gulf between the apparent piety of the worshipers and their conduct on other occasions. This would be more in line with the critique of sacrifice in the preexilic prophets. Once again, there is no consensus as to the identity of the people who are being condemned. On the one hand, some scholars assume that these must be the same people who championed the rebuilding of the temple and were enthusiastic for the sacrificial cult. It is difficult to believe that priests would actually have engaged in rituals that involved drinking swine's blood, but we could allow for rhetorical exaggeration on the part of the prophet. On the other hand, it is possible that some (unidentified) people were actually guilty of murder and of heterodox practices.

One other passage in Isaiah 56–66 is relevant to the issue of inner-community polemics. Isaiah 56:1-7 reassures eunuchs and foreigners who had joined themselves to the Lord that they are welcome on the holy mountain to minister to the Lord, and that their burnt offerings will be accepted. (This passage shows, incidentally, that Third Isaiah did not reject the temple cult in principle.) This hospitable attitude is in conflict with Deut 23:1-8, which excludes from the assembly of the Lord anyone "whose testicles are crushed or whose penis is cut off." The same passage excludes Ammonites and Moabites (but not Edomites or Egyptians). Ezekiel 44:9 also decrees that "no foreigner, uncircumcised in heart and flesh, of all the foreigners who are among the people of Israel, shall enter my sanctuary." This statement is not technically contradictory to Isa 56:1-7. Both texts can be read as requiring that foreigners "join themselves to the Lord." But the tone of the two passages is very different, one emphasizing access and the other exclusion. Access to the temple was evidently a matter of contention in the early postexilic community. The people whose views are reflected in Isaiah 56–66 favored relatively open access and were at odds with those who demanded restrictions. (It is apparent from Ezekiel 44 that the latter party included the Zadokite priests.) It does not necessarily follow that the opponents of Third Isaiah should be identified with the Zadokite priests in all cases. The prophet may have been fighting on more than one front. It is quite apparent, however, that there were bitter divisions within the postexilic community.

The Hope for the Future

The party with which the prophet identifies is described variously as "those who tremble at the word of the LORD" (66:2, 5) and "my servants." The Hebrew word for "tremblers," *haredim*, is the same word that is used in modern Israel for the ultraorthodox, but of course there is no necessary affinity between ancient and modern "tremblers." We shall find a group of people "trembling" again in the story of Ezra (Ezra 10:9). The servants are presumably the heirs of "the servant" of Second Isaiah. These people evidently did not enjoy much power in the early postexilic community, but they entertained hopes of a dramatic reversal of fortune. Isaiah 65:13 tells the opponents:

> "Therefore thus says the Lord GOD:
> My servants shall eat, but you shall be
> hungry;
> my servants shall drink, but you shall be
> thirsty;
> my servants shall rejoice, but you shall be
> put to shame."

The logic of the passage is similar to the Sermon on the Mount in the New Testament (Matthew 5–7): those who hunger and mourn in the present will have plenty and joy in the future.

The expectation of a radical reversal of fortunes is one of the key elements in apocalyptic literature, as we shall see later in connection with the book of Daniel. These chapters of the book of Isaiah anticipate some motifs that are characteristic of that literature. The prophet appeals to God to "tear open the heavens and come down, so that the mountains would quake at your presence" (Isa 64:1). There is no hope of salvation by human means, so the hope is for direct divine intervention, in the style of the theophanies of old. (There is another appeal to God as divine warrior in 59:16-17.) Most striking of all is the prophecy of a new heaven and a new earth in 65:17-25. Here the prophet looks forward to a new creation, in which life will be different. No longer shall there be "an infant who lives only a few days or an old person who does not live out a lifetime, for one who dies at a hundred years will be considered a youth, and one who falls short of a hundred will be considered accursed." Life will be longer and better, but not essentially different in kind. It is important to note that Third Isaiah does not envision resurrection of the dead or eternal life, as the later apocalyptic writings do. (In this respect, the new heavens and new earth have a quite different connotation in the New Testament Apocalypse, Rev 21:1.) His vision of the future remains close to what we found in the mythological utopia of Isaiah 11, where "the wolf and the lamb shall feed together, the lion shall eat straw like the ox" (65:23).

This section of the book of Isaiah ends on a jarring note. We are told that people will look at the dead bodies of the people who have rebelled against God, "for their worm shall not die, their fire shall not be quenched, and they shall be an abhorrence to all flesh" (66:24). This is not the idea of hell as it would emerge some centuries later. There is no suggestion that the wicked are alive to experience unending torment. Rather, the righteous and their descendants will derive satisfaction from the spectacle of the destruction of the bodies of the wicked. This is certainly a step on the road to hell, so to speak, and it appeals to the more vindictive side of human nature. This note is not characteristic of Third Isaiah, however. What we find in Isaiah 56–66 is the range of emotion experienced by the followers of Second Isaiah in the years after the return from Babylon, ranging from euphoric and idealistic hope to bitter recrimination and appeals for God to intervene. The idea of a new creation would be developed later and would become an important motif in apocalyptic literature in the period 200 B.C.E. to 100 C.E.

The So-Called Isaiah Apocalypse (Isaiah 24–27)

Cosmic Destruction

Apocalyptic imagery, imagery of cosmic destruction and renewal associated with apocalyptic writings such as the book of Revelation, figures even more prominently in Isaiah 24–27. For that reason, these chapters have often been singled out from the rest of the book and dubbed "the Isaiah Apocalypse." The designation is misleading. These chapters do not have the literary form of an apocalypse (which we shall see when we discuss the book of Daniel) and indeed are not necessarily a literary unit at all. They are not marked off as a separate section in the text. They do, however, contain a remarkable concentration of images of cosmic destruction. They differ from the preceding chapters of Isaiah, which contain oracles against various nations, insofar as they do not clearly refer to specific places, except for a reference to Moab (25:10), a couple of references to Jerusalem (24:23; 26:1), and an epilogue alluding to the restoration of the lost tribes (27:12-13).

This lack of explicit and specific references is typical of some of the later passages in the prophetic books. We find an extreme example of the phenomenon in Zechariah 9–14. It is possible that these oracles originally referred to highly specific occasions that we can no longer identify. For example, when Isa 24:10 says that "the city of chaos is broken down," the reference may be to the destruction of Babylon by King Xerxes of Persia in 482 B.C.E., as many scholars believe. But several other occasions have also been proposed, ranging from the eighth to the second centuries, and the text itself provides no specific identification of the city. It is possible, as other scholars have argued, that the reference is not to one specific city but to a type that represents all cities opposed to God, such as the capital cities of empires that oppressed Israel. This type is then contrasted with the strong city of Judah, Jerusalem, in 26:1-2. There is a somewhat similar contrast between Babylon and Jerusalem in the book of Revelation in the New Testament, where Babylon has come to stand for any city opposed to God. It should be noted, however, that in the original historical context of the book of Revelation, Babylon referred quite specifically to Rome.

In any case, it is not now possible to relate these chapters of the book of Isaiah to any specific historical crisis with any confidence. Instead, like the ancient myths, they evoke a type of situation that can be applied to various historical crises or can be taken as a foreshadowing of the end of the world. The ancient myths, such as *Enuma Elish* or the Baal myth, were myths of beginnings, or at least of events that were supposed to have happened long ago, even if they might be repeated periodically.

These chapters of Isaiah, in contrast, but like the book of Revelation and other apocalyptic writings, provide myths of ending, or at least of cataclysmic future events. Hermann Gunkel, one of the great biblical scholars of the late nineteenth and early twentieth century, coined the phrase "Urzeit gleicht Endzeit"—"the primeval time is like the end-time"—to explain the use of ancient myths in apocalyptic writings. In Isaiah 24–27 we recognize several allusions to the old "myths of beginnings," but they are now projected into the future.

Isaiah 24 provides an exceptionally vivid picture of the destruction of the physical world. Already Jeremiah had seen "the earth, and it was waste and void" (Jer 4:23), using the same language that refers to the state of the earth at the beginning of creation in Gen 1:2. Isaiah 24:1 uses different language to similar effect. Verse 2 suggests that the cosmic upheaval is a metaphor for social disruption, when roles are overturned. The manner in which the earth dries up in vv. 4-13 recalls the sad state of the earth in the Ugaritic myths when Baal, god of fertility, is taken prisoner by Mot (Death). In Isaiah 24 the distress of the earth is attributed to pollution because its inhabitants have violated "the eternal covenant," the phrase used for God's covenant with Noah in Gen 9:16. The covenant with Noah involved all living creatures, not only Israel, which had not yet come to be. There are also other allusions here to the early chapters of Genesis. The "city of chaos" in Isa 24:10 is described with the word *tohu*, which is used for the primeval void in Genesis 1. The windows of heaven are opened in Isa 24:18, as they were for the flood in Gen 7:11. God is said to scatter the inhabitants of the earth (Isa 24:1) as he scattered the people of Babylon in the story of the tower (Gen 11:8).

But the prophet also draws on other myths, some of which are not attested elsewhere in the Bible. At the end, "on that day the LORD will punish the host of heaven in heaven, and on earth the kings of the earth. They will be gathered together like prisoners in a pit; they will be shut up in a prison, and after many days they will be punished" (Isa 24:21-22). This passage seems to presuppose a myth about the host of heaven and a place where they are punished. Later this myth is spelled out in *1 Enoch*, an apocalyptic writing from the Hellenistic period that is not part of the canon but is classified with the Jewish pseudepigrapha (books attributed to people who did not in fact compose them). (Reference to the prison for the host of heaven is found in 1 En 18:14). We do not know what form of this myth was known to the author of Isaiah 24. The allusion reminds us again that the Bible preserves only a small fragment of the literature and stories that were known in ancient Israel.

The disruption described in Isaiah 24 leads ultimately to the triumph of YHWH on Mount Zion. There is a pattern here that is reflected in some of the Psalms (e.g., Psalm 93) that celebrate the triumph of YHWH over the chaotic forces of nature. This view of the kingship of YHWH was at home in the Jerusalem cult under the Davidic monarchy. The violence of the disruption here, however, and the projection into the future, are typical rather of the increased interest in eschatology in the Second Temple period, especially in the later additions to the prophetic books.

The Defeat of Death

Mythic themes appear again in Isaiah 25. Here we are told that God will prepare a feast for all peoples "on this mountain" (Mount Zion). Mythic conflicts often end with a triumphal feast. We have seen such a banquet in Ezekiel 39, and that is echoed in Rev 19:17-21. The banquets in Ezekiel and Revelation have a gruesome character, as the flesh of the enemy is devoured. The feast in Isaiah 25 has a more joyful (if high-cholesterol) character (rich food, aged wines). The most powerful image in this passage, however, is the statement that God will destroy "the shroud that is cast over all peoples, the sheet that is spread over all nations; he will swallow up death forever" (25:7-8). In the Ugaritic myths, Death (Mot) swallowed up Baal, with one lip to earth and one lip to heaven. The mythological figure of Mot symbolizes here everything that is wrong and distressful with human life. It is not apparent from this passage that resurrection or eternal life is envisioned. It may be that the prophet dreamed of a time when death would be no more, but this may be a metaphor for more general relief from the problems of life. Perhaps more than any other passage in the prophetic corpus, this one conveys the sense that the problems confronting Judah, or humanity, are not just local conflicts that are peculiar to a specific time and place, but are inherent in the fabric of creation. It is somewhat ironic then that this moving poetic oracle should be followed by a prediction that the Moabites shall be trodden down like straw in a dung pit. Death may be the ultimate human problem, but the next-door neighbor is usually a more pressing cause of aggravation.

The question of death is raised again in chapter 26. The prophet makes a contrast between other peoples and the people of YHWH:

> O Lord our God, other lords besides
>   you have ruled over us
> but we acknowledge your name alone.
> They are dead; they do not live; shades,
>   they do not rise,
> because you have punished and destroyed
>   them,
> and wiped out all memory of them.
> But you have increased the nation, O
>   Lord,
> you have increased the nation; you are
>   glorified;
> you have enlarged the boundaries of the
>   land. (26:13-15)

Then, after a few verses comparing the people to a woman in labor who produces only wind, the prophet continues:

> Your dead shall live, their corpses shall
>   rise.
> O dwellers in the dust, awake and sing
>   for joy!
> For your dew is a radiant dew,
> and the earth will give birth to those long
>   dead. (26:19)

Many scholars regard this passage as the first attestation of the hope for individual resurrection in the Hebrew Bible. In the context, however, it seems more likely that the resurrection language is metaphorical, as it was in Ezekiel 37, and that the reference is to the restoration of the people. The passage is concerned with the Jewish people rather than with individuals. The following verses tell the people to lie low until the wrath of God against the earth passes. Then they will rise again. That the prophet speaks of the resurrection of the dead, even metaphorically, is significant, however. Like Ezekiel 37, this passage affirms that God can raise the dead. Death is not necessarily final. There is certainly no expectation here that the resurrection of the dead, in any sense, is guaranteed. People live or die at the pleasure of the Lord. But the use of resurrection language would contribute in time to a growing belief that God would exercise his power over death on behalf of his servants. We must wait until the book of Daniel, however, to find an unambiguous affirmation of the hope that individual righteous people would not languish forever in the netherworld (Sheol) but would be raised to eternal life.

Leviathan

There is yet another allusion to ancient myth in Isa 27:1: "On that day, the LORD with his cruel, great, and strong sword will punish Leviathan the fleeing serpent, Leviathan the twisting serpent, and he will kill the dragon that is in the sea." There are several allusions in the Hebrew Bible to a battle between God and a monster in the context of creation. For example, Job 26:12 says, "By his power he stilled the Sea; by his understanding he struck down Rahab." Isaiah 51:9 asks, "Was it not you who cut Rahab in pieces, who pierced the dragon?" In Ps 74:13-14 the monster is called Leviathan: "You divided the sea by your might; you broke the heads of the dragons on the waters. You crushed the heads of Leviathan; you gave him as food for the creatures of the wilderness" (Leviathan is also mentioned as a primeval monster in Job 3:8; 41:4). The story of this battle is never told in the Bible,

but it is illuminated by the Canaanite myths from Ugarit, where the god Baal does battle with Yamm, the Sea. Associated with the Sea are monsters called Lotan, the dragon, and the crooked serpent. It is not clear whether these are distinct embodiments of chaos or different names for the same mythic figure. It is apparent that a variant of this story was told in ancient Israel, in which YHWH, not Baal, was the victorious deity. In the Canaanite myths, this battle is located in the beginnings of history. In Isa 27:1 it is projected into the future, to express the hope that "on that day" the Lord will eradicate the source of all the problems in the world. This use of ancient myth to describe a future crisis is one of the characteristic features of apocalyptic literature. We shall meet it again in Daniel 7, and it figures prominently in the book of Revelation, especially in chapters 12 and 13.

The Future of Israel

Isaiah 27 consists of a series of prophecies introduced by the phrase "on that day." The oracles in 27:2-12 are not necessarily of a piece with chapters 24–26. The first of these oracles picks up the motif of the vineyard from Isaiah 5, but now the condemnation is conditional. The vineyard will be destroyed if it grows brambles, but it has the option of making peace.

The reference to the "fortified city" in v. 10 was surely intended as a reference to a specific place. It is often identified as Samaria, in view of the references to "Jacob" elsewhere in the chapter. There is no consensus, however, as to the occasion of the prophecy: it has been related variously to the destruction of Samaria by the Assyrians or to that by Alexander the

Great four centuries later. Some scholars have even related it to the destruction of Samaria by the Jewish king John Hyrcanus in 108 B.C.E., although the latter date is certainly too late. As with many passages in the prophetic books, the original reference can no longer be identified with any confidence. What we have is a theological assessment of the history of northern Israel. The "guilt of Jacob" is due to the proliferation of altars and sacred poles. It is removed by adherence to the theology of Deuteronomy and the reforms of King Josiah. The future of Israel lies in worship at the Jerusalem temple. Even the lost tribes will be rallied to the holy mountain "on that day."

The Final Edition of Isaiah

Isaiah 24–27 may well be the latest part of the book of Isaiah. At least in one respect it is typical of the book as a whole: a central theme is the reign of YHWH on Mount Zion. The images of cosmic conflict and final victory might have made a fitting culmination to the book, but they were not placed at the end by the editors. Instead, they were associated with the oracles against foreign nations that dominate chapters 13–23.

The book of Isaiah was compiled over the space of several hundred years. Because of the oldest manuscript of the book in the Dead Sea Scrolls, we know it was completed by the mid-third century B.C.E. There are certainly continuities that run through the book, such as the centrality of Zion and the holy mountain, the references to YHWH as the Holy One of Israel, and the imagery of light. It is unlikely that these continuities are due to any "school of Isaiah" or other group that endured

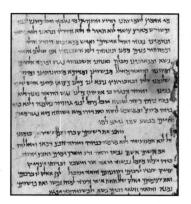

Fig. 19.2   Isaiah 53, from the Isaiah scroll from Qumran (1QIsa); now in the Israel Museum. Commons.wikimedia.org

over this lengthy span of time. It is more likely that the later authors were aware of the older Isaianic oracles and had some hand in shaping even the early chapters of the book. As it stands, the historical prophet is relativized. Even his call is moved away from the beginning of the book. Instead, the oracles of judgment with which the book begins stand as a timeless warning, not only to Jerusalem, but to all who regard themselves as the people of YHWH. Equally, the promises of hope and restoration go beyond the historical context of the return from the Babylonian exile and stand as paradigms of hope for all generations. There is clearly a movement from judgment to restoration in the book as a whole, but it remains a collection of oracles. The placement of individual prophecies is often associative (as when chaps. 24–27 are associated with the oracles against the nations). It is not tightly ordered in the manner that we might expect from a modern composition. Nonetheless, the editors succeeded in fashioning a book that would speak to many generations long after the time of Isaiah or even of the Babylonian exile.

FOR FURTHER READING

Commentaries

K. Baltzer, *Deutero-Isaiah: A Commentary on Isaiah 40–55* (trans. M. Kohl; Hermeneia; Minneapolis: Fortress Press, 2001). Extensive commentary but very speculative.

J. Blenkinsopp, *Isaiah 40–55* (AB 19A; New York: Doubleday, 2002). Excellent historical-critical commentary.

B. S. Childs, *Isaiah* (OTL; Louisville: Westminster John Knox, 2001). Attempt to read Isaiah 40–66 in the context of the book as a whole.

J. Goldingay, *The Message of Isaiah 40–55: A Literary-Theological Commentary* (London: T&T Clark, 2005). Supplements the more technical Goldingay and Payne commentary.

J. Goldingay and D. Payne, *Isaiah 40–55: A Critical and Exegetical Commentary* (ICC; 2 vols.; London: T&T Clark, 2006). Detailed textual, philological, and exegetical commentary.

P. D. Hanson, *Isaiah 40–66* (Interpretation; Louisville: Westminster John Knox, 1995). Focus on the prophet in his historical and sociological context, with homiletical insights.

S. Paul, *Isaiah 40–66. A Commentary* (Grand Rapids: Eerdmans, 2012). Attributes all 40–66 to Second Isaiah. Chapters 40–48 written in Babylon.

C. R. Seitz, "The Book of Isaiah 40–66," *NIB* 6:309–552. Theological commentary from a canonical perspective.

C. Westermann, *Isaiah 40–66* (trans. M. Kohl; OTL; Philadelphia: Westminster, 1969). Classic form-critical analysis.

Other Studies

H. Clifford, "Deutero-Isaiah and Monotheism," in J. Day, ed., *Prophecy and the Prophets in Ancient Israel* (London: T&T Clark, 2010), 267–89. Idol polemic and claims for exclusivity constitute a basis for monotheism.

R. J. Clifford, *Fair Spoken and Persuading: An Interpretation of Second Isaiah* (New York: Paulist, 1984). Elegant, concise analysis of the literary structure of Isaiah 40–45.

———, "Isaiah, Book of (Second Isaiah)," *ABD* 3:490–501. Summary of the critical issues.

P. D. Hanson, *The Dawn of Apocalyptic* (Philadelphia: Fortress Press, 1975), 32–208. Groundbreaking sociological analysis of Third Isaiah with detailed textual analysis.

W. R. Millar, "Isaiah, Book of (Chaps. 24–27)," *ABD* 3:488–90. Summary of critical issues in the so-called Apocalypse of Isaiah.

D. C. Polaski, *Authorizing an End: The Isaiah Apocalypse and Intertextuality* (Bib Int 50; Leiden: Brill, 2001). Use of allusions in Isaiah 24–27.

B. Schramm, *Opponents of Third Isaiah. Reconstructing the Cultic History of the Restoration* (Sheffield: Sheffield Academic Press, 1995. Sustained critique of Hanson, *The Dawn of Apocalyptic*. Denies opposition between Third Isaiah and the Zadokite priesthood.

C. R. Seitz, "How Is the Prophet Isaiah Present in the Latter Half of the Book? The Logic of Chapters 40–66 within the Book of Isaiah," *JBL* 115 (1996): 219–40. Attempt to relate chapters 40–66 to the earlier part of the book.

B. D. Sommer, *A Prophet Reads Scripture: Allusion in Isaiah 40–66* (Stanford: Stanford University Press, 1998). Careful analysis of allusions to earlier prophecy in these chapters.

J. Stromberg, *Isaiah after Exile: The Author of Third Isaiah as Reader and Redactor of the Book* (Oxford: Oxford University Press, 2011). Study in the redaction of Isaiah.

Lena Sofia Tiemeyer, *For the Comfort of Zion: The Geographical and Theological Location of Isaiah 40–55* (Leiden: Brill, 2010). Sees Second Isaiah as a product of Judahite rather than exilic community.

CHAPTER 20

Postexilic Prophecy
Haggai, Zechariah, Malachi, Joel

INTRODUCTION

In this chapter, we will look at some of the minor prophets from the period after the exile: Haggai, Zechariah, Malachi, and Joel.

The prophets Haggai and Zechariah are mentioned in the book of Ezra (5:1–2) in connection with the rebuilding of the Jerusalem temple: "Now the prophets, Haggai and Zechariah son of Iddo, prophesied to the Jews who were in Judah and Jerusalem, in the name of the God of Israel who was over them. Then Zerubbabel son of Shealtiel and Jeshua son of Jozadak set out to rebuild the house of God in Jerusalem, and with them were the prophets of God, helping them." In the following chapter we are told that "the elders of the Jews built and prospered, through the prophesying of the prophet Haggai and Zechariah son of Iddo. They finished their building by command of the God of Israel and by the decree of Cyrus, Darius, and King Artaxerxes of Persia, and this house was finished on the third day of the month of Adar, in the sixth year of King Darius" (Ezra 6:14-15). As we shall see when we discuss the book of Ezra, the account of

the restoration bristles with problems. If the temple was finished in the sixth year of Darius (516 B.C.E.), then Artaxerxes cannot have had anything to do with it (Artaxerxes I reigned 465–423 B.C.E.). For the present, however, we can accept the report that Haggai and Zechariah were active in the reign of Darius (522–486) and supported the rebuilding of the temple. The oracles of Haggai and those of Zechariah 1–8 fit well in this context.

It is apparent both from the account in Ezra and from the book of Haggai that a considerable time (approximately twenty years) elapsed between the first return, in the reign of Cyrus, and the eventual rebuilding. The exiles returned to an impoverished land, and building a temple was not the highest priority for many of them. The problems are reflected in Haggai 1, which is dated by its editors to the second year of Darius (520). At this point, the governor of Judah was Zerubbabel, son

Fig. 20.1 Darius I receives a foreign delegation; bas-relief from the walls of the treasury in Persepolis. Photo by Marcus Cyron; commons.wikimedia.org

of Shealtiel, who was a descendant of David according to 1 Chron 3:19. (According to Ezra 1:8, 11, the original leader of the returning exiles was Sheshbazzar, the prince of Judah, who was probably also a Davidic descendant; he may be identical with Shenazzar, who is listed in 1 Chron 3:18.) But the governor was not sole ruler; he shared authority with the high priest Joshua, son of Jehozadak. The new prominence of the high priest as a political leader is one of the key differences between postexilic Judah and the preexilic monarchy.

Haggai

Haggai 1 reports a dispute between the prophet and people who argued that "the time has not yet come to rebuild the LORD's house." It is quite possible that these people argued in good faith. The prophet Jeremiah had prophesied that Jerusalem would be desolate for seventy years (Jer 25:11; 29:10). The actual completion of the temple in 516 B.C.E. came almost exactly seventy years after the destruction. Some people may have believed that any earlier restoration would have been premature. Haggai, however, suggests a more mundane

reasoning: "Is it a time for you yourselves to live in your paneled houses, while this house lies in ruins?" The implication that the returnees were living in luxury is almost certainly unwarranted. The prophet himself emphasizes their lack of prosperity. But the charge that they put their own needs first focuses attention on an interesting problem in the sociology of religion. In a community where resources are scarce, should people attend first to basic human needs, such as housing, or should they devote their resources first to providing for worship and a temple? The importance of a temple, even from a purely sociological point of view, should not be underestimated. By devoting their resources to the temple, the people put the community as a whole ahead of individual needs and created an important symbol of their own identity, as well as of their religious commitments. The importance of such symbols can be seen in modern US history: immigrant communities repeatedly built impressive churches even though the individuals who contributed to the projects had very limited means.

Haggai is unequivocal in his demand that the temple be given the highest priority. His reasoning is not sociological, but is grounded in ancient mythological ideas about the relationship between cult and fertility. In the period since the return from Babylon, the people had planted much but harvested little and never had enough. The prophet's diagnosis is simple: it is because the house of the Lord is in ruins. Therefore the heavens have withheld their rain and the earth its produce. This kind of reasoning is completely at odds with modern pragmatism and strikes the modern reader as superstitious. More remarkably, it is also at odds with the prophetic tradition reflected in the Hebrew Bible. Prophets like Amos and Micah were extremely skeptical of the value of sacrifice and cultic worship, and accused the cultic establishments of their day of distorting the demands of the Lord. Jeremiah had derided those who set their hopes on "the temple of the LORD, the temple of the LORD." That tradition was continued in Haggai's own time by the prophet of Isaiah 66, who declared that heaven is God's throne and earth his footstool, and asked, "What is this house that you would build for me?" Evidently, not everyone in Judah shared Haggai's confidence in the efficacy of temple worship.

At the urging of the prophets, the rebuilding of the temple was begun. Haggai 2 describes the rather anticlimactic reaction to the foundations: "Who is left among you that saw this house in its former glory? How does it look to you now? Is it not in your sight as nothing?" Ezra 3:12-13 reports that many old people who remembered the first temple wept when they saw the foundations of the new one, so that one could not distinguish between the joyful shout of the younger people and the weeping of their elders. Haggai was unabashed. It was only a matter of time until the glory of the Lord would be revealed:

"Once again, in a little while, I will shake the heavens and the earth and the sea and the dry land, and I will shake all the nations, so that the treasure of all the nations shall come, and I will fill this house with splendor, says the LORD of hosts" (2:7). The splendor of the new temple would be greater than that of its predecessor. It should be noted that this prophecy is dated less than two months after the opening oracle in chapter 1.

Haggai's prophecy was not fulfilled. The second chapter of his book attempts to deal with this problem. The prophet briefly suggests that the offerings of the people are unclean, but his basic response is to reaffirm his prediction; it has not happened yet, but it will certainly happen soon, "from this day on." The failure of prophecy is often associated with apocalyptic and millenarian predictions of a later era. We shall find an example in the book of Daniel. But prophets had always made predictions that did not succeed. What is remarkable here is that such a prophecy should still be accepted as inspired and canonical by later generations. The reason, perhaps, was that Haggai had succeeded in his mission to have the temple rebuilt. In so doing, he contributed enormously to the stability of the Judean community in the Second Temple period. His contribution was not negated by the fact that the splendor he prophesied was hyperbolic and far in excess of anything experienced by the community in the Persian period. If the various dates supplied by the editors are correct, his entire career lasted only a few months, in the second year of Darius, or 520 B.C.E.

The final oracle in the book of Haggai is especially intriguing. Here again the prophet insists that the Lord is about to overthrow the kingdoms of the earth, but in this case, he goes further: "On that day, says the LORD of hosts, I will take you, O Zerubbabel, my servant, son of Shealtiel, says the LORD, and make you like a signet ring, for I have chosen you, says the LORD of hosts." The signet ring was the means by which a seal was imprinted. The royal seal, in particular, was the means by which deeds were stamped with the authority of the king. To say that Zerubbabel was "like a signet ring" was to say that he was the medium by which God's authority was exercised. The designation "my servant" has a similar force. (Jeremiah said that Nebuchadnezzar was the servant of the Lord; Second Isaiah cast Cyrus of Persia in this role.) Jeremiah 22:23-25 says that even if Coniah (Jehoiachin), king of Judah, were YHWH's signet ring, he would be torn off and cast away. The intriguing question here is whether Haggai meant that Zerubbabel would be restored to the kingship, and so that he was, in effect, the messiah, the one who would restore the kingdom of David.

The oracles of Haggai are dated to 520 B.C.E., the second year of Darius. Darius did not come to the throne by peaceful succession. A man named Gaumata had usurped the throne in 522. Darius, who was a member of the ruling Achaemenid family, led a conspiracy to overthrow the usurper. He then had to put down revolts in Media and Babylon and, eventually (519), in Egypt. Many scholars have suspected that the outpouring of spirit in Judah in the second year of Darius was a byproduct of these revolts and reflected hopes of independence under a restored monarchy. These hopes, of course, were quite unrealistic. The Persians were not about to allow Judah to become an independent state on the border of Egypt. Some scholars doubt that Zerubbabel and Joshua, whose power derived directly from the Persians, would have endorsed such hopes, but it does not follow that the prophets

Fig. 20.2   Persian warriors; painted relief from the palace of Darius I at Susa; at the Pergamon Museum, Berlin.
Commons.wikimedia.org

could not have entertained them. We have no record of the thoughts of the governor or the high priest. Haggai 2:23 is most easily explained on the assumption that the prophet was hoping for a restoration of the Davidic monarchy under Zerubbabel, whether the governor shared that hope or not.

The hope for Davidic restoration, however, did not necessarily imply rebellion against Persia. Up to this point, the Persians had been the benefactors of the Jews, allowing them to return to their homeland and permitting them to rebuild their temple. They had allowed a descendant of David to function as governor. It may be that the prophet hoped that they would also allow a renewal of the kingship. If so, this hope was unfounded, but it was nonetheless real for that. We shall reflect further on this issue in connection with the prophecies of Zechariah.

Zechariah 1–8

Zechariah is closely associated with Haggai. The opening verse dates the beginning of his career to "the eighth month, in the second year of Darius." (It should be noted that this verse confuses Zechariah son of Iddo, as the prophet is called elsewhere, with Zechariah son of Jeberechiah, who is mentioned in Isa 8:2. So also Zech 1:7.) The first vision account is dated to the eleventh month of the same year, two months after the last dated oracle of Haggai. All these dates were added by editors, and their accuracy may be questioned. (The concern for precise dates is reminiscent of Ezekiel and of the priestly tradition in general.) There is no doubt, however, that Zechariah was active about the same time as Haggai,

while Zerubbabel was governor and Joshua was high priest.

The prophecies that may be attributed to Zechariah are in chapters 1–6, more precisely in 1:7—6:15. Within this block of material are eight visions and one oracle. These prophecies are framed by sermonic material in 1:1-6 and chapters 7 and 8 that resembles the Deuteronomistic writings in language and theme. Chapters 1–8 are often referred to as First Zechariah, and they seem to constitute a coherent book, of which the visions of Zechariah form the core. Zechariah 9–14 is exceptionally obscure material, and we shall return to it below.

The introductory passage in 1:1-6 strikes a typically Deuteronomic theme by asserting that "the LORD was angry with your ancestors," and that the Lord would return to Judah if the people returned to him. Moreover, the Lord had given warning through "my servants the prophets," but the people had failed to heed it. This introduction serves a dual purpose of justifying God's punishment of Judah and of warning the reader to pay serious attention to the words of the prophet that follow in this book.

The Earth at Peace

The revelations of Zechariah typically take the form of visions seen in the night. These are not called dreams, perhaps because dreams were often disparaged in the traditions that were influenced by Deuteronomy. (Compare Deuteronomy 13 and Jer 23:28: "Let the prophet who has a dream tell the dream, but let the one who has my word speak my word faithfully.") These visions are innovative in another respect: they are interpreted for the prophet by an angel (who is often called "the inter-preting angel" or *angelus interpres* in modern scholarship). There is some precedent for this kind of vision in the book of Amos, where the Lord asks Amos what he sees and then explains it to him (e.g., Amos 8:1-2, where a basket of summer fruit symbolizes the "end" that is coming on Israel). Zechariah's visions are more elaborate than those of Amos but less elaborate than what we will find in the later apocalyptic visions of the book of Daniel. It may be significant that symbolic visions of this kind are also known in Persian tradition. (In the Bahman Yasht, Zoroaster sees a tree with metal branches, which is explained to him by the god Ahura Mazda.) It is possible that Zechariah's visions reflect Persian influ-ence, but the point cannot be proven. In any case, the introduction of the interpreting angel is a significant innovation in the Hebrew pro-phetic tradition. With respect to their literary form, the visions of Zechariah may be said to mark a transitional stage between the visions of the older prophets and the later apocalyptic writers.

In his first vision, Zechariah sees a man riding on a red horse, with red, sorrel, and white horses. The angel informs him that these are they whom the Lord has sent to patrol the earth. They report that the earth is at peace. The imagery of this vision is inspired by the elaborate system of surveillance in the Persian Empire. (The intelligence agents were called "the eyes of the king." Compare "the eyes of the Lord" in Zech 4:10.) The trademarks of this system were speed and secrecy. In this vision, the element of secrecy is conveyed by the shadows of the myrtle trees and the fact that the vision is at night. In 520, Darius had suppressed most of the revolts in his realm.

Egypt was not yet subdued, but in Mesopota-mia the earth was again at peace. The prophet imagines the rule of YHWH over the universe by analogy with the Persian Empire, and may well have believed that the rule of YHWH was implemented through the Persian system. The point of the vision is that the enemies of YHWH, most notably Babylon, are subdued. Consequently, the time is right to broach the question of the plight of Jerusalem, "with which you have been angry these seventy years." The time of desolation predicted by Jeremiah is nearing completion. And indeed, the Lord replies "with gracious and comfort-ing words." He had been angry with Judah for a little while, but the nations had made the disaster worse, and so he is extremely angry with them. The tide has turned in Judah's favor. The point is reinforced by the brief sec-ond vision (1:18-21), where the prophet sees blacksmiths prepared to strike down the horns of the nations. It is not apparent, however, that Zechariah includes Persia among the nations whose horns are to be broken. Rather, the Per-sian Empire seems to be the means by which the horns of Israel's traditional enemies are broken.

A City without Walls

In the third vision, the prophet sees "a man with a measuring line in his hand" (2:1). The image brings to mind the angel with a mea-suring rod in Ezekiel 40. The New Jerusalem of Ezekiel's vision, however, was a walled city where different zones were carefully marked off from one another. In contrast, Zecha-riah proclaims that Jerusalem will be inhab-ited like a village without walls, because God himself will be a wall of fire all around it. The implications of this vision are twofold. On the one hand, Jerusalem and the other cities of Judah were without walls in this period. More than half a century later, Nehemiah would build a wall around Jerusalem, with much difficulty. A city without walls was vulnerable and had little status. The prophet, however, finds positive significance in the image. Jerusalem would be without walls so that it could expand more easily. On the other hand, there was a quite different analogy for the city without walls. Pasargadae, the royal city of the Achaemenid, Persian, kings, was without walls but had in and around it a number of fire altars that symbolized the presence of the god Ahura Mazda. This is most probably the source of Zechariah's image of the protective wall of fire. The prophet, then, takes a situation that would have indicated weakness to most people and makes it into a symbol of divine protection and strength.

The oracle that follows this vision in chapter 2 is reminiscent of Second Isaiah. The prophet urges Jews who are still in Babylon to flee. Babylon will become plunder for its own slaves. The background of this oracle is the suppression of revolts in Babylonia and the destruction of Babylon by Darius. Babylon's difficulty was Judah's opportunity. At no point in the oracles of Zechariah (or in those of Second Isaiah) is Persia perceived as the enemy. Rather, Persia makes possible the restoration of Judah by subjugating Babylon. The prophet may have been naïve about the reality of Persian domination. From his point of view, Persia was the instrument of YHWH in bringing about the restoration of Judah. The Lord of history had roused himself, and everything was happening in accordance with his plan. The Persians, needless to say, had their own agenda, in which Judah was important mainly because of its location near the Egyptian frontier.

The High Priest and the Branch

The fourth vision, in Zech 3:1-10, addresses an issue that was internal to the Jewish community. The prophet sees the high priest Joshua standing before the angel of the Lord

Fig. 20.3 **Babylonians bring tribute to the Persian court; detail from an extensive bas-relief on the Apadana staircase showing tribute from many nations flowing to Darius; Persepolis.** Photo by Marcus Cyron. Commons.wikimedia.org

and "the Satan" standing at his right hand to accuse him. This is one of three cases in the Hebrew Bible where a figure called "Satan" appears. The others are in the prologue of Job and 1 Chron 21:1, where Satan, without the definite article, incites David to take a census of the Israelites. (To these cases may be added Num 22:22, where the angel of the Lord stands before Balaam "as an adversary [*satan*] to him." The word is used in the general sense of adversary in Ps 109:6.) In none of these cases can Satan be equated with the devil of later mythology. In Job, Satan attends a gathering of "the sons of God" and appears to be a member of the heavenly council. Both in Job and in Zechariah he is the heavenly accuser or adversary, a divinely appointed prosecutor, whose function is to bring to light the wrongdoings of human beings. The noun "Satan" has no cognates in ancient Semitic texts, but there are legal terms in Akkadian (such as *bel dababi*) that may indicate either a human or a divine legal opponent. The office of accuser, or prosecutor, first appears in Mesopotamia in the Neo-Babylonian period, and it was taken over by the Persians. It is related to the function of "the eyes of the king," whereby informers gave reports to those in power, and people might be accused on the basis of this information. In Zechariah 3, the scene implies that some people have brought an accusation against the high priest. The scene is not an earthly court but a heavenly one. The earthly reality may be no more than gossip. By setting the accusation in a heavenly tribunal, Zechariah in effect appeals the case to the supreme court. We are not told precisely what the accusation is. It evidently entails some form of unworthiness, symbolized by the filthy garments that have to be removed. There is no argument that

Joshua is not actually guilty; the Lord rebukes the Satan for bringing any accusation against him, because he is "a brand plucked from the fire." In view of the precarious situation of the Jewish community after the exile, the high priest must be affirmed and supported, not criticized. So the Lord invests Joshua with clean garments, thereby forestalling any further accusations.

The investiture is followed by an oracle that makes a twofold promise to Joshua. First, if he observes the Lord's requirements, he will be confirmed in the high priesthood, and given access "among those who are standing here," that is, the divine council. The requirements are not spelled out. We should expect that they would include both cultic and moral provisions. Access to the heavenly council is a privilege granted to prophets in the Hebrew Bible (e.g., Jer 23:18). Here it is extended to the high priest, who becomes the dominant religious functionary in Second Temple Judaism. The access is temporary, as it was in the case of the prophets. The apocalyptic literature of the Hellenistic period (Daniel, *1 Enoch*, Dead Sea Scrolls) will extend this privilege to the righteous after death, in the form of eternal life, but this is not yet the case in Zechariah.

The second promise is that God is about to bring "my servant the Branch." The word "branch" (Hebrew *tsemach*) occurs in Jer 23:5 and 33:15, where it refers explicitly to the Davidic line: "The days are surely coming, says the Lord, when I will raise up for David a righteous Branch, and he shall reign as king and deal wisely, and shall exercise justice and righteousness in the land" (Jer 23:5). The term is also found with reference to the legitimate heir to the throne in a Phoenician inscription from the third century B.C.E. A different term, but essentially the same image, is used in Isaiah 11, which refers to a shoot from the stump of Jesse. There is no doubt then that Zechariah is predicting a restoration of the Davidic line. Many scholars think that the choice of image, a branch, is a play on the name Zerubbabel, which means "seed of Babylon." In the context of Zechariah, the branch who is expected can only be Zerubbabel. The objection that the Persians would not allow Zerubbabel to become king is beside the point. The prophet is not giving a realistic assessment of Persian policy, but expecting a miraculous divine intervention. The colleagues of Joshua mentioned in v. 8 are taken as a sign of the coming of the messianic king. Unfortunately, it is not at all clear just who these people are or why they function as a sign.

It may be that the oracle about the branch is a secondary insertion in this chapter. It seems to interrupt an oracle about Joshua, which resumes in v. 9 with a reference to the high priest's breastplate (the stone that is set before him). If the oracle is an insertion, it must have been a very early one. As we shall see, the messianic hopes centered on Zerubbabel were short-lived. If this passage is an insertion, however, it may indicate that there was an upsurge of interest in the renewal of the monarchy. There is a related insertion in the following chapter, again heightening the focus on Zerubbabel.

Two Sons of Oil

In his fifth vision (4:1-7; 10b-14), Zechariah sees a lampstand or menorah of pure gold with seven lamps flanked by two olive trees. The angel asks if he knows what they are (that is, what they represent), and he replies

that he does not. The angel's explanation follows in v. 10b. In between, there is another oracle about Zerubbabel, which is an obvious insertion.

The original vision focuses on the menorah, which is well-known as part of the furniture of the temple (cf. 1 Kgs 7:49). The lampstand of the tabernacle in Exod 25:31-40 has seven lights. The one in Zechariah's vision has seven lamps with seven lips on each, so forty-nine lights in all. The lights are said to symbolize the eyes of the Lord that range through the whole earth—the heavenly counterpart to the eyes of the king in the Persian imperial system. The choice of the menorah, however, draws attention also to the temple cult. The lampstand symbolizes the presence of the Lord.

The two olive trees are said to symbolize "two sons of oil" (4:14). The word for oil here is *yitshar,* which refers to new olive oil, rather than *shemen,* the word usually used in connection with anointing. The olive trees provide oil for the lampstand. The two "sons of oil" apparently ensure that provision is made for the temple cult. There is little doubt that the two figures in question are the high priest Joshua and the governor Zerubbabel, both of whom played leading roles in the rebuilding of the temple. (Compare also the roles of the high priest and the "prince" in the New Jerusalem in Ezekiel 40–48.) What is disputed is whether the phrase "two sons of oil" implies that they were anointed (so NRSV: "two anointed ones"). Both the king and the high priest were anointed in ancient Israel. If the governor were anointed, this would imply a claim to royal status. Here again the objection that the Persians would not allow the governor to be anointed misses the point. The text does not imply that the anointing actually took place. The reference to oil, even if the word is *yitshar* rather than *shemen*, could hardly fail to suggest anointing when used in connection with a high priest and a Davidic ruler. The functions of these figures are conceived primarily with reference to the temple and its cult, as is also the case in Ezekiel 40–48. They also imply a different kind of community structure from that of the preexilic monarchy. The new order is a dyarchy, in which high priest and king share power. This new order is later reflected in the messianic expectations of the Dead Sea Scrolls, which speak of two messiahs, one from Aaron and one from Israel.

The insertion in Zech 4:6-10a sharpens the focus on Zerubbabel. He will rule not by (human) might or power but by the Spirit of the Lord. (Compare the prophecy of the shoot from the stump of Jesse in Isaiah 11.) In the postexilic context, this oracle forestalls the objection that Zerubbabel could not hope to lead a successful rebellion against the Persian Empire. There is no suggestion that rebellion would be necessary. The hope that Zerubbabel would restore the kingship was obviously fueled by his role in the rebuilding of the temple. In the ancient Near East, kings were regarded as the founders of temples, and they usually performed symbolic roles. When a new temple was being built, a brick was first taken from the old one, presumably to provide continuity. This may be the point of the reference to "the first stone" (NRSV "top stone") in Zech 4:7. Since Zerubbabel was performing traditional royal functions in connection with the rebuilding of the temple, it is not surprising that hopes surged that he would restore the monarchy, with or without Persian permission.

A Crown or Crowns?

Zechariah has three further visions. Two of those are in chapter 5. First the prophet sees a flying scroll that enters the houses of thieves and consumes them. Theft was presumably a problem in the impoverished Judean community. The scroll represents the curses of the covenantal law, such as we find in Lev 26:14-39. In the other vision in Zechariah 5, Wickedness, personified as a woman, is placed in a basket and transported to Shinar (an old name for Babylon; cf. Gen 11:2). We are reminded of the scapegoat in Leviticus 16, which carries sin away to the wilderness. We need not suppose that any ritual is implied in Zechariah. Instead of the wilderness, in this case, wickedness is transported to Babylon. That a house is built for it in Babylon may be taken to imply that the Babylonians worship wickedness.

The final vision of Zechariah picks up the motif of the horses from the first vision to form a neat *inclusio*. Here there are four chariots patrolling the earth. The Lord's Spirit is at rest in the north country. Babylon was traditionally the land of the north, because people coming from Babylon approached Israel from the north. Again, the enemies of the Lord are subdued.

Chapter 6 concludes with a narrative that relates directly to the messianic hopes of chapters 3 and 4. The prophet is told to collect silver and gold from the exiles who have returned from Babylon. With these precious materials, he is told to make crowns. (The plural is usually emended to the singular in English translations.) Then he is told to set it (singular) on the head of the high priest Joshua. The oracle that follows, however, seems much more appropriate for Zerubbabel: "Here is a man whose name is Branch; for he shall branch out in his place, and he shall build the temple of the LORD. It is he that shall build the temple of the LORD; he shall bear royal honor, and shall sit upon his throne and rule. There shall be a priest by his throne, with peaceful understanding between the two of them." It is clear from the last verse that the figure whose name is Branch is not a priest; therefore the oracle cannot refer to Joshua. Like chapter 4, this passage envisions dyarchy, in which power is shared between king and priest, although the king seems to have primacy. The anomaly of the passage is that no crown is placed on the head of the royal figure, only on that of the priest.

It seems clear that we no longer have the original form of Zechariah 6. Most probably, the plural "crowns" is correct; the prophet would have made crowns both for Zerubbabel and for Joshua. Zerubbabel, however, was edited out of the text. The idea of crowning the governor was probably too explosive. The crowning of Zerubbabel was either prevented or suppressed, and the text emended accordingly. We do not know what became of Zerubbabel. The Persian authorities may have realized that he was giving rise to messianic hopes (whether he wished it or not) and may have removed him from the scene.

It is typical of the way that biblical texts were edited that loose ends were allowed to stand. There was no systematic revision of the text to remove all reference to Zerubbabel. This may seem like careless editing from a modern point of view, but it has the advantage of allowing us to see several layers in the text and to reconstruct something of its history.

Zechariah 7–8

The excitement and turmoil about the restoration of the monarchy that dominate much of Zechariah 1–6 disappear completely in the concluding chapters, 7 and 8. Chapter 7 reports how people from Bethel came to Jerusalem to inquire about mourning and fasting. The response attributed to Zechariah is reminiscent both of Deuteronomy and of older prophets, from Amos to Jeremiah: the Lord is not concerned with fasting, but with kindness and mercy, and the protection of the widow, the orphan, and the alien. The woes that have befallen the people are due to the fact that they have not obeyed the Law and the words of the prophets. The tone of this chapter is quite different from the visions of Zechariah and is similar to that of the sermonic prose (C) sections of Jeremiah.

Zechariah 8 also brings to mind prose passages in the book of Jeremiah, especially the oracles of hope and consolation in Jeremiah 33. These hopeful predictions probably concluded the original book of Zechariah, as it was edited not long after the time of the prophet.

The Additions to Zechariah

The last six chapters of the book of Zechariah are among the most obscure and difficult passages in the Hebrew Bible. Although they have been classified as part of the book of Zechariah since the Middle Ages, the attribution is coincidental. There is no mention of Zechariah in these chapters. They were simply copied after the oracles of Zechariah in ancient manuscripts. Conversely, it is not apparent that the book of Malachi was originally distinguished from the preceding oracles, or that Malachi ("my messenger") was the name of a prophet. All the material in Zechariah 9–14 and Malachi may be regarded as a collection of anonymous oracles that was appended to the collection of Minor Prophets. The chapters conventionally attributed to Malachi are more coherent than Zechariah 9–14.

These chapters are punctuated by markers at three points. The heading "an oracle" appears at Zech 9:1; 12:1; and Mal 1:1. These headings suggest a division of the text, but they by no means guarantee that the material in between is coherent. Most of these oracles appear to have been written with specific situations in mind, but it is no longer possible to reconstruct with any confidence what these situations were. Zechariah 9–14 contains numerous echoes of and allusions to earlier biblical books, and some scholars have tried to view them as a kind of early biblical interpretation. But while the allusions to earlier literature are an important part of the fabric of these chapters, they do not present a clear or coherent interpretation of any older texts. These oracles were not composed as works of interpretation, but to address problems of their own time and place that are now lost from view. In some cases, however, they may have been composed as purely eschatological scenarios that had no reference to any historical events. Here I comment only on some of the more striking elements in these chapters.

Zechariah 9

The first of these oracles, in Zechariah 9, begins with an oracle against Israel's neighbors, moving from Syria (Hadrach, Damascus) to Tyre and Sidon, and down the coast to the Philistine cities. It is noteworthy, however, that only Tyre is said to be destroyed. The oracle asserts the sovereignty of YHWH over Syria but pronounces no judgment against it. Philistia will lose its identity and be inhabited by a mongrel people. Ekron, the furthest inland of the Philistine cities, will be absorbed in Judah as the Jebusites had been.

Many scholars regard Zech 9:1-8 as a distinct oracle, but the whole chapter can be read as a unit. Verses 9-10 are a transitional passage, describing the coming of a king to Jerusalem, "humble and riding on a donkey." The remainder of the chapter describes how God will liberate Israel "because of the blood of my covenant with you," and will manifest himself as a warrior to save them.

Attempts to locate this chapter historically have led to widely divergent results, ranging from the Assyrian period to the time of Alexander the Great (332 B.C.E.). Much depends on the interpretation of 9:13: "I will arouse your sons, O Zion, against your sons, O Greece, and wield you like a warrior's sword." There are valid reasons for questioning the authenticity of the phrase "against your sons, O Greece." The other verses in the poem all have two lines (bicola); this is the only one with three (a tricolon). Moreover, the word for Greece, *yawan,* is similar enough to Zion in Hebrew that it could be explained as a scribal error. Even if the reading is accepted, there is no agreement as to what that implies. Greece was involved in wars against Persia in the fifth century, and so many scholars argue for a date in the Persian period. Others think the most likely occasion is the campaign of Alexander the Great. Alexander destroyed Tyre. The Philistine cities had by then lost their identity,

Fig. 20.4 **Alexander the Great (left) faces Darius III at the Battle of Issus; Roman mosaic, copy of a Greek original, at the National Archaeological Museum, Naples.** Commons.wikimedia.org

and some, such as Ashkelon, became Hellenistic cities (cf. the "mongrel population" of Zech 9:6). If the chapter were indeed written in response to Alexander's campaign, it could be read as a fantasy of victory over Greece by the power of the divine warrior, and the restoration of a kind of kingship that contrasted sharply with that of Alexander. Nonetheless, the historical setting remains doubtful because of the uncertainty of the text.

The main importance of this chapter for later tradition lies in the picture of the messianic king. The humble king, riding on a donkey, is a throwback to the days of the judges. Such a king would contrast sharply with Alexander the Great, but also with every victorious monarch who ever invaded the region. But we should also note that prophetic oracles about a restored monarchy often picture the king who is humble, in contrast to the arrogance of most actual monarchs. So, for example, Mic 4:2

looks to Bethlehem, home of David but one of the little clans of Judah, for a future king. Isaiah 11 pictures a king who will be guided by the Spirit, and fear, of the Lord.

There is very little evidence of messianic hope in Judah between the time of Zerubbabel and the first century B.C.E., and for this reason it would be interesting to know the date of Zechariah 9. When messianism emerges in the Dead Sea Scrolls, we usually find a more militant picture of the Messiah, and Zechariah 9 is not among the biblical texts cited. It is cited, however, in the New Testament in Matt 21:5 and John 12:14-15.

The Theme of Kingship

The theme of kingship appears several other times in Zechariah 9–14 and is one of the elements that link these oracles to those of Zechariah. Zechariah 10 complains that "the people wander like sheep; they suffer for lack of a shepherd," and proceeds to express the anger of the Lord against "the shepherds." The reference is presumably to the foreign rulers who do not care for Judah as the Lord does. The theme of the shepherd is taken up again in chapter 11. Like much of Zechariah 9–14, this passage is obscure. It seems to report a symbolic action by the prophet, in which he acts out the attempt of YHWH to be a shepherd to Israel, ending in the payment of thirty shekels of silver, the price of a slave (Exod 21:32). The prophet is then told to resume the role of the shepherd because "a worthless shepherd will arise in the land." All too many rulers of Judah (or of anywhere else) would fit this description. There is another enigmatic oracle against a shepherd in 13:7-9. The passage about the thirty pieces of silver is cited loosely in Matt 27:9 (the story of Judas), where it is attributed to Jeremiah.

The house of David comes to the fore in Zechariah 12. This passage evokes the traditional theme of the assault of the nations against Jerusalem or Mount Zion (cf., for example, Psalm 2). In Zech 12:3—13:6 we have a series of oracles introduced by the phrase "in that day." This formula often indicates an editorial addition in other prophetic books, notably in the book of Isaiah. A few elements in these oracles are notable, even if they remain obscure. The Lord will give victory to Judah first so that the glory of the house of David and of Jerusalem should not be exalted. This passage reflects an awareness of tension between city and countryside that is completely lacking in Zechariah 1–8. Nonetheless, it affirms that the house of David will be "like the angel of the LORD." Another striking passage, 13:10-14, speaks of

a spirit of compassion on the house of David and the inhabitants of Jerusalem: "When they look on the one whom they have pierced, they shall mourn for him as one mourns for an only child." The Hebrew text actually reads: "on me, the one whom they have pierced." Nonetheless, commentators have tried repeatedly to identify a human figure, or figures, here. King Josiah, who was killed by the Egyptians at Megiddo, is the figure most often proposed, but it is difficult to see the relevance of Josiah to any conceivable context for this oracle. Other scholars have suggested that the reference is to some people who had been rejected by the Jerusalem establishment, or perhaps to the prophets, who were repeatedly rejected by kings and peoples alike. The passage suggests that there will be reconciliation at some future time. It is unlikely that the house of David was an active force in Jerusalem when this oracle was written, and so the whole passage must be read as a hypothetical, eschatological scenario. The "one whom they have pierced" is identified as the crucified Jesus in John 19:37.

The End of Prophecy

One of the most intriguing passages in Zechariah 9–14 is 13:2-6, which envisions a time when prophets will be ashamed of their calling and refuse to acknowledge it. Verse 6 refers incidentally to one of the more colorful aspects of prophecy when it raises the possibility that someone might ask about "these wounds on your chest." Canaanite and Syrian prophets were known to gash themselves as a way of inducing ecstasy (see the story of the prophets of Baal in 1 Kgs 18:28). The practice is not otherwise recorded with regard to

Israelite prophets, but there must have been some basis for the allusion in the postexilic period. The shame surrounding the profession of prophecy probably arose from the conflicts between the prophets in the time of Jeremiah and the discrediting of prophecy because of failed predictions. Too many prophets had spoken lies in the name of the Lord. Prophecy lost its authority in the Persian period. We do not know the names of any Hebrew prophets after Haggai and Zechariah. In the Hellenistic period, revelatory writings were attributed to ancient worthies such as Enoch or Daniel, not to their real authors. Increasingly in the Second Temple period, religious authority was vested in the scribes who were the authoritative interpreters of the Torah. Sometimes these people claimed inspiration. The Teacher of Righteousness, who was the most authoritative figure in the sect known from the Dead Sea Scrolls, was a case in point.

The Final Battle

The book of Zechariah as it is now constituted ends on a note that resembles such passages as Ezekiel's oracle against Gog or some later apocalyptic visions. This is a purely eschatological fantasy. It has no reference to any historical event. Again, the myth of the assault of the Gentiles on Mount Zion provides the framework. In this case, the city will be taken, as it was by the Babylonians, but then the Lord shall rouse himself. His appearance shall be followed by an earthquake and cosmic convulsions. The Lord will strike all the peoples who fight against Jerusalem so that their flesh and even their eyes will rot. This rather violent image of revenge on the nations is followed by a more peaceful conclusion. All who survive of

the nations will go up year after year to worship YHWH as king at the Festival of Booths, and Jerusalem will be a holy city.

This concluding oracle is in some ways typical of the anonymous oracles that have survived from the Second Temple period. Increasingly, these oracles are concerned not with the events of the time when they were composed, but with the final resolution of history, the end of days. They reflect the dissonance between the glorious promises of the Scriptures and the diminished existence of Judah under the Persians and later the Greeks, and a yearning for a time when the kingship of YHWH God of Israel would be revealed in all its splendor. Such oracles are sometimes called "proto-apocalyptic," and they bear some resemblance to apocalyptic visions. We shall see, however, when we consider the book of Daniel, that apocalyptic visions were firmly rooted in specific historical events and were quite different from these late prophetic oracles in some crucial respects.

Malachi

The oracles attributed to Malachi were probably also transmitted anonymously. The name is probably taken from Mal 3:1, where it means simply "my messenger." In this case, however, we encounter the voice of a distinct prophet. The book consists of six speeches or disputations, with two brief appendices at the end. The units are 1:2-5; 1:6—2:9; 2:10-16; 2:17—3:5; 3:6-12; and 3:13—4:3 (Heb. 3:13-21). The appendices are found in 4:4 (3:22) and 4:3 (3:23-24). (Note that the Hebrew text is divided into only three chapters, not four as in the English translations: Eng 4:1-5 = MT 3:19-24.)

There is some precedent for the disputation form in earlier prophecy (e.g., Micah 6). Some scholars have regarded it as an adaptation of a legal form, but it can be understood on the analogy of normal disputes between people.

Against Edom

The first oracle (1:1-5) addresses the skeptical question about God's love for Judah by contrasting her fate with that of neighboring Edom, which will be reduced to permanent desolation. Edom had not been destroyed by Nebuchadnezzar and incurred the hatred of Judah by looting and gloating over its fallen neighbor (see especially Obad 8-14). There are several bitter oracles against Edom in the prophetic corpus (Isaiah 34; 63:1-6; Jer 49:7-22; Ezek 25:12-14). The kingdom of Edom seems to have been brought to an end, however, by Nabonidus, the last king of Babylon, in the mid-sixth century B.C.E. Its desolate state in the Persian period was seen as evidence of the power of YHWH by Malachi.

A Critique of the Priesthood

The long disputation in 1:6—2:9 is a critique of the Jerusalem priesthood in the Persian period. Unlike preexilic prophets such as Amos or Micah, or even the postexilic prophet of Isaiah 66, Malachi does not question the value or validity of sacrifice. He only demands that it be done properly, and argues that it would be better to close up the temple than to offend the Lord with unworthy offerings. No one would offer a blind or lame animal as a present to the governor. Neither should one use the cult of YHWH to dispose of sick or blemished animals. (Incidentally, the reference to a governor, combined with the fact that the temple is functioning, is one of the indications of the Persian date of Malachi.)

In Mal 1:11 Malachi makes a remarkable claim: "From the rising of the sun to its setting my name is great among the nations, and in every place incense is offered to my name, and a pure offering." This remarkable claim has been explained in various ways. There were some Jewish temples outside the land of Israel in the Second Temple period. The best known were the shrine of Jewish mercenaries at Elephantine in southern Egypt in the fifth century, and the temple at Leontopolis in northern Egypt, built by the disinherited high priest Onias IV in the mid-second century B.C.E. These temples were, of course, in violation of the law of Deuteronomy, which forbade sacrificial worship outside Jerusalem. It is unlikely that Malachi had them in mind. Some have suggested that the passage anticipates the eschatological age when all nations will worship the true God. Yet the claim is not in the future tense, but in the present. It is possible that the prophet regarded the worship of the highest God in any religion as tantamount to the worship of YHWH. In the book of Ezra, King Cyrus of Persia is said to identify YHWH with "the God of heaven" (Ezra 1:2; in Persian religion the God of heaven was Ahura Mazda). We know of some Jewish writers in the Hellenistic period who held this view (the philosopher Aristobulus and the author of the *Letter of Aristeas*), and we find a similar idea in St. Paul's comments on "the unknown God" in the Areopagus of Athens in Acts 17. It may be that the prophet took the Persian professions of respect for "the God of heaven" at face value. It should be noted that this claim is made as part of a polemic against the inadequacy of the sacrifices offered in Jerusalem, and it may be deliberate hyperbole.

The primary concern of the prophet was with the integrity of Jewish worship. In Mal 2:4-9 he upbraids the priests of his day by reminding them of "the covenant with Levi." There is no account of such a covenant in the Hebrew Bible. Its existence may have been inferred from the blessing of Levi in Deut 33:9-11, which says that the Levites "observed your word, and kept your covenant." That passage goes on to speak of the teaching role of the Levites, as does Mal 2:6. There is a perpetual covenant with Phinehas in Numbers 25. Jeremiah 33:21 speaks of "my covenant with my ministers the Levites," which cannot be broken, just like the covenant with David. Nehemiah 13:29 refers to "the covenant of the priests and the Levites." From the last two passages, it seems that by the Persian period there was believed to be a covenant with Levi, or the Levites, even if it was not explicitly narrated in the Bible. Malachi is insistent that this is a conditional covenant that requires reverence and fidelity on the part of the priests. Here again he is not questioning the importance of the priesthood or the sacrificial cult, but he is holding them to a higher standard than was observed in Jerusalem in his time.

Infidelity and Divorce

The third disputation in 2:10-16 is the most difficult passage in Malachi and one of the most difficult in all the Hebrew Bible. The opening verse hints at division in the community, which results from "profaning the covenant of our ancestors." Judah, we are told, has profaned the sanctuary of the Lord, and "married the daughter of a foreign god." Some scholars take "the daughter of a foreign god" to be a goddess. The mention of a foreign god implies some involvement in pagan worship. The usual view of commentators is that the passage refers to marriage with foreign women, a problem that figures prominently in the book of Ezra. Those who married foreign women were likely to give some recognition to the religious practices of their wives (cf. the story of Solomon in 1 Kgs 11:1-8). It is clear from the passage that the offenders had not abandoned the worship of YHWH but were engaging in syncretistic, or mixed, worship.

In Mal 2:13 the prophet moves on to a second problem. The Lord "was a witness between you and the wife of your youth, to whom you have been faithless, though she is your companion and your wife by covenant." In view of the reference to the daughter of a foreign god in the previous passage, it is often suggested that Jewish men were divorcing their Jewish wives to marry foreign women, but there is no actual evidence that this was the case. If it were, we should expect that the divorce would be mentioned first, before "the daughter of a foreign god," as the divorce would have cleared the way for the idolatrous marriage. The prophet does not call for the divorce of foreign women or give approval to divorce in any context.

There is explicit mention of divorce in 2:16, but it is obscured by textual difficulties. The usual translation, "I hate divorce," attempts to make sense of a difficult phrase, but there is no first person pronoun in the sentence. The word "hate" is commonly used in marriage contracts in connection with divorce; it means to repudiate one's spouse. Accordingly, the phrase should be translated,

"For one has repudiated, sent away . . . and covered his garment with violence." The subject is indefinite. The force of the statement is that to repudiate and divorce (send away) is to commit flagrant injustice. According to Malachi, YHWH disapproves. So even if the ringing phrase "I hate divorce" is a mistranslation, the passage is nonetheless a remarkable condemnation of divorce. Divorce was perfectly acceptable in traditional Israelite religion (see Deuteronomy 24), although the right to divorce was restricted to the husband. (There was an exception to this in the Jewish military colony in Elephantine in southern Egypt in the fifth century, where wives also had the right to divorce their husbands.)

Despite a common assumption, there is no indication that Malachi was condemning only the divorce of Jewish wives. The basis for the condemnation is given in 2:15, but the verse is unfortunately corrupt. Literally it reads, "And not one did, and had a remnant of spirit. And what does the one seek? Godly offspring. Guard your spirits, and let no one be faithless to the wife of your youth." The NRSV takes the "one" as God: "did not one God make her?" This rendering echoes 2:10, "Have we not all one father?" The more usual interpretation takes the "one" as the object: "Did not he [God] make one?" By slight emendation, the word "remnant" (*she'ar*)' can be read as "flesh" (*she'er*)'. The question would then read, "Has he not made one, which has flesh and spirit?" This would be a reference to Gen 2:24, which says that man and wife became "one flesh." The remainder of the verse, "and what does the one seek? Godly offspring," can also be read against the background of Genesis. In Gen 1:28 the only command given to the primal

couple is to "be fruitful and fill the earth." On this reading, Malachi sees marriage as a covenant to which God is the witness, and which has as its goal the procreation of godly children. He does not appear to have anyplace for divorce. The opening statement in Mal 2:16 can now be read in a new light: "Have we not all one father?" The appeal is to creation and is meant to unify the community, not tear it apart.

The discussion of divorce in Malachi inevitably brings to mind an episode in Ezra 10, which is most probably dated to 458 B.C.E. On his return to Jerusalem, Ezra was horrified to find that Jewish men had married foreign women, and he compelled them to divorce the women and send them away with their children. We do not know the exact date of Malachi, but it clearly dates from the Persian period. If the reading of Malachi proposed here is correct, the prophet would have agreed with Ezra in condemning marriage with foreign women because of the potential for idolatry. But he would have disagreed emphatically with Ezra's solution because he saw divorce as contrary to the order of creation in Genesis. Marriage to foreign women was regrettable, but the solution was to raise godly children, not send them away. We are not sure, however, whether Malachi had Ezra in mind at all.

Malachi's pronouncements on divorce mark a change in traditional Jewish attitudes to marriage. Divorce would still be accepted by mainstream Judaism, but Malachi points to the emergence of a stricter view of marriage as indissoluble. The basis for that view was found in the statement in Genesis that man and wife were one flesh. This stricter view was later developed in the Dead Sea Scrolls and receives a famous endorsement in the New Testament in the saying attributed to Jesus, "What God has joined together, let no one separate" (Matt 19:6).

Like a Refiner's Fire

The fifth oracle in the book of Malachi (2:17—3:5) predicts the coming of the Lord to his temple in judgment in response to the people's complaint, "Where is the God of justice?" The "messenger" or angel sent to prepare the way recalls the angel sent before Israel in the exodus (Exod 23:20) but more directly Isaiah 40, where a figure in the divine council is told to prepare the way in the wilderness. In Isaiah 40 the context is one of consolation. In Malachi it is one of judgment. The main issue in dispute in this passage is the identity of "the messenger of the covenant." In the context it is difficult to distinguish this messenger from the Lord himself. In Genesis "the angel of the LORD" is similarly difficult to distinguish from the Lord himself. The focus of the passage, in any case, is on the terror and danger associated with the coming of the Lord. The theophany may be understood as a variant of "the Day of the LORD," which we have encountered repeatedly in the preexilic prophets. What is remarkable here is that the main purpose of the Lord's coming is to purify the temple. The judgment is not on the nations but on the center of the Lord's own cult.

The final oracle (Mal 3:6-12) repeats some of the charges that made the judgment on the cult necessary. Malachi has no objection to sacrifice or offerings. His problem is that people are "cheating God" by not bringing the full offerings and tithes. He also accuses people of cynicism in saying that their worship is for nothing. In 3:16, however, he distinguishes a group of "those who revered the LORD," who seem to be exempt from these charges. As in Isaiah 56–66, we see here signs of emerging sectarianism: the elect group that will be saved is not all of Israel or Judah, but only the righteous. The tendency to identify such an elect group within Israel becomes clearer later in the apocalyptic literature, and becomes fully explicit in the Dead Sea Scrolls.

The Epilogues

The book of Malachi ends with two brief epilogues. The first is a reminder to heed the teaching of "my servant Moses" (Heb 3:22; Eng 4:4). The oracles of Malachi were rather selective in their attention to the Mosaic law. The epilogue was added by an editor who wanted to affirm the primacy of the Torah. This epilogue may have been intended as a conclusion to the entire book of the Twelve.

The second epilogue (Heb 3:22-23; Eng 4:5-6) is more specifically related to the oracles of Malachi. In effect, it identifies the messenger who would prepare the way of the Lord with Elijah. Elijah had not died but had been taken up alive to heaven. He was therefore available to return and play a part in the end of history. This passage in Malachi is the earliest evidence of the expectation that Elijah would return. There is an allusion to this expectation in Sir 48:10 and again in the Dead Sea Scrolls (4Q558). It figures prominently in the New Testament, where John the Baptist is identified as Elijah who is to come (Matt 11:14; 17:10-13). In Jewish tradition, a place is set for Elijah at the celebration of the Passover.

Joel

We conclude our survey of the Minor Prophets with the books of Joel and Jonah, which appear out of chronological order in the canon.

In Joel, again there is a discrepancy between the Hebrew and English versification. The verses that appear as 2:28-32 in English are designated 3:1-5 in the Hebrew Bible. English chapter 3 corresponds to Hebrew chapter 4.

Joel is placed second in the Hebrew Bible, between Hosea and Amos, and fourth in the Greek Bible (LXX). The arrangement of the Book of the Twelve (Minor Prophets) follows a rough chronological order (Hosea, Amos, and Micah occur near the beginning; Haggai, Zechariah, and Malachi at the end). Consequently, it was traditionally assumed that Joel was a preexilic prophet. It is now recognized, however, that the placement of Joel in the Hebrew Bible is due to thematic contacts with the book of Amos. (The opening couplet of Joel 4:16 [Eng. 3:16], "The LORD roars from Zion and utters his voice from Jerusalem," is also found in Amos 1:2. The two books share the theme of the Day of the Lord.) The book provides little internal evidence for its date, but most scholars now agree that it belongs in the postexilic period and is one of the latest books in the collection of Minor Prophets, if not the latest.

Discussion of the origin of the book is complicated by the question of its literary unity. Joel 1:1—2:17 contains a description of a plague of locusts, with exhortations and prayers for deliverance. Joel 2:18-27 gives a reply and reassurance from God. Joel 2:28—3:21 (Hebrew chapters 3 and 4 are concerned with a future time when God will pour out his Spirit, save a remnant of his people, and judge the nations.)

The Plague of Locusts

There is no historical allusion in the first two chapters that might throw any light on their provenance. One striking feature of these chapters is their liturgical or cultic character. The prophet calls on the people to "sanctify a fast, call a solemn assembly" (1:14), and calls on the priests to put on sackcloth. It is unusual in the Hebrew Bible to find a prophet advocating liturgical acts in this way. Prophets were often associated with temples in the ancient Near East, and there may have been such prophets in preexilic Israel or Judah. The prophets most closely associated with the temple in the Hebrew Bible, however, are postexilic, most notably Haggai and Zechariah. Many scholars assume that Joel's account of the locust plague also comes from this later period, but the evidence is not decisive. It should be noted that the prophet does not prescribe ritual actions exclusively. The call to "return to me" (2:12) has a Deuteronomic ring to it, while the call to "rend your hearts, not your garments" (2:13), is a classic expression of the prophetic view of proper ritual.

The second striking feature of Joel 1–2 is the use of the motif of "the Day of the Lord." As we have seen earlier, this phrase originally referred to a festival day but was transformed by Amos into a day of judgment. The judgment is usually either direct intervention of God, or it is exercised by an invading army. Joel is exceptional in using the phrase of a plague of locusts, which he describes as an invading army with the Lord at their head

(2:11). The impact of such a plague was catastrophic. In the words of 2:3, it transformed the land from a garden of Eden to a desert waste. Such a natural disaster was perceived as a divine judgment no less than a Babylonian invasion.

The Final Judgment

The "Day of the Lord" is used quite differently in Joel 3:14 (Hebrew 4:14). Here it refers to the day of judgment against all peoples in the Valley of Jehoshaphat (which means, "YHWH judged"). We have a brief indication of the context in 3:4-8. Tyre, Sidon, and all the region of Philistia are accused of pillaging Judah. Specifically they are accused of selling boys and girls as slaves to the Greeks in exchange for prostitutes and wine. The reference to the Greeks does not require a date after Alexander the Great, but it surely requires a date in the postexilic period. Trade with Greece increased throughout this period. We know that there was an active slave trade in the Hellenistic period (third century B.C.E.).

The judgment in the Valley of Jehoshaphat goes far beyond revenge on a few neighboring cities. It is a judgment on all nations. This kind of vision of vengeance reappears continually in the later prophetic books: compare Ezekiel 38–39 or Zechariah 14. It reflects the resentment and anger of a people at the mercy of its neighbors. It is not the noblest sentiment in the Bible, but it is understandable. It is a sentiment shared by many people in the Third World in modern times as they look toward the more prosperous and dominant West.

Joel's vision for the future is not all vengeance, however. At the end of chapter 2, after the description of the locust plague, the prophet promises the people that "you shall eat in plenty and be satisfied." In chapter 4 he looks for a time when "the mountains shall drip sweet wine, the hills shall flow with milk." In part, his oracles reflect the universal human yearning for peace and plenty. A more specifically Jewish hope is articulated in 3:17: Jerusalem shall be holy and strangers shall never again pass through it. If this prophecy seems xenophobic, we should bear in mind that strangers who passed through Jerusalem had too often done so to pillage it.

Perhaps the most distinctive part of Joel's eschatological prediction is found in 2:28-32 (Hebrew 3:1-5). In the end of days, the Spirit of the Lord will be poured out on all flesh so that all have the gift of prophecy. This unusual prophecy is cited in the New Testament in Acts 2 in connection with the outpouring of the Spirit at Pentecost.

Jonah

The book of Jonah is unlike any other in the prophetic corpus. It is not a collection of oracles but a story about a prophet, and it provides an unusual perspective on the prophetic tradition. The subject, Jonah son of Amittai, is presumably the individual mentioned in 2 Kgs 14:25, who is said to have prophesied in the reign of King Jeroboam II of Israel in the eighth century B.C.E. From the passage in 2 Kings, we may infer that this Jonah was a prophet of hope who prophesied the restoration of the boundaries of Israel. The prophet described in the book of Jonah has nothing in common with this figure except his name. He is almost certainly a fictional character, invented several centuries after the reign of Jeroboam.

This Jonah, indeed, is something of an anti-prophet. When the word of the Lord comes to him, bidding him go to Nineveh and cry out against it, he goes instead in the opposite direction, to Tarshish (Spain), to flee from the presence of the Lord. His adventures are the stuff of comic legend. When a storm rises at sea, the sailors cry, each to his own deity. Ecumenical to a fault, they urge Jonah also to pray to his god. This cacophony of prayer fails to produce the desired result, so they resort to lots to determine the cause of the storm. (We might compare the procedure followed by Joshua when he was defeated in his initial attack on Ai in Joshua 7. The assumption that adversity reflects the displeasure of a deity was commonplace in the ancient Near East.) The lot falls on Jonah, who confesses that he is fleeing from his God. He urges the sailors to cast him overboard as a human sacrifice to appease the deity. They are reluctant to do so but eventually comply out of desperation. The storm is calmed. Such an extreme sacrifice might be expected to be efficacious. Compare

the story of the king of Moab, who turned the tide of battle by sacrificing his son (2 Kgs 3:27). Moreover, the miraculous result has the added effect of inducing the sailors to fear YHWH and worship him.

Jonah, however, does not die, as might be expected. A large fish swallows him, and he remains in its belly for three days and three nights. Inevitably, this story was taken by early Christians as prefiguring the resurrection of Christ on the third day (see Matt 12:39-41). More generally, Jonah became a symbol of resurrection in early Christian art. Jonah's resurrection, however, is rather ignominious: the fish vomits him out on the dry land.

While in the belly of the fish, Jonah prays to the Lord. His prayer takes the form of a psalm of thanksgiving, which presupposes that the Lord has already responded. Although many scholars defend its authenticity here, it is scarcely appropriate to Jonah's situation. He has not been driven away from YHWH's sight—he has deliberately fled from it. His life has not yet been brought up from the Pit. It is true that the book Jonah is full of irony, and it is conceivable that the author deliberately included a psalm that was inappropriate to the context to add to the humor of the situation. It is easier to suppose, however, that the psalm was added by a later editor. There are several clear examples of inserted prayers in the books of Esther and Daniel, where the prayers are found only in the Greek translations, not in the Masoretic text. These include the Song of the Three Young Men and the Prayer of Azariah in the story of the fiery furnace in Daniel 3, a story that is analogous to Jonah insofar as it involves miraculous protection from certain death. The prayer allows for a pause in the narrative between Jonah's descent into the fish

Fig. 20.5 Jonah thrown from the belly of the fish; early Christian fresco from the cubiculum of the Arenario, Rome. Scala/ArtResource, NY

and his reemergence, and so helps the pace of the story. This particular psalm was chosen because of its imagery: "the waters closed in over me; the deep surrounded me." In the idiom of the Psalms, however, such language is metaphorical and simply indicates extreme distress. Compare Ps 69:2: "I have come into deep waters, and the flood sweeps over me."

His deliverance from the fish allows Jonah a new beginning. Chapter 3 resumes the narrative by having the word of the Lord come to Jonah a second time. This time Jonah obeys and goes to Nineveh. In accordance with the hyperbolic style of Jonah, the size of the city is exaggerated. The ruins of Nineveh are roughly three miles across, certainly not three days' walk. Most surprising, however, is the response of the Ninevites. They immediately believe the prophet and repent with sackcloth and fasting. Never in the history of prophecy had a proclamation produced such a dramatic response. Even the animals fast and are clothed with sackcloth. We are reminded of the words of God to the prophet Ezekiel: "you are not sent to a people of obscure speech and difficult language . . . surely, if I sent you to them, they would listen to you" (Ezek 3:5-6). Ezekiel does not test that supposition. In both Jonah and Ezekiel, however, the supposed responsiveness of the pagan people serves to highlight the stubbornness of Israel. The text does not say explicitly that the God to whom the Ninevites cried was the God of Israel, although that may be implied, since this was the God in whose name Jonah spoke. Needless to say, there is no historical record of any such repentance by any Assyrian city.

There is yet another ironic twist in the story of Jonah, however. Jonah is not happy about the conversion of Nineveh. It should have been destroyed, as it deserved. The Lord is too merciful. That is why Jonah tried to run away. So now he goes out of the city. At first the Lord provides him with a bush for shelter, but then it withers. At this point, Jonah prays for death, as Elijah had done in the wilderness in 1 Kings 19. Jonah, of course, is no Elijah, although he shares some of Elijah's zeal for destroying the enemy. The destruction of the bush provides a final parable: if Jonah is concerned for the bush that withered, should he not be more concerned for Nineveh, "that great city in which there are more than a hundred and twenty thousand persons who do not know their right hand from their left, and also many animals?" (4:11).

The biblical prophets are often critical of the traditions and beliefs of Israel and Judah, and the tendency of "the chosen people" to be complacent and self-righteous (Amos is an obvious example). In most cases, however, they maintain a sharp distinction between Israel and the other nations, and often call down the wrath of God on Israel's enemies. The book of Jonah is exceptional in its compassion for the Ninevites, who are human beings like any other, and most of whom have little knowledge of the schemes of their rulers. It is even more exceptional in treating a prophet as a figure of fun. (Admittedly, Jonah is never actually called a prophet, but he is called to speak in the name of the Lord.) The author is suggesting, gently, that Hebrew prophets should not take themselves quite so seriously.

The universalistic message of the book, which makes little if any distinction between Jew and Gentile, is generally thought to point to a date in the postexilic period. It has sometimes been construed as a polemic against the particularism of Ezra and Nehemiah, but there is nothing in Jonah to suggest an allusion to those books. The statement that Nineveh *was* a great city has been taken as a clue that it no longer existed—that is, that the book was written after 612 B.C.E. when Nineveh was destroyed. None of this is conclusive, by any means. More significant, perhaps, is the impression that this is "belated" literature, written in reaction to the stereotypes of the Torah and the Prophets. It can hardly be later than the Persian period, since it was included in the collection of prophetic writings. It is somewhat ironic that the book found a place in the Twelve Minor Prophets. That it seemed to tell the story of a prophet seems to have eclipsed the irony with which it portrayed the prophetic office.

This was not the last irony that attended the transmission of the book of Jonah. For many conservative Christians, that it had the status of Scripture was taken to mean that the book was historically accurate. And so it became a virtue to believe that Jonah was swallowed by a big fish. But such credulity was never a real virtue. It merely indicated a tin ear in the matter of literary genre. This is a whimsical, ironic, and amusing fable. To take it as history is simply to miss the point.

Epilogue: The Book of the Twelve Minor Prophets

In the preceding chapters we have considered the books of the Minor Prophets as individual compositions, each in its own historical setting. The books are in fact so distinguished in the Hebrew Bible, and in most cases there is also an indication of the historical context of the prophet in question. But the Book of the

Twelve has also been regarded as a unit from ancient times. Ben Sira, in the early second century B.C.E., refers to "the Twelve Prophets" as a group (Sir 49:10), and the twelve books were copied on a single scroll at Qumran. Originally, these books were grouped together for a practical reason, so that the shorter books, such as Malachi, would not be lost. As noted already, there is a rough but inexact chronological order, and there are minor differences in order between the Hebrew and Greek Bibles. As we have seen in the discussion of Zechariah, the division of books in the latter part of the corpus is somewhat artificial. The scribes may have decided to distinguish twelve books because of the traditional association of the number twelve with the tribes of Israel. There are some indications of thoughtful arrangement in the Book of the Twelve, but the book remains a collection of writings that originated over several centuries, and its unity should not be exaggerated.

The most important common trait running through these books concerns the prominence of eschatology. All the books except Nahum and Jonah refer explicitly to the Day of the Lord, and Nahum refers to a coming divine judgment. The role of eschatology changes, however, in the later books of the collection. The book of Joel reflects a typical pattern, insofar as it starts out with a specific situation and moves to a much wider horizon of cosmic judgment. The same is true of the book of Zechariah. The older prophets were distinguished by their specificity. Think, for example, of Amos upbraiding the rich for selling the poor for a pair of sandals. Already in these books we found some passages that looked to an indefinite future, "at the end of days." In the later prophetic books these passages become more common. When the prophetic oracles were gathered in books and read as Scripture, the original context was often lost from view. Eschatological passages such as what we find in Joel 3–4 were not tied to any particular situation. They looked beyond history for a definitive judgment of all nations and a definitive restoration of Israel. None of these oracles, however, envisions the end of the world in the literal sense, as it is found later in apocalyptic writings. The idea of universal judgment is certainly important in the apocalypses, but it is only one of several motifs that characterize that literature. What we find in Joel or in Zechariah 9–14 is quite different from what we find in Daniel, although it is also significantly different from the prophecy of Amos or Jeremiah.

Joel is among the later prophetic books chronologically, but it is placed second in the Book of the Twelve in the Hebrew Bible. The emphasis on the more general kind of eschatology is typical of the editing of the whole collection. It is significant, in this respect, that the Book of the Twelve ends with the prediction of the coming of Elijah before the great and terrible Day of the Lord.

The eschatological focus of the Book of the Twelve receives additional emphasis in the Christian Old Testament, where it is placed at the end of the canon, so that it is taken to point forward directly to the New Testament. In the Hebrew Bible, it only concludes the works of the prophets and is followed by the Writings.

FOR FURTHER READING

General Studies of the Period

P. R. Bedford, *Temple Restoration in Early Achaemenid Judah* (JSJSup 65; Leiden: Brill, 2001). A rigorous attempt to consider the books of Haggai and Zechariah in their historical context.

P. Briant, *From Cyrus to Alexander: A History of the Persian Empire* (Winona Lake, IN: Eisenbrauns, 2002). Authoritative account of the historical context.

S. L. Cook, *Prophecy and Apocalypticism: The Postexilic Social Setting* (Minneapolis: Fortress Press, 1995). A study of postexilic prophecy in light of sociology and anthropology, emphasizing the diversity of social roles, in opposition to P. D. Hanson.

P. D. Hanson, *The Dawn of Apocalyptic* (Philadelphia: Fortress Press, 1975). Groundbreaking sociological study of postexilic prophecy.

Haggai, Zechariah, Malachi

M. J. Boda, *Haggai, Zechariah* (The NIV Application Commentary: Grand Rapids: Zondervan, 2004). A homiletical commentary but contains valuable exegetical observations.

M. J. Boda and M. H. Floyd, eds., *Tradition in Transition: Haggai and Zechariah 1–8 in the Trajectory of Hebrew Theology* (London: T&T Clark, 2008). Essays on various aspects of Haggai and Zechariah.

A. Finitsis, *Visions and Eschatology: A Socio-Historical Analysis of Zechariah 1–6* (London: T&T Clark, 2011). Emphasizes the prophetic (rather than apocalyptic) character of Zechariah's visions.

M. H. Floyd, *Minor Prophets, Part 2* (FOTL 22; Grand Rapids: Eerdmans, 2000), 251–626. Form-critical commentary.

A. D. Hill, *Malachi* (AB 25D; New York: Doubleday, 1998). Historical and philological commentary.

J. Kessler, *The Book of Haggai: Prophecy and Society in Early Persian Yehud* (VTSup 91; Leiden: Brill, 2002). Study of Haggai in historical context, with extensive commentary on the text.

W. E. March, "The Book of Haggai," *NIB* 7:707–32. Brief homiletical commentary.

C. L. Meyers and E. M. Meyers, *Haggai, Zechariah 1–8* (AB 25 B; New York: Doubleday, 1987); *Zechariah 9–14* (AB 25C; New York: Doubleday, 1993). Detailed historical and philological commentary.

B. C. Ollenburger, "The Book of Zechariah," *NIB* 7:735–840. Useful commentary with homiletical reflections.

D. L. Petersen, *Haggai and Zechariah 1–8* (OTL; Philadelphia: Westminster, 1985); *Zechariah 9–14 and Malachi* (OTL; Louisville: Westminster, 1995). More concise than Meyers and Meyers, but also an excellent historical-critical commentary.

P. L. Redditt, *Haggai, Zechariah, Malachi* (New Century Bible; Grand Rapids: Eerdmans, 1995). Brief, scholarly commentary.

E. M. Schuller, "The Book of Malachi," *NIB* 7:843–77. Brief commentary with homiletical reflections.

M. A. Sweeney, *The Twelve Prophets* (Berit Olam; Collegeville, MN, 2000), 2:527–752. Helpful exegetical commentary.

H. W. Wolff, *Haggai* (trans. M. Kohl; CC; Minneapolis: Augsburg, 1988). Classic commentary in the German tradition.

Joel

E. Achtemeier, "The Book of Joel," *NIB* 7:301–36. Brief homiletical commentary.

J. L. Crenshaw, *Joel* (AB 24C; New York: Doubleday, 1995). Historical and philological commentary.

T. Hiebert, "Joel, Book of," *ABD* 3:873–80. Concise summary of critical issues.

M. A. Sweeney, *The Twelve Prophets* (Berit Olam; Collegeville, MN, 2000), 1:145–87. Helpful exegetical commentary.

H. W. Wolff, *Joel and Amos* (trans. W. Janzen, S. D. McBride, and C. A. Muenchow; Hermeneia; Philadelphia: Fortress Press, 1977). Classic form- and redaction-critical commentary on Joel.

Jonah

J. Limburg, *Jonah* (OTL; Louisville: Westminster John Knox, 1993). Special interest in the afterlife of Jonah in literature and art.

D. Marcus. From *Balaam to Jonah: Anti-Prophetic Satire in the Hebrew Bible* (Brown Judaic Studies 301; Atlanta: Scholars Press, 1995). Reconstructs a tradition of prophetic satire from the Balaam story, some stories in Kings, and Jonah.

J. Sasson, *Jonah* (AB 24B; New York: Doubleday, 1990). Comprehensive commentary with special attention to folkloric elements.

Y. Sherwood, *A Biblical Text and Its Afterlife: The Survival of Jonah in Western Culture* (Cambridge: Cambridge University Press, 2000). Wide-ranging history of interpretation with emphasis on diversity.

P. Trible, "Jonah," *NIB* 7:463–529. Excellent commentary, with an excursus on the afterlife of Jonah.

———, "Jonah, Book of," *ABD* 3:936–42. Overview of the critical issues.

———, *Rhetorical Criticism: Context, Method, and the Book of Jonah* (Guides to Biblical Scholarship; Minneapolis: Fortress Press, 1994). Excellent exposition of the literary features of the book.

H. W. Wolff, *Obadiah and Jonah* (trans. M. Kohl; CC; Minneapolis: Augsburg, 1977). Classic commentary in the German tradition.

On the Unity of the Book of the Twelve

P. House, *The Unity of the Twelve* (JSOTSup 97; Sheffield: Sheffield Academic Press, 1990).

B. A. Jones, *The Formation of the Book of the Twelve: A Study in Text and Canon* (SBLDS 149; Atlanta: Scholars Press, 1995).

J. Nogalski, *Redactional Processes in the Book of the Twelve* (Berlin: de Gruyter, 1993).

J. Nogalski and M. Sweeney, eds., *Reading and Hearing the Book of the Twelve* (Symposium series; Atlanta: SBL, 2000).

D. L. Petersen, *The Prophetic Literature: An Introduction* (Louisville: Westminster John Knox, 2002), 169–214.

P. L. Redditt and A. Schart, eds., *Thematic Threads in the Book of the Twelve* (BZAW 325; Berlin: de Gruyter, 2003).

C. R. Seitz, *Prophecy and Hermeneutics: Toward a New Introduction to the Prophets* (Grand Rapids: Baker, 2007), 204–19.

Ben Zvi, E. and J. Nogalski, *Two Sides of a Coin: Juxtaposing Views on Interpreting the Book of the Twelve/The Twelve Prophetic Books* (Piscataway, NJ: Gorgias, 2009). Debate about the unity of the Book of the Twelve.

PART 4

The Writings

The last section of the Hebrew Bible consists of the Writings (*K^etubim*). This is something of a catchall category that includes historical books (Ezra, Nehemiah, Chronicles), poetic compositions (Psalms, Song of Songs, Lamentations), wisdom books (Job, Proverbs, Qoheleth), short stories (Ruth, Esther), and one prophetic or apocalyptic composition (Daniel). The Greek Bible also includes the deuterocanonical books, which are accepted as canonical in the Catholic tradition and are separated out as Apocrypha in Protestantism. The order of these books differs in the various Bibles. In the Hebrew Bible the order is Psalms, Job, Proverbs, Ruth, Song of Songs, Qoheleth, Lamentations, Esther, Daniel, Ezra, Nehemiah, and Chronicles. In the Greek Bible, Lamentations is appended to Jeremiah, and Daniel is also found in the Prophets. Ruth, Esther, Ezra, Nehemiah, and Chronicles are grouped with the historical books (as also are Judith, Tobit, and the books of Maccabees). Here we will begin with Ezra, Nehemiah, and Chronicles, which are close in time to the later prophets. Then we shall turn to the Psalms and wisdom books. Ruth and Esther, and also the book of Jonah from the Prophets, will be treated as short stories, a category that also includes the deuterocanonical books of Tobit and Judith. The book of Daniel will be discussed with the books of Maccabees, which provide the appropriate historical context. Finally, we will consider the deuterocanonical wisdom books of Ben Sira and the Wisdom of Solomon.

CHAPTER 21
Ezra and Nehemiah

INTRODUCTION

Our examination of Ezra-Nehemiah in this chapter will involve a review of the initial return of exiles under the authority of Persia, the career of Ezra, and the "memoir" of Nehemiah.

Ezra-Nehemiah

The books of Ezra and Nehemiah were originally counted as one book, under the name of Ezra, and were still regarded as a unit in Hebrew Bibles down through the Middle Ages. In the Greek tradition, they were distinguished as two books from the third century C.E., and in the Latin from the translation of Jerome's Vulgate in the fourth century. There are several other books associated with the name of Ezra. Most closely related to the canonical books is the apocryphal book of 1 Esdras (sometimes called 3 Ezra). This is a Greek translation of 2 Chronicles 35–36, Ezra 1–10, and Neh 8:1-13, with some differences in the order of material and an additional story about three youths at court, including Zerubbabel, who became governor of Judah after the restoration. It is of interest as a witness to a different arrangement of much of the material in Ezra and Nehemiah. Another apocryphal book, 2 Esdras, contains an important Jewish apocalypse from around 100 C.E. (better known as *4 Ezra*), as well as two shorter works of Christian origin, *5 Ezra* (2 Esdras 1-2) and *6 Ezra* (2 Esdras 15-16). In this chapter, we shall restrict our attention to the canonical books of Ezra and Nehemiah but shall also keep 1 Esdras in mind. Ezra and Nehemiah are two separate books in all modern Bibles, but they are closely bound together and are evidently the work of one author or editor. Accordingly they are often referred to together as Ezra-Nehemiah.

In modern times, the books of Ezra and Nehemiah have often been regarded as part of the Chronicler's History. The concluding verses of 2 Chronicles (2 Chron 36:22-23) are virtually identical with the opening verses of Ezra (Ezra 1:1-3a). Moreover, there are numerous points of affinity between the language and idiom of Chronicles and that of

Ezra-Nehemiah; both show great interest in the temple cult and matters related to it, such as liturgical music and the temple vessels. Some scholars argue that these similarities only reflect the common interests of Second Temple Judaism, and note that there are also differences in terminology. For example, the high priest is called *hakkohen haggadol* (the great priest) in Ezra-Nehemiah, but *hakkohen haro'sh* (the head priest) in Chronicles. Those who accept the common authorship of these books respond that the variation in terminology is determined by the context—for example, that Ezra-Nehemiah uses the usual postexilic designation for the high priest while Chronicles uses the older title appropriately for the period of the monarchy. The evidence is not decisive either way. It seems safer to regard Ezra-Nehemiah as an independent composition that has much in common with Chronicles but deals with a distinct period of Jewish history and has its own distinctive concerns.

The content of Ezra-Nehemiah may be outlined as follows.

Ezra 1–6: the return of the exiles and the building of the temple. These events took place more than half a century before the time of Ezra and are reported here on the basis of source documents. The sources include the decree of King Cyrus of Persia authorizing the return (1:2-4, Hebrew; 6:3-5, Aramaic; 5:13-15, Aramaic paraphrase), the list of returnees (2:1-67), and various correspondence with the Persian court (4:7-22; 5:6-17; 6:6-12). All of 4:8—6:18 is in Aramaic, but this section cannot be regarded as a single source. Rather, it seems that the author cited an Aramaic document and then simply continued in Aramaic. We must assume that the author and the intended readership were bilingual. We shall meet a similar phenomenon in the book of Daniel. This section is complicated by the fact that the author groups together related material at the cost of disrupting the historical sequence. At the end of chapter 1, the leader of the Judean community at the time of Cyrus's decree in 539 B.C.E. is named Sheshbazzar. In chapter 3, the rebuilding of the temple is undertaken by the high priest Joshua and Zerubbabel son of Shealtiel, with no mention of Sheshbazzar. These events can be dated to the reign of King Darius (520 B.C.E.). Yet in 5:16 we are told that Sheshbazzar came and laid the foundations of the temple. In between we find correspondence addressed to King Artaxerxes (486–465) and Darius (522–486). Evidently, the principle governing the composition is thematic rather than chronological. These chapters, which are largely a patchwork of source documents, are invaluable as a source of historical information, but it is clear that they are by no means a simple, straightforward narrative of the events.

The Ezra memoir. The account of the mission of Ezra is found in Ezra 7–10 and continued in Nehemiah 8–9 (actually beginning in Neh 7:73b). This account contains both first and third person narratives. Sources incorporated in this account include the commission of King Artaxerxes to Ezra (Ezra 7:12-26), the list of those who returned with Ezra (8:1-14), and the list of those who had been involved in mixed marriages (10:8-43).

The Nehemiah memoir. The account of the career of Nehemiah is found in the first person account in Neh 1:1—7:73a. Nehemiah 11–13 also pertains to the career of Nehemiah. These chapters include material from various sources, including a first person memoir (e.g., 12:31-43 and 13:4-31).

It is apparent from this summary that Ezra-Nehemiah reports events from three distinct episodes in the first century after the return from the exile: the initial return and rebuilding of the temple, the career of Ezra, and the career of Nehemiah. It is generally believed that these reports were compiled and edited sometime after the mission of Nehemiah, probably around 400 B.C.E.

The Initial Return

Fig. 21.1 The tomb of Cyrus in Pasargades, Iran. Commons.wikimedia.org

The decree of Cyrus, with which the book of Ezra begins, accords well with what we know of Persian policy toward the conquered peoples. An inscription on a clay barrel known as the Cyrus Cylinder (*ANET*, 315–16) reflects the way the Persian king presented himself to the people of Babylon. Marduk, god of Babylon, he claimed, had grown angry with the Babylonian king Nabonidus for neglecting his cult, and had summoned Cyrus to set things right. According to the decree in Ezra 1, he told the Judeans that it was "YHWH the God of heaven" who had given him the kingdoms of the earth and had charged him to build the temple in Jerusalem. Some scholars believe that the Hebrew edict in Ezra 1 is the text of a proclamation by a herald; others suspect that it is the composition of the author of Ezra-Nehemiah, based on the Aramaic edict preserved in Ezra 6:3-5. The latter edict says nothing about Cyrus's indebtedness to YHWH but simply orders that the temple be rebuilt to certain specifications and that the vessels taken by Nebuchadnezzar be restored. The authenticity of the Aramaic edict is not in dispute.

A noteworthy feature of the initial restoration is the designation of Sheshbazzar as "Prince of Judah." "Prince" (Hebrew *nasi'*) is the old title for the leader of the tribes in the Priestly strand of the Pentateuch and is also the preferred title for the Davidic ruler in Ezekiel (e.g., Ezek 34:23-24; 37:24-25). The use of this title strongly suggests that Sheshbazzar was descended from the line of David and so was a potential heir to the throne. His name does not appear in the genealogies of Chronicles, however. He has sometimes been identified with Shenazzar, who is listed as a son of Jeconiah, the exiled king of Judah, in 1 Chron 3:18. The names are different, but the suspicion that Sheshbazzar must have been a Davidide remains. Zerubbabel, who appears to have succeeded Sheshbazzar as governor of Judah, is listed as a grandson of Jeconiah in 1 Chron 3:19, but as son of Pedaiah rather than of Shealtiel as in the books of Ezra and Haggai. Interestingly enough, Ezra draws no attention to Zerubbabel's Davidic ancestry. The editors of Ezra-Nehemiah were loyal Persian subjects with no sympathy for messianic dreams. The predominance of priests and Levites in the list of returned exiles presumably reflects the historical reality but also reflects the priestly

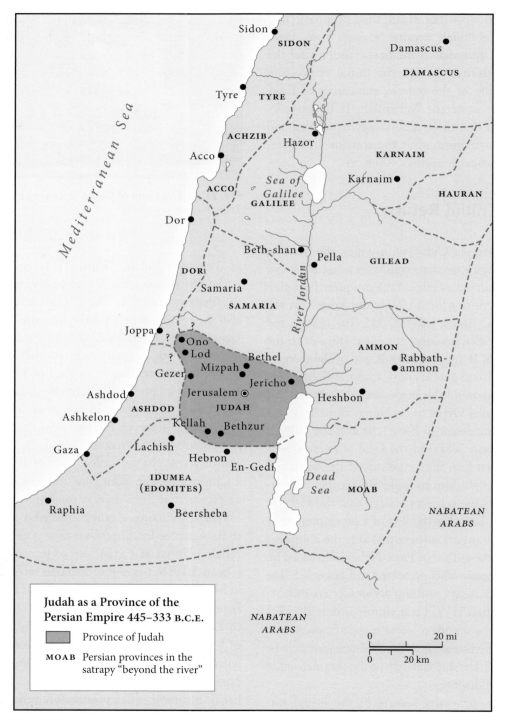

Judah as a Province of the Persian Empire 445–333 B.C.E.

    Province of Judah

MOAB Persian provinces in the satrapy "beyond the river"

Map 21.1

orientation of the author or editor, which is similar to that of Chronicles.

Sheshbazzar disappears quickly and silently from the stage of history. According to Ezra 5:16, it was he who laid the foundation of the temple. Yet in Ezra 3 it is Joshua and Zerubbabel who take the lead in rebuilding the temple, and the book of Zechariah explicitly credits Zerubbabel with laying the foundation (Zech 4:9). Zerubbabel's activity was in the reign of Darius, nearly two decades after the return. The book of Ezra, however, obscures the lapse of time. The uncritical reader most readily supposes that the "seventh month" of Ezra 3:1, when Joshua and Zerubbabel build the altar, is in the year of the initial return. Similarly Ezra 3:8 says that Zerubbabel and Joshua laid the foundation "in the second year after their return." If this is true, however, then Joshua and Zerubbabel must have been part of a second return some eighteen years after the initial one. The description of the mixed reaction of the people when they saw the foundation of the new temple (Ezra 3:12-13) is paralleled in Hag 2:3, which also notes that some people were disappointed with its reduced size.

The account in Ezra obscures the fact that there was a lapse of approximately twenty years between the initial return and the eventual building of the temple. The book of Haggai explains this delay by suggesting that people were more concerned to build their own houses than to rebuild the temple. In the book of Ezra, any delay in the rebuilding is explained by the opposition of "the adversaries of Judah" (4:1). These people offered to join in the building, "for we worship your God as you do, and we have been sacrificing to him ever since the days of King Esarhaddon of Assyria

who brought us here." The implication is that the people who were in the land when the exiles returned were the descendants of the settlers brought to northern Israel by the Assyrians (2 Kgs 17:24; the king is identified in the context as Shalmaneser). It is indeed likely that the people of Samaria, who had their own governor, hoped to exercise influence over Jerusalem. But there must also have been some people who were native Judeans who had not been deported and who expected, reasonably enough, to be included in the community around the Second Temple. The leaders of the exiles, however, took a strictly exclusivist position: "But Zerubbabel, Jeshua, and the rest of the heads of families in Israel said to them, 'You shall have no part with us in building a house to our God; but we alone will build to the LORD, the God of Israel, as King Cyrus of Persia has commanded us'" (Ezra 4:3). The exiles evidently regarded themselves as a pure community, which should not be mingled with "the people of the land." This rejection of cooperation, even from fellow Yahwists, was a fateful decision, and set the stage for centuries of tensions between the Jewish community that was centered on the temple and its neighbors.

The correspondence cited to show the opposition to the returnees is out of chronological order. The letter in Ezra 4:11-22 is addressed to King Artaxerxes (probably Artaxerxes I, 465–424 B.C.E.) and is concerned with the rebuilding of the city walls, not with the temple. The city walls were the great preoccupation of Nehemiah, who was active in Jerusalem in the reign of Artaxerxes. This document is inserted into the account of the building of the temple to explain the delay in the construction. According to Ezra

4:17-22, the king ordered that the work be stopped. In contrast, the second letter, in 5:6-17, is addressed to Darius and concerns the rebuilding of the temple. Ezra 6 records the response of Darius, authorizing the continuation of the building of the temple. The impression is given that the Persian authorities vacillated, whether through indecision or simply through bureaucratic incompetence. If the letter to Artaxerxes is restored to its proper context, however, there is no indecision on the part of the Persians with regard to the temple. The rebuilding had been authorized, and the objections were overruled. We shall return to the question of the walls when we discuss the career of Nehemiah.

The Career of Ezra

In Ezra 7:1 the narrative jumps back to the reign of Artaxerxes. Ezra, we are told, went up from Babylon to Jerusalem in the seventh year of that king. The date is ambiguous. There were three Persian kings named Artaxerxes: Artaxerxes I (465–424 B.C.E.), Artaxerxes II (405/404–359/358) and Artaxerxes III (359/358–338). Most scholars assume that the reference in Ezra is to Artaxerxes I. The mission of Nehemiah can be dated with confidence to the twentieth year of Artaxerxes I (445), and the biblical record places Ezra before Nehemiah. Nonetheless, there are problems with this dating, and a significant minority of scholars believes that Nehemiah came first and that Ezra was commissioned by Artaxerxes II in 398. If Ezra came first, then Nehemiah came a mere thirteen years later. Yet he encountered many of the same problems that had occupied Ezra, notably the problem of intermarriage with the neighboring peoples. We should have to assume then that Ezra's reforms were short-lived, and moreover that he had failed to ensure the security of Jerusalem by restoring the city walls. As we shall see, however, it is likely that his reforms *were* short-lived. Nehemiah complains that his policies were flouted when he returned to the royal court for a time between his two terms as governor. Ezra's policies, which required widespread divorce, must have been resented by many people. Moreover, Ezra was a religious reformer, and so it is not surprising that he failed to concern himself with the city walls. The evidence is not conclusive, but the biblical order of Ezra and Nehemiah remains the more probable.

Ezra is introduced as "a scribe skilled in the law of Moses" (Ezra 7:6). He was also a priest descended from Zadok and Aaron (7:1-6). He is sent to Jerusalem by the Persian king "to make inquiries about Judah and Jerusalem according to the law of your God, which is in your hand," and also to convey an offering of silver and gold to the temple of YHWH. This mission makes good sense in light of general Persian policy. The Persian king Darius I spoke often in his inscriptions of his laws and his "ordinance of good relations." He was widely revered as a legislator in antiquity. The Persians, however, did not impose uniform laws on all their subjects. Rather, their policy was to support local priests and cults, and thereby win their loyalty and that of the local populations.

In the year 519 BCE, Darius ordered his satrap in Egypt to assemble a commission of priests, soldiers and scribes, to gather in writing all the laws of Egypt from the time before the Persian conquest. Many scholars have assumed that this was part of a program to codify the local laws within the empire, and that he would have demanded Judeans also to collect their laws. If this is correct, then the Torah was produced at the behest of the Persian rulers. But there is no record of such collection of laws outside of Egypt. The Egyptian scribes produced two copies of their laws, one in Demotic (late Egyptian) and one in Aramaic. The Torah was only produced in Hebrew and could not be read by the Persians without the aid of a translator. Nonetheless, there is good evidence that the Persians allowed their subjects to live by their traditional laws. According to Ezra 7, the initiative for Ezra's mission seems to have come from Ezra rather than from the king, but royal authorization would have been necessary in order for Ezra's law to be proclaimed in Jerusalem.

An example of Persian authorization of the regulation of Jewish cult has survived in the form of the so-called Passover Papyrus, from 419 B.C.E., which is part of an archive of Aramaic papyri relating to a Jewish community at Elephantine in southern Egypt. This papyrus gives instructions for the observance of the Feast of Unleavened Bread, conveyed to the satrap by authority of Darius II. It is unlikely that any Persian king had much interest in the details of Jewish law. The initiative surely came from Jewish leaders, but they required Persian authorization to enforce their regulations. There is a parallel to the career of Ezra in the case of an Egyptian priest named Udjahoressnet, who collaborated with the Persian king Cambyses and used his influence to restore a sanctuary. Udjahoressnet was subsequently taken to Persia, presumably as an adviser on Egyptian affairs. He was eventually sent back to Egypt with the mission of restoring the scribal houses. The mission of Ezra must be seen in the context of this Persian policy of co-opting loyal subjects and allowing them to regulate their local cults.

The Law of Ezra

The identity of the law that Ezra brought from Babylon is a question of great interest. In Jewish tradition Ezra is revered as the person who restored the law of Moses, and it is generally assumed that his law was the Torah as we have it. Some modern scholars also credit Ezra with the final edition of the Pentateuch, incorporating the Priestly strand. There are numerous echoes of Deuteronomic law in Ezra and Nehemiah. These are especially prominent in connection with the issue of intermarriage, as we shall see below. The prayers in Ezra 9 and Nehemiah 9 have a strongly Deuteronomic character. But it is also clear that Ezra knew some form of the Priestly legislation. This appears especially in

Fig. 21.2 The Behistun relief of Darius I, depicting him giving orders to captives from various nations and describing his conquests in Old Persian, Elamite, and Babylonian languages; Mount Behistun, Iran. Commons .wikimedia.org

the regulations for the observation of the festivals of Tabernacles (Sukkoth) and Passover. But there are also some details that do not conform either to Deuteronomic or to Priestly law. The most important example concerns the festivals of the seventh month (Tishri) in Nehemiah 8–9. On the first day of the month, Ezra conducts a solemn reading and explanation of the Torah. This is the date set for Rosh Hashanah, the New Year's Festival, in Lev 23:24. Leviticus speaks of a holy convocation, accompanied by trumpet blasts, but does not mention a reading of the law. There are no trumpet blasts in Nehemiah. In Neh 8:13-17 we are told that on the second day of the month the people discovered the commandment about the Festival of Tabernacles and proceeded to observe it by making booths and living in them. We are told that this practice had not been observed since the time of Joshua, son of Nun. In Lev 23:34 this festival is supposed to be observed on the fifteenth of the month. Most notable is the discrepancy concerning Yom Kippur, the Day of Atonement, which is legislated for the tenth of the month in Lev 23:27. There is no mention of Yom Kippur in Nehemiah, and there is no observance on the tenth of the month. There is, however, a day of fasting and repentance on the twenty-fourth day of the seventh month in Neh 9:1. The simplest explanation of these discrepancies is that the cultic calendar had not yet taken its final shape when the books of Ezra and Nehemiah were edited. There are several other minor discrepancies, such as the variation in the amount of the temple tax (one-third of a shekel in Neh 10:32 but one half in P, Exod 30:11-16). Since taxation tends to increase rather than decrease, this is probably another indication that the Priestly

legislation had not reached its final form in the time of Ezra. Nonetheless, it remains true that the law of Ezra corresponds substantially to the Torah as we know it, including both Deuteronomy and some form of the Priestly code.

According to the account of Ezra-Nehemiah, the people of Jerusalem had no knowledge of the book of the law before Ezra's arrival. In fact, the prophetic oracles of Haggai, Zechariah, and Third Isaiah, which date to the period before Ezra, never appeal to such a book. Yet at some point, the book of the Torah was recognized as the law of Judah. Ezra is the person credited with this momentous innovation in the biblical tradition.

The Problem of Intermarriage

The dominant issue in Ezra's time in Jerusalem, however, is not the cultic calendar but intermarriage. According to Ezra 9:1-2, after Ezra had arrived in Jerusalem and presented his credentials, "the officials approached me and said, 'The people of Israel, the priests, and the Levites have not separated themselves from the peoples of the lands with their abominations, from the Canaanites, the Hittites, the Perizzites, the Jebusites, the Ammonites, the Moabites, the Egyptians, and the Amorites. For they have taken some of their daughters as wives for themselves and for their sons. Thus the holy seed has mixed itself with the peoples of the lands, and in this faithlessness the officials and leaders have led the way.'"

We do not know exactly who the officials were who made the complaint. They were evidently not identical with the officials who led the way "in this faithlessness." The practice of intermarriage was evidently a cause of some division within the community even before Ezra arrived. The "peoples of the lands" are identified in traditional biblical terms (cf. the lists in Gen 15:19-21; Exod 3:8, 17; Deut 7:1; et al.). Some of the names on this list were of immediate relevance (Ammonites, Moabites, Edomites), while others were obsolete, as the peoples no longer existed (Jebusites, Hittites). We must assume, however, that the primary temptation to intermarriage came from the descendants of the Judeans who had never gone into exile and from the Samaritans. These people were not regarded as members of the Jewish community, at least by purists such as Ezra. The attraction of intermarriage, apart from the normal development of human relations, was compounded by the economic situation. The returning exiles presumably hoped to recover their ancestral property in Judah. Those who had occupied the land in the meantime presumably did not want to cede possession of it now. (The book of Ezekiel touches on an early stage of this problem in Ezek 11:15: "your own kinsfolk, your own kin, your fellow exiles, the whole house of Israel, all of them, are those of whom the inhabitants of Jerusalem have said, 'They have gone far from the Lord; to us this land is given as a possession.'") We are never told whether the returnees were allowed to take possession of their ancestral lands. One way in which they might recover rights of inheritance in Judah was by intermarriage.

It is noteworthy that Ezra is only concerned about Jewish men who take foreign wives (note, however, that Nehemiah also objects to intermarriage with foreign men, Neh 13:25). Jewish women who married outside the community did not endanger the patrimony, since they inherited only if there were no male heirs (Numbers 27). Such women were no longer part of the Jewish community. Jewish men who married foreign women, however, brought them into the community and so "mixed the holy seed." An alternative explanation is also possible. In later Judaism a child was recognized as Jewish if his or her mother was Jewish (this is called the "matrilineal principle"). We do not know whether this principle was in effect in the time of Ezra. If it was, then the children of Jewish women would still be Jewish, even if the fathers were not, whereas the children of foreign women would not be so.

The prohibition of intermarriage is based on two passages in Deuteronomy. Chapter 7 orders the Israelites to destroy utterly the seven nations who inhabited the land before them: Hittites, Girgashites, Ammonites, Canaanites, Perizzites, Hivites, and Jebusites. It adds, "Do not intermarry with them, giving your daughters to their sons or taking their daughters for your sons, for that would turn away your children from following me, to serve other gods." In this case, idolatry seems to be the issue, and the prohibition applies equally whether the marriage is with foreign men or foreign women. Deuteronomy 23:3-8 declares categorically: "No Ammonite or Moabite shall be admitted to the assembly of the Lord." But the passage continues in 23:7-8: "You shall not abhor any of the Edomites, for they are your kin. You shall not abhor any of the Egyptians, because you were an alien residing in their land. The children of the third generation that are born to them may be admitted to the assembly of the Lord." It is apparent that Ezra's prohibition of intermarriage is broader than either of these, because it includes the Egyptians. The point, then, is not just strict observance of the law, but bespeaks a more extreme fear of contact with outsiders. Moreover, Ezra provides a new rationale for the prohibition. The danger is not just that those who worship other gods might lead the Israelites into idolatry, but that the "holy seed" would be defiled by the union itself. This is quite a novel idea in the Hebrew Bible and presupposes a greater gulf between Jew and Gentile than anything we have seen hitherto. This idea is rooted in the self-identity of the exilic community as a pure and holy remnant, and its determination to keep that character pristine.

Ezra, we are told, reacted to this situation dramatically. "When I heard this, I tore my garment and my mantle, and pulled hair from my head and beard, and sat appalled." The people who shared his outrage are described as "those who trembled at the words of the God of Israel" (Ezra 9:4; the Hebrew word for "tremblers," *haredim,* is the same word that is used for the ultraorthodox in modern Israel). The same word is used for the pious in Isa 66:2, 5, in a passage that also dates from the postexilic period. It is reasonable to suppose that there was a continuous party of rigorists in this period, but they were evidently in the minority and lacked political strength until Ezra arrived. Ezra makes a public prayer that bears a strong imprint of Deuteronomic theology. Israel is unworthy, but God has shown mercy. Yet Israel has again been unfaithful. At the center of the prayer is a loose paraphrase of Lev 18:24-30, claiming that the previous inhabitants of the land had defiled themselves, and of Deut 7:3-4, forbidding intermarriage with either men or women of these peoples. Ezra assumes, as had those who made the complaint in Ezra 9:1, that those outside the community of the returned exiles can be equated with the ancient Canaanites who had occupied the land before the emergence of Israel. This assumption is never justified.

The solution to the problem is allegedly proposed to Ezra by one Shecaniah, son of Jehiel, of the descendants of Elam. Elam was a province of Persia (cf. Dan 8:2). A large contingent of "descendants of Elam" had been part of the initial return from the exile (Ezra 2:7). Interestingly enough, the list of those who had married foreign women in Ezra 10 has six descendants of Elam, including Jehiel. If this is indeed the father of Shecaniah, we need not assume that the foreign woman in question was the latter's mother. Jehiel may have taken more than one wife. We can easily imagine how the son might have resented this arrangement, whether his mother had been divorced or just forced to accept a cowife. If this was the case, there may have been more to the dispute than zeal for purity. Rights of inheritance may also have been at issue. It is possible, however, that there was more than one Jehiel among the descendants of Elam.

The solution proposed by Shecaniah was drastic: "Let us make a covenant with our God to send away all these wives and their children" (Ezra 10:3). This action was not taken without some coercion. Members of "the congregation of the exiles" were ordered to appear in Jerusalem within three days or have their property forfeited. Then they were made to assemble in the open square before the temple in inclement weather until they "trembled" not only because of the matter at hand but also because of the heavy rain. Finally, the people agreed to separate from their foreign wives but pleaded that they not have to stand in the rain. A commission was established to oversee the matter, and within two months all foreign wives had been divorced. Ezra 10 provides a long list of the transgressors. The chapter ends on a chilling note: "All these had married foreign women, and they sent them away with their children" (10:44). We are not told where they went; presumably they returned to their fathers' houses. Ezra claims that only two citizens, supported by two Levites, opposed this solution. We may wonder, however, whether there was such near-unanimity on such a contentious issue. I have suggested in chapter 20 on the postexilic prophets that Mal 2:10-16, which condemns divorce, can be read as a protest against Ezra's enforced policy. There is no evidence in Ezra that these people had divorced Jewish wives before they married the foreign women. While Malachi disapproved of the marriage to women who worshiped other gods ("the daughter of a foreign god," Mal 2:11), he insisted that what God wanted was "godly offspring." Ezra, however, made no attempt to convert the foreign women or their children. Both women and children were sent away.

Ezra and Nehemiah

Further material relating to Ezra can be found in Nehemiah 8–9. (In 1 Esdras the material in Neh 8:1-13 follows directly on that of Ezra 1–10.) Nehemiah 8 deals with the festivals of the seventh month, a subject we have already discussed. Some have suggested that this material may have originally belonged after Ezra 8, before the incident with the foreign wives. Nehemiah 9 contains another long prayer in the tradition of Deuteronomic theology, confessing that Israel was rightly punished for failing to keep the covenant. This prayer is ascribed to Ezra in the text, but it may be a traditional theme. It fails conspicuously to focus on the problem of mixed marriages that is so central to the concerns of Ezra. Like the prayer in Ezra 9, it is representative of a kind of prayer that is widespread and typical of Second Temple Judaism. Another biblical example is found in Daniel 9, and yet another in Bar 2:11—3:8. All these prayers are profoundly informed by Deuteronomic theology, according to which the fortunes of the people of Israel are closely tied to their obedience or disobedience with respect to the Torah.

We do not know how long Ezra remained in Jerusalem. Nehemiah 8:9 claims that he and Nehemiah acted together in leading the people in the celebration of the first day of the seventh month (Rosh Hashanah). On the usual chronology, Nehemiah came to Jerusalem thirteen years after Ezra. It is inconceivable, however, that Ezra would have waited until then to attend to the observance of the festivals of the seventh month. Ezra and Nehemiah are mentioned together again in Neh 12:26, in a note associating them with the high priest Joiakim, and in 12:36, which claims that Ezra was present at the dedication of Nehemiah's walls. It is clear that the editor of Ezra-Nehemiah wanted to give the impression that they were contemporaries. Yet Nehemiah plays no part in Ezra's reform, and Ezra plays no part in Nehemiah's attempt to fortify Jerusalem. Most scholars conclude that the two men were not active in Jerusalem at the same time.

It does not seem that Ezra's reform had any lasting impact in Jerusalem. Nehemiah also had to deal with mixed marriages. If Ezra preceded him by thirteen years, as is usually supposed, then Ezra's influence must have been short-lived. Even if we suppose that Ezra came later, his reform had no lasting effect, as we hear even of high priests who intermarried and adopted Gentile ways in later times. Some scholars have supposed that Ezra was removed abruptly by the Persians, in response to complaints by citizens whose lives he had disrupted. This is certainly possible, but there is no evidence to support it. Later, in rabbinic tradition, Ezra was revered, but he receives little attention before the end of the Second Temple period. Ben Sira, the Jerusalem scribe who wrote his book of wisdom in the early second century B.C.E., appended to it a long "Praise of the Fathers," in which he sang the praises of the great men of Israel and Judah down to his own time. Nehemiah is included, but Ezra is not. We can only guess at the reason for the omission. It is possible that Ezra did not always enjoy the reputation that he later did in the rabbinic writings.

The Nehemiah Memoir

The core of the book of Nehemiah is provided by a first person account, known as the "Nehemiah memoir," which gives a forceful account of Nehemiah's career from his own point of view. Various analogies have been proposed to illustrate the genre of this account. Ancient Near Eastern kings often set up inscriptions to record and glorify their deeds. Nehemiah's account, however, is distinguished by its apologetic character. It is largely an attempt to justify himself and his actions. He appeals frequently to God to "remember for my good . . . all that I have done for this people" (Neh 5:19; cf. 13:14, 22, 31). A closer parallel than the royal inscriptions may be found in Egyptian autobiographical texts that were addressed to a deity and deposited in a temple (examples can be found in M. Lichtheim, *Ancient Egyptian Literature*, vol. 3: *The Late Period* [Berkeley: Univ. of California Press, 1980], 13–65). The call on a god to "remember" is common in dedicatory or votive inscriptions, especially in Aramaic. Finally, comparisons have been made with the psalms of individual complaint (Psalms 3, 5, 7, et al.), in which the psalmist complains that he is unjustly accused. Neither the inscriptions nor the psalms, however, provide a close analogy for Nehemiah's account. It has also been suggested that Nehemiah was required to write a report for the Persian court in response to the complaints of his enemies. Nehemiah's defense, however, is addressed to God rather than to the king, and so we must assume that such a report, if it existed, was adapted by Nehemiah so as to present his case in the context of the Jewish community.

Nehemiah's account begins in "the twentieth year" of Artaxerxes. Since some of the figures who appear in the account (notably Sanballat of Samaria, and possibly Nehemiah's brother Hanani) are also known from the Elephantine papyri, there is no doubt that the reference is to Artaxerxes I, and so the mission of Nehemiah can be dated with confidence to 445 B.C.E. (The Elephantine papyri are Aramaic documents pertaining to a Jewish community in the south of Egypt in the fifth century B.C.E.) At the outset of the narrative, Nehemiah is a cupbearer to the king. This was a position of considerable importance. The cupbearer had immediate access to the king and was in a position to give him informal advice. One of the most famous, legendary wise men of antiquity, Ahikar, is said to have been cupbearer to the Assyrian king

Esarhaddon (Tob 1:22). Some manuscripts of the Greek (LXX) translation of Nehemiah say that he was a eunuch, but this is evidently a scribal error. (The Greek word for "cupbearer" is *oinochoos;* "eunuch" is *eunouchos.* Some cupbearers in antiquity were eunuchs, but not all. Ministers at court were required to be eunuchs if they had significant responsibilities for the royal harem.)

The impetus for Nehemiah's mission comes from a report from his brother Hanani, who had visited Judah, that the people there were in great trouble, that the wall was broken down, and that the gates had been destroyed by fire. Some scholars have supposed that the reference here is to some recent act of destruction. One ingenious proposal links this event to the letter that is found out of context in Ezra 4, and which preserves a complaint addressed to Artaxerxes about attempts to rebuild the walls of Jerusalem. On that occasion, the king issued an order that the work be stopped, and those who had made the complaint made the Judeans comply "by force and power" (4:23). The book of Nehemiah implies that Nehemiah had Persian authorization for rebuilding the wall, and so the correspondence in Ezra 4 cannot relate to his mission. There is no evidence that the walls of Jerusalem had been rebuilt after the destruction by Nebuchadnezzar. Hanani's report may have been that the wall was still broken down more than a hundred years later.

The mission of Nehemiah is undertaken at his own request. His purpose is specifically to rebuild the walls of Jerusalem. He is granted the commission, and also a military escort, because of his personal standing with the king. At first, it would seem that a brief mission was envisioned. In Neh 5:14, however,

we learn that he was appointed governor of Judah, and that he occupied the position for twelve years. Then he returned to the court, but shortly afterward he returned for a second stint, of uncertain duration (13:6-7). It is evident that Nehemiah had a forceful personality, and it is not clear how far his actions were actually authorized by the Persians. In any case, he prevailed over his opponents and retained the approval of the king.

Nehemiah's great preoccupation on his first visit to Jerusalem was the rebuilding of the city walls. He did not announce publicly his intention of rebuilding. He inspected the walls by night and tried to present his adversaries with a fait accompli. The opposition was led by "Sanballat the Horonite and Tobiah the Ammonite official, and Geshem the Arab" (2:19). Sanballat is known from the Elephantine papyri as governor of Samaria. The name Tobiah is associated with the powerful family of the Tobiads, who lived in Transjordan (modern Jordan) and who were still a powerful force in Judean politics in the second century B.C.E. The name Sanballat honors the Babylonian moon-god, Sin, but this is not necessarily significant, as some Yahwistic Jews also had Babylonian names (e.g., Zerubbabel). The name Tobiah, in contrast, means "Yahweh is good," and suggests that its bearer worshiped the God of the Jews.

Sanballat, Tobiah, and their friends express concern that Nehemiah was rebelling against the king (2:19). Later they claimed that Nehemiah wanted to make himself king (6:6-7). Significantly, however, they are not said to complain to the Persian court. They appear to have accepted Nehemiah's royal authorization. Instead, the opponents only ridiculed the endeavor (4:1-3) and allegedly

Fig. 21.3 A petition from the Jewish community in Elephantine, Egypt, to the governor of Judah concerning the rebuilding of a temple that had been destroyed by pagans; ca. 407 B.C.E. letter from the Elephantine Papyri, The Passover Letter from Elephantine, Egypt, ca. 419 C.E.; now in the Brooklyn Museum. Commons.wikimedia.org

set a trap for Nehemiah, which he was smart enough to resist (6:1-9). These people were clearly involved in a power struggle with Nehemiah. His actions can be understood as an attempt to make Jerusalem independent of Samaria and Ammon, the home turf of Sanballat and Tobiah. He was not attempting to achieve independence from Persia. On the contrary, the distant Persian monarch was the source of his authority, by which he hoped to free Judah from the influence of its immediate neighbors.

In addition to political problems, Nehemiah also had to deal with a severe economic crisis because of a famine. According to Nehemiah 5, there was a great outcry because people had to pledge their fields and houses to get grain. Some were forced to sell sons and daughters as slaves, and some daughters were ravished. The root of the problem (apart from drought, which probably precipitated the crisis) was "the king's tax" (5:4). We do not have

much specific information about Persian taxation in Judah, but it was evidently oppressive.

Nehemiah was not about to challenge the king's tax, since his own authority derived from the king. He did, however, challenge the practices of Jews who took pledges from their brethren. Already the Book of the Covenant (Exod 22:25-27) forbade taking interest from the poor or holding their belongings. ("If you take your neighbor's coat in pawn you shall restore it before the sun goes down. . . . In what else shall that person sleep?") There is a similar provision in Deut 24:10-13. Nonetheless, debt was an endemic problem in ancient Israel and Judah, in both the monarchic and the postexilic periods, sometimes leading to the loss of ancestral property and sometimes to slavery (cf. Amos 8:6; Isa 5:8). The word that the NRSV translates as "interest" in Neh 5:11 is literally "the percentage, or one-hundredth." It has been suggested that this reflects a rate of one percent per month, or 12 percent per annum. This would be a relatively modest rate by ancient standards. In the Persian period the accepted rate was 20 percent, and higher rates were also known. Nonetheless, it is clear that the rate taken in Judah was more than the people could afford.

Leviticus 25:47-55 provides for the redemption of slaves and stipulates that any slaves who had not been redeemed should go free in the Jubilee Year. Nehemiah claims that he, or the Jewish community, had redeemed Jews who had been sold to other nations. It is not clear to what this claim refers. It may have been a practice either in Babylon or in Judah. Moreover, Nehemiah admits that his own family and servants have been lending at interest. This confession reduces the antagonism of his proposal and makes it easier to win the sympathy of the offenders. Nehemiah's proposal amounts to a remission of debt and restoration of property, such as was envisioned in the Jubilee Year in Leviticus 25. Such remissions were granted periodically in the ancient Near East, often at the beginning of the reign of a new king. There is a famous example in the case of King Ammisaduqa of Babylon in the seventeenth century B.C.E. (*ANET* 526–28). During the Babylonian crisis, Zedekiah made a covenant with the people so that they should set free their Hebrew slaves, but subsequently they took them back again (Jer 34:8-11). The problem was that such reforms tended to be short-lived. We do not know how long Nehemiah's reforms remained in effect. It is unlikely that they outlived his governorship.

The problem of intermarriage appears again in the second term of Nehemiah. In Nehemiah 13 we are told that "on the day they read from the book of Moses . . . it was found written that no Ammonite or Moabite should ever enter the assembly of God. . . . When the people heard the law they separated from Israel all those of foreign descent." It seems incredible that anyone would have been unaware of this law less than a generation after Ezra's reform. This passage, however, only serves as an introduction to a confrontation between Nehemiah and "the priest Eliashib" who had given a room in the temple to Tobiah the Ammonite, to whom he was related. The episode illustrates the violent character of Nehemiah: "I threw all the household furniture of Tobiah out of the room" (Neh 13:8). It also shows the difficulty of instituting any lasting reform. Tobiah had been ensconced in the temple when Nehemiah was recalled to the Persian court. We learn in 13:28 that one of the grandsons of Eliashib

was the son-in-law of Sanballat of Samaria. The purist policies of Ezra and Nehemiah could not erase the ties that bound the high priesthood in Jerusalem to the upper classes of the neighboring peoples.

It appears that Nehemiah's first term as governor was largely occupied with the security of Jerusalem and the building of the wall. In his second term he devoted more of his attention to religious problems. In 13:15-22 we read of his attempts to enforce the observance of the Sabbath. The book ends with yet another problem involving intermarriage. "In those days also I saw Jews who had married women of Ashdod, Ammon, and Moab, and half of their children spoke the language of Ashdod, and they could not speak the language of Judah. . . . And I contended with them and cursed them and beat some of them and pulled out their hair" (13:23-27). We can appreciate Nehemiah's concern for the erosion of Jewish identity. His tactics in beating people who did not conform, however, are uncomfortably reminiscent of the behavior of the Taliban when they were in control of Afghanistan.

Nehemiah emerges from his memoir as a person of great integrity. We should bear in mind, of course, that we only have his own account and that it has a clear apologetic character. If Eliashib had left a memoir, he would presumably have shown things in a quite different light. Nonetheless, we cannot doubt Nehemiah's sincerity. He insists that he sought no personal gain and did not even avail of the allowance traditionally given to the governor (Neh 5:14-19). His legacy was less controversial than that of Ezra. In the words of Ben Sira: "The memory of Nehemiah also is lasting; he raised our fallen walls" (Sir 49:13).

Conclusion

The most controversial issue in the books of Ezra and Nehemiah is undoubtedly the attempts to deal with the problem of intermarriage, especially in the case of Ezra. Ezra's action in expelling the "foreign" women and their children must be understood in the context of a small community that felt itself to be beleaguered and was struggling to maintain its identity. While this particular measure may not have had any lasting effect, the policy of separatism, the insistence of firm boundaries between Jew and Gentile, laid the foundation for the preservation of Jewish identity from antiquity to the present. The Ammonites, Moabites, and Edomites have long since disappeared from history. Ezra, then, must be given credit for his efforts to preserve the heritage of Judaism. Nonetheless,

the treatment of the women and children in Ezra 10 is one of the lower points of the biblical record. It does not offend modern sensibilities to the same extent as the slaughter of the Canaanites in Deuteronomy and Joshua, but it is nonetheless offensive. It is one of the more egregious cases in the Bible where considerations of purity and religious belief of one group (the "holy seed") take precedence over the basic rights of those who do not belong to that group. Such actions are not only offensive to modern sensibilities but are also counter to the teaching of the prophets and to some strands, at least, of the Torah. The book of Malachi can be read in part as a protest against these policies. We find a very different approach to the Gentile world in the stories of Ruth and Jonah. Ezra's career in Jerusalem was short-lived. His purist interpretation of Judaism is contested even with the Hebrew Bible itself.

FOR FURTHER READING

Commentaries

J. Blenkinsopp, *Ezra-Nehemiah* (OTL; Philadelphia: Westminster, 1988). Defends the coherence of these books with Chronicles.

D. J. A. Clines, *Ezra, Nehemiah* (NCB; Grand Rapids: Eerdmans, 1984). Insightful and readable.

L. L. Grabbe, *Ezra-Nehemiah* (London: Routledge, 1998). Readable commentary with historical focus.

R. W. Klein, "The Books of Ezra and Nehemiah," *NIB* 3:663–851. Reliable historical commentary with homiletical reflections.

H. G. M. Williamson, *Ezra, Nehemiah* (WBC 16; Waco: Word, 1985). Detailed philological commentary. Assumes that Ezra and Nehemiah are independent of Chronicles.

Historical Background

J. L. Berquist, *Judaism in Persia's Shadow: A Social and Historical Approach* (Minneapolis: Fortress Press, 1995). Readable account of the Persian period.

J. Blenkinsopp, *Judaism. The First Phase: The Place of Ezra and Nehemiah in the Origins of Judaism* (Grand Rapids: Eerdmans, 2009). Historical issues in Ezra and Nehemiah.

P. Briant, *From Cyrus to Alexander: A History of the Persian Empire* (Winona Lake, IN: Eisenbrauns, 2002). Authoritative account of the historical context.

L. L. Grabbe, *A History of the Jews and Judaism in the Second Temple Period. Vol. 1. Yehud: A History of the Persian Province of Judah* (London: T&T Clark, 2004). Sourcebook with extensive bibliographies.

K. G. Hoglund, *Achaemenid Imperial Administration in Syria-Palestine and the Missions of Ezra and Nehemiah* (SBLDS 125; Atlanta: Scholars Press, 1992). Important discussion of the Persian context, drawing on archaeology.

On the question of Persian authorization of the Torah

G. N. Knoppers and B. M. Levinson, *The Pentateuch as Torah. New Models for Its Promulgation and Acceptance* (Winona Lake, IN: Eisenbrauns, 2007). Wide spectrum of positions on Persian authorization.

Kyong-Jin Lee, *The Authority and Authorization of the Torah in the Persian Period* (Leuven: Peeters, 2011). Comprehensive presentation of the evidence.

J. W. Watts, ed., *Persia and Torah* (Symposium series; Atlanta: SBL, 2001). Seminal collection of essays.

Other Studies

C. Hayes, *Gentile Impurities and Jewish Identities* (Oxford: Oxford University Press, 2002), 19–44. Shows the novel character of Ezra's notion of a "holy seed."

D. Janzen, *Witch-Hunts, Purity and Social Boundaries: The Expulsion of Foreign Women in Ezra 9–10* (Sheffield: Sheffield Academic Press, 2002). Sociological and anthropological analysis of the marriage crisis.

J. Pakkala, *Ezra the Scribe*: *The Development of Ezra 7–10 and Nehemiah 8* (BZAW 347; Berlin: de Gruyter, 2004). Minute analysis of compositional strata.

K. E. Southwood, *Ethnicity and the Mixed Marriage Crisis in Ezra 9–10: An Anthropological Approach* (Oxford: Oxford University Press, 2012). Brings recent study of ethnicity to bear on Ezra's reform.

J. L. Wright, *Rebuilding Identity: The Nehemiah-Memoir and Its Earliest Readers* (BZAW 348; Berlin: de Gruyter, 2004). Minute analysis of compositional strata in Nehemiah memoir.

CHAPTER 22

The Books of Chronicles

INTRODUCTION

In this chapter, we will see how the distinctive themes and interests of the Chronicler stand in contrast with those of the Deuteronomistic History.

The books of 1 and 2 Chronicles constitute an alternative account of the history in the books of 2 Samuel and 1-2 Kings. They contain some material not found in the earlier books and apparently drew on some additional sources. The character of Chronicles, however, is most easily seen by comparing its narrative with that of Samuel and Kings. The secondary character of these books is recognized already in the Septuagint, where they are given the title *Paralipomena*, which means "things omitted" or "passed over." This characterization offers a justification of sorts for the inclusion of a second historical narrative in the biblical corpus. It is not an accurate description of Chronicles, as it is in fact a highly selective retelling of the older material. The title in the Hebrew Bible is *divrey hayyamim*, "the events of the days." The title "Chronicles" can be traced back to St. Jerome, who referred to the books as "Chronicon Totius Divinae Historiae," "the chronicle of the complete divine history."

The two books provide a continuous history, which can be divided into three parts:

- 1 Chronicles 1–9: Introduction;
- 1 Chronicles 10–2 Chronicles 9: the reigns of David and Solomon;
- 2 Chronicles 10–36: the history of Judah from the separation of the northern tribes.

Since 2 Chronicles concludes with a reference to the restoration of the Jews after the Babylonian exile by Cyrus of Persia (2 Chron 36:22-23 = Ezra 1:1-3a), this account was completed in the postexilic period. The genealogy of the house of David points to a date no earlier than 400 B.C.E. While there is no conclusive evidence as to the date, the late Persian period (early fourth century) is plausible. As we shall see, the history is colored to a great degree by the concerns of its time.

The character of Chronicles can be seen most readily by comparison and contrast with the books of Samuel and Kings. Most scholars see Chronicles as a rewriting of these books. A minority view holds that both histories drew on a common source, which would explain why Chronicles preserves independent traditions about the period of the monarchy.

1 Chronicles 1–9

The introductory material in 1 Chronicles 1–9 consists of extensive genealogies beginning with Adam and continuing down to postexilic times. The lists in the opening chapter derive primarily from Genesis and presuppose the Priestly edition of the primeval and patriarchal histories. The lists are highly condensed and move rapidly to Abraham and his descendants. The main focus is on the tribes of Israel. Although Judah is listed fourth among the sons of Jacob, his genealogy is presented first and at greatest length (2:3—4:23). The Chronicler acknowledges the sin of Er but skips over the episode of Onan and the encounter of Judah and Tamar. A few genealogies in this list have no biblical source: Caleb son of Hezron (2:18-24), Jerahmeel (2:25-41), and Caleb again (2:42-50). We do not know whether the Chronicler derived these genealogies from other sources or how old those putative sources might be. Chapter 3 is entirely devoted to the Davidic line. All the rulers of Judah are listed except Athaliah, the princess from northern Israel who usurped the throne (2 Kings 11). Most interesting here is the continuation of the genealogy after the end of the monarchy. The descendants of Jeconiah are listed for seven generations. Zerubbabel, the governor of Judah after the restoration, is listed as the grandson of Jeconiah. The extension of the list for five generations after Zerubbabel requires a date toward the end of the fifth century. It is also of interest that the Davidic line was known and traced well into the Persian period.

The other tribes that are accorded prominence in these genealogies are Levi and Benjamin. These were the tribes that remained faithful to the Davidic line and were also significant in the restoration of the postexilic period. The Levitical line is treated at length in 1 Chron 6:1-81. Benjamin is also treated at length in 8:1-40. Saul, the first king of Israel, is listed in the genealogy of Benjamin but receives no particular emphasis. The Chronicler returns to Saul, however, at the end of the genealogies in 9:35-44, where the notice prepares for the transition to the historical narrative proper, which begins with the death of Saul and the rise of David in chapter 10.

The remaining tribes are treated more briefly. The southern tribe of Simeon and the Transjordan tribes (Reuben, Gad, and the half-tribe of Manasseh) are discussed between Judah and Levi. The northern tribes west of the Jordan are compressed into 7:1-40. (There are some problems: Zebulun and Dan are missing, while there is an intrusive, duplicate genealogy of Benjamin.) Nonetheless, the inclusion of the northern tribes shows that the Chronicler conceived Israel as including them and did not equate it with the southern state of Judah.

The genealogical introduction concludes with a list of those who returned to form the postexilic community of Judah (9:1-44). These, we are told, included people of Judah, Benjamin, Ephraim, and Manasseh. The bulk of the list, however, is made up of priests, Levites, and various temple functionaries. The temple cult is given great prominence in the history that follows.

The Reigns of David and Solomon (1 Chronicles 10— 2 Chronicles 9)

David (1 Chronicles 10–29)

The history proper begins with the death of Saul. The Chronicler omits David's reaction to this event but adds his own evaluation: Saul died for his unfaithfulness and because he had consulted a medium for advice rather than relying on the Lord. He skips over the civil war between David and the house of Saul, and proceeds directly to the anointing of David as king at Hebron and the capture of Jerusalem. At this point, he inserts a list of David's officials that is an expanded form of the list in 2 Samuel 23. First Chronicles 12:1-22 tells of various people from Benjamin and Gad who joined with David while Saul was still alive. This passage has no basis in Samuel. This is followed by further lists of David's forces. Zadok, better known as a priest, appears here as "a young warrior" (12:28). The decision to bring the ark up to Jerusalem is reported in more detail than in 2 Samuel 6, with emphasis on the involvement of priests and Levites. The procession with the ark is interrupted when the unfortunate Uzzah touches it and dies (as in 2 Samuel 6–7), and is only resumed in 1 Chronicles 15, after the congratulations of Hiram of Tyre, reference to David's marriages and children in Jerusalem, and a Philistine campaign (1 Chronicles 14; cf. 2 Sam 5:11-25).

The interruption of the ark narrative allows time for David to prepare a place and pitch a tent for it. The completion of the narrative provides the occasion for the first major expansion of the narrative by the Chronicler. David decrees that no one but the Levites are to carry the ark. The Chronicler then provides lists of priests and Levites who are entrusted with this task, and also of the singers and cultic musicians. David, we are told, wore a robe of fine linen and a linen ephod. This rather dignified apparel does not fit well with the picture of the king leaping and dancing, thereby incurring the contempt of his wife Michal in 15:29 (cf. 2 Sam 5:20-23). Chronicles, however, omits the complaint of Michal that he had exposed himself and David's consequent rejection of her. The installation of the ark is followed by the singing of praise illustrated by a medley of passages from the Psalms (cf. Psalms 96, 106).

The report of Nathan's oracle, promising an everlasting dynasty to David, in 1 Chronicles 17 closely follows 2 Samuel 7. There are some crucial differences, however. First, Chronicles does not say that the Lord had given David rest (and therefore provided conditions suitable for building a temple). Second, there is no mention of punishment in the event of sin, as there is in the Deuteronomistic account in 2 Sam 7:14. Finally, the oracle concludes with an emphatic promise to "confirm him in my house and in my kingdom forever, and his throne shall be established forever" (1 Chron 17:14). The use of the first person pronoun here may be significant. "My house," spoken by God, can be understood as the temple. In that case the promise to the Davidic line may be linked to the temple in a way that was not at all the case in 2 Samuel 7.

There follows an account of David's wars in 1 Chronicles 18–20, drawn from 2 Samuel 8, 10, and 19–22. Most notable are the omissions. The entire episode with Bathsheba

(2 Samuel 11–12) is passed over, as is the rape of Tamar by Amnon and the subsequent rebellion of Absalom (2 Samuel 13–19). Also omitted are the stories of David's kindness to Saul's son Mephibosheth (2 Samuel 9), the rebellion of Sheba the Benjaminite (2 Samuel 20), and the psalms of David in 2 Samuel 22–23. While some of these passages would have reflected well on David, there seems to be a clear tendency to avoid stories that might be regarded as embarrassing or might detract from the portrayal of David as an ideal king.

Chronicles does, however, pick up the story of the census from 2 Samuel 24. Several discrepancies catch the eye. First, it is Satan who incites David to count the people. Satan is not yet here the devil, which he becomes in later Jewish and Christian mythology, but he is an adversary who puts people to the test. We have already encountered him in Zechariah 3. His most famous appearance in the Hebrew Bible is in the book of Job. Nothing more is said of his role here. In 2 Sam 24:1, David was incited by "the anger of the Lord."

Second, Levi and Benjamin are not included in the census. This may be due to their association with Jerusalem, which was subsequently exempted from the plague.

Third, the numbers in Chronicles are problematic. According to 2 Samuel there were 800,000 potential soldiers in Israel and 500,000 in Judah. In Chronicles there are 1,100,000 in all Israel. This figure can be explained as the sum of the two figures given in 2 Samuel minus 100,000 for each of the two tribes that were not counted. But then we are told that there were 470,000 in Judah. It may be that 500,000 was considered too round a number to seem authentic. Finally, in 2 Samuel David's heart smote him immediately after the census. In Chronicles we are told that God was displeased, and that he struck Israel. Only then does David repent.

In both narratives the hand of the angel of the Lord is stayed before he reaches Jerusalem, and the story has a happy outcome in the purchase of the site for the future temple. In 2 Samuel David got it as something of a bargain, for 50 shekels of silver. By the time Chronicles was written, inflation had taken its toll. The price now was 600 shekels of gold.

The last days of David in Chronicles have quite a different character from the account in 1 Kings 1–2. There is no intrigue surrounding the succession. Solomon is the only heir apparent. In 1 Kings 2, David's parting instructions had a Macchiavellian character, advising his son to eliminate potential enemies such as Joab. In Chronicles, his thoughts are entirely on the task of building the temple. David facilitates this task by providing materials for it in great quantity. The final activities of David in chapters 23–29 have no parallel in 2 Samuel and reflect the concerns of the Chronicler and his time. David ensures that the kingdom is fully organized before he passes it on to Solomon. The priorities of the Chronicler are shown by the relative space given to cultic and secular matters. The organization of the Levites and of the temple cult occupies chapters 23–26. We are told that 24,000 Levites are given charge of the work in the house of the Lord. There are 6,000 officers and judges, 4,000 gatekeepers, and 4,000 musicians. These numbers seem inflated to the point of absurdity (1 Chron 12:28 says that 4,600 Levites came to make David king at Hebron; in Ezra 8:15-20, fewer than 300 Levites return from Babylon).

Two factors are noteworthy in the organization of the clergy. First, the role of the Levites is to attend the Aaronide priests. The subordination of Levites to priests was a consequence of the centralization of the cult in Jerusalem. We have already seen that it was a contentious issue at the time of the restoration after the exile (see especially Ezekiel 44). Second, the priests are divided into twenty-four courses, to take turns at the temple service. This was a new development after the Babylonian exile. It was made necessary by the number of priests in Jerusalem in the Second Temple period. It should also be noted that the musicians are said to "prophesy" (25:1). Prophecy seems to be subsumed into liturgy in the Chronicler's vision. In contrast with this elaborate organization of the priests and Levites, the organization of the temporal affairs of the kingdom is described quite briefly in chapter 27.

In 1 Chronicles 28 David makes a speech to the assembled officials. He rehearses the promise conveyed by Nathan, designates Solomon as the chosen heir, and identifies his main task as building the temple. He then gives Solomon the plan for the temple. There is an analogy here with Moses, who is given a blueprint for the tabernacle in the book of Exodus. In 1 Chronicles 29 David challenges the people to contribute to the temple by recounting his own contributions from his personal treasury. Here again there is an analogy with Exodus, where the people are called on to make offerings for the tabernacle (Exod 25:1-7; 35:4-9, 20-29). David concludes with a prayer in which he praises God, gives thanks for the abundance from which the offerings are made, and prays for the people and for Solomon. It is typical of Chronicles that

Fig. 22.1 *Solomon Dedicates the Temple* by James Tissot (ca. 1896–1902); at the Jewish Museum, New York. Commons.wikimedia.org

the prayer for Solomon concludes: "that he may build the temple for which I have made provision."

First Chronicles concludes with a summary of David's reign and a list of alleged sources: the records of the seer Samuel, those of the prophet Nathan, and those of Gad the seer. There can be little doubt that the main actual source was 2 Samuel. By claiming that his source was the work of prophets who were contemporaries of David, the Chronicler is making a strong theological claim for the authenticity of his account. As we have seen, however, he exercised considerable freedom in adapting his sources, in order to project his ideal of temple worship into the early history of Israel.

Solomon (2 Chronicles 1–9)

The account of Solomon's reign is idealized in a way similar to that of David, and focuses on the building of the temple. It begins with Solomon's dream at Gibeon, in which he asks for wisdom. The choice of Gibeon is justified by the statement that the tent of meeting was there (in 1 Kgs 3:4 it was "the great high place"). Nothing is said of Solomon's elimination of his rivals (1 Kings 2). Neither is there any mention of his dubious display of wisdom in judging between the two prostitutes who claimed the same child (1 Kgs 3:16-28). Solomon is presented in Chronicles as a model of piety, and so his worthiness for building the temple is not jeopardized.

In 2 Chronicles 2 Solomon turns his attention to building the temple. As in 1 Kings, he makes an arrangement with Hiram (Huram in Chronicles) of Tyre for supplies of wood and craftsmen. According to 1 Kgs 9:20-22, Solomon conscripted the Amorites and other peoples who were left in the land for slave labor but did not make slaves of the Israelites. In 1 Kgs 5:13, however, we read that Solomon conscripted forced labor out of Israel, thirty thousand men, specifically in connection with the temple project. Chronicles makes no mention of forced labor from Israel and has Solomon take a census of aliens before he embarks on the temple building. In Chronicles, then, all the forced labor is imposed on aliens, whatever their origin.

The construction of the temple (2 Chron 3:1—5:1) is the centerpiece of the Chronicler's account of Solomon. Unlike the Deuteronomist in 1 Kings, the Chronicler attaches great importance to the location of the temple. He identifies it with Mount Moriah, scene of the near-sacrifice of Isaac, and with the threshing floor of Ornan the Jebusite, where the Lord had appeared to David, and which David had designated as the site for the temple (cf. 1 Chronicles 21, where it is *the angel* of the Lord who appears to David). Chronicles also goes beyond Kings in emphasizing the quantity of gold used in the temple (2 Chron 3:8-9).

The account of the dedication of the temple in 2 Chron 5:2—7:22 proceeds as follows:

1. The introduction of the ark into the temple (5:2—6:2). This section derives largely from 1 Kgs 8:1-13.
2. Solomon's address after this event (6:3-11), blessing the assembly and thanking God for fulfillment of some of the promises to David.
3. Solomon's prayer (6:12-42), closely following 1 Kgs 8:22-53. The temple is not the dwelling place of God, but the place where people may bring their petitions.
4. The conclusion of the ceremonies (7:1-11). Chronicles has fire come down from heaven to consume the sacrifices. This sign of divine approval was not found in Kings.
5. Finally, the Lord appears again to Solomon at night, as he had at Gibeon (7:12-22), confirming the choice of the place as a house of sacrifice, and affirming that he will establish Solomon's throne "if you walk before me as your father David walked." This passage follows 1 Kgs 9:1-5.

Second Chronicles 8 summarizes the other building projects of Solomon. Only at this point do we learn incidentally of his marriage to Pharaoh's daughter. Chapter 9 recounts the visit of the queen of Sheba and emphasizes Solomon's wealth (cf. 1 Kings 10). There is no mention in Chronicles, however, of his love for foreign women or of the multitude of his wives (1 Kings 11).

As in the case of David, the Chronicler claims to have derived his information from the writings of prophets.

The History of Judah (2 Chronicles 10–36)

In the older history, the Lord decided to tear the kingdom from Solomon because he had turned away under the influence of his many wives. This apostasy is not acknowledged in Chronicles. Neither does the Chronicler recount the reason for Jeroboam's original rebellion (the forced labor). He does follow Kings in recounting Rehoboam's refusal to lighten the load of the people. The conclusion, however, places the blame primarily on the northerners who seceded: "So Israel has been in rebellion against the house of David to this day" (10:18). Despite this statement, however, Chronicles does not simply identify "Israel" with the northern kingdom. Second Chronicles 11:3 refers to "all Israel in Benjamin and Judah." Thereafter Chronicles pays little attention to the northern kingdom, except insofar as it impinges on Judah. The Chronicler does not share the Deuteronomist's obsession with "the sin of Jeroboam" in setting up places of worship outside Jerusalem.

Rehoboam

The account of the reign of Rehoboam (11:5—12:16) illustrates the Chronicler's understanding of history. At first the king abides by the law of the Lord under the influence of the priests and Levites. During this period he prospers (he takes eighteen wives and sixty concubines, and begets twenty-eight sons and sixty daughters). But then he abandons the law of the Lord, and so the Lord sends Shishak of Egypt to punish him. Then Rehoboam humbles himself, and so the wrath of the Lord turns from him. Again, the Chronicler appeals to the authority of prophets for his account of Rehoboam's reign.

The history of the subsequent kings of Judah differs from the account in 1–2 Kings in various ways.

Abijah

Abijah (Abijam) received a brief and negative notice in the earlier history (1 Kgs 15:1-8). In 2 Chronicles he receives a whole chapter (13) and is represented as a staunch defender of Davidic sovereignty over all Israel. In accordance with the typical emphasis of Chronicles, he denounces Jeroboam for having "driven out the priests of the LORD, the descendants of Aaron, and the Levites" (13:9).

Asa

The treatment of Asa (14:1—16:14) is almost three times as long as that of 1 Kgs 15:9-24. His reign is divided into two periods: a long phase of fidelity and a much shorter phase of infidelity. The first phase is marked by complete reliance on the Lord and consequent success. The turning point comes when he is attacked by King Baasha of Israel and is moved to rely on Ben-hadad of Aram. For this he is rebuked by a prophet, and he retaliates by confining his critic. The displeasure of the Lord with this later phase is reflected in the disease of Asa's feet. The basic outline of this career is already found in 1 Kings, where Asa is credited with reform of the cult in his early years but is said to have relied on Ben-hadad after Baasha's attack. The account in Chronicles, however, is more elaborate and has a clearer moral message.

Jehoshaphat

Jehoshaphat is overshadowed by Ahab of Samaria in 1 Kings. He receives much more extensive treatment here (2 Chron 17:1—21:1). The notice in Kings is positive, except for the fact that he did not remove the high places (1 Kgs 22:41-44). Kings also says that he removed the remaining male prostitutes from the land (22:46). Chronicles credits him with much more extensive reforms. He allegedly sent officials, priests, and Levites to all the cities of Judah "having the book of the law of the LORD with them" (2 Chron 17:9). This would not have been possible in the Deuteronomistic History, since the book was only discovered later, in the reign of King Josiah. Because of this virtuous conduct, we are told, the fear of the Lord fell on neighboring kingdoms, and they did not make war on Jehoshaphat.

First Kings 22 reports that Jehoshaphat was allied with Ahab of Samaria in the campaign against Ramoth-gilead. This episode is the occasion of the prophecy of Micaiah ben Imlah, which is repeated in full in 2 Chronicles 18. Jehoshaphat has only a minor role in the story in Kings, although it is notable that he is the one who insists that Micaiah

be consulted. The statement in 1 Kgs 22:44, that "Jehoshaphat also made peace with the king of Israel," implies a positive judgment. In Chronicles, however, when Jehoshaphat returns to Jerusalem, he is met by a seer, Jehu son of Hanani, who asks, "Should you help the wicked and love those who hate the LORD?" (2 Chron 19:2). Jehoshaphat recovers from this false step but repeats his mistake later by joining with Ahaziah of Israel (20:35-37). Here the Chronicler alters the account of 1 Kings. According to the older history (1 Kgs 22:48-49), Jehoshaphat built ships to go to Ophir for gold, but they were wrecked at Ezion-geber. Then Ahaziah proposed that his servants go with those of Jehoshaphat in the ships, but Jehoshaphat declined the offer. Chronicles, in contrast, claims that he had joined with Ahaziah in building the ships, and was denounced by a prophet, Eliezer of Mareshah. It was because of this that he suffered the shipwreck (2 Chron 20:35-37).

The account of Jehoshaphat also includes a report of a spectacular victory over Moabites and Ammonites that has no parallel in Kings. The story drives home the point that victory in battle is by the power of God, not of human armies. First, Jehoshaphat prays for divine assistance (20:6-12). Then he is reassured by a prophet, Jahaziel son of Zechariah, a Levite. All Jehoshaphat has to do is stand still and see the victory of the Lord on his behalf. Singers go before the army, giving thanks to the Lord. Then the Ammonites and Moabites attack the inhabitants of Mount Seir and end up not only destroying the people of Mount Seir but themselves as well. Jehoshaphat and his army have only to collect the booty and return to Jerusalem with much fanfare. The emphasis, then, is on ritual, and the battle is entirely miraculous. The story must be regarded as a theological fiction, designed to display the Chronicler's ideas about the proper conduct of a battle. (Compare the highly ritualized story of the fall of Jericho in Joshua 6.)

Jehoram

Jehoshaphat's successor, Joram or Jehoram, receives a brief but negative notice in 2 Kings 16–24. He was married to a daughter of Ahab, and "walked in the way of the kings of Israel." Chronicles expands this account and portrays Jehoram as the first entirely negative figure in the Davidic line. He begins his reign by slaughtering his brothers. Such bloodbaths were not unusual in the ancient Near East at times of transition. The Chronicler may have had an independent source for this information, or may have invented it to illustrate Jehoram's bad character. The main embellishment of the account of Jehoram comes in the form of a letter from the prophet Elijah, threatening a plague on the people and an affliction of the king's own bowels because he had not followed the example of the kings of Judah but walked in the way of the kings of Israel. After this Judah is invaded by Philistines and Arabs, and the king dies in agony because of the disease in his bowels. This is the only mention of Elijah in Chronicles. Elisha is not mentioned at all. The reference to a letter is anachronistic. The use of letters only becomes common in Israel after the Babylonian exile. This feature, combined with the Judean, pro-Davidic character of its content, shows that this episode, like so many of the additions to the Deuteronomistic account, is a fiction, reflecting the theology of the Chronicler.

From Ahaziah to Joash (2 Chronicles 22–24)

Alliances between Judah and Israel are viewed negatively by the Chronicler because of the dominance of the northern kingdom. In the Chronicler's view, Israel should have been subject to Judah; moreover, the northern kings engaged in the worship of Baal. Ahaziah, son of Jehoram, had allied himself with Jehoram son of Ahab. When the northern king was wounded in battle, Ahaziah went to visit him and fell victim to Jehu's coup. In 2 Kings the killing of Ahaziah is told incidentally (2 Kgs 9:27). In Chronicles it is the main focus of the story: "It was ordained by God that the downfall of Ahaziah should come about through his going to visit Joram" (2 Chron 22:7).

After the death of Ahaziah, his mother Athaliah, daughter of Ahab, seized power in Judah. According to 2 Kgs 11:1-3 (and 2 Chron 22:10-12), she tried to destroy all the royal family, but the king's son Jehoash (Joash) was rescued and hidden. In the seventh year, a priest named Jehoiada organized a coup to put Joash on the throne. The account in Chronicles differs mainly in the new prominence given to the Levites as the bodyguards of the new king. Joash is praised in both Kings and Chronicles, although Kings notes that the high places were not dismantled. He is credited with carrying out repairs in the temple. The older history notes, however, that he had to give all the votive gifts from the temple and all the gold to the king of Aram (Syria) to induce him to withdraw from Jerusalem. Chronicles gives a more elaborate account of the change in this king's fortunes. After the death of Jehoiada, the officials of Judah persuaded Joash to abandon the house of the

Lord and serve idols. This led to a prophetic rebuke from Zechariah, son of Jehoiada. Joash, we are told, did not remember the kindness of Jehoiada, but killed his son. It was after this that the king of Aram came up against Joash. After the Arameans had withdrawn, Joash was killed by his servants (2 Chron 24:25-27; cf. 2 Kgs 12:19-21). The murder of the prophet provides a more satisfactory theological explanation for the downfall of Joash than was found in 2 Kings. For this very reason, we must suspect that the Chronicler invented the story.

From Amaziah to Ahaz (2 Chronicles 25–28)

Like Joash, Amaziah initially served the Lord but later fell from the true way, with disastrous results. The main deviation in Chronicles from the account in Kings is that Amaziah is said to have hired warriors from Israel early in his career. For this he was rebuked by a man of God, "for the LORD is not with Israel—all these Ephraimites" (2 Chron 25:7). Later he did battle with the northern kingdom and lost, and he was eventually killed in a coup.

The long reign of Uzziah (Azariah) is treated briefly in 2 Kgs 15:1-7. He was afflicted with leprosy and had to cede the task of governing to his son Jotham. In 2 Chronicles he receives a whole chapter (chap. 26). According to the latter account, he prospered at first and enjoyed success against the Philistines and the Ammonites. He fortified Jerusalem and built up his army. But then he became proud and attempted to usurp the role of the priests in offering sacrifice. It was at this point that he became leprous. Here again the additional material in Chronicles serves a theological

agenda and must be taken as the author's invention. It is noteworthy that Chronicles insists on the priority of the priests over the king in cultic matters.

Jotham receives a positive notice in both histories. Chronicles expands the account in 2 Kings, claiming that he received tribute from the Ammonites. His success, we are told, was due to the fact that he ordered his ways before the Lord.

Jotham's son Ahaz, however, receives a scathing report in both books. He is accused of deviant cultic practice, even human sacrifice. The most notable event in his reign was the Syro-Ephraimite war (2 Kings 16; cf. Isaiah 7). Ahaz took the controversial step of appealing, successfully, to Assyria for help. He subsequently brought a new altar from Damascus and made various changes in the temple furniture. Chronicles claims that before he turned to Assyria, Ahaz had been defeated by both Aram and Israel, and many people had been taken captive. (A prophet intervenes to free the captives in Samaria.) Chronicles claims that the appeal to Assyria was caused by incursions of Philistines and Edomites, and that Assyria oppressed him rather than helped him, as he had to pay tribute. Chronicles is unwilling to admit that a king of Judah could be helped at all by a foreign power. It further claims that Ahaz not only brought an altar from Damascus, but worshiped the gods of the king of Aram. Finally, the Chronicler contradicts the statement of 2 Kgs 16:20 that Ahaz was buried with his ancestors.

Hezekiah (2 Chronicles 29–32)

In the Deuteronomistic History, Hezekiah ranks second only to Josiah among the kings of Judah. In Chronicles, he surpasses the later ruler. According to 2 Kgs 18:3-7, he removed the high places, tore down the sacred pillars and poles, and smashed the bronze serpent that Moses had made. Chronicles credits him with a much more extensive reform. First he repaired the doors of the temple. Then he enlisted the Levites to cleanse the temple. When this was completed, he offered sacrifices and restored the Levites to their liturgical tasks, as prescribed by David.

Then in chapter 30 we are told that "Hezekiah sent word to all Israel and Judah, and wrote letters also to Ephraim and Manasseh, that they should come to the house of the Lord at Jerusalem, to keep the Passover to the Lord." There is a famous letter from Elephantine in Egypt in the late fifth century B.C.E. regarding the observance of the Passover, but letters are anachronistic in the time of Hezekiah, some three hundred years earlier. The fact that emissaries are sent to Ephraim and Manasseh presupposes that the northern kingdom of Israel is no more. Yet, amazingly, the Chronicler has not even mentioned the destruction of Samaria by the Assyrians.

According to 2 Kings, it was Josiah who first celebrated the Passover as a centralized feast in Jerusalem. We are told emphatically that no such Passover had been kept since the days of the judges (2 Kgs 23:22). Chronicles claims that Hezekiah kept the festival in this way and also prolonged the festival for seven days, presumably incorporating the observance of *Matstsoth*, or Unleavened Bread. We are told that there had been nothing like this since the time of David and Solomon. Hezekiah also appointed priests and Levites as David had done. It is unlikely that the Chronicler was drawing on ancient sources here. The tendency to project the full cult of the Second Temple back into earlier history is evident throughout his work. Hezekiah is cast as an entirely faithful king. Therefore the Chronicler assumes that he must have done everything as it should be done.

The account of the invasion of Sennacherib is presented in condensed form. There is no mention of stripping the temple to pay tribute to Sennacherib, as in 2 Kgs 18:13-16. Even the miraculous deliverance by the angel of the Lord is presented in a terse, matter-of-fact way, as a response to the prayers of Hezekiah and Isaiah (2 Chron 32:20).

The glowingly positive account of Hezekiah contains one discordant note. According to 2 Chron 32:24-26, Hezekiah did not respond properly when he was healed from his illness. Therefore "wrath came upon him." When he humbled himself, however, the wrath was deferred to a later time. There is only an indirect basis for this in 2 Kings. There, when Hezekiah shows his treasury to the Babylonian envoys, Isaiah prophesies that all that is in his house will be carried off to Babylon. Hezekiah is not troubled, since there will be peace in his days. In 2 Kings he is guilty at most of imprudence. The Chronicler requires

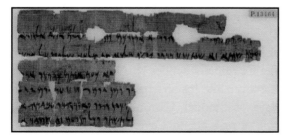

Fig. 22.2 The Passover papyrus from Elephantine, ca. 419 B.C.E., now in the Staatliche Museen zu Berlin. Center for Online Judaic Studies

a more theological explanation. The wrath of God must be punishment for a sin—in this case, pride.

The account of Hezekiah ends on a positive note, however, emphasizing the wealth and prosperity he enjoyed. There is archaeological evidence for the prosperity of Judah in Hezekiah's reign. The Chronicler's account, however, may owe more to theology and ideology than to historical memory.

Manasseh (2 Chron 33:1-20)

In the Deuteronomistic History (2 Kgs 21:1-18), Manasseh is the bad king *par excellence*. He is guilty of all sorts of idolatry and even of human sacrifice. It is specifically because of his sins that Jerusalem is destroyed. Chronicles repeats all the charges against Manasseh but then continues with a surprising narrative. The king is taken captive to Babylon by the king of Assyria. There he is moved to repentance and recognizes the Lord. Accordingly, he is restored to Jerusalem. He proceeds to fortify the city and remove the pagan cults that he himself had installed. The concluding summary (33:19) makes reference to his prayer to God. A composition called "The Prayer of Manasseh" is preserved in Greek and Latin, and included in the LXX and in Protestant editions of the Apocrypha, but this is certainly a much later prayer, inspired, no doubt, by the references in Chronicles.

This rehabilitation of Manasseh by the Chronicler is puzzling. Nothing is said of rebellion against Assyria, and so there is no apparent reason for him to have been taken prisoner to Babylon. (Moreover, the Assyrians would presumably have taken him to Nineveh.) It may be that the Chronicler was troubled by the fact that divine punishment did not follow immediately on Manasseh's misdeeds. His supposed conversion is required to explain his peaceful death. Nonetheless, it is puzzling that the wrath of God should be related to the pride of the good Hezekiah rather than to the manifest sins of Manasseh.

Josiah (2 Chronicles 34–35)

The brief, and evil, reign of Amon is more significant in Chronicles than in 2 Kings, as it serves to undo the repentance of Manasseh. It is, nonetheless, a brief interlude. The account of Josiah differs from that of Kings in several ways. In Kings the first reforming activity of the young king is dated to his eighteenth year. In Chronicles he begins to seek the Lord already in his eighth year, when he becomes king, and he begins to purge Judah and Jerusalem of the high places in his twelfth year. These reforms are carried out in Ephraim and Manasseh as well as in Judah. The repair of the temple, in his eighteenth year, is therefore viewed as part of an ongoing reform. Chronicles, typically, emphasizes the participation of Levites, some of whom were musicians and scribes. The account of the discovery of the book follows 2 Kgs 22:8-20. The novelty of Josiah's Passover has been preempted by Hezekiah in the Chronicler's account. Here again Chronicles emphasizes the role of the Levites. Despite the lengthy account of Hezekiah's Passover, the Chronicler echoes Kings in saying that no Passover like Josiah's had been kept since the days of Samuel. Chronicles emphasizes the role of priests and Levites, and the participation of Israel as well as Judah.

In 2 Kings, the manner of Josiah's death is obscure. We are simply told that when

Pharaoh Neco met Josiah at Megiddo, he killed him (2 Kgs 23:29). Chronicles clarifies the situation by saying explicitly that Josiah was fatally wounded in battle. (The account in Kings could be interpreted as an execution.) More surprisingly, Chronicles faults Josiah for fighting against the pharaoh. Neco pleaded with him not to oppose him, because God had commanded him to hurry. But, we are told, Josiah did not listen to Neco's words, which were from the mouth of God (2 Chron 35:22). Josiah's death, then, is not merely an act of divine mercy, so that he would not see the fall of Jerusalem, but is also in some part a punishment for his own disobedience. All of this has clear theological significance in the context of Chronicles. It is doubtful that the Chronicler had any independent historical information.

The Conclusion

The last years of Judah are narrated more briefly in Chronicles than in 2 Kings. The Deuteronomist blamed the misfortune on the sins of Manasseh (2 Kgs 24:3). The Chronicler puts the blame more broadly on the infidelity of rulers, priests, and people, and their refusal to listen to the prophets. The desecration and despoliation of the temple provides an appropriate conclusion to the Chronicler's history. Yet the book ends on a hopeful note, pointing forward to the restoration under Cyrus of Persia. The last verse of Chronicles is also the first verse of the book of Ezra. As we have seen in the context of Ezra, the relationship between the two books is disputed. Modern scholarship has long held that Ezra and Nehemiah are the work of the Chronicler, but that view has been widely disputed in recent years.

The Date and Purpose of the Chronicler

The central concerns of Chronicles should be evident from the preceding summary. The covenant with David is foundational, and northern Israel is culpable for failing to respect it. The focus of that covenant is on the temple, at least as much as on the kingship. The proper care of the temple is the responsibility of the priests and Levites, and the Chronicler never tires of emphasizing the roles of the clergy. When the cult is properly maintained and practiced, all is well. Apostasy, worship of other gods, and other cultic irregularities lead to disaster. There is a strict principle of retribution in history. So the peaceful death of Manasseh must be explained by his conversion, while the violent death of the reformer Josiah betrays disobedience on his part. Prophets figure prominently in the story, but their function is limited to reminding people of what they already know through the Torah. Some of the prophets are identified as Levites. The music of the temple is associated with prophecy, and prophets are credited with compiling historical records. The Chronicler is concerned with "Israel," which includes the northern territory, but he shows little interest in the northern kingdom and does not even bother to report its destruction. Judean kings are faulted for making alliances with their northern counterparts, as these alliances lead only to apostasy.

The purpose one ascribes to the Chronicler's History depends in part on the date to which one assigns it. The concluding reference to Cyrus of Persia requires a postexilic date. The extension of David's genealogy in 1 Chronicles points to a date around 400 B.C.E. or slightly later. Several scholars, however, have argued for the existence of earlier editions of the Chronicler's History. Some have proposed that a form of the history was drafted in the time of Hezekiah, in view of the prominence accorded to that king. But the portrayal of Hezekiah seems quite anachronistic. In large part, the Chronicler seems to have assumed that Hezekiah, as a good king, would have done all the things Josiah is said to have done, although some of these things, such as the celebration of the Passover in Jerusalem, make better historical sense in the time of Josiah. Other scholars have argued for an edition of the Chronicler's History around 520 B.C.E., in the time of Zerubbabel. This might explain the interest in the building of the temple and organization of the cult and could be understood as an affirmation of the leadership of the Davidic line. But the building of the temple and the organization of the cult are described in terms that are highly idealized and cannot be reliably tied to any historical events. The suggestions of earlier editions of the Chronicler's work remain hypothetical. The language of Chronicles is generally regarded as Late Biblical Hebrew, which is to say, later than the Priestly source of the Pentateuch and the book of Ezekiel. There is no clear Hellenistic influence that would point to a date later than the fourth century B.C.E. Only a very small fragment of Chronicles has been found among the Dead Sea Scrolls, but at least it verifies the existence of the book before the turn of the era.

Much of the Chronicler's History can be seen to derive from biblical materials, especially from 2 Samuel and 1–2 Kings. Whether the author also had other, nonbiblical sources has been much debated. The Chronicler had a particular fondness for lists. Some of these may have derived from old sources (e.g., some of the tribal genealogies in 1 Chronicles 2); others, such as the lists of temple functionaries, are more probably postexilic. While the Chronicler may have had occasional access to independent historical information, the great bulk of the cases where he departs from the Deuteronomistic History can be explained by his theological and ideological preferences. In many cases, such as the reign of Manasseh, he displays astonishing freedom in manipulating the historical record. Chronicles describes history as the author thought it should have been. It is not a reliable source for historical information about preexilic Israel or Judah.

Some suggest that the Chronicler cherished messianic hopes for the restoration of the Davidic kingdom. However, the author seems much more interested in the temple cult than in the monarchy. The primary role of the king is to provide for the temple and its cult, whether by building the temple and organizing the cult in the case of David and Solomon, or by maintaining or restoring it in the case of later kings (cf. the role of the king in Ezekiel 40–48). No doubt, the author would have welcomed the restoration of the Davidic line, but there is little sense in Chronicles of political aspiration. The proper functioning of the cult was much more important than political independence.

The aim of the Chronicler was to promote a view of Judaism that centered primarily on the temple cult and on the active leadership of priests and Levites. The great contribution of David and Solomon was that they put the cultic system in place. Other kings are evaluated by the degree to which they maintained it. This temple-centered, cultic view of Judaism, with its great emphasis on the leadership of priests and Levites, is characteristic of Second Temple Judaism. The Chronicler wanted to claim that this view of the cult of YHWH dated back to the time of David and Solomon, and was supported by consistent divine retribution in the history of Judah. The aim of the history was to legitimize and lend authority to this view of Judaism.

FOR FURTHER READING

Commentaries

L. C. Allen, "The First and Second Books of Chronicles," *NIB* 3:299–659. Well-informed commentary with homiletical reflections.

S. Japhet, *I and II Chronicles* (OTL; Louisville: Westminster John Knox. 1993). Important critical commentary. Rejects attribution of Ezra and Nehemiah to the Chronicler.

R. W. Klein, *1 Chronicles* (Hermeneia; Minneapolis: Fortress, 2006); 2 Chronicles (2012). Thorough, comprehensive commentary.

G. N. Knoppers, *1 Chronicles 1–9* (AB 12; New York: Doubleday, 2004); *1 Chronicles 10–29* (AB 12A; 2004). Balanced authoritative commentary.

S. L. McKenzie, *1-2 Chronicles* (Nashville: Abingdon Press, 2004). Nontechnical exposition of Chronicles use of its sources.

S. J. de Vries, *1 and 2 Chronicles* (FOTL 11; Grand Rapids: Eerdmans, 1989). Form-critical breakdown of the text.

Other Studies

A. G. Auld, *Kings without Privilege: David and Moses in the Story of the Bible's Kings* (Edinburgh: T&T Clark, 1994). Influential argument that Chronicles and Samuel-Kings drew on a common source.

I. Kalimi, *The Book of Chronicles. Historical Writing and Literary Devices* (Jerusalem: Bialik, 2000); *The Reshaping of Ancient Israelite History in Chronicles* (Winona Lake, IN: Eisenbrauns, 2005). Detailed study of the Chronicler's use of Samuel and Kings. Views Chronicles as history writing and a unified work.

G. N. Knoppers, "Greek Historiography and the Chronicler's History: A Reexamination of an Alleged Non-relationship," *JBL* 122 (2003): 627–50. Argues that features of the genealogies in Chronicles have parallels in classical sources.

R. F. Person, *The Deuteronomic History and the Book of Chronicles* (Atlanta: SBL, 2010). Posits common source for Chronicles and Samuel-Kings.

H. G. M. Williamson, *Israel in the Books of Chronicles* (Cambridge: Cambridge University Press, 1977). Important treatment of the Chronicler's view of Israel.

CHAPTER 23

The Psalms and Song of Songs

INTRODUCTION

Two poetic books among the Writings occupy us in this chapter: the book of Psalms and the Song of Songs (or Song of Solomon).

The book of Psalms (the Psalter) contains 150 psalms in the Hebrew Bible and modern Christian Old Testament. The name "Psalms" is derived from the Greek *Psalmoi* (Latin *Psalmi*), from the verb *psallein*, to sing to the accompaniment of a harp or lyre. In Hebrew tradition the book is called *t'hillim*, "praises." The root word, *hll*, is reflected in the acclamation "Hallelujah," which in the Hebrew Bible occurs only in the Psalter, at the beginning or end of several psalms. The closest Hebrew equivalent for "psalm" is *mizmor*, which occurs fifty-seven times. Individual psalms are also called *shir* (song) or even *t'pillah* (prayer) among other terms, some of which are no longer intelligible, such as *miktam*. The Greek Bible (LXX) contains an additional psalm (151), in which David celebrates his victory over Goliath. The Greek psalms are also numbered differently. In two cases, consecutive Hebrew psalms (9–10; 114–115) are combined in the Greek (as Psalms 9 and 113), while Hebrew Psalms 116 and 147 are each divided into two psalms (114–115 and 146–147) in the Greek.

The book of Psalms is traditionally attributed to King David. In the books of Samuel, David is depicted as a musician (1 Sam 16:16-23) who composes a lament (for Saul and Jonathan, 2 Sam 1:17), a song of thanksgiving (2 Samuel 22 = Psalm 18), and poetic "last words" (2 Sam 23:1-7). His name appears in the superscriptions of seventy-three psalms. In thirteen instances (3, 7, 18, 34, 51, 52, 54, 56, 57, 59, 60, 63, 142) the psalm is associated with an event in David's life. One of these, Psalm 18, appears in 2 Samuel 22. It is now generally accepted that these references were added by an editor long after the time of David, but they contributed to the tendency to see all the Psalms as Davidic. Several psalms are associated with other people in the Hebrew text: Solomon (72, 127), Asaph (50, 73–83), the Korahites (42, 44–49, 84–85, 87–88), Heman (88), Ethan (89), Moses (90), and Jeduthun, one of David's musicians (39, 62, 77). Nonetheless, the association with David was strengthened in the later tradition. In the LXX eighty-five psalms are ascribed to David. In 2 Chron 16:7 David "appointed the singing of praises to the Lord by Asaph and his kindred," and this is followed by a medley of passages from the Psalms. The Psalms Scroll from Qumran Cave 11 claims that David wrote 3,600 psalms. By the time the Dead Sea Scrolls were written in the first century B.C.E., it was possible to refer to "David" in the same context as Moses and the prophets, to indicate an authoritative body of Scripture (4QMMT C 10). Similarly in the New Testament, citations from Psalms can be introduced as sayings of David (see, e.g., Acts 2:25, 31, 34).

The book of Psalms as found in the Hebrew Bible is divided into five books: 1–41; 42–72; 73–89; 90–106; 107–50. Each book ends with a doxology, or short hymn of praise: 41:13; 72:20; 89:52; 106:48. Psalm 150 is a doxology in its entirety, to mark the end of the Psalter. According to the Midrash on Psalm 1, the five books of David correspond to the five books of Moses (the Pentateuch). Nonetheless, there is evidence that this arrangement of the Psalms was made at a relatively late time. One indication of this is the presence of several smaller clusters that reflect earlier groupings of psalms, such as the Psalms of Asaph and of the Korahites, noted above, or the "Songs of Ascent" (130–134). In the first book (1–41), all but 1, 2, 10, and 33 have superscriptions that mention David. Another cluster of psalms with Davidic superscriptions is found in Psalms 51–70 (of which only 66–67 are exceptions). Moreover, Psalm 72 is followed by an epilogue, which says that the prayers of Jesse, son of David, are ended. This statement would seem to mark the end of an earlier collection. Psalms 42–83 (that is, the second book and most of the third) are sometimes called the Elohistic Psalter, since in these psalms God is called *elohim* more than four times as often as YHWH, whereas

Fig. 23.1   David plays the lyre; mosaic from the synagogue in Gaza, sixth century C.E.; Photo: Israel Museum.

the latter name predominates in the rest of the Psalter by a ratio of better than 2:1. It should be noted that this Elohistic Psalter overlaps the second and third books of the canonical collection.

Important new light has been shed on the history of the book of Psalms by a Psalms Scroll from Qumran Cave 11 (11Q5), edited by J. A. Sanders in 1965. This scroll contains most of the last third of the biblical Psalter, but in an unconventional arrangement (101–3, 109, 118, 104, 147, 105, 146–8, et al.). It also includes a poem identical with 2 Sam 23:1-7 ("the last words of David") and several apocryphal psalms: Psalm 151 (a variant of the corresponding psalm in the Greek Psalter); Psalms 154–5, which are also found in the Syriac Bible; and a poem related to Ben Sira 51:13-19, 30. There are also three psalms that were previously unknown: "A Plea for Deliverance," "Apostrophe to Zion," and a "Hymn to the Creator." And there is a prose catalog of David's compositions placed toward the end of the collection but followed by four psalms. Several other manuscripts of the Psalms found at Qumran also show differences in the order of the psalms (4Q83, 4Q84, 4Q86, 4Q87, 4Q92, 4Q95, 4Q98). A few others include material that is not found in the Masoretic Bible (4Q88 contains the "Apostrophe to Zion"). In all, thirty-nine manuscripts of the Dead Sea Scrolls contain portions of the Psalms, but most of these manuscripts are very fragmentary. It should be noted that the Dead Sea Psalms scrolls show only a few differences from the Masoretic Psalter in the first three books of the canonical collection (Psalms 1–89). The great majority of the variations are found in the last third of the Psalter. This evidence strongly suggests that the order, and even the content, of the latter part of the Psalter was still fluid in the second century B.C.E. and can only have been settled finally after that time.

The Different Kinds of Psalms

Despite the traditional association with David, it is now generally agreed that these psalms were composed over many centuries to serve the needs of the worshiping community in Jerusalem. The foundational research in this respect was done by the German scholar Hermann Gunkel early in the twentieth century. He argued that the psalms were not the spontaneous prayers of individuals, but reflect fixed forms that were transmitted from generation to generation. (These forms could be adapted, however, in ways that were quite original.) The truth of this insight is confirmed by the fact that the same forms of religious poetry appear all over the ancient Near East. In accordance with the method of form criticism, which he pioneered, Gunkel sought to establish the *Sitz im Leben* or "setting in life" of the psalms, by trying to discover the ways in which they were used in worship. For example, he suggested that psalms of thanksgiving should be related to sacrifices of thanksgiving that are prescribed in the laws. Subsequent scholars have modified Gunkel's analysis in various ways, and it is now widely recognized that psalms cannot always be tied to one specific setting. Gunkel made an enduring contribution, however, by drawing attention to the different literary forms and genres in the Psalms, and by showing that many, though not necessarily all, were originally designed for use in the context of worship.

CLASSIFICATION OF PSALMS IN THE HEBREW BIBLE	
Hymns	8, 19, 29, 33, 65, 67, 68, 96, 98, 100, 103–5, 111, 113, 114, 117, 135, 145–50
Psalms of YHWH's Enthronement	93, 97, 99
Psalms of Individual Complaint	3, 5–7, 13, 17, 22, 25–28, 32, 38, 39, 42, 43, 51, 54–57, 59, 61, 63, 64, 69–71, 86, 88, 102, 109, 120, 130, 140–43.
Psalms of Communal Complaint	44, 74, 79, 80, 83, 89
Psalms of Thanksgiving	18, 30, 34, 40:1-11, 41, 66, 92, 116, 118, 138
Royal Psalms	2, 18, 20, 21, 45, 72, 101, 110, 132, 144:1-11
Wisdom Psalms	1, 14, 37, 73, 91, 112, 119, 128

(Many psalms are difficult to classify and are omitted from this list.)

Hymns

A hymn is a song of praise. The Hebrew name for the Psalter (*t*hillim) reflects the prominence of this kind of composition in the collection, especially toward its end (the imperative "Hallelujah!" is found in 104–6, 111–13, 115–17, 135, and 146–50). Gunkel listed the following psalms as hymns: 8, 19, 29, 33, 65, 67, 68, 96, 98, 100, 103–5, 111, 113, 114, 117, 135, 145–50. Hymnic elements can also be found in many other psalms, especially in thanksgiving hymns but also in laments. Hymns may begin by calling on the Lord, as in Psalm 8 ("O LORD our Sovereign, how majestic is your name in all the earth!") or simply by calling on the congregation to praise the Lord, as in Psalms 146–50. They typically give the reasons for praising God, his works in creation or history, or his character. Psalms 8 and 104 put the emphasis on the works of creation. Psalm 114 recalls the exodus. Psalm 146 praises the Lord for liberating prisoners and opening the eyes of the blind. The hymn

may conclude by echoing the introductory affirmation (Psalm 8) or call to praise (Psalms 146–50) or by pronouncing a wish (104:31: "may the glory of the LORD endure forever"; 29:11: "May the LORD bless his people with peace!"). The form allows some variation from one hymn to another, but nonetheless it is not difficult to recognize.

Hymns praising deities figure prominently in all religions of the ancient Near East, and probably in all religions. Psalm 104 has a close parallel in the Egyptian Hymn to Aten (the deity represented by the solar disk, venerated by the heretical, "monotheistic" Pharaoh Akhenaten: *ANET*, 369–71). There are numerous examples of Mesopotamian hymns to various deities, some dating back to ancient Sumer, including the goddess Ishtar, Marduk, the moon-god, and the sun-god (*ANET*, 383–92).

Hymns were sung on a wide variety of occasions but were especially associated with the temple and holy places, and with the celebration of festivals. "Happy are those who live in your house, ever singing your praise" (Ps 84:4). "Enter his gates with thanksgiving, and his courts with praise" (100:4; in this case, the singing of hymns is associated with liturgical processions). According to 1 Chron 16:4-7, David appointed Levites as ministers before the ark to invoke, thank, and praise the God of Israel. The singing of praise seems to have been a prominent part of the temple worship throughout the history of Israel and Judah.

Psalms of YHWH's Enthronement

A distinct group of hymns celebrate the kingship of YHWH. Psalms 93, 97, and 99 begin with the acclamation "YHWH is king!" Psalms 47 and 96:10-13 also contain this statement, but not as the introduction to the psalm. In 10:16 it appears in the context of a psalm of complaint. The classic kingship of YHWH psalms (93, 97, 99) are simple hymns that affirm the greatness of YHWH as king. He is more majestic than the mighty waters (93:4), and his decrees are sure (93:5). The heavens proclaim his righteousness (97:6). He is also glorified in the history of Israel by the service of Moses, Aaron, and Samuel (99:6-7). The psalmist occasionally bids the assembly to "extol our God" (99:9), but these psalms can also consist of simple declarative sentences (as in Psalm 93).

Two aspects of these psalms have given rise to controversy in modern scholarship. The first is the translation of the opening acclamation, which may be rendered either as "YHWH is king" or "YHWH has become king." The argument for the latter translation is that similar acclamations are found in biblical narratives when a human king ascends the throne or lays claim to the kingship (2

Sam 15:10: "Absalom has become king"; 2 Kgs 9:13: "Jehu has become king"). The second controversy is related to this. A great Norwegian scholar, Sigmund Mowinckel, argued that these psalms reflect a festival celebrating the enthronement of YHWH. We may recall that the Babylonian creation myth, *Enuma Elish*, told how Marduk had become king of the gods and celebrated his kingship. *Enuma Elish* was recited annually at the Babylonian New Year's festival. The Canaanite Baal Cycle of myths celebrated how Baal became king of the gods by his victories over Yamm (Sea) and Death (Mot). It is possible that these psalms reflect a tradition that YHWH had to assert his kingship by a primordial victory. Psalm 93 emphasizes that YHWH rules over the roaring of the sea and the mighty waters, although it does not say that he defeated them. There is no explicit reference in the Hebrew Bible, however, to a festival of YHWH's enthronement, and it is unlikely that there was a special festival with this theme. It may well be, however, that the kingship of YHWH was celebrated in connection with the New Year, like the kingship of Marduk in Babylon, or in connection with the Festival of Sukkoth, or Tabernacles, which was also known as "the feast of YHWH." There are many echoes in the Bible of a combat myth, in which YHWH was said to have overcome a sea monster in the process of creation (e.g., Job 26:12; Isa 51:9). This myth is never told as a narrative in the Bible, however. It may be that at one time YHWH was thought to have become king, as Baal or Marduk had. In the biblical text as we have it, however, the emphasis is on the permanence, even eternity, of YHWH's kingship rather than on its origin.

Individual and Communal Complaints

The kind of psalm most commonly found in the Psalter is the individual complaint, which Gunkel called "the basic material of the Psalter." He listed the following examples: Psalms 3, 5–7, 13, 17, 22, 25–28, 32, 38, 39, 42, 43, 51, 54–57, 59, 61, 63, 64, 69–71, 86, 88, 102, 109, 120, 130, 140–43. There are also several psalms of mixed genres that include elements of complaint. The so-called confessions of Jeremiah (Jer 11:18-20; 15:15-21; 18:19-23; 20:7-12, 14-19) conform to this genre, and there are many echoes of it in the book of Job. At one time, some scholars argued that the "I" of the psalmist should be understood as collective, so that all these psalms could be appropriated by the community. There is some basis for this view, in that these psalms have often been recited communally in Jewish and Christian worship, and they may have been so recited in biblical times. Nonetheless, they seem to be designed primarily to articulate individual experiences. For this reason, it was easy to suppose that they had been written by David, and some are even assigned to particular occasions in David's life. (Psalm 3 bears the superscription "A psalm of David when he fled from Absalom"; Psalm 51 is presented as his prayer for forgiveness after his affair with Bathsheba.) Their language is often stereotypical, and so they could be appropriated by numerous individuals over the centuries. There are many examples of this kind of psalm from ancient Babylon; some even provide for the person praying the psalm to insert his or her own name. One should not, then, regard them purely as expressions of individual experience, but rather as formulaic expressions of typical individual experiences that could be appropriated by a wide range of people (Ps 22:1 is put on the lips of Jesus on the cross in Matt 27:46; Mark 15:34). There are occasional references in these psalms to ritual actions, and this is also the case in the corresponding Babylonian psalms. For example, Ps 51:7 says, "Purge me with hyssop and I shall be clean."

The typical elements of these complaints are as follows:

1. They often begin with a plea to God to hear the prayer: "Give ear to my words, O Lord" (5:1); "Have mercy on me, O God, according to your steadfast mercy" (52:1).
2. There is often a complaint about the psalmist's condition: "My God, my God, why have you forsaken me?" (22:1); "More in number than the hairs of my head are those who hate me without cause" (69:4).
3. There may a confession of sin, as in Psalm 51, or an assertion of innocence, as in Psalm 69.
4. Invariably, the psalmist appeals to God for help. In many cases, this takes the form of a request for vengeance. "Rise up, O Lord, in your anger; lift yourself up against the fury of my enemies" (7:6); "Pour out your indignation on them, and let your burning anger overtake them" (69:24).
5. Some psalms go on to acknowledge a divine response. "The Lord has heard the sound of my weeping. The Lord accepts my prayer" (6:9); "From the horns of the wild oxen you have rescued me" (22:21). Sometimes this is followed by a vow or promise to give

Fig. 23.2 Laments over the Ruin of Ur; cuneiform tablet from the late third millennium B.C.E.; at the Louvre. Commons.wikimedia.org

thanks: "I will give to the LORD the thanks due to his righteousness" (7:17); "With a freewill offering I will sacrifice to you" (54:6). The psalm may conclude with an expression of praise or thanks: "Let heaven and earth praise him, the seas and everything that moves in them" (65:34).

The communal complaints are similar in form but arise from the fate of the people rather than the experience of individuals. Examples include Psalms 44, 74, 79, 80, 83, 89 (Psalm 89 can also be considered as a royal psalm, but there is a lament over the neglected state of the kingship in vv. 38-52). Communal laments are also found in the narrative books of the Bible, for example, Ezra 9:6-15; Neh 9:6-37; Dan 9:4-19. They mark calamities of various sorts, war, exile, pestilence, famine. A nice illustration of a ritual context can be found in Joel 1:3-14, where the occasion is a plague of locusts: "Put on sackcloth and lament, you priests; wail you ministers of the altar . . . sanctify a fast, call a solemn assembly. Gather the elders and all the inhabitants of the land to the house of the LORD your God, and cry out to the LORD." In numerous instances, people call a fast in response to some adversity (Judg 20:23; 1 Sam 7:6; et al.). A late example of a communal lament in reaction to military adversity can be found in 1 Macc 3:50-54.

There is a whole genre of laments in the ancient Near East that bewails the destruction of cities. The biblical complaints have much in common with this genre, notably in Psalm 137, where the psalmist weeps at the memory of Zion "by the rivers of Babylon."

Individual and Communal Thanksgiving

The psalms of thanksgiving are integrally related to the psalms of complaint, and as we have seen, the latter often conclude by giving thanks for deliverance, whether actual or anticipated. Again, the psalms of individuals are quite common in the Psalter, while the very existence of communal psalms of thanksgiving has been disputed. Examples of individual thanksgiving are found in Psalms 18, 30, 32, 34, 40:1-11, 41, 66, 92, 116, 118, 138. These psalms would usually have been accompanied by a thanksgiving sacrifice. The same Hebrew word, *todah*, is used for both prayer and sacrifice of thanksgiving.

The typical elements in a thanksgiving psalm are as follows:

1. An invitation to give thanks or praise: "O give thanks to the LORD, for he is good" (118:1); or an affirmation of the intention to give thanks: "I will bless the LORD at all times" (34:1); or of the propriety of giving thanks: "It is good to give thanks to the LORD, to sing praises to your name, O Most High" (92:1).
2. The psalmist recounts the distress from which he or she was rescued: "While I kept silence, my body wasted away . . . for day and night your hand was heavy upon me" (32:4).
3. The heart of these psalms is the thanks rendered to God. "O LORD my God, I will give thanks to you forever" (30:12). For this reason, psalms of thanksgiving are often very much like hymns.

In many cases, there are indications of the ritual context. These include references to processions. Psalm 118 refers to "the gate of the LORD" through which the righteous enter (118:20) and instructs the participants: "Bind the festal procession with branches, up to the horns of the altar." Psalm 40 says that God has not required sacrifice or burnt offering, but the psalmist tells "the glad news of deliverance in the great congregation" (40:6, 9). The bystanders are often bidden to join in the praise and thanks: "Be glad in the LORD and rejoice, O righteous, and shout for joy all you upright of heart" (32:11). Here again, these psalms have a collective aspect. While they express the thanksgiving of an individual, others are invited to identify with the one who has been delivered and share in the celebration. Once more, the exemplary aspect of the psalms can be expressed by associating them with episodes in the life of David. Psalm 18

is introduced as a psalm of David on the day that the Lord delivered him from the hand of his enemies and from Saul.

Communal psalms of thanksgiving are hard to find in the Psalter. The clearest examples are found in the narrative books of the Bible, for example, in Exodus 15, after the deliverance from Egypt. There are, however, a few in the Psalter. Psalm 68 is probably the clearest example, as it recounts at length how God went forth before his people. Another clear example is found in Psalm 124. There is also a communal context in Psalms 66 and 67.

Other Kinds of Psalms

The complaints, thanksgivings, and hymns are the major kinds of cultic poetry in the Psalter. There is a good deal of variation in the individual psalms, and several combine elements of complaint or lament with elements of praise and thanksgiving. Examples of mixed forms can be found in Psalms 19, 33, and 129. Some psalms that do not fit any of these classifications nonetheless seem designed for ritual occasions. Psalm 24 is a liturgy for people entering the temple: "Who shall ascend the hill of the LORD, and who shall stand in his holy place?" Psalm 15 is similar: "O LORD, who may abide in your tent? Who may dwell on your holy hill?" The Psalms of Ascent (Psalms 130–34) are presumably named because they were used by pilgrims, but the individual psalms are of different kinds. Psalm 132 commemorates the bringing of the ark to Jerusalem, and may have been associated with a festival. In contrast, Psalm 131 is a simple, and beautiful, prayer of trust, while Psalm 133 is a meditation on the pleasures of harmonious fellowship.

One of the most important of the smaller categories is that of the royal psalms, in which Gunkel included 2, 18, 20, 21, 45, 72, 101, 110, 132, and 144:1-11, while he regarded 89:47-52 as related. "Royal psalms" is not a form-critical category—these psalms do not share a common literary form but only the theme of kingship. We have already considered their importance for the ideology of kingship in Israel in connection with the story of Solomon in 1 Kings. Psalms 2 and 110 are plausibly understood as coronation psalms. Psalm 45 is composed for a royal wedding. Some of the royal psalms fit the categories of complaint or thanksgiving (18, 89, 144).

Wisdom Psalms

The final category of psalms to be discussed is that of wisdom psalms. These psalms are distinguished by their reflective, meditative tone and didactic character. They often reflect on the fate of the righteous and the wicked, a typical theme of wisdom literature such as we find in the book of Proverbs. Examples of wisdom psalms are 1, 14, 37, 73, 91, 112, 119, and 128. Gunkel felt that these poems did not originate in the context of worship. Others hold that they are liturgical pieces, and that they reflect the changed character of worship after the Babylonian exile. It is also possible that they originated in the synagogue, where study of the Torah replaced sacrifice as the focal point of worship. It is noteworthy that the Torah figures prominently in some of these psalms, most obviously in Psalm 119 ("Happy are those whose way is blameless, who walk in the law of the LORD. Happy are those who keep his decrees, who seek him with their whole heart"). Similarly in Psalm 1,

the righteous are those whose delight is in the law of the Lord. Psalm 19 declares that "the law of the LORD is perfect, reviving the soul." The Torah was not an object of study in the older wisdom literature (Proverbs, Qoheleth). It first finds a place in wisdom instruction in the book of Ben Sira, in the early second century B.C.E., and again in the Dead Sea Scrolls. The wisdom psalms that refer to the Torah as the source of wisdom par excellence are likely to be relatively late (Hellenistic period).

The inclusion of the wisdom psalms had a significant impact on the shape and character of the Psalter. As the opening psalm in the collection, Psalm 1 sets the tone for what follows, and suggests that the Psalter should be read in light of the Torah as a source for wisdom. Psalm 119 has an impact on the impression made by the Psalter as a whole because of its sheer length (176 verses). These psalms give the Psalter a didactic character. At the same time, they make the point that study is a form of worship in Second Temple Judaism and testify to the growing importance of the Torah for Jewish religious life. The attribution of roughly half the psalms to David also had the effect of relating the Psalter to the narrative books of the Scriptures, and encouraged the practice of intertextuality, that is, of reading one book in the light of others.

The Psalms as Poetry

Most, if not all, of the Psalms were originally meant to be sung. They are written in rhythmic style and are usually regarded as poetry, although they do not necessarily conform to modern Western ideas of poetry. The most prominent feature of Hebrew poetry is parallelism, the correspondence between the second line of a poetic verse and the first. This correspondence may be of different kinds. The most typical kind of correspondence is synonymous parallelism, where both parts of the verse say essentially the same thing. For example, 1:1 declares blessed

> "those who do not follow the advice of
>   the wicked,
> or take the path that sinners tread,
> or sit in the seat of scoffers."

The verse here says the same thing in three different ways. But even when there is a very close correspondence between the different parts of a verse, the later part is not necessarily identical with the first. In 1:2 the statement that "on his law they meditate day and night" is not strictly synonymous with the preceding statement that "their delight is in the law of the Lord." The second part of the verse provides some additional information. Hebrew parallelism complements the thought of the first line of a verse, and this may be done in various ways.

A number of other literary devices are exhibited in the Psalms. Several psalms are acrostics, that is, each verse begins with a different letter of the alphabet, in sequence (Psalms 9–10, 25, 34, 37, 111–12, 119, 145). Acrostics show deliberate attention to the aesthetics of the psalms, a concern for pleasing the eye and ear as well as for communicating thought. Other common devices include repetition of a word or line to form an *inclusio* (that is, causing the psalm to end in the same way that it began). For example, Psalm 136 begins and ends with the verse: "O give thanks to the Lord for he is good, for his steadfast love endures forever." Chiastic arrangements

(ABBA or ABCBA) are also common, both in individual lines and in larger units. For a simple example, see 1:5-7, where the sequence is "wicked-righteous-righteous-wicked."

Perhaps the most important poetic characteristic of the Psalter, however, is the use of metaphor and figurative language. Consider, for example, Psalm 65:

> "Save me, O God, for the waters have
>   come up to my neck.
> I sink in deep mire, where there is no
>   foothold;
> I have come into deep waters and the
>   flood sweeps over me."

Later in the psalm it becomes clear that certain people hate the psalmist without cause and insult him. The language of drowning is entirely metaphorical and quite evocative. Metaphorical language is especially important in the attempt to speak about God (as, for example, in 23:1, "the Lord is my shepherd"). In other cases, the poets rely on simile, where the analogies are explicit, as when the author of Psalm 131 compares his peace of soul to that of a weaned child with its mother, or as when Psalm 49 says that human beings are like beasts that perish (49:20).

The Theology of the Psalms

The book of Psalms is not a unified composition in the sense of a modern treatise. It is a loosely edited anthology, in which certain themes are highlighted by the frequency with which they occur and by their placement in the collection. Nonetheless, they provide an ample window on Israelite and ancient Jewish spirituality. Since the psalms lend themselves to liturgical use, they have been used constantly over the centuries. Succeeding generations of Jews and Christians have found in the Psalms the language to help them express both their existential anxiety and their wonder and admiration for the God of creation.

The Human Situation

As noted above, the most typical kind of psalm in the Psalter is the individual complaint or lament. These psalms, by definition, arise from situations of distress, "out of the depths" in the phrase of Psalm 130. They often address particular experiences of adversity; many are prayers for deliverance from enemies. They are often expressed, however, in hyperbolic terms that picture the plaintiff before the jaws of death:

> "For my soul is full of troubles, and my
>   life draws near to Sheol.
> I am counted among those who go down
>   to the Pit . . .
> like those whom you remember no more,
> for they are cut off from your hand.
> You have put me in the depths of the Pit,
> in the regions dark and deep." (88:3-6)
> "The waters have come up to my neck.
> I sink in deep mire where there is no
>   foothold. . . .
> Do not let the flood sweep over me,
> or the deep swallow me up,
> or the Pit close its mouth over me."
>   (69:2, 15)

Sheol and the Pit are the netherworld, where the shade of the person goes after death. (The *nephesh* or soul survives after death as a shadowy spirit, like a ghost, but is not really alive). There is no joy or vitality in Sheol.

> "The dead do not praise the LORD,
> nor do any that go down into the
>   silence." (115:17)
> "For in death there is no remembrance
>   of you;
> in Sheol who can give you praise?" (6:5)

This is the common destiny of all humankind in most of the Hebrew Bible. Even though the psalmist often thanks God for deliverance from the jaws of death, the reprieve is of necessity short-lived.

> "O LORD, what are human beings that
>   you regard them,
> or mortals that you think of them?
> They are like a breath;
> their days are like a passing shadow."
>   (144:4)
> "You have made my days a few
>   handbreadths,
> and my lifetime is as nothing in your
>   sight.
> Surely everyone stands as a mere breath.
> Surely everyone goes about like a shadow.
> Surely for nothing they are in turmoil;
> they heap up and do not know who will
>   gather." (39:5-6; cf. 90:3-6; 103:15-16)

In light of this rather gloomy prospect, we might expect the Psalms to be somewhat depressing, but this is not at all the case. The psalms of complaint do not focus on the ultimacy of death, but on more immediate dangers from which deliverance is possible. Sometimes the deliverance is already effected. In Psalm 18 the psalmist confesses that when "the cords of Sheol entangled me," God "reached down from on high, he took me; he drew me out of mighty waters" (18:5, 16). Consequently, the psalms as a whole are animated by trust rather than fear.

"Even though I walk in the valley of the
   shadow of death,
I fear no evil; for you are with me." (23:4)
"The Lord is my light and my salvation.
Whom shall I fear?" (27:1)

Despite the inevitability of death and the abject circumstances implied in many complaints, the psalmists seldom indulge in self-abasement. The famous phrase of 22:6, "But I am a worm and not human," is atypical. (In contrast, the poet of the *Hodayot*, or Thanksgiving Hymns, in the Dead Sea Scrolls, typically belittles himself as "a creature of clay, fashioned with water, foundation of shame, source of impurity, oven of iniquity, building of sin," 1QH[a] 9:22, trans. F. García Martínez and E. J. Tigchelaar, *The Dead Sea Scrolls Study Edition* [Leiden: Brill, 1997], 159). The confidence of the psalmists is grounded in belief in a benevolent creator God. Psalm 8 echoes the account of creation in Genesis 1. The psalmist marvels at the majesty of the heavens, and asks:

"What are human beings (*adam*) that you
   are mindful of them,
mortals (*ben adam*, 'son of man') that you
   care for them?"

But he goes on:

"Yet you have made them a little lower
   than God [or 'divine beings,' *elohim*],
   and crowned them with glory and
   honor.
You have given them dominion over the
   works of your hands;
you have put all things under their feet."

The value of life is ensured primarily by the possibility of a relationship with God, as can be seen especially in the expressions of trust cited above. This relationship reaches its fullest potential in connection with the presence of God in the temple.

"O God, you are my God,
I seek you, my soul thirsts for you,
my flesh faints for you as in a dry and
   weary land
where there is no water." (63:1)

This thirst is satisfied to some degree by gazing on the presence of God in the sanctuary, "beholding your power and your glory" (63:2). In Psalm 84 the psalmist declares, "My soul longs, it faints for the courts of the Lord," and adds that "a day in your courts is better than a thousand elsewhere." We find here an indication of a transcendent experience, an experience of ultimate value that is not negated by human mortality. We shall find a similar kind of experience in the celebration of human love in the Song of Songs, which declares that "love is as strong as death" (Song 8:6).

In some psalms the confidence in divine deliverance and the sense of fellowship with the divine seem to suggest that death may not be final after all, at least in special cases. Psalm 16:9-10 affirms:

"Therefore my heart is glad and my soul
   rejoices;
my body also rests secure.
For you do not give me up to Sheol
or let your faithful one see the Pit."

In the New Testament this passage is taken to refer to the Messiah and is cited as a proof text for the resurrection of Jesus (Acts 2:24-28). In the context of the Hebrew Psalter, the passage may mean only that the psalmist is confident that God will not let him "see the Pit" on this occasion, or before his life has run its natural course. A more intriguing case is provided by Ps 49:15 (MT 49:16): "But God will ransom my soul from the power of Sheol, for he will take me." The expression "take me" recalls the exceptional case of Enoch in Gen 5:24: "Enoch walked with God and he was not, for God took him." It was assumed, already in antiquity, that God had taken Enoch up to heaven, granting him an exception to the common human fate. It is possible that the psalmist hoped for a similar exception. The same verb is used in Ps 73:23-26:

> "Nevertheless I am continually with you;
> you hold my right hand.
> You guide me with your counsel,
> and afterward you will take me in
>   glory. . . .
> My flesh and my heart may fail,
> but God is the strength of my heart and
>   my portion forever."

Here again the psalmist seems to hope that the relationship with God will not be terminated by death, as would be the case in Sheol. Immortality may also be envisioned in the case of the king. According to 21:4, "he asked you for life, you gave it to him—length of days forever and ever."

It should be emphasized, however, that these cases are exceptional. The normal expectation in the Psalms is that people go to Sheol after death, and that when the Pit closes over them they can no longer even praise God. None of the psalms cited here offers any description of what eternal life might be like. They simply express confidence that God will "take" them. That they entertain such a hope at all is highly significant, however. Belief in

the possibility of eternal life would eventually emerge in Judaism in the Hellenistic period, in the apocalyptic literature and the Dead Sea Scrolls. This belief would be highly important for early Christianity.

The Kingship of God

There is never any doubt in the Psalms that God has the power to kill or to give life, to save or to destroy. The central image used to portray God is that of kingship, and the emphasis is on majesty and power: "The Lord is king, he is robed in majesty; the Lord is robed, he is girded with strength" (93:1). This theology is associated specifically with Zion, the holy mountain in Jerusalem (e.g., 48:1; 97:8; 99:2), and is probably continuous with the old Canaanite cult of El Elyon that was associated with Melchizedek in Genesis 14 (cf. Psalm 110).

In the psalms celebrating his kingship, YHWH is said to manifest his power by thunder, lightning, and earthquake. This kind of storm language was often used to describe theophanies in the Ugaritic myths, although it is associated with Baal, "the rider of the clouds," rather than with El. A classic example of this kind of storm theophany is found in Psalm 29:

> "The voice of the Lord is over the
>   waters;
> the God of glory thunders,
> the Lord, over mighty waters.
> The voice of the Lord is powerful;
> the voice of the Lord is full of majesty."

It has been suggested that this psalm was a lightly adapted Canaanite hymn; apart from the name YHWH there is nothing in it that could not have been said of Baal. Again in Psalm 97 we are told:

> "Clouds and thick darkness are all
> around him;
> righteousness and justice are the founda-
> tion of his throne.
> Fire goes before him and consumes his
> adversaries on every side.
> His lightnings light up the world; the
> earth sees and trembles.
> The mountains melt like wax before the
> Lord,
> before the Lord of all the earth."

It should be noted that the association of a deity with justice and righteousness was not peculiarly Israelite, but was rather part of the common theology of the ancient Near East. *Tsedeq*, "Justice," was even the name of a minor Canaanite deity.

Several of these hymns note that YHWH is exalted above the flood and is more majestic than the mighty waters (e.g., Psalm 93). This motif echoes the old Canaanite myth whereby Baal attained the kingship by defeating Yamm, the Sea. There is a more explicit allusion to this myth in 89:9-10:

> "You rule the raging of the sea;
> when its waves rise, you still them.
> You crushed Rahab like a carcass;
> you scattered your enemies with your
> mighty arm."

Some psalms suggest that the same myth is reflected in the Israelite story of the Exodus. In Ps 77:16 the waters saw YHWH and were afraid at the time of the Exodus. In Psalm 114 the sea looked and fled.

With the exception of the reference to Rahab in Psalm 89, the Psalms may be said to demythologize the old combat myth. The sea is normally viewed as part of nature, even if it is personified on occasion. YHWH's mastery over the sea and over the natural world in general is rooted in his role as creator. The fullest description of creation in the Psalms is found in Psalm 104, a hymn that has many points of analogy not only with Ugaritic mythology but also with the Egyptian hymn of Akhenaten (the "monotheistic" pharaoh) to the solar disk (*ANET*, 369–71). Psalm 104 begins by describing the majesty of God, "wrapped in light as with a garment." It goes on to say that YHWH stretched out the heavens like a tent and set the beams of his chambers on the waters. Then he set the earth on its foundations so that it should never be shaken. Then he covered it with the deep. At first the waters covered the mountains, but they fled at the rebuke of the Creator. "You set a boundary that they may not pass, so that they might not again cover the earth" (104:9). The process of creation, then, involved confining the sea within limits. A somewhat similar poetic account of creation is found in Job 26, which says that God "stretches out Zaphon [the mythical mountain of the north] over the void, and hangs the earth upon nothing." Job retains a clearer reference to the conflict with Rahab and the Sea. Both the psalm and the passage in Job draw on a tradition about creation that is not preserved in Genesis but appears to play a vital role in the Jerusalem cult. (It is also reflected in some prophetic passages such as Isa 51:9-11.)

The kingship of YHWH then derives from his role as creator and is attested by nature itself: "The heavens are telling the glory of God and the firmament proclaims his handiwork" (Ps 19:1; cf. 8:3). Consequently,

YHWH's kingship is supposed to be universal. "The heavens proclaim his righteousness and all the peoples behold his glory" (97:6). He is Lord of all the earth. All the ends of the earth have allegedly seen the victory of this God (98:3). The psalmists were surely aware that the kingship of YHWH was not, in fact, universally recognized. Consequently, the motif of the universal kingship of YHWH takes on eschatological implications, much like the motif of the "Day of the Lord" in the Prophets, which may itself have been inspired by the celebration of the kingship of YHWH in the cult. So Psalm 96 calls on all nature to rejoice

> "before the Lord; for he is coming,
> for he is coming to judge the earth.
> He will judge the earth with
>   righteousness,
> and the peoples with his truth."

Psalm 146 affirms:

> "The Lord will reign forever, your God,
> O Zion, for all generations."

We do not find in the Psalms the critique of present political realities that is characteristic of the prophets. The Psalter does, however, have an eschatological dimension in so far as it points to an ideal of the universal kingship of YHWH that has not yet been realized.

The Theology of Human Kingship

The kingship of YHWH has its earthly counterpart in the rule of the Davidic dynasty in Jerusalem. The relationship is pictured vividly in Psalm 2, where the Lord proclaims: "I have set my king on Zion, my holy mountain," and in Psalm 110, where the king is invited to sit at the right hand of YHWH. The king is YHWH's son and his vicar on earth. He may even be addressed as *elohim*, "god," although he is clearly subordinate to the Most High (45:7). The promise to David, reported in 2 Samuel 7, is reflected in Psalms 89 and 132.

All of this can be viewed rather easily as political propaganda, and no doubt it functioned this way in ancient Judah. The remarkable stability of the Davidic line over four centuries testifies to the effectiveness of the claim that YHWH had endorsed the royal house as the instrument of his rule. Of course the monarchy is not the only political system that receives divine endorsement in the Hebrew Scriptures. Early Israel had allegedly survived for some two centuries without a monarchy, and after the Babylonian exile Jews were obliged to find another form of governance. The Bible does not ultimately indicate preference for any one form of government. We have already seen sharp criticism of the monarchy both in the historical books and in the Prophets.

Some comments should be made, however, about the portrayal of kingship in the Psalms. First, like his divine counterpart, the king is committed to justice and righteousness. Psalm 72 prays:

> "Give the king your justice, O God,
> and your righteousness to a king's son.
> May he judge your people with
>   righteousness,
> and your poor with justice."

To be sure, this was the common theology of the ancient Near East. Hammurabi, no less than David or Josiah, proclaimed, in the prologue to his famous code, his purpose "to cause justice to prevail in the land, to destroy the wicked and the evil, that the strong might not oppress the weak" (*ANET*, 164). In the biblical context, however, the ideal of justice and righteousness was refined by the preaching of the prophets and eventually by the reforms of the Deuteronomists. The Deuteronomic understanding of kingship is probably reflected in Ps 89:27-37, which echoes 2 Samuel 7 in insisting that kings who break the law will be punished, even though the promise will not be revoked. Psalm 132:12 goes further, in apparently making the promise conditional on observance of the law.

Just as the kingship of YHWH had an eschatological aspect, so too did the rule of the Davidic dynasty. Psalm 2 implies a universal rule over "the nations" that was never realized historically. After the Babylonian exile, the eschatological aspect of the royal psalms became more pronounced. When there was no longer a king on the throne, these psalms became monuments to the hope of restoration. Psalm 2, which explicitly uses the Hebrew word *mashiach* (anointed one), would provide a basis for the view that the Messiah should be the son of God. This idea plays a central role in Christianity but is also attested in Jewish texts, in the Dead Sea Scrolls (4Q174 = the Florilegium; 4Q246 = the *Aramaic Apocalypse* or *Son of God* text), and again in *4 Ezra*. (Neither the Scrolls nor *4 Ezra* cites Psalm 2 as a proof text for the sonship of the Messiah, but *4 Ezra* 13 alludes to the psalm in a messianic context.) Psalm 110 is cited in Acts 2:34 as a proof text for the ascension of Jesus to heaven ("The Lord said to my Lord, 'Sit at my right hand'"). The royal psalms were generally understood as messianic in later Jewish and Christian tradition.

The Character of God

By definition, the God of the psalmists is a God who is expected to answer prayer. Naturally, the psalmists tend to emphasize the mercy of God:

> "The Lord is gracious and merciful,
> slow to anger and abounding in steadfast love.
> The Lord is good to all,
> and his compassion is over all that he has made." (Ps 145:9)

This is essentially the same characterization of God that is found in Exod 34:6 and repeated several times in the Scriptures (e.g., Ps 103:8). The psalmists praise the faithfulness of God: in the words of the refrain of Psalm 136, "His steadfast love endures forever." The mercy and fidelity of God are the basis for the psalmists' appeals "from the depths" and the subject of profuse thanksgiving. The Lord sets prisoners free, opens the eyes of the blind, and upholds the orphan and the widow (Psalm 146). All creation depends on him for its food in due season (145:15).

There is, however, another aspect of the character of God implied in several psalms. In many cases, the psalmists pray not only for deliverance but also for vengeance. So we read in Psalm 94:

> "O Lord, you God of vengeance, you God of vengeance, shine forth!
> Rise up, O judge of the earth; give to the proud what they deserve."

The psalmists' idea of what the wicked deserve is sometimes expressed quite vividly:

"O God, break the teeth in their mouths;
    tear out the fangs of the young lions, O
        Lord! . . .
Let them be like the snail that dissolves
    into slime;
like the untimely birth that never sees
    the sun." (Ps 58:6, 8)

Perhaps the most chilling prayer in the Psalter is found in 137:8-9:

"O daughter Babylon, you devastator!
    Happy shall they be who pay you back
    what you have done to us!
Happy shall they be who take your little
    ones
    and dash them against the rock!"

The sentiment is quite understandable, in view of what the Babylonians had done to Jerusalem, but it is none the more edifying for that. Again in 139:19–22 the psalmist prays:

"O that you would kill the wicked, O
    God,"

and goes on to plead,

"Do I not hate those who hate you, O
    Lord? . . . I hate them with perfect hatred."

Perhaps the first thing to be said about these psalms is that they are presented explicitly as expressions of human sentiments. There is no assurance that God shares these sentiments. But it is clear that at least some psalmists see God as a God of vengeance, just as surely as they see him as a God of mercy. The two sides of the divine character were stated explicitly in Exod 34:6-7: the same God who is gracious and merciful by no means acquits the guilty but visits the iniquity of the parents on their children even to the third and fourth generation. The Psalms are by no means exceptional in the Bible in depicting God as a God of vengeance. The justice of God typically entails a threat of violence toward wrongdoers. The Psalms routinely affirm that God will destroy the wicked, even when they are not at all vengeful in tone (e.g., Ps 145:20: "The Lord watches over all who love him, but all the wicked he will destroy").

Emotion or Instruction?

The problem with the psalms that ask for vengeance is not so much a matter of the character of God, who is a judge as well as a deliverer. The vengeance of God can even be a reason for human restraint if it is understood that vengeance is something that should be left to God, not pursued by human beings. The problem is rather with the kind of human character that these psalms seem to project. It makes a difference here whether we view these psalms as emotive expressions or as moral instructions. There can be little doubt that most of the psalms originated as emotive expressions. Their strength lies precisely in their ability to articulate the full range of human emotions, from anguish to joy. But anger and the desire for vengeance are also basic human emotions that should not be denied or suppressed. For victims of Babylonian terror, or victims of analogous terror in the modern world, Psalm 137 is cathartic. To be sure, it does not express the noblest of sentiments, but it is at least honest and forthright. By providing verbal expression for anger and vengeance, the psalm can act as a kind of safety valve that acknowledges the feelings without necessarily acting on them. If the psalmist took it upon himself to take Babylonian children and dash their heads against the rock, that would be quite a different matter. The power of the Psalms is that they depict human nature as it is. They do not necessarily depict human nature as it should be or as we would wish it to be.

Many argue, with much justification, that the editors of the Psalter wished to present it precisely as a book of instruction. This argument derives primarily from the inclusion of the wisdom psalms, and especially from the placement of Psalm 1 at the beginning of the collection and from the sheer length of the Torah psalm, Psalm 119. No doubt there is much to be learned from the Psalms. They teach the majesty of God and the needfulness of humanity, and encourage people to trust in the mercy and fidelity of God. Yet the prayers for vengeance serve as a reminder that the Psalms must also be read critically. The book of Psalms is not a book of moral instruction. It is primarily a record of ancient Israel and Judah at prayer. Countless generations of Jews and Christians have felt the words of the Psalter appropriate to express their own prayers and feelings. The need to express feelings, however, is no guarantee that those feelings are edifying or that they can serve as moral guidelines.

The Song of Songs

The Song of Songs (that is, "the greatest of songs," often called the Song of Solomon or Canticles in English Bibles) resembles the Psalms only insofar as both are collections of poems. In the Hebrew Bible it is placed among the Writings, after Job, as the first of the five Scrolls or Megillot: Song of Songs, Ruth, Lamentations, Qoheleth, Esther. This grouping of shorter books is based on their use in the liturgy: Song of Songs is read at Passover, Ruth at the Feast of Weeks, Lamentations on the ninth of Ab (marking the destruction of the temple), Qoheleth at Sukkoth, and Esther at Purim. In Christian Bibles it is usually grouped with Proverbs and Qoheleth on the grounds that all three are supposed to be Solomonic compositions. In fact, however, the Song (or Canticle, from the Latin *Canticum* in the Vulgate translation) is a unique composition, without any close analogy elsewhere in the biblical corpus. It is a collection of love songs, a celebration of erotic love between man and woman.

Because of its exceptional character in the biblical corpus, the Song has always been controversial. Fragments of three copies of the work have been found in the Dead Sea Scrolls. Two of these copies appear to have omitted some passages, even though these passages are attested in one or other of the copies. One copy omits the material from 4:8 to 6:11, while another omits the material between 3:5 and 3:9. The reason for these omissions is not clear. There was some dispute among the rabbis as to whether the Song should be included in the canon of Scripture. The great Rabbi Akiba, who died about 135 c.e., is said to have declared that the whole world was not worth the day on which the Song was given to Israel, "for all the scriptures are holy, but the Song of Songs is the Holy of Holies" (Mishnah *Yadaim* 3:5). But the rabbis preserved the sanctity of the Song by interpreting it as an allegory for the love between YHWH and Israel (despite the fact that the Song never mentions God). According to another rabbinic saying, anyone who sang the Song in a banquet house like a profane song would have no share in the world to come (Babylonian Talmud *Sanhedrin* 101a; Tosefta *Sanhedrin* 12.10). In Christian tradition the Song was most often read as an allegory for the love between Christ and the church.

The association of the Song with Solomon is due to the fact that his name is mentioned six times (1:5; 3:7, 9, 11; 8:11-12), while there are references to a "king" in 1:4, 12, and 7:5. These references led the editor to ascribe the Song to Solomon in the superscription. Solomon is never the speaker in any of the passages that mention him. In some cases, he is introduced in the context of explicit comparison (1:5; 8:11-12). In chapter 3, and in the references to a king, there is most probably an implicit comparison between the beloved and Solomon. Opinions vary widely on the actual date of the poems. The appearance of a Persian word, *pardes,* "garden," in 4:13, requires a postexilic date. Some scholars place it as late as the Hellenistic period, but decisive evidence is lacking.

Besides the traditional allegorical interpretation, the major modern interpretations of the Song see it as (1) a drama with either two or three main characters, (2) a cycle of wedding songs, (3) a remnant of a fertility cult, (4) a single love poem, or (5) a collection of love poems. Neither the dramatic interpretation nor the theory that relates the Song to a fertility cult can be maintained without distorting or rearranging the poems. Neither is there any clear indication of a wedding context. The crucial factor in appreciating the literary structure of the text is the recognition that there are several changes of speaker. Most often the speaker is a woman, sometimes addressing the beloved directly, sometimes speaking to "the daughters of Jerusalem." In 1:7—2:7 there is a dialogue between male and female. In 4:1-15 the voice is that of the man, and this is again the case in 6:1-10 and 7:1-9. In view of the changing voices and perspectives, it is difficult to defend the structural unity of the poem. Even those who argue for an overarching unity still distinguish a number of songs within the composition.

The number of songs is also a matter of disagreement, ranging from as few as six to more than thirty. The analysis followed here distinguishes eleven units:

I. 1:2-6: the woman expresses her longing for the beloved and introduces herself to "the daughters of Jerusalem." She compares herself to a vineyard, which she "has not kept."

II. 1:7—2:7: a dialogue between man and woman, which starts by making inquiries about a rendezvous and culminates in mutual admiration.

III. 2:8-17: a poem describing an encounter with the beloved.

IV. 3:1-5: a description of the search for and discovery of the beloved.

V. 3:6-11: a poem describing a wedding procession of King Solomon, which may be an implicit analogy, comparing the splendor of the beloved to the glory of Solomon.

VI. 4:1—5:1: a poem describing the physical beauty of the woman. This kind of poem is called a *wasf* and is typical of Near Eastern love poetry.

VII. 5:2—6:4: a dialogue between the woman and the daughters of Jerusalem, which includes a description of the man in the style of a *wasf.*

VIII. 6:5-12: a poem spoken by the man in praise of the woman. Again, there are elements of a *wasf* here.

IX. 7:1-9: another *wasf* in praise of the woman.

X. 7:10—8:4: a poem by the woman expressing her desire.

XI. 8:5-14: a series of very short poems that serve as an epilogue or conclusion. The woman refers to "my vineyard, my very own," in 8:12, thereby echoing the introductory verses.

The Song of Songs contains some of the most beautiful poetry in the Bible. It is rich in similes and repeatedly evokes scenes from nature. The beloved is compared to a rose of Sharon, a lily of the valley, a lily among brambles (2:1-2), or to a dove in the clefts of the rock (2:14). The beloved speaks at a time when winter is past, flowers appear on the earth, and the sound of the turtledove is heard in the land (2:10-12). Most striking is the appreciation of physical beauty in the *wasf* poems. (For comparable emphasis on physical beauty in the Jewish tradition, we must go to the postbiblical Genesis Apocryphon from Qumran, which praises the beauty of Sarah in similar detail.) Admittedly, some of the similes are startling to the ears of an urban, Western reader: "I compare you, my love, to a mare among Pharaoh's chariots" (1:9). "Your hair is like a flock of goats moving down the slopes of Gilead. Your teeth are like a flock of shorn ewes that have come up from the washing. . . . Your two breasts are like two fawns, twins of a gazelle" (4:1-5). The poetry reflects a bucolic, rural setting, with a ready appreciation of the beauty of animal life. (This is not negated by the references to a city. City life in ancient

Israel and Judah was never far removed from the rural context.) Another feature of the poetry is the frequent evocation of fruits and spices: "Your channel is an orchard of pomegranates with all the choicest fruits, henna with nard, nard and saffron, calamus and cinnamon, with all trees of frankincense, myrrh and aloes, with all chief spices" (4:13-15).

The most striking aspect of the Song, however, is its uninhibited celebration of sexual love. Just how uninhibited it is, is a matter of interpretation. Several passages lend themselves readily to sexual interpretations (e.g., 5:4: "my beloved thrust his hand into the opening, and my inmost being yearned for him"). But even if one does not explore the full range of metaphorical allusions, it is clear that physical love is joyfully affirmed. There is little to indicate that the lovers are married. The poem in 3:6-11 may celebrate a wedding procession, but in most of the poems the lovers evidently do not live together. This is why the woman has to go in search of the man. In 1:7, she asks where he pastures his flock. In 3:2, she rises from her bed and goes around the city to seek him. When she finds him, she brings him to her mother's house. On another occasion she is beaten by the sentinels as she searches for her lover (5:7). In 7:10-13 she urges him to go with her to the vineyards, so that "there I will give you my love." The impropriety of this love is reflected in 8:1: "O that you were like a brother to me, who nursed at my mother's breast! If I met you outside, I would kiss you, and no one would despise me." It is clear then that the love envisioned is not protected by the institution of marriage. There is no indication that it is adulterous (that either party is married to anyone else). Most probably, the lovers are young and unmarried.

The woman appeals to "the daughters of Jerusalem" as coconspirators, and this again suggests clandestine arrangements.

All of this contrasts sharply with the kind of sexual ethic that we meet elsewhere in the Bible, which is usually concerned to impose penalties (often draconian) for sexual irregularities. The primary concern in the biblical laws is with the institution of marriage. According to Deuteronomy 22, if a man is caught lying with the wife of another, both must die. Also if a man lies with a woman who is betrothed, both are subject to the death penalty, except that if the incident happens in an isolated area the woman is not held accountable. In the case of a woman who is neither married nor betrothed, however, the penalty is much less severe: "The man who lay with her shall give fifty shekels of silver to the young woman's father, and she shall become his wife. Because he violated her he shall not be permitted to divorce her as long as he lives" (Deut 22:29). The formulation in Deuteronomy implies that the young woman was forced. It does not appear, however, that premarital sex was regarded as a grievous matter so long as a marriage ensued.

The perspective from which the Song of Songs is written, however, differs greatly from that of Deuteronomy. Deuteronomy is concerned with social control, from the viewpoint of the authorities in the society. The Song of Songs articulates the viewpoint of the lovers, who find love intoxicating, delightful, and irresistible. From this perspective there can be no question of condemnation, regardless of social disapproval. The Song is unique in the Bible in giving expression to the romantic and erotic feelings of a woman.

The Song is one of only two books in the Hebrew Bible that does not mention God (the other is the book of Esther). Nonetheless, Rabbi Akiba declared it to be "the Holy of Holies." The reason, perhaps, was the purity of the love expressed, which validates itself by its strength and beauty. Love is affirmed as an ultimate value in life. Nowhere is this expressed more powerfully than in 8:6-7: "Set me as a seal upon your heart, as a seal upon your arm; for love is strong as death, passion fierce as the grave. . . . Many waters cannot quench love, neither can floods drown it. If one offered for love all the wealth of one's house, it would be utterly scorned."

In the New Testament, the author of the Johannine epistles wrote: "If we love one another, God lives in us, and his love is perfected in us" (1 John 4:12). No doubt, the author had a less passionate kind of love in mind. Nonetheless, the saying might also be applied to the love expressed in the Song of Songs. Love so intense is perhaps as close as mortals can come to participation in something divine.

FOR FURTHER READING

Psalms

Commentaries

L. C. Allen, *Psalms 101–150* (WBC 21; Waco: Word, 1983). Theological commentary with discussion of previous scholarship.

P. Craigie, *Psalms 1–50* (WBC 19; Waco: Word, 1983). Form-critical commentary with use of ancient Near Eastern parallels.

E. S. Gerstenberger, *Psalms, Part 1; with an Introduction to Cultic Poetry* (FOTL 14; Grand Rapids: Eerdmans, 1988); *Psalms, Part 2; Lamentations* (FOTL 15; Grand Rapids: Eerdmans, 2001). Acute form-critical analysis.

F.-L. Hossfeld and E. Zenger, Psalms 2. *A Commentary on Psalms 51–100* (Hermeneia: Minneapolis: Fortress Press, 2005); Psalms 3. *A Commentary on Psalms 101–150* (2011). Full critical commentary.

H.-J. Kraus, *Psalms* (2 vols.; trans. H. C. Oswald; CC; Minneapolis: Augsburg, 1988–1989). Classic form- and redaction-critical commentary.

J. C. McCann, "The Book of Psalms," *NIB* 4:641–1280. Thorough commentary with homiletical reflections.

M. E. Tate, *Psalms 51–100* (WBC 20; Dallas: Word, 1990). Theological commentary with attention to the final form of the Psalter.

Other studies

H. W. Attridge and M. Fassler, eds., *The Psalms in Community: Jewish and Christian Textual, Liturgical, and Artistic Traditions* (Symposium series; Atlanta: SBL, 2003). Wide-ranging collection of essays on ancient, medieval, and modern use of the Psalms.

W. P. Brown, ed. *The Oxford Handbook on the Psalms* (New York: Oxford University Press, 2014). Diverse essays from traditional and contemporary perspectives.

W. P. Brown, *Seeing the Psalms: A Theology of Metaphor* (Louisville, KY: Westminster John Knox, 2002). Insightful treatment of metaphors in the Psalms.

W. Brueggemann, *The Psalms and the Life of Faith* (Minneapolis: Fortress Press, 1995). Theological and homiletical study.

P. W. Ferris, *The Genre of Communal Lament in the Bible and the Ancient Near East* (SBLDS 127; Atlanta: Scholars Press, 1992). Comparative study of the lament genre.

P. W. Flint, *The Dead Sea Psalms Scrolls and the Book of Psalms* (Leiden: Brill, 1997). Important study of the evidence of the Dead Sea Scrolls on the formation of the Psalter.

S. Gillingham, *Psalms through the Centuries* (Oxford: Blackwell, 2008). First of two volumes on the reception history of the Psalms.

H. Gunkel, *An Introduction to the Psalms: The Genres of the Religious Lyric of Israel* (completed by J. Begrich; trans. J. D. Nogalski; Macon, GA: Mercer University Press, 1998). Foundational study of the Psalms. Indispensable.

F. Lindström, *Suffering and Sin: Interpretations of Illness in the Individual Complaint Psalms* (Stockholm: Almqvist & Wiksell, 1994). Detailed exegetical study of views of suffering in the Psalms.

J. C. McCann, *A Theological Introduction to the Psalms: The Psalms as Torah* (Nashville: Abingdon, 1993). Theological discussion from the perspective of the canonical approach.

P. D. Miller, *They Cried to the Lord: The Form and Theology of Israelite Prayer* (Minneapolis: Fortress Press, 1994). Major discussion of the theology of the Psalter.

S. Mowinckel, *The Psalms in Israel's Worship* (trans. D. R. Ap-Thomas; 2 vols.; Nashville: Abingdon, 1962). Classic discussion of the cultic setting of the Psalms.

H. P. Nasuti, *Defining the Sacred Songs: Genre, Tradition and the Post-Critical Interpretation of the Psalms* (JSOTSup 218; Sheffield: Sheffield Academic Press, 1999). Argues for the continued importance of genre in interpretation.

S. R. A. Starbuck, *Court Oracles in the Psalms. The So-Called Royal Psalms in Their Ancient Near Eastern Context* (SBLDS 172; Atlanta: SBL, 1999). Useful review of scholarship on the royal psalms.

C. Westermann, *Praise and Lament in the Psalms* (trans. K. R. Crim and R. N. Soulen; Atlanta: John Knox, 1981). Classic form-critical discussion.

G. H. Wilson, *The Editing of the Hebrew Psalter* (SBLDS 76; Chico, CA: Scholars Press, 1985). Important study of the editorial shaping and final shape of the canonical Psalter.

E. Zenger, *A God of Vengeance? Understanding the Psalms of Divine Wrath* (Louisville: Westminster John Knox, 1996). Theological attempt to grapple with a problematic aspect of the Psalms.

———, ed., *The Composition of the Book of Psalms* (Leuven: Peeters, 2010). Diverse essays on the composition and redaction of Psalms.

Song of Songs

Commentaries

J. C. Exum, *Song of Songs: A Commentary* (OTL; Louisville: Westminster, 2005). Balanced discussion of gender relationships.

M. V. Fox, *The Song of Songs and the Ancient Egyptian Love Songs* (Madison: University of Wisconsin Press, 1985). Discussion of the Song in the context of ancient Near Eastern love poetry.

O. Keel, *Song of Songs* (CC; Minneapolis: Fortress Press, 1994). Well illustrated with textual and iconographic parallels from ancient Near East.

R. E. Murphy, *The Song of Songs* (Hermeneia; Minneapolis: Fortress Press, 1990). Full commentary with good discussion of medieval interpretation.

M. H. Pope, *Song of Songs* (AB 7C; New York: Doubleday, 1977). Rich commentary against ancient Near Eastern background, highlighting the erotic character of the book.

R. J. Weems, "The Song of Songs," *NIB* 5:361–431. Well-informed commentary from a feminist perspective.

Other studies

A. Brenner, ed., *A Feminist Companion to the Song of Songs* (The Feminist Companion to the Bible 1; Sheffield: Sheffield Academic Press, 1993). A collection of essays from a feminist perspective.

D. Carr, *The Erotic Word: Sexuality, Spirituality, and the Bible* (New York: Oxford University Press, 2005). Positive construal of biblical views of sexuality. Pp. 89–154 on Song of Songs.

R. E. Murphy, "Song of Songs, Book of," *ABD* 6:150–55. Good overview of the scholarly discussion.

C. E. Walsh, *Exquisite Desire: Religion, the Erotic, and the Song of Songs* (Minneapolis: Fortress Press, 2000). Lively celebration of the eroticism of the Song.

CHAPTER 24
Proverbs

INTRODUCTION

This chapter addresses a form of literature different from those we've studied previously: the book of Proverbs. We will examine the traditional link between wisdom and King Solomon, the origins of wisdom literature, the composition of the book of Proverbs, and the nature of proverbial wisdom, as well as the contents of Proverbs.

In the book of Proverbs, we encounter a kind of literature that is quite different from the Torah, Prophets, or historical books. Conspicuously absent is any reference whatever to Israel and any interest in history at all. The book is in part a collection of proverbs or traditional sayings, which, almost by definition, have a timeless quality. In part it is instructional literature, presented as the teaching of a father to his son. This kind of literature is called "wisdom literature" because of the frequency with which words for wisdom and folly occur. While it appears only toward the end of the Hebrew Bible, it was an ancient and widespread form of literature in the Near East, and it may well be more representative of popular thought in ancient Israel than the more cultic and distinctively Israelite literature. In the Hebrew Bible, the wisdom literature is represented by Proverbs, Qoheleth (Ecclesiastes), and Job, and by some Psalms, such as Psalm 1. The deuterocanonical books, or Apocrypha, include two major wisdom books, that of Ben Sira and the Wisdom of Solomon. There is also a hymn to wisdom in the book of Baruch.

Wisdom and Solomon

The book of Proverbs is introduced as "the proverbs of Solomon, the son of David, king of Israel." We have already seen in 1 Kings that the wisdom of Solomon was legendary. In part, this was exemplified in his judgments (1 Kings 3), but it also involved a prodigious mastery of proverbs and knowledge of the natural world (1 Kgs 4:29-34; MT 5:9-14). Significantly, he is compared with "the wisdom of all the people of the east, and all the wisdom of Egypt."

This kind of lore was international and not specifically religious. Few scholars now would accept Solomonic authorship for any part of Proverbs. Solomon was the traditional patron of wisdom, as David was the traditional composer of psalms. We shall find later that the book of Qoheleth, which is certainly postexilic and probably Hellenistic in date, also adopts the persona of Solomon, even though it does not use his name. The Wisdom of Solomon, which invokes his name explicitly, was written in Greek around the turn of the era. The association with Solomon, then, is not a claim of authorship in the modern sense. It rather indicates that Proverbs represents a tradition that can be traced back to Solomon. It should be noted that Proverbs includes some sayings that are not attributed to Solomon: the "words of the wise" in chapters 22–23, the words of Agur in chapter 30, and the words of Lemuel in chapter 31.

Some scholars have supposed that Solomon was responsible for initiating the wisdom tradition in Israel by setting up scribal schools in Jerusalem. He would presumably have needed scribes for the service of his kingdom, and such scribal schools are known from other parts of the ancient Near East. Since Solomon is said to have married Pharaoh's daughter, this would account for the influence of Egyptian wisdom traditions on Proverbs and for the general affinities between Israelite and Egyptian wisdom. In recent years, however, skepticism has grown about the historicity of Solomon's empire because of the lack of archaeological evidence for it. To be sure, the primary area where such evidence might be found is safely buried under the Temple Mount in Jerusalem, and arguments from silence must be treated with caution. But it is now generally agreed that Jerusalem was a small town in Solomon's time and expanded significantly only two centuries later, in the time of Hezekiah. The evidence for literacy in ancient Israel before the time of Hezekiah is meager. It is of interest that the book of Proverbs itself says that one section of the book beginning in 25:1 consists of "proverbs of Solomon that the men of Hezekiah copied." Kingship is a prominent theme throughout chapters 10–29 of Proverbs, especially in chapters 28–29. This strengthens the impression that this literature was associated in some way with the royal court, whether this was already the case in the time of Solomon or not.

The Origins of Wisdom Literature

Basically, two kinds of setting have been proposed for the origin of wisdom literature. On the one hand, proverbs form part of the oral tradition of peoples all over the world. Presumably, Israel also had its folk proverbs that circulated in the tribes and families before ever the monarchy came to be. Such proverbs are essentially oral and are used contextually. A famous example is found in Ezek 18:2: "The parents have eaten sour grapes, and the children's teeth are set on edge." The riddles of Samson in Judges 14 are a similar phenomenon. It seems plausible that some of the sayings in the book of Proverbs would have originated in this way. In most cases, the individual saying is a unit in itself. Consequently, Proverbs is not a book that lends itself to continuous reading. Rather, it is a collection of wise sayings, and wisdom consists in knowing when to use an individual saying aptly in context.

On the other hand there is a well-attested genre of wisdom instruction, especially in Egypt, that dates back to the third millennium B.C.E. Examples include the teachings of Amenemhet and Ptahhotep (third millennium), those of Amenemope and Ani (second millennium), and numerous others. (Translations of these texts can be found in *ANET*, 412–24; and in M. Lichtheim, *Ancient Egyptian Literature* 1:58–80; 2:135–63). These instructions were copied in the scribal schools, and new instructions were composed, down to Hellenistic times. They consist of maxims relating to proper behavior and success in life. They typically deal with relations with other people, both superiors and inferiors, friends and enemies. They often caution about relations with women. They are by no means opportunistic. On the contrary, they seek to inculcate moral virtues in the belief that

these ultimately lead to success. Self-control is essential. Composure and reserve are recommended. The "heated man" is the antithesis of the wise. The Instruction of Amenemope is especially noteworthy for its reverence for "the Lord of all" and for the protection of the weak. The publication of the teaching of Amenemope in 1923 led to the discovery of close parallels between this work and Prov 22:17—23:11, and to the conclusion that the Hebrew composition was modeled on the Egyptian. The Egyptian instructions were copied for the instruction of scribes in schools sponsored by the pharaohs. It is not clear, however, whether such schools existed in Jerusalem before the exile. The earliest clear reference to a school in Jerusalem is found in the book of Ben Sira, from the early second century B.C.E. (Sir 51:23). Nonetheless, the analogy with the Egyptian instructions suggest that this

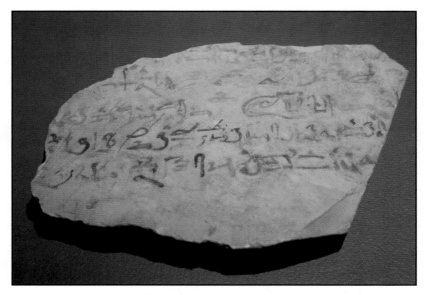

Fig. 24.1 Ostracon containing some of the teachings of Amenemhet, from Thebes; now in the Römer-und-Pelizaeus Museum, Hildesheim, Germany. Commons.wikimedia.org

literature was developed under the monarchy to serve the needs of the court. This suggestion receives some support from the reference to the men of Hezekiah in Prov 25:1. A court setting is also suggested by the Words of the Wise Ahikar (*ANET*, 427-30), an Aramaic wisdom book that circulated very widely in the ancient Near East (a copy was found in the Jewish archive at Elephantine in southern Egypt). Ahikar was supposedly an adviser to the king of Assyria. His name also appears in the book of Tobit.

These two kinds of settings, of course, are not mutually exclusive. It may be that the men of Hezekiah made a collection of popular proverbs or incorporated them into their compositions. There can be little doubt that the material in Proverbs evolved over several centuries. It may have served as material for education both in the home and in the court. It is usually assumed that the book was finally put together in the postexilic period, although the evidence is far from clear. By that time the monarchy no longer existed, and the wisdom instructions must be presumed to have served more general educational purposes.

If we may extrapolate from the case of Ben Sira, we might suppose that sages in Jerusalem offered instruction, whether on a tutorial basis or in a more formal school. The book of Proverbs would have provided material for such instruction. This kind of education was evidently distinct from that offered by the Levites, who taught from the Torah (according to 2 Chron 17:7-9). There are no explicit references to the Torah in the books of Proverbs, Qoheleth, and Job. Ben Sira, early in the second century B.C.E., appears to have been the first Jewish wisdom teacher to include the Torah in his curriculum.

The Composition of Proverbs

Within the book of Proverbs, there are seven distinct collections introduced by distinct headings or superscriptions:

The numerical sayings in 30:15-33 and the poem on the capable woman in 31:10-31 also appear to be distinct units.

It appears then that the book is made up of several collections. These appear in different

COLLECTIONS IN THE BOOK OF PROVERBS	
1:1—9:18	The proverbs of Solomon, son of David, king of Israel
10:1—22:16	The proverbs of Solomon
22:17—24:22	The words of the wise
24:23-34	These also belong to the wise
25:1—29:17	Other proverbs of Solomon that the men of Hezekiah collected
30:1-14	The words of Agur, son of Jakeh
31:1-9	The words of King Lemuel, with which his mother instructed him

order in the Greek translation (LXX), where the sequence is: 22:17—24:22; 30:1-14; 24:23-34; 30:15-33; 31:1-9; 25:1—29:27; 31:10-31. In part this different order may reflect an attempt to group together material of foreign origin: the words of the wise, which are influenced by Egyptian wisdom, and the sayings of Agur and Lemuel. There are also several additional verses in the LXX.

The proverbial core of the book is found in chapters 10–29. Chapters 1–9 contain more developed instructions and more general reflections on the nature of wisdom. Chapters 30–31 contain miscellaneous additions to the book, including the sayings of two individuals who are otherwise unknown and are not evidently Israelites (Agur and Lemuel).

The Nature of Proverbial Wisdom

Perhaps the most fundamental objective of proverbial wisdom is simply to make observations. Several sayings have the character of simple propositional statements. "Anxiety weighs down the human heart, but a good word cheers it up" (Prov 12:25). "Hope deferred makes the heart sick" (13:12). "The poor are disliked even by their neighbors, but the rich have many friends" (13:20). "'Bad, bad,' says the buyer, then goes away and boasts" (20:14). The numerical sayings in chapter 30 are likewise attempts to observe and categorize phenomena. Four things are small but exceedingly wise (ants, badgers, locusts, the lizard). Four are stately in their gait (the lion, the rooster, the he-goat, and the king). This latter kind of observation is related to riddles: Name four things that are small and wise, or what do

these four things have in common? How is a king like a rooster? There is, of course, also an element of humor in noting the similarity between his majesty and the farmyard fowl.

Observational sayings implicitly appeal to experience. This appeal is only rarely made explicit. Proverbs 24:30-34 is a case in point: "I passed by the field of one who was lazy...." In most cases, these observations were passed on from father to son, or from teacher to student, and accepted on the authority of tradition. We shall find that Qoheleth was exceptional in attempting to verify traditional wisdom for himself. Moreover, observations are often quite tendentious. They may attempt to pre-empt discussion by stating that something is simply the case, when it may not in fact be so obvious. Perhaps the most blatant example of such a tendentious observation is found in Ps 37:25: "I have been young, and now am old, yet I have never seen the righteous forsaken or their children begging bread." Either the psalmist had not looked very far, or he simply assumed that anyone whose children were begging bread was not righteous. Many assertions in Proverbs also are debatable, but express what the author wanted the reader to believe. "Riches do not profit in the day of wrath, but righteousness delivers from death" (11:4); "The righteous are delivered from trouble, and the wicked get into it instead" (11:8). "Those who spare the rod hate their children" (13:24). Many of the assertions are attempts to define what it means to be wise or foolish. "A wise child loves discipline," we are told (13:1); "a fool despises a parent's instruction" (15:5). Nonetheless, it is important that none of these observations claims to derive from revelation or any kind of divine authority. In principle, these are claims that any human person should be able to verify by observation. To be sure, tradition carries enormous weight. In the words of Bildad in the book of Job, "Inquire now of bygone generations, and consider what the ancestors have found; for we are but of yesterday, and we know nothing, for our days on earth are but a shadow." Yet in principle this tradition is human knowledge, and therefore open to verification and dispute. It can also be insightful, humorous, and on target. See, for example, the description of the drunkard in 23:29-35.

The observations of traditional wisdom are extended by the use of analogies. We have touched on this point in connection with the numerical sayings. One of the objectives is to establish what different phenomena have in common, and thereby bring order to experience. But again, comparisons can be tendentious. They are in effect invitations to look at the world in a certain way (they also provide opportunities for biting humor). "Like a gold ring in a pig's snout is a beautiful woman without good sense" (11:22). "Like clouds and wind without rain is one who boasts of a gift never given" (25:14). "Like a dog that returns to its vomit is a fool that reverts to his folly" (26:11). "A continual dripping on a rainy day and a contentious wife are alike" (27:15). However tendentious they may be, comparisons are a way of finding order in experience and enabling the wise person to master the confusion of experience.

Another important way in which things are linked together is the chain of cause and effect. "Whoever digs a pit will fall into it, and a stone will come back on the one who starts it rolling" (26:27). Drunkenness leads to "wounds without cause" and "redness of eyes" (23:29). Laziness and idleness lead to poverty (24:30-34). Wisdom consists, in no small measure, in understanding the consequences of various courses of action. Moreover, one must be wary of hasty judgments. "Sometimes there is a way that seems to be right, but in the end it is the way of death" (16:25). Here again, the alleged consequences may be tendentious. We are assured repeatedly that "treasures gained by wickedness do not profit, but righteousness delivers from death" (10:2). It is all too obvious that generalizations such as this admit of many exceptions. The connection between act and consequence, however, is crucial to the ethics of proverbial wisdom. Virtue is not recommended as an end in itself, or at least not only as an end in itself. The sages seek to convince us that righteousness is ultimately the most profitable course of action. Herein lies the main problem of wisdom ethics, since the profitability of righteousness is not always in evidence. This problem is treated at length in the book of Job.

The ethical teaching of Proverbs is highly pragmatic. This literature was designed to help the student succeed in life. It was not narrowly religious. Proverbs 23:1-8 (in the section modeled on the Instruction of Amenemope) gives advice on table manners if one is invited to eat with a ruler. There is scarcely a moral issue involved here, but social behavior could have a huge impact on the career of a scribe. Concern for practical results informs the advice of the sages on ethical issues. Even though it is good to help one's neighbor, it is folly to go surety for the debt of another: "If you have nothing with which to pay, why should your bed be taken from under you?" (22:27). A bribe, we are told, "is like a magic stone in the eyes of those who give it; wherever they turn they prosper" (17:8; cf. 18:16). This pragmatic attitude is often considered to be typical of "old wisdom" before it was tempered by the moralistic tendency of the postexilic period. Sometimes this kind of pragmatism is viewed negatively, as cynical. In 2 Samuel 13, when David's son Amnon is tormented by desire for his sister Tamar, his friend Jonadab, who is described as "a very crafty man" (2 Sam 13:3), contrives a way to put the young woman at his mercy. Advisers to kings and rulers were supposed to be "wise," and no doubt their wisdom was no more preoccupied with morality than is the case with political advisers in the modern world. It has even been suggested that the wisdom of the serpent in the story of Adam and Eve is a caricature of pragmatic wisdom. Pragmatism, however, should not be equated with cynicism. The opportunism of the wise in the book of Proverbs is always limited by "the fear of the LORD." The concern for practical results is one of the more appealing aspects of this literature because of its down-to-earth, realistic character.

We do, however, also find moments of idealism in Proverbs, when the conduct recommended cannot easily be identified with self-interest. This appears especially in the form of concern for the poor. There is, to be sure, some tension within Proverbs on this subject. On the one hand, there is a tendency to blame the poor for their condition and to assume that poverty is the result of laziness. "A slack hand causes poverty, but the hand of the diligent makes rich" (10:4). "Poverty and disgrace are for the one who ignores instruction, but one who heeds reproof is honored" (13:18). Yet Proverbs also warns frequently against oppressing the poor. This is one of the few occasions where Proverbs appeals to YHWH. "Those who oppress the poor insult their Maker, but those who are kind to the

needy honor him" (14:31). "Whoever is kind to the poor lends to the LORD, and will be repaid in full" (19:17). "Do not rob the poor because they are poor, or crush the afflicted at the gate; for the LORD pleads their cause" (22:22-23). We need not suppose that this concern arises from the influence of the Torah or the Prophets. We find a similar concern in the Egyptian Instruction of Amenemope: "Beware of robbing a wretch, of attacking a cripple; don't stretch out your hand to touch an old man. . . . He who does evil, the shore rejects him, the floodwater carries him away" (Lichtheim, *Ancient Egyptian Literature,* 2:150). The idea that justice required the protection of the needy was recognized throughout the ancient Near East from very early times.

The tension between pragmatism and idealism in Proverbs sometimes results in contradictory advice. According to Prov 26:17, someone who meddles in the quarrel of another is "like somebody who takes a passing dog by the ears." Yet we are told in 24:11–12: "If you hold back from rescuing those taken away to death, those who go staggering to

Fig. 24.2 **Gold mask of Amenemope of Egypt, 21st Dynasty; now in the Cairo Museum.** Commons.wikimedia.org

the slaughter; if you say, 'Look, we did not know this'—does not he who weighs the heart perceive it?" Again, some sayings seem to condone bribery. "A gift in secret averts anger; and a concealed bribe in the bosom, strong wrath" (21:14). Yet we are told that "the wicked accept a concealed bribe to pervert the ways of justice" (17:23). Presumably, not all bribes lead to perversion of justice. It is of the essence of the wisdom literature, however, that advice that is right for one situation may be wrong for another. As Qoheleth will say, there is a time for everything. Proverbs 26:4-5 emphasizes this point by juxtaposing two contradictory sayings: "Do not answer fools according to their folly, or you will be a fool yourself. Answer fools according to their folly, or they will be wise in their own eyes." Wisdom is not a matter of knowing a stock of universal truths. It is a matter of knowing the right response on a specific occasion. "To make an apt answer is a joy to anyone, and a word in season, how good it is!" (15:23). Conversely, a proverb in the mouth of a fool is said to hang limp like the legs of a cripple (26:7).

There is also some tension in Proverbs between the pragmatic, hardheaded wisdom that we have considered and a moralizing tendency that appears in other sayings. Several such sayings appear in chapter 10. "The LORD does not let the righteous go hungry, but he thwarts the craving of the wicked" (10:3). "Blessings are on the head of the righteous" (10:6). "Whoever walks in integrity walks securely" (10:9), and so on. Some scholars suppose that these sayings reflect a secondary redaction of Proverbs. The "old wisdom" was pragmatic, geared toward practical success in life. Later, when Proverbs came to be viewed primarily as religious instruction, the

moralistic element was introduced, to inculcate obedience and deference to tradition, without regard to practical results. It is certainly true that the two distinct tendencies can be found in this literature. It is also true that the function of the literature changed over time. In the preexilic period it was used in the training of people for service at court. In postexilic times it was still used for the training of scribes but was also increasingly used as religious education. Nonetheless, other scholars regard the separation of editorial strata as too simple and suppose that both elements were present in the tradition from early times.

The name of YHWH is invoked in Proverbs much less frequently than in the Torah or the Prophets, and there is no reference at all to the history of Israel or to a revealed Torah. The Deity functions in the wisdom literature primarily in two ways. First, God guarantees the cosmic order, which ensures that the chain of cause and effect takes its course. "The eyes of the LORD are in every place, keeping watch on the evil and the good" (15:3). Proverbs has no place for miraculous interventions in history, nor does it encourage prayer for extraordinary deliverance. The chain of cause and effect is automatic, to a great degree. The role of the deity in this kind of universe has been compared to that of a midwife. God sees to it that nature takes its course. God is also creator, and so there is no suggestion that nature is independent of God. But the divine role in human affairs is obviously more restrained than was the case in the Prophets. Second, God is encountered in human affairs as the power that limits human capability. "The plans of the mind belong to mortals, but the answer of the tongue is from the LORD" (16:1). "Do not boast about tomorrow, for you do not know what a day may bring" (27:1). Human beings are not in control of their own destiny; not even fully in control of what they say. Hence the beginning of wisdom is the fear of the Lord, an attitude of humility and reverence that recognizes our dependent status as creatures. Arrogance and self-reliance are the antithesis of wisdom. This belief that true wisdom requires humility and caution is also characteristic of Egyptian wisdom. Only rarely does Proverbs hint at divine judgment, as when it says that the Lord pleads the cause of the poor (22:23), and even in those cases we need not suppose that any miraculous intervention is envisioned.

Proverbs 30–31

The words of Agur and Lemuel at the end of the collection are consistent with the character of Proverbs 10–29. The words of Agur are remarkable for their skepticism, which anticipates the more developed reflections that we will find in the book of Qoheleth. "Who has ascended to heaven and come down?" Agur asks (30:4). Presumably, he would have been skeptical about prophets who claimed to have stood in the council of the Lord, not to mention the later apocalyptic visionaries who claimed to have enjoyed tours of heaven. But the so-called proverbs of Solomon have no place for such special revelations either. The words of Lemuel touch on the duties of a king. He should refrain from strong drink. Drink, however, has its own proper use, to enable the wretched to forget their misery for a while. The main duty of the king is to judge righteously and defend the rights of the poor.

Proverbs ends with a remarkable poem on "the capable wife." This poem is a valuable counterbalance to the picture of the "strange woman" in Proverbs 1–9. It shows that the sages were not misogynistic; they were critical of some female behavior, not of women as such. But for all its professed praise of women, 31:10-31 is unabashedly patriarchal in its perspective. It reflects the crucial contributions of women to agricultural society in antiquity and shows high respect for their competence. In the end, however, much of the glory redounds to the husband, who is a gentleman of leisure because of her labors and can take his place among the elders of the city gates. The role of women in a traditional society in antiquity was light-years away from modern feminism, but it was not entirely negative either. Even if the husband in Proverbs 31 does not rise early to help her, he at least joins in the praise of his wife and appreciates what an asset she is.

Proverbs 1–9

In contrast to Proverbs 10–31, chapters 1–9 are made up of lengthy instructions, which reflect on the nature of wisdom in a more abstract way. The purpose of the collection is expressed as follows:

"For learning about wisdom and
    instruction,
    for understanding words of insight,
for gaining instruction in wise dealing,
    righteousness, justice, and equity;
to teach shrewdness to the simple,
    knowledge and prudence to the
    young—
let the wise also hear and gain in
    learning,
    and the discerning acquire skill,

to understand a proverb and a figure,
  the words of the wise and their riddles." (Prov 1:2-6)

We may compare the introduction to the Instruction of Amenemope:

"Beginning of the teaching for life,
the instructions for well-being,
every rule for relations with elders,
for conduct toward magistrates;
knowing how to answer one who speaks,
to reply to one who sends a message,
so as to direct him on the paths of life,
to make him prosper on the earth."
(Lichtheim, *Ancient Egyptian Literature,*
  2:148)

The Egyptian instruction places more emphasis on professional training and preparation for life in the service of officials. Both texts, however, emphasize that understanding is related to moral training. Both also emphasize the primacy of understanding: right action only follows from a grasp of the way things are.

Proverbs 1:7 might serve as a summary of the theology of Proverbs: The fear of the Lord is the beginning of knowledge. Whatever else the phrase may mean, it entails recognition of one's own limitation and reliance on a higher power. This attitude was not peculiar to ancient Israel, but was broadly typical of ancient Near Eastern wisdom. It is, nonetheless, characteristic of Hebrew wisdom. Linked to this "fear of the Lord" is a similar deferential disposition toward parents and teachers. "Hear, my son, your father's instruction, and do not reject your mother's teaching" (1:8). The student is warned repeatedly of the dire fate that awaits those who do not pay heed to authority: "At

the end of your life you will groan, when your flesh and body are consumed, and you say, 'Oh, how I hated discipline, and my heart despised reproof! I did not listen to the voice of my teachers or incline my ear to my instructors. Now I am at the point of utter ruin in the public assembly'" (5:12-14).

Two themes predominate in Proverbs 1–9. One consists of repeated warnings against various temptations that beset the young. The other is the praise of wisdom itself. These themes reach a climax in chapters 7–9, where both folly and wisdom are personified in female form.

The theme of warning is introduced in 1:8-19, in an admonition that is rather typical of the concerns of parents for their teenage children. They worry that the son (or daughter) may "get in with the wrong crowd" and so come to grief. The warning is typically dire. These "sinners" are plotting murder, and in the end they will lose their own lives. The real issue, both in ancient and in modern times, is one of control and influence. Will the young person be guided by his or her parents, or succumb to the pressures of the peer group? Such concerns are timeless and not peculiar to any historical period. They are, perhaps, more typical of urban than of rural society, insofar as the youth are exposed to more influences and less likely to be restrained by the force of tradition. Most scholars have assumed that these chapters were written in Jerusalem in the Second Temple (probably Persian) period, but the evidence is not conclusive.

The "Strange Woman"

The primary image of temptation in these chapters, however, is "the strange woman" (*'ishah zarah*). This figure is first introduced in 2:16-19, where she is associated with the adulteress: "You will be saved from the strange woman, from the adulteress with her smooth words, who forsakes the partner of her youth, and forgets her sacred covenant." Again in 5:3-4 we are told that "the lips of a strange woman drip honey, and her speech is smoother than oil, but in the end she is bitter as wormwood, sharp as a two-edged sword." The most elaborate description is in chapter 7. The author claims to see "a young man without sense" who is accosted by a woman "decked out like a prostitute, wily of heart. She is loud and wayward; her feet do not stay at home." She seduces the young man, who goes with her like an ox to the slaughter. The chapter ends on a somber note: "her house is the way to Sheol, going down to the chambers of death" (7:27). Each of the passages dealing with the strange woman similarly ends with a warning that her ways lead to death (cf. 2:18-19; 5:5).

The "strange woman" of Proverbs has given rise to a multitude of interpretations. The claim that her ways lead down to Sheol leads some commentators to conclude that she is a mythological figure, or at least that she is depicted in a way that is modeled on certain goddesses in Near Eastern literature. In the Epic of Gilgamesh, the goddess Ishtar proposes marriage to Gilgamesh. In the Ugaritic Epic of Aqhat, the goddess Anat offers eternal life to Aqhat. In each case, the human hero refuses. There may be some mythological influence in the portrayal of the strange woman in Proverbs, in that she seems to offer the fullness of life but delivers only death. Nonetheless, it is clear that the strange woman is a human figure, not a goddess.

Another line of interpretation suggests that the woman is a cult prostitute who entices the young man to participate in the worship of a goddess. The whole idea of cultic prostitution, which was long thought to have been a feature of Canaanite religion, is now viewed with considerable skepticism. In any case, there is really nothing to suggest that the strange woman is involved in any kind of cultic ritual. Moreover, in chapter 7 she is "decked out like a prostitute," which suggests that she is not actually a prostitute.

Many scholars have supposed that the adjective "strange" here means that the reference is to foreign women. Jewish young men are warned then not to succumb to the attractions of foreigners. The warnings against the strange woman might then be related to the crisis over intermarriage in the time of Ezra. Yet Proverbs never indicates that the problem is that she belongs to a different people. In contrast, a passage from the Egyptian Instruction of Ani warns of "a woman from abroad, who is not known in her (own) town" (Ani iii [13], *ANET*, 420). In the Egyptian instruction, the problem is not ethnic (she is not said to be non-Egyptian) but the fact that she is away from home. The woman in Proverbs 7, however, is at home. It is her husband who is out of town.

The most satisfactory explanation of the strange woman is simply that she is the wife of another. This is explicitly the case in chapter 7, which says that her husband has gone on a journey. Moreover, there is an explicit warning against "the wife of another" in 6:24-35. (The Hebrew text reads "an evil woman." The Greek has "a married woman." It is clear from the context that the reference is to a married woman in either case.) The passage in Proverbs 6 gives a quite mundane account of the dangers of adultery. The adulterer gets wounds and dishonor, and his disgrace will not be wiped away, "for jealousy arouses a husband's fury and he shows no restraint when he takes revenge" (6:34). Deuteronomy stipulates that if a man is caught lying with the wife of another man, both of them must die (Deut 22:22). Proverbs assumes that this law was not in force. The aggrieved husband might in principle accept compensation. The *de facto* penalty seems to be "wounds and dishonor." It should be noted that the objection is not to extramarital sex as such. "A prostitute's fee is only a loaf of bread, but the wife of another stalks a man's very life" (6:26). The problem with adultery is that it transgresses a social boundary and leads to conflict and danger.

The speech of the "strange woman" in chapter 7 includes an intriguing detail that has defied commentators. She tells the young man that "I had to offer sacrifices, and today I have paid my vows, so now I have come out to meet you" (7:14-15). Some scholars have supposed that the woman had vowed to have sexual intercourse with a stranger. There is a story in the Greek historian Herodotus about the "foul custom" of the Babylonians by which a woman had to give herself to a stranger before marriage (Herodotus 1.99). Modern scholars, however, regard this story as evidence of the credulity of Herodotus, rather than of a Babylonian custom. Moreover, the woman in Proverbs 7 is already married. Alternatively, it has been suggested that a woman needed money to pay for her vows, and that the action of the "strange woman" is due to the fact that her husband is away and has taken his money with him. (Compare Numbers 30, which insists that a woman's vows may be canceled by her father or her husband, who would actually bear the cost.) Perhaps the most plausible explanation, however, is that the woman wants to celebrate having fulfilled her vows while her husband is away.

The strange woman, then, is first of all the adulteress, who is perceived as a threat to the social order (from an explicitly male point of view). In Proverbs, however, this figure takes on symbolic significance so that she represents all deviation from the way of wisdom.

The Figure of Wisdom

In contrast to the "strange woman" stands the figure of Lady Wisdom. Wisdom first appears in Prov 1:20, crying out in the street and at the city gates. Wisdom is not secret. It is available to anyone who is willing to take instruction. The public preaching of Wisdom and its admonitory tone bring to mind the prophets such as Jeremiah, who roamed the streets of Jerusalem calling on people to repent. The repentance that Wisdom seeks is repentance of folly and attention to the teachings of Wisdom. In the Hellenistic world, teachers and philosophers sometimes sought pupils in public places. Whether any teachers in Jerusalem in the Persian period similarly sought out students, we do not know. The thrust of Wisdom's speech is that people need to submit to instruction, and it implies that such instruction is available, whether in a formal school or by individual tutorial. It is not simply a matter of changing one's behavior, although this would surely follow from right understanding. The call of the sage differs from that of the prophet in emphasizing the priority of understanding over action.

Perhaps the most surprising aspect of Wisdom's first speech is its vindictive tone: "I also will laugh at your calamity; I will mock when panic strikes you" (1:26). Later, in 8:17, Wisdom says, "I love those who love me," and she repeatedly promises that those who listen to her will prosper. But she has little sympathy for the foolish. Qoheleth will later remark that the Lord "has no pleasure in fools" (Qoh 5:4). The statement that Wisdom will laugh at the calamity of the foolish is echoed in the book of Job, even more harshly, when Job claims that God mocks the calamity of the innocent (Job 9:23). This charge may not be justified, but it coheres with the belief in the wisdom literature that actions breed their own consequences. People who ignore instruction and then come to grief have no one to blame but themselves.

A different aspect of wisdom is highlighted in Prov 2:19: "The Lord by wisdom founded the earth; by understanding he established the heavens." Since the earth was founded with wisdom, nature is rational and admits of understanding. This is the basis for a kind of natural theology, whereby one can arrive at knowledge of the Creator by studying the order of the universe. There is no suggestion here that nature is out of joint or spoiled by sin.

The role of Wisdom in creation is developed at length in the great Wisdom poem in Proverbs 8. Wisdom is again portrayed as crying out at the crossroads and the city gate. Her words are righteous, but they are also better than jewels. Education is also profitable.

Perhaps the most startling aspect of this poem is the degree to which Wisdom praises herself. Elsewhere in the Hebrew Bible only the Most High makes such grandiose claims (see especially Isaiah 40–55). This manner of speech has led many scholars to suspect that Wisdom was originally conceived as a goddess. The closest analogies to her speech are found in inscriptions in which the Egyptian goddess Isis sings her own praises (these are called *aretalogies* of Isis). Isis claims, for example, to be the eldest daughter of the sun-god Re, to be the ruler of all lands, to have set down laws for humanity, to control the rise and fall of kings, and many other accomplishments. (Compare Prov 8:15-16: "By me kings reign and rulers decree what is just; by me rulers rule, and nobles, all who govern rightly.") These aretalogies of Isis are known from Greek inscriptions, which are no earlier than the first century B.C.E., and therefore too late to have influenced the book of Proverbs. It may be, however, that similar praises of Isis

Fig. 24.3   Isis nurses her son Horus (representing the ascendant pharaoh); bronze, ca. 680–640 B.C.E.; at the Walters Art Museum, Baltimore. Commons.wikimedia.org

were known in Egyptian tradition at an earlier date. In any case, the similarity is noteworthy.

Wisdom has also been compared to another Egyptian goddess, Maat, the goddess of truth and justice. Maat was the foundation principle of Egyptian society, and her role in Egyptian religion is somewhat similar to that of Wisdom in Proverbs. But Maat never sings her own praises and is not even portrayed as speaking.

To say that the portrayal of Wisdom is influenced by that of a goddess or goddesses is not necessarily to say that Wisdom was thought to be a goddess herself. Wisdom is first of all an attribute of (some) human beings, which is also presumed to be an attribute of God in a higher degree. When wisdom is depicted as a female figure who speaks, this is the literary device of personification. There are many examples of such personification in the Hebrew Bible and in other literature, ancient and modern. Compare, for example, Ps 85:10-11: "Steadfast love and faithfulness will meet; righteousness and peace will kiss each other. Faithfulness will spring up from the ground, and righteousness will look down from the sky." Sometimes personifications of this sort could be regarded as divinities. In the Ugaritic texts, Righteousness sometimes appears as a minor deity. The Egyptian goddess Maat is to some degree a personification of truth and righteousness. It has been suggested that Wisdom was also a goddess in this way, specifically that she was the patron goddess of wisdom schools. There is no real evidence that Wisdom was regarded as a goddess either in Israel or in Canaan. It is probably true, however, that the way that Wisdom is portrayed is influenced by the depictions of goddesses, especially Isis and Maat.

The role of Wisdom in creation is addressed most explicitly in 8:22-31. Here we are told: "The LORD created me at the beginning of his work, the first of his acts of long ago" (v. 22). The Hebrew word that is translated "created" is *qanah,* which normally has the meaning "purchase" or "acquire." It is used with reference to human beings acquiring wisdom in 1:5; 4:7; and several other places. The question then arises whether wisdom was created, or whether it existed independently and was acquired by YHWH. It should be noted that in Job 28 God is said to know where Wisdom can be found but is not said to create her. The later tradition, however, is unanimous in understanding this verse to say that YHWH created Wisdom (this is how the verse is translated in the Greek). Proverbs 8:25 uses birth imagery to speak of how Wisdom was brought forth. Interestingly, the verb *qanah* is used with reference to the birth of Cain in Gen 4:1, where Eve says, "I have acquired a man with YHWH." In any case, Wisdom is clearly subordinate to YHWH in Proverbs 8, and is used for his purposes.

Wisdom, we are told, is created, or acquired, before the creation of the world. The Hebrew word for "beginning" (*re'eshith*) can mean "best" or "most important" as well as temporally first, and the two meanings are complementary. In later rabbinic tradition, six things were said to be created or contemplated before the creation of the world: the Torah, the throne of glory, the patriarchs, Israel, the temple, and the name of the Messiah (Midrash Rabbah on Genesis 1:4; the midrash assumes that Prov 8:22 refers to the creation of the Torah). In Proverbs 8 the implication is that Wisdom was then involved in the work of creation. The NRSV translates 8:30: "Then I was beside him as a master worker; and I was daily his delight, rejoicing before him always." The word translated "master worker" is *amon*, and the meaning is disputed. The translation "master worker" understands the term in the light of the Akkadian word *ummanu*. This meaning is probably assumed in the Greek translation and is certainly found in the Wisdom of Solomon, a later wisdom book, written in Greek around the turn of the era (Wis 7:22). An alternative explanation relates the word to the Hebrew *amen* and translates "continually, steadfastly." Yet another understands the word as "ward, nursling," and takes it to portray Wisdom as a child. The last interpretation accords well with the following lines, which refer to rejoicing and delight. In any case, Wisdom accompanies God in the work of creation and ensures that wisdom is embedded in the order of the universe.

Wisdom thus forms a bridge between the creation and the created. By acquiring wisdom, human beings can grasp the order of the universe and the purpose of life, but they can also share in the wisdom of God. Wisdom thus provides a rather different model for understanding the relations between God and the universe from what we find in the Torah and the Prophets, where the emphasis is on obedience. This kind of natural theology, or creation theology, is further developed in the deuterocanonical wisdom books of Ben Sira and the Wisdom of Solomon.

One other feature of the figure of Wisdom should be noted. Wisdom claims to give life, just as the "strange woman" leads to death. It is not implied that those who acquire wisdom will enjoy eternal life. The reference is rather to the fullness of life in this world— long life and prosperity (cf. Prov 3:16: "Long life is in her right hand; in her left hand are riches and honor"). Eventually, this promise of fullness of life would be one of the factors that contributed to the rise of a hope for immortality. Among the biblical and deuterocanonical wisdom books, however, this hope is only found in the Wisdom of Solomon.

Proverbs 1–9 concludes by juxtaposing the contrasting figures of Wisdom and "the foolish woman." Wisdom is constructive and nourishing. She builds a house for shelter, and she provides food and drink. (The imagery of food and drink in connection with wisdom will appear again in Ben Sira 24, and plays an important role in the New Testament in the Gospel of John.) The foolish woman resembles Wisdom insofar as she makes her appeal in public places and she also promises nourishment, but her promise is deceptive. Her way leads to death. These contrasting figures sum up the teaching of Proverbs 1–9. There are two ways, but only one delivers what it promises. We are reminded of the story of Adam and Eve, and the false promise of the tree of the knowledge of good and evil.

Conclusion

Later Jewish tradition would identify the way of Wisdom with obedience to the Torah. The identification of Wisdom and Torah is found explicitly in Ben Sira (chap. 24) in the early second century B.C.E. (Both Deuteronomy and Ezra had earlier claimed that the Torah constitutes wisdom.) There is nothing to indicate, however, that this identification was implied in Proverbs. The book makes absolutely no mention of Israel or of Mount Sinai. There is overlap, to be sure, between the commandments of wisdom and those of the Torah, but there is nothing here to correspond to the ritual Torah or the more distinctively Israelite commandments. The instruction was based not on any distinctive revelation to Israel, but rather on the common wisdom of the ancient Near East. Thus Proverbs draws on a tradition of instruction that was different from the cultic traditions of Sinai and Zion and that had its roots partly in popular proverbial wisdom and partly in the tradition of instruction at the royal court. The latter kind of instruction is best known from Egypt, but analogous instruction was given to scribes and courtiers throughout the ancient Near East. This tradition took shape in Jerusalem and can be traced back with some confidence to the time of Hezekiah. In the postexilic period, the focus was more heavily on moral instruction, as can be seen especially in Proverbs 1–9. This tradition of instruction would continue down to the Hellenistic period. Only in the time of Ben Sira was the Torah clearly included in the curriculum.

FOR FURTHER READING

Commentaries

R. J. Clifford, *Proverbs* (OTL; Louisville: Westminster, 1999). Careful exegesis with close attention to textual problems.

M. V. Fox, *Proverbs 1–9* (AB 18A; New York: Doubleday, 2000); *Proverbs 10–31* (Yale Anchor Bible 18B; New Haven: Yale University Press, 2009). Excellent philological commentary, with incisive critiques of scholarly theories.

W. McKane, *Proverbs* (OTL; Philadelphia: Westminster, 1970). Substantial commentary, with extensive introduction. Sharp distinction between pragmatic "old wisdom" and later "moralizing" stratum.

R. E. Murphy, *Proverbs* (WBC; Dallas: Word, 1998). Emphasizes coherence with biblical worldview.

R. C. Van Leeuwen, "Proverbs," *NIB* 5:17–264. Scholarly commentary with homiletical suggestions.

Other Studies on Proverbs

C. Camp, *Wisdom and the Feminine in the Book of Proverbs* (Bible and Literature 11; Sheffield: Almond, 1995). Feminist reading of Proverbs.

J.J. Collins, "The Biblical Precedent for Natural Theology," in idem, *Encounters with Biblical Theology* (Minneapolis: Fortress Press, 2005), 91–104. Wisdom as reflection on the order of nature.

J. L. Crenshaw, "Proverbs, Book of," *ABD* 5:513–20. Good summary of critical issues.

K. J. Dell, *The Book of Proverbs in Social and Theological Context* (Cambridge: Cambridge University Press, 2006). Study of social setting of Proverbs. Emphasizes its theological character.

T. Sandoval, *The Discourse of Wealth and Poverty in the Book of Proverbs* (Leiden: Brill, 2005). Distinguishes three related discourses on wealth and poverty.

H. C. Washington, *Wealth and Poverty in the Instruction of Amenemope and the Hebrew Proverbs* (SBLDS 142; Atlanta: Scholars Press, 1994). Comparison of Proverbs and Amenemope.

S. Weeks, *Instruction and Imagery in Proverbs 1-9* (Oxford: Oxford University Press, 2007). Appreciation of Proverbs 1–9 as a poetic work.

General Introductions to Wisdom Literature

W. P. Brown, *Character in Crisis: A Fresh Approach to the Wisdom Literature of the Old Testament* (Grand Rapids: Eerdmans, 1996). Introduction to the wisdom literature as character formation.

D. M. Carr, *Writing on the Tablet of the Heart. Origins of Scripture and Literature* (New York: Oxford University Press, 2005). Good discussion of scribal education in the ancient Near East.

J. L. Crenshaw, *Old Testament Wisdom: An Introduction* (rev. ed.; Louisville: Westminster John Knox, 2010). Readable and reliable mid-level introduction.

C. Fontaine, *Traditional Sayings in the Old Testament* (Bible and Literature 5; Sheffield: Almond, 1982). Excellent study of contextual use of proverbs in the Old Testament.

K. Koch, "Is There a Principle of Retribution in the Old Testament?" trans. T. H. Trapp, in J. L. Crenshaw, ed., *Theodicy in the Old Testament* (Issues in Religion and Theology 4; Philadelphia: Fortress Press, 1983). Groundbreaking study of the chain of act and consequence, especially in the wisdom literature.

M. Lichtheim, *Ancient Egyptian Literature* (3 vols.; Berkeley: University of California Press, 1976). Authoritative translation of Egyptian wisdom texts in vol. 1:58–82, 134–92; vol. 2:135–66; vol. 3:159–217.

R. E. Murphy, *Wisdom Literature: Job, Proverbs, Ruth, Canticles, Ecclesiastes, Esther* (FOTL 13; Grand Rapids: Eerdmans, 1981). Concise guide to literary forms in the wisdom books.

D. Penchansky, *Understanding the Wisdom Literature. Conflict and Dissonance in the Hebrew Text* (Grand Rapids: Eerdmans, 2012). Wisdom literature as record of disputes, with diverse positions.

L. G. Perdue, *Wisdom and Creation: The Theology of the Wisdom Literature* (Nashville: Abingdon, 1994). Comprehensive theology of the wisdom literature.

———, *Wisdom Literature. A Theological History* (Louisville: Westminster John Knox, 2007). Introductory survey to the biblical books, including the Deutero-Canonical books.

———, *The Sword and the Stylus. An Introduction to Wisdom in the Age of Empires* (Grand Rapids: Eerdmans, 2008). Introductory survey with attention to historical context.

G. von Rad, *Wisdom in Israel* (trans. J. D. Martin; Nashville: Abingdon, 1972). Classic exposition of wisdom theology.

S. Weeks, *An Introduction to the Study of Wisdom Literature* (London: T&T Clark, 2010). Brief, lively, introduction.

C. Westermann, *Roots of Wisdom: The Oldest Proverbs of Israel and Other Peoples* (trans. J. D. Charles; Louisville: Westminster John Knox, 1995). Insightful analysis of proverbial wisdom.

CHAPTER 25

Job and Qoheleth

We turn in this chapter to two other expressions of wisdom in ancient Israel, both very different from Proverbs: the books of Job and Qoheleth.

The book of Proverbs represents "normal" wisdom in ancient Israel. It has much in common with the instructional literature of the ancient Near East, and it is characterized by a positive view of the world and confidence in its order and justice. This worldview was open to criticism, however, and already in antiquity some scribes found the traditional claims of wisdom problematic. The wisdom tradition gave rise to two great works that questioned the assumptions on which the world of Proverbs was built. These works are the books of Job and Qoheleth.

Job

More than any other book in the Old Testament, the book of Job is recognized as a classic of world literature. The impatient saint, festering on his dunghill, has served as a symbol for the human condition for such diverse luminaries as Martin Luther, Immanuel Kant, William Blake, and D. H. Lawrence. Modern poets, authors, and dramatists (Robert Frost, Archibald MacLeish, Elie Wiesel) continued to find inspiration in his story. The power of the book lies not so much in its poetic language, powerful though it is, as in the directness with which it addresses a basic human problem: the righteous suffer while the wicked prosper. Job provides no easy answers, and indeed there has been endless debate as to just what answers the book does provide. But it plumbs the depths of the problem in a way that is without rival in the biblical corpus.

The book consists of a narrative introduction or prologue followed by a series of poetic dialogues and a narrative conclusion or epilogue. The prologue sets the stage by telling how Job lost everything in a single day because of an arrangement between God and Satan. At first, Job's piety is not shaken. Then three friends, Eliphaz the Temanite, Bildad the Shuhite, and Zophar the Naamathite, come to visit him. The greater part of the book is

Fig. 25.1 *Job*, by Léon Bonnat (1880), emphasizes the afflicted man's anguish.

Commons.wikimedia.org

taken up with their exchanges with Job. These fall into three cycles. Job speaks first in chapter 3. Then each of the friends takes a turn (Eliphaz in chaps. 4 and 5; Bildad in chap. 8, Zophar in chap. 11). Job answers each in turn (chaps. 6–7, 9–10, 12–14). The cycle starts over in chapter 15, with Eliphaz, followed by Bildad in chapter 18 and Zophar in chapter 20. Again Job answers each in turn (16–17, 19, 21). The third cycle starts in chapter 22 with the speech of Eliphaz, followed by the response of Job in chapters 23–24. In this case, however, the speech of Bildad in chapter 25 is exceptionally short, and there is no speech of Zophar. Moreover, parts of the speech attributed to Job in chapters 26 and 27 match the arguments of the friends rather than those of Job. These incongruities have led to various proposals. A typical solution is to regard 26:5–14 as the conclusion of Bildad's speech,

and to supply the missing speech of Zophar from 27:8-23. Some verses in chapter 24 (18-20, 23-25) must also be attributed either to Bildad or to Zophar.

Chapter 28 interrupts the dialogues with a poem on wisdom that is quite appropriate to the overall message of the book but seems out of place here and was probably added later. Job concludes the dialogue with his friends with a lengthy speech in chapters 29–31.

At this point, a new character, Elihu son of Barachel the Buzite, enters the fray, angry both at Job and at the three friends because of their failure to silence him. Elihu's speech runs to the end of chapter 37, but it adds little or nothing to the arguments of the three friends. Moreover, Elihu is not mentioned in the epilogue to the book. The consensus of scholarship is that Elihu is a secondary addition to the book, although some critics defend the originality of the speech. Attempts to find a literary justification for the inclusion of this speech are not persuasive, however. Most probably, it was added by a scribe who shared the viewpoint of the friends and was dissatisfied at their apparent failure in their argument with Job. The name Elihu brings to mind the prophet Elijah, although the speech of Elihu has little in common with the famous prophet.

The book reaches its climax in chapters 38–39, when God speaks to Job out of the whirlwind. Job responds submissively in 40:3-5, but God continues with another speech in 40:6—41:34. Again, Job submits with a brief response (42:1-6). The book concludes with a prose epilogue.

It is apparent then that, despite its literary reputation, the book has its share of literary problems. Some of those (the disruption of the third cycle of the dialogues) are due to accidents of transmission (the Hebrew text of Job is notoriously difficult and corrupt). Others may be explained by secondary additions (chap. 28; the speech of Elihu). The additions scarcely alter the shape or meaning of the book, however. In this respect, Job has aptly been compared to a medieval cathedral that grew gradually over centuries. It is also apparent that *redundancy* is a feature of the book's style. Hebrew poetry is inherently redundant, as it often attains its effect by saying the same thing in different ways. The three cycles of speeches in the dialogues do not so much advance the argument as reinforce it by repetition. Similarly, the two speeches of God reinforce each other. The repetition enhances the rhetorical effect. The people who translated Job into Greek were apparently not so enamored of repetition and produced a much shorter version of the book. But redundancy in itself is not an argument against authenticity—quite the contrary. It is one of the characteristics of the book.

The main problem presented by the book is the tension between the dialogues and the prose narratives that frame them. Prose introductions are not unusual in wisdom writings of the ancient Near East. The story of Ahikar, which was popular throughout the Near East and was copied by the Jews of Elephantine in Egypt in the fifth century B.C.E., provides a famous example. The sayings of Ahikar are embedded in the story of the sage's life. In the case of Job, however, the narratives depict the hero in a way that is very different from what emerges in the dialogues. In the prologue, Job is a model of patience and resignation. This is the story that gives rise to the famous reference in the Epistle of James (Jas 5:11) to the patience of Job. At the beginning of the

dialogues, however, Job explodes by cursing the day he was born and coming close to cursing God. Throughout the dialogues, the friends defend the justice of God as axiomatic, while Job questions it at every turn. Yet in the epilogue God rebukes the friends, telling them that "you have not spoken of me what is right, as my servant Job has" (42:7). Most scholars assume that the prose frame reflects an older folktale, in which Job was consistently patient. No such narrative has survived as an independent composition, although a Christian bishop, Theodore of Mopsuestia, is said to have known such a story in oral form around 400 C.E. In the book of Job as we have it, however, the introductory story sets up a problem but does not resolve it. Moreover, the epilogue does not quite match the introduction, since it is concerned with the friends rather than with Satan. The traditional story is used as a building block in a new composition, in which both narratives and dialogues play integral parts. The tensions between them are essential to the message of the book as they

Fig. 25.2   Job feasts with his children, enjoying the rewards of his faithfulness to God; illustrated manuscript of the Book of Job (MS Grec 135) in the Bibliothéque Nationale de France. Commons.wikimedia.org

correspond to tensions within the religion of Israel and biblical theology.

The book provides no clear evidence of its date. The language of the prose tale points to a date no earlier than the sixth century B.C.E. The language of the dialogues is archaic, but this may be a matter of poetic style rather than an indication of date. The best parallels to the poetry of the dialogues are found in Second Isaiah and Jeremiah (sixth century). The role of Satan points to postexilic sources (Zechariah, Chronicles), and the use of the definite article with Satan may suggest a date before Chronicles, where the word is used as a proper name. An Aramaic paraphrase, the Targum of Job, from Qumran dates to the third or second century B.C.E., so the biblical book must be older than that. Most scholars date it to the sixth or fifth century. There is an obvious analogy between the experience of Job and that of Judeans who lived through the destruction of Jerusalem, but Job contains no trace of an allusion to the national disaster. Like the wisdom of Proverbs, Job has a timeless quality that has enabled it to speak directly to people of different eras.

The Prologue (1:1—2:13)

Job is exceptional among the characters in the Hebrew Bible in that he is not an Israelite. He is located in "the land of Uz." Uz appears as a personal name among the sons of Seir in Edom in Gen 36:28, and it is mentioned in parallelism with Edom in Lam 4:21. Consequently, most scholars assume that the land of Uz was located south of Israel, in the region of Edom. An addition to the Greek translation of Job locates him on the border of Idumea and Arabia (LXX Job 42:17b). But the name Uz also appears among the descendants of Aram (Syria) in Gen 10:23 and among the children of Abraham's brother Nahor in Gen 22:21. The specific location is not important to the story, except insofar as Job is situated in "the east" (1:3), and not in Israel. The international perspective is typical of the older wisdom literature. It may be that the story of Job was drawn from international lore. In Ezek 14:14 Job is linked with Noah and Danel (Daniel) as legendary righteous men. Noah is a biblical figure but prior to Abraham and not properly an Israelite. Danel is known from the legend of King Keret in Ugaritic (Canaanite) lore. The Jewish origin of this form of the story of Job, however, is shown by use of the name YHWH for God.

When we first meet Job, he is "the greatest of all the people of the east." His greatness is shown by his wealth, which was generally accepted as a sign of divine favor. He had an ideal family, seven sons and three daughters. Moreover, he was scrupulously devout, even offering sacrifices as insurance, lest his children sin even inadvertently. There is no hint of hypocrisy. Even the Deity acknowledges that he is blameless and a model of the prime virtue of the wisdom tradition, the fear of the Lord.

Job's life changes, however, because of the intervention of Satan, or "the Satan" as he is called in the Hebrew. We have already encountered this figure in Zechariah 3, where he is the adversary who brings accusations against the high priest Joshua. In 1 Chron 21:1, where Satan is used as a proper name, he incites David to take a census of Israel. Both of these texts are postexilic, a fact that lends some support to the view that Job is postexilic too. In none of these cases is Satan the demonic figure or devil of later mythology (he has that character in texts from around the turn of the era, including the New Testament). Here he appears to be a member of the heavenly council in good standing. At least he has the right of access at meetings of "the sons of God" or lesser divinities (who are demoted to the rank of angels in later Judaism and Christianity). His job, however, is distinctive. He is a roving prosecuting attorney who goes to and fro upon the earth to ferret out wrongdoing and put humanity to the test.

Satan's attention is drawn to Job by the boast of YHWH: "Have you considered my servant Job? There is no one like him on the earth, a blameless and upright man who fears God and turns away from evil" (1:8). Satan's response cuts to the heart of the popular theology of the ancient world: "Does Job fear God for nothing?" All over the ancient Near East the reigning assumption was that wealth and prosperity went hand in hand with right living. These were the fruits of wisdom in the book of Proverbs (e.g., Prov 8:18). Satan suggests that true righteousness should be disinterested. The Greek philosopher Plato made the same point in his discussion of justice in his *Republic*, book 2: the just man can only be recognized as such if he perseveres when his justice brings him no reward, but rather ignominy and even death. YHWH, rather chillingly, hands his faithful servant over to Satan to be tested. The first test involves not only the loss of all his property, but also the death of his children. Job remains unfazed: "the LORD gave and the LORD has taken away; blessed be the name of the Lord" (1:20). Satan, however, is not impressed: "Skin for skin, all that a man has he will give for his life" (2:4). Satan wagers that if God touches Job's person, Job will curse

him to his face. The Lord, obligingly, says, "He is in your power; only spare his life." The test is not quite as dire as that in Plato's *Republic*. Job must be kept alive, so that the result of the experiment may be seen. Even his personal affliction, however, does not immediately break down Job's patience, despite the taunting of his wife. "Shall we receive the good at the hand of God, and not receive the bad?" he asks (2:10). Only when he is confronted by his "friends" does his piety crack.

The significance of this opening scene should not be missed, however. God admits to Satan that "you incited me against him to destroy him for no reason" (2:3). This admission must be kept in mind throughout the dialogues. Job, of course, does not know why he is being afflicted. A Hellenistic Jewish writing called the *Testament of Job* thought that this was inappropriate and had God reveal to Job in advance what he was going to do. Armed with that knowledge, Job has no problem in maintaining his composure. In the biblical book, however, Job enjoys no such revelation, but the reader is privileged with the "inside story" of what is really going on.

The Dialogues 3:1—27:23

Job initiates the dialogues with a bitter complaint against God. He does not address the Deity directly here but uses the third person. There is no appeal for mercy, only curses and imprecations. Job stops short of fulfilling Satan's prediction that he will curse God to his face. Instead, he curses the day of his birth. The idea that it would have been better to have died at birth is extraordinary in the biblical corpus for its pessimism and recalls the frequent motif in Greek tragedy that "not to be born is the best thing." In mentioning those who curse the Sea and those who rouse up Leviathan (3:8), Job touches on mythological themes that will reappear toward the end of the book.

Job's opening salvo belongs to the general tradition of lament literature, although it is exceptional in its bitterness. The closest analogies come from Mesopotamian literature. A Sumerian text from the second millennium B.C.E. called "A Man and His God" (*ANET*, 589–91) reports the complaint of a man who claims to have suffered injustice. This composition, however, is unfailingly respectful in its address to the deity, and in the end "his bitter weeping was heard by his god." It is closer to the psalms of individual complaint than to the raging of Job. The Babylonian poem "I Will Praise the Lord of Wisdom" (*ANET*, 434–37) is likewise respectful and greatly emphasizes the need to perform proper cultic acts. The analogy to Job lies in the distress of the poet ("I spend the night in my dung, like an ox") and in the recognition that the god's ways are inscrutable. The closest parallel to Job is found in the Babylonian Theodicy, from about 1100 B.C.E. (*ANET*, 601–4). In this composition the sufferer engages in a dispute with a friend. The sufferer observes that those who do not worship the gods prosper, while those who do become impoverished. His friend grants that "Narru, king of the gods, who created mankind . . . gave twisted speech to the human race, with lies, not truth, they endowed him forever." But in this case, the dialogue partners are cordial and mutually respectful. Nothing in any of this literature prepares us for the heated exchanges between Job and his friends.

The viewpoint of the friends is grounded in traditional wisdom. "Think now," asks Eliphaz, "who that was innocent ever perished? Or where were the righteous cut off?" (4:7). He appeals to his own experience, but one suspects that his belief is based on dogma rather than on observation. To counter Job's protestations of innocence, Eliphaz recounts a revelation he received at night that no human being is innocent: "Can mortals be righteous before God? Can human beings be pure before their Maker?" (4:17). Job may not be a great sinner, but he cannot be completely innocent. Therefore Eliphaz recommends that Job confess his sin and appeal to God's mercy. God's punishment is beneficial in the long run: "Happy is the one whom God reproves" (5:17).

Job reacts with unexpected anger: "Those who withhold kindness from a friend forsake the fear of the Almighty. My companions are treacherous like a torrent-bed, like freshets that pass away" (6:14-15). The offense of Eliphaz is that he has assumed Job's guilt without evidence. He is thinking deductively: if Job is suffering, he must be guilty. Job demands an inductive approach: "Teach me, and I will be silent; make me understand how I have gone wrong. How forceful are honest words! but your reproof, what does it reprove? Do you think that you can reprove with words, as if the speech of the desperate were wind?" (6:25-26). Job appeals for honesty, and he is nothing less than candid himself. "Therefore I will not restrain my mouth; I will speak in the anguish of my spirit; I will complain in the bitterness of my soul" (7:11).

At this point, he turns to address God directly. His complaint is not, as we might have expected, that God is absent or negligent with regard to humanity. Quite the contrary. Job complains that God is oppressing him as if he were the Sea or the Dragon, the cosmic enemies of ancient mythology. "What is man that you make so much of him?" Job asks (7:17). The question inverts the well-known psalm: "What is man that you are mindful of him? a human being [literally, 'son of man'] that you attend to him?" (Ps 8:4).

For Job, the attention of God is not a good or desirable thing, but an affliction. God should not be affected by human sin and should be able to overlook it. Instead, he is the "watcher of humanity" who targets a human being who will all too soon be dead.

Bildad responds to the challenge in chapter 8. He is not as conciliatory as Eliphaz: "The words of your mouth are a great wind" (8:2). For Bildad, the issue is simple: "Does God pervert justice? Or does the Almighty pervert the right?" (8:3). These are rhetorical questions. The answer is axiomatic and negative. It is reinforced by the wisdom of the ages: "Inquire now of bygone generations, and consider what their ancestors have found; for we are but of yesterday, and we know nothing" (8:8-9). Bildad affirms the chain of act and consequence that was basic to proverbial wisdom: "Can papyrus grow where there is no marsh?" (8:11). Job must be guilty, and God must be proven right.

Job's reply to Bildad is a pivotal passage, as it anticipates much of what will happen at the end of the book. When Job asks, "How can a mortal be just before God?" (9:1), his point is different from that of Eliphaz, who asked a similar question in 4:17. Job is not speaking about the inner state of a person, but about juridical acquittal. The problem is that God is both accuser and judge, and so it is impossible to win one's case before him. God prevailed over the Sea and over the mythical monster Rahab. How can a human being hope to withstand him? Where Bildad affirmed the justice of God, Job acknowledges only the raw power of the Creator. At issue is the very nature of justice. Is justice simply the will of the all-powerful Creator? Or can it be measured by standards that humanity can recognize?

Job does not waver in protesting his innocence, but he shows little hope of winning satisfaction: "Though I am innocent, my own mouth would condemn me; though I am blameless; he would prove me perverse" (9:20). This prediction must be borne in mind when we come to the eventual encounter between God and Job at the end of the book. For the present, despair leads to candor: "It is all one; therefore I say, he destroys both the blameless and the wicked. When disaster brings sudden death, he mocks at the calamity of the innocent. The earth is given into the hand of the wicked; he covers the eyes of its judges—if it is not he, who then is it?" (9:24). Job, no less than Bildad, has biblical precedent on his side. The prophets had argued consistently that the one God YHWH was responsible for everything that happened, good and bad. "Does disaster befall a city," asked Amos, "unless the LORD has done it?" (Amos 3:6). In the words of Second Isaiah: "I am the LORD, and there is no other. I form light and create darkness, I make weal and create woe; I the LORD do all these things" (Isa 45:6-7). Job draws the logical conclusion. YHWH must also be responsible for the injustice that is rampant on earth.

The remainder of Job's response to Bildad raises two further important issues. In 9:26 Job complains that "there is no umpire between us." Here he touches again on the problem of getting a fair trial before God. The

Fig. 25.3 William Blake evokes the power of the accusations leveled against Job in an illustration in *Job's Evil Dreams* (1821). Commons. wikimedia.org

second issue is an appeal to God's mercy. God must know that Job is not guilty (as indeed he does, in the narrative of the book). God should transcend the limitations of human beings ("Do you see as humans see?" 10:4). Why then should God destroy the work of his own hands? We may compare Hos 11:9, where God resolves not to destroy Ephraim again, "for I am God and no mortal." In the end, of course, God will not destroy Job, but he has already destroyed Job's children and servants. Why should an all-powerful God need to inflict such suffering on mere mortals?

The last friend to speak, Zophar, is quite brief. As between God and Job, there can be no contest. "Can you find out the deep things of God? Can you find out the limit of the Almighty?" (11:7). Like Eliphaz, Zophar counsels submission. His argument rests on the unfathomable superiority of the Deity.

Job does not dispute this point; he complains that he does not need to be told this: "What you know, I also know; I am not inferior to you" (13:2). He goes on to draw a sharp contrast between himself and his friends. Job wants to get to the heart of the issue, to argue his case with God. The friends, he claims, are trying "to whitewash with lies" (13:4). They "speak falsely for God, and speak deceitfully for him" (13:7). Job recognizes that they are trying to speak "for God," to defend God's good name, as religious people typically do. If evidence is thought to be damaging to God's good name, it must be explained away, and pious dogma must be maintained. Not only does Job reject that approach, but he claims that God does too: "Will it be well with you when he searches you out? Or can you deceive him, as one person deceives another? He will surely rebuke you if in secret you show partiality" (13:9-10). This claim too will be tested when God finally appears on stage at the end of the book.

In the conclusion of this speech, Job dwells again on the wretched state of humanity and on how God should not need to afflict such creatures. He insists especially on the finality of death. There is hope for a tree that is cut down (14:7), but when mortals expire they are laid low. While this denial of resurrection, or of meaningful afterlife, was the standard view of ancient Israel, it must be noted here, as it is crucial to the problem of Job. The Hellenistic *Testament of Job* has Job rewarded in heaven for his sufferings on earth. No such easy solution is available to the author of the Hebrew book.

The second and third cycles of dialogue add rhetorical weight to the dispute between Job and his friends, but they add little by way of new argument. Here it will suffice to highlight two passages: 19:23-26 and 26:7-14.

Job 19:23-26 was made famous by its rendition in Handel's *Messiah:* "I know that my redeemer liveth." For traditional Christianity, the redeemer is Christ, but messianic prophecy has no place in the worldview of Job. The relevant passage is translated as follows in the NRSV:

> O that my words were written down!
>   O that they were inscribed in a book!
> O that with an iron pen and with lead
>   they were engraved on a rock forever!
> For I know that my Redeemer lives,
>   and that at the last he will stand upon
>   the earth;
> and after my skin has been thus
>   destroyed
>   then in my flesh I shall see God,
> whom I shall see on my side.

The Hebrew text of this passage is very difficult and probably corrupt at some points; but the general idea is clear enough. Job expresses his conviction that sooner or later his innocence will be vindicated. Since this may happen later rather than sooner, he wishes for his words to be preserved. Two points in the passage are controversial.

The first concerns the identity of the redeemer (Hebrew *go'el*), who will at last stand forth upon the earth (literally, "dust"). Some scholars take the redeemer to be God, who is often called redeemer elsewhere in the Hebrew Bible (Pss 69:19; 103:4; Isa 43:1, 14). But throughout the book, Job regards God as his adversary, and so it would make no sense to expect God to be the redeemer. More likely the reference is to an intermediary figure, such as the "umpire" hoped for in 9:33, or, more pertinently, the heavenly witness who is mentioned in 16:19, where Job exclaims: "O earth, do not cover my blood; let my outcry find no resting place. Even now, in fact, my witness is in heaven, and he that vouches for me is on high." The witness is presumably a member of the heavenly council (cf. also 33:23). The focus, however, both in 16:19 and in 19:25, is not on the person of the redeemer, but on the hope of redemption.

The second issue in this passage is whether it implies a belief in resurrection. Job 19:26 is difficult. The Hebrew reads "from [or 'without'] my flesh," not "in" as translated in the NRSV. Hence the passage has been taken to express the hope for a vision of God after death. We have seen, however, that in chapter 14 Job emphatically rejects any hope of resurrection. It is unlikely, then, that he endorses such a hope in chapter 19. The passage expresses a clear conviction that Job will eventually be granted the encounter with God that he had sought throughout the dialogues. In fact, such an encounter takes place at the end of the book, although Job hears rather than sees God. The expression "from my flesh" remains obscure, but it is unlikely that it involves life after death.

Job 26:7-14 is attributed to Job as the text stands but is likely to have been part of a speech of Zophar. In any case, it provides a fine example of the kind of mythological view of creation that must have been widely held in ancient Israel. In this account, creation involved stilling the Sea (Yamm) and striking down the sea monster Rahab. This description of creation goes farther than most of the allusions in the Psalms. God hangs the earth on nothing and draws a circle on the waters at the separation of light and darkness. Heaven is supported by pillars. This passage ranks with Psalm 104 as one of the major witnesses to an important account of creation that is quite different from anything in the book of Genesis.

Job's Self-Justification (Chapters 29–31)

The final speech of Job in chapters 29–31 differs from his earlier outbursts. Up to this point, he had complained that his suffering was unjust but had not discussed his past conduct. Here he paints a picture of his prime, "when the Almighty was still with me, when my children were around me" (29:5). By his own account, he was a champion of righteousness: "eyes to the blind, and feet to the lame . . . a father to the needy, and I championed the cause of the stranger" (29:15-16). In return, he enjoyed respect: "Young men saw me and withdrew, and the aged rose up and stood" (29:8). Moreover, he thought he had a deal with God: "Then I thought, 'I shall die in my nest, and I shall multiply my days like the phoenix; my roots spread out to the waters, with the dew all night on my branches'" (29:18-19). In chapter 30, however, he expresses his profound disillusionment: "But now they make sport of me, those who are younger than I, whose fathers I would have disdained to set with the dogs of my flock" (30:1). He continues, in chapter 31, to set out what might have been fair punishment for various crimes: "If my heart has been enticed by a woman, and I have lain in wait at my neighbor's door, then let my wife grind for another, and let other men kneel over her" (31:9-10); or: "if I have raised my hand against the orphan . . . then let my shoulder blade fall from my shoulder" (31:21-22).

But there is considerable irony in all of this. Job is in no position to bargain with God. The fate that has already befallen him is worse than any of his imprecations. Moreover, he comes across as not only righteous but self-righteous. His contempt for the people he would not put with the dogs of his flock is damning. We need not doubt that Job is genuinely righteous in his behavior. His concern for his slaves is grounded in their common humanity: "Did not he who made me in the womb make them?" (31:15). He plays by the rules in life. But he also expects life to keep the rules as he understands them.

Elihu (32:1—37:24)

Despite the length and vehemence of his intervention, Elihu brings nothing new to the discussion. The burden of his speech was already stated by Bildad in chapter 8: "The Almighty will not pervert justice" (34:12). The end of Elihu's speech (36:24—37:24) extols the God of nature in a way that anticipates, to a degree, the revelation that is to follow. It may be that this speech was meant to fuse together some of the arguments of the friends, which were less than successful, with the appeal to the power of nature, which ultimately prevails. One feature of Elihu's speech, however, deserves special attention. At the beginning of his speech, he justifies his intervention, despite his youth: "Truly it is the spirit in a mortal, the breath of the Almighty, that makes for understanding. It is not the old that are wise, nor the aged that understand what is right" (32:8-9). This assertion marks a major shift in the Hebrew wisdom tradition. Even though Elihu holds to very traditional positions, he has in principle opened the door to the questioning, or rejection, of tradition. In this much, at least, Elihu resembles Job. He is unwilling to defer to authority. The content of his speech, however, is not so much a repudiation of the arguments of the friends as a restatement of them.

The Speeches from the Whirlwind

The book reaches its climax in chapters 38–41, with the speeches from the whirlwind. As both Job and his friends had predicted, YHWH is overpowering. The experience of the theophany, however, surpasses any idea of it that mortals might have entertained and overwhelms Job in a way that no speeches could.

At no point does YHWH respond to the question raised by Job about his guilt or innocence. How could he? In the phrase of Robert Frost, he was "just showing off to the Devil, as is set forth in chapters One and Two." Instead, he hurls at Job a series of impossible questions: "Where were you when I laid the foundation of the earth?" The speeches of God present a catalog of concerns that are far beyond the reach of humanity but are vital to the running of the universe, from the birth times of mountain goats to the control of the mythical monsters Behemoth and Leviathan. The implication is clear. Humanity is only one small part of a huge universe. Job had complained that God was paying too much attention to humanity and its faults. Not so, is the divine reply. On the contrary, God has too many things on his mind to regard Job's fate as of great importance. The lesson then is not only the limits of Job's human knowledge or the invincible power of God. Job is given a lesson in perspective. Neither he nor humanity in general is as important as he had thought. Job gets the point when he answers meekly: "See, I am of small account" (40:4).

The Epilogue

If the book of Job ended at 42:6, it would be rather depressing. Job had predicted, in chapter 9, that God would make him condemn himself, even though he was innocent. While he does not exactly abandon his plea of innocence, Job repents, at least of his audacity in speaking of things he did not understand. But essentially Job has been crushed, as if by a thunderbolt. He has been shown that he does not understand the universe, but he has not been given any reassurance that it pays any attention to a moral law, as he had originally assumed.

The book does not end at 42:6, however. Instead, we have a brief, but surprising, prose epilogue. After Job's submission, we might have expected that God would thank the friends for their efforts on his behalf. Instead, he tells Eliphaz: "My wrath is kindled against you and against your two friends; for you have not spoken of me what is right, as my servant Job has" (42:7). The friends, we must recall, had insisted that God does not pervert justice. Job, in contrast, had asserted that "he destroys both the blameless and the wicked" (9:22). God agrees with Job. Job had warned the friends that God would not be pleased that they were speaking falsely on his behalf, and in this he was right. We should not necessarily conclude that, in the view of the author, God does pervert justice. Rather, the point is that God does not comply with human conceptions of justice and is under no obligation to do so. The poet Robert Frost, in his play, *A Masque of Reason*, has God return after one thousand years to thank Job for his services:

> God, I've had you on my mind a thou-
> sand years
> To thank you someday for the way you
> helped me
> Establish once for all the principle

There's no connection man can reason
    out
Between his just deserts and what he
    gets.

This insight flew in the face of traditional wisdom, and indeed of much of the Hebrew Bible. The point was not lost on Frost:

You realize by now the part you played
To stultify the Deuteronomist
And change the tenor of religious
    thought.
My thanks are to you for releasing me
From moral bondage to the human race.

The friends are not treated harshly, although they are subjected to the indignity of having to rely on the intercession of Job. The epilogue provides a happy ending all around, in the manner of comedy rather than tragedy. Job's fortunes are restored. Now all his relatives, and those who had known him before, all of whom were conspicuous by their absence up to this point, come out of the woodwork to show him sympathy. Each gives him a piece of money and a gold ring. Job's wealth is doubled, and he is given a new family to replace the old one, with the nice touch that the daughters are now given an inheritance with their brothers. (Even the daughters of Zelophehad in Numbers 27 were allowed to inherit only because they had no brothers.)

We might think, initially, that Job was restored to his original state, with some enhancement. But he ought to have learned something from the experience. No great confidence could be placed in people who professed their friendship when he was restored, when they had been absent in his time of need. And he should know from experience that all the newfound wealth and family that he is given at the end could be lost again in one bad day. Never again should Job be so confident that he would grow old in his own nest, or that other people were not worthy to be put with the dogs of his flock.

The book of Job has more than one lesson. As between Job and his friends, Job is vindicated. He was not being punished for any sins, as the reader knew from the beginning. Moreover, his near-blasphemous candor is preferred to the piety of those who would lie for God. His honesty, however, is not tantamount to wisdom. He has to live with the fact that the universe does not revolve around humanity, let alone around Job. The justice of God, if that be the proper term, cannot be measured by human standards.

The Wisdom Poem (Chapter 28)

The latter point is reinforced by the great poem on wisdom that is inserted at chapter 28, and that serves as a commentary on the drama in the manner of a Greek chorus. In sharp contrast to Proverbs 8, where Wisdom cries out in the street, this poem emphasizes the elusiveness of Wisdom. Humanity knows all kinds of wonderful things and can extract precious metals from the bowels of the earth, "but where shall wisdom be found?" (28:12). Even Abaddon and Death, the underworld personified, do not know where Wisdom is hidden. Only God knows its place, because he established it at creation. It should be noted here that Job 28 does not say that God created Wisdom (although the point is unclear). It may be that Wisdom is something primeval. Neither does it say that God used Wisdom to create the world, in the manner of Proverbs

8. Rather, Wisdom is something jealously guarded by God: "And he said to humankind, 'Truly, the fear of the Lord, that is wisdom; and to depart from evil is understanding'" (Job 28:28). Wisdom, strictly speaking, is inaccessible to humanity. To fear the Lord is to accept human limitation, and to recognize that we are not the center of the universe. In this much, at least, Job affirms a central teaching of traditional wisdom, even if he questions the usual assumptions of order and consequences on which that tradition was based.

Qoheleth (Ecclesiastes)

The book of Job may be said to represent a crisis in the wisdom tradition, arising from the realization that some of the most hallowed assumptions are proven false by experience. As we have seen in the case of Proverbs, the wisdom tradition does not rely on revelation of the kind that one finds in the Prophets. Essentially, it is an attempt to generalize on the basis of experience. But in traditional wisdom, students are not supposed to rely on their own experience. Rather, as Bildad put it, they should "inquire of bygone generations, and consider what their ancestors have found" (Job 8:8). Consequently, the supposedly empirical findings of past generations often hardened into dogma. In a sense, Job was recalling the tradition to its roots by reexamining its basis. It should be noted that even the conservative Elihu shows impatience with assumptions about the wisdom of age and tradition.

The skeptical questioning of tradition in the biblical corpus reaches its high point in the book of Qoheleth or Ecclesiastes. The inclusion of this book in the canon of Scriptures is remarkable and was a matter of some controversy in antiquity. In the first century C.E. the rival schools of Shammai and Hillel were divided on the issue. The more conservative school of Shammai rejected it, but the Hillelites prevailed. Objections continued to be raised against the book as late as the fourth century C.E. because of its lack of coherence and its radical questioning of tradition.

The name Qoheleth has never been satisfactorily explained. It has the form of a feminine participle but is used with reference to a man (the son of David, Qoh 1:1). It appears both with and without the definite article. The Greek form, "Ecclesiastes," "member of an assembly," assumes that the word is derived from *qahal*, "assembly." A modern suggestion takes the word to mean "gatherer" or "assembler," a designation that is reasonably appropriate in light of the content of the book. But the meaning is uncertain and remains obscure.

The superscription of the book identifies Qoheleth as "the son of David, king in Jerusalem." Qoheleth 1:12 repeats that he was king over Israel. He was traditionally identified as Solomon. (Jewish tradition held that Solomon composed the book in his old age. The attribution may help explain why the book became canonical.) But even if that identification was implied in the opening chapter, it was not maintained consistently. In most of the book, the speaker appears as a teacher who is acutely aware of the injustice of high officials but is unable to do anything about it. At the end of the book, we are told that Qoheleth was a wise man who taught the people knowledge, weighing and studying and arranging many proverbs. This description suggests that he was a teacher, the occupation that is usually assumed for the authors and tradents of wisdom books. Qoheleth is exceptionally critical of traditional wisdom, but this need not be incompatible with his role as a teacher. That he is said to teach "the people" may suggest that he cast his net more widely than sages of earlier generations.

In any case, the language of the book shows that it cannot have been written in the age of Solomon. This is Late Biblical Hebrew, heavily influenced by Aramaic, and with many points of affinity with the later Hebrew of the Mishnah. There are two clear Persian loanwords: *pardes* ("garden," 2:5, the word from which Eng. "paradise" derives) and *pitgam* ("response, sentence," 8:11). Dates proposed for the book range from the Persian (fifth-fourth century B.C.E.) to the Hellenistic period (third or early second century B.C.E.). There are no Greek loanwords, but then Greek words are very rare in admittedly later writings such as Ben Sira, Daniel, and the Dead Sea Scrolls. Some scholars have held that Qoheleth is influenced by Greek philosophy, especially Epicureanism, but the similarities are superficial. One possible indication of date may be that the author takes issue with belief in life after death: "Who knows whether the human spirit goes upward and the spirit of animals goes downward to the earth?" (3:21). The view that the human spirit goes upward after death is not attested in Judaism before the Hellenistic period, when it appears in the apocalypses of the books of Enoch and Daniel. That this view merits refutation in Qoheleth shows that it must have been current, and this is unlikely before the late third century B.C.E. As in the case of other wisdom books, however, exact dating is not crucial here. Qoheleth is primarily concerned with aspects of life and death that are pertinent to all times and places.

Attempts to find a literary structure in the book have not been very successful. There is a clear editorial frame, consisting of a superscription in 1:1 and two epilogues, in 12:9-11 and 12-14. Moreover, the book begins and ends with two poems (1:2-11 and 11:7—12:7). The refrain "vanity of vanities" in 12:8 picks up the refrain of the opening poem. One can distinguish roughly between the two halves of the book. The first half is punctuated by the refrain "All this is vanity and chasing after wind," which marks off sections 2:1-11; 2:12-17; 2:18-26; 3:1—4:6; and 4:7—6:19. Qoheleth 6:10-12 wraps up the first half by picking up the theme of the opening poem, that there is nothing new under the sun. The second half of the book is marked by the phrases "not find out" and "who can find out," and "cannot know." Other refrains are repeated throughout the book: the advice that one should eat, drink, and be merry occurs seven times in all. Concern over the finality of death also runs throughout the book. Several attempts to find a more elaborate literary structure have not proven persuasive.

Several analogies can be found both for Qoheleth's pessimism and for his advice for the enjoyment of life in wisdom literature of the ancient Near East. Many of these derive from Egypt. The most important are "The Dispute of a Man with His Ba" and the "Songs of the Harpers." In the "Dispute," a man who has become disillusioned with life contemplates suicide. His *ba,* or soul, tries to convince him that life is still preferable to death. The "Harpers' Songs" are tomb inscriptions that reflect on death and call for the enjoyment of life. Qoheleth is also reminiscent of the *Epic of*

Gilgamesh, in which the hero fails in his quest for everlasting life and is advised to enjoy the life that is given to him.

Vanity of Vanities

The first two verses of Qoheleth (1:2-3) introduce two of the basic themes of the book. The first is summed up in the famous phrase "vanity of vanities." The Hebrew word that is traditionally translated as "vanity" here *(hebel)* literally means "vapor." The Midrash, Qoheleth Rabbah, takes it to mean "like the steam from an oven." Some commentators offer "absurd" as a modern equivalent, but while this term captures some of Qoheleth's frustration, it does not convey the key aspect of *hebel,* which is transitoriness. As we shall see repeatedly in the book, what makes life "vanity" is the finality of death. Nothing lasts.

The second basic theme has the form of a question: "What profit do people have from all the toil at which they toil under the sun?" (1:2). The idea of "profit" comes from business and perhaps reflects the growing commercialization of Jerusalem in the Hellenistic period. The Hebrew term is *yitron,* "that which is left over." The quest for a "profit" from life defines the problem that concerns Qoheleth to a great degree. Again, this problem is impermanence or transitoriness. However much people may seem to gain for a while, in the end it all dissolves like vapor.

The poem in 1:2-11 expresses another aspect of Qoheleth's view of the world: "There is nothing new under the sun." The Hebrew Bible is often said to have a linear view of time, in contrast to the cyclic view of ancient Near Eastern myth; that is, the Bible supposedly allows for a sense of progress and direction in history. This is true of some parts of the biblical corpus. The early history of Israel is constructed as a "history of salvation," the journey of Israel to the promised land. Again, the prophets often look forward to a Day of the Lord, or to a time of restoration. But the prophets also knew that "all flesh is grass, and all its beauty is like the flower of the field" (Isa 40:6). The wisdom books of Proverbs, Job, and Qoheleth have no sense of a goal in history. Rather, as the Greek historian Thucydides saw, the same or similar things happen over and over again. Novelty is an illusion that results from our ignorance of history. Obviously, Qoheleth's insight here has its limitation. The Hebrew sage never dreamed of the technological innovations of the modern world. But he might not have been impressed. While life in the ancient world was very tradition-bound, there was considerable innovation in the Hellenistic age. Yet no innovation, ancient or modern, has ever changed the basic constraints that govern human life. Moreover, the great advances in human understanding, by a Plato or a Shakespeare, are not accomplished once and for all but must be appreciated and understood anew by every generation. Understanding and insight cannot be accumulated.

The fact that people of long ago are not remembered undermines a common hope in the ancient world that one might live on through one's reputation and good name. This hope is what a modern psychologist might call an "immortality symbol," a means by which we may hope to live on after we die. Qoheleth underlines the futility of such hope. Only a few people are remembered, and even they may not be remembered accurately. Qoheleth insists that there is no transcendence of death and no way out of the cyclical existence in which humanity is trapped.

Qoheleth's Experiments in Living

In 1:12—2:24 Qoheleth adopts the persona of a king leaving a record of his experiences. (The fiction may be influenced by royal inscriptions from the ancient Near East.) He claims that he conducted a series of experiments, "to search out by wisdom all that is done under heaven." The novelty of this procedure should not be missed. Normally, wisdom teachers in the ancient Near East were content to pass on the traditional wisdom they had learned from their own teachers. Qoheleth breaks the mold by insisting on finding out for himself. (Note the frequency of the first person pronoun, "I.") He makes trial of pleasure, wealth, and even wisdom. What he finds is that "all is vanity and a chasing after wind."

Qoheleth's experiments reflect the persona of Solomon. The king was famous for the number of his wives, for his wealth, and for his wisdom. What Qoheleth adds to the persona, however, is an angle of inquiry: What profit does a person have from all of this? Pleasure, by its nature, is transitory; it cannot be accumulated. Wealth can be accumulated, but to what purpose, if one does not enjoy it? In the end the person who accumulates wealth must leave it to someone who did not toil for it (2:21). We are reminded of the parable of the rich man in Luke 12:16-20, who built his barns but never lived to enjoy them. Wisdom, Qoheleth asserts, is better than folly just as light is better than darkness, yet the same fate befalls the wise and the fool. Here is precisely the core of the problem. Wise and fool alike die, and there is no enduring remembrance of either one. Even wisdom, then, yields no enduring profit. Human labor is simply "the business that God has given to human beings to be busy with" (1:13).

Yet Qoheleth's conclusion from his experiments is not as negative as we might have expected. "There is nothing better for mortals than to eat and drink, and find enjoyment in their toil. This also, I saw, is from the hand of God" (2:24). To reach this conclusion, however, is to give up on the quest for a "profit" in life. There is no profit, but life can still be enjoyed. The point is not to attain a destination, but to enjoy the journey. This, in a nutshell, is the message of Qoheleth. People who spend their lives gathering and heaping are "sinners" who miss the mark of what life is about. Those who enjoy life as it passes are those who please God.

It is unclear whether the last sentence of chapter 2, "This also is vanity," applies to the work of gathering and heaping, or to the conclusion that Qoheleth has just enunciated. In this passage, the vanity is most probably the gathering and heaping. But it is typical of Qoheleth that he undermines anything that might be taken for certainty. So we must reckon with the possibility that even his own conclusions are reckoned as "vanity" and "chasing after wind." Certainty is not given to human beings, and even when we hold convictions we should not lose sight of their ephemeral character.

A Time for Everything

The limits of human wisdom are set out clearly in a famous passage in 3:1-9: "For everything there is a season, and a time for every matter under heaven." The passage goes on to list fourteen pairs of opposites: to be born and to die, to kill and to heal, to love and to hate, and so on. The assertion that there is a time for each of these may seem shocking at first: should there be a time to kill and a time to hate? But in this respect, Qoheleth is quite faithful to the tradition of biblical ethics. As we saw in chapter 6, on the book of Exodus, the absolute prohibitions of the Ten Commandments are relativized in practice in the "book of the covenant" (Exodus 21–24), the casuistic laws that take specific circumstances into account. There are lots of situations where killing is not only permitted but commanded. The psalmist has no qualms about "hating" God's enemies. Where Qoheleth differs from the rest of the biblical tradition is in his lack of confidence that human beings can know the right time. In Proverbs, as we have seen, timing is what distinguishes the wise person from the fool. For Qoheleth, however, this wisdom is beyond the human grasp.

According to Qoh 3:11, God has put eternity into the human heart. The meaning of this verse is controversial. The word for "eternity" ('olam) is most familiar from the phrase "forever and ever" or the like. Accordingly, the NRSV translates: "a sense of past and future," but this is far too weak. The 'olam is the primeval past or the distant future. The word can also mean "that which is hidden." In Qoheleth the idea is that humanity has the desire to know the full scope of God's plan for the world, or the full meaning of things, but cannot find it out. In accordance with the wisdom tradition, Qoheleth does not entertain the possibility of revelation, of the kind associated with Mount Sinai, but the skeptical view of the limits of wisdom also sets Qoheleth apart from Proverbs.

Since humanity cannot figure it all out, what are people to do? Qoheleth reiterates the message that one should eat and drink and enjoy the life that is available. He also repeats the key observation that leads to his conclusion: "the fate of humans and the fate of animals is the same . . . who knows whether the human spirit goes upward and the spirit of animals goes downward to the earth?" (3:19-21). The traditional Hebrew belief was that the shade of human beings lived on in Sheol. Only in the apocalyptic literature (Daniel, and the noncanonical books attributed to Enoch) do we find a belief that the human spirit goes upward after death. Qoheleth is probably taking issue here with beliefs that were just beginning to emerge in his time. His appeal, however, is not to traditional belief but to personal experience. Strictly speaking, no one knows what happens after death, but the common human experience is that people do not come back. More than any other biblical author, Qoheleth is resolutely empirical in his approach to life. There is no leap of faith here, no wager based on hope without evidence. Qoheleth's philosophy of life is that we should base our lives on the evidence that we have. This means that we should make the most of life in the here and now, rather than live in the uncertain hope of the hereafter. Whether Qoheleth was engaged in direct dispute with apocalyptic writers or not, his philosophy was the exact opposite of what we find in the book of Daniel.

Sayings of the Wise

The book of Qoheleth does not exhibit a clear progression of thought (any more than the world according to Qoheleth exhibits any purposeful progression). Rather, it returns again and again to the basic themes we have found in the opening chapters. In chapters 4–6 some interesting observations are interspersed with the reflections.

The statement in 4:2-3 that the dead are more fortunate than the living, and that those who have not been born are more fortunate still, is atypical of the Hebrew Bible, and extreme even in the context of Qoheleth. The sentiment is quite typical of Greek tragedy, and Job comes close to it in his complaints against God.

In 4:9-12 Qoheleth ventures one of his occasional affirmations: two are better than one. The statement that if two lie together they at least keep each other warm implies a sexual ethic that is far removed from that of Leviticus, or even Deuteronomy, and presupposes a society, probably urban, where individuals are not surrounded by their extended families. The point is not developed.

The cautionary comment on vows, in contrast, is very close to Deut 23:21-22. Qoheleth shows no interest in cultic matters, but the blunt warning that God has no pleasure in fools is typical of the pragmatic wisdom tradition. Neither does Qoheleth have any time for dreams (5:7). In this respect, he had a noteworthy precedent in Jer 23:28 but again is in sharp contrast to what we will find in the book of Daniel.

Qoheleth 7:1-14 differs from all that precedes it, in that it is primarily a collection of proverbial sayings, such as we might find in Proverbs. (There is another collection of traditional material in chap. 10.) Qoheleth 7:1, "Better is a good name than precious ointment," contains a wordplay in Hebrew ("name" is *shem;* "ointment" is *shemen*), and

echoes the sentiment of Prov 22:1. Yet in Qoh 7:6 we meet the familiar refrain "This also is vanity." Here again it is not immediately clear whether the vanity applies only to the laughter of fools in the preceding verse or to the collection of sayings as a whole. It may well be that Qoheleth is deliberately qualifying the confident-sounding proverbs. Such advice has some value, but in the end it too is mere human opinion and therefore vanity, like all human wisdom. There is distinct irony in the statement in 7:12 that "the protection of wisdom is like the protection of money." True, but we need only remind ourselves of the story of Job to see that this too is vanity. Again in 8:10-13, we must wonder whether the confident statement that "it will not be well with the wicked" is ironic. Throughout these chapters, Qoheleth seems to be reciting traditional wisdom and occasionally reminding himself and the reader that it is all vanity.

One of the most striking statements in Qoheleth is in 7:16-17: "Do not be too righteous, and do not act too wise. . . . Do not be too wicked, and do not be a fool." Here the Hebrew sage adopts the advice of the Delphic oracle: "nothing too much." In part, the advice may be directed against pretense, against those who are righteous or wise in their own eyes. Such a warning would be quite in line with the teaching of the prophets. But Qoheleth's warning must also apply to the kind of zeal that is so often praised in the Hebrew Bible. (The paradigm examples are Phinehas, in Numbers 25, and Elijah.) The point can be illustrated by a postbiblical, noncanonical Jewish story, the *Testament of Abraham*. According to this story, an archangel took Abraham for a ride on a heavenly chariot before he died. Whenever Abraham saw people sinning, he asked God to strike them down, for Abraham had never sinned and had no compassion for sinners. Eventually, God intervened and told the archangel to take Abraham back to earth, lest he destroy all creation. The comment of Qoheleth is apt: "Surely there is no one on earth so righteous as to do good without ever sinning" (7:20).

Another striking saying in chapter 7 is less enlightened. "One man among a thousand I found, but a woman among all these I have not found" (7:28). Jewish sages in antiquity (all men) were not especially friendly to the opposite sex. Ben Sira is a much worse offender than Qoheleth in this regard, but the two sages share the prejudices of a male profession in a patriarchal society.

Qoheleth returns to his basic insights in chapter 9. The same fate comes to everyone, righeous and wicked. The conclusion follows: eat your bread with enjoyment, and drink your wine with a merry heart. The wording of this passage is especially reminiscent of the story of Gilgamesh, where the hero fails in his quest for eternal life but is told by the barmaid Siduri that the gods have reserved eternal life for themselves and that he should enjoy the life that is given to him (the passage is cited in chapter 1 above).

The Concluding Poem

Perhaps the most moving part of Qoheleth is the poem on old age at the end of the book. This poem balances the opening poem in 1:1-11 and shares the same theme: all is vanity or vapor. Qoheleth 12:1-8 is widely recognized as an allegory of old age, but there is no agreement on how the details should be interpreted. The reference to old age is clear in 12:1: "the years draw near when you will say, 'I have no pleasure in them.'" Some commentators have attempted to see each phrase as a description of the failure of some bodily organ. So in 12:3 the "keepers of the house" and the "strong men" might refer to the arms and legs, the "grinders" to the teeth, and "those that look through the windows" to the eyes. The almond tree that blossoms in 12:5 might refer to the graying of the hair. Other details of the poem, however, do not easily fit this line of interpretation. Other commentators take the passage as an account of a storm, nightfall, or the ruin of an estate, any of which could serve as a metaphor for old age. The passage is not a sustained allegory, but an allusive poem that conveys a cumulative impression of collapse, culminating in the conclusion that all things pass, all is vapor.

The purpose of the poem is stated at the outset: "Remember your creator in the days of your youth." The word for "creator" (*boreyka*) is a wordplay. It is very similar to "pit, grave" (*bor*), and "well, source" (*b^e'er*). There is a rabbinic saying, attributed to one Akabya ben Mahalalel, that one should "know whence you came [your source], whither you are going [your grave], and before whom you are destined to give an accounting [your creator]" (*Abot* 3:1). From the perspective of Qoheleth, the three ideas are closely related. To remember either one's birth or one's death is to remember that one is a creature.

The poem in Qoh 12:1-8 suggests not only the decline of the individual in old age, but also the end of the world, with the failure of the sun and moon and cosmic light. It is interesting to compare the imagery of the poem with a passage from an apocalypse, *Syriac* or *2 Baruch*, written about 100 C.E.: "For the youth of the world is passed and the strength of the creation is already exhausted . . . and the pitcher is near to the cistern and the ship to the port, and the course of the journey to the city and life to its consummation" (*2 Bar.* 85:10). Qoheleth does not expect an end of the world; see Qoh 1:4, "A generation comes and a generation goes, but the earth remains forever." He uses the imagery of collapse to convey the sense of an ending. For the present world is always passing away.

The Epilogues

The book of Qoheleth concludes with three epilogues that clearly do not come from the author of the main part of the book. The first, in 12:9-10, describes the author, in the third person, as a teacher of traditional wisdom, although he must have been an unusual one. The second, in vv. 11-12, comes from an editor who was troubled by the skeptical sayings of the sage. He justifies them by comparing them to goads, but adds quickly: "Of anything beyond these, my child, beware. Of making many books there is no end, and much study is a weariness of the flesh" (as any student can testify). Here we see the canonical impulse at work in the attempt to limit the number of books that can be accepted as authoritative.

The final epilogue, in 12:13-14, does most violence to the spirit of the book. It picks up a verse from 8:17, where the sage says in his heart that God will judge the righteous, but that verse is followed by a passage that explains that human beings and animals have the same fate. There is no irony in the epilogue: all one has to do is fear God and keep his commandments. This is the only time that the commandments are mentioned in Qoheleth. The epilogue practically tells the reader not to pay too much attention to the book. One does not need wisdom; it is sufficient to keep the commandments. We find a somewhat similar attitude later in the book of Baruch (see chapter 28 below). Qoheleth, in contrast, never suggested that "the whole duty of everyone" could be identified so simply.

It is not surprising, however, that some scribes found Qoheleth troubling and tried to limit its influence. The greater surprise is surely that it was included in the canon of Scripture at all. Its inclusion may have been due to its supposed Solomonic authorship, but it also testifies to the critical spirit that pervades so much of the Hebrew Scriptures.

FOR FURTHER READING

Job

Commentaries

S. E. Balentine, *Job* (Macon, GA: Smyth & Helwys, 2006). Well-illustrated theological commentary.

N. C. Habel, *The Book of Job* (OTL; Philadelphia: Westminster, 1985). Detailed commentary. Distinctive for defending the authenticity of the Elihu speeches.

J. G. Janzen, *Job* (Interpretation; Atlanta: John Knox, 1985). Theological consideration of existential questions raised by Job.

C. A. Newsom, "The Book of Job," *NIB* 4:319–637. Elegant, literate commentary with theological reflections.

M. H. Pope, *Job* (AB 15; New York: Doubleday, 1979). Classic philological commentary, rich in parallels with ancient Near Eastern literature.

C.-L. Seow, *Job 1–21. Interpretation and Commentary* (Grand Rapids: Eerdmans, 2013). Literary-theological commentary with attention to reception history.

Studies

J. L. Crenshaw, "Job, Book of," *ABD* 3:858–68. Excellent overview of the critical issues.

———, *Reading Job* (Macon, GA: Smyth & Helwys, 2011). Literary and theological commentary.

K. J. Dell, *The Book of Job as Sceptical Literature* (BZAW 197; Berlin: de Gruyter, 1991). Categorizes Job as different from Proverbs/Wisdom.

G. Gutiérrez, *On Job: God-Talk and the Suffering of the Innocent* (Maryknoll, NY: Orbis, 1987). Interpretation of Job in light of liberation theology.

Avi Hurvitz, "The Date of the Prose Tale of Job Linguistically Reconsidered," *HTR* 67 (1974): 17–34. Argument for the date of the prologue on the basis of language.

C. A. Newsom, *The Book of Job: A Contest of Moral Imaginations* (New York: Oxford University Press, 2003). Sophisticated literary and moral analysis.

L. G. Perdue, *Wisdom in Revolt: Metaphorical Theology in the Book of Job* (JSOTSup 112; Sheffield: JSOT Press, 1991). Good discussion of the critical issues.

S. Terrien, *The Iconography of Job through the Centuries* (University Park: Pennsylvania State University Press, 1996). Superb illustrated volume.

J. W. Whedbee, *The Bible and the Comic Vision* (Minneapolis: Fortress Press, 2002), 221–62. Job as comedy.

Modern adaptations

R. Frost, *A Masque of Reason* (New York: Holt, Rinehart and Winston, 1945). Witty and insightful retelling of Job.

A. MacLeish, *J. B. A Play in Verse* (Boston: Houghton Mifflin, 1958). Modern dramatization of Job.

E. Wiesel, *The Trial of God: A Play in Three Acts* (New York: Schocken, 1979). The theme of Job, set in a pogrom in seventeenth-century Russia.

Qoheleth

Commentaries

J. L. Crenshaw, *Ecclesiastes* (OTL; Philadelphia: Westminster, 1987). Excellent, concise commentary.

T. Krüger, *Qoheleth* (Hermeneia; Minneapolis: Fortress Press, 2004). Full scholarly commentary.

N. Lohfink, *Qoheleth* (trans. S. McEvenue; CC; Minneapolis: Fortress Press, 2003). Sensitive literary and theological commentary.

R. E. Murphy, *Ecclesiastes* (WBC 23A; Waco: Word, 1992). Rich, detailed exegetical commentary.

C.-L. Seow, *Ecclesiastes* (AB 18C; New York: Doubleday, 1997). Detailed philological commentary, with attention to socioeconomic background. Dates the book to the Persian period.

W. S. Towner, "The Book of Ecclesiastes," *NIB* 5:267–360. An erudite homiletical commentary.

Studies

J. Barbour, *The Story of Israel in the Book of Qohelet: Ecclesiastes as Cultural Memory* (Oxford: Oxford University Press, 2012). Argues that Qoheleth is haunted by the decline and fall of the nation and the Babylonian exile.

M. J. Boda, T. Longman III, and C. G. Rata, *The Words of the Wise are Like Goads: Engaging Qohelet in the 21st Century* (Winona Lake, IN: Eisenbrauns, 2013).

S. Burkes, *Death in Qoheleth and Egyptian Biographies of the Late Period* (SBLDS 170; Atlanta: SBL, 1999). Comparative study of the central issue in Qoheleth.

J. L. Crenshaw, "Ecclesiastes, Book of," *ABD* 2:271–80. A good overview of the issues.

M. Fox, *A Time to Tear Down and a Time to Build Up: A Rereading of Ecclesiastes* (Grand Rapids: Eerdmans, 1999; reprint, Eugene, OR: Wipf and Stock, 2010). Penetrating study of the thought of Qoheleth.

E. P. Lee, *The Vitality of Enjoyment in Qohelet's Theological Rhetoric* (BZAW 353; Berlin: de Gruyter, 2005). Positive construal of Qoheleth's theology.

C. J. Sharp, "Ironic Representation, Authorial Voice and Meaning in Qohelet," in C.J. Sharp, *Irony and Meaning in the Hebrew Bible* (Bloomington: University of Indiana, 2009), 196–220. Argues that Qohelet is ironic and that the epilogue gives the true message of the book.

M. A. Shields, *The End of Wisdom: A Reappraisal of the Historical and Canonical Function of Ecclesiastes* (Winona Lake, IN: Eisenbrauns, 2006). The epilogue reflects a negative judgment on the value of wisdom. Wide-ranging essays on all aspects of Qoheleth.

S. Weeks, *Ecclesiastes and Scepticism* (London: T&T Clark, 2012). Comprehensive study of thought of Qoheleth.

CHAPTER 26

The Hebrew Short Story
Ruth, Esther, Tobit, Judith

INTRODUCTION

In this chapter, we shall consider two books of the Hebrew Bible that are entire short stories: the books of Ruth and Esther; and two others, Tobit and Judith, that are preserved in the Apocrypha and recognized as canonical in the Catholic Church.

One of the great contributions of the Hebrew Bible to world literature lies in the development of prose fiction, specifically of the novella, or short story. We have already seen that many of the quasi-historical narratives in the Bible could be viewed as fictional compositions, even if they contain reminiscences of historical events. This is true of the stories of Genesis, which are artful compositions that reflect on human dilemmas (think of the story of Abraham and Isaac in Genesis 22 or that of Judah and Tamar in Genesis 38). Much of the books of Samuel reads like a historical novel. Regardless of the historical basis, which cannot be verified in any case, the portrayal of characters (such as David's) and the plotting of the narrative require the kind of imaginative construction that we associate with prose fiction. The story of Joseph is an especially rich and complex narrative that provided a model, to some degree, for the later stories of Esther and Daniel. All these stories are relatively simple narratives, that describe a situation of tension or crisis and proceed to its resolution. Their power lies both in the initial complication of the situation and in the manner of the resolution.

In addition to these narratives that are embedded in longer biblical books, there are also several that constitute books in themselves. In this chapter, we shall consider five such books.

Ruth

The book of Ruth is exceptional in the Hebrew Scriptures insofar as its heroine is a Moabite woman who marries an Israelite and returns to Israel with her mother-in-law.

Moabites do not usually get good press in the Hebrew Bible. In Numbers 25, the Israelites incite the wrath of YHWH by having sexual relations with Moabite women and joining in the worship of their gods. Deuteronomy 23:3 decrees that no Ammonite or Moabite should be admitted to the assembly of the Lord, even to the tenth generation. Ruth, however, is an exemplary character. Although the story is related to Israelite history at the beginning and at the end, it is primarily the story of family relationships. On this level of interaction between individuals, ethnic origin recedes in importance. What matters is how people behave toward one another. Like the parables of Jesus in the New Testament, the story uses concrete, specific situations to illuminate human behavior in a way that transcends the particularity of time and place. It is a story of human action, with little appeal to divine intervention. The occasional references to the Lord, however, are enough to suggest that the entire action is being guided to a happy conclusion by divine providence.

The story of Ruth is divided into four chapters. The first chapter sets up the situation of crisis. As in some of the stories in Genesis, the action is set in motion by a famine in the land of Israel. A man from Bethlehem named Elimelech, in the time of the judges, goes to live in Moab. (Mention of Bethlehem helps to link the story with two incidents at the end of the book of Judges, the story of the Levite from Bethlehem, beginning in Judg 17:7, and that of the concubine from Bethlehem in Judges 19. These stories, however, are very different from that of Ruth.) The man's sons marry Moabite women named Orpah and Ruth. Elimelech dies, and some years afterward his sons die too.

Throughout the ancient Near East the situation of widows and orphans was especially precarious, as indeed it has also been in other times and places, including the modern world. The situation of a widow who had no son was especially dire, as there would be no one to inherit the family property. According to Deut 25:5-10, if a man died without a son, his brother should marry the widow and raise up an heir to the deceased (this is known as the levirate law). The brother could refuse but would then be put to shame before the elders of the town. The purpose of this law was to prevent the widow from marrying outside the family, thereby alienating the family property, but it also was a way of ensuring that the widow would be taken care of. There are only two stories in the Hebrew Bible that illustrate the working of the levirate. One is the story of Judah and Tamar in Genesis, where Judah refuses to honor the practice and Tamar takes matters into her own hands. The other is the story of Ruth.

In the case of Ruth, we are not told which brother died first, or why the other did not take the widow to wife. For the purposes of the story, the two seem to have died at the same time. Naomi plaintively tells her daughters-in-law that she has no sons in her womb that they could hope to marry. Accordingly, she urges them to return to the houses of their parents until they should find new husbands. Orpah is persuaded to do this, but Ruth persists in going with Naomi: "Where you go, I will go; and where you lodge, I will lodge; your people shall be my people, and your God my God." Ruth thereby abandons the relative security of staying with her own people in an act of fidelity to her mother-in-law and to the family of her dead husband. The first chapter ends with the return of the two destitute women to Bethlehem (which literally means "house of bread") and the lament of Naomi that although she went away full the Lord has brought her back empty. Her emptiness is all the more striking in the context of the barley harvest that was about to begin.

The second chapter introduces another character who has a crucial role in the story. Elimelech has a rich kinsman named Boaz. Naomi had not mentioned the existence of this relative to Ruth in chapter 1. The levirate law, as formulated in Deuteronomy, applied only to brothers. Boaz would not have been under any legal obligation to help a distant kinswoman, nor do the women claim anything from him as a matter of right. Instead, Ruth proposes to support the women for a while by gathering ears of grain left by the reapers. (Biblical law requires the reapers to leave something for the poor and the alien: Lev 19:9-10; 23:22; Deut 24:19-22.) When she comes to the field of Boaz, he notices her and protects her because of her fidelity to her mother-in-law. He allows her to eat at his table and instructs the reapers to let her glean even among the standing sheaves. Only at the end of the day does Naomi tell Ruth of her relationship to Boaz and suggest that her meeting Boaz is a sign of the Lord's providential care. Ruth and Naomi are now secure until the end of the barley and wheat harvests, but their long-term future is still precarious.

Chapter 3 brings the drama of the story to a climax. Naomi realizes that the best hope for long-term security is to have Boaz marry Ruth. Her plan for bringing this about, however, is remarkable. She does not instruct Ruth to ask Boaz to marry her, but rather to seduce him. The scene is the threshing floor,

Fig. 26.1 *Ruth in the Field of Boaz* by Julius Schnorr von Carolsfeld (1828). Commons.wikimedia.org

where Boaz is winnowing barley. The threshing floor was not only a workplace but also a place of celebration, where men relaxed at the end of the work of harvest. The prophet Hosea accuses Israel of acting like a prostitute on all the threshing floors (Hos 9:1). These were apparently places where prostitutes might expect to find customers. Ruth is told to wash and anoint herself and to put on her best clothes. We may compare the more elaborate preparations of the girls from the king's harem in Esth 2:12, or Judith's preparation for seducing Holofernes in Jdt 10:3. Already in Mesopotamian mythology, the goddess Inanna washes and perfumes herself before she meets Dumuzi (*ANET,* 639). Ruth waits until Boaz has eaten and drunk and lies down in contentment. There is perhaps an implication that he is slightly drunk. In Gen 19:30-38 the daughters of Lot get their father drunk and then sleep with him. The eldest becomes the mother of Moab. Holofernes becomes drunk in his attempt to seduce Judith. Unlike these figures, however, Boaz is not drunk to the point of unconsciousness. He is merely in a receptive mood.

When the time was right, Ruth "came stealthily and uncovered his feet and lay down" (Ruth 3:7). The reference to feet is a euphemism. Ruth initiates a sexual encounter. It has been objected that nowhere else in the Hebrew Bible does a woman uncover a man, but herein lies precisely the boldness of Ruth's action. Boaz, naturally, is somewhat startled to find a woman at his "feet," but he is pleased to discover her identity. It is not clear, however, whether the sexual encounter is consummated. Ruth asks him to "spread your cloak over your servant, for you are next-of-kin" (3:9). Spreading the cloak signifies protection. More specifically, in the context, Ruth is requesting that Boaz marry her. Compare Ezek 16:8, where YHWH spreads the edge of his cloak over Israel and covers her nakedness and enters into a covenant with her. Obviously, Ruth's action entails considerable risk, although she also puts considerable pressure on Boaz (note his concern that it not be known that she slept with him). We must assume that Boaz lets her stay the night because he finds her attractive, but he handles the question of marriage with all due propriety. There is another man who is more closely related to Naomi, but if he declines to marry Ruth, Boaz will do so as next of kin.

The final chapter provides the resolution of the crisis. Boaz convenes the elders in the city gate. The closer relative is willing to buy Naomi's field but backs out when he finds that he must take Ruth as part of the bargain. He then formally renounces his right in the matter by removing his sandal (cf. Deut 25:9, where the rejected widow is supposed to pull the sandal from his foot). Boaz marries Ruth,

and the story reaches its happy ending. When Ruth bears a child, Naomi nurses him and the people say, "A son has been born to Naomi." The emptiness of which she complained at the end of chapter 1 has been filled.

The conclusion of chapter 4 attempts to locate Ruth in the context of biblical history. The people pray that she may be like Rachel and Leah, and that the house of Boaz be like the house of Perez, whom Tamar bore to Judah. It is natural enough that Ruth should be linked with Tamar. Both are widows who take bold sexual initiatives so that they can have children. Moreover, we are told that Ruth's child became the father of Jesse, the father of David. Lest the full significance of this be lost, the book concludes with a genealogy of Perez, who turns out to be a direct ancestor of Boaz. Some scholars argue that this genealogy is the premise and starting point for the story of Ruth. On this reading, the purpose of the book is to put a positive spin on the fact that David's great-grandmother was Moabite by showing how she won the Lord's favor. The story of Ruth would then be analogous to some of the stories in 2 Samuel that have also been thought to deflect criticism of the Davidic line. But while the stories in 2 Samuel are overtly political, Ruth is not. David is only mentioned at the end, in a virtual appendix. It seems much more likely that the genealogies were added secondarily, to justify the inclusion of a story about a Moabite woman in the Scriptures of Israel. The similarities between Ruth and Tamar would have suggested the link with the genealogy of Perez. Ruth is placed after Judges in the LXX because the story is set in the period of the judges (1:1). In the Hebrew Bible it is associated neither with Judges nor with the books of Samuel, but is placed among the Writings. It seems very unlikely that the story of Ruth can be used as a source for David's family history.

The actual date and provenance of the story remain in dispute. At one extreme, scholars who regard the Davidic genealogy as an intrinsic part of the story tend to date it very early, perhaps in the time of Solomon. But the view that there was extensive literary activity in the time of Solomon has been largely discredited in recent scholarship. At the other extreme, many scholars have assumed a postexilic setting because of its focus on a marriage between an Israelite and a Moabite woman. On this latter reading, the story was composed as a polemic against the stringent rejection of marriage to foreign women by Ezra and his ilk. The placement of the book in the Writings lends some support to a postexilic date, since many of the Writings can be shown to date from this period. Against this view, however, it must be said that Ruth does not read like a polemic, and that the point of the story is not to affirm mixed marriages. Mixed marriage, in fact, is not acknowledged as a problem at all. It seems entirely natural that the sons of a man from Judah who grow up in Moab should marry Moabite women. When the women accept the God of Israel, as Ruth does, there is no problem whatsoever. The viewpoint of Ruth is entirely different from that of Ezra, and the difference could not have gone unnoticed in the postexilic era, but it does not necessarily follow that Ruth was composed as a polemic against Ezra.

The story of Ruth presupposes an agrarian society, where people moved easily between Judah and Moab. It is written in classical Hebrew prose. It seems somewhat more likely that such a story would have been written before the exile rather than after, but the date remains quite uncertain. While the levirate law is known to us primarily from Deuteronomy, Ruth does not necessarily depend on the biblical law code. The practice of levirate marriage was presumably traditional, and Deuteronomy does not specify the obligation of the next of kin, other than the brother. The action of Boaz is not constrained by legal obligation, but is motivated by kindness toward a destitute kinswoman, who also happens to be attractive and adventuresome.

The message of the story, in any case, should not be tied too closely to any hypothesis about its date. The view that it is political propaganda, whether for David or against Ezra, does not do justice to this gentle and humane story. The message is simply that people who act with fidelity and compassion are ultimately blessed by God, even if they have to endure difficult circumstances for a while. Ethnic origins are of little importance, and sexual propriety can be adapted to the needs of a situation. Ruth wins favor, both with Boaz and with God, because she did not abandon her mother-in-law in her time of need but was willing to do whatever was necessary to ensure the continuation of her husband's family.

Esther

The book of Esther differs from Ruth and Jonah insofar as its heroine is located in the Diaspora at the Persian court. In this respect, it resembles the stories of Joseph (at the Egyptian court) and Daniel (Babylonian and Persian courts), and the apocryphal book of 3 Maccabees (Ptolemaic Egyptian court). The "court tale" is often distinguished as a sub-genre of the Jewish short story in antiquity. A rich fund of stories set at the Persian court can be found in the Greek historian Herodotus. The stories of Joseph, Esther, and Daniel are especially closely related, although each has its own distinctive emphases.

The form of the story of Esther that is found in the Hebrew Bible (MT) is not the only form known. The Greek (LXX) translation contains six extended passages (107 verses) that have no counterpart in the Hebrew. These passages are regarded as part of the canonical text in the Roman Catholic tradition, but they are clearly secondary additions to the MT. There is also another Greek recension (or edition) of Esther known as the Greek Alpha Text (AT). This recension is found in five medieval manuscripts, but many scholars believe that it contains a form of the text that is older than the MT. The AT includes the Greek additions, and so it is not older than the MT in its present form. Apart from those additions, however, it is notable for lacking several passages found in the MT. These omissions are difficult to explain hence the view that the AT preserves a very old form of the text. Some scholars, nonetheless, still hold to the view that the AT is a revision of the LXX translation.

The book of Esther is divided into ten chapters. The first chapter locates the story "in the days of Ahasuerus, the same Ahasuerus who ruled over 127 provinces from India to Ethiopia." The king in question is better known by the anglicized version of his Greek name, Xerxes. Xerxes I (485–465 b.c.e.) did in fact rule from India to Ethiopia. The historical number of satrapies is variously given as twenty or twenty three. Dan 6:2 gives it as 120. Ahasuerus is said to give two banquets, one for all his officials and ministers lasting 180 days, and one for all the people of Susa, the capital, lasting 7 days. The queen, Vashti, gives a banquet for the women at the same time. Persian kings were famous for their banquets, but the description given in Esther is clearly hyperbolic. No banquet would have lasted for 180 days (half a year!). In all, Esther describes no fewer than seven banquets at the royal court. Banquets become, in effect, a major structuring device of the story, which also includes three Jewish feasts toward the end of the narrative.

The feasting, however, takes an unpleasant turn. The king orders the queen to appear before him "wearing the royal crown, in order to show the peoples and the officials her beauty" (1:11). Vashti refuses. The king's desire to put his wife on display is of a piece with the ostentatiousness of his banquet. Herodotus tells a story about a Lydian king, Candaules, who was so proud of the beauty of his wife that he insisted that his bodyguard, Gyges, should see her naked (Herodotus 1.8-12). The queen was enraged when she discovered the plot and insisted that Gyges murder Candaules. Some ancient commentators supposed that Vashti was ordered to appear wearing only her crown, but this is not necessarily so. The idea of being put on display before a roomful of drunken men was offensive enough, even if she was fully clothed. The honor of the queen required that she refuse, but by so doing she slighted the honor of the king.

Vashti's refusal is elevated into an issue of imperial concern: if the queen can disobey her husband with impunity, so might any wife disobey her husband. So Vashti is banished from the king's presence by a law of the Medes and the Persians that cannot be altered. The notion that a royal decree cannot be altered is a folkloric motif, found also in the book of Daniel. It heightens the drama of the story by creating circumstances that are beyond the king's control (this motif is absent from the AT). The removal of Vashti sets the story of Esther in motion by creating the vacancy at the royal court that she would fill.

The second chapter explains how Esther was chosen to be a member of the royal harem and then crowned as queen in place of Vashti (this becomes the occasion of another banquet). Several features of this story are striking in a Jewish context. Esther appears to have no qualms about being taken into the royal harem. Unlike the later story of Judith, she shows no concern for observing distinctive Jewish practices. In fact, she conceals her Jewish identity on the advice of her cousin and mentor, Mordecai. Mordecai is a loyal subject of the king and proves this by uncovering a plot against the king's person and communicating it to the king through the new queen.

Chapter 3 introduces another character who is essential to the plot: Haman, who is appointed over all other officials. Conflict develops between Haman and Mordecai when Mordecai refuses to prostrate himself before Haman in the Persian manner. It is apparent from Esther 3:4 that prostration was not in accordance with Jewish custom, although the religious basis for the refusal is not made explicit. Again, the honor of both characters is at stake. Haman attributes the slight to the fact that Mordecai is a Jew, and resolves to destroy all the Jews in the kingdom. The excessive character of this reaction is typical of the hyperbolic style of Esther. Haman appeals

to the king, but does not mention the Jews by name. Instead, he characterizes them as "a certain people . . . whose laws are different from those of every other people, and who do not keep the king's laws" (2:8). These people are evidently not assimilated, but retain their distinct identity within the empire. As typically happens in stories of this sort, the king is entirely gullible and gives his assent without question. Thus the crisis of the story develops: a decree is issued for the destruction of all the Jews of the kingdom.

The fasting of the Jews at the beginning of chapter 4 is in pointed contrast to the constant feasting of the royal court. The crisis facing the Jewish people presents a special dilemma for Queen Esther. Mordecai asks her to go to the king to intercede. She responds that no one may enter the presence of the king without being summoned. This is another folkloric motif, analogous to the irrevocable laws of the Medes and Persians, that heightens the drama of the story. Mordecai's reply goes to the heart of the predicament: "Do not think that in the king's palace you will escape any more than all the other Jews. For if you keep silence at such a time as this, relief and deliverance will arise for the Jews from another quarter, but you and your father's family will perish. Who knows? Perhaps you have come to royal dignity for just such a time as this" (4:14). Esther resolves to risk her life and calls on all the Jews of Susa to join her in a fast.

The danger to Esther's life is quickly dispelled in chapter 5. The king receives her warmly and offers to grant anything she might ask. At first she requests only that the king and Haman join her in a banquet. Haman is elated, but he is still galled by the insubordination of Mordecai, so he gives orders that a gallows be prepared for him. From this point forward, however, the story is marked by the repeated reversal of expectations. In chapter 6 the king has a sleepless night and remembers that Mordecai has not been rewarded. He asks Haman what should be done for the man the king wishes to honor. Haman, thinking that he himself is the man, recommends lavish honors. Consequently, he has to attire Mordecai with robes and lead him on horseback around the city, to his great chagrin. But a worse fate awaits him. In chapter 7, when the king and Haman come to her banquet, Esther tells the king about the plot against the Jews, whom she now identifies as "my people." When the king asks who is responsible, she identifies Haman. When the king storms out in anger, Haman throws himself on Esther to beg for his life, but the king returns and thinks it is a sexual assault. Haman is hanged on the gallows he had prepared for Mordecai.

The story now moves to its conclusion. In chapter 8 Esther asks the king to revoke the decree against the Jews. The king tells her and Mordecai that they may write as they please and seal it with his seal (so much for the unchangeable decrees of the Medes and Persians). The letters, written by Mordecai, give the Jews permission to kill any people who might attack them, throughout the provinces. So on the very day on which the Jews were to be destroyed, they slaughtered their enemies by the thousand, with the knowledge and permission of the king (chap. 9). Furthermore, they instituted the Festival of Purim to commemorate the occasion. The book ends with a brief epilogue (chap. 10) claiming that the honors given to Mordecai are recorded in the annals of the kings of Media and Persia.

Fig. 26.2   Scenes from the book of Esther, illustrated in a fresco from the third-century c.e. **synagogue at Dura-Europos.** Commons.wikimedia.org

Esther and History

Despite the reference to the annals at the end, it is quite clear that the events recorded in Esther are not historical. Several details in the book are historically problematic. Mordecai was supposedly among the exiles taken to Babylon by Nebuchadnezzar. Yet he is active in the reign of Xerxes a century later. The number of provinces, or satrapies, is inaccurate. There is no historical evidence for the deposition of a Persian queen, and so forth. But the fictional character of Esther should be quite clear from the style of the book, which is full of hyperbole and stock characters, such as the gullible king and the wicked courtier. The idea that a Persian king would give the Jews in his kingdom unlimited authority to slaughter their enemies is simply incredible. Perhaps the crowning irony of the book is that so many Jews and Christians over the centuries accepted it as historical. Scholars who try to salvage a historical core from this fantastic story are only slightly less gullible than their precritical ancestors.

As presented in the Hebrew Bible, the book appears to be a festal legend: a story told to explain why a festival (Purim) is celebrated. The actual origin of this festival is unclear. It is not strictly a religious festival. No prayers or sacrifices are prescribed, but drinking to inebriation is permitted by the Babylonian Talmud (*Megillah* 7b). The name Purim is explained in Esth 3:7 as referring to the casting of lots (cf. 9:26). The fact that lots were cast before Haman to establish the day, even before he secured the decree from the king, may suggest that Purim was a pagan festival before it became a Jewish one. Many scholars, however, think that this explanation of the name is not its original meaning. The LXX gives the name as *phrourai* (watchers or guards). The first attestation of the festival is in 2 Macc 15:36, where it is called Mordecai's day. It should be noted that the provision for a festival is not found in the Greek AT. Some scholars take this as evidence that the link with Purim was not part of the original story, but it is possible that it was omitted by Christian scribes, for whom the festival was irrelevant. The idea of a festival commemorating a slaughter has a parallel in Herodotus, who says that the Persians celebrated a festival called Magophonia to commemorate the slaughter of the magi who seized power after the death of King Cambyses (Herodotus 3.79). The story of Esther has very little in common with the story of the magi, but the Jewish festival may have been suggested by the Persian one.

The reference in 2 Maccabees is also the earliest attestation of the story of Esther. No trace of the book has been found in the Dead Sea Scrolls. This may be a matter of chance; only a small scrap of Chronicles is found there. But in view of the number of texts that have been found in the Scrolls, the absence of Esther must be regarded as significant. Some scholars have argued that Esther would have been rejected by the Qumran sect for theological reasons, but this is not convincing. The Scrolls include many texts that never attained the status of Scripture. One fragmentary Aramaic document, 4Q550, is a tale set at the court of Xerxes, which was dubbed "Proto-Esther" by its editor. In fact, it has no specific links with Esther that would justify that label, but it appears to be a tale of the same general type. If the Essenes of Qumran found that story acceptable, it is not apparent why they should object to Esther. The reference in 2 Maccabees shows that the book was known in Israel before the turn of the era, but it was probably not yet widely accepted as Scripture. There is some evidence that its status was still disputed by some Jews in rabbinic times (see the talmudic tractate *Megillah* 7), and it is missing from many Christian lists of canonical books. The book was probably composed somewhere in the eastern Diaspora around the fourth century B.C.E. The historical inaccuracies of the book suggest that it is considerably later than the time of Xerxes, but there is no trace of Hellenistic influence in it.

While the events recorded in Esther are fictional, the book is of considerable historical interest. It is the earliest known narrative of an attempt to wipe out a Jewish community in a Gentile environment. In later history such stories become all too familiar, down to the Holocaust in the twentieth century. The attempt of Antiochus Epiphanes to suppress the Jewish cult in Jerusalem in the time of the Maccabees, which we consider in the next chapter, was not really analogous. Epiphanes was not trying to wipe out a community. One possible parallel in the Persian period concerns the Jewish community at Elephantine in southern Egypt, whose temple was burned down by their Gentile neighbors. We do not know the full details of what happened. In that case, the situation of the Jews was complicated by the fact that they were a Persian garrison attacked by native Egyptians. For closer analogies to the situation in Esther, we have to wait until the first century c.e., when the Jewish community in Alexandria came under attack. The novelistic account in 3 Maccabees may reflect that situation indirectly, or it may be a fictional account from an earlier time. We do not, however, have any evidence for attacks on the Jewish communities in Persia or Babylonia in the Persian or early Hellenistic periods. Persian kings are generally depicted as protectors of the Jews in biblical sources (Second Isaiah, Ezra-Nehemiah), and indeed the king in Esther is also benign, even if somewhat impulsive. Why then should the author of Esther have conjured up the nightmarish fantasy of a plot by a Persian courtier to wipe out the Jews?

The reason given by Haman for his plot against the Jews is that "their laws are different from those of every other people, and they do not keep the king's laws" (3:8). The latter part of this charge is a calumny: Mordecai is a loyal subject of the king. But the perception that the Jews were a people set apart, who refused to assimilate fully into the Gentile culture, is a constant factor in conflicts between Jews and Gentiles in later times, beginning in the Hellenistic era. Most fundamentally, Jews, with relatively few exceptions, refused to worship the same deities as other people. They also had peculiar customs in the matter of food, which inhibited social relations. Because they were "a people set apart," they felt, and were, especially vulnerable, even in a relatively tolerant culture

such as that of Persia. If conflicts arose, such as that between Haman and Mordecai, the distinctive, alien character of the Jews made them an easy target for resentment and suspicion. Hence the fear of attack by Gentiles was present even before it became a reality. Some scholars use the word *anti-Semitic* with reference to Haman and other enemies of the Jews in antiquity, but this is anachronistic. Haman's hostility is not based on any theory of racial superiority. It is rather a matter of conflicting interests and power struggles and the attempt of one group to secure its own advancement at the expense of another.

The perception of Jewish difference is all the more surprising in this story, since Mordecai and Esther appear to be quite assimilated. Their names echo those of Babylonian deities Marduk and Ishtar. Esther has no qualms about entering the king's harem, and there is no indication that she attempts to observe any distinctive Jewish laws. The only religious observances in the book are fasts (but no prayers) in times of crisis. Most strikingly, the book of Esther, as found in the Hebrew Bible, never refers to God (this omission was noted and corrected by the Greek translators). Yet Haman's charge shows that the community at large must have observed distinctive laws. And while Mordecai encourages Esther to make herself available to the king, he is adamant on the need for solidarity with the Jewish people.

The Religious Character of Esther

The reason for Esther's silence about God is much debated. To describe the book as secular would be anachronistic. The hand of the God of Israel may be hidden, but it is nonetheless present. Mordecai tells Esther that if she does not act, "deliverance will rise for the Jews from another quarter" (4:14), and suggests that Esther's royal rank was providential. Later Haman's friends advise him that he cannot hope to prevail against the Jewish people. These statements can hardly be explained without the tacit acknowledgment of the God of Israel. Yet it is striking that the Jews are not even said to thank the Lord for their deliverance. The silence of Esther on this subject can only be explained by the theology of the author, which bears some analogy to the wisdom literature, where God acts as the midwife behind the scenes of history. The stories of Joseph and Ruth are also somewhat reticent about divine intervention, although neither is entirely silent on the subject. Esther differs from the wisdom literature, however, in its unabashed focus on the Jewish people and defense of their interests. This interest does not extend to the land of Israel. This is Diaspora Judaism, which has its own integrity and identity, quite apart from the land of Judah or the temple. We need not suppose that all Diaspora Judaism was of this sort. We know that many Jews from abroad went to Jerusalem on pilgrimage. Esther suggests, however, that at least some Jews did not regard life in the Diaspora as a state of exile and nonetheless maintained a vigorous Jewish identity.

It should be noted that the Greek AT does refer to God in the narrative. Some scholars have drawn the conclusion that the editor of the MT omitted references to the Deity that were included in the original story. This seems highly improbable. The AT appears to be based on a variant Hebrew form of the story. It does not follow, however, that this was the form of the story known to the editor of the canonical text. It is unlikely that any Jewish editors would have excised references to the Deity from the form of the text that they knew.

The absence of the Deity from the narrative of Esther has given offense to some scholars over the centuries. Even more problematic, however, is the conclusion of the book, where the Jews slaughter their enemies and then establish a festival to celebrate the occasion. To be sure, the slaughter is a fantasy, but that hardly makes the vengefulness any less distasteful. The glorification of violence is not exceptional in the Hebrew Bible. At least in Esther, the Jews are attacking people who wanted to attack them, although their actions go well beyond the bounds of self-defense. The conquest narratives in Joshua, which may be equally fictional, are even more problematic, since the slaughter is unprovoked. But Esther cannot be held up as a model for relations between ethnic groups. It seems to view the options in a situation of conflict as either to kill or to be killed. There is no attempt at reconciliation. This is all the more remarkable since Esther shows no desire for Jewish independence. The sovereignty of the Persian king is not questioned. The ideal situation is one where the king can be manipulated to advance the interests of the Jews. In the fantasy of Esther, the Jews are triumphant. The politics of ethnic antagonism, however, seldom yield such a clear-cut result. Violence, and even the fantasy of violence, most often begets just more violence.

The Additions to Esther

The Additions to Esther make the religious aspects of the text much more explicit than they were in the Hebrew form of the text. The passages are usually identified by the letters A-F. Addition A describes a dream of Mordecai, in which he sees "what God had determined to do" in the coming conflict between Jews and Gentiles. Addition B contains the royal edict ordering the massacre of the Jews. C has prayers of Mordecai and Esther. D describes Esther's unsummoned appearance before the king. E contains the royal edict drafted by Mordecai, revoking the edict sent by Haman, and F has the interpretation of Mordecai's dream, which says that God made two lots, one for Israel and one for the nations. The primary effect of these additions is to make the characters more pious and to leave no doubt about the role of God in the story. They do not necessarily all come from the same hand. A, C, and D are probably translations from Hebrew, while B and E are probably composed in Greek. At the end of F there is a statement that the Greek translation was brought into Egypt "in the fourth year of Ptolemy and Cleopatra." Unfortunately, several Ptolemies who reigned for at least four years had wives named Cleopatra. The most probable date is either 114 B.C.E. (Ptolemy VIII) or 77 B.C.E. (Ptolemy XII).

Tobit

A very different kind of story from the eastern Diaspora is found in the deuterocanonical book of Tobit. This book was not included in the Hebrew Bible, but it was originally composed in a Semitic language. Fragments of one Hebrew and four Aramaic manuscripts have been found in the Dead Sea Scrolls. The story is preserved in the Greek and Latin Bibles,

and it is regarded as canonical in the Roman Catholic Church.

Tobit was allegedly a man from the tribe of Naphtali in northern Israel, who was taken captive to Assyria when King Shalmaneser destroyed Samaria in 722 B.C.E. (2 Kgs 17:1-6). Even in exile he refrained from eating the food of the Gentiles. Nonetheless, he found favor with the king, and conducted business for him in Media, where at one time he left ten talents of silver on deposit. He lost favor with the king however, because of his practice of burying the dead who had been executed. Because of this he had to flee and lose all his property. He was restored after the death of Shalmaneser, through the intercession of his nephew Ahikar.

Tobit meets with further misfortune, however, when bird droppings fall into his eyes and cause him to go blind. He is supported by his wife, but in his righteous zeal he accuses her of stealing. She retorts that his righteousness has done him little good. At this point, Tobit prays for death. At the same time, in Media a young woman, Sarah daughter of Raguel, a kinsman of Tobit, was praying for death because she had been married seven times and each husband had been killed by a demon before the marriage was consummated. The prayers of both are answered, not by death but by the sending of the angel Raphael to heal them.

Tobit now remembers the money he had left on deposit in Media and sends his son Tobias to fetch it. He charges the young man not to marry any Gentile woman but to take a wife from his own kindred. The son looks for a man to go with him and finds Raphael, disguised as a human being, and hires him. So the young man and the angel set out, and the

Fig. 26.3 *Tobias Heals His Blind Father* by Andrea Vaccaro (1640). Museu Nacional d'Art de Catalunya. Commons.wikimedia.org

dog goes with them. On the way a large fish leaps out to attack Tobias. Raphael instructs him to open the fish and take out its gall, heart, and liver and keep them as medicines. Raphael guides Tobias to the house of Raguel, and tells him about Sarah. He urges the young man to seek her hand in marriage, since he is her next of kin. Tobias knows about Sarah's previous husbands and is wary, but Raphael, tells him how he can repel the demon, using the fish's liver and heart. Sarah's parents are reluctant because of her previous history, but Tobias insists. Then Raguel gives her to him "in accordance with the decree in the book of Moses." The young couple pray before they retire for the night. The parents are so sure that Tobias will die that they dig his grave, but in the morning he is found alive and well.

Tobias now retrieves the silver but remains with his in-laws for fourteen days of wedding celebration. In the meantime, his parents are sick with worry because of his prolonged absence. Tobias hurries home when the feast is ended. Raphael instructs him to smear the gall of the fish on his father's eyes, and sure

enough, his sight is restored. Tobit proposes to give Raphael half of the silver in gratitude, but the angel finally reveals his true identity. Tobit thereupon bursts into praise of God (chap. 13). Before he dies he prophesies that all Israel, including Jerusalem, will be made desolate, but that Jerusalem will subsequently be restored and the exiles will return to the land. The book ends with a brief notice about the deaths of Tobit and his wife, and says that Tobias lived to see the destruction of Nineveh.

The story of Tobit is no more historical than the other stories we have reviewed. Its fanciful nature is apparent in the roles of the angel, the demon, and the magical cures. Even though it is set in Assyria before the Deuteronomic reform, it clearly reflects the piety of Second Temple Judaism. The story is a romance; in large part it is the story of the quest of a young man for a bride and the trials he encounters. More broadly, the plot is that of a traditional folktale. At the beginning, the protagonists are in a state of lack (Tobit is blind, Tobias needs a wife, and Sarah needs a husband). Their needs are met and their problems are resolved through the aid of a wonderful helper (Raphael). The story draws on widespread folkloric motifs such as the Grateful Dead and the Dangerous Bride. Tobit's ultimate good fortune is clearly related to his piety in burying the dead, even if the link is not made explicit. The mention of Ahikar also links Tobit to the world of Near Eastern folklore. Ahikar was a legendary wise man at the Assyrian court. His story, which included a collection of proverbs, circulated in several languages. An Aramaic version was preserved by the Jewish community in Elephantine in southern Egypt in the fifth century B.C.E. All these folkloric elements are woven together by a master storyteller with a good sense of humor. What other Israelite hero is undone by bird droppings? One of the delightful touches of the story is the role of the dog, which is quite unnecessary for the plot but adds a dimension of realism.

Unlike the story of Esther, Tobit is not lacking in explicit piety. The protagonists miss no opportunity to praise the God of heaven. The piety, however, involves a strange mix of elements. On the one hand, Tobit gives a rare glimpse of popular Jewish piety in the Second Temple period. This involved a lively faith in angels and demons and in cures that we would regard as superstitious, or even magical. There is great appreciation of spontaneous virtue and common humanity. The piety of burying the dead has a pivotal role in the Greek tragedy *Antigone*. Almsgiving and care for the poor are widespread, if not universal, human values. On the other hand, there are repeated references to the law of Moses, strictly interpreted in the Deuteronomic tradition. Tobit refuses to eat Gentile food and insists that his son not marry a Gentile. He also deplores the "sin of Jeroboam," who rebelled against the house of David (Tob 1:4-5), and claims to have worshiped in Jerusalem when he lived in the land of Israel. His final testament at the end, about the coming desolation and restoration of Jerusalem, also has a distinctly Deuteronomic ring to it. It seems likely then that a popular folktale was reworked by an author who was deeply committed to the law of Moses. It is remarkable, however, that the folkloric, and even magical, elements in the story were allowed to stand.

Tobit's indebtedness to the Torah is not confined to legal issues. The journey of Tobias in quest of a wife from his own people recalls the stories of Isaac and Jacob in Genesis. The prayer of Tobias on his wedding night draws explicitly on Genesis: "You said, 'It is not good that the man should be alone; let us make a helper for him like himself'" (Tob 8:6). This is one of the earliest citations of the opening chapters of Genesis (the others are in Ben Sira and the Dead Sea Scrolls). The view of marriage that it expresses, which emphasizes the role of the wife as helpmate, is much more positive than what we find in Ben Sira.

We cannot be sure when or where Tobit was written. That it was current both in Hebrew and Aramaic in the Dead Sea Scrolls suggests that it can be no later than the second, or more likely the third, century b.c.e. Tobit's prediction of the course of Israel's history at the end shows no awareness of the upheavals in Jerusalem in the time of the Maccabees.

This is one of the most entertaining stories in the biblical corpus, and we must assume that entertainment was one of the purposes for which it was composed. The author of the story as we have it used the entertaining romance as an occasion for conventional moral instruction. In his deathbed speech in chapter 14, Tobit assures his son that righteousness is rewarded and wickedness punished. And so it is in this story, but only if one takes a long-term view and watches out for bird droppings along the way.

Judith

The final novella under review in this chapter is set in the land of Israel. Like the others, it has the superficial trappings of historical narrative. It gives dates and places in great detail. But the expectation that this is a reliable history is quickly dispelled. In the very first verse we read that Nebuchadnezzar ruled over the Assyrians and lived in Nineveh. What Jewish person in the Second Temple period could possibly have been so ignorant about the king who destroyed Jerusalem? It has been suggested that the author falsified history intentionally for comic effect. More plausibly, he may have wished to associate Nebuchadnezzar with Assyria because the real threat to Judea when the story was written came from Syria, the home of the great persecutor of the Jews in the second century B.C.E., Antiochus Epiphanes.

The story begins with a fictional account of a battle between Nebuchadnezzar and the completely fictitious Arphaxad of Media. The western provinces refuse to come to the aid of the Assyrian king, and so he resolves to destroy them. After he has subdued the Medes, he sends his general Holofernes westward. Most of the peoples submit to him, but the Israelites prepare to resist. The fictional town of Bethulia becomes the focal point of the attack (the name recalls Bethel, but also the Hebrew word *bᵉtulah,* "virgin," which is used several times in connection with Zion). When Holofernes hears of their preparation, he makes inquiries about them from Achior the Ammonite (the name recalls the famous Assyrian sage Ahikar, who was mentioned in the book of Tobit). Achior provides a summary of the history of Israel and assures Holofernes, in Deuteronomic fashion, that Israel will only be conquered if the people have offended their God. Holofernes responds indignantly, "Who is God but Nebuchadnezzar?" (6:2). Achior is bound and left outside Bethulia until he is rescued by the Jews, who welcome him. Holofernes now lays siege to Bethulia. Some of the people lose heart and reproach their rulers for not making peace with the Assyrians.

Only at this point, approximately halfway through the narrative in chapter 8, is the heroine Judith introduced. The name Judith means simply "woman of Judah" or "Jewish woman." It also recalls the name of Judah the Maccabee, the great champion of freedom in the Maccabean era. Judith is a widow of exemplary character and beautiful to boot. She rebukes the people who have proposed surrender and tells them that she is going to do a great deed, but they must not try to find out what she is doing. Before she goes out of Bethulia, she prays, asking God to make her "deceitful words" to the Assyrians successful.

Judith now goes to the Assyrian camp. She gains admission by promising advice on the best way to attack Bethulia, but also by her beauty. She tells Holofernes that the food supply of the Jews is exhausted, and that they are ready to outrage their God by eating forbidden food. She proposes to stay with Holofernes but to go each night to the valley to pray so that she may learn from God when the Jews have sinned. Holofernes offers her delicacies, but she refuses to eat the food of Gentiles lest she offend her God. Holofernes tolerates her observances. On the fourth night, he makes a banquet and summons her to his presence. She beautifies herself and agrees to drink with him. When they are alone in his tent, however, Holofernes falls into a drunken sleep, and Judith cuts off his head and puts it in her bag. The guards let her out, as they are accustomed to her nightly excursions. When she returns to Bethulia, she is praised above all other women. The Assyrian army panics and is defeated, Achior is circumcised and converts to Judaism, and Judith leads the women in a

Fig. 26.4 *Judith and the Head of Holofernes* by Cristofano Allori (1577–1621); Pitti Palace, Florence. Commons.wikimedia.org

festive dance. The book concludes with a song of praise on the lips of Judith.

The story of Judith lacks the comic character of Tobit or even of Esther. The heroine resembles Esther, in that she risks her life for her people, and the two books share a militant attitude toward the Gentiles. Judith and Esther also share a rather unconventional mode of action in their willingness to go to the bed of a Gentile ruler (Ruth also flouted sexual convention). Judith, however, is preserved from transgression by the drunkenness of the king. She is, in fact, exemplary in her observance of Jewish law, quite in contrast to the more cavalier approach of Esther. The great scandal of the story, however, is her willingness to deceive the Assyrian general, violate his trust, and kill him in a gruesome manner. There is a biblical precedent for her action in Judges 4–5, where Jael the Kenite shelters Sisera in her tent and then drives a tent peg into his skull. There is no apology for the violence of the action. The survival of the people is at stake, and Judith is a heroine. That a woman performs this great deed accords with the theology of the book of Judges, where God effects his deliverance through improbable means to show that it is not an achievement of human power.

The book of Judith is blatantly nationalistic. It is preserved only in Greek, Latin, and other translations, but the idiom suggests that it was composed in Hebrew. No trace of it has been found in the Dead Sea Scrolls. The spirit of the book is very similar to that of 1 Maccabees, which also celebrates militant Jewish resistance to foreign oppressors. It is widely supposed that Judith, too, is Maccabean literature, written toward the end of the second century B.C.E., when the heirs of the Maccabees, the Hasmoneans, ruled in Jerusalem. First Maccabees was also written in Hebrew but preserved only in Greek and other translations. It was not included in the Dead Sea Scrolls, probably because the Dead Sea sect was not sympathetic to the Maccabees, who were less than scrupulous in their observance of the Law. It is somewhat ironic that these two books, which celebrate militant Jewish nationalism, did not find a place in the canon of Jewish Scriptures, but were included in the Greek Bible and remain canonical in the Roman Catholic Church.

FOR FURTHER READING

General

A. Brenner, *A Feminist Companion to Esther, Judith and Susanna* (The Feminist Companion to the Bible 7; Sheffield: Sheffield Academic Press, 1995). A collection of feminist articles on these stories.

A. Lacocque, *The Feminine Unconventional: Four Subversive Figures in Israel's Tradition* (OBT; Minneapolis: Fortress Press, 1990). A study of female characters in Jewish stories: Ruth, Esther, Judith, Susanna.

L. M. Wills, *The Jewish Novel in the Ancient World* (Ithaca, NY: Cornell University Press, 1995). An introduction to the Jewish novel or short story, including several works that are not included in any canon.

Ruth

E. F. Campbell, *Ruth* (AB 7; Garden City, NY: Doubleday, 1975). Argues for Solomonic dating and sets Ruth in a covenantal context.

K. Farmer, "The Book of Ruth," *NIB* 2:891–946. Takes Ruth as more parable than apologia.

D. N. Fewell and D. M. Gunn, *Compromising Redemption: Relating Characters in the Book of Ruth* (Louisville: Westminster John Knox, 1990). Questions the exemplary nature of the characters in Ruth.

T. Linafelt, *Ruth*, and T. K. Beal, *Esther* (Berith Olam; Collegeville, MN: Liturgical Press, 1999). Literary commentary.

V. H. Matthews, *Judges and Ruth* (New Cambridge Bible Commentary; Cambridge: Cambridge University Press, 2004). Literary commentary with attention to cultural context.

K. Nielsen, *Ruth* (OTL; Louisville: Westminster John Knox, 1997). Regards the story as political propaganda for David.

J. M. Sasson, *Ruth: A New Translation with a Philological Commentary and a Formalist-Folklorist Interpretation* (Baltimore: Johns Hopkins University Press, 1979). Uses Vladimir Propp's *Morphology of the Folk-Tale* to shed light on the structure of Ruth.

P. Trible, *God and the Rhetoric of Sexuality* (OBT; Philadelphia: Fortress Press, 1978), 166–99. Sensitive literary reading.

———, "Ruth, Book of," *ABD* 5:842–47. Good overview of the critical issues.

Esther

T. K. Beal (see Linafelt, *Ruth*, above).

A. Berlin, *Esther: The Traditional Hebrew Text with the New JPS Translation* (Philadelphia: Jewish Publication Society, 2001). Concise commentary, emphasizing comic elements and literary artistry.

D. J. A. Clines, *The Esther Scroll: The Story of the Story* (JSOTSup 30; Sheffield: JSOT Press, 1984). A study of the formation of the book.

S. White Crawford, "The Book of Esther," *NIB* 3:853–972. Comprehensive commentary, including the Additions.

L. M. Day, *Esther* (Nashville: Abingdon, 2005). Literary-theological commentary.

M. V. Fox, *Character and Ideology in the Book of Esther* (2nd ed.; Eugene, OR: Wipf and Stock, 2010). Focuses on the depiction of character but also contains a good discussion of the texts of Esther.

J. D. Levenson, *Esther* (OTL; Louisville: Westminster John Knox, 1997). Defends the religious character of Esther.

C. A. Moore, *Daniel, Esther, and Jeremiah: The Additions* (AB 44; Garden City, NY: Doubleday, 1977). Thorough commentary on the Greek Additions.

———, *Esther* (AB 7B; New York: Doubleday, 1971). Standard comprehensive commentary.

———, "Esther, Book of," *ABD* 2:633–43. Review of the critical issues.

Tobit

D. A. deSilva, *Introducing the Apocrypha* (Grand Rapids: Baker, 2002), 63–84. Good discussion of all aspects of the story.

J. A. Fitzmyer, *Tobit* (CEJL; Berlin: de Gruyter, 2003). Thorough commentary, using the textual evidence from the Dead Sea Scrolls.

C. A. Moore, *Tobit* (AB 40A; New York: Doubleday, 1996). Comprehensive commentary.

G. W. E. Nickelsburg, "Tobit," in *The HarperCollins Bible Commentary* (ed. J. L. Mays; San Francisco: HarperCollins, 2000), 719–31. Concise commentary, in the context of the apocryphal literature.

I. Nowell, "The Book of Tobit," *NIB* 3:973–1071. Full commentary, with attention to the theology of the story.

G. G. Xeravits and J. Zsengellér, *The Book of Tobit: Text, Tradition, Theology* (Leiden: Brill, 2005). Essays on various aspects of Tobit.

Judith

T. Craven, *Artistry and Faith in the Book of Judith* (SBLDS 70; Chico, CA: Scholars Press, 1983). Pioneering literary study.

D. A. deSilva, *Introducing the Apocrypha* (Grand Rapids: Baker, 2002), 85–109. Readable review of the literary and theological issues.

A. J. Levine, "Judith," *The Oxford Bible Commentary* (ed. J. Barton and J. Muddiman; Oxford: Oxford University Press, 2001), 632–41. Concise commentary with feminist sensitivity.

C. A. Moore, *Judith* (AB 40; Garden City, NY: Doubleday, 1985). Standard, comprehensive commentary.

J. C. VanderKam, ed., *"No One Spoke Ill of Her": Essays on Judith* (SBLEJL 2; Atlanta: Scholars Press, 1992). A collection of excellent essays.

L. M. Wills, "The Book of Judith," *NIB* 3:1075–1183. Literate treatment in light of the conventions of ancient fiction.

CHAPTER 27

Daniel, 1–2 Maccabees

INTRODUCTION

This chapter concerns Jewish writings composed in the Hellenistic era: the book of Daniel (and Greek additions to the book), and 1 and 2 Maccabees.

The book of Daniel is exceptional in many respects. It is probably the latest composition in the Hebrew Bible. Like the book of Ezra, it is written partly in Hebrew and partly in Aramaic. The Greek edition of the book includes passages and whole stories that are not attested in the Hebrew Bible version. Moreover, it contains the only example in the Hebrew Bible of a genre, apocalypse, that was of great importance for Judaism in the Hellenistic and Roman periods and also for early Christianity. In the Greek and Latin Bibles, and in Christian tradition, Daniel is regarded as the fourth of the Major Prophets, and the book follows those of Isaiah, Jeremiah, and Ezekiel. In the Hebrew Bible, however, Daniel is placed among the Writings. It may be that the canon of prophetic writings was already closed when Daniel was written. It may also be that the rabbis saw the book as having more in common with the Writings than with the Prophets.

As found in the Hebrew Bible, the book falls into two sections. The first six chapters are stories about Daniel and his friends, who were allegedly among the exiles deported from Jerusalem by Nebuchadnezzar, at the Babylonian and Persian courts. The second half of the book, chapters 7–12, consists of a series of revelations to Daniel, which are explained to him by an angel. Strictly speaking, only the second half of the book is an apocalypse, but the stories in chapters 1–6 form an introduction that sets the scene. One of the oddities of the book is that the division by language does not fully coincide with the division by genre. Chapters 2–7 (strictly, 2:4b—7:28) are in Aramaic. Chapter 1 and chapters 8–12 are in Hebrew. It seems clear that the book was written in stages. The Aramaic stories in chapters 2–6 originally circulated independently. Chapter 1 was written as an introduction to these stories, presumably in Aramaic. The first of the visions, in chapter 7, was composed in Aramaic for continuity with the tales. The remaining chapters were added in Hebrew, presumably because of patriotic fervor at the time of the Maccabean revolt. The opening chapter was then translated into Hebrew so that the beginning and end of the book would be in Hebrew, forming an *inclusio.* This explanation is, of course, hypothetical, but it gives a plausible account of the way the book took shape.

The Greek Additions to the book are of two kinds. Two poetic compositions, the Prayer of Azariah and the Song of the Three Young Men, are inserted into chapter 3. The stories of Bel and the Dragon and of Susanna are free-standing stories analogous to the stories in chapters 1–6.

The Court Tales

The stories in Daniel 1–6 have much in common with the short stories in the Hebrew Bible, especially those of Joseph and Esther. Like these stories, they are "court tales": stories about Jews at the court of a foreign king. Like Esther, the stories in Daniel are set in the eastern Diaspora, and most probably originated there. Unlike Esther, however, Daniel is overtly pious, and the stories are punctuated with prayer and praise. Nonetheless, they share with Esther the concern about maintaining Jewish identity in a foreign land, in the service of a foreign king.

The tales ostensibly tell the story of a group of young Judeans who were deported after the conquest of Jerusalem by Nebuchadnezzar. Any attempt to derive historical information from these stories, however, encounters insuperable problems. The opening verse dates the siege of Jerusalem to the third year of King Jehoiakim (606 B.C.E.). We know from other sources, both biblical and Babylonian, that Nebuchadnezzar did not besiege Jerusalem until 598/597, and Jehoiakim died before the siege began. His son Jehoiachin submitted to the Babylonians in 597 and was deported to Babylon. Chapter 2 is set in the second year of the reign of Nebuchadnezzar, which would require that he had conquered Jerusalem in his first year (one Greek manuscript resolves the problem by dating chapter 2 to the twelfth year). Later chapters present problems that are even more glaring. Daniel 4 claims that Nebuchadnezzar was transformed into a beast for seven years. There is no historical corroboration of such an extraordinary event. Chapter 5 presents a king of Babylon named Belshazzar. There was in fact a historical Belshazzar, who was son of the last king of Babylon, Nabonidus, and who governed Babylon in the absence of his father. He was never king, however. Daniel goes on to say that after the death of Belshazzar, "Darius the Mede" received the kingdom. No such figure is known to history. Conservative Christian scholars have expended enormous energy in efforts to salvage the historicity of Darius the Mede and other problematic data in Daniel. These efforts are misdirected. These stories are not exercises in history writing. They are legends, full of miraculous elements (the fiery furnace, the lions' den). They are meant to inspire awe and wonder, and are not to be taken as factual accounts. In fact, it is unlikely that Daniel ever existed. The name Daniel (Danel) was attached to a legendary figure from antiquity, who is known from the Ugaritic Epic of Aqhat, and who is mentioned in Ezek 14:14, 20, in conjunction with Noah and Job, as a paradigmatic righteous person. He is also mentioned in Ezek 28:3 as a paradigmatic wise man ("Are you wiser than Daniel?"). The Daniel of the book of Daniel, however, would have been a younger contemporary of Ezekiel. It is likely that the biblical author borrowed the name of the legendary hero and assigned it to a fictional Judean in the Babylonian exile.

The story of Daniel, then, is not historical. It is, however, meant to be exemplary. Daniel is an exceptional Jew who does things that the ordinary person cannot hope to imitate, but he models a lifestyle for Jews in the Diaspora. He strikes a fine balance between loyalty to his pagan rulers and fidelity to his God and to his religious tradition.

Daniel 1

The opening chapter introduces the main characters in the tales and establishes their setting in the exile. When the exiles are taken to Babylon (together with the vessels that will reappear in chap. 5), some of them are selected to be trained for service at the royal court. Their training involves "the language and literature of the Chaldeans." In effect, they are to be scribes or wise men. In the following chapter, it appears that they are called upon to do the same kinds of things that Chaldean wise men did. The Chaldeans were a people who lived south of Babylon and who came to power in the late seventh century B.C.E. From that time on, the name is commonly used to refer to Babylonians. In the Hellenistic period, however, the name is used for a class of diviners and astrologers, and "Chaldean arts" comes to mean divination. Daniel appears in the following chapters primarily as a dream interpreter and as one who can decipher signs (the writing on the wall in chap. 5). This kind of skill is sometimes called "mantic wisdom." Like prophecy, it is a way of receiving messages from God, but the method of reception is different. The Hebrew prophets are often derisive about dreams (see Jer 23:25-32) and about Babylonian wisdom in general (Isa 44:25; 47:13). The book of Daniel, however, claims that Jews can outdo the Chaldeans in their own wisdom because of the power of their God.

There is another issue raised in Daniel 1, however. Daniel and his companions refuse to partake of the king's rations lest they defile themselves. Presumably, the reference is to the laws of *kashrut*, or purity, although these laws do not figure otherwise in Daniel. (Esther, in contrast, seems to have had no such scruples.) It may be that this introductory chapter was written in the time of the Maccabees when the food laws became an issue of principle because of the attempt of the king to force Jews to violate them. But Daniel's abstinence has broader significance. It indicates his refusal to assimilate completely at the Gentile court. Even though Daniel and his companions are loyal subjects of the king, they retain this independence throughout. They also have an overriding loyalty to the God of Israel.

The Jewish youths prosper on their vegetarian diet. The point, of course, is not to recommend vegetarianism, but to indicate that God looks after those who keep his laws. Equally, when the youths succeed spectacularly and surpass all the wise men of Babylon, this is attributed not to their native intelligence but to the favor of their God.

Daniel 2

Comparison between Daniel and the Babylonian wise men is at the heart of chapter 2. The king has a dream and summons the Chaldeans to interpret it. (The narrative switches to Aramaic at this point.) He does not, however, tell them the dream, but demands that they prove their trustworthiness by telling the dream as well as interpreting it. The Chaldeans respond, reasonably enough, that no king has ever made such a request. In fact, the demand is, in human terms, impossible to satisfy. It creates a problem that can be resolved only by divine revelation. The episode thus becomes not a test of interpretive ability but of the power of the gods on whom each party relies.

The king flies into a rage and orders that all the wise men be killed. This kind of hyperbolic reaction is typical of the portrayal of kings in these stories. The king is a stock figure, like a character in a fairy tale. The execution order applies even to Daniel and his companions, who have not been consulted at all up to this point. Daniel, however, manages to get a stay of execution so that he can attempt to resolve the problem.

The Chaldean wise men, insofar as we are told, are helpless in the face of the king's demand. Daniel, however, has a resource on which he can draw. He and his companions pray to the God of heaven, and the mystery is revealed to him in a dream or "vision of the night."

Nebuchadnezzar's dream concerns a giant statue composed of different metals: gold, silver, bronze, and iron mixed with clay. These are interpreted as representing a series of kingdoms. Nebuchadnezzar's Babylonian kingdom is the head of gold—the golden age. Each of the succeeding kingdoms is inferior to the one that precedes it. The fourth kingdom is strong as iron and crushes everything, but it is mixed with clay, and so has a fatal weakness. In the end the entire statue is destroyed by a stone

that becomes a mountain. Daniel interprets this to mean that "the God of heaven will set up a kingdom that will never be destroyed, and will never be left to another people."

There are ancient parallels for the representation of history by a sequence of metals of declining value, even if they are not in the form of a statue. The Greek poet Hesiod, who wrote about 700 B.C.E., described history as a sequence of five ages—golden, silver, bronze, a fourth that is not identified with a metal, and iron. The fourth age breaks the pattern of decline and is inserted to provide space for the heroes of Greek legend. It would seem, then, that Hesiod was adapting a scheme that he did not invent. A closer parallel to Daniel is found in a Persian text, the Bahman Yasht, chapter 1. There we read that the supreme god, Ahura Mazda, revealed to Zoroaster "the wisdom of all-knowledge" in a vision of a tree with four branches. One branch was of gold, one of silver, one of bronze, and the fourth of mixed iron. The golden age was the time of Zoroaster. The iron age would be dominated by "the divs with disheveled hair," which is generally taken as a reference to the Greeks. The Bahman Yasht in its current form is relatively late (after the sixth century C.E.), but it is likely that the original Yasht dates from the early Hellenistic period. We need not assume, however, that Daniel was directly influenced by the Persian text, although this is possible. More likely, the schema by which ages or kingdoms were represented by metals was widely known in the ancient Near East.

Daniel's interpretation of the statue also draws on another widely known pattern: the idea that a sequence of four kingdoms would be followed by a lasting fifth one. Several Greek and Roman sources describe the sequence as follows: first Assyria, second Media, third Persia, fourth Greece, and finally Rome. This view of history seems to have developed in Persia, since Media never had an important role in the west. People in the Near East would not have looked to Rome as the final kingdom, but would rather have hoped for a restoration of their native kingship, which had been overrun by Alexander the Great in 334–323 B.C.E.

Daniel does not identify the four kingdoms, but their identity becomes clear as the book progresses. When the Babylonian kingdom falls at the end of chapter 5, the new ruler is called Darius the Mede. He is followed by Cyrus of Persia (6:28). The sequence starts over in chapter 7, which is dated to the first year of Belshazzar of Babylon. He is followed by Darius the Mede (9:1) and Cyrus of Persia (10:1), and Daniel is told that after the prince of Persia, the prince of Greece will come (10:20). The four kingdoms, then, are Babylon, Media, Persia, and Greece. Babylon replaces Assyria because it was the Babylonians who conquered Jerusalem. The presence of Media, however, can be explained only by reference to the schema of the four kingdoms. Media never ruled over the Jews, and no such person as Darius the Mede ever existed. (There were three Persian kings called Darius, all after Cyrus.) Darius the Mede, then, is invented to fit the traditional pattern of the sequence of kingdoms.

It is somewhat surprising in a Jewish text to find the reign of Nebuchadnezzar, the king who had destroyed Jerusalem, depicted as a golden age. To be sure, Nebuchadnezzar is Daniel's king, and some flattery is in order. Nonetheless, it is difficult to avoid the suspicion that Daniel is adapting a Babylonian prophecy here, which looked back to the glory days of Nebuchadnezzar and hoped for a restoration of a lasting Babylonian kingdom in the future. (A small number of Babylonian prophetic texts were published in the second half of the twentieth century. At least one, the Uruk prophecy, predicts a lasting Babylonian kingdom.) Daniel, however, is adapting this prophecy for Jewish purposes. He does not tell Nebuchadnezzar that the final kingdom will be Jewish; the king is free to think that it will be a Babylonian restoration. But Jewish readers know better. The mountain that develops out of the stone is Mount Zion, and the God of heaven is sure to favor his own people. Moreover, the whole statue, representing all Gentile sovereignty, will be brought crashing down. Nonetheless, Daniel is not suggesting rebellion. The promised kingdom will only come about long after the reign of Nebuchadnezzar. Eschatology is deferred. For the present, the Jews in Babylon are quite content in the service of the Gentile king. The political order will be set right in God's good time.

Nebuchadnezzar expresses admiration for Daniel's god and appoints Daniel ruler over the whole province of Babylon. He does not seem to perceive the threatening character of the prophecy. But then the exaltation of the hero is part of the genre, a stock ending to a tale such as this. We shall see an even more incongruous ending in the story of Belshazzar in chapter 5.

Daniel 3

Daniel's companions, Shadrach, Meshach, and Abednego, play no role in chapter 2, although they are said to be promoted at the end, at Daniel's request. Conversely, Daniel plays no role in chapter 3. Most probably, these stories were originally independent of each other.

The drama of chapter 3 revolves around a demand by King Nebuchadnezzar that all the officials of his kingdom worship a giant statue that he had set up (it is not clear whether the statue represents a god or Nebuchadnezzar himself). Babylonian kings are not otherwise known to have made such demands. The Jews, alone among the king's officials, are presented with a dilemma, because of the exclusive character of their religion. We do no know of any incidents where Jews were confronted with such a problem before the second century B.C.E. and the persecution initiated by Antiochus Epiphanes of Syria that led to the Maccabean revolt. Since Daniel 7–12 clearly reflects the Maccabean era (168–164 B.C.E.), some scholars have argued that Daniel 3 comes from the same time. But there are notable differences between the two situations. Worship of a statue was not an issue in the Maccabean crisis. (Later, in the first century C.E., the Roman emperor Caligula provoked a crisis by trying to install his statue in the Jerusalem temple.) More importantly, the martyrs of the Maccabean era were not rescued from death: their hope was for vindication after death by resurrection and exaltation. Daniel 3, like the book of Esther, reflects the inherent vulnerability of Jewish life in the Diaspora. The Jews were a people set apart who did not follow the same customs as other people, especially in matters of religion, and therefore were always viewed with suspicion and often with hostility. As in Esther, professional rivalry plays a part in the accusation against the Jews. Unlike Esther, however, the substance of the accusation concerns a religious issue, their refusal to worship an idol.

The confrontation between the king and the three Jews anticipates a genre of martyr story that becomes common from the time of the Maccabees onward. The king, as usual, is a stock character who becomes filled with rage at the slightest provocation. He frames the issue as a test of divine power: "Who is the god that will deliver you out of my hands?" The answer of the young men is striking: "O Nebuchadnezzar, we have no need to present a defense to you in this matter. If our God whom we serve is able to deliver us from the furnace of blazing fire and out of your hand, O king, let him deliver us. But if not, be it known to you, O king, that we will not serve your gods and we will not worship the golden statue that you have set up" (3:16-18). We are not to suppose that the youths seriously doubted the ability of their God to deliver them, but their refusal to worship the idol is not contingent on any guarantee of deliverance. The deliverance in question is before death, not after. Regardless of the power of God, deliverance can never be taken for granted. The youths realize that their God might allow them to die. Their refusal is a matter of principle, not of expediency. This stance is important to keep in mind when we turn to the visions of Daniel in the Maccabean period. There the resolution of the martyrs is strengthened by the promise of resurrection. But the decision to resist the king's command does not depend on that promise. Those who are faithful to their God have to be faithful even at the cost of their lives.

In Daniel 3, of course, the heroes are delivered unscathed. The king sees a fourth person in the furnace who has the appearance of a god. The Greek edition of the story has a fuller text at this point: "The angel of the LORD came down into the furnace . . . and made the inside of the furnace as though a moist wind were whistling through it." The Greek version also contains two long prayers, the Prayer of Azariah and the Song of the Three Young Men, which have no counterpart in the Hebrew. When the three men emerge from the furnace, the king acclaims their God and issues a decree forbidding anyone to utter blasphemy against him. This is what Jews in the Diaspora hoped for and sometimes received: the patronage of the king for the protection of their religion.

Daniel 4

In chapters 4–6 two quite different texts of Daniel exist. The LXX translation has a very different form of these stories. Here we confine our attention to the form of Daniel 4 found in the Hebrew Bible. This form of the story is presented as a decree of Nebuchadnezzar in acknowledgment of the Most High God and recounting the wonderful experience that had befallen him. (There is a discrepancy in versification between the MT and the English Bibles. English 4:1-3 = MT 3:31-33l.)

Fig. 27.1 **The three young men in the fiery furnace; late third- or early fourth-century fresco in the Christian catacomb of Priscilla, Rome.** Commons.wikimedia.org

As in chapter 2, Daniel has a dream. The Chaldeans fail to interpret the dream, although in this case, the king narrates it to them. Given the content of the dream, they might well be reluctant to explain it in any case. The dream concerns a great tree, which gives shelter to birds and beasts. Then "a watcher and a holy one" appears from heaven and decrees that the tree be cut down and its stump left in the earth. At this point, however, the image is switched. The watcher decrees, "Let his lot be with the beasts of the field in the grass of the earth and let the mind of an animal be given to him until seven times pass over him." (At this point, part of the interpretation seems to be given already in the dream.)

Daniel explains the dream with some diffidence: "May the dream be for those who hate you and its interpretation for your enemies." Later rabbinic interpreters found Daniel's concern for Nebuchadnezzar scandalous: Why should a Jew be so concerned for the destroyer of Jerusalem? But Daniel's goodwill toward his master is consistent throughout. He goes on, however, to explain to the king that he will be driven away from human society and be made to eat grass like oxen, "until seven times pass over you" (that is, for seven years). He advises the king to "atone for your sins with righteousness" (4:27; MT 4:24). The word for "righteousness" was commonly used for "almsgiving" in later Judaism. Daniel's advice was a subject of controversy at the time of the Reformation, as Lutheran interpreters objected to the implication that the welfare of the king depended on good works (rather than faith).

Nebuchadnezzar undergoes the transformation and is ultimately restored. He learns his lesson, that the Most High alone is sovereign and that he can raise up and put down kings at his pleasure. Nebuchadnezzar stops short of converting to Judaism, but he is unstinting in his praise of the God of heaven.

Needless to say, there is no evidence that the historical Nebuchadnezzar was ever forced to eat grass like the beasts of the field. Attempts to diagnose his medical condition are beside the point. Indeed, we know something of the way in which this story developed. The last king of Babylon, Nabonidus, was absent from Babylon for several years. He spent the time in Teima, in the Arabian wilderness, and devoted himself to the worship of the moon-god. Because of his absence, he was reviled by the priests of Marduk in Babylon. Scholars have long suspected that the story of Nebuchadnezzar's madness was originally a story about Nabonidus. This suspicion was confirmed by the discovery among the Dead Sea Scrolls of an Aramaic text called the Prayer of Nabonidus. This text is introduced as "the words of the prayer that Nabonidus . . . prayed," but the fragments do not preserve a prayer. Instead, they preserve Nabonidus's account of how he was "stricken with an evil disease by the decree of God in Teima." He was smitten for seven years but was eventually restored when a Jewish diviner explained to him that he should pray, not to idols, but to the true God. The story in Daniel 4 is evidently an elaboration of this tradition. The name of Nebuchadnezzar was substituted for that of Nabonidus because he was much better known.

Like all the stories in Daniel 1–6, the tale of Nebuchadnezzar's madness is designed to show the sovereign power of the Most High God. One can imagine that Jews would take some delight in the idea of the mighty king of Babylon eating grass like an ox. Nonetheless,

the portrayal of Nebuchadnezzar is not hostile. In the end, he comes to his senses and acknowledges the power of the God of Daniel.

Daniel 5

Daniel 5 is the only story in this collection that gives a really unsympathetic account of a pagan king. Belshazzar, historically, was the son of Nabonidus, and he governed Babylon while his father was away in Teima. The Babylonian sources, however, continue to distinguish between "the king" (Nabonidus) and "the king's son" (Belshazzar).

The story of Belshazzar's feast is notable for two striking images. The first is the luxurious, even decadent, feast, which involves the sacrilegious use of the sacred vessels from Jerusalem. The luxury of the feast is ironically inappropriate, in view of the imminent fall of Babylon. The second is the mysterious writing on the wall, which the Chaldeans fail to interpret but Daniel deciphers. It announces the imminent fall of Babylon, which then takes place that night. The "writing on the wall" has become a proverbial expression for imminent disaster.

Daniel is not nearly as deferential to Belshazzar as he was to Nebuchadnezzar. He rudely refuses the king's rewards (5:17) and draws a sharp contrast between Nebuchadnezzar, who learned his lesson, and Belshazzar, who reverted to idolatry. Perhaps Daniel is emboldened by the king's imminent demise. The implication is clear in any case: Gentile rule is not necessarily either good or bad. There are good kings (after they have been chastised!) and bad ones. The destruction of Babylon is taken to reflect the punishment of God for Belshazzar's idolatry.

Fig. 27.2 *Belshazzar's Feast* by Rembrandt (ca. 1635–1638); in the National Gallery, London. Commons.wikimedia.org

Daniel 6

The final tale of the collection again presents a sympathetic pagan king. As noted already, no such figure as Darius the Mede is known to history. Darius I of Persia (522–485 B.C.E.) was famous for dividing the empire into administrative districts called satrapies (cf. Dan 6:1). Daniel, however, would have been a very old man when Darius I came to the throne.

The story in chapter 6 strongly resembles that in chapter 3. Here Daniel is the hero, and he is thrown into the lions' den rather than the fiery furnace. The charge against him arises from his religion but is contrived by his professional rivals at court. The king, typically, is gullible and passes a foolish "law of the Medes and Persians" that cannot be changed. He is entirely sympathetic to Daniel, however, and even prays that Daniel's God may save him. He is scarcely surprised when Daniel is found alive. He promptly orders Daniel's accusers thrown to

the lions. Since the beasts have been abstaining from Daniel, they promptly devour the Chaldeans, together with their wives and children.

Here again the power of this story lies in its striking imagery. The lions' den has become proverbial for any situation of adversity.

The Purpose of the Tales

The tales in Daniel 1–6 have been aptly said to present "a lifestyle for the Diaspora." Their message to the Jews in exile is twofold: participate in the life of the Gentile world and be loyal to the king, but realize that your ultimate success depends on your fidelity to your God and his laws. These tales have much in common with Esther but are much more overtly religious. They were most probably composed in the Diaspora, but if so they must have been brought back to Israel at some point. The second half of the book of Daniel was certainly composed in or around Jerusalem. These stories probably developed over time. Daniel 2 presupposes a setting no earlier than the Hellenistic period. The iron mixed with clay in the statue is taken as a reference to interdynastic marriage, between the Seleucids of Syria and the Ptolemies of Egypt. There were two such marriages: one in 252 B.C.E. and one in 193 B.C.E. Daniel 2, then, can be dated no earlier than 252 B.C.E. The late third century is a reasonable guess as to the date of composition.

In the context of the book, the tales in chapters 1–6 establish the identity of Daniel, the figure who presents his own visions in chapters 7–12. The way Daniel is described may provide a clue to the kind of people who produced this literature. Daniel is portrayed as a wise man who does some of the same things as the Chaldeans but relies on the power of his God to reveal mysteries. He is not a prophet, and he only rarely strikes a prophetic note in addressing the Gentile kings. Neither is he the kind of wise man portrayed in Proverbs or Qoheleth. His kind of wisdom is sometimes described as mantic wisdom: it chiefly consists in his ability to interpret dreams and other mysteries such as the writing on the wall (compare the story of Joseph). He has no quarrel with Gentile rule as such, for the present, although the interpretation of Nebuchadnezzar's dream in chapter 2 expresses the hope that the Gentile kingdoms will eventually be overthrown.

The Visions (Daniel 7–12)

The visions in the second half of the book of Daniel differ from the tales in chapters 1–6 both in genre and in setting. Daniel 7–12 consists of four literary units, each of which reports a revelation. Chapters 7 and 8 are symbolic visions in the prophetic tradition (cf. especially the visions of Zechariah). In each case, the visions are interpreted to Daniel by an angel. In chapter 9, the revelation takes the form of the interpretation of an older prophecy from Jeremiah, but again the interpretation is given by an angel. In chapters 10–12, Daniel has a vision of an angel, who then narrates the revelation to him. In each case, the revelation is eschatological in focus. The final revelation culminates with a prediction of resurrection and judgment. This is the only passage in the Hebrew Bible that speaks unambiguously of individual resurrection. This hope is also expressed in the apocryphal, or deuterocanonical, books of 2 Maccabees and the Wisdom of Solomon, which are part of the Old Testament in the Catholic tradition but are not included in the Hebrew Bible, since they were written in Greek.

The Genre Apocalypse

While angelic interpreters are also found in the prophetic visions of Zechariah, the combination of angelic revelation and transcendent eschatology (characterized by the judgment of individuals after death) constitutes a new and distinct genre in biblical literature. This genre, apocalypse, takes its name from the book of Revelation in the New Testament. There is extensive apocalyptic literature from Judaism in the Hellenistic and Roman periods. The book of *1 Enoch* contains no fewer than five apocalypses, all attributed to Enoch, who supposedly lived before the flood. Some of the Enoch apocalypses are older than Daniel, some roughly contemporary, and one, known as the *Similitudes of Enoch,* is later, most probably from the first century C.E. *First Enoch* is fully preserved only in Ethiopic, but fragments of the Aramaic original have been found in the Dead Sea Scrolls. Another apocalypse of Enoch, *2 Enoch,* is preserved in Slavonic. The date is uncertain, but it may have been composed in the first century C.E. Another cluster of apocalypses, *4 Ezra* and *2 and 3 Baruch,* were composed at the end of the first century C.E., at about the same time as the book of Revelation. Several of these apocalypses, especially the *Similitudes of Enoch, 4 Ezra,* and Revelation, were directly influenced by Daniel. All the Jewish apocalypses are pseudepigraphic: their real authors are not named, but the works are attributed to famous people who had lived centuries earlier (or in the case of Enoch, thousands of years earlier). This device presumably added to the authority of the compositions. It also allowed the seer to "predict" many things that had actually happened by the time the book was written, and thereby to strengthen confidence in the real predictions.

The apocalypses fall into two types. One type, represented by *1 Enoch* 1–36 and by *2 Enoch* and *3 Baruch,* describes a wonderful journey to places that are normally beyond the range of human experience, or an ascent through the heavens. In these apocalypses the emphasis is on cosmology, and the visionary typically sees the abodes of the dead and the places of judgment. The other type of apocalypse has its paradigmatic example in the Book of Daniel. In this case, the emphasis is on history, which is typically divided into a specific number of periods (four kingdoms, seventy weeks of years). In apocalypses of this type, the focus is on the time of the end, when

God will intervene for judgment. The judgment in these apocalypses involves a public judgment of the nations, but it also involves the judgment of individuals, followed by a blessed afterlife or everlasting punishment. Both types of apocalypses give great prominence to angels or demons, and all expect a final judgment of the dead. The judgment of the individual dead is the motif that most clearly distinguishes the expectations of the apocalypses from biblical prophecy. The view of the world found in these books is also found in other literary genres of the time and is very influential in the Dead Sea Scrolls and in the New Testament.

The Setting of the Visions

The setting of Daniel 7–12 also differs from that of chapters 1–6. The tales are set in the Diaspora and generally reflect an acceptance of Gentile rule. The visions, in contrast, are focused on events in Jerusalem and reflect a time of persecution. While no names are mentioned and the allusions are veiled, they point quite clearly to the persecution instigated by the Syrian king Antiochus IV Epiphanes in 168–164 B.C.E., which provoked the Maccabean revolt and which is described in 1 and 2 Maccabees. At that time, Syrian forces occupied the Jerusalem temple and installed a pagan altar on top of the sacrificial altar there. The pagan altar becomes known as "the desolating abomination" or "abomination of desolation" both in Dan 11:31 and in 1 Macc 1:54. Some Jews were put to death for observing the law of Moses (e.g., by having their sons circumcised) or for refusing to participate in pagan sacrifices. According to Deuteronomy, those who kept the Law should prosper and live long lives. Now Jews were confronted with a situation where those who broke the Law prospered and those who observed it risked losing their lives. It is against this backdrop that the visions of Daniel must be read.

Daniel 7

In chapter 7, Daniel has a terrifying dream, which is really a nightmare. He sees four great beasts rising from the sea. The fourth is especially terrifying. It has iron teeth and stamps with its feet. This last beast grows horns, including one final upstart horn that is especially offensive. Then the scene changes to a heavenly throne room, where a judgment is held and the beasts are condemned. Then Daniel sees "one like a son of man," that is, one like a human being, coming on the clouds of heaven. This figure is given dominion and a kingdom that will never pass away.

This vision clearly resembles Daniel 2 in some respects. Both visions involve four kingdoms and a final kingdom that will not pass away. But the imagery is very different. The first kingdom in chapter 2 was represented by a head of gold, and so could be thought to be a golden age. In chapter 7 all the kingdoms are beasts that arise from the sea.

This imagery draws on old mythic traditions that can be traced back to the Canaanite texts from Ugarit but that are also often reflected in the Hebrew Bible. In the Ugaritic myths, the Sea, Yamm, is a monster who challenges the authority of the god Baal and is crushed by him. In ancient Israel, YHWH, not Baal, is the God of life, and there are numerous allusions to a battle between him and the Sea and a monster that is called Rahab or Leviathan. According to Job 26:12-13, YHWH "stilled the sea, by his power he smote Rahab." Isaiah 51:9-11 asks: "Was it not you who cut Rahab in pieces, who pierced the dragon? Was it not you who dried up the sea?" In Isa 27:1 the battle is projected into the future: "On that day the LORD with his cruel and great and strong sword will punish Leviathan the fleeing serpent, Leviathan the twisting serpent, and he will kill the dragon that is in the sea." In this myth, which is quite different from the account of creation in Genesis but very similar to creation myths of the ancient Near East, the work of creation involves subduing the sea and killing its monsters. In Daniel 7 the beasts rise up again. The four kingdoms are portrayed as manifestations of primeval anarchy let loose upon the world.

In Dan 7:9 thrones are set up and a white-haired "Ancient of Days" appears, surrounded by thousands of servants. This figure is evidently God. It is surprising, then, when another figure appears "with the clouds of heaven." In the Hebrew Bible, the figure who rides on the clouds is always YHWH, the God of Israel (cf. Pss 68:5; 104:3). Yet in Daniel 7 this figure is clearly subordinate to the Ancient of Days. The juxtaposition of two divine figures can be understood against the background of the Canaanite myth. There the high god was El, a venerable figure with a white beard. The young fertility god was Baal, who is called the "rider of the clouds" in the Ugaritic texts. In the Hebrew Bible, YHWH usually combines the roles of El and Baal. In Daniel 7, however, they are separated. The influence of the Canaanite mythic tradition is clearly evident in the pattern of relationships between the Ancient of Days, the rider of the clouds, and the beasts from the sea. We do not know in what form the author of Daniel

7 knew this tradition. Some of it is reflected in biblical poetry, but the author probably had sources that are no longer available to us. Of course he adapted the tradition. The rider of the clouds does not attack the Sea as Baal had attacked Yamm. The conflict is resolved by a divine judgment. And of course the Jewish author would not have identified the Ancient One and the rider of the clouds as El and Baal.

The identity of the "one like a son of man" in its Jewish context is the most controversial issue in the book of Daniel, and one of the most controversial in the entire Bible. Traditional Christian exegesis assumed that this figure was Christ because of the way the phrase "Son of Man" is used in the Gospels. This understanding of the figure could not have been available to Jews before the Christian era, but they could have taken the figure as the Messiah. This understanding of the phrase was in fact standard in both Jewish and Christian exegesis for many centuries. But there is no other reference in Daniel to a messiah (a king who would restore the kingdom of David). Over the last century or so, there have been two main interpretations of the "one like a son of man." Many scholars assume that this figure is simply a symbol for the Jewish people. The alternative, and more satisfactory, interpretation is that he is an angel, most probably the archangel Michael, who represents the Jewish people on the heavenly level.

The argument that the "one like a son of man" is the Jewish people takes the angel's interpretation as the point of departure. According to the interpretation, the four beasts are four kings or kingdoms. Then, "the holy ones of the Most High" will receive the kingdom. Some scholars assume that the "one like a son of man" is a symbol for the holy ones, who are then identified with the Jewish people. In the literature of this period, however, holy ones are nearly always angels. (Compare the "watcher and holy one" who announced Nebuchadnezzar's fate in Daniel 4.) Whenever else Daniel sees a "man" in his vision, the figure turns out to be an angel (see Dan 8:15; 9:21; 12:6-7). Moreover, the interpretation that says that the four beasts are four kings is clearly inadequate. It gives the reference of the beasts but not their significance. They are not only kingdoms, but kingdoms that arise out of the primeval chaos represented by the sea. In short, they suggest that these kingdoms embody some kind of mythical, supernatural power. The figure riding on the clouds and the reference to "holy ones of the Most High" suggest that the Jews, too, are not alone in their time of struggle. We shall see in Daniel 10 that each people was thought to have a heavenly "prince" or protector. The "prince" of Israel was the archangel Michael. Most probably, it is Michael who is depicted as "one like a son of man" coming with the clouds of heaven.

Of course, the vision in chapter 7 is still addressed to the situation of the Jewish people. The offensive "little horn" is Antiochus Epiphanes, who attempted to change the sacred festivals and the law (7:25). The Jews are given into his power for "a time, two times, and half a time," or three and a half years. But eventually Israel's heavenly allies, the holy ones, prevail. The Jewish people are "the people of the holy ones of the Most High" who receive the lasting kingdom in 7:27.

Daniel's vision dramatizes the conflict in which the Jews found themselves in the time of Antiochus Epiphanes. On the one hand, it claims that this crisis is worse than might be

Fig. 27.3 Bust of Antiochus IV ("Epiphanes") from Syria; now in the Altes Museum, Berlin.

Commons.wikimedia.org

thought: it is nothing less than an eruption of primordial chaos. But it is also reassuring, for the end of the story is known. The holy ones will eventually prevail, and the Most High will pronounce judgment. The conflict will be resolved on the heavenly level. The appropriate response on the part of the Jewish people is not to take up arms in its own defense but to wait for the deliverance from heaven. All of this will be spelled out more clearly in the last revelation of the book.

Daniel 8

The vision in chapter 8 resembles chapter 7 in that it develops the image of the little horn. In this case, however, there are no beasts from the sea. At first Daniel sees a fight between a ram, representing Persia, and a goat, representing Greece. The goat wins, but "at the height of its power, the great horn was broken," a reference to the early death of Alexander the Great. In its place grew four horns,

representing the successors of Alexander in the separate kingdoms of Greece, Asia Minor, Syria, and Egypt. One of these (Syria) sprouts the little horn that becomes Antiochus Epiphanes. This little horn grows as high as the host of heaven and casts some of the host and some of the stars to the ground and tramples on them. It then challenges "the prince of the host" (God).

The meaning of this vision in terms of "plain history" is indicated by the question of the angel in 8:13. The little horn is Antiochus Epiphanes, and his assault on the stars, and on God, takes the form of desecrating the temple and disrupting the sacrificial cult. In Daniel's vision, however, it is depicted as a rebellion in heaven, in terms drawn from an ancient myth. This myth is reflected in Isa 14:12-15, where the king of Babylon is compared to the Day Star (Lucifer), the son of Dawn: "You said in your heart, 'I will ascend to heaven; I will raise my throne above the stars of God . . . I will ascend to the tops of the clouds, I will make myself like the Most High.' But you are brought down to Sheol, to the depths of the Pit." The myth of the Day Star was itself an old Canaanite myth. It describes the danger of arrogance, or hubris, which is also the primary sin in Greek tragedy. The one who tries to rise too high will end by losing everything. Antiochus's attack on the Jerusalem temple is understood as an attack on heaven. In the end, we are told by the interpreting angel, "he shall be broken, and not by human hands" (8:25).

One other detail in Daniel 8 requires comment. In vv. 13-14 one angel asks another, "For how long is this vision concerning the regular burnt offering?" The answer is, "For two thousand three hundred evenings and mornings," that is, 1,150 days (sacrifices were offered twice a day). This is an attempt to predict the number of days that remain until the end of the desolation of the temple. We shall find further attempts to calculate the time of the end in Daniel 12.

Daniel 9

Revelation takes a different form in chapter 9. Daniel is pondering the prophecy of Jeremiah (Jer 25:11-12; 29:10-14) that Jerusalem would be desolate for seventy years. By the time the book was written (although not by the time Daniel was supposed to live), much more than seventy years had elapsed, and Jerusalem was desolate again.

The prayer of Daniel in this context is a traditional prayer of repentance, of the Deuteronomic type (cf. the prayers in Ezra 9 and Nehemiah 9). Its theology does not match that of the book of Daniel. In the prayer, the suffering of the Jewish people is viewed as a punishment for sin. The revelations given to Daniel, however, understand it differently, as a consequence of the sinful rebellion of Antiochus Epiphanes against God.

After Daniel has finished his prayer, an angel appears to him and explains the prophecy. The seventy years are really seventy weeks of years, or 490 years. After seven weeks, the initial restoration of Jerusalem takes place. Then 62 weeks pass uneventfully. At the end of this period, an anointed one is cut off. The reference is not to the Messiah in the usual sense of the term, but to the anointed high priest Onias III, who was murdered in 171 B.C.E. (see 2 Macc 4:23-28). Then, in the last week, troops come to destroy the city and the sanctuary. They disrupt the sacrificial cult for half of the week. The implication is that from the time the cult is disrupted and the "desolating abomination" is installed in the temple, the time remaining is half a week or three and a half years (a time, times, and half a time).

The interpretation of Jeremiah's prophecy is an important text for the history of apocalyptic speculation about the time of the end. It serves as the basis for such calculations already in the Dead Sea Scrolls. By modern calculations, the 490 years from the destruction of the temple should have ended in 96 B.C.E., but Daniel was written some seventy years after that. We do not know how the author calculated the length of time between the Babylonian exile and the Maccabean revolt. The Jewish historian Josephus, writing in the late first century C.E., said that Daniel was the greatest of the prophets because he not only said what would happen, but when it would happen. We might wonder how Josephus could believe in the accuracy of Daniel's calculations, so long after the 490 years had elapsed by any reckoning. But in fact Daniel had discovered a way to defend the reliability of any prediction. If seventy years could mean seventy weeks of years, could not the weeks of years also have a symbolic value? Speculation as to when the prediction would be fulfilled continued down through the Middle Ages.

Daniel 10–12

The final revelation of the book spans chapters 10–12. Daniel 10:2-9 describes how Daniel has his vision. He fasts for three weeks. Fasting can indeed lead to visionary experience. Whether the author of the book actually had visions in this way is something we cannot be sure of, but it seems plausible. Other apocalypses describe other techniques for inducing visions. For example, in *4 Ezra,* Ezra eats "the flower that is in the field" (2 Esd 9:24) and subsequently has a wonderful vision.

Daniel's vision in this case resembles that of Ezekiel in Ezek 8:2: a wonderful gleaming man, who turns out to be an angel. He is dressed in linen like a priest. He explains to Daniel the real nature of conflicts on earth. He is engaged in combat with the "prince of Persia," and after that the "prince of Greece" will come. Nobody helps him except "Michael your prince." Michael, prince of Israel, is the archangel. The princes of Persia and Greece are presumably the patron angels of those peoples. In earlier times they would be called simply the gods of those peoples (cf. the speech of the Assyrian Rabshakeh in Isaiah 36). The implication is that conflicts on earth are decided not just by human actions but by the actions of the gods or patron angels.

The angel proceeds to tell Daniel what is written in "the book of truth," a heavenly writing that is analogous to the tablets of destiny in Babylonian mythology. (In the Babylonian creation story, *Enuma Elish,* Marduk gets to fix the destinies and so determine the course of history.) The implication is that the course of history is predetermined. The history in question begins with the last kings of Persia and extends down to the second century b.c.e. No names are mentioned, in accordance with prophetic style, so that the impression is given that the future is perceived dimly, though in detail. (Akkadian predictions have a similar style.) Kings of Syria (the Seleucids, in the Hellenistic period) are called "the king of the north." Kings of Egypt (the Ptolemies) are called "the king of the south." In 11:21 we are told that "a contemptible person" will arise. This is Antiochus Epiphanes. Verses 25-28

describe Epiphanes' first invasion of Egypt, which took place in 170 c.e. and was relatively successful. Verse 29 describes his second invasion of Egypt, in 168, which was a disaster. He was confronted by the Romans (the Kittim) and ordered to withdraw. He obeyed. Daniel implies that he took out his frustration on Jerusalem. While the king was in Egypt, civil war had broken out in Jerusalem between the former high priest, Jason, and the current one, Menelaus (see 2 Macc 5:5-14). The king took it that Judea was in revolt and sent in the troops.

After this, for reasons that remain controversial, Antiochus attempted to suppress the Jewish cult. Some Jews collaborated. Daniel says, "He shall seduce with intrigue those who violate the covenant" (11:32). The people who know their God, however, stand firm. The real heroes, from the viewpoint of Daniel, are the "wise" (Hebrew *maskilim*) who instruct the common people, even though some of them do so at the cost of their lives.

It is reasonable to suppose that the authors of Daniel belonged to the circle of "the wise." The instruction they gave to the masses presumably corresponded to the revelations of Daniel: that the human conflicts were only a reflection of conflicts on the supernatural level, and that the outcome was assured. Some scholars have argued that "the wise" should be identified with a party known as the Hasidim, who are mentioned three times in the books of Maccabees (1 Macc 2:42; 7:12-13; 2 Macc 14:6). We know very little about these people, except that they were militant supporters of the Maccabees. Daniel, in contrast, says nothing about the Maccabees. Daniel 11:34 says that the wise shall receive little help. This has often been interpreted as a slighting reference to the Maccabees. It is not clear, however, that Daniel would have regarded the Maccabees as a help at all. In his view, the battle would be won by the archangel Michael. The role of the Jews was to keep themselves pure and not do anything to obstruct their heavenly deliverer.

Daniel 11:40-45 describes the downfall of the king. Verse 45 claims that he would meet his death between the sea and the holy mountain, that is, in the land of Israel. This prophecy was not fulfilled. Antiochus Epiphanes died in Persia late in 164 B.C.E. from wounds received in an attempt to rob a temple. The unfulfilled prophecy reveals the date of the composition of Daniel. All the "predictions" are correct down to the persecution. This part of the prophecy was presumably written after the fact and served to inspire confidence in the real prediction of the end of the story, which was yet to come. The prophecy must have been written before the news of Antiochus's death reached Jerusalem.

The death of the king is not the climax of the prophecy. According to Dan 12:1-3: "At that time Michael, the great prince, the protector of your people, shall arise." Then all those written in the book of life would be delivered. Some would rise to everlasting life and some to everlasting contempt. The wise would shine like the stars forever. We know from a passage in *1 Enoch* 104 that "to shine like the stars" means "to become companions of the angels." The idea of astral immortality, that some souls ascend to the stars after death, was well known in the Greek world. Daniel does not say that everyone will be raised, only the righteous and the wicked. Neither does he say that the resurrection will involve a body of flesh and blood. Daniel 12:2, which is usually taken to refer to "the dust of the earth," can better be translated as "the land of dust," or Sheol. The idea then is that the wise, at least, are lifted up from Sheol to heaven. No one writing in Hebrew or Aramaic would have imagined the soul as completely incorporeal. (This would also be true for most people writing in Greek.) Even souls had bodies of some sort, but they were spiritual bodies, such as we might associate with a ghost (cf. St. Paul's discussion of the resurrection in 1 Corinthians 15). For the wise, however, these bodies would be glorified so that they would shine like the stars.

The hope for resurrection explains why the wise could let themselves be killed in the time of persecution. The traditional hope in ancient Israel was for a long life and to see one's children's children. This hope was changed radically by the idea of resurrection to a glorious afterlife. The goal of life would henceforth be to become like the angels so that one could live with them forever. This new hope is central to the apocalyptic literature. It figures prominently in the Dead Sea Scrolls, and it was essential to the rise of Christianity. Of course the transition in the nature of Jewish hope was not instantaneous and complete. Not all Jews accepted the idea of resurrection (the Sadducees did not). Those who did believe in resurrection did not necessarily give up their old ideas about fulfillment on earth. But the idea of individual resurrection, which occurs in the Hebrew Bible for the first time in Daniel, introduced a kind of hope for the future that was radically new in the context of Jewish tradition, and that would have far-reaching consequences for the development of religion in the Western world.

Two final points from Daniel 10–12 require comment. In 12:4 Daniel is told to "keep the words secret and the book sealed until the time of the end." We should not infer that the book of Daniel was to be kept secret. The time of the end was the time when the book was actually written. The command to keep it secret explained why these visions had not been known before the Maccabean period.

The second point concerns the calculation of the time of the end in 12:11-12. The first of these verses says, happy are those who persevere and attain the 1,290 days. The second says, happy are those who persevere and attain the 1,335 days. Two different numbers are placed side by side. A third number, 1,150, was given in chapter 8, and in that case it was clear that the number was counted from the time that the temple was profaned. The simplest explanation of the different numbers is that when the shorter number passed, a new calculation was made. This phenomenon is well known from the case of the Millerites in nineteenth-century America, who recalculated the end several times. In the case of Daniel, however, there is a further complication. All the figures given amount to more than three years and may be taken as approximations of the time, times, and half a time, or three and a half years, mentioned elsewhere in the book. But according to 1 Maccabees, the temple was restored by Judas Maccabee exactly three years after it was profaned. It would seem that the author of Daniel's visions did not regard the Maccabean restoration as the "end." Most probably, he still awaited the resurrection of the dead.

The Additions

We have already noted that the Greek text of Daniel contains two long prayers in chapter 3 that are not found in the Aramaic. The Greek also contains two additional stories about Daniel: Bel and the Dragon, and Susanna. Both tales have elements of the detective story. Daniel does not rely on revelation as he does in the Aramaic tales, but uses his wits to solve problems.

Bel and the Dragon

Bel and the Dragon is closely related to Daniel 6. In both tales Daniel is thrown into the lions' den. Bel and the Dragon is set in the reign of Cyrus the Persian. The Babylonians allegedly believed that a statue of the god Bel ate the offerings that were placed before it (in real life, the Babylonians were not so gullible). Daniel shows that the priests and their families came at night to eat them. He does this by the simple stratagem of spreading ashes on the floor to show their footsteps. He then shows that a great snake or dragon, also worshiped by the Babylonians, is no god, by feeding it cakes that cause it to burst open. (Snakes were worshiped in ancient Greece, and possibly in ancient Egypt, but there is no evidence of snake worship in Babylon.)

The Babylonian priests become alarmed, reasonably enough, and complain that "the king has become a Jew." They compel the king to cast Daniel into the lions' den for six days. Daniel's survival is explained in a manner different from Daniel 6. The prophet Habakkuk is transported from Judea by an angel holding the hair of his head, to bring Daniel a stew and bread. Inevitably, Daniel's enemies are eventually fed to the lions.

The king in Bel and the Dragon is sympathetic to Daniel, just as Darius is in Daniel 6. Such a sympathetic portrayal of a pagan king

CHART OF DATES IN HELLENISTIC PERIOD	
336–323 B.C.E.	Campaigns of Alexander the Great
320–198	Judea ruled by Ptolemies of Egypt.
198-164	Judea conquered by Seleucids of Syria
175–164	Antiochus IV Epiphanes
175-168	Hellenistic reform in Jerusalem
168–167	Profanation of temple; Maccabean revolt
164	Rededication of temple by Judas Maccabee
164–63 B.C.E.	Judea independent under Hasmoneans (descendants of Maccabees)
63 B.C.E.	Conquest of Jerusalem by Roman general Pompey

is more likely to have been composed before the time of Antiochus Epiphanes than later. This story then may be roughly contemporary with the tales in Daniel 1–6, but it must have circulated in different circles. It is essentially a story making fun of Babylonian idolatry (cf. Isa 44:9-20). The story of the lions' den may have been a popular legend. The form of the story that we find here is not necessarily derived from Daniel 6.

Susanna

The story of Susanna gives a picture of Daniel that is quite different from what we find in the other stories. Here he is not a royal official, but a young man in a Jewish community in Babylon. (Nothing is said of a Jewish community in Daniel 1–6 or in Bel and the Dragon.) He comes to prominence because of the attempt of two lecherous old men to seduce the virtuous Susanna while she is bathing in her father's garden. (Outdoor bathing is convenient for the plot of such stories. Compare the story of David and Bathsheba in 2 Sam 11:2.) When Susanna refuses their advances, they accuse her of fornication with a young man (cf. the accusation brought against Joseph by Potiphar's wife in Genesis 39). Since they are judges and people of standing in the community, their accusation is believed and Susanna is condemned to death. Daniel, however, comes to the rescue by the simple device of cross-examining the two accusers. The judges are put to death instead of Susanna.

The story of Susanna has much in common with the tradition of Jewish short stories, which often resemble parables in the way they reverse expectations (cf. the story of Judah and Tamar in Genesis 38). It is dangerous to judge by appearances. Normally, two elderly male judges would be presumed to be wise and righteous. In this case, however, the young man is wiser, and the woman, all too often regarded as inferior in a patriarchal society, is the shining example of virtue.

1 and 2 Maccabees

The events in the time of Antiochus Epiphanes (175–164 B.C.E.), which form the backdrop of the visions of Daniel, are described in 1 and 2 Maccabees. First Maccabees was most probably written in Hebrew but is extant only in Greek and other translations. Second Maccabees was composed in Greek and was an abridgement of a longer history by one Jason of Cyrene. It is somewhat ironic that these stories of Jewish liberation are not represented in the Hebrew Bible and owe their preservation to the Christian churches. Both books are canonical in the Catholic tradition and part of the Protestant Apocrypha.

First Maccabees

First Maccabees tells the story of the Maccabee family and their immediate descendants, the Hasmonean dynasty, who ruled Judea for approximately a century, down to the conquest of Jerusalem by the Roman general Pompey in 63 B.C.E. The history in 1 Maccabees extends as far as the accession of John Hyrcanus in 135 B.C.E.

The events leading up to the Maccabean revolt are described rapidly in the opening chapter. Only brief notice is given to the "Hellenistic reform" by which "certain renegades" got permission from the king to follow the Gentile way of life. They then built a gymnasium in Jerusalem and "removed the marks of circumcision," presumably because they exercised nude in the Greek fashion (1:11-15). First Maccabees, however, pays little further attention to these people. In this account the trouble results from unprovoked aggression by the Syrian king Antiochus Epiphanes. First he pillaged Jerusalem (1 Macc 1:20 dates this event to the 143rd year of the Syrian era, or 169 B.C.E.). Two years later he sent a tax collector, who again plundered the city and established a citadel, in which he installed "a sinful people, men who were renegades" (1:34). Finally, "the king wrote to his whole kingdom that all should be one people and that all should give up their particular customs" (1:41-42). Consequently, a violent attempt was made to suppress the Jewish religion. Copies of the law were destroyed, people were put to death for having their sons circumcised, and the temple was profaned by the installation of the "profaning sacrilege," an altar on which pagan sacrifices were offered. We shall see that a much fuller and somewhat different account of these events is found in 2 Maccabees. The claim of 1 Maccabees, that the king tried to impose uniformity on his whole kingdom, cannot be sustained. In fact, Antiochus Epiphanes was known to celebrate the multiplicity of deities worshiped in his kingdom. His repressive measures were directed only against the Jews.

According to 1 Maccabees, the revolt that broke out was inspired by fidelity to the covenant and the resolve to die rather than be defiled by impure food. It was initiated by Mattathias, the father of the Maccabees, who refused to offer pagan sacrifice and killed a Jew who came forward to do so. Thus we are told, "He burned with zeal for the law as Phinehas did against Zimri the son of Salu" (2:26). (The reference is to the story in Numbers 25, where Phinehas, grandson of Aaron, kills an Israelite in the act of intercourse with

Fig. 27.4 A coin of Antiochus IV; the inscription reads, "King Antiochus, image of God, bearer of victory." Commons.wikimedia.org

a Midianite woman.) He then calls on all who are zealous for the law to follow him, and he retreats to the hills.

The Maccabees, however, were prepared to qualify their adherence to the Law. First Maccabees 2:29-38 tells of a group of pious Jews who withdrew to the wilderness to avoid the persecution. They were attacked on the Sabbath day. They refused to violate the Sabbath by defending themselves, and so they were slaughtered, calling on heaven and earth to witness that they were being killed unjustly. The invocation of heaven and earth is an allusion to Deuteronomy 32, which goes on to say, "Vengeance is mine, says the LORD" (Deut 32:35). Those who died on the Sabbath may have hoped that God would avenge them. Their mentality may have been similar to that of the "wise" in Daniel 11, who lay down their lives but are assured of vindication in the hereafter. A clearer parallel to the martyrs in 1 Maccabees can be found in another apocalyptic writing, the *Assumption* (or *Testament*) *of Moses,* where a man called Taxo and his seven sons lay down their lives in confidence that the kingdom of God is at hand.

When Mattathias and his friends heard of the slaughter on the Sabbath, they mourned for the victims, but they resolved that they would defend themselves on the Sabbath, lest the whole Jewish people be wiped from the earth. In doing so, they resolved to break the Law for the greater good of the people. Not all pious Jews agreed with this decision. The dilemma, however, is one that has continued to confront Judaism down to modern times (cf. the Arab attack on Israel on Yom Kippur in 1973). There has always been some division of opinion within Judaism between those who insist on absolute obedience to the Law and those who take a more pragmatic approach and give priority to the survival of the people.

The remainder of 1 Maccabees recounts the heroic exploits of the Maccabean family. Mattathias dies at the end of chapter 2. His son Judas, called Maccabeus, or "the hammer," replaces him as leader. First Maccabees describes him in terms reminiscent of the divine warrior in the Hebrew Bible (1 Macc 3:3-9; cf. Isa 59:15-20). He recaptures Jerusalem and purifies the temple, three years to the day after it had been defiled (1 Macc 4:36-61), and institutes the festival of Hanukkah to commemorate the occasion. He gathers Jews from outlying areas into Judea for safekeeping. In the process he pillages Gentile towns and slaughters their inhabitants (chap. 5). Antiochus Epiphanes is shaken by the news of these exploits, realizes that he has brought ruin on his own head by attacking Jerusalem, and dies in despair (chap. 6).

The Jews suffer some setbacks in this generally glorious history. One of Judas's brothers, Eleazar, dies heroically in battle while stabbing an elephant from underneath (6:43-47). When a new high priest from the line of Aaron, Alcimus, is appointed, one group of

Judas's followers, the Hasidim, appear before him to make peace, but he kills sixty of them in one day (7:16). Judas himself is eventually killed in battle (9:11-18).

Before his death, however, Judas took a remarkable action by sending an envoy to Rome (1 Maccabees 8). He was evidently aware of the broader international scene. The Romans made a treaty with the Jews, promising mutual support in the event of war. The Roman interest in this treaty was anti-Syrian rather than pro-Jewish. Rome did not intervene in the wars of the Maccabees and probably never intended to do so. Nonetheless, the occasion is noteworthy as the first official contact between Rome and the Jews. A century later, Rome would conquer Judea and would eventually bring destruction on Jerusalem on a far greater scale than any Syrian ruler ever could.

Judas was succeeded by his brother Jonathan. At this time there were various pretenders competing for the throne of Syria, and Jonathan was able to play them off against each other. Eventually, however, he was killed treacherously by a general named Trypho, who was plotting to seize the kingship (12:48). His brother Simon, who succeeded him, met a similar fate, when he and two of his sons were murdered at a banquet in Jericho (16:15). Simon was succeeded by his son, John Hyrcanus.

Neither Jonathan nor Simon claimed the title of king. Eventually, their successors would assume that rank, beginning with Aristobulus, the successor of John Hyrcanus, in 104–103 B.C.E. According to 1 Macc 14:30, Jonathan became high priest, presumably by exercising the high priest's functions. In the case of Simon, we are told that his rank as high priest was confirmed by public decree (13:41-42;

14:35). Not all Jews were happy with this arrangement, since the Maccabees were not from the traditional high priestly family. The legitimacy of the Maccabean high priesthood was criticized both by the Pharisees and by the sect that preserved the Dead Sea Scrolls (most probably the Essenes).

There is no hint of criticism of the Maccabees in 1 Maccabees, however. Even though Simon died a rather shameful death (he was drunk when he was murdered), his reign is described as a golden age, the fulfillment of prophecy. According to a poem in 1 Macc 14:4-15, "the land had rest all the days of Simon . . . all the people sat under their own vines and fig trees, and there was none to make them afraid" (cf. Mic 4:4). It is apparent from the ongoing story that any such period of peace was short-lived. First Maccabees, however, is the official chronicle of the Maccabean family, and it depicts the achievements of the family in utopian terms.

Second Maccabees

The book of 2 Maccabees offers a different perspective on the same events. The book begins with two letters to the Jews in Egypt, urging them to join in the celebration of the purification of the temple (Hanukkah). These letters are prefixed to the book proper, which begins at 2:19, with an explanation of the work of the author who abridged this story from a five-volume history by Jason of Cyrene.

Second Maccabees differs from 1 Maccabees in several respects:

1. It gives a much fuller account of the events leading up to the persecution,

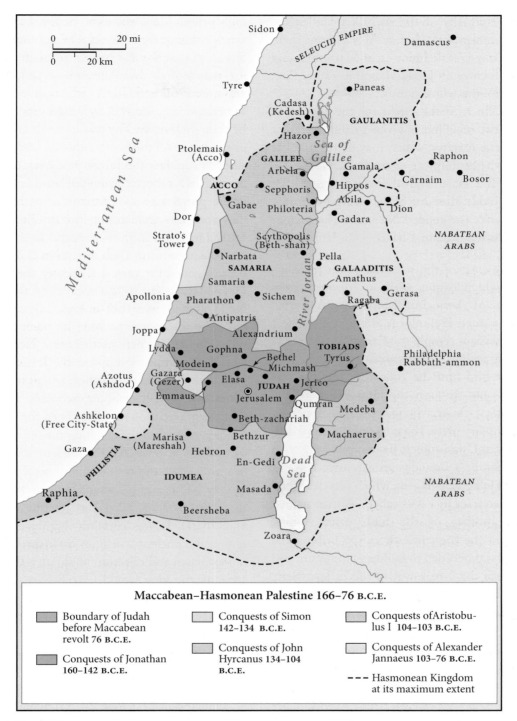

Maccabean–Hasmonean Palestine 166–76 B.C.E.

▨ Boundary of Judah before Maccabean revolt 76 B.C.E.	▨ Conquests of Simon 142–134 B.C.E.	▨ Conquests of Aristobulus I 104–103 B.C.E.
▨ Conquests of Jonathan 160–142 B.C.E.	▨ Conquests of John Hyrcanus 134–104 B.C.E.	▨ Conquests of Alexander Jannaeus 103–76 B.C.E.
		− − − Hasmonean Kingdom at its maximum extent

Map 27.1

especially of the so-called Hellenistic reform.

2. It makes no mention of Mattathias and focuses on Judas Maccabee rather than on the whole family.

3. Much of the credit for the success of the rebellion is given to the deaths of the martyrs, which may be regarded as the centerpiece of the book.

4. The story ends before the death of Judas, after one of his greatest victories, over the general Nicanor. (This victory is reported in 1 Macc 7:43-50.)

The tone of the narrative is set in chapter 3, which begins with an episode before the rise of Antiochus Epiphanes. A Syrian officer named Heliodorus attempted to enter the Jerusalem temple to seize its treasure. He was miraculously prevented by angels, who flogged him until he collapsed. His life was spared only through the intercession of the high priest Onias, who is depicted as a person of exemplary piety. The point of the story is to show that God protects his temple.

Chapter 4 provides an extensive account of the Hellenistic reform, which was described in a few verses in 1 Maccabees. A man named Jason, brother of the high priest Onias, obtained the high priesthood by bribing the king, and proceeded to build a gymnasium and introduce the Greek way of life in Jerusalem. (The word *hellēnismos*, "Hellenism," is used here for the first time to refer to the Greek way of life.) His innovations were greeted with enthusiasm by some people. Some priests, we are told, neglected the service of the temple in their eagerness for athletic contexts. Then a man named Menelaus, who was not of the high priestly family, outbid Jason and became high priest. Menelaus also contrived to have the legitimate high priest, Onias, murdered. When Antiochus Epiphanes invaded Egypt for the second time (in 168 B.C.E.), Jason attempted unsuccessfully to stage a coup. When the king heard of fighting in Jerusalem, he thought that the city was in revolt and sent in the troops. Shortly after this he took measures to suppress the Jewish religion. According to 2 Maccabees, the temple became a place where prostitutes had intercourse with Gentiles and Jews were compelled to celebrate a festival in honor of the Greek god Dionysus.

The account of these events in 2 Maccabees is generally more satisfactory than that of 1 Maccabees. It becomes clear that the king's actions were not entirely unprovoked but were a response to what he perceived as rebellion on the part of the Jews. Nonetheless, the attempt to suppress the Jewish religion is extraordinary in antiquity and remains extremely puzzling. Some scholars suspect that the persecution may have been the idea of Menelaus, as a way of crushing the opposition of traditional Jews. All the ancient accounts, however, place the responsibility on the king. It may be, as some ancient authors suggest, that the king regarded the Jewish religion as barbaric. It was certainly highly distinctive in the ancient world, in its insistence on monotheism and rejection of idolatry. On this account, the king would have been trying to make it like a Greek cult, in effect, to "normalize" it. But his actions are still hard to explain. There was no precedent in the Greek world for an attempt to suppress a cult in this manner. Better precedents, in fact, can be found in the biblical tradition, notably in the reform of King Josiah (2 Kings 22–23), which suppressed the cults of the Israelite high places.

In placing so much emphasis on the Hellenistic reform, 2 Maccabees represents the basic conflict as one between Hellenism and Judaism. Yet it should be noted that on any account the "reforms" of Jason and the building of the gymnasium encountered no significant opposition. It was only when the king attempted to suppress the traditional forms of Jewish worship that a revolt broke out. The essential conflict, then, was not over broad cultural issues but over the freedom of the Jewish people to practice their traditional religion as they saw fit.

Second Maccabees dwells at length on the deaths of the martyrs, those Jews who refused to violate their religion and suffered death instead. Second Maccabees 6:18-31 tells the story of an old man named Eleazar who refused to eat swine's flesh. The people supervising the persecution urged him to pretend to eat it, but he refused on the grounds that such pretense was not worthy of a man of his age. Eleazar

then chose death over dishonor as a matter of dignity. Second Maccabees tells in gruesome detail the story of a mother and seven sons. The first brother invokes Deuteronomy 32 by affirming that God will have compassion on his servants. The second is more specific: "The king of the universe will raise us up to an everlasting renewal of life because we have died for his laws" (2 Macc 7:9). The faith of the brothers, then, is essentially the same as that of the "wise" in Daniel: they give up their lives in this world in the hope of exaltation after death. In 2 Maccabees, however, the resurrection has a distinctly physical character. One brother offers his hands to be cut off because he is confident that he will get them back again (7:11). The emphasis on bodily resurrection seems to be inspired by the circumstances of the story, where the bodies of the young men are subjected to torture.

The words of the sixth brother shed light on another aspect of the situation. He tells the king that "we are suffering these things on our own account because of our sins against our own God" (7:18). Nonetheless, the king should not think that he will escape punishment. The theology of the brothers here follows a pattern familiar from the Hebrew Bible. Suffering is assumed to be a punishment for sin. Antiochus, like Assyria in Isaiah 10, is the rod of YHWH's anger. But his own motivation is evil, and he will not escape punishment.

Second Maccabees 8 proceeds with the story of Judas Maccabee. In this account, Judas begins by imploring God to respond to the blood of the innocent victims of the persecution. Then God's wrath was turned to mercy. Chapter 9 reports the death of Antiochus Epiphanes. As in 1 Maccabees, the dying king realizes the mistake he made

Fig. 27.5   A bronze coin issued under Antiogonos II, last of the Hasmonean kings, displays the seven-branched menorah from the Temple; Israel Museum. Erich Lessing/ArtResource, NY

in attacking the Jews. According to 2 Maccabees, however, he even vows to become a Jew if he recovers. His promises, however, are in vain. Second Maccabees 10 describes the recapture and purification of Jerusalem and the temple. The remainder of the book is devoted to the military exploits of Judas, up to the defeat of Nicanor. Chapter 13 reports that the arch-villain Menelaus met a fate worthy of his deeds. He was accused before the king as being responsible for all the troubles in Jerusalem and was thrown into a tower full of ashes. (This method of execution is not otherwise attested.)

One other episode from the story of Judas is worthy of note. In chapter 12, Judas and his men take up the bodies of Jews who had fallen in battle. All were found to be wearing idolatrous objects. The implication is that they would not have been killed if they had not sinned. Judas takes up a collection for a sin offering. The author of 2 Maccabees interprets this action as evidence of faith in resurrection: "For if he were not expecting that those who had fallen would rise again, it would have been superfluous and foolish to pray for the dead" (12:44). The action could be interpreted differently, as a way of protecting the army from divine punishment by atoning for the sins of some of its members. The new faith in resurrection, however, which we first encountered in the book of Daniel, is of pivotal importance for 2 Maccabees.

In general, 2 Maccabees places much more emphasis on divine assistance than was the case in 1 Maccabees. This is why the deaths of the martyrs are effective. Angelic horsemen appear to assist the Jews in battle (11:8), just as they had appeared to defeat Heliodorus. Before the battle with Nicanor, Judas sees the murdered high priest Onias and the prophet Jeremiah in a dream (15:12-16). He also recalls how the Lord had sent his angel to defeat the Assyrian Sennacherib. The glory, then, redounds to God. There is much less emphasis here on the human achievements of the Maccabees.

Perhaps the greatest legacy of 2 Maccabees, however, lies in the stories of the martyrs. These stories served as blueprints for numerous similar tales in later Judaism and especially in Christianity. An early example is found in the book of 4 Maccabees, which is sometimes included in the Apocrypha, although it is not part of the Catholic Bible. It is typical of these stories that the tyrant confronts the martyrs in person, and that the latter have an opportunity to affirm the beliefs for which they die. We have seen an early form of this kind of story in Daniel 3. Second Maccabees 7, however, differs from Daniel 3 in two crucial respects: the martyrs actually die, and their conviction is grounded in the hope of resurrection.

FOR FURTHER READING

Apocalyptic Literature

J. H. Charlesworth, ed., *The Old Testament Pseudepigrapha. Vol. 1. Apocalyptic Literature and Testaments* (Garden City, NY: Doubleday, 1983). The noncanonical apocalyptic texts in translation.

J. J. Collins, *The Apocalyptic Imagination* (2nd ed.; Grand Rapids: Eerdmans, 1998). Standard introduction to the apocalyptic literature.

———, ed., *The Encyclopedia of Apocalypticism. Vol. 1. The Origins of Apocalypticism in Judaism and Christianity* (New York: Continuum, 1998). Comprehensive treatment of apocalypticism in the ancient world, including early Christianity.

F. J. Murphy, *Apocalypticism in the Bible and Its World: A Comprehensive Introduction* (Grand Rapids: Baker, 2012). Introductory survey to Jewish apocalypses. Largely focused on New Testament.

B. H. Reynolds III, *Between Symbolism and Realism: The Use of Symbolic and Non-Symbolic Language in Ancient Jewish Apocalypses 333–63 B.C.E.* (Göttingen: Vandenhoeck & Ruprecht, 2011). Excellent discussion of apocalyptic symbolism.

C. Rowland, *The Open Heaven. A Study of Apocalyptic in Judaism and Early Christianity* (New York: Crossroad, 1982). Emphasizes the mystical aspects of apocalyptic literature.

Daniel

J. J. Collins, *Daniel* (Hermeneia; Minneapolis: Fortress Press, 1993). Comprehensive commentary on the full book, including the Additions.

———, *Daniel with an Introduction to Apocalyptic Literature* (FOTL 20; Grand Rapids: Eerdmans, 1984). Concise form-critical analysis.

J. J. Collins and P. W. Flint, eds., *The Book of Daniel: Composition and Reception* (VTSup 83; 2 vols.; Boston and Leiden: Brill, 2001). Collection of essays representing a wide range of views.

J. E. Goldingay, *Daniel* (WBC 30; Dallas: Word, 1989). Excellent commentary with extensive bibliography. Good discussion of the history of interpretation.

J. H. Han, *Daniel's Spiel. Apocalyptic Literacy in the Book of Daniel* (Lanham, MD: University Press of America, 2008). Emphasizes how apocalyptic language constructs an alternative view of reality.

L. F. Hartman and A. A. Di Lella, *The Book of Daniel* (AB 23; Garden City, NY: Doubleday, 1978). Strong on the textual criticism of the book.

A. Lacocque, *The Book of Daniel* (Atlanta: John Knox, 1979). Sensitive reading of the symbolism of the book.

J. A. Montgomery, *A Critical and Exegetical Commentary on the Book of Daniel* (ICC; Edinburgh: T&T Clark, 1927). Classic philological and text-critical commentary.

A. Portier-Young, *Apocalypse against Empire. Theologies of Resistance in Early Judaism* (Grand Rapids: Eerdmans, 2011). Excellent discussion of Daniel (and the early Enoch literature) in historical context.

C. L. Seow, *Daniel* (Westminster Bible Companion; Louisville: Westminster John Knox, 2003). Excellent popular commentary.

D. L. Smith-Christopher, "Daniel," *NIB* 7:17–194. Interesting reading of Daniel in light of postcolonialism.

A. S. van der Woude, ed., *The Book of Daniel* (BETL 106; Leuven: Peeters, 1993). Collection of wide-ranging technical articles.

A. C. Merrill Willis, *Dissonance and the Drama of Divine Sovereignty in the Book of Daniel* (London: T&T Clark, 2010). Theological reading of Daniel's visions.

L. M. Wills, *The Jew in the Court of the Foreign King* (Minneapolis: Fortress Press, 1990). The best treatment of the court tales.

1 and 2 Maccabees

E. J. Bickerman, *The God of the Maccabees* (reprint, Leiden: Brill, 1979). Classic study suggesting that Menelaus was the prime instigator of the persecution.

D. A. deSilva, *Introducing the Apocrypha* (Grand Rapids: Baker, 2002), 244–79. Concise treatment, highlighting the major themes.

R. Doran, "1 Maccabees," "2 Maccabees," *NIB* 4:1–299. Excellent readable commentaries, fully informed by up-to-date scholarship.

———, *2 Maccabees* (Hermeneia; Minneapolis: Fortress Press, 2012). Full critical commentary.

D. J. Harrington, *The Maccabean Revolt: Anatomy of a Biblical Revolution* (Wilmington, DE: Glazier, 1988). Lucid exposition of the differences between the two historical accounts.

M. Hengel, *Judaism and Hellenism* (trans. J. Bowden; 2 vols.; Philadelphia: Fortress Press, 1974) 1:267–309. Influential account. Follows Bickerman.

D. R. Schwartz, *2 Maccabees* (Berlin: de Gruyter, 2008). Full critical commentary.

V. Tcherikover, *Hellenistic Civilization and the Jews* (reprint, Peabody, MA: Hendrickson, 1999), 39–265. Alternative to Bickerman's account. Supposes that the persecution was a reaction to rebellion.

G. G. Xeravits and J. Zsengellér, eds. *The Books of Maccabees: History, Theology, Ideology* (Leiden: Brill, 2007). Essays on various aspects of the books of Maccabees.

CHAPTER 28

The Deuterocanonical Wisdom Books
Ben Sira, Wisdom of Solomon, Baruch

INTRODUCTION

This chapter examines two wisdom books included in the Catholic Old Testament but regarded as Apocrypha in Protestantism: Ben Sira and the Wisdom of Solomon.

The deuterocanonical books that make the greatest theological difference between the Catholic Old Testament and the Protestant and Hebrew Bibles are the wisdom books of Ben Sira and the Wisdom of Solomon. These books greatly increase the prominence of wisdom literature in the Catholic Bible, and this material is congenial to the traditional Catholic interest in natural theology. The Wisdom of Solomon is indebted to Greek philosophy in a way that distinguishes it from all other books of the Old Testament. It is also the only book of the Old Testament that professes a belief in the immortality of the soul, an idea that would have enormous importance in the history of the Christian West.

The Wisdom of Ben Sira (Ecclesiasticus)

The book of Ben Sira was written in Hebrew, in Jerusalem, in the first quarter of the second century B.C.E. It was well known in Judaism, and is the only book of the Apocrypha that is cited in rabbinic tradition. It was not included in the canon of Hebrew Scriptures, however. Its exclusion may be partly due to its late date, but the book of Daniel, which was included, is later. The obvious difference between the two books is that Daniel is pseudonymous—it supposedly contains the revelations given to Daniel in the Babylonian exile. Ben Sira, in contrast, is known by his own name. That he was known to be a latter-day writer, rather than anything in the content of his book, is likely to have prevented his inclusion in the Scriptures.

Ben Sira (Sirach in Greek) is identified in a preface written by his grandson, who translated the book into Greek. The grandson tells us that he arrived in Egypt in the thirty-eighth year of Ptolemy VIII Euergetes II, or 132 B.C.E. The translation was done some time later. According to the grandson, Ben Sira (whom he calls "my grandfather Jesus") had devoted himself to reading the Law and the Prophets, and the other books of the ancestors. The notice is important, as it shows that the Law and the Prophets were recognized canonical categories at this time. The other writings of the ancestors, however, constituted an open-ended category, and Ben Sira's book resembled them in kind.

The book is not fully preserved in Hebrew. Some Hebrew citations in the Talmud were always known, but in modern times several fragments of the Hebrew text have come to light. Fragments of six medieval manuscripts were recovered from the Cairo Geniza in the late nineteenth century. These cover most of chapters 3–16 and fragments of chapters 18–36. Much older fragments were found among the Dead Sea Scrolls. Some of these are very small fragments, but the poem in 51:13-20 is included in the Psalms Scroll from Qumran Cave 11. Finally, twenty-six leather fragments were found at Masada, the stronghold by the Dead Sea where the Jewish revolutionaries made their last stand against the Romans in 73 C.E. These fragments contain much of chapters 39–44. In all, about 68 percent of the book is now available in Hebrew.

The full text is preserved in Greek, Latin, and Syriac. The book enjoyed considerable popularity in Christianity, so that it became known as "the church book," *Liber Ecclesiasticus*.

As was the case in Proverbs, literary structure is difficult to discern in Ben Sira. The book is divided roughly in two by the great hymn to Wisdom in chapter 24. Much of the first half of the book is taken up with practical instructions, punctuated by poetic passages in praise of wisdom. The second half of the book contains longer, more theological reflections. The instructional part of the book is brought to conclusion with hymns to the Creator in 39:12-35 and 42:15—43:33. The "Praise of the Fathers," a long poem in praise of biblical heroes, follows as a kind of epilogue (chaps. 44–50). The book concludes with two poems in chapter 51.

Ben Sira on Women

The practical instruction, found mainly but not exclusively in the first half of the book, deals with matters familiar from ancient wisdom instructions: honor of parents, friendship, treatment of children and slaves, and so on. The most controversial part of this instruction is Ben Sira's view of women. The sage extols the virtues of the good wife in Sir 26:1-4, 13-18, in a manner similar to Proverbs 31. Admittedly, her virtues are assessed from the husband's point of view. She is praised for silence and modesty. There is no mention of substantial business activity on the part of the wife, such as we find in Proverbs 31. A more significant difference from Proverbs, however, is that Ben Sira sets this praise in contrast to a discourse on the wickedness of women (Sir 25:13-26; 26:6-12, 19-27). One might, perhaps, compare the portrayal of the "strange woman" in Proverbs 7, but Ben Sira is speaking of wives and daughters, not strangers or prostitutes, and his rhetoric is much more extreme. "Any iniquity," he declares, "is small compared to a woman's iniquity" (25:19). In 42:14 he goes further: "Better is the wickedness of a man than a woman who does good; it is a woman who brings shame and disgrace."

Much of Ben Sira's negative comment on women arises from a fear of being put to shame. In 42:9-14 he explains his feelings about daughters: "A daughter is a secret anxiety to her father, and worry over her robs him of sleep; when she is young, for fear she may not marry, or if married, for fear she may be rejected; while a virgin, for fear she may be seduced and become pregnant in her father's house; or having a husband, for fear she may go astray." In 22:3 he declares bluntly, "The birth of a daughter is a loss." Such sentiments were not unknown in ancient Judaism (or elsewhere in the ancient world). According to the Babylonian Talmud: "Without both male and female children the world could not exist, but blessed is he whose children are male and woe to him whose children are female" (*Baba Bathra* 16b). Yet Ben Sira is exceptional in his vehemence on the subject.

One of the sage's statements about women is especially unfortunate. In 25:24 he declares: "From a woman sin had its beginning, and because of her we all die." There can be little doubt that this is a reference to Eve, although the remark is not made in the context of a discussion of Genesis. Elsewhere, as we shall see, Ben Sira ignores the fall and suggests that God created humanity mortal from the start. In fact, this is the only time in Jewish literature before the Christian era that the woman is blamed for the origin of sin and death. There is a text in the Dead Sea Scrolls, 4Q184, "The Wiles of the Wicked Woman," that says "she is the start of all the ways of wickedness"; but that passage is clearly based on the portrayal of the "strange" woman in Proverbs 7 and cannot be taken either as a statement about the origin of sin or about women in general. Even the view that Adam was the source of sin and death emerges only in the literature of the first century c.e. (Rom 5:12-21; 1 Cor 15:22; Wis 2:23-24; et al.). For another expression of the view that the woman was more culpable than the man in the garden of Eden we have to wait until the Pastoral Epistles, toward the end of the New Testament, where we read in 1 Tim 2:14 that "Adam was not deceived, but the woman was deceived and became a transgressor." This view had a long and unfortunate history in Christianity. It is the dubious distinction of Ben Sira to have introduced it into the biblical tradition, in the course of one of his tirades against women.

Wisdom and the Law

Ben Sira, however, makes other contributions to the tradition that admit of a more positive response. In the tradition of Proverbs, he personifies the figure of Wisdom as a female intermediary between God and the world. The most important passage dealing with this figure is found in chapter 24. There we are told that "Wisdom praises herself" in the assembly of the Most High. It appears then that she is a heavenly figure, in the company of the heavenly hosts. The self-praise has a parallel in a series of inscriptions in which the Egyptian goddess Isis recites her own accomplishments. These inscriptions, called "aretalogies" of Isis, are all in Greek and date from a time later than Ben Sira, but they probably reflect an older tradition. There is good evidence for Egyptian influence on the book of Proverbs, and it is likely that Ben Sira, too, was influenced by an Egyptian model at this point.

The claims made by Wisdom are extraordinary. She came forth from the mouth of the Most High. That which comes forth from the mouth is either breath (spirit) or word. We are reminded of Genesis 1, where God creates the world by speaking. As we shall find in the Wisdom of Solomon, the Word (Greek *Logos*) was a very important concept in Hellenistic philosophy. The statement that Wisdom came forth from the mouth of God lays the foundation for the identification of Wisdom with the Word or Logos. Again, the statement that Wisdom covered the earth like a mist recalls the Spirit of God hovering over the deep in Genesis 1 and suggests a close association between Wisdom and the Spirit.

The statements in 24:4-5 are even more startling: "I dwelt in the highest heavens, and my throne was in a pillar of cloud. Alone I compassed the vault of heaven and traversed the depths of the abyss." In the Hebrew Bible, only YHWH could make such claims. The pillar of cloud was famously associated with the divine presence at the exodus. In Sirach 24 the presence of God in the world is mediated by Wisdom.

Wisdom held sway over all peoples and places (this was also one of the claims of Isis). But she sought a resting place. There may be an allusion here to a myth about Wisdom's search for a home on earth. In the Similitudes of Enoch, an apocalypse from the first century C.E., we read: "Wisdom found no place where she could dwell, and her dwelling

was in heaven. Wisdom went out in order to dwell among the sons of men but did not find a dwelling; wisdom returned to her place and took her seat in the midst of the angels" (*1 En.* 42:1-2). It is possible that *1 Enoch* was responding to Ben Sira, but it is more likely that both texts drew on a common myth. In Ben Sira, however, Wisdom does not return to heaven in frustration. Instead, the Creator commands her to "make your dwelling in Jacob, and in Israel receive your inheritance" (Sir 24:8). More specifically, we are told that she took root in the holy tent and was established in Zion. In short, Wisdom found its home in the Jerusalem temple, the place where God had made his name to dwell according to Deuteronomy 12. The idea of Wisdom finding

Fig. 28.1 Noah releases a dove from the ark in an early Christian fresco from the catacombs in Rome. As the dove searched for a resting place, so Ben Sira describes Wisdom seeking a place to alight on the earth—and finding it in Israel. Commons.wikimedia.org

a home on earth is important background for the prologue of the Gospel of John, which speaks of the Word becoming flesh and dwelling among us. Wisdom in Ben Sira does not become flesh. It is not embodied in a human being. But it does find a particular dwelling place on earth in Jerusalem and the temple.

The poem goes on to describe how Wisdom flourished in her new home by comparing it to various plants (palm trees, terebinths, vines). In vv. 19-22 Wisdom invites people to eat of her fruits and promises that those who partake of her will hunger and thirst for more. Here again we have language that is later taken up in the Gospel of John. In John 6:35 Jesus says: "I am the bread of life. Whoever comes to me will never be hungry, and whoever believes in me will never be thirsty." Although one speaks of hungering for more and the other of never being hungry again, the idea is basically the same. Both Wisdom in Ben Sira and Jesus in the Gospel offer a kind of food that is unlike any other.

The most surprising statement of all, however, is found in Sir 24:23: "All this is the book of the covenant of the Most High God, the law that Moses commanded us as an inheritance for the congregations of Jacob." Wisdom, in short, is nothing other than the Torah of Moses. Just as Wisdom was said to be created before all ages, later Jewish tradition would affirm that the Torah was created before the creation of the world (Midrash Rabbah on Genesis 1).

The identification of Wisdom and the Torah can be understood in two different ways. On the one hand, it can be taken to mean that the Torah is the exclusive source of wisdom; on the other, it may mean that the Torah is one privileged formulation of wisdom that in principle can be found anywhere. Hellenistic Judaism usually took the relation of the Torah and Greek wisdom in the latter sense. Plato, it was said, was Moses speaking Greek. Ben Sira was not as deeply immersed in Hellenistic culture as were the Jews of Alexandria, such as the author of the Wisdom of Solomon or the philosopher Philo. But he, too, recognized that the Torah was not the exclusive source of wisdom. In 39:4 he says that the scribe who devotes himself to the study of the law of the Most High "travels to foreign lands and learns what is good and evil in the human lot." The Torah is one valid source of wisdom, but it is not the only one.

The importance of Ben Sira in the development of the Jewish wisdom tradition lies precisely in the fact that he included the Torah of Moses among the sources of wisdom. The earlier wisdom books, Proverbs, Qoheleth, and Job, are distinguished by their lack of any explicit reference to the Torah. Wisdom represented an educational tradition in Israel that was quite distinct from the Levitical teaching associated with the cult. Both Deuteronomy (4:6) and Ezra (7:25) associated the law with wisdom, but Ben Sira was the first wisdom teacher to include the Torah in his curriculum. Deuteronomy may contain wise laws, but it is still in the form of a law code. Ben Sira is a book of wisdom instruction that uses the Torah as one of its sources.

The Interpretation of Genesis

Ben Sira's use of the Torah may be illustrated with reference to his interpretation of the creation stories in Genesis. In 15:11-20 he argues that God bears no responsibility for human sin. (In contrast, the Community Rule from

Qumran claims that God created two spirits for humanity, one of light and one of darkness.) Ben Sira continues: "It was he who created humankind in the beginning, and he left them in the power of their own inclination" (15:14; the Hebrew word is *yetser*, the rabbis taught that human beings have two *yetsers*, one good and one bad). The emphasis is on free will, and the language echoes Deuteronomy at some points: "Before each person are life and death, and whichever one chooses will be given" (Sir 15:17; cf. Deut 30:15, 19). The situation of Adam was no different from that of any Jew faced with the choice of observing the law.

Ben Sira continues with a fuller discussion of Genesis in chapter 17. The opening statement, "The LORD created human beings out of earth and makes them return to it again" (17:1), strongly implies that humanity was created mortal from the start (cf. v. 2: "He gave them a fixed number of days"). The account alludes both to Genesis 1 and to Genesis 2–3 but leans more heavily on Genesis 1 (Sir 17:3: "He made them in his own image"). Most remarkable, however, is the statement in 16:7: "He filled them with knowledge and understanding and showed them good and evil." Nothing is said of any command forbidding them to eat from the tree of the knowledge of good and evil. Ben Sira, in effect, has no concept of a fall. Human beings are created mortal and are given a choice between good and evil. So it was in the beginning and so it continues to be. Similarly in 41:4 we are told that death is the Lord's decree for all flesh. From Ben Sira's point of view, knowledge and wisdom are good, and it is inconceivable that God would ever have forbidden people to partake of them. In view of this understanding of the Genesis story, his statement in 25:24 that woman is the origin of sin and death becomes all the more perplexing and difficult to justify.

Theodicy

Ben Sira reflects at length on the problem of evil. He tries out various answers, and they are not all compatible with each other. Despite his vigorous defense of free will in chapters 15 and 17, he gives a rather different account in 33:7-13:

> All human beings come from the ground,
> and humankind [Adam] was created out
>   of the dust.
> In the fullness of his knowledge the
>   LORD distinguished them
> and appointed their different ways.
> Some he blessed and exalted,
> and some he made holy and brought near
>   to himself;
> some he cursed and brought low
> and turned them out of their place.
> Like clay in the hand of the potter
> to be molded as he pleases
> so all are in the hand of their Maker
> to be given whatever he decides.

On this account, there are good and bad people because that is how the Lord made them. In fact, creation is characterized by pairs of opposites: "Good is the opposite of evil and life is the opposite of death; so the sinner is the opposite of the godly. Look at all the works of the Most High; they come in pairs, one the opposite of the other" (33:14-15; cf. 42:24-25). The idea that evil has to exist because good must have its opposite derives from Stoic philosophy. The Stoic Chrysippus, who lived a little earlier than Ben Sira, wrote that there is nothing more foolish than those who think that good can exist without evil. Nothing exists without its matching opposite. This idea, however, does not sit easily with Ben Sira's insistence on human free will.

Ben Sira also borrows from the Stoics the idea of teleology: everything is created for a purpose, to meet some need. Everything is good in its appointed time. Storms and natural disasters are created to give vent to God's anger. Ben Sira rather blithely claims that "all these are good for the godly, but for sinners they turn into evils" (39:27). This idea is certainly in line with the claims of Genesis that God's creation is good, but it can hardly withstand serious reflection. The book of Job had already shown that disasters can strike the good and the bad without distinction.

The problem of evil was acute for Ben Sira because he resolutely resisted the idea of reward or punishment after death. Death is simply the Lord's decree for all flesh. Whether life is for ten or a hundred or a thousand years, there is no inquiry about it in Hades (41:1-4). In this respect, his view of life resembles that of Qoheleth. "Hard work was created for everyone, and a heavy yoke is laid on the children of Adam, from the day they come forth from their mother's womb until they return to the mother of all the living. Perplexities and fear of heart are theirs, and anxious thought of the day of their death" (40:1-2). Unlike Qoheleth, however, Ben Sira still wants to insist that there is justice in the world. So he suggests that while all creatures are troubled by anxiety, this affects sinners seven times more. Death and destruction were created for the wicked. He does not find a satisfactory explanation, however, for the fact that these things also befall the just.

Unlike Qoheleth, Ben Sira remains convinced that the world is in the power of a benevolent and all-powerful Deity. At the end of the great hymn to the Creator in chapter 43, he declares: "He is the all" (43:27). Taken at face value, the phrase sounds pantheistic. The Stoics believed that the world (*cosmos*) was the body of God and was animated by a Spirit or Logos. Ben Sira, however, hardly meant this rhetorical flourish to be taken literally. He clearly maintains a distinction between the Creator and creation. The more typical phrase is "God of all" (36:1). He does, however, see a very close relation between God and nature or creation. In this he is typical of the wisdom tradition.

The Praise of the Fathers

The long section in chapters 44–50 is devoted to the praise of famous men from Israel's past (Ben Sira includes no women in the list). This catalog differs from most reviews of biblical history. It is not focused on events or on the mighty acts of God. It is rather focused on individuals and their character. Primary attention is given to those who were leaders of their people. Ben Sira is especially interested in the priesthood. The praise of Aaron in chapter 45 is three times as long as that of Moses and is followed by praise of another priest, Phinehas. David and Solomon are praised at length, as are Elijah and Elisha. Mention is also made of Isaiah, Jeremiah, Ezekiel, and the Twelve (Ben Sira did not know Daniel). Surprisingly, there is no mention of Ezra, although Nehemiah is praised for raising up the fallen walls (49:13).

The series concludes with a figure who was a contemporary of Ben Sira. This was Simon the high priest, known as Simon the

Just, who was high priest from 219 to 196 B.C.E. During his time (in 198), Jerusalem passed from the control of the Ptolemies of Egypt to the Seleucids of Syria. Simon welcomed the Syrians and was rewarded for his loyalty. Ben Sira's admiration for Simon was undoubtedly colored by the success Simon enjoyed under Syrian patronage. He was able to repair the temple and the fortifications. Syrian favor, however, would be short-lived, as we know from the stories in the books of Maccabees, which describe events that began a mere quarter of a century after Simon welcomed the Syrians to Jerusalem.

The Role of the Scribe

Ben Sira gives us a clearer picture of his role in society than do most biblical writers, and certainly more than any other wisdom writer. In 38:24—39:11 he discusses the vocation of the scribe in contrast to other professions. This kind of contrast is modeled on a famous Egyptian composition from the second millennium, the Instruction of Duauf, also known as "The Satire on the Trades" (*ANET*, 432–34). Ben Sira is not as derisive of other professions as the Egyptian sage was, but he leaves no doubt about the superiority of the life of the scribe. After all, "how can one become wise who handles the plough . . . and whose talk is about bulls?" (38:25). As the sage realizes, one has to have leisure in order to acquire wisdom. Since he is not independently wealthy, he aspires to serve great men (39:4). He belongs, in short, to the class of retainers, who depend on the rich and powerful for their livelihood. It is not surprising, then, that he takes a conservative position on social ethics and seldom strikes a

prophetic note, although he sometimes claims to be inspired (see, for example, 24:33: "I will pour out teaching like prophecy and leave it to all future generations").

Ben Sira depicts the scribe as one who is devoted to the study of the Torah but also seeks out wisdom in all its forms and even travels to foreign lands to seek it out. He is pious and prays to the Most High (prayer is seldom mentioned in the earlier wisdom books). In the concluding poem of the book he describes how he prayed for wisdom "while I was still young, before I went on my travels" (51:13). The analogy with Solomon is obvious (1 Kings 3). His goal is to serve the great, win honor in his lifetime, and leave a glorious name after his death.

It seems likely that Ben Sira earned his living, at least in part, by teaching. Also in the final poem of the book he calls on the uneducated to come to him "and lodge in my house of instruction" (51:23; the Hebrew phrase is *bēt midrash*). This is the earliest reference to a school in Jewish tradition. (According to the Talmud, schools were established either in the reign of Alexander Jannaeus [103–76 B.C.E., Jerusalem Talmud *Kethuboth* 8.32c] or in the first century C.E., by Joshua ben Gamala [Babylonian Talmud *Baba Bathra* 21a].) Ben Sira's school was probably more like a tutorial system. Sirach 6:34-36 advises the aspiring student to find a wise teacher, attach oneself to him, and wear out his doorstep. Formal education in Judaism was still in its infancy. Ben Sira represents a milestone in the development, not only by the fact that he mentions a house of instruction but also by the fact that he combines the teaching of Torah with traditional wisdom.

The Wisdom of Solomon

The Wisdom of Solomon is a very different kind of wisdom book from Ben Sira. It was composed in Greek in Alexandria, Egypt, most probably in the early first century C.E. (The only other book in the Old Testament that was composed in Greek is the deuterocanonical 2 Maccabees.) Moreover, the author had evidently had a good Greek education and knew a great deal more about Greek philosophy than was the case with Ben Sira. Wisdom is not a philosophical tract; it is rather a rhetorical piece that draws on philosophical ideas. One of these ideas is the immortality of the soul, a concept that was quite alien to Ben Sira and the older wisdom tradition, and that makes a profound difference in the worldview of Wisdom.

The Jewish community in Alexandria took root shortly after the conquest of Egypt by the Greeks, at the end of the third century B.C.E. Jews prospered under the rule of the Ptolemies, the Greek dynasty that ruled Egypt down to the death of Cleopatra after the battle of Actium in 31 B.C.E. A Jewish high priest, Onias IV, who fled from Jerusalem at the time of the Maccabean revolt, became a general in the Ptolemaic army and was allowed to build a Jewish temple at Leontopolis. There is an extensive Jewish literature from Egypt, written in Greek. Most of this literature is believed to have been written in Alexandria. By the early first century C.E. there were no less than a million Jews in Egypt, according to the philosopher Philo. Philo's figures are not reliable, but there is no doubt that the Jewish population was very large.

The Romans took control of Egypt after the battle of Actium. Roman rule eventually brought difficulties for the Jews. The Roman system of taxation drew a sharp line between those who were citizens of the Greek cities, such as Alexandria, and those who were not. The Jews as a group were never citizens, although some individual Jews enjoyed that status. There was increasing friction between the Jews and the Greeks in Alexandria, and violence broke out in 38 C.E. In 41 C.E. the emperor Claudius issued a decree that ordered the Alexandrians to respect the rights of the Jews to live according to their own customs but also reminded the Jews that they lived in "a city not their own" and that they should not strive for more than what they had. Nonetheless, violence broke out again in 66 C.E., and the Jewish community suffered great losses. It was virtually wiped out in the course of a revolt against Rome in 115–117 C.E.

The Wisdom of Solomon was written against the backdrop of these events, most probably in the first half of the first century C.E. Its attitude to the Gentile world is ambivalent. On the one hand, it is thoroughly imbued with Greek culture. On the other hand, it shows signs of the increasing antagonism between the Jews and their neighbors.

The book falls into three sections: the "book of eschatology" in 1:1—6:21, the "book of wisdom" in 6:22—10:21, and the "book of history" in chapters 11–19. The transitions between these sections are not clear-cut. Some scholars define the book of eschatology simply as chapters 1–5, and chapter 10 is often included in the book of history. But while these passages are transitional, the differences between the different sections have

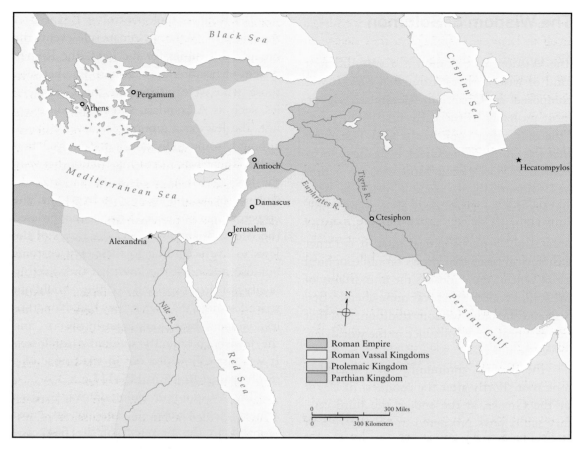

Map 28.1   The ancient Near East around 60 B.C.E.

led some scholars to suppose that the book is composite. The unity of the book is now generally accepted, however. The author drew on different kinds of source material in the various sections, but the book is held together by the central role of wisdom, which is most fully expressed in the second section.

The Book of Eschatology

The opening section of the book is presented as an address to the rulers of the earth, but

it is essentially an argument that justice ultimately prevails. The core of the argument is found in chapter 2. Here the philosophy of the unrighteous is laid out in a long speech. They reason that life is short and sorrowful, and that no one has been known to return from Hades. Thus far Qoheleth and even Ben Sira would agree. The wicked, however, draw an extreme inference. Not only do they resolve to enjoy the good things of creation, and to "crown ourselves with rosebuds before they wither," but they also resolve to "let our might be our law of right, for what is weak proves itself to be useless" (2:11). So they decide to "lie in wait for the righteous man, because he is inconvenient to us and opposes our actions; he reproaches us for sins against the law and accuses us of sins against our training" (2:12; the reference to the law suggests that the unrighteous in question are Jews who have abandoned their religion). They resolve to torture him to put him to the test, "for if the righteous man is God's child he will help him and will deliver him from the hand of his adversaries" (2:18). So they condemn the righteous to a shameful death. But, says the author of Wisdom, they reasoned wrongly, for they did not know the mysteries of God, that God "created us for incorruption and made us in the image of his own eternity" (2:23). The souls of the righteous are in the hand of God and no torment touches them. In the eyes of the wicked they seemed to die, but they are at peace (3:3). The contrasting fates of the righteous and the wicked are further dramatized in chapter 5, in a judgment scene. The unrighteous learn that they have been mistaken, and find that the righteous, whom they had held in derision, are numbered among the sons of God and that their lot is among the holy ones.

For the Wisdom of Solomon, then, the vindication of the righteous is awaited after death. In this respect, Wisdom breaks with the Hebrew wisdom tradition, as found in Proverbs, Qoheleth, and Ben Sira. (There is, however, a Hebrew wisdom book found at Qumran, called 4QInstruction, that also endorses the hope for eternal life, which it also regards as a "mystery.") There can be little doubt that the author of Wisdom was familiar with, and influenced by, apocalyptic literature. We have seen that the book of Daniel similarly

hoped for vindication after death (Dan 12:3). Even closer parallels to Wisdom can be found in the noncanonical Epistle of Enoch (*1 Enoch* 91–105), which also assures the righteous that they will be companions of the host of heaven. The language in Wisdom 5, which refers to the angelic host as sons of God and holy ones, also has many parallels in the Dead Sea Scrolls. It should also be noted that both Daniel and Wisdom adapt the figure of the Suffering Servant of Isa 52:13—53:12. In Isaiah the kings of the earth are astounded that one whom they despised is found in the end to be exalted and glorious. The Isaianic passage most probably referred to the hoped for restoration and exaltation of Israel. In Daniel and in Wisdom, however, the hope is for the vindication of individuals after death.

The apocalyptic literature provides one source for the hope for eternal life in the Wisdom of Solomon. Another source, however, is no less important. The Greek philosopher Plato provided a famous discussion of justice in his dialogue, the *Republic.* In the second book of the *Republic,* one of the figures in the dialogue, Glaucon, argues the injustice is more profitable that justice. He further argues that in order to compare the just and the unjust we must imagine them in their pure states. The unjust man must not be recognized as such, while the just must be a good person who is thought to be bad: "The just man who is thought unjust will be scourged, racked, bound—will have his eyes burnt out, and at last, after suffering every kind of evil, he will be impaled" (*Republic* 361). There is a similar separation of pure types in the Wisdom of Solomon. The wicked enjoy prosperity on earth, while the righteous are condemned to a shameful death. The analogy with Plato suggests that the author of Wisdom, too, is constructing a philosophical argument. The passage need not be taken to reflect any actual historical persecution of the righteous.

The most important influence of Platonic philosophy, however, is found in the understanding of immortality in Wisdom. The hope is not for resurrection but for the continued life of the soul, which is untouched by torment or death. According to the prayer of Solomon in Wis 9:15, "a perishable body weighs down the soul, and this tent of clay encumbers a mind full of cares." Plato had written that "so long as we have the body, and the soul is contaminated by such an evil, we shall never attain completely what we desire" (*Phaedo* 66B). Similar ideas can be found in the Jewish philosopher Philo. For Plato the soul was preexistent. Wisdom seems to play with that notion in 8:19-20: "I was indeed a child well-endowed, having had a noble soul fall to my lot, or rather being noble I entered an undefiled body." But Wisdom attaches no importance to the preexistence of the soul. Rather, the soul is immortal because it is made in the image of God (2:23), and it maintains that immortality through righteousness. Wisdom even goes so far as to say that God did not make death. Death entered the world through "the envy of the devil" (2:24; this may be the earliest attestation of the identification of the snake in the garden of Eden as the devil). Those who belong to the lot of the devil bring death on themselves by their conduct. Wisdom differs from Plato, then, in making the immortality of the soul dependent on righteousness. Nonetheless, the idea of the immortal soul is clearly derived from Platonic philosophy.

This section of the Wisdom of Solomon was especially influential in later Christian tradition. The righteous man claims to be the child of God, and so the wicked taunt him: "If the righteous man is God's child, he will help him and deliver him" (2:18). The Greek word translated "child" in the inclusive translation of the NRSV is *huios*, son. In the Gospel of Matthew, during the crucifixion, the chief priests and elders mock Jesus, saying, "He trusts in God; let God deliver him now, if he wants to, for he said, 'I am God's son.'" Jesus is identified as the righteous one of whom Wisdom spoke. Wisdom 3:1, "the souls of the righteous are in the hand of God," has traditionally been sung or recited as part of the liturgy of burial in the Roman Catholic Church.

The Book of Wisdom

In the opening chapter of the book, we are told that wisdom is a holy spirit (1:5). It is evidently identical with "the spirit of the Lord," which fills the world and holds all things together (1:7). The concept of wisdom in the Wisdom of Solomon is evidently indebted to such passages as Proverbs 8 and Sirach 24, but it is also influenced by Hellenistic philosophy. The Stoics conceived of the spirit (*pneuma*) as the soul of the universe. It was a fine, fiery substance that spread through all reality and brought it to life. It was identified with the Logos (Word or Reason) that was the rational principle in the universe. It could sometimes be called God. The description of wisdom in Wis 7:22—8:1 is heavily indebted to Stoic descriptions of the Logos. It is portrayed as a fine, pure substance that can penetrate all things and bring order to the universe. Wisdom differs from the Stoic Logos insofar as it is not itself an immanent God, but is rather the link between a transcendent God and the universe. It is a breath of the power of God and a pure emanation of his glory. This combination of the Stoic Logos with a transcendent God was not unusual in Hellenistic philosophy around the turn of the era, when Stoics and Platonists borrowed freely from each other's ideas. The philosophical context of the Wisdom of Solomon, and also of the philosopher Philo, is usually identified as Middle Platonism, which was a blending of Platonism with some elements of Stoicism.

In the Wisdom of Solomon, wisdom is conceived as a power that transforms people: "In every age she passes into holy souls and makes them friends of God and prophets" (7:27). Proverbs or Ben Sira might agree that it is by wisdom that people become pleasing to God. The Wisdom of Solomon, however, presents this idea in a more systematic way, as part of the working of the universe. Wisdom is a spirit, but it is also a fine substance that can actually enter into people and transform them. Later Christian theology would adapt this understanding of wisdom to develop the notion of grace as a spiritual substance that connects humanity with God. The idea of wisdom was also taken up and adapted in the Christian doctrine of the Trinity. On the one hand, wisdom is the Logos or Word with which Jesus is identified in the prologue to the Gospel of John. On the other hand, wisdom is the spirit of the Lord that fills the whole world. Wisdom 1:7, "the spirit of the Lord has filled the world," is traditionally sung at the beginning of the Catholic Mass for Pentecost, the primary celebration of the Holy Spirit in the Christian liturgical calendar.

The "book of wisdom" in 6:12—11:1 concludes with a recitation of the working of wisdom in history. We are told that wisdom delivered Adam from transgression, saved Noah from the flood, and kept Abraham blameless, even in face of his compassion for his son. No names are mentioned in this account, but the identifications are obvious. Noah is "the righteous man" who is saved when the earth is flooded (10:4). Lot is "the righteous man" who escapes the fire that descended on the Five Cities" (10:6), and so on. The implication is that wisdom will likewise rescue any other righteous person. The people of Israel, nonetheless, have a special place. While they are not named either, they are clearly recognizable as the "holy people and blameless race" that wisdom delivers from oppression (10:15). In all of this, the saving action attributed to YHWH in the Hebrew Bible is attributed to wisdom. Wisdom is the instrument through which God's presence in the world is actualized.

The Book of History

The so-called book of history in Wisdom 11–19 continues this rehearsal of biblical history, but beginning in 11:2 it no longer speaks of the role of wisdom but rather addresses God directly. The usual division between the two sections is due to this change in the manner of presentation. Nonetheless, there is obviously continuity between the paraphrase of biblical history in chapter 10 and the long discourse on the exodus in chapters 11–19.

Much of the discussion in this section has to do with idolatry. The author is scathing in his contempt for the Egyptians, who worshiped "irrational serpents and worthless animals" (11:15). He is much more sympathetic toward philosophers, who thought that the elements of nature were the gods who rule the universe. These people, he suggests, "are little to be blamed, for perhaps they go astray while seeking God and desiring to find him" (13:6). Yet they are not to be excused, for if they were able to know so much, why did they not arrive at a knowledge of God? Underlying this critique is the author's own view of the relation between God and the universe: "From the greatness and beauty of created things comes a corresponding perception of their creator" (13:5). This kind of argument had been made by Greek philosophers at least since the time of Plato (fourth century B.C.E.). In the *Timaeus,* Plato imagined a craftsman or demiurge who was responsible for the construction of the world. Aristotle reasoned from the phenomenon of motion that there must be a Prime Mover. Even the Stoics, who believed that God was immanent in the world, held that the regularity and beauty of nature could not be a product of accident, but must point to a supreme being. This kind of argument for the existence of God, on the basis of the regularity of nature, became a cornerstone of the kind of Christian theology that is called "natural theology." Natural theology was widely accepted in the Middle Ages and remains characteristic of theology in the Roman Catholic tradition.

Besides the denunciation of idolatry, the major theme of Wisdom 11–19 is that the judgments of God are proportional to the offense. Those who worshiped dumb animals perished by them in the plagues. God does not unleash his full power against the wicked, for "you are merciful to all . . . for you love all things that exist and detest none of the things that you have made" (11:23-24). Nonetheless, we are told that "those who lived long ago in your holy land you hated for their detestable practices" (12:3-4). Just as the soul may lose

its immortality because of unrighteousness, so, apparently, creatures can lose the love of God by their misdeeds. There is an undeniable element of nationalism in the author's castigation of the Canaanites and the Egyptians. Nonetheless, it is significant that he does not denounce them simply because they do not belong to the chosen people, but tries to justify his condemnation by reference to their actions.

The book concludes with the destruction of the Egyptians at the Red Sea. In this case, the misdeeds of the Egyptians are directly relevant to the situation in Alexandria when the book was written. The author complains that the crime of the Egyptians was especially heinous because they had "made slaves of those who were their benefactors," even though they had already shared the same rights. The first level of reference here is to the conduct of the pharaoh before the exodus. But there is also a second level. At the time that Wisdom was written, the Jews of Alexandria felt that they were deprived, in the Roman era, of rights that they had enjoyed under the Ptolemies. In recalling the story of the exodus, they were expressing their hope that God would intervene to judge their enemies as he had done in ancient times.

The Wisdom of Solomon reflects some of the ethnic tensions that prevailed in Alexandria in the first century C.E. Nonetheless, the book maintains a fundamentally positive attitude toward the Gentile world. The author shows his willingness to learn from Hellenistic philosophy and to use its categories. Wisdom is not confined to the Jewish law. The author insists, however, that all true philosophy should culminate in the acknowledgment of the one Creator, who is the God worshiped in biblical tradition as the God of Israel.

Fig. 28.2   The exodus from Egypt and the closing of the sea upon the Egyptian army; from the third-century C.E. synagogue at Dura-Europos. Commons.wikimedia.org

The Book of Baruch

One other important passage on wisdom is found in a deuterocanonical book, in Bar 3:9—4:4. The book of Baruch is introduced as "the words of the book that Baruch, son of Neriah . . . wrote in Babylon, in the fifth year . . . at the time when the Chaldeans took Jerusalem and burned it with fire." Already this notice gives rise to a problem: according to Jer 43:1-7, Baruch remained in Jerusalem with Jeremiah after the fall of the city and was later taken to Egypt. The tradition that he was taken to Babylon is reflected in later Jewish sources. This is not the only historical problem posed by this book. It refers to a high priest named Jehoiakim (1:7) who is otherwise unknown, and, like the book of Daniel, it regards Belshazzar as the son of Nebuchadnezzar (1:11). The consensus of scholarship dates the book to the second century B.C.E.

The book falls into two main sections, which may have originally been independent of each other. The first part contains an introduction in 1:1-14 and communal prayers in 1:15—3:8. It is generally agreed that this part of the book was composed in Hebrew. In the introduction, Baruch and his companions collect money to send to Jerusalem, together with the silver vessels that had been taken to Babylon. They instruct the recipients to offer sacrifices on the altar of the Lord for Nebuchadnezzar and his son Belshazzar. It is highly unlikely that Jews would have been able to collect money for Jerusalem a mere five years after the destruction, and the existence of an altar of the Lord in Jerusalem at that time is also problematic.

The communal prayer is in the Deuteronomic style: the Lord is in the right; we have sinned and done wrong; nonetheless, we ask for mercy. Similar prayers are found in Ezra 9, Nehemiah 9, and Daniel 9. The prayer in Baruch is especially closely related to Daniel 9. In view of the reference to Belshazzar in Baruch 1, dependence on Daniel is likely.

The second half of the book consists of the hymn in praise of wisdom (3:9—4:4), followed by an address by Jerusalem to the people of Israel (4:5-29) and an address to Jerusalem (4:30—5:9). It is uncertain whether the original language of these poems was Greek or Hebrew.

The hymn on wisdom begins as an address to Israel, bidding her hear the commandments of life (cf. Deut 30:15-20). Israel is in a foreign land because it neglected the wisdom of God. Already this passage implies that wisdom is to be found in the Torah.

The poem continues in a vein similar to Job 28. No one knows the place of wisdom. No one has gone up to heaven to bring her down (cf. the words of Agur in Prov 30:3-4). Only the Creator knows where to find her. In Job 28 God pointedly refused to reveal it to humanity. Rather, he said, "Fear of the LORD, that is wisdom, and to depart from evil is understanding." In other words, humanity does not have access to wisdom and should simply fear the Lord. According to Baruch, however, "he gave her to his servant Jacob, and to Israel, whom he loved. Afterward she appeared on earth, and lived with human-kind" (3:36-37). Baruch 4:1 echoes Sirach 24: "She is the book of the commandments of God, the law that endures forever." The poem concludes by asserting "Happy are we, O Israel, for we know what is pleasing to God" (Bar 4:4).

There can be little doubt that this poem presupposes Ben Sira's identification of wisdom and the law. The identification, however, may be understood in a different way. In Ben Sira wisdom is active in creation and can most probably be known through other means besides the Torah. Baruch, however, makes no mention of the role of wisdom in creation. Like Job 28, it emphasizes that wisdom is inaccessible to humanity. When it is given to Israel, then it becomes her exclusive posses-sion. The implication is that only Israel knows what is pleasing to God.

Conclusion

In the book of Baruch, wisdom is subordinated to the Law. Those who have the Law would seem to have little need of other wisdom. Ben Sira, in contrast, seems to have regarded other wisdom and the Torah as complemen-tary: the Torah was the source of wisdom par excellence, but it was not an exclusive source. The value of "alien wisdom" is most clearly affirmed in the Wisdom of Solomon, which scarcely refers to the Torah at all (there is a possible reference in Wis 2:12). Both Ben Sira and Wisdom affirm that wisdom is spread throughout creation, and that the study of nature can lead to knowledge of God. In this respect, they were continuous with the "cre-ation theology" or "natural theology" of the older wisdom tradition as found in Proverbs. The apocryphal wisdom books, however, are more systematic, and are informed in varying degrees by Greek philosophy (the Wisdom of Solomon is much more thoroughly informed than is Ben Sira). Much of later Christian theology, and some Jewish theology, consisted of an attempt to view the biblical tradition through lenses provided by Greek philoso-phy. (The great pioneer in this regard was the Jewish philosopher, Philo of Alexandria, who lived in the first half of the first century c.e.) The inclusion of the Wisdom of Solomon in the canon of Scriptures of Catholic Christian-ity provided an important precedent for this later theological development.

FOR FURTHER READING

Ben Sira

C. Camp, "Understanding a Patriarchy: Women in Second-Century Jerusalem through the Eyes of Ben Sira," in A. J. Levine, ed., *"Women Like This": New Perspectives on Jewish Women in the Greco-Roman World* (SBLEJL 1; Atlanta: Scholars Press, 1991), 1–39. Lucid exposition of Ben Sira's culture of honor and shame, and its implications for his view of women.

J. J. Collins, *Jewish Wisdom in the Hellenistic Age* (OTL; Louisville: Westminster, 1997), 21–111. Extensive discussion of the theology and ethical teaching of Ben Sira.

———, "The Wisdom of Jesus Son of Sirach," in J. Barton and J. Muddiman, eds., *The Oxford Bible Commentary* (Oxford: Oxford University Press, 2001), 667–98. Short commentary, emphasizing ethical and theological issues.

J. L. Crenshaw, "The Book of Sirach," *NIB* 5:603–867. Excellent theological commentary.

D. A. deSilva, *Introducing the Apocrypha* (Grand Rapids: Baker, 2002), 153–97. Good synthesis of recent scholarship on Sirach.

D. J. Harrington, *Jesus Ben Sira of Jerusalem: A Biblical Guide to Living Wisely* (Collegeville, MN: Liturgical Press, 2005). Popular introduction to Ben Sira.

L. G. Perdue, *Wisdom Literature: A Theological History* (Louisville: Westminster John Knox, 2007), 217–66. Well documented overview.

P. W. Skehan and A. A. Di Lella, *The Wisdom of Ben Sira* (AB 39; Garden City, NY: Doubleday, 1987). The most extensive commentary in English. Good discussion of textual problems.

G. G. Xeravits and J. Zsengellér, ed., *Studies in the Book of Ben Sira* (Leiden: Brill, 2008). Essays on various aspects of Ben Sira.

Wisdom of Solomon

J. J. Collins, *Jewish Wisdom in the Hellenistic Age* (OTL; Louisville: Westminster, 1997), 178–221. Fuller treatment of the comments in this volume.

D. A. deSilva, *Introducing the Apocrypha* (Grand Rapids: Baker, 2002), 127–52. Up-to-date discussion. Strong on the theology of the book.

W. Horbury, "The Wisdom of Solomon," in J. Barton and J. Muddiman, eds., *The Oxford Bible Commentary* (Oxford: Oxford University Press, 2001), 650–67. Brief but erudite commentary.

M. Kolarcik, "The Book of Wisdom," *NIB* 5:435–600. Fine literary and theological commentary.

L. G. Perdue, *Wisdom Literature* (above), 267–324. Well documented overview.

D. Winston, *The Wisdom of Solomon* (AB 43; Garden City, NY: Doubleday, 1979). Comprehensive commentary. Especially strong on the philosophical background of Wisdom.

G. G. Xeravits and J. Zsengellér, ed., *Studies in the Book of Wisdom* (Leiden: Brill, 2010).

Baruch

D. A. deSilva, *Introducing the Apocrypha* (Grand Rapids: Baker, 2002), 198–213. Discussion of the theological themes of the book.

D. Mendels, "Baruch, Book of," *ABD* 1:618–20. Concise summary of the critical issues.

C. A. Moore, *Daniel, Esther, and Jeremiah: The Additions* (AB 44; Garden City, NY: Doubleday, 1977), 253–316. Full philological commentary.

A. J. Saldarini, "The Book of Baruch," *NIB* 6:927–91. Brief commentary with up-to-date scholarship and theological reflections.

CHAPTER 29

From Tradition to Canon

The writings that make up the Hebrew Bible and the Old Testament are first of all the literary heritage of ancient Israel and Judah. These writings were composed and copied and revised over several hundred years. As we should expect of any corpus of writings that developed in this way, they are diverse in content and point of view as well as in literary form. Attempts of modern scholars to find a "center" of biblical theology have inevitably proved to be circular. Themes that are central to some books (for example, the covenant, in Deuteronomy) are absent from others (Proverbs, Qoheleth). Rather than impose principles of uniformity on this literature, we should recognize it for what it is: the literature of a people that reflects the ever-changing circumstances of that people's history.

The Bible does not preserve all the literature of ancient Judah. We know from the Dead Sea Scrolls, and from some of the Pseudepigrapha, that there were many other writings in circulation. We should like to know more of the principles of selection that led to the formation of the canon. In some cases, party politics may have played a role, but in general the writings that were included were those that were supported by a broad consensus. The Torah had been accepted as authoritative since the Persian period, and the Prophets since the beginning of the second century B.C.E. The only area where there was room for debate in the final selection of authoritative Scriptures was that of the Writings. Sectarian writings, such as the books of Enoch or some of the Dead Sea Scrolls, were not widely enough accepted to warrant inclusion. The books included were those that were cherished by the rabbis who laid the foundations of Judaism after the revolt against Rome in 66–70 C.E. The larger collection found in the Greek Bible reflects the more extensive corpus of writings that circulated in the Greek-speaking Diaspora.

The editors who gathered these books together made only very modest efforts to impose a meaningful shape on the collection. The different order of the Greek and Hebrew Bibles is a case in point. The fact that the Prophets are placed at the end of the Septuagint version supports the Christian view of the Old Testament as an essentially prophetic collection that points forward to the fulfillment of revelation in the New Testament. But, in fact, the editing of the biblical books, like their composition, was a gradual process that went on over several hundred years. The references to Moses and Elijah at the end of the book of Malachi mark the end of the collection of the prophets, but this collection was already closed at the beginning of the second century B.C.E. The warning at the end of Qoheleth against the multiplication of books of this kind was surely inserted by an editor, but not necessarily by anyone involved in finalizing the collection of sacred Scriptures. The "canonical shape of the text" is largely in the eye of the modern interpreter. The Bible consists of a collection of diverse writings that can be, and always have been, interpreted in various ways.

Sacred Scripture

On one level, then, the Hebrew Bible and Old Testament are collections of documents pertinent to the religious history of ancient Israel and Judah. For Jews and Christians over the centuries, however, they are more than that; they are also sacred Scriptures, which are in some way authoritative for how people live, even in the modern world. The understanding of these writings as sacred Scripture is bound up with claims of inspiration or revelation, and with the status of "canon" ascribed to the collection.

Claims of inspiration and revelation can scarcely be discussed profitably in an academic context. We can, however, say something about the way in which such claims arose and what they might entail.

The first thing to note is that such claims are made in some biblical books but by no means all. The laws of the Pentateuch supposedly originated in the revelation to Moses on Mount Sinai, although many of them are transparently of later origin. The prophets spoke their oracles in the name of the Lord. There is no claim of divine inspiration in the narrative and historical books, however, and the wisdom literature makes no pretense of being anything but human. Nonetheless, the claim of inspiration was gradually extended to the whole corpus, by analogy with the laws and the prophets.

To claim that the Bible is inspired or revealed is inevitably to claim authority for it. The nature and scope of that authority, however, are subject to debate. Many of the conflicts regarding the interpretation of the Bible have concerned discrepancies between the expectations of believers and the findings of critical scholarship. So, for example, it is often assumed that an inspired text must be historically accurate, whereas modern scholarship has repeatedly cast doubt on the veracity of biblical stories. (Think, for example, of the book of Joshua.) But the assumption begs questions of genre and intention. Joshua is not an exercise in historiography in the modern sense of the term. There is no reason, in principle, why a work of fiction should not be inspired as easily as a historical chronicle. Again, it is commonly assumed that an inspired text must be morally edifying. Many biblical texts most certainly are not, by any civilized measure. (Think again of Joshua and the alleged wholesale slaughter of Canaanites with divine approval.) But again, there is no reason in principle why a text that is shocking might not be inspired. Such a text can raise our moral consciousness by forcing us to confront the fact that immoral actions are often carried out in the name of religion. In fact, however, claims of inspiration and revelation often carry with them assumptions and presuppositions that turn out to be inappropriate to the texts. For this reason, they are problematic. Rather than ask whether a text is revealed (and by what criteria could we possibly decide?) it is better to ask whether a text is revelatory, whether we learn something from it about human nature or about the way the world works. A text that is neither historically reliable nor morally edifying, such as the book of Joshua, may be all too revelatory about human nature.

People who approach the Bible with strong presuppositions about its inspired or revealed character are often at pains to save the appearances of the text and explain away anything that might conflict with their presuppositions. In the ancient world, this was often done by means of allegory, the interpretation of a text as meaning something other than what it actually says. This method was originally developed by Greek scholars in Alexandria to explain away the scandalous behavior of the gods in Homer's epics. It was adapted by Jewish scholars in Alexandria around the turn of the era. The most famous practitioner was Philo of Alexandria, who wrote extensive commentaries on the Torah, interpreting it in terms of Platonic philosophy. Later this method was used by the Christian church fathers, and it was widely accepted as a legitimate method of interpretation in late antiquity. An allegorical interpretation might, for example, explain the commands to eradicate the Canaanites as commands to root out vice from the soul. Such interpretations have little credibility in the modern world, however, and often seem to smack of dishonesty. (We are reminded of Job's indictment of his friends, on the grounds that they would "lie for God" or distort the evidence to try to make God look good.) It is better to come to terms with the text in its own terms than to allegorize it so that it conforms to our ideas of propriety.

Canon

The term *canon* means "measuring stick," and it was used in the Hellenistic world for the standard or norm by which things were evaluated.

It was adapted in early Christianity to refer to "the rule of faith." To speak of the Bible as canon implies that the Bible is the standard by which everything else is judged. This idea has a more central place in Protestant Christianity than in Judaism or in Catholicism. The status of "canon" is not something that is inherent in the biblical text but reflects the kind of authority conferred on the text by a particular community.

The idea of a canon has become fashionable in secular literary criticism in recent years to denote the corpus of classic works that stand as benchmarks of excellence in a field. So one might say that Homer was canonical in ancient Greece, or Shakespeare in English literature. Canonical works are copied over and over again, and they become the standard reference works of their particular field. The biblical books can be said to be canonical in this sense for Judaism and Christianity. They provide a fund of stories and sayings that are shared by these traditions and provide the basis for a common discourse. They provide analogies by which new experiences can be understood and problems addressed. The biblical books are not necessarily benchmarks of literary excellence, although some of them may be, but they provide case studies in moral and religious reasoning. The case of the Bible, however, is somewhat different from that of a literary canon because of the claim of divine inspiration and the religious authority it implies.

The ways in which the Bible has functioned as canon have varied widely among religious communities. Biblical texts are not always laws to be obeyed or examples to be imitated. There are many subtler ways in which people may be informed by a canonical book. Some modern approaches to the canon have celebrated that diversity. In the phrase of James A. Sanders, the canon is "adaptable for life." It is not a tightly coherent, systematic collection that imposes one orthodox view of life. Rather, it is a smorgasbord of resources, some of which may be helpful at one time, others at another. From this perspective, what is important about the canon is the process whereby old texts are constantly used to address new situations. This process can be seen at work already in the Hebrew Bible; think, for example, of the theme of the new Exodus in the prophecies of Hosea and Second Isaiah. The fact that the texts continue to be used is more important than the way in which they are used. From this perspective, the canon is a resource rather than a norm, but the need to refer constantly to the canonical text inevitably places some restraints on the interpreter.

A different approach to the canon is associated with the work of Brevard Childs, who places greater emphasis on the authority of the text. Childs attaches great importance on the final form of the text rather than on the process whereby it reached that form or the different forms in which it was preserved. As we have seen, however, the idea that the text as a whole has a "canonical shape," or indeed that there is one "final form" of the text, is problematic. One of the effects of this approach is that it attaches greater weight to the work of the editors than to the words of the prophets or the original authors of a given book. So, for example, the book of Amos is read in light of its conclusion, which softens the message of the prophet by saying that God will not completely destroy the house of Israel, and by speaking of a Davidic restoration. Or

the skepticism of Qoheleth is undermined by the rather conservative warning at the end, to fear God and keep the commandments. In part, this preference for the "final form" of the book arises from skepticism about our ability to recover the original words of the prophets or sages. Any reading of a book that regards some parts of it as secondary is to some degree hypothetical. But there is also a theological, and even a political issue at stake. Prophets like Amos and sages like Qoheleth were fiercely critical of the institutions and authorities of their day. The editors, in contrast, tend to have an institutional perspective—in the book of Amos, an affirmation of the Davidic dynasty, in Qoheleth, an affirmation of the Law. The choice between the historical-critical quest for the original words of a prophet and the canonical preference for the "final form" of the text is often a choice between challenging religious tradition in the manner of the prophets and defending it in the manner of religious authorities, ancient and modern.

Enduring values

The importance that the Bible has enjoyed in the Western world is due in large part to its canonical status in Judaism and Christianity, and to the widespread belief in its inspiration. Be that as it may, the influence of these books on Western culture is enormous. Knowledge of biblical stories is indispensible for the appreciation of Western art and culture. Think, for example, of the Sistine Chapel paintings of Michelangelo, or of Milton's *Paradise Lost*. Even apart from its importance as a cultural aid, however, the Old Testament remains vital and engaging literature even from a purely humanistic perspective. Here it may suffice to mention two factors that render the Bible an important resource for humanistic education.

First, no other collection of documents from the ancient world, and scarcely any other documents at all, speak with such passionate urgency on the subject of social justice. The primary voices in this respect are those of the Hebrew prophets, but the law codes of the Pentateuch are also of fundamental importance for our understanding of human rights. To be sure, the biblical laws are not always satisfactory by modern standards. Biblical attitudes to slaves, women, and foreigners are all mired in the cultural assumptions of the ancient world, with only occasional flickers of enlightenment. Nonetheless, the concern for the unfortunate of society in these books is remarkable and often stands as a reproach to the modern Western world.

Second, it has been claimed that the biblical authors were the pioneers of prose fiction. Whatever the historical merits of this claim, and it is not without substance, the achievements of the biblical writers are not just a matter of literary form. The biblical narratives offer a warts-and-all picture of human nature that has seldom been surpassed. The realism of the narratives of Genesis or the story of David is widely recognized and appreciated. The account of the brutality of conquest is no less realistic, but has less often been appreciated, because it has too often been construed as moral example. When the Bible is read without moralistic presuppositions, however, it gives a picture of human nature that is not comforting but may well be said to be revelatory.

In the modern world, unfortunately, the Bible, and especially the Old Testament, is often viewed with suspicion because of its association with religious fundamentalism. There are, to be sure, laws in the Bible that can only be described as narrow-minded and intolerant, but the collection as a whole cannot be characterized in this way. As we have seen repeatedly, this is a collection of writings that is marked by lively internal debate and by a remarkable spirit of self-criticism, directed not only at the people of Israel but sometimes at the myths and certainties of the tradition. Think, for example of Job's critique of the premises of the wisdom tradition or of Deuteronomistic theology, or of Jonah's ironic portrayal of prophecy. It is somewhat ironic, then, that fundamentalistic readings of the Bible treat it so often as a bedrock of certainty. The portrayal of the Bible as a source of infallible truth does not arise from a reading of the Bible itself, but is a monstrous imposition upon it, even if it is one that is backed by a long tradition.

One of the most persistent themes of the Hebrew Bible is the critique of idolatry. This applies not only to carved or molten statues, but to the human tendency to absolutize things that are merely part of the created order. Perhaps the greatest irony in the history of the Bible is that it itself has so often been treated as an idol and venerated with a reverential attitude while its message is ignored. Biblical figures from Abraham to Job do not hesitate to argue with the Almighty. The least that might be expected of readers of the Bible is that they bring the same critical spirit to bear on the biblical text.

FURTHER READING

J. Barr, *Holy Scripture: Canon, Authority, Criticism* (Philadelphia: Westminster, 1983). Incisive critique of conservative views of biblical authority.

J. Barton, *Holy Writings, Sacred Text: The Canon in Early Christianity* (Louisville: Westminster John Knox, 1997). Thoughtful reflections on the origin of the biblical canon and its implications.

S. B. Chapman, *The Law and the Prophets: A Study in Old Testament Canon Formation* (Tübingen: Mohr Siebeck, 2001). Disputes the view that the Law was more important than the Prophets from an early time.

B. S. Childs, *Introduction to the Old Testament as Scripture* (Philadelphia: Fortress Press, 1979). Monumental treatment of the Old Testament, emphasizing the "canonical shape" as authoritative. Contains extensive summaries of scholarship that are useful quite apart from Childs's own perspective.

C. Helmer and C. Landmesser, *One Scripture or Many? Canon from Biblical, Theological and Philosophical Perspectives* (Oxford: Oxford University Press, 2004). Historical and theological essays on the canon.

T. H. Lim, *The Formation of the Jewish Canon* (Yale Anchor Reference Library; New Haven: Yale University Press, 2013). An up-to-date critical assessment of the formation of the canon, drawing especially on the evidence of the Dead Sea Scrolls.

L. M. McDonald and J. A. Sanders, *The Canon Debate* (Peabody, MA: Hendrickson, 2002). Wide-ranging collection of essays on questions relating to the canons of both testaments.

J. A. Sanders, "Adaptable for Life: The Nature and Function of Canon," in F. M. Cross et al., eds., *Magnalia Dei: The Mighty Acts of God: Essays on the Bible and Archaeology in Memory of G. E. Wright* (New York: Doubleday, 1976), 531–60. Excellent account of the "canonical process."

Glossary

Achaemenid—A dynasty of Persian kings (559–333 B.C.E.)

acrostic—A poem in which lines begin with the letters of the alphabet in sequence

Ahikar—A legendary Assyrian sage

Akhenaten—Pharaoh Amenophis IV (c. 1350 B.C.E.), whose devotion to the god Aten (the solar disk) was the closest thing to monotheism before the rise of Israel

Akiba—A rabbi of the early second century C.E.

Akitu—The Babylonian new year's festival

Akkadian—The language of ancient Babylon and Assyria

Amarna—The place on the Nile River where Akhenaten had his court

Amarna letters—Letters from vassals in Canaan to the Egyptian court, in the time of Akhenaten

Amenemope—The name associated with an Egyptian wisdom book that is thought to have influenced Proverbs

amphictyony—A league of tribes around a central shrine

Anat—A Canaanite goddess

Apiru—or *Habiru*, people on the fringes of society in the second millennium B.C.E., possibly related to Hebrews

apocalypse—Literary genre of revelations about the end-time

Apocrypha—Books that are included in the Catholic Bible, but are not found in the Hebrew Bible or in the Protestant canon

apodictic law—Absolute, declarative law (no ifs or buts)

Aram—Syria

Aramaic—The language of Syria, closely related to Hebrew; the standard language of diplomacy under the Persians

Arameans—People from ancient Syria

Asherah—A Canaanite goddess, also worshiped in Israel; also, the name for a sacred pole at cult sites

Astarte—A Canaanite goddess also worshiped in Israel

Aten heresy—The exclusive worship of Aten, the solar disk, by Akhenaten

Athtar—A god in Ugaritic myth; the morning star

Atrahasis—One of the Babylonian accounts of creation; the name of a wise human in that account

Baal—The Canaanite storm-god

Bahman Yasht—Persian apocalyptic text with a vision of four kingdoms

Ban (*herem*)—The custom of slaughtering the enemy as a sacrifice to the god of the victors

Bar Kokhba—The leader of the Jewish revolt against Rome in 132–135 B.C.E.

Book of the Covenant—Exodus, chapters 21–23

Canaan—The area including Palestine, Lebanon, and part of Syria in the second millennium B.C.E.

canon—The corpus of biblical books, viewed as sacred Scripture

canonical approach—Theological approach to the Old Testament as Scripture, regarding the final form of the text as authoritative

casuistic law—Case law, based on specific situations

centralization of cult—The prohibition of sacrifice outside of Jerusalem by King Josiah, 621 B.C.E.; also called the Deuteronomic Reform

Chemosh—A god of Moab

cherubim—Mythical winged creatures, portrayed in the Jerusalem temple

collar-rimmed jars—A type of pottery associated with early Israel

corvée—Forced labor

cosmogony—A story about the origin of the world

court narrative—The account of intrigues at David's court; 2 Sam 9—1 Kings 2 (= the Succession Document)

covenant—A solemn agreement; used especially of agreements between God and Israel

covenant form—The structure of covenant, understood on the model of ancient treaties

credo—"I believe"; a profession of faith

D—The Deuteronomic source in the Pentateuch

Dagon—A god of the Philistines

Day of the Lord—The day of divine intervention in prophetic texts

Dead Sea Scrolls—Texts found near Qumran by the Dead Sea, beginning in 1947

deuterocanonical—Books included in the Roman Catholic canon but relegated to the Apocrypha in Protestant Bibles

Deuteronomic reform—The reform of King Josiah, 621 B.C.E., which centralized the cult in accordance with Deuteronomy 12

Deuteronomistic History—The books of Joshua, Judges, Samuel, and Kings (= the Former Prophets)

demiurge—The maker of the world; creator

divination—A means of consulting the gods

Documentary Hypothesis—The theory that the Pentateuch was composed by combining four main strands or documents (J, E, D, P)

E (Elohist)—A narrative source in the Pentateuch

El—A Canaanite high god; the word El is a generic name for "god" in biblical Hebrew

Elephantine papyri—Aramaic documents from a Jewish garrison in the south of Egypt in the fifth century B.C.E.

Elohim—The Hebrew word for God; can be understood as either singular or plural

Enuma Elish—The Babylonian account of creation

Ephraim—Tribe named for a son of Joseph, in the central hill country of Israel; often used as a name for Israel

Epicureanism—A school of Greek philosophy that advocated the (sober) enjoyment of the present

epic—A story of human heroes, involving actions of the gods

eschatology—Discussion of the last things

etiology—A story that explains the cause of something

etymology—A story that explains the origin of a word or name

form criticism—Analysis of small units of biblical literature, with attention to genre and setting

Former Prophets—The books of Joshua, Judges, Samuel, Kings (= the Deuteronomistic History)

four-room house—The style of house typical of early Israel

Gerizim—A mountain near Shechem; site of the Samaritan temple in the Hellenistic period

Gilgamesh—The hero of a popular Mesopotamian epic

Grundschrift—German for "basic document"; used in the nineteenth century for what was later called the Priestly Writing (P)

Habiru—People on the fringes of society in the second millennium B.C.E., possibly related to Hebrews

Hadad—Another name for Baal

Hades—Greek name for the netherworld

Hasidim—A party of Jewish pietists during the Maccabean revolt

Hellenistic—An adjective referring to the Greek-speaking world after the conquests of Alexander the Great (who died in 323 B.C.E.)

Hellenistic reform—The introduction of Greek customs into Jerusalem, 175–168 B.C.E.

Herem **(ban)**—The custom of slaughtering the enemy as a sacrifice to the god of the victors

Hexateuch—The first six books of the Bible (the Pentateuch plus Joshua)

high places—Open-air places of worship

Hittites—A people of Asia Minor (modern Turkey) in the second millennium B.C.E.

Holiness Code (H)—Leviticus 17–26; closely related to the Priestly source

Horeb—The mountain of revelation in E and D traditions (instead of Sinai); the name means "wilderness"

Hyksos—A people from Syria who ruled Egypt for about a century (1650 to 1550 B.C.E.)

Immanuel—"God with us"; the name of child foretold in Isaiah 7

inclusio—A literary device wherein the ending corresponds to the beginning

Isaiah, First—Isaiah 1–39, or portions thereof

Isaiah, Second—Isaiah 40–55

Isaiah, Third—Isaiah 56–66

J (Yahwist)—A narrative source in the Pentateuch

Jebusites—Inhabitants of Jerusalem before the Israelites

Jeroboam, sin of—The erection of cult sites in northern Israel, at Bethel and Dan, contrary to Deuteronomic law

Josephus—A Jewish historian, late first century C.E.

Joseph, tribes of—Ephraim and Manasseh

K^etubim—"Writings"; the third part of the canon of Hebrew Scriptures

Levirate law—The law requiring the brother of a deceased man to marry his widow

Levites—Priests descended from Levi; subordinated to Zadokite priests in Jerusalem after the exile

LXX (Septuagint)—A Greek translation of the Old Testament

Marduk—The main god of Babylon

Mari—A place on the Euphrates where important texts from the second millennium were discovered

Marzeach—Feasting, related to the cult of the dead

mashal—A literary form involving analogy; can refer to a proverb, parable, or taunt song

Masoretic text (MT)—The traditional text of the Hebrew Bible, as fixed in the Middle Ages

Masseba—Sacred pillar or standing stone

Mesha Stele—*See* Moabite Stone

midbar—"Wilderness" (Hebrew)

Middle Platonism—A form of Greek philosophy that combined elements of Platonism and Stoicism

Midrash—Rabbinic commentaries on biblical texts

Milcom—A god of the Ammonites

Mishnah—A compilation of rabbinic law from the second century C.E.

Moabite Stone—(also known as the Mesha Stele); an inscription of King Mesha of Moab from the ninth century B.C.E., commemorating victory over Israel

Mot—Death; a god in Ugaritic myth

myth—Sacred story

nabi'—The Hebrew word for prophet

natural theology—Knowledge of God derived from the created order; typical of wisdom literature

nazirite—Person consecrated to God by a vow (see Numbers 6)

Negev/Negeb—An area south of the hill country of Judah

Nehushtan—The bronze serpent associated with Moses

Old Greek—The original Greek translation of the Bible, which is different in some cases from that preserved in the Septuagint

P—The Priestly strand in the Pentateuch

patriarchal—Relating to the patriarchs (Abraham, Isaac, and Jacob)

Pentateuch (Torah)—The first five books of the Bible, also called "the books of Moses"

Philo—Jewish philosopher in Alexandria in the early first century C.E.

pit—A term for the netherworld (Sheol)

Platonism—Greek philosophy influenced by the teachings of Plato

Pseudepigrapha—Books that are attributed to famous ancient people (such as Enoch) who did not actually write them

Qumran—Site where the Dead Sea Scrolls were discovered

Rabbinic Judaism—Refers to Judaism in the period ca. 150–650 C.E.

redaction criticism—The study of how books or blocks of material, such as the source documents of the Pentateuch, were edited

restoration—The return of Judean exiles from Babylon to Jerusalem, after the Babylonian exile

ribh—Accusation or lawsuit

Samaria—Capital of northern Israel

Samaritans—People who lived around Shechem in the Second Temple period; they had their temple on Mount Gerizim. They were rejected by Jerusalem as descendants of Assyrian settlers but worshiped the God of Israel

Sea Peoples—People who invaded the area of Palestine around 1200 B.C.E. and became the Philistines

Second Temple period—The period after the Babylonian exile, down to the first century C.E. (539 B.C.E. to 70 C.E.)

Septuagint (LXX)—A Greek translation of the Old Testament

Shamash—The sun, or sun-god

Sheol—Hebrew name for the netherworld; like the Greek Hades

Sitz im Leben—German for "setting in life"; a technical term in form criticism

Solomonic enlightenment—Supposed flowering of culture in the reign of Solomon, now doubted

source criticism—The attempt to distinguish different sources in the biblical text, especially in the Pentateuch

Stoicism—A school of Greek philosophy that emphasized the role of reason in the world

Succession Document—An account of intrigues at David's court, 2 Sam 9—1 Kings 2 (= Court narrative)

Suffering Servant—A figure described in Isaiah 53 whose suffering and death saves others; probably meant to describe Israel in the exile

Sukkoth—The Festival of Booths or Tabernacles

Suzerainty treaty—A treaty in which one party is subordinate to the other, the suzerain

Talmud—Either of two rabbinic compilation of commentaries on the Mishnah, the Jerusalem Talmud (Yerushalmi), which dates from the fifth century C.E., and the Babylonian (Bavli), from the sixth

targum—A paraphrastic Aramaic translation of biblical texts

Tel Dan inscription—Inscription from the ninth century B.C.E. mentioning the "house of David"

Tetragrammaton—The divine name YHWH, so called because it has four letters

theogony—A story about the birth of the gods

theophany—The manifestation of a god

Tiamat—The mother goddess in the Babylonian creation story *Enuma Elish*

Torah (Pentateuch)—The first five books of the Bible, also called "the books of Moses"

Tosefta—The collection of rabbinic laws that supplement the Mishnah

Transjordan—Area east of Jordan River

Twelve, Book of the—The Minor Prophets, Hosea to Malachi

Ugarit—Modern Ras Shamra, in northern Syria, where important tablets were discovered in 1929

Vassal treaty—A treaty in which one party (the vassal) is subordinate to the other

Writings—Hebrew *K^etubim*: the third part of the canon of Hebrew Scriptures

Yahwist (J)—A narrative source in the Pentateuch

YHWH—Proper name of the God of Israel, pronounced "Yahweh"; traditionally, Jews do not pronounce the divine name and do not insert the vowels when writing it; instead, they say "Adonai" ("the Lord") or "ha-Shem" ("the name")

Yamm—Sea; a god in Ugaritic myth

Yom Kippur—The Day of Atonement

Zadokites—Priests descended from Zadok (priest under David and Solomon); high priests in the Second Temple period were Zadokite, down to the Maccabean revolt

Zaphon—"North"; the name of a mountain in Syria, sacred to Baal

Zion—A hill in Jerusalem; the City of David

Zion theology—Belief that God had chosen Zion and would protect it

Zoroastrianism—Persian religion based on the teachings of Zoroaster (Zarathustra)